DOCUMENTARY CREDITS

for Lucy

Altogether elsewhere, vast
Herds of reindeer move across
Miles and miles of golden moss,
Silently and very fast.

W. H. Auden
The Fall of Rome

DOCUMENTARY CREDITS

the law and practice of documentary credits
including standby credits and demand guarantees

Second edition

by
Raymond Jack
one of Her Majesty's Counsel and Circuit Judges,
of Trinity College, Cambridge, and of the Inner Temple

Butterworths
London, Dublin, Edinburgh
1993

United Kingdom	Butterworth & Co (Publishers) Ltd, 88 Kingsway, LONDON WC2B 6AB and 4 Hill Street, EDINBURGH EH2 3JZ
Australia	Butterworths, SYDNEY, MELBOURNE, BRISBANE, ADELAIDE, PERTH, CANBERRA and HOBART
Belgium	Butterworth & Co (Publishers) Ltd, BRUSSELS
Canada	Butterworths Canada Ltd, TORONTO and VANCOUVER
Ireland	Butterworth (Ireland) Ltd, DUBLIN
Malaysia	Malayan Law Journal Sdn Bhd, KUALA LUMPUR
New Zealand	Butterworths of New Zealand Ltd, WELLINGTON and AUCKLAND
Puerto Rico	Butterworth of Puerto Rico, Inc, SAN JUAN
Singapore	Butterworths Asia, SINGAPORE
USA	Butterworth Legal Publishers, CARLSBAD, California, and SALEM, New Hampshire

A CIP Catalogue record for this book is available from the British Library.

First edition 1991

ISBN 0 406 02288 7

Typeset by Phoenix Photosetting, Chatham, Kent
Printed and bound in Great Britain by Mackays of Chatham PLC, Chatham, Kent

Foreword
to
First Edition

Some years ago a Queen's Bench Master, exasperated beyond endurance by the complexities of a case about bills of exchange, was driven to observe 'I *do* wish people wouldn't use these things, they cause nothing but trouble.'

The same ignoble thought must on occasion have occurred to practitioners and judges seeking to unravel the complex interlocking contracts involved in a documentary credit. Where were the rules and principles to be found? 'Oh that they were printed in a book!' (*Job* 19: 23).

Raymond Jack has answered Job's prayer and in doing so has brought to the task his characteristic gifts of lucidity, thoroughness and accurate scholarship. Here is a clear and intelligible account of the roles, rights and responsibilities of buyer and seller, buyer and issuing bank, issuing bank and confirming bank, confirming bank and seller, seller and issuing bank. Here is an accessible introduction to the leading cases decided here and abroad. Here is a detailed commentary on the Uniform Customs and the interpretations of the ICC Banking Commission, all-important in a field which (of all others) requires of traders, bankers and lawyers a truly international approach. Here is a comprehensive survey which is firmly rooted in the realities of the market-place but discusses the theoretical problems to which documentary credits give rise, suggesting the proper direction of travel where no clear signposts at present exist.

This book will be a boon to all practitioners in this field, whether commercial or legal, who may now await the next problem to come their way with confidence and even eagerness.

London
November 1990

T. H. Bingham

Preface
to
Second Edition

This second edition is occasioned by the publication of the 1993 Revision of the Uniform Customs, an event foreseen at the conclusion of my first preface. This has resulted in substantial rewriting, in particular to take account of the new treatment by the Uniform Customs of transport documents and of the duty of banks in connection with the acceptance or refusal of documents. The chapter on conflict of laws takes account of the coming into force of the Rome Convention. I have adopted the name, demand guarantees, from the ICC's Uniform Rules for Demand Guarantees, to refer to those instruments variously called performance bonds, first demand guarantees, and performance guarantees: the Uniform Rules are described in the text and appear as an appendix. I have taken account of cases decided since the preparation of the previous text.

There is some temptation to use this preface as an opportunity to appraise the new Uniform Customs. But, some comments apart, that would seem premature and inappropriate. The Working Group established to carry out the revision consisted of ten persons: three from the United States, including the Chairman and a professor of law; two from Germany; two from England; a professor of law from Italy; one member from Norway; and one from the ICC in Paris. There has been a shift from Europe and England to America: the two professors were also the first lawyers to be members. Like their predecessors the Group faced a task which was unique in this sense – that they were preparing rules intended to regulate an important aspect of international trade in much the same way as international conventions regulate other aspects: yet the Uniform Customs do not have the force of law and can only operate through the agreement of parties to credits. In short, the ICC cannot say what parties to credits may or may not agree to, save indirectly. It cannot legislate: this is forgotten at peril. Likewise, although the nature of the Working Group no doubt gave them some advantages over the framers of international conventions, the latter have advantages which the status of the Working Group meant they could not share. One is that the Working Group contained no one trained and experienced as a professional draftsman. This is apparent in the product: to take one clear example, there is the failure of the Article dealing with transfer and amendments to state the consequences of a first beneficiary's retention or non-retention of his right to refuse to allow the transferring bank to advise amendments to the second beneficiary.

The Chairman's Preface to the new Revision refers to surveys which show that it is still the case that up to half the documents presented under credits are rejected on first presentation. This means that there is something seriously wrong. It can no doubt be said that it is substantially the fault of those presenting documents. Banks can also be at fault in permitting credits to be issued which are not sufficiently clear or precise. And banks can be at fault by being over-zealous in applying the rule of strict compliance. That rule may itself sometimes properly be regarded as the villain. Whatever the causes, such a failure rate is time-consuming and expensive, and inhibits the flow of trade. It must detract from the useful-ness of credits. If it is not improved substantially, more commercial parties will be looking, as some already are, to more efficient ways of doing business. The new Uniform Customs have been prepared with this in mind.

Lastly I owe my thanks again to John Turnbull, now of the Swiss Bank Corporation, for his assistance on numerous points, also to John Richardson of P & O Containers, and to Nicholas Bennett of Hong Kong.

Ridge   RAYMOND JACK
26th October 1993

Preface
to
First Edition

The intention of this book is to set out the law and practice relating to documentary credits in a manner which will be of assistance to banks and to the commercial men who use credits, while also providing the more detailed discussion of the relevant law which lawyers may need. I have aimed to describe how documentary credits work and it is a natural step from the description of their contractual framework to the legal principles which govern their operation.

The main subject matter is the traditional type of credit, which in England is usually that intended when the older term, letter of credit, is used, and which provides a means of payment under a contract of international sale or, less commonly, services. The book also covers that species of credit with which the English courts have yet to become properly acquainted, called a standby credit, originating in the United States, which is in function more of a guarantee than a primary means of payment, and which is now expanding its role in relation to some commodities into the field occupied by traditional credits. In conjunction with standby credits I have included those guarantees which are called first demand guarantees or bonds and have set them in the wider context of guarantees generally.

The law and practice relating to documentary credits comes from four primary sources. They are first the general principles of contract law from which the legal rules relating specifically to documentary credits have been developed and to which reference must be made to understand those rules and to answer any problem which has not yet been resolved by the courts. Second, there are the decisions of the courts which specifically relate to documentary credits, and the rules laid down by such decisions. Third, and perhaps a non-lawyer might put this first, there are the Uniform Customs and Practice for Documentary Credits published by the International Chamber of Commerce. Lastly, there is the established practice of banks. There is a little to be said about each of these.

The law which I have set out is English law. While it would make a better book to provide a comparative description of relevant aspects of American and continental laws, time is a unique commodity and this must wait at least for a further edition. Not only because a number of important decisions in the field have come from the Privy Council, it is my hope that the law as stated can be taken as applicable in Commonwealth jurisdictions.

With a book of a wide ambit, such as one covering the whole of contract law, it is the author's function to separate from the thousands of reported decisions those that are worth citation, and to provide a distillation of the judgments, which is offered as a statement of the law. With documentary credits the number of decisions is relatively small. Decisions, which in another context might or might not secure a footnote, may deserve discussion simply because they are illustrative of what happens in practice.

There are often points which have not been decided, or which have not been decided in any authoritative manner. I have seen it as my function in this different situation to look for the problems which may arise but which are as yet undetermined and, by the application of general contractual principles and keeping in mind the commercial reality of each situation, to offer a view.

I had initially thought that the practice of banks should be a larger source of material than has been the case. In most litigation concerning credits the court hears evidence from bankers expert in credit operations. But unless an established and generally accepted practice is proved, such evidence cannot by itself be decisive, although it may greatly help the court in defining the issues and demonstrating the advantages of one view or another. For the practice of one bank is often not that of another, particularly if they are in different countries or continents. It became clear to me that, not having the power to summon up a committee of bankers to assist me, it could be dangerous to rely upon the practice of one bank to provide material which was of general application. A number of Opinions of the ICC Banking Commission show the differences which can exist on important questions. I have therefore limited the assistance which I have sought as to banking practice as an independent source of material. This may need to be stated so it is not asked, or at least not asked too fiercely, why a lawyer is writing about the practice of credits.

That said, I can now record my very considerable gratitude to John Turnbull of the Banque Paribas in London for reading my typescript, correcting at least some of what are politely called infelicities, and giving me his ideas and discussing a number of problems. It was a pleasure to work with him.

I trust that in writing this book I have taken my own line. But I am grateful that I have not been an explorer without maps. I acknowledge the great help which I have received in particular from the work of H. C. Gutteridge and Maurice Megrah, and that of Professor Ellinger.

The law is stated as at 1 December 1990. Meanwhile the judges of the Commercial Court and of the Court of Appeal proceed with their tasks, and the ICC has in train a further revision of the Uniform Customs, which may emerge in 1993. The advances of modern communications raise the possibility of credits without documents. The vitality of this creation of the high Victorian age grows rather than is diminished.

The Temple   RAYMOND JACK
December 1990

Acknowledgments

The publishers and author wish to thank the following for permission to reproduce material from the sources indicated:

Banking Commission Decisions (1975–79) on LC queries
ICC Publication No 371
Copyright © 1980

Uniform Customs & Practice for Documentary Credits (1983 Revision)
ICC Publication No 400
Copyright © 1983

UCP 1974/1983 Revisions Compared and Explained
ICC Publication No 411
Copyright © 1984

Uniform Rules for Demand Guarantees
ICC Publication No 458
Copyright © 1992

Case Studies on Documentary Credits
ICC Publication No 459
Copyright © 1989

Uniform Customs & Practice for Documentary Credits (1993 Revision)
ICC Publication No 500
Copyright © 1993

The above published by the International Chamber of Commerce, Paris
Available from ICC PUBLISHING SA, 38 Cours Albert 1er, 75008 Paris,
France and from ICC UNITED KINGDOM, 14/15 Belgrave Square,
London SW1X 8PS

Scrutton on Charterparties and Bills of Lading (19th edn, 1984)
  Sweet & Maxwell

Contents

The detailed contents of each chapter are set out at the head of each

Table of Statutes

References in this Table to *Statutes* are to Halsbury's Statutes of England (Fourth Edition) showing the volume and page at which the annotated text of the Act will be found. Para references in **bold** type indicate where the section of the Act is set out in part or in full.

Table of Cases

The Uniform Customs
Unless otherwise stated references
to the Articles of the Uniform
Customs are to the Articles of
the Uniform Customs and Practice
for Documentary Credits, 1993
Revision, ICC Publication No 500,
the text of which is set out as
Appendix 1 and is followed by an
index of the primary references to
each Article in this book as
Appendix 2. Appendix 2 also
relates the Articles of the
1993 Revision to those of the
1983 Revision.

Chapter 1

Introduction to Documentary Credits and to the Uniform Customs

A. General Introduction

1.1 *Outline of the chapter* The object of this chapter is to describe documentary credits, their function and how they are operated in practice so that Chapter 2 may describe particular kinds of credit and Chapter 3 may begin the sequence of chapters covering specific relationships which arise between the parties to documentary credits. The chapter has also to introduce the Uniform Customs and Practice for Documentary Credits. These contain provisions governing documentary credits, their operation and the rights and obligations to which they may give rise.

1.2 *The name* The terms 'documentary credit', 'letter of credit' and 'commercial credit' are all in current use and no distinction need be made between them. The Uniform Customs[1] refer to 'documentary credits' in Articles 1 and 2 and thereafter simply to 'credits', which term is used to include 'standby letters of credit'. Standby letters of credit have a different function to the credits with which this book is mainly concerned and they are considered in Chapter 12.

1 See para 1.21 below.

1.3 The general concept and function of documentary credits In simple transactions of sale such as may take place in a shop the buyer pays the seller in exchange for the goods. In commercial transactions where buyer and seller are in different countries and the goods must be transported by sea or road or air by a third party carrier, something more sophisticated is required. A documentary credit is a means of providing payment first by substituting a bank for the buyer as the party which will make payment to the seller. Secondly, payment is made not against the transfer of the goods but against the documents which represent the goods after they have been shipped and are in transit. In broad terms a documentary credit provides the promise by a bank of immediate or future payment against the presentation of documents to the bank or its agent, most commonly in connection with sale of goods. It is normally used in international transactions and it utilises the international banking system. The first advantage of credits as they are commonly operated is that they provide a seller with a promise of payment, often immediate payment, given by a bank in the seller's own country. Subject to the solvency of the bank, certainty of payment is achieved provided that the seller is able to meet the terms of the credit. That means in essence that he must be able to present the documents required by the credit within the time required by the credit. Credits may be used in different ways to achieve different results, in particular as to when the seller is paid and when the buyer has to provide reimbursement to the bank responsible for the payment. They may also be used, by the mechanism of transfer, to provide for payment to a party from whom the seller is himself acquiring the goods. The function of a credit may be thus not only to provide security of payment to the seller, but to arrange for the financing of the transaction.

1.4 Comparison with payment against documents The transaction whose development was probably the first step towards the documentary credit system, is that where the buyer agrees to pay cash against presentation of documents to him by the seller. In a CIF contract the documents to be presented to the buyer would be the invoice, the bills of lading, a policy or certificate of insurance, and such other documents as might be specified in the contract of sale. The feature in common with documentary credits is the promise to pay in return for the transfer of documents of the right description. The main difference from a documentary credit is that the seller has only the promise of the buyer to pay and not that of a bank: the buyer may renege on his promise because the market or his circumstances have changed, leaving the seller with a claim for damages for breach of contract against a buyer in another country. A second difference is that to receive payment the seller has to get the documents to the buyer. As the buyer is usually in another country and because the seller will wish to retain his security in the goods given by the documents he will need to use an agent whom he can trust to present the documents to the buyer. This will often be a bank. Because of this need to get the documents to the buyer there will be a delay before the seller gets paid. But if no bank is involved the banking charges which will be incurred if a credit is used will be saved.

1.5 The introduction of a bill of exchange into the payment-against-documents concept enables credit to be given to the buyer, and these long-established methods are also used in documentary credits. Where credit is to be given, the contract of sale provides not for the buyer to pay against documents but to accept a bill of exchange drawn on him by the seller and payable at a future date. When the seller receives back the accepted bill he may be able to discount the bill with his own bank or with a discount house. He will then not be out of pocket pending the maturity of the bill, although when fixing his price he will need to take account of the fact that when he discounts the bill he will only receive its discounted value.[1] But if the buyer in due course dishonours the bill, the seller will have to refund his bank or the discount house because he is liable as the drawer of a dishonoured bill. He will then also have parted with both documents and goods. Instead of the seller obtaining the buyer's acceptance of the bill prior to his negotiation of it, the seller's bank may be prepared to advance the seller against the price immediately by taking from him the bill drawn on the buyer together with the documents relating to the goods. His bank will then obtain the buyer's acceptance of the bill against the release to him of the documents. Again, if the bill is dishonoured by non-acceptance or by non-payment, the seller will have to reimburse the bank to which he negotiated the bill. In contrast with these transactions, where bills of exchange are used in conjunction with documentary credits a bank which undertakes by the credit to pay on, or to negotiate, a bill drawn on the buyer will normally have no recourse against the seller if the bill is dishonoured by the buyer.[2]

1 That is the amount of the bill less interest and the bank's margin.
2 A bank which negotiates (ie buys) documents under a negotiation credit and which is not obliged by the credit to do so, has a right of recourse: see para 7.9 below.

1.6 *Further outline of documentary credits* (a) The party who arranges for the opening of a credit is referred to as 'the applicant'. Where the underlying transaction which gives rise to the need for the credit is one of sale, this will be the buyer. The bank which is requested by the applicant to open the credit is referred to as 'the issuing bank', and the party to whom the credit is addressed may be referred to as 'the beneficiary'. This will be the seller where the underlying transaction is one of sale. The simplest form of credit is where the issuing bank at the request of the applicant undertakes to make payment to the beneficiary provided that the terms and conditions of the credit are met. The proviso will usually mean first that the documents must comply with the provisions of the credit, and second that they must be presented in accordance with its provisions as to time and place. No other bank is involved.

1.7 (b) The more complicated but more usual form is where the issuing bank instructs another bank which will usually be in the country of the seller or beneficiary to advise the credit to the seller and to pay when documents are presented to it. This enables the beneficiary to deal with a bank in his own country. The bank which performs this advising function is sometimes referred to as 'the advising bank' and sometimes as 'the correspondent bank'. It is given the latter name because it will usually be the issuing bank's correspondent in the country in question.

1.8 (c) The mere fact that the advising bank advises the credit to the beneficiary does not give the beneficiary rights against it unless it adds its own undertaking to that of the issuing bank. It is most desirable for the beneficiary that it should do so because he then has an enforceable undertaking from a bank in his own country as well as from the issuing bank in the buyer's country. The form which the undertaking of the advising bank then takes is that it 'confirms' the undertaking of the issuing bank or, as it is usually and more shortly put, it 'confirms the credit'. It is then called a 'confirming bank'.

1.9 These relationships can be set out diagrammatically as follows:

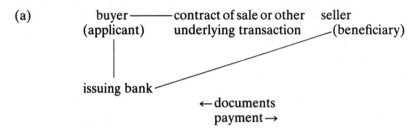

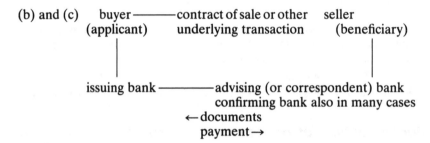

These are the basic forms which documentary credits take. The manner in which bills of exchange may be utilised in connection with them is considered as part of the discussion of the definition of documentary credits provided in the Uniform Customs.[1]

1 Para 1.37 below.

1.10 ***The setting up of a credit and its operation*** Behind every documentary credit there is an underlying transaction (or contract) which has earlier been entered into between the applicant for the credit and the beneficiary. As has been stated this is most commonly a contract of sale. One term of this underlying contract will be that the credit should be opened. It should specify the type of credit and so far as necessary its terms. It may identify the bank at which documents are to be presented. This contract is the origin of the credit, but it is separate from it and it does not form part of the credit. The credit will be operated in accordance with its own terms and without regard to the terms of the underlying contract or the performance of the underlying contract.[1]

1 This principle, called the 'autonomy of the credit' is enlarged upon in para 1.40 below.

1.11 The first stage in relation to the credit itself is the giving of instructions by the applicant (the seller) to a bank to open the credit in the particular manner which is required. The applicant will usually approach his own bank for this purpose.

1.12 The second stage will usually be the instruction by the issuing bank of a correspondent or advising bank in the beneficiary's country. But it is possible for this stage to be omitted.

1.13 The third stage is the advising of the credit to the beneficiary by the correspondent bank, or where there is no correspondent bank, by the issuing bank itself. As has been mentioned, where the correspondent bank has been so instructed by the issuing bank it will confirm the credit,[1] adding its undertaking to that of the issuing bank. This will be something that the seller/beneficiary is likely to have required when he made his contract with the buyer/applicant. The credit as advised to the beneficiary forms a contract between the issuing bank and the beneficiary, and also between the beneficiary and that correspondent bank if, but only if, the latter has added its confirmation and so become a 'confirming bank'.

1 Unless, having evaluated the credit risk, it declines to do so.

1.14 Next is the operation of the credit by the beneficiary. When the beneficiary has shipped the goods or done whatever else is necessary to bring into being or obtain the documents which are needed to operate the credit, he presents them to the bank to which presentation under the credit is to be made. This is usually the correspondent bank. If there is no correspondent bank and he has to present them to the issuing bank in the buyer's country, he is likely to use his own bank as agent for this purpose.[1] The bank to which documents are presented will check them to see that they comply with the credit and it will also check that presentation has been made as the credit requires. If all is in order, it will pay the beneficiary if that is what the credit provides for. Or it will conform with whatever other payment undertaking the credit provides. If the documents are not in order, it must refuse them. Before the refusal becomes final, at the seller's request it may take instructions from the issuing bank, or from the applicant direct if it is the issuing bank, to see whether the applicant is prepared to accept the documents even though the terms of the credit have not been met.[2] In practice, in very many cases the documents are found not to meet the terms of the credit, and it is common also for buyers to waive the discrepancies which have been notified to them because they want the goods.

1 The credit may permit presentation to banks other than the correspondent bank for negotiation, in which case it is called a 'negotiation credit'. Negotiation credits are described in Chapter 2, para 2.22 et seq.
2 The problems arising in connection with this under Article 14 of the Uniform Customs are considered in para 5.32 et seq.

1.15 If the credit provides for the documents to be presented to a correspondent bank, as is usually the case, and that bank has accepted the documents, it will then remit them to the issuing bank. It will then be the duty of the issuing bank in its turn to check that the documents conform to the credit. If it finds that they do so, it will reimburse the correspondent bank what it has paid to the beneficiary. If it considers that they do not do so it will send a notice of refusal to the correspondent bank and will return them to it unless the buyer is prepared to waive the discrepancies which have now been found.

1.16 The last step is for the issuing bank to present the documents to the applicant or buyer. This will be done against payment by the buyer to the bank or in accordance with whatever else may have been agreed between them. If the buyer finds that the banks have accepted documents which do not comply with the credit, he may reject them. When he has obtained the documents, the buyer may use them to obtain possession of the goods. The device of a trust receipt[1] can be used to enable the buyer to take possession of the documents and sell the goods, while retaining for the bank its security interest in the goods and in the proceeds of sale after they are sold.

1 See Chapter 11, para 11.11.

1.17 *A series of contractual relationships* The relationships established by the setting up of a letter of credit give rise to a number of contracts,[1] and the path down which the documents are passed can be seen as a chain of contracts. When the issuing bank agrees to act on the instructions of the applicant a contract comes into being between them involving rights and obligations on each side. When a correspondent bank agrees to act on the instructions of the issuing bank and to advise the credit and to take on whatever further roles the instructions require, a contract comes into being between the two banks with rights and obligations on each side. The advice of the credit to the beneficiary brings into being a contract between the issuing bank and the beneficiary. If the correspondent or advising bank confirms the credit, a contract also comes into being between this confirming bank and the beneficiary. But if the advising bank does not confirm the credit, no contract between it and the beneficiary is created: the beneficiary only has rights against the issuing bank. The majority of disputes which arise in connection with credits are concerned with whether the documents comply with the credit. More complex problems are often to be resolved by considering each contract in turn and spelling out the rights and obligations of the parties to it. Perhaps the most important aspect is the identification of the capacity in which a particular party is acting towards another. The source of the contract will almost always be documentary, and there will very often just be the one document to be examined, such as the applicant's completed form of application to the issuing bank, or the written instructions from the issuing bank to the confirming bank or the credit itself as between the issuing bank and the beneficiary, and as between a confirming bank and the beneficiary.

1 See also para 1.40 below.

1.18 *The construction of documentary credits and the relevance of banking practice* Under English law, where a contract is contained in a document and the meaning is clear, the basic rule is that no evidence in addition to the terms of the document, no extrinsic evidence, is admissible to modify the meaning of the words used. Extrinsic evidence is, however, always admissible to show that words have a particular meaning in their context, which differs from their ordinary meaning. Also, where the meaning is not clear, where there is ambiguity, evidence of the circumstances in which the contract was made is admissible to help to ascertain the meaning of the written words. As Lord Wilberforce stated in *Reardon Smith Line Ltd v Yngvar Hansen-Tangen*[1] 'No contracts are made in a vacuum: there is always a setting in which they have to be placed. The nature of what is legitimate to have regard to is usually described as "the surrounding circumstances" but this phrase is imprecise: it can be illustrated but hardly defined. In a commercial contract it is certainly right that the court should know the commercial purpose of the contract and this in turn presupposes knowledge of the genesis of the transaction, the background, the context, the market in which the parties are operating.' He went on to refer to the object of ascertaining the intention of the parties in an objective sense. He continued 'Similarly when one is speaking of aim, object or commercial purpose, one is speaking objectively of what reasonable persons would have in mind in the situation of the parties.'

1 [1976] 1 WLR 989 at 995.

1.19 In a commercial context the parties may be presumed to contract in accordance with any custom or usage of the particular trade. Evidence of custom in the trade is admissible to explain the terms used in the contract, and also to clarify ambiguities and to establish matters on which the contract is silent. In cases involving documentary credits it is common for the court to hear evidence from bankers of appropriate experience as to what customary banking practice is in the circumstances arising in the case.[1] The evidence on each side may not conflict, in which case it will be accepted by the court. Or the court may reject the evidence on one side. Or it may find that there is no established customary practice. This was the case in *Banque de l'Indochine et de Suez SA v JH Rayner (Mincing Lane)*[2] where Parker J stated 'It is clear from the evidence that no uniform banking practice exists either as to the form of the indemnity or guarantee which is used in the case of payment notwithstanding irregularities, nor as to the consequences of a payment being made under reserve.' In *Bank Negara Indonesia 1946 v Lariza (Singapore) Pte Ltd*[3] the Privy Council declined to determine whether an issuing bank was a bank to whom a request for the transfer of a transferable credit might be made under Article 46 of the 1974 Revision of the Uniform Customs, because there had been no expert evidence on relevant banking practice at the trial which could assist their Lordships.[4]

1 Compliance of documents with the terms of the credit is to be determined by 'international standard banking practice': Article 13.a of the Uniform Customs (considered further in paras 8.2 and 8.8 below).
2 [1983] QB 711.
3 [1988] AC 583.
4 See ibid at 598 H.

1.20 *The inclusion of bills of exchange* It is desirable to state at an early stage that the introduction of bills of exchange, or drafts as they are often called, into the arrangements constituting a documentary credit brings with it a separate group of rights and obligations arising on the bill itself between the parties to it, namely the drawer, the drawee/acceptor, the payee and any indorsers and indorsees. The terms of the credit which have been specified by the applicant pursuant to his agreement with the beneficiary will determine who are to be the parties to the bill and in what capacity. Thus the drawee/acceptor could be the issuing or the confirming bank, or the applicant,[1] or even a third party, as may have been specified and so has become a term of the credit. So the inclusion of a bill of exchange among the documents to be presented adds a complication which requires to be thought through: what is the function of the bill; what obligations are intended to and will result from it? It is suggested that bills of exchange should not be included among the documents required by a credit without reason. The question of recourse between parties to a bill is of particular importance. This is considered subsequently.[2] It can be stated at this point that issuing and confirming banks do not have a right of recourse against the drawer/beneficiary of the credit in the event of the bill's dishonour by non-acceptance or non-payment.

1 Now not permissible under the Uniform Customs: see Article 9 and para 5.17 below.
2 Para 5.68.

B. The Uniform Customs

1.21 *History*   The convenience if not the necessity of an international code governing the operation of documentary credits and providing uniformity is obvious given the internationality of credit transactions. By being incorporated into the contracts which come into being in connection with credits, a code can provide a uniformity in the rights and obligations to which those contracts give rise. It can encourage a uniformity of banking practice in relation to credits. It can reduce the differences which might otherwise emerge as a result of differences in national laws relating to credits. In 1933 the International Chamber of Commerce first published The Uniform Customs and Practice for Documentary Credits, often referred to in its various revisions as the UCP and referred to in this book as the Uniform Customs. This first code was only adopted by bankers in some European countries. A Revision was published in 1951, which met with greater success, including its adoption by banks in the United States. But it was only the 1962 Revision[1] that secured the approval of banks in the United Kingdom and most Commonwealth countries. This Revision made changes to matters which had previously been objectionable to British banks. The version came close to universal adoption. A third Revision, the 1974 Revision,[2] came into effect in 1975, and was more comprehensive than its predecessors. It was made necessary in particular by the spread of containerisation and the use of combined transport documents. The fourth Revision known as the 1983 Revision, came into effect on 1 October 1984.[3] The Introduction to the ICC's Case Studies on Documentary Credits[4] states that special note was taken for the 1983 Revision of:

'– the continuing revolution in transport technology, the geographical extension of containerisation and combined transport;
– the increasing influence of trade facilitation activities on development of new documents and new methods of producing documents;
– the communications revolution, replacing paper as a means of transmitting information (data) relating to a trading transaction by methods of automated or electronic data processing (ADP/EDP);
– the development of new types of documentary credits, such as the deferred payment credit and the standby credit;
– the increasing interest and influence in international trade of nations which are less developed and, therefore, less experienced in this area.'

The same factors lay behind the need for a further fifth Revision, the 1993 Revision,[5] which came into effect on 1st January 1994. In particular it was apparent that further attention was required to the matter of transport documents, the area where once the marine bill of lading once ruled uncontested. A further aim of the Revision was to simplify and to clarify. For it appeared that approximately 50% of sets of documents presented under credits were failing to meet the requirements of the credit upon first presentation. In short, as the Introduction to the 1993 Revision accepts, the 1983 Revision was failing to do its job. The Uniform Customs are accepted by banks in over 160 countries making their application to credits nearly universal. Unless it is stated otherwise all references in this book to the Uniform Customs are to the 1993 Revision.

1 ICC Brochure No 222.
2 ICC Publication No 290.
3 ICC Publication No 400.
4 ICC Publication No 459.
5 ICC Publication No 500.

1.22 *The nature of the Uniform Customs*   The Uniform Customs consist of 49 Articles which set out provisions which are intended to regulate many aspects of documentary credit operations. They are promulgated by the ICC and are made effective by their incorporation into credits[1] by the banks of countries whose banking associations have accepted them. They are not intended to be a code having the force of law. For the ICC cannot, and does not purport to, legislate. In this respect they are quite different in nature to the many international conventions, such as those on carriage, which have the force of law in the countries parties to them. In contrast the Uniform Customs must rely upon contract, that is, agreement, for their binding effect in each credit contract where they are incorporated. Their contractual nature is fundamental to their understanding. Secondly, although their coverage is growing more comprehensive with each Revision, the Uniform Customs do not purport to cover all questions which may arise in connection with credits. The title gives an indication of their nature, 'Uniform Customs and Practice'. They do not purport to be a code setting out the law relating to and governing credits in the way, for example, that the English Sale of Goods Act 1893 and its successor of 1979 intended to codify and also in some respects to change the English common law relating to sale of goods. Of course the Uniform Customs do have to deal with matters which are treated in an English court as matters of law, such as the legal rights and obligations to which credits may give rise. Thus in particular the Uniform Customs set out in Article 9 the undertakings which are given by issuing and by confirming banks. They are not, however, set out in legal language. Other rights and obligations which may arise in connection with credits are not referred to. Nor are the capacities in which banks act fully considered. Neither are the legal consequences. There is therefore a considerable area which is left to the national courts of whatever country is called upon to decide a dispute. Naturally the framers do take account of legal decisions. There may be one particular reason, in addition to others, why the Uniform Customs are not comprehensive, nor intended to be. It is that it is felt that some matters are best left to national courts. An example of this is the effect of fraud or forgery which is touched on by Article 15 but not directly dealt with.[2] Other matters may appear more mysterious. Thus the Uniform Customs do not deal fully with the important question of recourse.

1.23 ***The ICC Banking Commission and ICC Publications*** The Commission's full name is the ICC Commission on Banking Technique and Practice. It draws its members from countries where the ICC is represented by a National Committee. It meets twice a year, usually in Paris, 'to hear and decide on matters of banking technique and practice including UCP interpretation problems and questions'.[1] As a result of the considerations of the Committee five booklets are available containing their decisions or opinions on questions concerning the Uniform Customs:

> *Decisions (1975–1979) of the ICC Banking Commission*
> ICC Publication No 371
> *Opinions (1980–1981) of the ICC Banking Commission*
> ICC Publication No 399
> *Opinions of the ICC Banking Commission 1984–1986*
> ICC Publication No 434
> *Opinions of the ICC Banking Commission 1987–1988*
> ICC Publication No 469
> *Opinions of the ICC Banking Commission 1989–1991*
> ICC Publication No 494

These do not of course have the force of law, but they represent the views of considerable experts, and it is suggested that they should be given substantial weight by a court in accordance with the merits of the particular decision. They are often explanatory of the thinking behind the Uniform Customs, and they illustrate banking practice. Two further booklets, *Case Studies on Documentary Credits*, ICC Publication No 459, and *More Case Studies on Documentary Credits*, ICC Publication No 489 set out the answers to particular queries of a committee of experts to whom the Commission has delegated the task of dealing with questions and problems for the guidance of banks and commercial parties. 292 individual queries are considered, each allocated to an Article of the Uniform Customs. These too should be given weight by a court in accordance with their merits. It is interesting, but perhaps not surprising, that of 292 queries relating to the Uniform Customs and considered by the experts between October 1984 when the 1984 Revision came into force and December 1990 41% related to the documents to be presented, in particular to transport documents. This emphasises both the importance of transport documents and the difficulties caused by a period of change after one in which the marine bill of lading was almost the only transport document. None of these decisions or opinions are given or intended to be used as legal opinions, but are intended as interpretations of the Uniform Customs by non-legal experts according to banking practice. The ICC also publishes a comparison of the 1983 and 1993 Revisions of the Uniform Customs[2] which identifies and explains the changes which were made and contains important material. Lastly, there is a Guide to Documentary Credit Operations.[3]

1.24 *ICC Standard Forms* Since at least 1970 the ICC has published standard forms for use in connection with documentary credits (but not standby credits). The current forms make changes required by the 1993 Revision and are published with guide notes and recommendations.[1] The layout of the forms uses as its basis the United Nations layout key, which gives similarity to and alignment with a large number of other forms and documents whose use in international trade has been increasing over the years.

1 Standard Documentary Credit Forms, ICC Publication No 516.

1.25 *The application of the Uniform Customs: the need for incorporation* The Uniform Customs are intended to apply to all documentary credits, including, to the extent that they are applicable, standby credits. Article 1 of the Uniform Customs provides:

> ARTICLE 1[1] **Application of UCP**
> The Uniform Customs and Practice for Documentary Credits, 1993 Revision, ICC Publication No 500, shall apply to all Documentary Credits (including to the extent to which they may be applicable, Standby Letter(s) of Credit) where they are incorporated into the text of the Credit. They are binding on all parties thereto, unless otherwise expressly stipulated in the Credit.

Article 1 can only be self-effecting in a country where it is provided by the law of the country that the Uniform Customs shall apply to any credit to which the Uniform Customs intended that they shall apply. This is not the case in at least the great majority of countries, and it is not the case in the United Kingdom or in Commonwealth countries. Parties are free to adopt the Uniform Customs or to ignore them as they wish. Adherence to the Uniform Customs is effected by banks undertaking to the ICC, probably by a national banking organisation, that they will do so, meaning that they will incorporate the Uniform Customs in all credits which they issue.[2]

1 Article 1 is based on Article 1 in the 1983 Revision.
2 An example of the ICC's policing of the adherence is given in the Opinions of the ICC Banking Commission 1987–1988, Reference 147 – ICC Publication No 469. The ICC Spanish National Committee formed the view as a result of a court decision that Spanish banks were not bound by the Uniform Customs, and reported their concern to the Banking Commission. Correspondence between the Commission and the Consejo Superior Bancario Espanol elucidated that all credits issued by Spanish banks showed that they were subject to the Uniform Customs, and that the decision in the particular case arose on its special facts.

1.26 The means by which the Uniform Customs are made applicable to credits is by an express term in the credit that it is issued subject to the terms of the Customs. This is recognised and provided for in Article 1 by the words 'where they are incorporated into the text of the credit'. An attempt might be made to secure their application by means of a statement issued by an individual bank, or by an association of banks, in a country, that all credits issued by the bank, or by members of the association, were issued subject to the Uniform Customs. There must be serious doubts whether such a notice would be treated as effective, particularly in an international situation, and where it is so very straightforward for a bank's standard form document to carry the wording provided by Article 1 or an equivalent wording. An argument could be put forward for their application on the facts of a particular case if the parties had previously dealt on the basis of the Uniform Customs and it appeared that the absence of an express incorporation in the particular instance was through inadvertence. The inference in such a case would probably be that the parties intended that the current Revision should apply to the credit even where their previous dealings had been on the basis of an earlier Revision. Because the Uniform Customs are so universally incorporated, it is likely that even in a case where it cannot be established that they apply, if a point arises which is covered by the Uniform Customs, the solution provided by the Customs will be adopted as representing modern banking practice in relation to the principles underlying credits and as to documentary requirements. That would not be so where the terms of the credit in question were actually found to be to contrary effect, nor perhaps where a bank sought to rely on an exclusion of liability in the Uniform Customs.[1]

1 Cf *Attock Cement Co Ltd v Romanian Bank for Foreign Trade* [1989] 1 WLR 1147 at 1159B.

1.27 *Interpretation*   Given the manner in which the Uniform Customs have come into being, it is suggested that the sometimes narrow approach of English law to questions of construction, particularly statutory construction, should not be followed, at least in its full rigour.[1] A more purposive rather than literal interpretation or construction should be applied, namely that which will in the particular case give effect to the specific and general intentions of the Uniform Customs. This is in keeping with the likely approach of the civil-law countries of the Continent. In practice considerable attention is likely to be paid to the effect accorded to a particular provision in the Uniform Customs by established banking practice.[2]

1 Support for a practical, commercial, commonsense approach is to be found in the speech of Lord Diplock in *The Antaios* [1985] AC 191 at 200. But the most recent case in which the Court of Appeal was required to construe the detail of a provision of the Uniform Customs may tend to a literal approach: see *Bankers Trust Co v State Bank of India* [1991] 2 Lloyd's Rep 443.
2 See para 1.19 above.

1.28 *Relationships to which applicable*   Article 1 of the Uniform Customs provides that they 'are binding on all parties thereto', meaning all parties to credits. A credit is in turn defined by Article 2 in terms of an 'arrangement' whereby the issuing bank does certain things.[1] It is not defined in terms of a contract, and the choice of 'arrangement' indicates a wider and looser concept. Who are the parties to the arrangement constituting the credit? Clearly the issuing bank, any confirming bank and the beneficiary to whom the credit is addressed are included. For these are parties to the contract or contracts which constitute the credit. But what of an advising bank which does not confirm the credit; is it intended to be included as a party? It is suggested that the answer is that it is. Certainly as the credit is governed by the Uniform Customs, in carrying out its duties it is bound to take account of them. So while in one sense an advising bank which does not confirm the credit is not a party to it, its relations with the issuing bank are in every practical sense subject to the provisions of the Uniform Customs and it may be treated as falling within Article 1. This is surely the intention. A second difficulty may arise in respect of relations between the applicant and the issuing bank. If the credit is the arrangement instigated by the issuing bank the applicant is not a party to it. On the other hand the Uniform Customs contain important provisions which are intended to apply to the applicant, such as Articles 8, 9, 10, 11 and 12 among others. This confirms that 'credit' in Article 1 is to be read in a wide sense. The applicant is intended to be one of those referred to. The Uniform Customs are thus applicable to a number of relationships or contracts. But they will not apply to the underlying contract between the applicant and the beneficiary, which gives rise to the credit, such as that between a buyer and seller. The application of the Uniform Customs would be wholly inappropriate. But the Uniform Customs may nonetheless be relevant in determining particular obligations of the buyer regarding the opening of the credit.

1 See para 1.32 below.

1.29 ***The Uniform Customs and earlier court decisions*** The first Revision to be accepted by the United Kingdom banks, and therefore incorporated by wording on the credits which they issued, was the 1962 Revision. The subsequent revisions have made substantial changes. In cases decided by an English court prior to 1962 the court will not have been concerned with the Uniform Customs. What is the weight of such decisions today, when the Uniform Customs will invariably be applicable? The answer is that many of them remain good law, and the same result will often be reached today applying the Uniform Customs. This is because in many areas there is little conflict between the law and practice developed in relation to credits in the English cases and the Uniform Customs. The approach must now be to examine the Uniform Customs to see whether they provide an answer to the point at issue. If they do, that today is the answer which must be given by the court. An early case on the point may help to show the principle, and it may illustrate how it is to be applied. But the case cannot be applied to achieve a result which would be contrary to the relevant provisions of the Uniform Customs. Of course, if the Uniform Customs are silent on a point, then nothing stands in the way of applying a pre-1962 decision which covers it.

1.30 ***Conflicts between the terms of the credit and the Uniform Customs*** This is a subject of growing importance. For the Uniform Customs are now intended to determine some aspects of the rights and obligations under a credit regardless of what the parties have set out in the credit. This is intended to be subject only to the exclusion by the credit of the relevant provision in the Uniform Customs. One example is the problem of non-documentary conditions.[1] The Uniform Customs provide that they shall be ignored.[2] This could work to defeat the intention of the parties on a point important to them. Prima facie the parties to the various contracts arising in connection with a credit are free to make the arrangements which they desire, and to include such specific terms as they think appropriate. Article 1 ends 'unless otherwise expressly stipulated in the credit'. This recognises that the parties may expressly exclude some provisions of the Uniform Customs while incorporating the remainder. What is meant by an express provision is a provision expressly stating that, for example, a particular Article is not to apply.[3] In such situations no difficulty will arise, and this is the way in which a potential conflict should be avoided. A difficulty does arise where there is an apparent conflict between a provision of the Uniform Customs (which has not been expressly excluded) and a term of the credit. An English court will try first to find a resolution which gives effect to both without doing too much violence to the language of either. An example of this process is given by the *Forestal Mimosa* case.[3] Conflict may often be avoided by the words which occur in many Articles of the Uniform Customs, 'unless otherwise stipulated in the credit'.

1 See para 8.15 below.
2 Article 13.c.
3 *Forestal Mimosa Ltd v Oriental Credit Ltd* [1986] 1 WLR 631 at 639C.

1.31 If the conflict cannot be resolved, the general position in English law is that, where an express term of a contract conflicts with a provision of incorporated standard terms, the express term should normally be given effect on the ground that it is a term to which the parties have given their particular attention and so it should override a term which is incorporated only by reference and so is unlikely to have been considered by them.[1] Should a situation arise in which an English court does have to choose between giving effect to a provision of the Uniform Customs or to another term of the credit which is in express contradiction of it, the situation is one of real difficulty for the court. For the evidence of banking practice is likely to support the Uniform Customs provision, while sound and established principles of construction lead the court the other way. In *Royal Bank of Scotland plc v Cassa di Risparmio delle Provincie Lombarde*[2] Mustill LJ stated:

> 'Nevertheless, whilst not belittling the utility of the UCP, it must be recognized that their terms do not constitute a statutory code. As their title makes clear they contain a formulation of customs and practices, which the parties to a letter of credit transaction can incorporate into their contracts by reference. This being so, it seems to me that the obvious place to start, when searching for a contractual term material to a particular obligation, is the express agreement between the parties. If it is found that the parties have explicitly agreed such a term, then the search need go no further, since any contrary provision in UCP must yield to the parties' expressed intention. If on the other hand the agreement is silent in the material respect, then recourse must be had to UCP, and if a relevant term is found there, that term will govern the case.'

It is suggested that the *Royal Bank of Scotland* case did not present a conflict of the stark nature under consideration here, and so did not in fact give rise to the dilemma.

1 See, generally, *Chitty on Contracts* (26th Edn) General Principles, paras 826 and 833, and specifically the quotation following in the paragraph.
2 [1992] 1 Bank L R 251 at 256.

1.32 *The definition of documentary and standby credits in the Uniform Customs* A definition is provided by Article 2. Whereas Article 1 refers to 'all Documentary Credits, including . . . Standby Letter(s) of Credit', Article 2 appears to separate the two. Nonetheless it is clear that a standby credit is a form of documentary credit. Perhaps the problem is that there is no term which refers only to credits which perform the function which has already been described of securing payment in relation to an underlying contract, usually one of sale, rather than the different function which is performed by standby credits.[1] Although Articles 1 and 2 refer to 'documentary credits' rather than to 'documentary letters of credit', they both refer to 'standby letters of credit'. It is suggested that there is no significance in this.[2] Article 2 provides:

ARTICLE 2[3] **Meaning of Credit**

For the purposes of these Articles, the expressions 'Documentary Credit(s)' and 'Standby Letter(s) of Credit' (hereinafter referred to as 'Credit(s)') mean any arrangement, however named or described, whereby a bank (the 'Issuing Bank'), acting at the request and on the instructions of a customer (the 'Applicant') or on its own behalf.

i.   is to make a payment to or to the order of a third party (the 'Beneficiary'), or is to accept and pay bills of exchange (Draft(s)) drawn by the Beneficiary,
    or
ii. authorises another bank to effect such payment, or to accept and pay such bills of exchange (Draft(s)),
    or
iii. authorises another bank to negotiate,

against stipulated document(s), provided that the terms and conditions of the Credit are complied with.

For the purposes of these Articles, branches of a bank in different countries are considered another bank.

1 The function of standby credits is described in Chapter 12. In essence they provide for payment on receipt of documents evidencing default under the underlying contract. Sometimes the term 'commercial credit' is used to contrast with standby credits.
2 The notes on the Articles on pages 10, 11 and 12 of ICC Publication No 411 refer to 'standby credits' and it is suggested that this is the more usual name. It is curious that while the term 'letter of credit' may be falling into disuse, it is here retained in connection with the more modern standby credits.
3 Article 2 is based on Article 2 in the 1983 Revision.

1.33 The following elements may be extracted from this definition:

– an applicant (a customer of a bank) instructs the bank to make an arrangement;
– by the arrangement the bank is either to make a payment to the beneficiary of the arrangement, or to accept and pay drafts drawn by him, or the bank authorises a second bank to do these things, or it may authorise a second bank to negotiate (ie buy the documents);
– the payment or acceptance is to be against (that is, on the bank receiving) stipulated documents;
– the payment or acceptance will only be forthcoming if the terms and conditions of the credit are complied with.

It is to be remarked that the Article makes no reference to the existence of any underlying transaction between the applicant for the credit and the beneficiary, which is usually an essential pre-condition for the coming into being of a credit.[1] Nor is there any reference to the function of the payment to be made through the credit. These are essential to the understanding of the transaction though not to its definition.

1 Indeed the Article foresees that the issuing bank may 'act on its own behalf' rather than on instructions. This does not of course suggest that ordinarily an issuing bank acts on behalf of its customer, at least in the legal sense of an agent: it does so as a principal, although on instructions.

The ways in which credits may be operated considered in conjunction with the Uniform Customs definition

1.34 The simplest form has already been considered[1] and is that where the issuing bank at the request of its customer, the applicant, undertakes to pay to the beneficiary, or to his order, against documents. This is the arrangement foreseen by the first half of Article 2.i.

1 Para 1.6.

1.35 The more complicated but more usual form is where the issuing bank utilises the services of an advising bank or correspondent bank both to advise and to pay against conforming documents. This too has already been considered.[1] It is the arrangement primarily foreseen by the first half of Article 2.ii. It may be noted that the definition does not incorporate the concept of confirmation of the credit by the advising bank.

1 Para 1.7.

1.36 In each of these situations the issuing bank may promise to pay immediately following the examination of the documents, or at a deferred date, such as 90 days after date of shipment or two months after date of presentation of documents.

1.37 Article 2 allows for use of bills of exchange (drafts).[1] The arrangement may be that the issuing bank is to accept and pay drafts, or to authorise another bank to accept and pay or negotiate drafts. The drafts are always to be drawn by the beneficiary. The draft may:

– be drawn on one of the banks. In that case, if it is a sight bill, ie payable immediately on presentation, that bank will pay it if the documents are in order. Or, if it is a time or term draft, sometimes called a usuance draft, ie a draft payable at a future date such as three months after sight or 30 days after shipment, subject to the documents being in order the bank will accept it and pay it when it becomes due.
– be drawn on another bank or another party.[2] The credit may require that the banks negotiate such a bill, that is to say that they pay against it immediately[3] rather than waiting for it to become due following acceptance (but the applicant/buyer does not have to pay them until the draft is due). Or the credit may simply require that they pay when the bill becomes due if the drawee does not. This is not fully provided for by Article 2, but is spelt out in Article 9 which sets out the various undertakings which may be given by issuing and confirming banks.[4]

1 Draft is the word used in the ICC's Standard Forms.
2 Drafts are sometimes drawn on the applicant. This is 'prohibited' by the Uniform Customs: see the discussion of Article 9 in para 5.17 below. It is difficult to see what function such a draft performs save that acceptance of it will confirm the applicant's acceptance of the documents.
3 The beneficiary will receive payment of the amount of the bill discounted to reflect interest between the date of negotiation and the date that the bill becomes due. The beneficiary therefore pays for the financing of the transaction. In some cases the credit will provide for the beneficiary to receive the full amount of the bill. Then interest will be charged to the applicant for the credit, who is then the party paying for the financing the transaction.
4 Article 9 is considered in Chapter 5, para 5.13 et seq.

1.38 ***Arrangements falling outside the Uniform Customs definition***   The effect of Articles 1 and 2 of the Uniform Customs is that the Customs apply to credits as defined in Article 2. So it can at least be argued that, even though a document containing a payment undertaking states that it is subject to the Uniform Customs, it is not so subject because the Articles of the Uniform Customs only apply to credits as defined by Article 2 and the document falls outside that definition. A way in which the point could quite easily arise is if a credit was issued by a finance house which did not have, or arguably did not have, the status of 'bank'. 'Bank' is not defined by the Uniform Customs, and it is probably right that it is not. For the concept of a bank is not easy to define and it varies from one municipal law to another. It is suggested that if a finance house issues a letter of credit which states that it is subject to the Uniform Customs, the Customs should be applied to it regardless of whether the finance house is properly to be described as a bank. This would give effect to the intention of the credit.[1] The solution should be the same in any other situations in which the 'credit' states that it is subject to the Uniform Customs but falls outside the definitions provided by Article 2.

1 This approach follows the approach of the US Court of Appeals in *Barclays Bank DCO v Mercantile National Bank* [1973] 2 Lloyd's Rep 541 at 544.5 and 481 F 2d 1224. For an inconclusive discussion of the problem arising where a credit is issued by either a non-financial institution or a financial institution which may not strictly be a bank, see Ref 177, Opinions of the ICC Banking Commission, Publication No 494.

1.39   Chapter 12 considers standby credits and demand guarantees and bonds, and the application of the Uniform Customs to them is there also considered. It should, however, be pointed out at this point that the 1974 Revisions of the Uniform Customs contained no reference to standby credits. The express inclusion in the 1983 Revision apparently came about as a result of a reference to the ICC Banking Commission on which the Commission expressed the view that a standby credit fell within the definition of a credit provided in the 1973 Revision.[1] It was common for banks to incorporate the Uniform Customs into standby credits prior to this.

1 See Decisions (1975–1979) of the ICC Banking Commission, ICC Publication No 371, at R1, and ICC Publication No 411, page 10.

C.   The Autonomy of Documentary Credits[1]

1.40   In the context of documentary credits autonomy[2] is used to refer to the principle that the credit is to be treated as an independent transaction. In particular it is independent of the terms of the underlying transaction giving rise to it, and its performance is independent of the performance of that transaction. In *United City Merchants (Investments) Ltd v Royal Bank of Canada*[3] Lord Diplock stated[4] in relation to a confirmed credit 'It is trite law that there are four[5] autonomous though interconnected contractual relationships involved.' The principle is fundamental to credit transactions, and it is essential to the continuance of the documentary credit system as the primary means of payment in international trade that it should be scrupulously observed. The principle follows from what is sometimes stated as a second principle, that a documentary credit is a transaction in documents and in documents alone. It is suggested that, although the two principles can be separately stated, they are in reality so closely connected that they cannot be treated independently. Because credits are transactions in documents, if the documents are right, the bank must honour its payment obligations under the credit. This and the fact that the beneficiary of a credit has the promise of a bank give a documentary credit its special value. Transactions which would otherwise be unlikely to take place because the parties cannot trust one another are thereby made possible.

1 See also Chapter 8, para 8.11.
2 'Autonomous' is used in its sense of 'self-governing' or 'independent'.
3 [1983] 1 AC 168.
4 Ibid at 182.
5 There are in fact five where the credit is confirmed: Lord Diplock omitted the contract between the issuing bank and the beneficiary: thus—
    (i)   buyer/seller (applicant/beneficiary) – the underlying contract;
    (ii)   buyer (applicant)/issuing bank;
    (iii) issuing bank/confirming bank;
    (iv)   issuing bank/beneficiary;
    (v)   confirming bank/beneficiary.

1.41 The immediate and most important consequence of the principle is that the performance of the contract between the applicant and the beneficiary which underlies the credit, is irrelevant to the performance of the credit. It is irrelevant that it may be alleged that the goods are not of the standard required by the contract. The one exception is where there is fraud on the part of the beneficiary. That exception and the principle itself are examined more fully with citation of authority in Chapter 9.[1]

1 The autonomy principle is referred to in particular in paras 9.3 and 9.29.

1.42 The principle of autonomy is stated in Article 3 of the Uniform Customs. Article 4 provides that the parties to credits deal in documents alone. Article 15 makes clear that in credit operations banks have no responsibility for anything other than the conformity of the documents to the credit by listing, in a somewhat ragbag manner, some of the many things that can go wrong even though the documents are in order, and by absolving banks from responsibility for them. The Articles provide:

ARTICLE 3[1]   **Credits v Contracts**
            (a) Credits, by their nature, are separate transactions from the sales or other contract(s) on which they may be based and banks are in no way concerned with or bound by such contract(s), even if any reference whatsoever to such contract(s) is included in the Credit. Consequently, the undertaking of a bank to pay, accept and pay Draft(s) or negotiate and/or to fulfil any other obligation under the Credit, is not subject to claims or defences by the Applicant resulting from his relationships with the Issuing Bank or the Beneficiary.
            (b) A Beneficiary can in no case avail himself of the contractual relationships existing between the banks or between the Applicant and the Issuing Bank.
ARTICLE 4[2]   **Documents v Goods/Services/Performances**
            In Credit operations all parties concerned deal with documents, and not with goods, services and/or other performances to which the documents may relate.

ARTICLE 15[3]   **Disclaimer on Effectiveness of Documents**

Banks assume no liability or responsibility for the form, sufficiency, accuracy, genuineness, falsification or legal effect of any document(s), or for the general and/or particular conditions stipulated in the document(s) or superimposed thereon; nor do they assume any liability or responsibility for the description, quantity, weight, quality, condition, packing, delivery, value or existence of the goods represented by any document(s), or for the good faith or acts and/or omissions, solvency, performance or standing of the consignors, the carriers, the forwarders, the consignees or the insurers of the goods, or any other person whomsoever.

1 Article 3 derives from Articles 3 and 6 in the 1983 Revision.
2 Article 4 follows Article 4 in the 1983 Revision.
3 Article 15 follows Article 17 in the 1983 Revision.

Chapter 2

Types or Categorisations of
Documentary Credits

2.1 *Introduction* The rights and obligations created by a credit are to be found from its terms, and whether they are or are not typical of a particular type of credit must be treated with caution as a guide to their understanding. For a label may be helpful or it may be misleading if the credit is typical in some respects but not in others. Where, however, a categorisation is established by the Uniform Customs it is important because the rules applying to the category provided by the Customs will apply. This is of particular importance with the two primary categorisations of credits, namely into revocable and irrevocable credits, and into confirmed and unconfirmed credits. The discussion which follows is also a means of further introducing the differing obligations which may be undertaken in connection with credits.

A. Revocable and Irrevocable Credits

2.2 A revocable credit is one which may be cancelled or amended by the bank undertaking to pay without the beneficiary's consent. An irrevocable credit can be cancelled or amended only with the consent of the applicant, the issuing bank and the beneficiary. Article 6 of the Uniform Customs provides:

ARTICLE 6[1] **Revocable v Irrevocable Credits**
    a. A Credit may be either
      i. revocable,
        or
      ii. irrevocable.
    b. The Credit, therefore, should clearly indicate whether it is revocable or irrevocable.
    c. In the absence of such indication the Credit shall be deemed to be irrevocable.

1 Revocable credits were covered by Article 7 in the 1983 Revision.

2.3 Given the unsatisfactory nature of a revocable credit,[1] it is right that Article 6.c should provide that in the absence of indication a credit is deemed to be irrevocable. Previously, the position had been the other way.[2] Article 6.c is consistent with the view that it is suggested an English court would take, that an irrevocable credit must be provided where the underlying contract simply provides for payment by letter of credit. This is on the ground that a revocable credit provides no security.[3] In *International Banking Corpn v Barclays Bank Ltd*[4] Atkin LJ stated in respect of the admittedly unusual credit which he was considering 'And the other matter which I think quite plainly emerges is that a credit so announced is irrevocable unless it appears on the face of it that it is revocable.'[5]

1 See paras 2.8 and 2.9 below.
2 See the criticism of Article 7.c of the 1983 Revision in the first edition, para 2.3.
3 See paras 2.8, 2.9 and 3.8 below.
4 (1925) 5 Legal Decisions Affecting Bankers 1.
5 Ibid at 5.

2.4 What is the position where the credit does not use the words 'revocable' or 'irrevocable' but contains an undertaking such as 'We hereby engage that payment will be duly made against documents presented in conformity with the terms of this credit'? Article 6.c will now provide that it is to be treated as an irrevocable undertaking. But even without the Article it is suggested that it should be treated as irrevocable. For it appears in a commercial document and it will quite properly be understood by its recipient as giving him an irrevocable undertaking. This view appears to be accepted by Gutteridge.[1]

1 See Gutteridge & Megrah *The Law of Bankers' Commercial Credits* (7th edn) pp 21, 22.

2.5 Although revocable credits and their advantages for buyers featured prominently in the ICC's Guide to Documentary Credit Operations,[1] the ICC's Standard Forms[2] and The Guidance Notes included with them make no reference to revocable credits and therefore assume that the applicant requires an irrevocable credit to be opened.

1 ICC Publication No 415, page 10.
2 ICC Publication No 516.

2.6 ***Revocable credits*** Article 8 of the Uniform Customs relates to revocable credits and is as follows:

ARTICLE 8[1] **Revocation of a Credit**
    a. A revocable Credit may be amended or cancelled by the Issuing Bank at any moment and without prior notice to the Beneficiary.
    b. However, the Issuing Bank must:
        i. reimburse another bank with which a revocable Credit has been made available for sight payment, acceptance or negotiation – for any payment, acceptance or negotiation made by such bank – prior to receipt by it of notice of amendment or cancellation, against documents which appear on their face to be in compliance with the terms and conditions of the Credit;

      ii. reimburse another bank with which a revocable Credit has been made available for deferred payment, if such a bank has, prior to receipt by it of notice of amendment or cancellation, taken up documents which appear on their face to be in compliance with the terms and conditions of the Credit.

1 Article 8 is taken from Article 9 in the 1983 Revision.

2.7 Although Article 8 may at first sight suggest that a bank can never come under an obligation to a beneficiary in respect of a revocable credit, it is clear that where the credit provides for payment by means of a time draft or for deferred payment in the sense explained in paragraph 2.19 below and the beneficiary has presented documents which are accepted by the bank, an obligation will come into being. For Article 8.b assumes that the bank for whose reimbursement it is providing has become obliged to the beneficiary. In any event it would be wholly unacceptable for a bank to be able to reject its payment obligation to the beneficiary after it had accepted the documents and the beneficiary had lost control of them.

2.8 Apart from this very limited protection a revocable credit provides no undertaking by the issuing bank to the beneficiary at all. For even if the correct documents are presented and the bank has not until then decided to revoke the credit, it may do so and reject the documents.[1] It might for instance do that if it thought that the financial circumstances of its customer, the applicant, had deteriorated since the credit was opened. For this reason a confirmed revocable credit would ordinarily be a contradiction in terms, there being no effective undertaking to confirm. A confirmation would mean something, however, where the credit provided for payment to be deferred: then the confirming bank would add its undertaking to that of the issuing bank which becomes irrevocable after documents have been accepted, that payment will be made in due course.

1 This is confirmed in the commentary on the Article in the ICC's Documentary Credits: UCP 500 and 400 Compared; Publication No 511.

2.9 The serious disadvantage of revocable credits is shown by *Cape Asbestos Co Ltd v Lloyds Bank Ltd*.[1] There the plaintiffs agreed to sell 30 tons of asbestos to buyers in Warsaw, who opened a revocable credit through Lloyds Bank in London. Lloyds informed the plaintiffs 'This is merely an advice of the opening of the above-mentioned credit, and is not a confirmation of the same.' The first shipment of 17 tons was duly paid for through the credit. The plaintiffs then shipped the remaining 13 tons. Meanwhile, unknown to them Lloyds had been informed of the cancellation of the credit. The documents were presented to Lloyds in London and refused. The action was brought against them on the basis that it was their duty to give reasonable notice of the withdrawal of the credit. The evidence established that it was usual for the defendants to give notice of the withdrawal of credits, but here they had omitted to do so. The court held that there was no legal obligation on the bank to give notice. So the credit turned out to be a delusory security, and, as the plaintiffs were unable to recover from their buyers, they went unpaid. The position where an unnotified amendment took place, for example one involving the adding of a document to those to be presented to get payment, would be no less galling.

1 [1921] WN 274.

2.10 *Irrevocable credits* Almost all credits issued today are irrevocable, and it is only they which will provide the security which the seller has no doubt sought in specifying that payment shall be by letter of credit. Where a contract specifies payment by letter of credit, an irrevocable credit is required.[1] When a bank issues an irrevocable credit the bank gives its undertaking that the beneficiary will receive payment as the credit may provide. The forms that the undertaking may take are set out in Article 9.a of the Uniform Customs. In summary, the issuing bank undertakes to pay where the credit provides for sight payment or deferred payment; it undertakes to accept drafts drawn on it, or to be responsible for their acceptance and payment at maturity if they are to be drawn on another bank;[2] where the credit provides for negotiation, it undertakes to pay against appropriate drafts without recourse to drawers or bona fide holders, or to provide for negotiation by another bank and to pay if negotiation is not effected. Article 9.b sets out the equivalent undertakings which are given by a confirming bank. These undertakings are further considered in Chapter 5.[3] They are at the heart of a documentary credit, and they make the instrument the secure means of payment which it is intended to provide. Article 9.d sets out that the undertakings cannot be amended or cancelled without the agreement of the issuing bank, any confirming bank, and the beneficiary. Obviously the agreement of the applicant (who has ultimately to fund the operation) is also needed. The amendment of a credit is considered in detail in Chapter 3.[4]

1 See Chapter 3, para 3.8.
2 The Uniform Customs prohibit drafts drawn on the applicant; see Articles 9.a.iv and 9.b.iv and para 5.17 below.
3 Para 5.12 et seq.
4 Para 3.33 et seq.

2.11 It may be questioned at what point the relevant undertaking becomes binding on the issuing and confirming banks. Clearly the credit must be communicated to the beneficiary, and it is suggested that it becomes binding at that moment. This is consistent with Article 9.a which implicitly suggests that the undertakings which it sets out become binding when they are given. This must surely be the intention of the parties. It is also confirmed by Article 9.d.ii which provides that an issuing bank is bound by an amendment from the moment of its issue. There can be no distinction in this respect between the issue of a credit and the issue of an amendment. The alternative is that the credit becomes binding when the seller has acted on it by doing something towards the performance of his contract – which might be the making of an arrangement to ship the goods, or commencing to manufacture or continuing to manufacture them. This was the suggestion of Rowlatt J in *Urquhart, Lindsay & Co Ltd v Eastern Bank Ltd.*[1] But in *Dexters Ltd v Schenker & Co*[2] Greer J pointed out[3] that on receipt of the credit the seller becomes bound to proceed with the contract (for the provision of the credit is normally a condition precedent to the seller's obligation to ship), and he appeared to consider a bank bound from that moment. These cases are considered further in connection with the consideration for the bank's undertaking.[4]

1 [1922] 1 KB 318 at 321,2.
2 (1923) 14 Ll L Rep 586.
3 Ibid at 588.
4 See paras 5.3, 5.6 et seq below.

2.12 Where a contract of sale calls for an irrevocable credit to be opened in London, a credit which is advised through a London bank which does not confirm it, does not meet the contract as the London bank gives no undertaking: *Enrico Furst & Co v WE Fischer Ltd*.[1]

1 [1960] 2 Lloyd's Rep 340.

2.13 *Irrevocable credits with partial responsibility* Credits are sometimes issued as irrevocable credits in respect of the full invoice value of the goods to be sold, which contain a statement that the issuing bank will be responsible for part of the payment only. In one example 40% of the invoice price was to be paid against presentation of documents, the remainder by means of a 90-day draft drawn on the applicant for the credit. The credit stated the deferred part was without responsibility or engagement on the part of the bank. It also appears that it was a growing practice for credits payable in Egypt, although expressed to cover the full invoice price, to provide that 10% only should be paid by the bank against documents, the remainder to be settled directly between the applicant and the beneficiary's agent in Cairo without responsibility on the part of the bank. Clearly the limitation imposed by the bank on its undertaking is effective: there are no grounds for suggesting that the bank should nonetheless bear responsibility for the full amount. It may be thought undesirable because it is in effect an invitation to the buyer to argue with the seller over that part of the price not secured by the credit and to obtain a discount whether or not the seller has in actuality correctly performed his side of the contract. The Board of Directors of the Banks' Association of Egypt has disapproved the practice.[1]

1 See Case Studies on Documentary Credits, ICC Publication No 459, Case 12, and Opinions of the ICC Banking Commission 1987–88, ICC Publication No 469, Ref 148.

B. Confirmed and Unconfirmed Credits

2.14 The use of these terms assumes the existence of an advising bank (also called the correspondent bank), and the distinction depends upon the position taken by that bank. In short, with a confirmed credit the advising bank adds its undertaking to that of the issuing bank that payment (if that is what the credit provides for) will be made. If the credit is unconfirmed, it does not: the sole undertaking is that of the issuing bank.

2.15 *Unconfirmed credits* Where the credit is unconfirmed the advising bank acts solely as the agent of the issuing bank. It will be instructed by the issuing bank to notify the credit to the seller. The credit is likely to provide for the documents to be presented to the advising or correspondent bank, and it will receive them as agent for the issuing bank. If it is to pay, it will pay simply as the agent of the issuing bank and not because of any obligation existing between it and the seller. The position of the advising bank as agent is considered in greater detail subsequently.[1] The important feature where the credit is unconfirmed is that, if the documents are wrongfully refused by the bank to whom they are presented, the seller has normally a remedy only against the issuing bank, which is usually abroad, and so proceedings may be more difficult than if he had an undertaking from a bank in his own country.

1 Para 6.4.

2.16 *Confirmed credits* Where a credit is confirmed, the advising or correspondent bank adds its own undertaking to that of the issuing bank to pay, or to accept or negotiate bills as the case may be. This then gives the beneficiary the advantage of having a paymaster in his own country. The credit will also be an irrevocable credit (see above),[1] so the beneficiary will have the full benefits which the developed form of documentary credits can provide. Article 9.b of the Uniform Customs sets out the undertaking of a confirming bank in the same terms as Article 9.a sets out the undertaking of the issuing bank in relation to an irrevocable credit, with appropriate changes. Thus the confirming bank undertakes as appropriate to pay at sight or on a deferred date, to accept bills drawn on itself, and to be responsible for the acceptance of bills drawn on other drawees, and to negotiate without recourse bills drawn by the beneficiary on any drawee apart from itself. Where an advising bank purports to confirm a credit but reserves for itself a right of recourse against the seller, the two are inconsistent and the advising bank is not giving an absolute undertaking. The credit is not to be treated as a confirmed credit: see *Wahbe Tamari & Sons Ltd v Colprogeca*.[2] The position of the confirming banker is further discussed in Chapters 5 and 6.[3] *Silent confirmations* and *confirmations on request* are considered in paragraphs 6.14 and 6.15 in Chapter 6.

1 Para 2.8.
2 [1969] 2 Lloyd's Rep 18.
3 See Chapter 5 generally and Chapter 6, para 6.13.

C. Categorisation of Credit by Payment Obligation

2.17 Article 10.a of the Uniform Customs provides:

> ARTICLE 10.a All Credits must clearly indicate whether they are available by sight payment, by deferred payment, by acceptance or by negotiation.

This provides an important and convenient means of categorising credits in accordance with the type of payment obligation which is undertaken by the obligated banks. Although it does not expressly say so, Article 10.a covers two situations, namely where the credit does not include a bill of exchange or draft among the documents to be presented, and where it does.

2.18 *Where no bill of exchange: sight credits and deferred payment credits* Where the credit does not include a bill of exchange (or draft) among the documents to be presented, it may provide for payment on presentation of documents – after allowing time, of course, for them to be examined for compliance with the credit. Then it can be called a *sight credit*. Or the credit may provide for payment to be made at the conclusion of a period measured from the presentation of documents or, for example, from the date of the transport document. Then the credit is called a *deferred payment credit*.

2.19 The introduction to ICC Publication No 411 refers to 'the development of new types of documentary credits, such as the deferred payment credit and the standby credit'. It may be thought that any credit which does not provide for payment against presentation of documents to the issuing or advising bank provides for deferred payment and so is entitled to that name. In the past deferred payment has commonly been provided for by the use of a time draft, on the maturity of which payment is due. More recently the practice has developed of dispensing with a draft and having the credit provide that payment under it shall be due after the required period from, for example, the date of presentation of documents to the advising bank, or from the date of the transport document, as the credit may provide. It is this streamlined form of the transaction that is commonly called a deferred payment credit. The main change which was made from the 1974 Revision of the Uniform Customs to accommodate deferred payment credits was the addition of what are now Articles 9.a.ii and 9.b.ii. Articles 10.a and 14.a also refer to deferred payments, and Article 8.b.ii provides for the reimbursement of a bank which has incurred a deferred payment obligation under a revocable credit. Where payment is deferred, the beneficiary has the security of the bank's undertaking; but if the applicant is in the meantime to receive and to be able to deal with the goods, the bank will have to release the documents to him. The loss of security for the bank which would otherwise occur can be avoided by the use of a trust receipt as described in Chapter 11.[1]

1 Para 11.11.

2.20 ***With bills of exchange: credits available by acceptance or negotiation*** If the bill or draft is a sight bill, that is one payable at sight, it must be presented to the party on whom it is drawn for payment to be triggered. This will normally be the bank to which documents are to be presented under the credit and which is to make payment. Then the beneficiary will receive payment on presentation of documents following their examination. But if the bill is a sight bill drawn on the issuing bank or another bank, then, unless the credit otherwise provides, the strict position is that payment is only due on presentation of the bill to the party on whom it is drawn. The issuing bank and any confirming bank are of course obliged to ensure payment, whether or not payment is forthcoming from the party on whom the bill is drawn. If the bill is what may be called a time draft or a usuance draft and provides for payment after a period from acceptance of the bill, then, again unless the credit otherwise provides, payment will only be forthcoming when that time comes. Where payment is only forthcoming under the credit when the bill is due at the end of a period after acceptance, the credit may be called an *acceptance credit*.

2.21 The credit may provide that payment is to be forthcoming immediately by providing that payment is available *by negotiation*. Article 10.b.ii provides:

ARTICLE 10.b.ii Negotiation means the giving of value for Draft(s) and/or document(s) by the bank authorised to negotiate. Mere examination of the documents without giving of value does not constitute a negotiation.

The term 'negotiation' is sometimes used where a bank accepts and pays against documents where the credit provides for immediate payment in the full amount. This is a misuse. Negotiation is better used only when the paying bank pays less than the full amount by reason of a time element. Thus, if a credit calls for a bill drawn on the issuing bank payable 30 days after acceptance and provides that the credit is available by negotiation at the correspondent bank, the correspondent bank will take off from the sum due under the credit interest to reflect the number of days between payment and payment under the bill. It is preferable to call a credit of this nature 'available by negotiation' and to keep the term 'negotiation credit' for credits which invite any bank, or any description of bank, to negotiate documents under them as is considered next.

D. Straight and Negotiation Credits

2.22 A straight credit is one under which the undertaking of the issuing bank, or, if it is a confirmed credit, the undertakings of the issuing and confirming banks, are directed to the named beneficiary alone, and only he may rely on them. With a negotiation credit the undertakings are directed to any bank, or to any bank of a description stated in the credit, which becomes a bona fide holder of any bill of exchange and the other documents which are stipulated by the credit. The purpose of making a credit a negotiation credit is that it enables a bank to negotiate (or buy) the documents from the beneficiary and then to present them under the credit and to receive payment in due course. In this way the beneficiary gets his money immediately from the negotiating bank, and the negotiating bank has the undertakings given by the credit available to it, and will present the documents under the credit as the party entitled in due course to payment. It can, if need be, sue in its own name. It is apparent that there will only be need for this where the credit does not provide for immediate payment: if it does, the beneficiary may just as well present the documents to the paying bank himself either directly or using his own bank as his agent for collection.

2.23 The practice of making credits negotiable by other banks in this way is recognised by Article 10.b of the Uniform Customs:

ARTICLE 10.b.i Unless the Credit stipulates that it is available only with the Issuing Bank, all Credits must nominate the bank (the 'Nominated Bank') which is authorised to pay, to incur a deferred payment undertaking, to accept Draft(s) or to negotiate. In a freely negotiable Credit, any bank is a Nominated Bank. Presentation of documents must be made to the Issuing Bank or the Confirming Bank, if any, or any other Nominated Bank.

2.24 Negotiation by a bank which is not the issuing or advising bank and which does so under a negotiation credit as has been described may be distinguished from negotiation by a bank which does so as the issuing or advising bank under a credit which provides for payment to be available from it 'by negotiation'.[1]

1 See para 2.21 above.

2.25 What is necessary to make a credit a negotiation credit so that the promise held out by it may be accepted by any bank of appropriate description, which negotiates documents complying with the credit? This is a matter of construing the words of the credit, and if the credit is carefully worded there will be no problem. If it does not appear that the undertaking embodied in the credit is to be construed more widely, the credit must be given effect to as a straight credit. The answer may be provided as a matter of necessary implication as it was in the old case of *Re Agra and Masterman's Bank, ex p Asiatic Banking Corpn.*[1] There was there an undertaking to honour drafts drawn on the bank, together with this statement 'This credit will remain in force for twelve months and parties negotiating bills under it are requested to indorse particulars on the back hereof.' It was held that this anticipated the negotiation of bills by other parties, and hence that there was an undertaking to them. The credit was not a documentary credit, but was simply a facility to obtain funds by drawing bills. But the logic of the construction was in no way dependent on that, and would apply equally to a documentary credit. In *Sassoon & Sons Ltd v International Banking Corpn*[2] a similar argument was presented based on a wording which was less clear. The Board merely noted the argument observing 'and it is a very summary way of converting the terms of a discount offer by one bank into an undertaking applicable to actual discounts by any other bank . . .'. The ground of decision in the case, however, was that the seller had discounted the draft to the plaintiff not on terms that it was a negotiation pursuant to the credit, but on terms that the plaintiff should present the bill and documents to the buyer and so obtain payment. The buyer accepted the bill but later dishonoured it by non-payment, and the plaintiff was held to be entitled to recover from the seller as the drawer of a dishonoured bill.

1 (1867) 2 Ch App 391.
2 [1927] AC 711, PC.

2.26 Suppose that a credit simply states 'negotiation is permitted', and an undertaking is given 'We undertake to honour all drafts drawn under and in conformity with the terms of this credit': would such wording make the credit generally negotiable? There is no authority on such a wording in English law. A meaning has to be found for the words 'negotiation is permitted'. Their placing and context within the credit will be relevant. It may simply mean negotiation by a bank named in the credit. But if that does not appear possible, then probably the credit should be construed as permitting negotiation by any party.[1,2] What is the position where the credit does not nominate a bank authorised to accept, pay or negotiate nor allow negotiation by any bank? It is suggested in the ICC's More Case Studies on Documentary Credits[3] that it is a normal practice in this event to deem the credit freely negotiable. It is then stated 'However this is not without risk'. It is suggested that it would indeed be a risky assumption to make. For such a credit contains nothing in its wording to suggest that it is freely negotiable and the sounder assumption must be that it is available only with the issuing bank. Article 10.b.i begins 'Unless the credit stipulates that it is available only with the Issuing Bank, all Credits must nominate the bank (the 'Nominated Bank') which . . .'. It does not follow that, if the credit does not so stipulate and if there is no nomination, the credit is freely available.

1 A different position is taken in *Benjamin's Sale of Goods* (4th edn) para 23–027. While it is accepted that without words that are sufficient to indicate that the credit should be generally negotiable, it must be construed as a straight credit, it is suggested that, contrary to *Benjamin*, if clear words are not used, it is a question of construing the words in accordance with the practice of international banking, and that there is and should be today no tendency in the courts in favour of straight credits in cases of uncertainty.
2. See also *Udharam Rapchand (Sons) HK Ltd v Mercantile Bank Ltd* [1985] HKLY 52.
3. Case 191, Publication No 489.

2.27 *European Asian Bank AG v Punjab and Sind Bank (No 2)*[1] demonstrates the difficulties which may arise as well as the principles to be applied in resolving them, and is worth some detailed consideration. The Singaporean sellers, Bentrex, sold cloves to the Indian buyers, Jain, c. and f. Bombay. At Jain's request the Punjab Bank in New Delhi opened a letter of credit through their correspondents in Singapore, the Allgemene Bank, which was advised to Bentrex through the European Asian Bank. The credit was available by Bentrex's drafts at 180 days after bill of lading date. Clause 6 provided 'Letter of credit should be advised through European Asian Bank . . . and should be divisionable and unrestricted for negotiation.' Clause 9 provided 'We hereby engage with drawers, endorsers and bona fide holders of drafts drawn under and in compliance with the terms of this credit that such drafts will be honoured on presentation and delivery of documents as specified above. Negotiations under this credit are restricted [to Allgemene Bank, Singapore].' Reimbursement was to be effected from the Irving Trust, New York. Bentrex presented to the European Asian Bank documents and a draft drawn on Jain made payable to the order of the European Asian Bank. The bank sent the documents directly to the Punjab Bank in India, where the draft was accepted by Jain. Jain were then informed that the vessel and cargo had been lost, and claimed on their insurers who repudiated liability: there had been a fraud, and no goods had been shipped at all. Meanwhile Bentrex had been paid by the European Asian Bank who were therefore out of pocket. The Irving Trust were not put in funds. Both the Punjab Bank and the Allgemene Bank (who had confirmed the credit) refused to pay the European Asian Bank. The main points decided by the Court of Appeal were these. It was held first that the European Asian Bank had negotiated the documents[2] and draft and were seeking payment on their own behalf: they were not acting as agents of Bentrex and so were unaffected by the fraud of Bentrex. Second, the apparent contradiction between clause 6 and clause 9 was to be resolved as follows. In clause 6 'divisionable' was an error for 'divisible' and the clause meant that the credit was transferable in whole or in part (clause 7 permitted part shipments). 'Unrestricted for negotiation' meant that documents could be presented under the credit by any transferee of the credit. Clause 9 meant that whoever presented the documents (Bentrex or their transferee) could only do so through the Allgemene Bank who would then negotiate the documents as the only authorised negotiator. It was therefore not a negotiation credit, and under the terms of the credit the European Asian Bank had no rights against the Punjab Bank. By reason, however, of the communications between the two banks at the time of the delivery of the documents to the Punjab Bank and Jain's acceptance of the bill, the Punjab Bank was estopped from denying that they were responsible for ensuring payment to the European Asian Bank at maturity. So they had to pay.[3]

1 [1983] 1 WLR 642, [1983] 1 Lloyd's Rep 611.
2 That is, the bank had bought the documents.
3 This may be compared with the view expressed by the ICC Banking Commission, Opinions 1984–86, Ref 95 that documents may be presented direct to an issuing bank which must accept them and pay even though it has specified another bank as the negotiating bank in the credit advised to the beneficiary. It is suggested that, if a bank specifies negotiation through a particular bank as a term of the credit, it is surely entitled to insist on such negotiation (unless the bank specified has refused negotiation) and to reject documents presented to it direct.

2.28 As the *Sassoon* and *European Bank* cases[1] demonstrate, in order to claim under a negotiation credit, the holder of the documents must have acquired them by a negotiation pursuant to the credit and not by other means. The wording of the credit is in any event likely so to provide.

1 Supra, paras 2.24 and 2.26.

2.29 Other aspects relating to the position of a negotiating bank are considered subsequently in Chapter 7, Part B, and the questions of recourse are referred to in paras 5.69, 6.28, 7.7 and 7.9 according to context.

E. Transferable and Non-transferable Credits

2.30 Where a credit is designated as transferable, the beneficiary has the right to request the appropriate bank to make the credit available in whole or in part to one or more other parties, and perhaps at some other place. It is important to emphasise at the start that the right is only a right to request, and the bank is not obliged to accede to the request if it does not wish to. The credit must be expressly designated as transferable. The object of transfer is to enable the beneficiary nominated in the credit to use the credit to provide a means of payment to a party, or to the parties, from whom he in his turn is buying the goods. He may have contracted to provide a credit. He can then satisfy his obligation by the transfer of so much of the credit opened in his favour as is required to pay his seller. He must, however, ensure that the terms of the contract which he has made with the party from whom he is buying will be met by the transfer of the credit which he has contracted for with his buyer. He must ensure that the documents which he is entitled to from the party from whom he is buying will meet the terms of the contract with his buyer. Where the credit which the beneficiary receives is not designated as transferable, or if the bank does not accede to the request for transfer, the seller has the alternative of arranging a back-to-back credit. Article 48 of the Uniform Customs governs transferable credits, and the transfer of credits is fully discussed in Chapter 10.

F. Back-to-back Credits and Counter Credits

2.31 A credit may be described as back-to-back when it is intended that the documents which are received through the operation of it may be presented, with substitution of invoices (and possibly other documents), to obtain payment under another credit. Thus a seller of goods, the beneficiary of a credit opened in his favour by his buyer, may approach the bank which has advised the credit to him and request it to open a second credit in favour of his own suppliers, on the security of the first credit. This is likely to be possible only if he already banks with that bank. Alternatively he may approach his own bank and request them to do so using the credit already opened in his favour as a 'counter'. In the latter case the second credit may be called a counter credit. In each case the credit which the buyer has secured in favour of his own suppliers is a separate credit for which he is in the position of applicant. When conforming documents are presented, he will have to reimburse the bank and take up the documents regardless of the position between him and his buyer and under the credit of which he is beneficiary. In contrast, if he is able to arrange for transfer, he will avoid this area of risk. Back-to-back credits also carry a risk for banks for a similar reason: the bank which is in the middle of the chain has an obligation to pay the beneficiary of the credit which it has opened regardless of whether its customer is able to obtain payment under the backing credit. For this reason banks may prefer to use a transferable credit. It is essential that the documents required under the backing credit will be provided by the second credit. This may be difficult or even impossible where the basis of sale is different, for example, where the bank's customer is buying FOB but selling C and F or CIF and a long voyage is involved. Here the second credit is likely to need to be in place before the backing credit is available. There is also room for differences of interpretation where the backing credit and the second credit are payable by different banks, which may create a further difficulty.

2.32 In *Ian Stach Ltd v Baker Bosley Ltd*[1] Devlin J described the manner in which transferable credits and back-to-back credits may be used to provide payment in a string of contracts:

> 'Where, as in the present case, there is a string of merchants' contracts between the manufacturer or stockist and the ultimate user, the normal mechanism for carrying out the various contracts is the familiar one which was intended to be used in this case: the ultimate user, under the terms of his contract of sale, opens a transferable, divisible credit in favour of his seller for his purchase price: his seller in turn transfers so much of the credit as corresponds to his own purchase price to his seller or, more probably, if his own contract with another merchant also calls for a transferable, divisible credit, procures his own banker to issue a back-to-back credit – that is to say, he lodges the credit in his favour with his own banker, who in his turn issues a transferable, divisible credit for the amount of his purchase price to his own seller; and so on, through the string of merchants, until the banker of the last merchant in the string issues the credit in favour of the actual manufacturer or stockist. The reason why they issue fresh credits is that in banking practice a transferable credit is regarded as transferable once only, and, also as is obvious in this sort of trade, it is desired, naturally enough, by any merchant in the string to conceal from his buyer and his seller who his own customer is. That is the way, as both parties to the present transactions knew, in which this type of business is normally carried on.'[2]

1 [1958] 2 QB 130.
2 Ibid at 138.

2.33 It has been suggested[1] that if a credit is not transferable it may be wrong for the advising bank to open a back-to-back credit at the seller's request upon the strength of it. Two reasons are suggested. The first is that the opening of a back-to-back credit is equivalent to transfer, and that as the first credit is non-transferable transfer is prohibited. It may be thought more precise to say that transfer is not permitted: it may not be permitted simply because, for reasons of his own, the seller did not contract for a transferable credit. Secondly, it is said that the buyer wants the seller's own goods and not those of a third party; so the bank should not facilitate supply from another source. But often the seller is not a producer of goods, and some goods, such as commodities, may be expected by their nature to be purchased by the seller for the purpose of the contract to which the credit relates. If the buyer requires the seller's own goods, he should ensure that the contract between them reflects this: he may also be able to provide that the documents to be presented under the credit also confirm it, which will give some further protection. It is concluded that the practice whereby correspondent banks open back-to-back credits is perfectly acceptable in law and in practice.

1 See *Benjamin's Sale of Goods* (4th edn) para 23–044.

2.34 The difficulties which may befall banks which find themselves in what may be called a quasi back-to-back situation, in particular where the object of the transaction is to trade goods between countries which forbid trade with each other, are well illustrated by the case of *Mannesman Handel AG v Kaunlaren Shipping Corpn*.[1] In this action before the London Commercial Court it was held that in the special circumstances of the case it would be contrary to the principle of good faith in Swiss law for a bank which had received the assigned proceeds of a backing credit to refuse to pay out on documents presented to it under the credit which it had itself opened although there were discrepancies.

1 [1993] 1 Lloyd's Rep 89.

G.   Revolving Credits

2.35 A revolving credit is one in which the credit limit, that is, the invoice value of the goods in respect of which documents can be presented under it, is not limited to a fixed overall amount. It is one where the maximum value is restored in a manner provided by the credit. Thus it may be provided that the limit is restored each time a shipment is made: so, if the limit is £100,000 and a shipment of £95,000 is made, the limit is immediately restored to £100,000, but no shipment may exceed £100,000. Alternatively the limit may be restored after an appropriate period of time: so there could be a limit of £100,000 per month, which would limit the goods to be shipped to that figure in any month. Such a revolving credit may be arranged on a cumulative basis, meaning that any sum not utilised during one month is carried forward and may be utilised subsequently. This is to be contrasted with a non-cumulative instalment credit containing no such provision, which requires a specific shipment each month. Then Article 41 of the Uniform Customs will apply to provide that if any instalment is not drawn in the period allowed for, the credit ceases to be available for that and any subsequent instalments (unless otherwise provided by the credit). As the term 'revolving credit' may mean such different things and as the operation of such a credit can be complicated, it is particularly important that the buyer and seller should spell out in the underlying contract precisely what they intend, and that this should be fully and accurately set out in the credit itself.

H. 'Red Clause' and 'Green Clause' Credits (sometimes called anticipatory credits)

2.36 Red clause credits contain a clause traditionally printed in red enabling the seller to draw on the credit in advance of the shipment of the goods. It may be used to finance the seller's own purchase or production of the goods. The buyer may obtain security if the advance is only to be made against documents such as a warehouseman's receipt (though the seller must retain his ability to deal with the goods for the purpose of shipment, which may also enable him to deal with them in other less desirable ways). The inclusion of a red clause represents a considerable display of trust by the buyer in his seller. As to the type of documents which at one time a seller might be required to deposit with the paying bank, see *South African Reserve Bank v Samuel & Co*.[1] The red clause was developed in the Australian, New Zealand and South African wool trades. One modern use, and of green clause[2] credits, has been in the Zaire coffee trade.

1 (1931) 40 Ll L Rep 291.
2 See para 2.38.

2.37 A modern example of a red clause credit is given by *Tukan Timber Ltd v Barclays Bank plc*.[1] Tukan were importers of timber from Brazil and in order to finance the trade they opened a letter of credit in favour of their suppliers which appears to have been a form of revolving credit: it was referred to as an 'umbrella credit'. It contained a 'red clause' which enabled the suppliers to draw on the credit simply by presenting receipts countersigned by one or other of two directors of Tukan. Each advance was to state what lot it referred to and the amount was to be deducted from the payment to be made when the lot was shipped and documents presented in respect of it. When a dispute developed between Tukan and their suppliers, the suppliers sought to take advantage of the red clause by presenting receipts which bore the forged signature of a director. The bank did not pay, but Tukan brought proceedings to secure their own position by an injunction. The claim failed on the ground that Tukan had not established that there was a sufficient risk of yet further fraudulent claims being made.

1 [1987] 1 Lloyd's Rep 171.

2.38 A refinement of the red clause is the 'green clause'. This allows pre-shipment advances but provides for storage in the name of the bank, thus hopefully providing the bank with security.

I. Standby Credits[1]

2.39 Documentary credits may be divided under two heads according to function. The first head covers the traditional function of credits, as has already been described, namely to provide payment to the seller of goods or less commonly to the seller of services when he performs his contract by delivering documents to the bank.[2] Standby credits most commonly fulfil the function of providing security against the non-performance of a party to a contract, who may sometimes be a seller, and sometimes may have a different capacity. Standby credits provide for payment to the beneficiary by a bank against delivery of documents to the bank. But it follows from their function that the documents required will be very different from those under a traditional credit: they may comprise only a statement in a specified form that the other party to the underlying contract has failed to fulfil his obligations.

1 Standby credits are considered in Part B of Chapter 12.
2 Sometimes called commercial credits in contrast with standby credits.

Chapter 3

Buyer and Seller
(Applicant and Beneficiary)

A.   The Obligation to Open a Documentary Credit

3.1 *The origin of the obligation* A documentary credit comes into being, or is opened, in nearly every case because of the existence of an underlying contract which provides that it should be opened. The most common such contract is one of sale. Hence the title of this chapter, which deals with the relations of the applicant of the credit and its beneficiary. The obligations of the buyer and seller in relation to the credit arise from this underlying contract, and what their obligations are is primarily a matter of construing that contract.

3.2 *The provisions of the underlying contract*   The underlying contract should spell out with sufficient particularity what the credit should be. It should state the type of credit, in particular whether it should be revocable or irrevocable, confirmed or unconfirmed, whether it is to be transferable. The amount and currency will normally follow automatically from the price provisions of the sale contract, but if they do not this must be specified. The description of the goods, quantity and unit price, if there is one, will also be found elsewhere in the sale contract. It is advisable to provide where the credit is to be opened or where advised and confirmed (if to be confirmed). It should provide when it is to be opened and the period for which it is to be available. The documents against which the credit is to be payable should be listed. In a formal contract, whose terms have been fully considered, these and other matters can all be spelt out leaving no room for uncertainty as to the credit that is required. But this is seldom the case. Very often the term as to payment is very brief. It may be no more than 'Payment: by confirmed letter of credit'. What then is the seller's obligation as to the credit which he opens?

3.3 *The credit to be opened*   Where the terms of the credit to be opened are not spelt out in the underlying contract, or are not fully spelt out, the choice is either to find them by other means or to hold that the contract is void for uncertainty. Some can be filled in from other provisions in the contract of sale. Custom of the trade, the past dealings of the parties and reasonableness may also be relied upon. It may be that the buyer will send to the seller a pre-advice of the credit which he proposes to open: if the seller agrees to the terms, they will become the terms to be complied with. Or the buyer may go ahead and open the credit in terms which seem to him appropriate. The seller then has the opportunity to object to them if he thinks he has grounds for doing so. But, if he does not, depending upon his conduct, he may be held to have accepted the terms of the credit so that its terms have become the terms to be provided pursuant to the underlying contract. Or he may be held to have waived his right to object. These processes are illustrated by two cases.

3.4   In *Soproma SpA v Marine and Animal By-Products Corpn*[1] the contract of sale provided 'Payment: Against letter of credit, confirmed irrevocable, with Marine and Midland Trust Co, New York.' The credit which was opened was not confirmed, and it did not cover the whole of the shipment period provided by the contract of sale. The former was a contravention of an express term of the payment clause. The latter can be described as in breach of a term to be implied that the credit should cover the whole of the shipment period permitted by the contract. It was also alleged that the credit was defective in that it called for documents which were not specified in the contract of sale. In respect of this last contention McNair J stated '. . . I should not feel disposed to accept this conclusion.

It seems to me to be a necessary implication from the use of the words "payment against letters of credit" that the credit itself should set out in detail the specific conditions under which it can be operated including the period of its availability and that so long as these conditions are fair and reasonable and are not inconsistent with the terms of the contract itself no objection can be taken to them by the sellers.'[2] But the sellers had not objected to the credit as opened, and were held to have waived their right to do so.

1 [1966] 1 Lloyd's Rep 367.
2 Ibid at 386.1.

3.5 In *Ficom SA v Sociedad Cadex Ltda*[1] the underlying contract was for the sale of coffee beans. Again the payment provision was shortly stated 'Payment: by immediate irrevocable letter of credit to be opened in favour of sellers with the Banco Mercantil, La Paz, Bolivia . . .'. The credit which was opened required a quality certificate in a particular form. No objection to the credit was taken by the sellers but they did object to one of three amendments proposed to it. The judge (Robert Goff J) held that there was a binding agreement between the parties as to the form of the credit and that as the sellers were unable to present documents which met its terms they were at fault. In reaching his conclusion he examined the ways in which the correct terms of a credit might become established:

'I approach the matter in this way. It is plain on the authorities that parties to a contract of sale, under which payment is to be made by means of a letter of credit, can, by subsequently agreeing to terms of the letter of credit which differ from those specified in the sale contract, thereby vary their contractual obligation under the sale contract: see *W J Alan & Co Ltd v El Nasr Export and Import Co* [1972] 2 QB 189, [1972] 1 Lloyd's Rep 313. A somewhat similar case may arise where the parties do not, in their sale contract, define the terms of the proposed letter of credit. Where that occurs the letter of credit, as subsequently agreed between the parties, may fill the contractual gap and so supplement the terms of the sale contract;[2] if that is not done, for example, where the parties are unable to agree on the terms of a letter of credit to be issued under a contract of sale, then the dispute may have to be resolved by defining where possible, by means of implication or by resort to any approved custom of the trade, the terms upon which the parties must be taken to have agreed that the letter of credit should in due course be issued.

Now, whether there has, in any particular case, been a binding agreement between the parties either to vary the terms of the original sale contract, or to supplement its express terms, is to be ascertained by asking the question whether the parties intended so to do – their intention to be ascertained objectively in the usual way from their words and actions at the relevant time. Furthermore, in considering whether there has, in any particular case, been any such binding agreement, it is important to bear in mind the possibility that there has been no more than a forbearance by one party, under which he forbears to enforce his strict legal rights under the sale contract, which will at most give rise to no more than an equitable estoppel, and may be capable of withdrawal by him upon giving reasonable notice to the other party.

In the present case, I am concerned with a contract of sale in which the terms of the letter of credit – and in particular of the documents to be presented under the letter of credit – were undefined in the sale contract. Now, in such a case, it is a commonplace that a letter of credit will be opened thereafter – sometimes preceded by a pre-advice by the buyer of the terms of the proposed credit followed by detailed negotiations of the terms so proposed – resulting in a letter of credit being issued in precise terms acceptable to both parties. Often the letter of credit so agreed will take the form which is usually employed in the particular trade. Now, although it is impossible to formulate any general rule, in such a case the terms of the letter of credit so agreed may well become binding contractually upon the parties. If so, and if they depart in any respect from the terms (express or implied) of the original sale contract, they will constitute a binding variation of that contract: if they simply fill a gap in the original sale contract, then they will operate to supplement that contract. It is of importance to the parties that the terms of the letter of credit, if so agreed by them, should become binding, because on that basis the buyer will enter into a binding arrangement with his own bank, which in turn will enter into a binding arrangement with the issuing bank instructed to issue the letter of credit to the seller, the terms of which will in their turn become binding as between the issuing bank and the seller. An example of a case in which such a binding variation of a sale contract was entered into is the case of *Alan v El Nasr*, to which I have previously referred; I refer in particular to the judgment of Lord Justice Megaw in that case at pp 327 and 217–218 of the respective reports.

Such a case may be contrasted with a case where the letter of credit established departs in some particular respect from the terms required by the sale contract, and the sellers forbear from insisting upon precise compliance with the terms of the sale contract in that particular respect. In such a case, particularly where the contract contemplates deliveries by instalments and therefore drawing on the letter of credit by instalments, such a forbearance may well give rise to no more than equitable estoppel, which the buyers may be able to resile from subsequently by giving reasonable notice to the sellers that they intend to resume their strict legal rights under the contract. Examples of cases of that kind are *Panoutsos v Raymond Hadley Corpn of New York* [1917] 2 KB 473, and *Enrico Furst & Co v W E Fischer Ltd* [1960] 2 Lloyd's Rep 340.

Now what happened in the present case? First of all, we have a sale contract which was silent on the terms upon which the letter of credit was to be opened. It is possible that this gap in the sale contract could, if necessary, have been filled, by implication, by reference to the custom of the trade – although I observe that in the award (in par 3(c) of the special case) the Committee of Appeal in this connection refer only to the "normal" custom of the trade. But, be that as it may, I am satisfied, on the special case and the documents exhibited to the case, that the parties by agreement filled the gap in the sale contract. This is not a case where, on the documents before me, there was a pre-advice of the letter of credit terms, followed by negotiation, leading up to an agreement on those terms; it appears that the buyers simply opened a letter of credit in certain terms. But it is plain that the sellers agreed to the letter of credit so opened as being acceptable to them. In reaching that conclusion, I do not rely simply upon the finding of fact in the award that there was no objection to these terms raised on behalf of the sellers. I rely also on the subsequent conduct of the parties, and in particular on the occasion when the buyers subsequently proposed an amendment to that letter of credit relating to the quality certificate, which was rejected by the seller "because it was not agreed initially".'[3]

1 [1980] 2 Lloyd's Rep 118.
2 This passage was cited and applied by Bingham J in *Shamsher Jute Mills Ltd v Sethia (London) Ltd* [1987] 1 Lloyd's Rep 388 at 392.
3 [1980] 2 Lloyd's Rep 118 at 131,2.

3.6 In response to an argument that the term in the credit as to the certificate involved an agreement which was unsupported by consideration Robert Goff J stated 'Where, as here, the sale contract is silent as to the terms of the letter of credit contemplated by the sale contract, the definition of those terms is a matter of mutal benefit and acceptance of the terms by each party is therefore supported by consideration moving from the other.'[1]

1 [1980] 2 Lloyd's Rep 118 at 132.

3.7 *Terms as to revocability and confirmation*   These are matters which should be, and usually are, covered by the underlying contract. If the credit should be confirmed, a revocable credit will not do.[1] Nor will an irrevocable but unconfirmed credit.[2] Where a credit is required to be confirmed and the advising banker purports to confirm it but at the same time reserves a right of recourse against the seller on his bills of exchange, this will not do: for the right of recourse is inconsistent with the conception of a confirmed credit.[3] Where the contract provides for the irrevocable credit to be opened in London, an irrevocable credit advised by a London bank which does not add its confirmation is not an irrevocable credit opened in London because the London bank can resile at any time.[4]

1 *Panoutsos v Raymond Hadley Corpn of New York* [1917] 2 KB 473.
2 *Soproma SpA v Marine and Animal By-Products Corpn* [1986] 1 Lloyd's Rep 367.
3 *Wahbe Tamari & Sons Ltd v Colprogeca* [1969] 2 Lloyd's Rep 18.
4 *Enrico Furst & Co v WE Fischer Ltd* [1960] 2 Lloyd's Rep 340.

3.8   The contract may be silent as to whether the credit is to be revocable or irrevocable, confirmed or unconfirmed. If there is a previous course of dealing between the parties, the court may resolve the question by reference to it. But what if there is not? Because a revocable credit offers no security and because it may be presumed to be the intention of the parties to provide the seller with security, there is a strong argument that the credit must be at least irrevocable. In *Giddens v Anglo African Produce*[1] the contract called for a credit to be established with the National Bank of South Africa. The credit opened by the bank provided for drafts to be negotiated with recourse. Bailhache J remarked 'How that can be called an established credit in any sense of the word absolutely passes my comprehension.' While this is strictly an authority on the meaning of established, it indicates a view of a revocable credit which is likely to be adopted by the court today.

1 (1923) 14 Ll L Rep 230.

3.9   Where the underlying contract does not state that the credit is to be a confirmed credit, prima facie the buyer will fulfil his obligation if he opens an irrevocable credit with his own bank as the issuing bank which is either advised direct to the seller by that bank or is advised to him through a correspondent bank in the seller's country. The seller might argue that he was entitled to a confirmed credit on the ground that, arguably, the preponderance of credits issued are now confirmed credits, reflecting the function of a credit as being not only to give the seller the security of a bank undertaking but the undertaking of a bank in his own country. As Denning LJ began his judgment in *Pavia & Co SpA v Thurmann-Nielsen*[1] 'The sale of goods across the world is now usually arranged by means of confirmed credits.' Such an argument does not appear to have been considered by an English court. It is suggested that it should fail. If the seller requires a confirmed credit, it is for him to say so and have the requirement included in the contract of sale. The seller might adopt a fall-back argument that he was at least entitled to have the credit advised to him by a bank in his own country to which the seller could present documents. He could rely on the fact that in the particular trade it is rare that a credit is advised direct to the seller by the issuing bank in another country. (In some trades, for example the oil trade, it is common.) It is therefore to be reasonably anticipated, he would argue, that in the ordinary course a credit in his trade will be advised through an appropriate correspondent bank. Such an argument may have a greater chance of success, but appears untried.

1 [1952] 2 QB 84.

3.10 *Documents to be required*   It is dangerous to generalise because any contract may have its own particularities. Obviously with a CIF contract the documents to be presented will include the bills of lading or other transport document, invoice and an insurance document. But what as to documents such as packing lists, certificates of origin, or inspection certificates? Here, in the absence of prior dealings between the parties, one may be thrown back upon what is reasonable as being usual in the trade. A packing list and a certificate of origin may seem innocuous enough – though in some circumstances the latter could cause difficulties. Though it will often work to the seller's advantage the requirement for a certificate of inspection by a specified agency would be more difficult unless it can be supported by prior dealings between the parties or is usual in the trade in question. An example of a document which clearly the buyer is not entitled to include among those to be presented under the credit in the absence of a contractual stipulation is a guarantee of the machine, the subject of the contract.[1]

1 See *Newman Industries Ltd v Indo-British Industries* [1956] 2 Lloyd's Rep 219.

3.11 *Correcting defects*   If the credit as opened does not comply with the contract the seller may be able to treat this as a breach entitling him to terminate even though the period for the opening of the credit has not expired, if it is reasonable to deduce that the buyer does not intend to remedy the defect. But, otherwise, if the buyer corrects a defect within the period, the seller must accept the credit. In *Kronman & Co v Steinberger*[1] the sellers tried to take advantage of an obvious mistake in the credit as initially opened which the buyers corrected, and to call the contract off. The court held them liable in damages.

1 (1922) 10 Ll L Rep 39.

3.12 *The possibility of no enforceable contract*   Where there is no agreement as to the terms of the credit to be opened, it may be held that the parties were never ad idem, and so there is no enforceable contract. This occurred in *Schijveshuurder v Canon (Export) Ltd*[1] where the parties were in disagreement whether a bill of lading was required to be among the documents to be presented, or whether a goods receipt would be sufficient. Obviously where the parties in their negotiations leading to the alleged contract are in actual disagreement over some feature and this has not been resolved, it is difficult for the court to find a concluded contract. But where the parties to a commercial transaction have intended to bind themselves, the court will be loathe to conclude that they have failed to do so, and will ordinarily find a contract and flesh it out by means of reasonable implication where it is necessary to do so. Thus in *Scammell and Nephew Ltd v Ouston*[2] Lord Maugham stated[3] 'In commercial documents connected with dealings in a trade with which the parties are perfectly familiar the court is very willing, if satisfied that the parties thought they had made a binding contract, to imply terms and in particular terms as to the method of carrying out the contract which it would be impossible to supply in other kinds of contract', citing *Hillas & Co Ltd v Arcos Ltd*.[4]

1 [1952] 2 Lloyd's Rep 196.
2 [1941] AC 251.
3 Ibid at 255.
4 (1932) 147 LT 503.

3.13 ***No legal duty to cooperate to finalise the terms of a credit*** It was argued in *Siporex Trade SA v Bank Indosuez*[1] that there is a duty resting on a seller to cooperate with the buyer and perhaps also with the bank in negotiating and finalising the terms of a credit. The case was mainly concerned with a performance bond which was payable if no credit was opened. It was held that the bank was bound to pay against an appropriately worded demand on the bond, and that the bank was not concerned with the underlying dispute between the buyers and sellers as to the credit. Hirst J, however, went on to consider the arguments which arose if he was wrong on that primary finding, and in doing so he considered and rejected the suggestion of a duty to cooperate. After referring to the *Ficom* case[2] he stated:[3]

> 'I shall deal with the buyer's position first. I do not for a moment doubt that in the world of everyday commerce such cooperation frequently occurs, nor do I doubt that it is highly desirable particularly where important matters are left outstanding. But proof of normality of practice, or even of a high degree of desirability, falls far short of establishing the existence of a contractual duty owed by the buyer to be implied as a contractual term. . . . In my judgment, under the normal well-established principles of letters of credit, it is for the buyer to establish the letter of credit as required by the contract. If the contract terms are themselves incomplete, and unresolvable by reference to custom, the supposed duty to cooperate would in effect be no more than an agreement to agree, which is not a workable contractual term. Moreover the scope of the proposed duty in any given case would be impossible to define with the degree of precision required for a workable term. . . . I am not prepared to hold that there is any legal duty imposed on the seller to cooperate with the buyer.'

1 [1986] 2 Lloyd's Rep 146.
2 Supra, para 3.5.
3 At [1986] 2 Lloyd's Rep 162.

B. The Time for the Credit to be Opened

(1) General

3.14 A credit must be opened in due time. That must include its communication to the beneficiary. It is not enough for the applicant to instruct a bank within the time. If the credit is to be confirmed, the confirmation must also be communicated in due time. So, in short, the beneficiary must have binding promises from the banks within the appropriate period.[1] The situations relating to that period can be categorised into three. There are those where the contract of sale makes an express provision as to the date by which the credit is to be opened. This may be done by naming a date or by providing a mechanism for it to be ascertained.[2] Secondly, the contract may have no such provision but it may be of a type, namely a CIF or FOB contract, or one of their variations, where the time can be stated in accordance with principles established in previous cases. These are considered in paragraphs 3.16 to 3.21 below. Lastly, one may be thrown back upon a test of reasonableness.

1 See *Bunge Corpn v Vegetable Vitamin Foods Private Ltd* [1985] 1 Lloyd's Rep 613 at 617.
2 For a particular point of construction of a term of a contract as to when a credit was required to be opened, held to be arguable by the Court of Appeal, see *Sohio Supply Co v Gatoil (USA) Inc* [1989] 1 Lloyd's Rep 588, and for a case where the term as to the time for opening the credit gave no difficulty, but which was dependent for its operation on a clause which gave rise to dispute, see *Transpetrol Ltd v Transol Olieprodukten Nederland BV* [1989] 1 Lloyd's Rep 309.

3.15 Where the contract provides for the credit to be opened immediately, 'that means that the buyer must have such time as is needed by a person of reasonable diligence to get that credit established'.[1] In *Etablissements Chainbaux SARL v Harbormaster Ltd*[2] Devlin J had to consider the nature of the obligation to provide a credit within a reasonable time.[3] He cited from Lord Watson's speech in *Hick v Raymond and Reid*[4] that, where the law implies that a contract should be performed within a reasonable time, it 'has invariably been held to mean that the party upon whom it is incumbent duly fulfils his obligation, notwithstanding protracted delay, so long as such delay is attributable to causes beyond his control, and he has neither acted negligently nor unreasonably'. Devlin J went on to point out that only time taken directly in the arranging of the credit could be considered and not, for example, time taken in obtaining currency required to enable the credit to be opened.

1 Per Porter J in *Garcia v Page & Co Ltd* (1936) 55 Ll L Rep 391.
2 [1955] 1 Lloyd's Rep 303.
3 Ibid at 311.
4 [1893] AC 22.

(2) CIF and FOB Contracts

3.16 (a) CIF contracts Where the sale is a CIF contract, frequently nothing is said in the contract as to the time for opening the credit, but usually a period for shipment is stated. It is established that in such circumstances the credit must be opened at the latest by the first date for shipment. But there is some authority which suggests that it should be opened earlier.

3.17 In *Pavia & Co SpA v Thurmann-Nielsen*[1] the Court of Appeal (Somervell and Denning LJJ) held that with a CIF contract the credit must be opened for the whole of the shipping period. It had been argued for the buyers that it was sufficient if the credit was opened by the time that the sellers had actually got the documents ready for presentation. The sellers were not called upon to argue in the Court of Appeal: in the court below they had simply argued that the credit must be opened by the start of the shipment period and had not taken the argument to the stage of suggesting that it must be opened a reasonable period before that time.[2]

1 [1952] 2 QB 84.
2 See [1951] 2 Lloyd's Rep 328.

3.18 The next case was *Plasticmoda SpA v Davidsons (Manchester) Ltd.*[1] Here there were to be two shipments on CIF terms 'the first one month from today and the next to follow sixty days later'. Denning LJ began his judgment stating that *Pavia* established that 'when nothing is said the buyer must establish the credit at the beginning of the shipment period. There was in this case no shipment period but only a shipment date. The letter of credit ought no doubt to have been established a reasonable time before that date.'[2] The other judgments do not refer to the point.

1 [1952] 1 Lloyd's Rep 527.
2 The fact that the contract provision as to shipment was in terms of a specific date rather than a period (which gives the seller some leeway) may be a ground for distinguishing the *Plasticmoda* case from *Pavia*.

3.19 A question similar to that in *Pavia* arose in *Sinason-Teicher v Oilcakes and Oilseeds Trading Co*[1] where the obligation was to provide not a letter of credit but a bankers' guarantee covering payment. The contest was between the sellers' argument that the guarantee had to be provided as soon as reasonably possible and the buyers' arguments that it had to be provided by the first shipment date, alternatively within a reasonable time before the first shipment date. Devlin J held that the bank guarantee was to be treated in the same manner as a letter of credit, and that *Pavia* did not decide that the buyer could delay until the first date for shipment before opening the credit. He concluded that the buyers' second argument was right. But he did not spell out how the reasonable period was to be measured. Is it a reasonable period for the seller to get the goods to the vessel? Does it include time for the seller to do other things to the goods which he may need to do to get them ready for shipment? What if he had substantial work to do to them, or even if he is to manufacture them? In the Court of Appeal Denning LJ agreed that *Pavia* did not decide that the buyer could delay right up to the first date for shipment, and stated that the credit must be provided a reasonable time before that date. Birkett LJ did not refer to *Pavia*. Morris LJ did, and, though his judgment is not wholly clear, it tends to uphold the first date of shipment as the date by which a guarantee or letter of credit should be provided.

1 [1954] 1 WLR 935; affd [1954] 1 WLR 1394, [1954] 2 Lloyd's Rep 327.

3.20 *(b) FOB contracts* The argument was continued into the field of FOB contracts in the case of *Ian Stach Ltd v Baker Bosley Ltd.*[1] Diplock J held that the FOB contract he had to consider was in classic form and the buyer had the right and responsibility of making arrangements for shipment and choosing the date of shipment. He appears to have held that *Pavia* was a binding authority with regard to CIF contracts and thought that the remarks of Denning LJ concerning it in *Sinason-Teicher* were obiter. He rejected the buyers' argument that the credit must be opened a reasonable time before the shipping instructions take effect, and held that with a classic FOB contract the credit must be opened at the latest by the earliest shipping date. He stated that for the purpose of the case before him he need go no further.

1 [1958] 2 QB 130.

3.21 *(c) A view* It can well be argued that the law has been determined at least so far as the Court of Appeal by the decision in *Pavia*[1] as Diplock J appears to have held in *Ian Stach*.[2,3] This view which follows is advanced on the basis that the point is still open to argument. If the purpose of the credit extends to enabling the seller to do whatever he has to do to the goods prior to shipment in the knowledge that the credit has been opened, the credit should be opened 'a reasonable time' before the period for shipment. But it cannot be said that this is the clear intention of both parties. The buyer may well not know what the seller has to do: he may well not be in a position to judge what a reasonable time will be, particularly in a case where there are special circumstances affecting the seller. He may well consider that, if the credit is opened prior to the first date for shipment, this should be sufficient for the seller. Also the introduction of an additional 'reasonable period' introduces an undesirable uncertainty, undesirable in particular if the timely opening of the credit is a matter where default can be treated as a repudiation of the contract. Further, if an element of reasonable time is introduced, time ceases to that extent to be of the essence and it becomes necessary for the seller to serve a notice specifying a particular date by which the credit must be opened before he can cancel for default if he desires to cancel before the earliest date for shipment.[4] This last difficulty will not arise if, as may well be the case, time remains of the essence and it remains a condition of the contract that the credit be opened by the reasonable date. The problems which the introduction of an indefinite period of time may introduce have not been considered in the cases, and its introduction appears undesirable. If a seller wants the credit to be opened before the time for shipment, he can include a term in the contract of sale providing for that and stating how long before the time for shipment it is to be opened.

1 Supra, para 3.20.
2 Supra.
3 For a contrary view, see *Alexandria Cotton & Trading Co (Sudan) Ltd v Cotton Co of Ethiopia* [1963] 1 Lloyd's Rep 576 at 589 per Roskill J.
4 See para 3.25 below.

(3) Where there is No Shipment Date

3.22 In the absence of any express provision it is to be implied that the credit shall be opened within a reasonable time of the contract being made.[1] This would be assessed with the expected or likely date of shipment in mind, among such other relevant factors as might exist. Thus in *Baltimex Ltd v Metallo Chemical Refining Co Ltd*[2] both parties had anticipated that there might be delays, and the sellers could not complain of them.

1 As to the assessment of a reasonable time, see para 3.15 above.
2 [1955] 2 Lloyd's Rep 438.

(4) Where the Seller lets time go by

3.23 Often the seller does not cancel the contract when the time for opening the credit is first passed: he continues with the contract in the hope that the buyer will perform. What is the position then? Once he has done anything to affirm the contract after his right to cancel has accrued, he has waived the right. He may even be treated in appropriate circumstances as having affirmed it by his silence. His position following affirmation is as stated by Devlin J in *Etablissements Chainbaux SARL v Harbormaster Ltd:*[1]

> 'Now, the position of a party who has started out with a contract where time is of the essence and has allowed the time to go by is, I think, quite clearly laid down in the authorities. He has got to make time of the essence of the contract again in the normal case, and that means that he has to give a notice giving the other side what is a reasonable time in all the circumstances to comply with their obligations, and it is only after they fail to do that that he is entitled to cancel the contract.'

He continued, '. . . the notice is not always essential. If the seller . . . fails to give it, it is still open to him to prove that if he had given a reasonable notice it would have been of no use to the plaintiff.' Applying these principles, suppose that the contract provides that the credit is to be opened by the beginning of May and shipment is to be in June. The buyer fails to open it and the seller urges him to do so. By mid-May he has still not done so. The seller serves a notice calling upon him to do so within seven days. If no credit is provided within that period, the seller may then cancel the contract, provided that seven days was reasonable – as prima facie it would be. Alternatively the seller may feel that there is now no hope of the buyer providing the credit, so he does not serve notice, he simply cancels. So long as he can establish that the further time would not have assisted the buyer, he is within his rights. Other examples of cases involving waiver of the time for opening the credit first set by the contract are *Ian Stach Ltd v Baker Bosley Ltd;*[2] *Plasticmoda SpA v Davidsons (Manchester) Ltd;*[3] *Baltimex Ltd v Metallo Chemical Refining Co Ltd;*[4] *State Trading Corpn of India Ltd v Compagnie Française*[5] and *Wahbe Tamari & Sons Ltd v Colprogeca.*[6]

1 [1955] 1 Lloyd's Rep 303 at 312.
2 [1958] 2 QB 130.
3 [1952] 1 Lloyd's Rep 527.
4 [1955] 2 Lloyd's Rep 438.
5 [1983] 2 Lloyd's Rep 679.
6 [1969] 2 Lloyd's Rep 18.

C.   The Opening of the Credit a Condition Precedent to the Seller's Obligation to Ship

3.24 The obligation on the buyer to open a credit which conforms to the requirements of the contract of sale is a condition of that contract in the sense that if it is not performed in due time, the seller may accept the buyer's breach of contract as a repudiation of the contract and terminate it. Secondly, the performance of the buyer's duty is a condition precedent to the seller's obligation to ship the goods, in the sense that until it is performed the seller is under no duty to perform his obligation. In *Trans*

Trust SPRL v Danubian Trading Co[1] Denning LJ first pointed out that the stipulation for a credit may be a condition precedent to the formation of the contract of sale.[2] It is suggested that, while this is possible, it is rare. He went on 'In other cases a contract is concluded and the stipulation for a credit is a condition which is an essential term of the contract. In those cases the provision of the credit is a condition precedent, not to the formation of a contract, but to the obligation of the seller to deliver the goods. If the buyer fails to provide the credit, the seller can treat himself as discharged from any further performance of the contract and can sue the buyer for damages for not providing the credit.' This passage has been cited with approval[3] and is supported by previous authority.[4] It is suggested that it sets out the usual position.

1 [1952] 2 QB 297.
2 Ibid at 304.
3 *Lindsay & Co Ltd v Cook* [1953] 1 Lloyd's Rep 328 at 335; *Plasticmoda SpA v Davidsons (Manchester) Ltd* [1952] 1 Lloyd's Rep 527 at 536.
4 *Garcia v Page & Co Ltd* (1936) 55 Ll L Rep 391; *Dix v Grainger* (1922) 10 Ll L Rep 496; *Soproma SpA v Marine and Animal By-Products Corpn* [1966] 1 Lloyd's Rep 367 at 386.

3.25 ***The seller's right to terminate***   It is clear that the seller is not obliged to ship the goods until a credit conforming to the contract of sale has been opened. It is clear that where the credit is to be opened by a fixed date, either fixed expressly by the contract, or which may be determined from it, and it is not opened by the date, the seller may terminate the contract.[1] Time is then 'of the essence', and any failure to meet the obligation entitles cancellation.[2] But it may be that the time for the opening of the credit can only be assessed in terms of what would be a reasonable time.[3] Then the seller can obtain a right to terminate the contract by serving a notice giving the buyer a date by which the credit must be provided, which must be a reasonable one. If the buyer defaults, the seller may then cancel the contract and claim damages. In *British and Commonwealth Holdings plc v Quadrex Holdings Inc*[4] Sir Nicholas Brown-Wilkinson V-C giving the judgment of the Court of Appeal stated[5] '. . . where, if a time for completion had been specified in the contract, time would have been of the essence, the innocent party can make time of the essence by serving a reasonable notice to complete even though the guilty party has not been guilty of improper or undue delay'. Where the obligation on the buyer is to open the credit within a reasonable time, it must also be open to the seller to terminate the contract where the buyer lets so much time go by without opening the credit in comparison with what would be reasonable, that his conduct amounts to a repudiation of the contract.

1 The time for the opening of a credit is considered in paras 3.14 to 3.23 above.
2 See the cases cited in para 3.24 and *Wahbe Tamari & Sons Ltd v Colprogeca* [1969] 2 Lloyd's Rep 18.
3 See inter alia para 3.22 above.
4 [1989] QB 842.
5 Ibid at 858.

3.26 ***Cases where an act by the seller is a pre-condition***   In some instances the buyer's duty to open the credit may not arise until the seller has done some act, and in the event of the seller failing to do so, it will be he who is at fault and not the buyer. Thus in *Knotz v Fairclough Dodd and Jones Ltd*[1] the contract provided 'Payment by letter of credit for 97% of sellers' provisional invoice . . .', and it was held that the supply of the provisional invoice was a condition precedent to the buyer's obligation to open the credit. In *Nicolene Ltd v Simmonds*,[2] the buyers had repeatedly offered to open a letter of credit, but the defendants had failed to give any instructions to do so and were held to be the party at fault. This case is also authority (if it be needed) for the proposition that a seller cannot be required to provide a letter from his bank stating that a facility for the credit is available. In *State Trading Corpn of India Ltd v M Golodetz Ltd*[3] the underlying contract was for the sale of a cargo of sugar by Golodetz to STC. Payment was to be by irrevocable letter of credit in a standard form, which was to be procured by STC not later than seven days after the conclusion of the contract and irrespective of the opening of a perform-ance guarantee by Golodetz. The performance guarantee was to be provided within seven days of the conclusion of the deal. Golodetz also undertook to provide a performance guarantee relating to a counter-trade, and this was to be done within seven days of the finalisation of the contract. Golodetz opened the performance guarantee but not the counter-trade guarantee. STC did not open a credit and argued that the opening of the counter-trade guarantee was a condition precedent to their obligation to do so. The Court of Appeal rejected this argument and held STC liable in damages. The main reason was that the obligation to open the credit was not conditional upon the opening of the performance guarantee, and the counter-trade guarantee was the less important of the two guarantees.

1 [1952] 1 Lloyd's Rep 226.
2 [1952] 2 Lloyd's Rep 419; affd [1953] 1 QB 543.
3 [1989] 2 Lloyd's Rep 277.

3.27 *The buyer's duty to open the credit in due time is abso-lute* Subject to such latitude as an obligation to provide a credit within a reasonable time may give him, the buyer's duty to provide a credit in time is absolute. Thus, if the communication of the credit is held up by delay on the part of a bank, the buyer is responsible: *A E Lindsay & Co Ltd v Cook*.[1]

1 [1953] 1 Lloyd's Rep 328.

3.28 *The seller's remedies against the buyer for damages* The seller's right to cancel the contract where no credit conforming to the underlying contract has been opened in due time, has already been referred to. It has also been stated that where no conforming credit is opened in time, unless a non-conforming credit is opened which is none-theless acceptable to the seller, the seller's obligation to ship never becomes effective. Where the contract is not performed because of the buyer's failure to open a conforming credit, the seller may sue him for damages. Such damages are to be assessed in accordance with the same general principles which apply in any other situation where a buyer repudiates the contract of sale, and reference should be made elsewhere for a full treatment.[1] In brief the seller's loss will usually be assessed as the difference between the price under the contract and the price obtainable for the goods in the open market, assuming that there is an available market.[2] In special circumstances which were known to the buyer when the contract was made, the seller may recover an alternative measure.

Thus in *Trans Trust SPRL v Danubian Trading Co Ltd*[3] the buyers knew that if they failed to procure the opening of the credit the sellers would be unable to buy in the goods. The sellers were held to be entitled to recover the actual profit which they would have made had the transaction gone through. They were held not to be entitled to be indemnified against a claim against them by the sellers to them, because the circumstances giving rise to such a claim were not known to the buyers. In *Ian Stach Ltd v Baker Bosley Ltd*[4] the plaintiff sellers were entitled to recover the difference between the contract price and the market price (which they had in fact obtained on a re-sale of the goods).

1 See inter alia *Benjamin's Sale of Goods* (4th edn) paragraphs 16–050 and following.
2 See Sale of Goods Act 1979, s 50.
3 [1952] 2 QB 297.
4 [1958] 2 QB 130.

D. The Seller Proceeding as if a Non-conforming Credit were Conforming

3.29 Where the credit as opened conforms to the underlying contract, the seller has no right to object to its terms. It frequently happens that a seller likewise takes no objection to a credit which does not conform but proceeds as if it were a conforming credit. What is the position then? There are three possibilities. First, he may be held to have waived the irregularity. Second, he may be held to be estopped from complaining of it. The cases make little distinction between these two and tend to concentrate more on the former. Third, there may be held to have been a variation of the underlying contract, that is, it is to be deduced from the conduct of the parties that they have agreed to vary the terms of the contract between them to provide that the credit shall be in the form in which it has in fact been opened. Where there has been a waiver or an estoppel, in appropriate circumstances the seller may give notice to the buyer that despite his previous acceptance of the position he now requires it to be remedied.[1] This is not possible where there has been a variation. A variation must be supported by consideration. It is suggested that this is to be found in the fact that, for better or worse, both the parties have become bound by the new term.[2]

1 The notice must permit a reasonable time for this to be effected.
2 Cf *Ficom SA v Sociedad Cadex Ltda* [1980] 2 Lloyd's Rep 118 at 132.2, supra para 3.6.

3.30 A leading case on waiver is *Panoutsos v Raymond Hadley Corpn of New York*.[1] The contract provided for a number of shipments, payment to be by 'confirmed banker's credit'. The credit was not confirmed, but the sellers made some shipments and operated the credit. They then cancelled the contract without previous notice on the ground that the credit did not accord with the contract. It was held that 'the seller, by waiving for a time the condition as to a confirmed credit, was not thereby bound to act upon that credit up to the end of the contract, but that he was not entitled to cancel the contract without giving the buyer reasonable notice of his intention to cancel so as to give the buyer an opportunity of complying with the condition'.[2]

1 [1917] 2 KB 473.
2 Headnote.

3.31 In *Enrico Furst & Co v W E Fischer Ltd*[1] the credit was to be an irrevocable credit opened in London and payable in London. But the London advising bank did not add their confirmation. Nor did the credit provide for a weight certificate as the contract required. But the sellers treated it as valid and asked for an extension of the time provided by it for the presentation of documents. Diplock J held that there had been a waiver of the contract requirements citing section 11(1) of the Sale of Goods Act 1893.[2]

1 [1960] 2 Lloyd's Rep 340.
2 'Where a contract of sale is subject to any condition to be fulfilled by the seller the buyer may waive the condition, or may elect to treat the breach of condition as a breach of warranty and not as a ground for treating the contract as repudiated.' See now s 11(2) of the Sale of Goods Act 1979.

3.32 *W J Alan & Co Ltd v El Nasr Export*[1] concerned the export of coffee from Kenya to Egypt. The contract was priced in Kenyan shillings, but the letter of credit was held to have been opened in sterling. Trouble arose because sterling was devalued causing the credit to be less valuable than it would have been if expressed in Kenyan shillings. This occurred after the documents in respect of a first shipment had been negotiated under it and just prior to the presentation of documents in respect of a second shipment. The sellers attempted to recover the difference between the currencies directly from the buyers. Lord Denning MR held that the case was one of waiver. Megaw LJ held that there had been a variation and not a waiver of the obligation in the underlying contract of sale. He held that the sellers had accepted the bank's offer contained in the credit on the buyers' instructions by acting on the credit in presenting documents. So the banks became bound and the credit unalterable except by the consent of all parties concerned 'all of whose legal rights and liabilities have necessarily been affected by the establishment of the credit'. So the currency of the sale contract was irrevocably altered.[2] He also held that, if there had not been a variation, there had been a waiver which the sellers could not unilaterally abrogate. Stephenson LJ simply held that the sellers could not now claim against the buyers because 'they were attempting to assert a liability which, whether by variation or waiver, they had allowed the buyers to alter'.[3]

1 [1972] 2 QB 189.
2 Ibid at 218.
3 Ibid at 221.

E.　The Amendment of the Credit

3.33 *Introduction*　The amendment of a credit should be a matter which is instigated by the applicant either with the agreement of the beneficiary or at his request. In that sense it is a matter which arises between them, and it is therefore considered in this chapter. The amendment itself is effected between the issuing bank and the beneficiary, probably through an advising bank. So it also involves them and could equally be considered in the chapters which are concerned with their relations.

3.34 *The legal position*　A bank undertaking contained in a letter of credit constitutes a binding contract between the bank and the beneficiary. So, just as any contract can only be amended by the agreement of all parties to it, a bank undertaking contained in a documentary credit can only be amended by the agreement of the parties to the undertaking, namely the bank giving the undertaking and the beneficiary. Where the credit is confirmed by the advising bank, its consent is also needed. As the credit is issued on the instructions of the applicant, it would be a breach of the agreement between the applicant and the issuing bank for the carrying out of those instructions, if the credit were to be amended without the agreement of the applicant. In practice the amendment of a credit is initiated by instructions from the applicant to the issuing bank. These instructions may have been preceded by a request for the amendment by the beneficiary. Such a request will be made where the beneficiary considers when the terms of the credit are advised to him, that they are inappropriate and should be changed. Or it may be made subsequently, perhaps to take account of events, as where a need to extend the shipping period arises or there are found to be difficulties in obtaining a certificate in the form required by the credit as opened. Where the request arises because the terms of the credit as advised to the beneficiary are unacceptable to him, in most cases it will amount to a rejection of the credit as opened. He will not want to object to an amendment which he has requested and, depending on the precise circumstances, it may not be open to him to do so. Likewise where the amendment follows from his request to amend a credit which had previously been acceptable. The difficulty arises where the applicant initiates an amendment which is not acceptable to the beneficiary. Then it is clear that the beneficiary is entitled to reject the amendment when it is advised to him, and the credit remains unchanged.[1]

1 For an example of amendments being accepted and rejected, see *Ficom SA v Sociedad Cadex Ltda* [1980] 2 Lloyd's Rep 118 at 127, and of amendments simply not being accepted, see *United City Merchants v Royal Bank of Canada* [1979] 1 Lloyd's Rep 267 at 275 – Mocotta J.

3.35 *The Uniform Customs* Articles 9.a and .b of the Uniform Customs set out the undertakings which may be given by issuing and confirming banks. Article 9.d provides that the undertakings cannot be amended without the consent of the banks and the beneficiary. It states:

ARTICLE 9.d[1]   i.   Except as otherwise provided by Article 48,[2] an irrevocable Credit can neither be amended nor cancelled without the agreement of the Issuing Bank, the Confirming Bank, if any, and the Beneficiary.

ii. The Issuing Bank shall be irrevocably bound by an amendment(s) issued by it from the time of the issuance of such amendment(s). A Confirming Bank may extend its confirmation to an amendment and shall be irrevocably bound as of the time of its advice of the amendment. A Confirming Bank may, however, choose to advise an amendment to the Beneficiary without extending its confirmation and if so, must inform the Issuing Bank and the Beneficiary without delay.

iii. The terms of the original Credit (or a Credit incorporating previously accepted amendment(s)) will remain in force for the Beneficiary until the Beneficiary communicates his acceptance of the amendment to the bank that advised such amendment. The Beneficiary should give notification of acceptance or rejection of amendment(s). If the Beneficiary fails to give such notification, the tender of documents to the Nominated Bank or Issuing Bank, that conform to the Credit and to not yet accepted amendment(s), will be deemed to be notification of acceptance by the Beneficiary of such amendment(s) and as of that moment the Credit will be amended.

iv. Partial acceptance of amendments contained in one and the same advice of amendment is not allowed and consequently will not be given any effect.

It will be noticed that the Article refers only to the parties to the credit itself and does not mention the applicant and the need for him to instigate the amendment.[3] In relation to the advice of an amendment Article 11.b provides:

ARTICLE 11.b[4]   If a bank uses the services of an Advising Bank to have the Credit advised to the Beneficiary, it must also use the services of the same bank for advising an amendment(s).

1 Article 9.d was preceded by the much shorter Article 10.d in the 1983 Revision.
2 Article 48 relates to transfer.   3 See para 3.34 above.
4 Article 11.b closely follows Article 12.d in the 1983 Revision.

3.36 *Problems in practice*   When the issuing bank receives instructions from the applicant to make an amendment, provided that it is happy with it, it will instruct the advising bank of the amendment, and the amendment will then be advised to the beneficiary usually in the form of a statement that the credit is thereby amended. This may or may not be accompanied by a request that the beneficiary inform the bank whether the amendment is acceptable. It is frequently not, and it is then for the beneficiary to object to the amendment of his own accord if he so wishes. This, of course, assumes that he is aware of his right to object to unacceptable amendments. The position was illustrated by the standard form for amendments issued by the ICC.[1] This included the following statements: 'The above mentioned credit is amended as follows', and 'This amendment is to be considered as part of the above mentioned credit and must be attached thereto'. There was nothing on the document to suggest that it was in effect an offer from the bank to the beneficiary that the credit should be so amended. As a result of this situation it is probable that some beneficiaries do not appreciate that they have any right to refuse an amendment. Even those who do may be fearful that, if they do so, when they present documents which comply with the credit as unamended the documents will be rejected.[2] Where a seller is faced with an amendment to a credit, which is unacceptable, he should inform the bank that it is unacceptable to him stating that he intends to comply with the credit as originally advised in accordance with Article 9.d. If the bank replies insisting on the amendment, he is likely to be able to treat that as a repudiation of the credit entitling him to damages against the bank. Alternatively he may prefer to remonstrate with his buyer insisting that the buyer withdraw the instructions for the amendment. If that is refused, the seller's position will be the clearer against both. Alternatively again, the seller can present documents to the bank in compliance with the unamended credit: if the bank refuses them, it will be liable to the seller.[3]

1 ICC Publication No 416, page 47. The new forms, Publication No 516, were not available at the time of finalisation of this paragraph.

2 As an example of an amendment which beneficiaries felt bound to accept even though it was strongly against their interest to do so, see *Astro Exito Navegacion SA v Chase Manhattan Bank NA* [1983] 2 AC 787, headnote.
3 See para 5.61 et seq below for a discussion of the seller's remedies.

3.37 *Where the beneficiary is silent following receipt of an amendment* The position is now covered by the new Article 9.d.iii, which, it is suggested, does not alter the previous position as established by legal principle. If an amendment is advised and the beneficiary does nothing to indicate his acceptance of it nor his rejection of it, either by his words or conduct, the Article provides that his silence is not to be taken as an acceptance of it. The legal justification is that the advice of the amendment from the bank is to be construed as an offer from the bank to him: unless something can be found which is to be taken as indicating his acceptance of that offer, it remains simply an offer.[1] Where the beneficiary remains silent following receipt of an amendment, it will in ordinary circumstances also be open to him in due course to present documents conforming to the credit as amended, thereby accepting the bank's offer made by the advice of the amendment.

1 Compare Opinions (1980–1981) of the ICC Banking Commission, ICC Publication No 399, Reference 71, where the Commission decided by a majority that the beneficiary's consent to an amendment had to be an express acceptance and could not be implied merely from his silence.

3.38 *Amendment and the Confirming Bank* Paragraphs ii and iii of Article 9.d are new. The first sentence of paragraph ii shows that an issuing bank cannot withdraw an amendment which it has advised even though the credit itself has not yet become amended as a result of the beneficiary's acceptance of the amendment. Although paragraph ii does not say so in terms, it is clear from its last sentence that if a confirming bank simply passes on an amendment (which is what happens in the great majority of cases) it will be bound by it. It will only not be bound if it states that it is advising it without adding its confirmation. If it does so, then a novel situation arises. For until the amendment is accepted the credit remains unamended and the bank remains a confirming bank in respect of it. But once it is accepted, the credit is amended, and the confirming bank must cease to be bound by its confirmation. In this situation, therefore, the beneficiary has not only to choose whether it wants the amendment: it has also to choose whether it wishes to continue to have a confirmed credit.

3.39 *Several amendments in the one advice* It frequently happens that the beneficiary is advised of several amendments in the one advice. Is it open to him to accept those he finds acceptable and to refuse the others? Article 9.d.iv makes it clear that he cannot. The contractual analysis is that the bank's offer to amend is a single offer only capable of acceptance as a whole. The beneficiary's request to accept some but not all of the amendments offered would have to be treated as a counter-offer by him, which the banks in their turn may accept or refuse. But whereas the previous Article 10.d allowed for this by concluding 'without the agreement of all the above named parties', this possibility is now not covered expressly. Nonetheless, if agreement was reached by all involved on a partial acceptance, it is suggested that it would become binding.[1] Article 9.d.iv does not provide that a partial acceptance is to be treated as a refusal of the amendments, but that it 'will not be given any effect'. It therefore appears that following a partial acceptance the position will be as it would be if the beneficiary had remained silent, that is to say, in effect his options still remain open.

1 The commentary on the Article in the ICC's Documentary Credits: UCP 500 and 400 Compared, Publication No 511, states that such an agreement would be ineffective unless a new amendment covering only the agreed portion of the previous amendment was issued and agreed upon. But the Article does not state that: it states that partial acceptance [by a beneficiary] is not allowed; it does not rule out an agreement by all on one part of a proposed amendment.

3.40 *Amendment and transfer*　The problems created by the amendment of a credit which has been transferred are considered in Chapter 10.[1]

1 Para 10.27.

F.　The Operation of the Credit

3.41　Where a credit is opened by the buyer which conforms to the contract of sale or which is accepted by the seller and the contract of sale varied to conform with the credit, or the discrepancies waived, it is the seller's duty to the buyer to ship the goods and present documents to the bank which accord with the terms of the credit. He will then receive payment in accordance with the terms of the credit. If he does not present documents to the bank or if he presents documents which do not accord with the terms of the credit and which are rejected by the bank, he is liable in damages to the buyer for failing to perform his side of the contract.[1] It is necessary to add 'and which are rejected by the bank' because a high proportion of sets of documents presented under credits do not accord with the terms of the credit and, in the great majority of these cases, on the buyer being informed of the discrepancies he will decide that they do not merit the rejection of the documents and he will instruct the bank to accept them. In such a situation he will retain his right to claim damages against the seller for such breach of the contract of sale as may have occurred by reason of the documents not complying with the contract, but he will receive the goods and the seller will receive the price.

1 See among other cases *Soproma SpA v Marine and Animal By-Products Corpn* [1966] 1 Lloyd's Rep 367.

3.42 *Where the cooperation of the buyer is required*　The operation of the credit may require the cooperation of the buyer. One way in which this may arise is if the credit provides that shipment is to be on a vessel nominated by the buyer or contains some other term of a similar nature.[1] If no vessel is nominated, the seller cannot ship the goods, nor operate the credit: the buyer will be in breach of contract with the seller by reason of his failure. The credit may provide for the bank to be informed of the nomination by the buyer. This having occurred, if the shipping documents show shipment on the vessel and otherwise conform to the credit the bank will be in a position to pay. It may otherwise be necessary for the seller to provide documentary evidence to the bank that the vessel named in the shipping documents has been nominated by the buyer.[2] Another way in which the cooperation of the buyer may be required is in the completion of the documentation to be presented under the credit. Thus the buyer or his representative may be required to sign a certificate of inspection of the goods. If he fails to do so when he should, he will place himself in breach of contract with the seller. But he will have rendered the credit inoperable. In an appropriate case, an order may be obtained from the court that he complete the document, and in the event of his failure to comply a court official may be empowered to do so in his place.[3]

1 Where the credit is opened in terms that require a further advice, or an amendment, nominating the vessel in order for it to become operative, it has been suggested that the bank may be in breach of its undertaking if no such advice or amendment is forthcoming, because it has opened an inoperable credit and failed to secure that it becomes operable. But that cannot be so. The credit as opened is only operable if the advice or amendment is forthcoming, and so the bank's undertaking to pay is conditional upon that. The bank gives no express undertaking that the condition will be satisfied. It is also clear that such an undertaking is not to be implied, because it is not within the bank's hands to procure its satisfaction, nor will the applicant be liable to the bank for failing to nominate a vessel and satisfy the condition. But the applicant will be liable to the beneficiary on the underlying contract of sale, and it is here that the remedy lies.

2 Compare the requirement in the credit in *Banque de l'Indochine et de Suez SA v JH Rayner (Mincing Lane) Ltd* [1983] QB 711 that 'Shipment to be effected on vessel belonging to Shipping Company that member of an International Shipping Conference'. It was held by Parker J that reasonable documentary proof was required: page 719B, confirmed by the Court of Appeal on this point at [1983] QB 728, 729.

3 See *Astro Exito Navegacion SA v Chase Manhattan Bank NA* [1983] 2 AC 787 considered in para 9.42 below.

G.   The Failure of the Credit to Provide Payment

3.43 It may happen that the seller is unable to obtain payment through the credit which the buyer has opened even though he presents, or is in a position to present, documents in accordance with the terms and conditions of the credit. This may come about because the bank becomes insolvent. It may come about because the bank wrongly refuses to accept the documents. There is a variety of possible situations, not all of which have been touched on in the cases. It is an area where caution is necessary in the making of general statements.

Credits as Absolute or Conditional Payment

3.44 It has on occasion been suggested on particular facts that the provision by the buyer of the letter of credit is absolute payment, that is to say, once the credit has been provided the buyer has no further duty in connection with payment and the seller's only right to payment is through the letter of credit whatever may happen. The alternative is that the credit is provided as conditional or provisional payment. Where the credit is conditional payment, if the conditions are not, or cease to be, satisfied, the seller has a right to claim payment from the buyer. The condition which is most evident is that the relevant bank must be solvent and able to pay. A second possible condition is that it should accept conforming documents and should pay (whether or not any failure arises from an inability to pay). It will be appreciated that where a credit provides for immediate payment and the bank fails to pay, the seller's position is very different to where payment is deferred. For the seller will be able to retain the documents and the control of the goods. Where the credit provides for deferred payment (whether or not a bill of exchange is involved) the seller will have parted with his documents on the strength of the bank's promise and the goods are likely to have reached their destination and may have passed into the buyer's possession. The fact that the buyer has received the goods is likely to be important. The main English authorities and one Australian authority on this area are the following. They are taken in order of date.

3.45 In *Newman Industries Ltd v Indo-British Industries*[1] after the credit had been opened the buyers instructed the bank not to pay unless a form of guarantee which was possibly not required by the letter of credit (but certainly not required by the contract of sale) was provided. The bank rejected the documents. The sellers were not the shippers on the bill of lading nor was it to their order and they had lost possession of the goods, a generator, which had been shipped to Bombay and attracted charges almost equal to its price. Sellars J held that the sellers could recover the price from the buyers. He said 'I do not think that there is any evidence to establish, or any inference to be drawn, that the draft under the letter of credit was to be taken in absolute payment. I see no reason why the plaintiffs, in the circumstances which have so unfortunately and unnecessarily arisen, should not look to the defendants, as buyers, for payment.'[2] The letter of credit had been taken in place of a bank guarantee of the payment of the price at the request of the buyers and was a confirmed irrevocable credit. It was not decided whether the credit did in fact require as a document to be presented the kind of guarantee the buyers wanted, and so it was not decided whether the bank was right to refuse the documents. The goods conformed with the contract and the property had passed to the buyers though they had not taken up their right to possession. It would seem essential to an analysis of the situation to determine whether the bank had rightly rejected the documents. The point which emerges most clearly from the judgment is that the court considered it right that the sellers should be entitled to recover in the circumstances which had arisen. In the Court of Appeal the decision was reversed on the ground that no concluded agreement between the parties for the sale of the generator had been reached.[3]

1 [1956] 2 Lloyd's Rep 219.
2 [1956] 2 Lloyd's Rep 219 at 236.
3 See [1957] 1 Lloyd's Rep 211.

3.46 Next in time is the decision of the High Court of Australia in *Saffron v Société Minière Cafrika*.[1] Here the contract provided 'payment: by opening a letter of credit with the Banque de l'Indochine . . .'. The bank correctly refused to pay because the tonnage of chromium shipped was below the minimum and because the bill of lading was not blank endorsed. The goods were received by a sub-buyer, but the buyer had himself received no payment. The court stated 'It is not reasonable to suppose that the parties here intended that in the unlikely circumstances that the buyer got the chrome but payment therefor against the letter of credit was refused, the seller should not be paid. The trial judge reached the conclusion that the letter of credit was not intended to be the exclusive source of payment, with the assistance by way of analogy of the rules relating to the acceptance of negotiable instruments. This analogy is no doubt useful . . .'[2] The trial judge's decision was upheld. The court did not need to consider what the position would have been if it had been the seller's sole fault that the letter of credit had failed as the primary source of payment because, the court reasoned, the buyer had been responsible for the bill of lading being as it was and he had accepted delivery of the tonnage loaded.

1 (1958) 100 CLR 231.
2 Ibid at 244.

3.47 In *Soproma SpA v Marine and Animal By-Products Corpn*[1] the sellers sued the buyers for damages. The documents had been rejected by the bank as not being in order, and the goods, Chilean fishmeal, had been sold for the seller's account on arrival. The documents had also been presented direct to the buyers. McNair J stated:

> 'Under this form of contract, as it seems to me, the buyer performs his obligation as to payment if he provides for the sellers a reliable and solvent paymaster from whom he can obtain payment – if necessary by suit – although it may well be that if the banker fails to pay by reason of his insolvency the buyer would be liable; but in such a case, as at present advised, I think that the basis of the liability must in principle be his failure to provide a proper letter of credit which involves *inter alia* that the obligee under the letter of credit is financially solvent. (This point as to the buyers' liability for the insolvency of the bank was not fully argued before me and I prefer to express no concluded opinion upon it as I understand that it may arise for decision in other cases pending in this Court.) It seems to me to be quite inconsistent with the express terms of a contract such as this to hold that the sellers have an alternative right to obtain payment from the buyers by presenting the documents direct to the buyers. Assuming that a letter of credit has been opened by the buyer for the opening of which the buyer would normally be required to provide the bank either with cash or some form of authority, could the seller at his option disregard the contractual letter of credit and present documents direct to the buyer? As it seems to me, the answer must plainly be in the negative.'

He went on to hold that the credit as opened was not in accordance with the contract of sale but the divergencies had been waived by the sellers. He held that the documents they had presented did not accord with the credit, and so the sellers were the party liable in damages. It may well be that in the light of those findings he did not need to enter upon a discussion of the nature of the credit.

1 [1966] 1 Lloyd's Rep 367.

3.48 *WJ Alan & Co Ltd v El Nasr Export and Import Co*,[1] a decision of the Court of Appeal, is probably the leading authority even though the court's observations on the nature of the credit as conditional payment were not necessary to the decision. The underlying contract was for the sale of coffee by Kenyan sellers to Egyptian buyers. The contract provided for payment in Kenyan shillings. A credit was opened which provided for payment in sterling, and the sellers were paid accordingly. But meanwhile sterling had been devalued, and they sued the buyers for the difference between the contract price in Kenyan shillings and the sterling they had received through the credit. It was held that by accepting the sterling credit the sellers had either agreed to a variation of the contractual term for payment in Kenyan currency or had waived it. So the question of the nature of the payment provided by the credit did not in fact arise. But counsel had researched the question of absolute or conditional payment, and this led to at least Lord Denning making some general statements. The contract provided 'Payment, By confirmed irrevocable letter of credit . . .'. Lord Denning stated 'In my opinion a letter of credit is not to be regarded as absolute payment unless the seller stipulates, expressly or impliedly, that it should be so. He may do it impliedly if he stipulates for the credit to be issued by a particular banker in such circumstances that it is to be inferred that the seller looks to that particular banker to the exclusion of the buyer.'[2] He concluded that in the ordinary way a contract providing for a confirmed irrevocable credit provided it as a conditional method of payment.[3] Megaw LJ asked 'Does the mere establishment of the credit, completed by confirmation, discharge the buyer's liability completely? Or does it discharge it provisionally, and, if so, subject to precisely what provision?' He went on to point out the danger of formulating general principles unless they were so hedged about with qualifications and reservations that they were useless. (It is suggested that this last is an over-statement of the difficulties.) He then found that on the simple form of provision for payment involved the sellers had no right to require payment other than in accordance with the credit so long as no default was made by the bank in the performance of its obligations.[4] Stephenson LJ stated that if the confirming bank had defaulted the sellers might have been able to sue the buyers, 'For the buyers promise to pay by a letter of credit, not to provide by a letter of credit a source which did not pay.' He agreed that the credit there operated as a conditional payment.[5]

1 [1972] 2 QB 189.
2 Ibid at 210.
3 Ibid at 212.
4 Ibid at 218, 219.
5 Ibid at 220, 221.

3.49 *Maran Road Saw Mill v Austin Taylor & Co Ltd*[1] is one of the two reported cases arising from the collapse of Sale & Co, a London merchant bank involved in the finance of the Malaysian timber trade. The defendants who acted as sellers' agents in London opened a letter of credit through Sale & Co in favour of the plaintiff sellers providing for payment by 90-day drafts. The defendants received payment from the buyers against documents and put Sale & Co in funds. But the bill accepted by Sale & Co under the credit was dishonoured. Ackner J accepted from *W J Alan & Co v El Nasr*[2] that 'in the ordinary way a letter of credit operates as a conditional payment of the price and not as absolute'[3] and applied the same principle to a letter of credit providing for payment by an agent to his principal. He held the defendants liable. So they had to pay twice.[4]

1 [1975] 1 Lloyd's Rep 156.
2 Supra.
3 [1975] 1 Lloyd's Rep 156 at 159.
4 For discussion of another aspect of this case, see para 6.35.

3.50 Ackner J had also to decide the next case, *E D and F Man Ltd v Nigerian Sweets and Confectionery Co Ltd*.[1] Here an irrevocable credit was opened in London by the Nigerian buyers at a bank which was substantially in common ownership with them. Payment was by 90-day drafts. The buyers received the goods, and it appears that they paid the bank. But the bank became insolvent. In holding the buyers liable Ackner J stated 'The fact that the sellers have agreed on the identity of the issuing bank is but one of the factors to be taken into account when considering whether there are circumstances from which it can properly be inferred that the sellers look to that particular bank to the exclusion of the buyer. It is in no way conclusive. In this case unlike the United States case of *Ornstein v Hickerson* 40 F Supp 305 (1941), referred to by Lord Denning MR which was the basis of Mr Evans' submission, there were other circumstances which clearly supported the presumption that the letters of credit were not given as absolute payment but as conditional payment.'[2] The sellers therefore succeeded against the buyers for the price.

1 [1977] 2 Lloyd's Rep 50.
2 Ibid at 56.

3.51 In *Shamsher Jute Mills Ltd v Sethia (London) Ltd*[1] the FOB sellers shipped goods and presented documents. The documents were rightly rejected by the bank as they did not conform to the credit. The sellers then sued the buyers direct for the contract price or damages. It was unclear what had happened to the goods: they had been shipped to Antwerp where they were sold, perhaps in satisfaction of charges: neither buyer nor seller had benefited. It was argued that if a letter of credit was a conditional payment and if goods conforming to the original contract (which these did) were shipped, the seller could sue the buyer. Bingham J held that by accepting the credit terms the sellers were to be taken as having varied the contract or to have waived any right to rely on the earlier contract terms. He held that, as the sellers had failed to comply with the credit terms, they could not recover against the buyers. This case may be contrasted with *Newman Industries Ltd v Indo-British Industries*.[2] It may be thought that the reasoning in *Shamsher Jute* is to be preferred if the two cases are not to be distinguished on their facts.

1 [1987] 1 Lloyd's Rep 388.
2 [1956] 2 Lloyd's Rep 219, para 3.45 above.

3.52 It is suggested that these authorities support the following propositions:
(1) The question whether the establishment of a letter of credit is an absolute or conditional discharge of the buyer's obligation as to payment is strictly a question of construction of the contract between the buyer and the seller. The contract will however normally be silent and it will be a matter of deduction for a court or arbitrator what the intentions of the parties should be taken to be in all the circumstances.[1]

1 See *W J Alan & Co v El Nasr Export and Import* [1972] 2 QB 189; *Newman Industries Ltd v Indo-British Industries Ltd* [1956] 2 Lloyd's Rep 219; *Saffron v Société Minière Cafrika* (1958) 100 CLR 231; *Re Charge Card Services Ltd* [1987] Ch 150 at 165 et seq (Millett J) and [1989] Ch 497 at 511, 512 (Court of Appeal).

3.53 (2) In the absence of a clear indication that the seller intended to look to a particular bank to the exclusion of the buyer, the credit will be presumed to be a conditional payment only. Such an indication might possibly be found in the express terms of the contract or it might more likely be found in the manner in which the bank or banks and machinery of payment were chosen.[1]

1 See the cases cited for the first proposition, and *Soproma SpA v Marine and Animal By-Products* [1966] 1 Lloyd's Rep 367; *Maran Road Saw Mill v Austin Taylor & Co Ltd* [1975] 1 Lloyd's Rep 156 and *E D and F Man Ltd v Nigerian Sweets and Confectionery* [1977] 2 Lloyd's Rep 50.

3.54 (3) Where a credit is absolute payment and is correctly established or is accepted by the seller, the seller will normally have no rights against the buyer if the seller presents conforming documents but nonetheless remains unpaid. His only remedy is against the bank or banks. There may be two exceptions to this. Firstly, if the buyer induces the banks not to pay, the buyer may be liable for inducing breach of contract depending on his appreciation that a breach was involved. Secondly, if the buyer has received the goods, that may give rise to remedies against him – as to which, see below.[1] No case has touched on the problem of what should happen if the bank fails before the documents can be presented. For the contractual means of transfer of the documents to the buyer has been lost. In such circumstances the contract could be argued to have been frustrated.

1 Para 3.60.

3.55 (4) If the credit is conditional payment and the time for payment is deferred and 'the bank' becomes insolvent after the documents have been presented, the buyer must pay the seller whether or not he has already paid the bank.[1] Where there is only one bank, the issuing bank, undertaking to pay, as there was in the cases cited, the position is straightforward. But what if the credit is a confirmed credit? If the confirming bank becomes insolvent, the seller can sue[2] the issuing bank to recover payment. It is arguable that the seller is obliged to do so before he can pursue the buyer, because the buyer's conditional obligation to pay is to be the last resort for the seller if the banking machinery fails. The insolvency of the issuing bank will not affect the seller if the credit is confirmed because the confirming bank is obliged to pay him even though its right of recoupation from the issuing bank may be worthless.

1 See *Maran Road Saw Mill v Austin Taylor & Co Ltd* [1975] 1 Lloyd's Rep 156 and *E D and F Man Ltd v Nigerian Sweets and Confectionery* [1977] 2 Lloyd's Rep 50.
2 Cf presentation of documents to the issuing bank, as to which see para 3.58 below. As to the possibility of fresh drafts being drawn where the drawee bank has refused acceptance, see para 5.16 below.

3.56 (5) Where the credit is conditional payment and the seller has not received payment because the bank has wrongly rejected the documents, has a condition of the credit being payment failed, and can the seller sue the buyer as an alternative to suing the bank should he wish? No definite answer can be given. The passage in the judgment of McNair J in the *Soproma* case[1] suggests not. On the other hand in *Alan v El Nasr*[2] Megaw LJ stated[3] that the seller had no right to claim payment from the buyer 'so long, at any rate, as no default is made by the bank in its performance of the letter of credit obligations'. Stephenson LJ stated that if the confirming bank had defaulted the sellers might have looked to the buyers: 'For the buyers promised to pay by letter of credit, not to provide by a letter of credit a source of payment which did not pay.' If the documents have been rejected, the property in the goods and the control of them is likely to have remained with the seller. It can be argued to be sufficient that he has a remedy against a bank which is likely to be a confirming bank in his own country. Where the buyer has induced the bank to refuse the documents wrongfully by, for example, taking some specious point which is to the buyer's advantage, the buyer will be liable in damages for inducing breach of contract. If the buyer has obtained the goods, other considerations may apply.[4]

1 [1966] 1 Lloyd's Rep 367 at 386.1, para 3.47 above.
2 [1972] 2 QB 189 at 219, para 3.48 above.
3 At page 220.
4 See para 3.60 below.

3.57 (6) Whether the credit is conditional or absolute payment, if the seller presents documents to the bank which do not conform to the credit and are rejected, the seller cannot sue the buyer direct unless the buyer has obtained the goods. This is so whether or not the goods conform to the contract. This is the clear outcome of the *Soproma* case[1] and *Shamsher Jute*.[2]

1 [1966] 1 Lloyd's Rep 367, para 3.47 above.
2 [1987] 1 Lloyd's Rep 388, para 3.51 above.

3.58 (7) A separate point arises where the rejection of the documents is by a confirming bank. Is the buyer bound to present them to the issuing bank before pursuing such remedy as he may have against the buyer (if any)? It is suggested not. As between the two banks the confirming bank is the agent of the issuing bank. Further the credit is likely expressly to provide that the documents are to be presented to the confirming bank.[1]

1 See para 6.9 below.

3.59 (8) Where the seller does have a claim against the buyer it may be for the price. Alternatively it might be for the price but framed in damages for breach of the obligation that the bank should pay, in which case there seems to be no objection to adding to the damages expenses incurred in trying to get the bank to pay. In some circumstances a claim for the price whether as the price or by way of damages may not be appropriate, and the claim should be framed in terms of damages calculated on the seller's loss on the transaction. Reference is made to the discussion of the seller's remedies against the bank in Chapter 5 below.[1]

1 Para 5.61.

3.60 ***Where the buyer has received the goods*** The buyer may receive the goods and the seller remain unpaid in two constrasting situations. One is where the credit provides for deferred payment, and the documents go through and get taken up by the buyer and are used by him to obtain the goods. The other is where the documents do not go through, perhaps because the bank rightly rejects them but the seller obtains the goods nonetheless. He may, for example, obtain them by giving an indemnity to the ship in the absence of the bill of lading. It may even come about as part of a fraud set up by the buyer. He may, for example, have ensured that the letter of credit requires a document which the seller is unlikely to be able to provide, or he may have failed to extend the period of the credit to cover a late shipment which the parties have arranged.

3.61 In the former situation, if the reason why the seller has not been paid is the bank's insolvency and the credit is conditional payment, whether or not the buyer put the bank in funds, the buyer will have to pay the seller himself.[1] It is suggested that in the rare case of a credit which is absolute payment, if the insolvency of the bank has terminated the buyer's obligation to put it in funds,[2] the buyer should be obliged to pay the seller even though the credit is an absolute payment: otherwise the buyer has got the goods for nothing.

1 See para 3.55 above.
2 As to which see *Sale Continuation Ltd v Austin Taylor & Co Ltd* [1968] 2 QB 849 discussed in para 11.14 below.

3.62 Where the documents have not passed through the credit and the buyer has got the goods, one may be confident that the buyer will be held liable for the price though the legal basis may be difficult to predict without knowledge of the precise circumstances. It might be held that by instructing the bank not to pay against the documents because of the discrepancies (the bank will usually request the buyer's instructions), the buyer has waived any right to treat the credit as payment. Where, as is likely, the seller has retained the right to possession of the goods, he has an alternative to his action for the price, which is to sue in conversion for the value of the goods. The buyer will have converted the goods by taking them if he had no title to them and no right to possession. This is of use where the market has risen and so the damages may exceed the price. In such a situation, if the buyer has himself sold the goods – perhaps for a higher price – the seller may alternatively sue in quasi-contract to recover the amount received by the buyer as the proceeds of his tort.[1] If the goods have been delivered to the buyer without the buyer having the bills of lading, the seller, if he retains the bills, will have a right of action against the carrier for misdelivery, in English law for conversion. For an example of such a claim being made against a carrier and accepted by him in exchange for an assignment of the seller's rights under the credit, see *Mannesman Handel AG v Kaunlaran Shipping.*[2]

1 See Goff & Jones *The Law of Restitution* (3nd edn) ch 32.
2 [1993] 1 Lloyd's Rep 89 at 91.2.

H. The Buyer's Claims against the Seller

3.63 It is beyond the ambit of this book to deal with the rights and obligations of the buyer and seller arising from the contract of sale save in relation to the letter of credit. It may simply be mentioned that where such a contract provides for the seller to supply both goods and documents, there are separate rights and obligations in relation to each. Both must conform to the contract, and even if one conforms the seller will be liable if the other does not.[1]

1 See generally *Benjamin on Sale of Goods* (4th edn) para 19–164 et seq.

I.   Restraining the Seller from Operating the Credit

3.64 The buyer may come to believe that the seller has shipped goods which
do not accord with the terms of the contract of sale, or even that the
seller intends a fraud and has shipped rubbish. In such circumstances he
may consider the possibility of preventing the seller from presenting
documents to the bank and obtaining payment under the credit by
obtaining a court order preventing him from doing so. This will only be
possible if the documents have not yet got into the banking chain. It may
well also raise the problem that the seller is in a foreign country. Or the
buyer may consider the possibility of obtaining an order against the
bank preventing it from paying. The essential rule has been described
under the heading of 'the autonomy of documentary credits' in paragraph 1.40 above, namely that the performance of the contract of sale
between the applicant for the credit and its beneficiary is irrelevant to
the operation of the credit. The credit is a transaction in documents and
allegations concerning the goods to which they relate are not to be used
as a ground for interfering with the operation of the credit. There is one
exception to this, which is where there is fraud on the part of the
beneficiary. This and the considerable difficulties in obtaining an injunction are considered in detail in Chapter 9.

Chapter 4

The Applicant and the Issuing Bank

A. The Contract

4.1 When a bank accepts instructions from the applicant for a credit to open the credit, a contract comes into being between the applicant and the bank. It is this contract which defines their relations. It is the second of the 'four autonomous though interconnected contractual relationships' referred to by Lord Diplock in *United City Merchants (Investments) Ltd v Royal Bank of Canada*.[1] He described it as follows:

> 'the contract between the buyer and the issuing bank under which the latter agrees to issue the credit and either itself or through a confirming bank to notify the credit to the seller and to make payments to or to the order of the seller (or to pay, accept or negotiate bills of exchange drawn by the seller) against presentation of stipulated documents; and the buyer agrees to reimburse the issuing bank for payments made under the credit. For such reimbursement the stipulated documents, if they include a document of title such as a bill of lading, constitute a security available to the issuing bank.'

1 [1983] 1 AC 168 at 182, 3.

B. The Application to Open the Credit

4.2 *The application* In accordance with his duty to open a credit arising from his contract with the seller, the buyer will apply to a bank to issue a

credit in appropriate form. It may be that the buyer will have an arrangement with his bank entitling him to open credits through the bank up to a
given value at any one time. The documentation relating to such an
arrangement is likely to include a right of indemnity in favour of the bank
and an authority to debit the applicant's account. If the applicant's
business is such that he frequently needs to open credits, such an arrangement is advisable because it may make a formal application for the credit
to the bank on one of the bank's standard application forms unnecessary,
an application by telex being acceptable, and it may save the need for the
bank to examine the merits of each individual application. Otherwise the
applicant will usually be required to make an application on one of the
bank's standard application forms. If the applicant has not already done
so as part of his arrangements with the bank, he is likely also to be
required to complete a form of indemnity and an authority to debit his
account.

4.3 If, as is often the case, the underlying contract of sale has been no more
specific in its payment provision than, for example, 'Payment: by confirmed irrevocable letter of credit', it is at this point that the buyer must
first specify precisely the type of credit that he requires and list the
documents against which it is to be payable. It is essential that the
application should set out in clear terms what is wanted. The relevant
provision in the Uniform Customs is Article 5:

> ARTICLE 5   **Instructions to Issue/Amend Credits**
> a. Instructions for the issuance of a Credit, the Credit itself,
>   instructions for an amendment thereto, and the amendment
>   itself, must be complete and precise.
>   In order to guard against confusion and misunderstanding,
>   banks should discourage any attempt:
>   i. to include excessive detail in the Credit or in any amend-
>   ment thereto;
>   ii. to give instructions to issue, advise or confirm a Credit by
>   reference to a Credit previously issued (similar Credit)
>   where such previous Credit has been subject to accepted
>   amendment(s), and/or unaccepted amendment(s).
> b. All instructions for the issuance of a Credit and the Credit itself
>   and, where applicable, all instructions for an amendment
>   thereto and the amendment itself, must state precisely the
>   document(s) against which payment, acceptance or negotia-
>   tion is to be made.

Article 5 in the 1983 Revision contained the substance of the present
Article 5.a up to and including 5.a.i. The previous Article 13 covered the
subject matter of Article 5.a.ii.[1] Article 5.b is taken from the previous
Article 22.a which was in section D entitled Documents. Many of the
provisions relating to documents are capable of being relevant to the
applicant's instructions to the issuing bank because they contain provisions stating which documents will be acceptable under a credit in the
absence of stipulation in the credit to the contrary. Reference should be
made to Chapter 8, in particular to Part C.

1 See para 4.8 below.

4.4 The main matters for the applicant to consider in connection with his instructions to the issuing bank are:

(1) whether the credit is to be revocable or irrevocable, confirmed or unconfirmed;

(2) whether the credit is to be transferable;

(3) whether the credit is to be available by sight payment, deferred payment, acceptance or negotiation – Article 10.a of the Uniform Customs (this involves a decision as to whether the documents to be presented should include a bill of exchange and consideration of the function, if any, which it will fulfil);

(4) the sum to be available under the credit, currency, unit prices;

(5) the advising (confirming) bank – it is most often left to the issuing bank to choose its own correspondent in the country of the beneficiary;

(6) the description of the goods: this will be required to be stated on the invoice – see Article 37.c of the Uniform Customs and paragraphs 8.27 and 8.52 below;

(7) the documents to be presented, which should be concisely but sufficiently described – the description of the transport document is of particular importance;

(8) latest date for shipment, period for presentation from date of transport document, last date of validity of credit;

(9) are part shipments to be allowed;

(10) is there any need to prohibit transhipment;[1]

(11) the means of transmission of the credit: whether by airmail or a form of teletransmission.

(12) whether it is necessary to exclude any of the Articles of the Uniform Customs because their effect would be contrary to the intention of the parties.[2]

1 This must be considered in conjunction with the transhipment provisions of the relevant Article among Articles 23 to 28. As to transhipment, see para 8.76 et seq below.
2 See para 1.30 above.

4.5 ***The bank and its instructions; unclear instructions*** If on checking the application a bank is not happy with the instructions which it has received, it should decline to open the credit until satisfactory instructions have been achieved. The bank should in particular check that the instructions are clear and will not give rise to difficulties in the operation of the credit, and that there are no contradictory terms. There is often an urgency in getting the advice of the credit to the seller, and so delay due to the clarification of instructions may give rise to difficulty. Article 12 of the Uniform Customs may assist an advising bank in such a situation. It provides:

> ARTICLE 12   **Incomplete or Unclear Instructions**
> If incomplete or unclear instructions are received to advise, confirm or amend a Credit, the bank requested to act on such instructions may give preliminary notification to the Beneficiary for information only and without responsibility. This preliminary notification should state clearly that the notification is provided for information only and without the responsibility of the Advising Bank. In any event, the Advising Bank must inform the Issuing Bank of the action taken and request it to provide the necessary information.

> The Issuing Bank must provide the necessary information without delay. The Credit will be advised, confirmed or amended, only when complete and clear instructions have been received and if the Advising Bank is then prepared to act on the instructions.

Article 14 in the 1983 Revision from which Article 12 is derived, began 'if incomplete or unclear instructions are received to issue, confirm, advise or amend a credit . . .'. Article 12 does not refer to 'issue', and the issuing bank is now excluded from the ambit of the Article. This must be on the basis that it deals direct with the applicant and so should not need to give a preliminary notification as provided for by Article 12. A preliminary notification is issued under Article 12 without responsibility.[1] If further information necessary to clarify the position is not received, the bank seeking it is not obliged to do anything further. No doubt as a matter of courtesy it will want to inform the potential beneficiary of this position. But no question of any liability on the part of the bank to the potential beneficiary can arise.

1 In contrast with a preliminary advice issued under Article 11.c; see para 5.4 below.

4.6 *Clarification after issue of the credit*　If the bank finds itself in a situation where it has accepted instructions which are later found to be unclear, it should take further instructions to clarify them, if it is still open to it to do so. But if the credit has been notified to the beneficiary, a contract between the bank and the beneficiary will have come into being, which cannot be modified without the beneficiary's consent. The ambiguity may only have been observed following the presentation of documents by the beneficiary. Suppose the credit as opened can be read as requiring possibly a document of type A among those to be presented, or possibly type B: it is not immediately clear which. If the 'correct' construction of the credit as notified is that document A is required, it cannot be open to the bank to take instructions from the buyer to clarify the position that it is in fact B that the buyer wants and to refuse to accept documents which include A. The passage which is sometimes relied upon as suggesting that instructions must be taken occurs in *European Asian Bank v Punjab and Sind Bank (No 2)*.[1] The case has already been considered in Chapter 2 above[2] and the facts set out. It will be remembered that there was an apparent conflict between clauses (6) and (9) of the credit as to whether it was a negotiation credit. After referring to the principle in *Ireland v Livingston* (1872)[3] the court stated:

> 'But even if the principle were capable of applying to a case as the present, the conflict between clauses (6) and (9) was apparent on the fact of the letter of credit. Given this state of affairs, and the obvious nature of this conflict, the proper course of any bank, considering whether to act as negotiating bank, would be to inquire of the issuing bank whether it was intended that negotiation should be regarded as unrestricted, or as restricted to ABN. It cannot be right that, on facts such as these, a bank should be able to rely on one part of the document, ignoring another part which is inconsistent, without making any inquiry of the issuing bank, by telex or otherwise.'

However the position of a bank considering whether to act as a negotiating bank is different to that of a bank which has actually issued a credit and to which documents may have been presented in reliance on the credit as issued. In practice, where documents have not been presented, an ambiguity which is observed in time can often be covered by an amendment acceptable to the beneficiary.

1 [1983] 1 WLR 642 at 656.
2 Para 2.27.
3 (1872) LR 5 HL 395 and see para 4.7 below.

4.7 *The bank acting on ambiguous instructions* The principle in *Ireland v Livingston*[1] is that where an agent has received instructions which are ambiguous he may adopt a reasonable interpretation of them, and it is not then open to his principal to say that he intended the other meaning. *Midland Bank Ltd v Seymour*[2] applied this principle to the position of an issuing bank and referred to the issuing bank as the buyer's agent, which as was pointed out in the *European Asian Bank* case[3] is not strictly correct. In *Commercial Banking Co v Jalsard*[4] the Board of the Privy Council stated:[5]

'It is a well-established principle in relation to commercial credits that if the instructions given by the customer to the issuing banker as to the documents to be tendered by the beneficiary are ambiguous or are capable of covering more than one kind of document, the banker is not in default if he acts upon a reasonable meaning of the ambiguous expression or accepts any kind of document which fairly falls within the wide description used: see *Midland Bank Ltd v Seymour* [1955] 2 Lloyd's Rep 147.

There is good reason for this. By issuing the credit, the banker does not only enter into a contractual obligation to his own customer, the buyer, to honour the seller's drafts if they are accompanied by the specified documents. By confirming the credit to the seller through his correspondent at the place of shipment he assumes a contractual obligation to the seller that his drafts on the correspondent bank will be accepted if accompanied by the specified documents, and a contractual obligation to his correspondent bank to reimburse it for accepting the seller's drafts. The banker is not concerned as to whether the documents for which the buyer has stipulated serve any useful commercial purpose or as to why the customer called for tender of a document of a particular description. Both the issuing banker and his correspondent bank have to make quick decisions as to whether a document which has been tendered by the seller complies with the requirements of a credit at the risk of incurring liability to one or other of the parties to the transaction if the decision is wrong. Delay in deciding may in itself result in a breach of his contractual obligations to the buyer or to the seller. This is the reason for the rule that where the banker's instructions from his customer are ambiguous or unclear he commits no breach of his contract with the buyer if he has construed them in a reasonable sense, even though upon the closer consideration which can be given to questions of construction in an action in a court of law, it is possible to say that some other meaning is to be preferred.'

Thus it appears that the bank will be acting correctly and entitled to be indemnified by the buyer if it accepts documents which accord with the true construction of the credit or which give a reasonable meaning to an ambiguous expression. But, so far as the seller is concerned, if the bank refuses documents on the strength of an ambiguity which it is later found to have misconstrued, the bank will be liable to the seller for refusing documents which were in accordance with the terms of the credit as correctly construed.

1 Supra.
2 [1955] 2 Lloyd's Rep 147 at 153.
3 Supra at 656.
4 [1973] AC 279.
5 Ibid at 285, 6.

4.8 *Instructions referring to previous credits* Sometimes the instructions may refer to a previous credit or credits. As Article 5.a.ii[1] provides, this is to be discouraged because first the ease of making such a reference may mean that the applicant has not fully thought through whether the previous terms are in fact fully applicable. Secondly, there is the problem of amendments to the earlier credit. Article 13 in the 1983 Revision (from which Article 5.a.ii[1] is derived) provided that where instructions were given to issue a credit by reference to a previous credit, amendments were to be disregarded. This might have been criticised because an applicant's unfamiliarity with the Article might have permitted him to think that a reference to a previous credit should be taken as being to the credit in its final form. But the Uniform Customs do not now seek to resolve this problem. ICC Publication 511, UCP 500 and 400 Compared, explains that this is because of the divergence of views on how to handle it. It was best simply to discourage such instructions where the previous credit had been subject to amendment, whether or not accepted.

1 See para 4.3 above for text.

C. The Issuing Bank's Duties

4.9 There are three functions which the issuing bank performs and in relation to which it owes duties to the buyer, the applicant.

(1) Following the bank's acceptance of the applicant's instructions it is its duty to arrange that a credit according with those instructions is duly opened. Depending on the instructions this may be done by itself advising the opening of the credit direct to the beneficiary, or, and more likely, it will be done by instructing a correspondent bank in the country of the beneficiary to advise the credit.

(2) It has to receive and examine documents under the credit.

(3) It is obliged to pay as required by the credit.

4.10 *The duty* The bank must follow its instructions precisely, both in the opening of the credit and in the acceptance or rejection of documents which are presented under it. In that sense, but in that sense alone, it is under an absolute duty.

(a) The nature of the duty in the opening of the credit has not been fully examined by the courts. But it is suggested that it is not absolute, in the sense that the bank does not guarantee that it will procure that a credit is opened in accordance with its instructions. Thus it does not guarantee to procure that the credit will be confirmed. It may be that, unknown to it, the proposed beneficiary is of such a reputation that no bank in its own country is prepared to confirm a credit to it. The issuing bank would fully perform its duty to the applicant if, having taken all reasonable steps to procure a confirmed credit, it reported to the applicant that it was unable to do so. But it is difficult to see how something might otherwise go wrong without the fault of the issuing bank or of the advising bank acting as its agent. This suggestion is supported by the decision of the House of Lords in *Equitable Trust Co of New York v Dawson Partners Ltd*.[1] The provisions of the Uniform Customs which are relevant to an issuing bank's responsibility for the acts or omissions of its correspondent bank are considered below, as are the provisions relevant to errors of transmission.[2]

(b) The nature of the duty in connection with the examination and acceptance or rejection of documents is examined in Chapter 8.[3] It is a duty to examine with reasonable care to ascertain that the documents appear on their face to be in compliance with the provisions of the credit.

1 (1926) 27 Ll L Rep 49, and the next paragraph below.
2 Paras 4.15 to 4.18.
3 Para 8.2 et seq.

4.11 ***Equitable Trust Co of New York v Dawson Partners Ltd***[1] This case is best known for the passage from the speech of Viscount Sumner as to the need for the documents presented to comply strictly with the terms of the credit, quoted subsequently in paragraph 8.20. The facts were that Dawson Partners asked the Equitable Trust Company to open a confirmed credit through their correspondents in Batavia, the Hongkong & Shanghai Bank. The instructions given by Dawson Partners required that payment should be against documents which included 'a certificate of quality to be issued by experts who are sworn brokers, signed by the Chamber of Commerce'. The underlying contract was for the sale of '3000 kilos Java vanilla beans, sound, sweet and of prime quality'. It was alleged that instead the seller had shipped a quantity of sticks, stones and old iron. Nonetheless documents including a certificate signed by a single sworn broker and countersigned by the institution which performed the functions of the chamber of commerce were presented. They were accepted by the Hongkong & Shanghai Bank, who in their turn were reimbursed by the Equitable Trust Company. The latter brought proceedings against Dawson Partners when they refused to pay. The reason why the certificate signed by one broker had been accepted was that the telegraphic codes used by the banks did not distinguish between singular and plural and so what should have been 'experts' was transcribed as 'expert'. The main basis of the House of Lords' decision in favour of Dawson Partners was that they had undertaken to reimburse the bank against documents which included a certificate with the signatures of at least two experts, and that the signature of one would not do: the bank's entitlement to reimbursement was dependent on strict compliance with its instructions. The bank put forward a number of arguments, all of which were rejected. Among them was one that, as the buyers had requested the transmission of the credit by cable, the transmission should be at their risk. One conclusive answer to that was that the problem to which the use of the code in question gave rise was an obvious one and surmountable.[2] Today the case would in this respect have turned on consideration of Article 16 of the Uniform Customs.[3] It would be argued that the Article is not intended to protect a bank from its own negligence but from liability arising from transmission faults coming about without the bank's fault, and that the use of such a code without taking steps to clarify the ambiguity between singular and plural was negligence. It is suggested that the Article would not have affected the outcome of the case.

1 (1926) 27 Ll L Rep 49.
2 Ibid at 53.2, per Viscount Sumner.
3 Set out at para 4.15 below.

4.12 Most of the cases involving an allegation by the buyer that the issuing bank has failed to comply with instructions involve payment by the bank against documents which were alleged not to comply with the buyer's instructions and the terms of the credit as opened. A rather different example arose in *Midland Bank Ltd v Seymour*.[1] In that case the credit was to be available in Hong Kong, but the bills drawn on the bank pursuant to it had been passed from Hong Kong to London and accepted there. Devlin J held[2] that, if the bank was authorised to pay or accept only in Hong Kong, 'then although the place of payment may be commercially immaterial, the bank has exceeded its mandate and cannot recover'. He went on to hold that acceptance in London was also within the bank's mandate.

1 [1955] 2 Lloyd's Rep 147.
2 Ibid at 168.

4.13 *The consequences of failure*   The consequences of a failure by an issuing bank to comply with its instructions may take two forms. First, it may be liable to the buyer for damages sustained by the buyer as a result of the failure for breach of contract. Thus, if an issuing bank failed to request the advising bank to confirm the credit and in consequence the seller was entitled to and did cancel the contract, prima facie the bank would be liable in damages both to the buyer, its applicant, for his own loss and for what the buyer might have himself to pay the seller in damages. Such a situation is unlikely to arise because the usual course of events would be a complaint by the seller to the buyer that the credit was not confirmed in conformity with the contract between them, which would result in the correction of the bank's error. Secondly, and more commonly, the consequence of an issuing bank failing to comply with its instructions may be that it is left with documents on its hands in respect of which it has paid the beneficiary or the correspondent bank but which the buyer is not obliged to take up or to pay for. That will come about where the credit has been operated in accordance with its terms but the terms do not comply with the bank's mandate from its customer, as occurred in the *Equitable Trust* case.[1] Or, and this is the more common situation, it comes about where the credit has been correctly opened but the bank is found to have accepted documents which it should have rejected as not complying with the terms of the credit.

1 (1926) 27 Ll L Rep 49.

Exclusions of liability
4.14 *General – the bank's own terms*   The application forms provided by banks frequently contain clauses exempting them from liability, and this is unobjectionable where the purpose is to exempt the bank from liability for matters outside its control. But sometimes they attempt to go further and excuse themselves from errors within their own offices. A clause which purported to entitle the bank to be reimbursed against documents which had been accepted through its own negligence and which did not comply with the terms of the credit, would be aimed at defeating the purpose of the transaction. Unless such a clause was drafted in the most clear and unambiguous terms it would not be construed as achieving that effect in English law. Reference should be made to the law

concerning the construction of exemption clauses in the text books on the law of contract.[1] A bank might also be prevented from relying on such a clause by reason of section 3 of the Unfair Contract Terms Act 1977.

1 For example, *Chitty* (26th edn) 'General Principles', paras 945 to 962.

4.15 *Transmissions* Article 16 of the Uniform Customs provides as follows:

ARTICLE 16[1] **Disclaimer on the Transmission of Messages**
Banks assume no liability or responsibility for the consequences arising out of delay and/or loss in transit of any message(s), letter(s) or document(s), or for delay, mutilation or other error(s) arising in the transmission of any telecommunication. Banks assume no liability or responsibility for errors in translation and/or interpretation of technical terms, and reserve the right to transmit Credit terms without translating them.

The Article covers two subjects: the transmission of any messages, letters or documents, or telecommunication, and the translation of technical terms with a general right to decline translation. The matters referred to in the first sentence of the Article are matters which it may be thought will ordinarily arise without an involvement on the part of the bank. There is no suggestion in it that the purpose is to absolve the bank where it has itself been negligent.[2] It is suggested that the Article should not be construed as exempting a bank from liability from its own negligence. This conclusion would be supported by the application of the tests contained in the opinion of the Privy Council in *Canada SS Lines v The King*[3] as to when in English law an exemption clause should be construed as excluding liability for negligence. It may, however, be questioned how far such peculiarly English tests should be applied to the construction of such an international document.[4] But here, it is suggested, they provide the correct answer. The reference to documents may include documents presented to a bank under a credit which have to be transmitted to another bank. The beneficiary will usually be entitled to payment by reason of his presentation of the documents to the first bank. But where this is not the case, and, for example the documents are lost in transmission between banks without negligence on their part, prima facie the loss will fail on the beneficiary.

1 Taken unchanged from Article 18 in the 1983 Revision.
2 See also para 4.11 above.
3 [1952] AC 192 at 208.
4 As to the principles to be applied in the construction of exemption clauses in relation to negligence, see generally *Chitty on Contract* (26th edn) 'General Principles' para 950 et seq.

4.16 *Acts of God, riots, etc* Article 17 of the Uniform Customs provides:

ARTICLE 17[1] **Force Majeure**
Banks assume no liability or responsibility for the consequences arising out of the interruption of their business by Acts of God, riots, civil commotions, insurrections, wars or any other causes beyond their control, or by any strikes or lockouts. Unless specifically authorised, banks will not, upon resumption of their business, pay, incur a deferred payment undertaking, accept Draft(s) or negotiate under Credits which expired during such interruption of their business.

So an interruption of the bank's business by such a cause may bring about the loss of the benefit of the credit.

1 Taken largely unchanged from Article 19 of the 1983 Revision.

4.17 *The acts and omissions of the advising bank*   This involves first understanding the relationship between the issuing and the advising bank, which is considered in Chapter 6. In essence, so far as the applicant for the credit is concerned (the buyer), the advising bank is to be treated as the agent of the issuing bank. The acts of the advising bank are therefore to be taken as those of the issuing bank for the purpose of determining any liability which the issuing bank may have to the applicant. So, if the advising bank fails correctly to perform its function of advising the credit to the beneficiary and the applicant for the credit is thereby caused loss, it appears that the issuing bank would be liable at common law. It cannot be said that this is as yet clearly established by case law. It is certainly consistent with the decision of the House of Lords in the *Equitable Trust* case[1] and follows as a matter of principle from the advising bank's position as agent.[2] It is also possible for there to be an intermediate position, that an issuing bank should not be automatically liable for the acts of its advising or correspondent bank on the ground that such a bank is its agent, but should be liable only where the issuing bank is itself negligent. The position is now likely to be determined by the application of Article 18 of the Uniform Customs.

1 (1926) 27 Ll L Rep 49.
2 See para 6.4 below.

4.18   Article 18 provides:

ARTICLE 18[1]   **Disclaimer for Acts of an Instructed Party**
a. Banks utilising the services of another bank or other banks for the purpose of giving effect to the instructions of the Applicant do so for the account and at the risk of such Applicant.
b. Banks assume no liability or responsibility should the instructions they transmit not be carried out, even if they have themselves taken the initiative in the choice of such other bank(s).
c.i. A party instructing another party to perform services is liable for any charges, including commissions, fees, costs or expenses incurred by the instructed party in connection with its instructions.
  ii. Where a Credit stipulates that such charges are for the account of a party other than the instructing party, and charges cannot be collected, the instructing party remains ultimately liable for the payment thereof.
d. The Applicant shall be bound by and liable to indemnify the banks against all obligations and responsibilities imposed by foreign laws and usages.

At a first reading the intended effect appears to be that, whatever the advising bank does, it does at the risk of the applicant and not of the issuing bank. It is to be remembered that the applicant has no contract with the advising bank, and it is at the best doubtful whether it has any rights against it.[2] The most common error made by advising banks is to pay against documents which do not conform to the credit. When that happens, it should be picked up by the issuing bank when it in its turn receives and inspects the documents. The consequence then will be that, unless the applicant is nonetheless prepared to accept the documents, the issuing bank will return them to the advising bank and will refuse to reimburse the advising bank. If the issuing bank fails to spot the error, the applicant will be entitled to refuse the documents when it receives and examines them. It cannot be the intention of Article 18 to alter the outcome in either of those situations. It will be noted that they resolve themselves because the bank at fault carries the loss because it has paid out and has no right to reimbursement. Where it is another bank which is to pay, Article 18 can be argued to shift the loss onto an innocent party, the applicant. Where the advising bank advises the credit with an error, such as the omission of one of the documents which the applicant specified to be those against which payment should be made, and the credit provides for payment to be made not by the advising bank but by the issuing bank or another bank nominated by it, the issuing bank will be bound by the advice of the credit. For it will have been made by its agent acting within that agent's ostensible authority.[3] The beneficiary will be entitled to payment. Article 18.a appears to have the effect that in such a situation the payment would be 'for the account and at the risk of' the applicant. If so, he would be bound to accept and pay for documents which did not comply with his mandate to the issuing bank, despite the fact that the clear negligence of the correspondent or advising bank as the agent of the issuing bank would give the issuing bank a right of reimbursement against it. Had the issuing bank made such an error itself, the liability would of course rest with it. A similar situation arises where the error by the advising bank is not as to the terms of the credit but in accepting documents which do not in fact comply with the terms as correctly advised, and payment is to be made by another bank. In accepting the documents the advising bank will have acted as the agent of the issuing bank and will bind it, and the beneficiary will be entitled to his payment. Again, Article 18 may be argued to have the effect that the applicant for the credit would be bound to accept and pay for documents which did not comply with his instructions, and even though the issuing bank would have a remedy against the bank actually at fault. It is surprising if it is the intention of Article 18.a to enable banks to avoid responsibility in these situations. Unless its wording clearly requires that result, it is suggested that it should not be construed as doing so. An alternative construction of the Article is that its effect is to prevent an applicant holding an issuing bank liable in damages for any loss caused to the applicant by the action of a bank instructed by the issuing bank: it does not enable the issuing bank to pass on to the applicant liability which would otherwise rest with the banks.[4] The issue is touched on in terms which support this second construction in a very brief decision of the ICC Banking Commission[5] where the Commission stated that the Article's predecessor exonerated the issuing bank for the errors of the advising bank, provided that the issuing bank had not been guilty of negligence itself. The word 'exonerated' does not suggest that the Article enables a bank to require an applicant to accept and pay for documents which do not comply with the applicant's instructions. 'Exoneration' and 'immunity' are the words in the commentary on the Article in the ICC's UCP 500 and 400 Compared.[6] This confirms that the intended effect is only to prevent the issuing bank from being liable in respect of the errors of a correspondent bank unless the issuing bank has itself been negligent.

1 Article 18.a, .b and .d is taken from Article 20 in the 1983 Revision. Article 18.c is new.
2 See below, paras 6.36 and 9.34.
3 See paras 6.4 and 6.5 post.
4 See also Chapter 6, paras 6.5 and 6.28 et seq. For a contrary view, see *Benjamin's Sale of Goods* (4th edn) para 23–136.
5 Decisions, 1975–1979, Ref 17.
6 Publication No 511.

4.19 *May the bank waive terms appearing to be inserted for its benefit?* It is a part of the general law of contract that a party may waive compliance with a term in the contract which has been inserted solely for his benefit, and enforce the contract as if the provision had been omitted.[1] In *Guaranty Trust of New York v Van Den Berghs Ltd*[2] the buyer's application for the credit required a bill of lading made out to the bank's order. It was held that the buyer was bound to accept a bill made out to the buyer's order as this was a better document from his point of view. As the provision that the bill be made out to the bank's order was inserted for the bank's benefit, the bank was entitled to waive it. It is suggested that it will often be difficult to be sure that a provision has been inserted solely for the benefit of the bank. Thus, although on the particular facts in the *Guaranty Trust* case[3] it may have been clear, it is possible to think of situations in which the buyer would have reason for wanting the bill made to the bank's order.[4] It may be doubted whether there is room today for the principle in relation to the documents to be supplied under a documentary credit: the buyer should be entitled to precisely the documents which he has asked for in his application form, and to which the bank has agreed. In any event the principle must be one having a very limited application.

1 See *Chitty on Contract* (26th edn) 'General Principles', para 1611.
2 (1925) 22 Ll L Rep 447.
3 Ibid at 458, per Sargant LJ.
4 Such as where the buyer is on-selling in a different name.

4.20 *The issuing bank's general duty of care to the buyer in connection with the credit* If the transaction financed by the credit goes wrong, for example, if the seller ships rubbish and having presented the documents and received payment, effectively disappears, the buyer may sometimes seek to blame the bank for having failed to advise as to the terms of a credit which would have protected him, for example, for failing to advise that the documents to be presented under the credit should include a certificate of inspection by an independent and reliable agency. It is suggested that the validity of such a contention is to be determined by an examination of the particular facts of the case, looking in particular to see what duty the bank has undertaken towards its customer by express agreement or by implication. Thus a bank may well have a greater understanding and knowledge of letters of credit than its customer. If, in such a situation, the customer seeks advice and the bank gives it and does so without any exclusion of liability, the bank is likely to be liable if it fails to act with the reasonable skill and care to be expected of such a bank. On the other hand if a customer does not seek the bank's advice but simply puts forward its application for a credit, it is unlikely to succeed in an allegation that the bank should have issued a warning or given advice. Two cases are illustrative of the position.

4.21 In *Midland Bank Ltd v Seymour*[1] Mr Seymour had asked the bank for inquiries to be made about sellers in Hong Kong who were ultimately to ship him rubbish instead of ducks' feathers. The bank made inquiries, passed on the response and suggested a surveyor's inspection certificate, which Mr Seymour thought was unnecessary. The bank then received a further report which they failed to pass on. Mr Seymour complained about that, and also alleged that the bank should have made fuller inquiries at an earlier stage. Devlin J held that the bank was acting on a contractual basis in connection with its inquiries. He went on to consider what the bank's duty was. Firstly, it was a duty to take care not to supply misleading information. Secondly, he suggested, but did not decide, that there was no duty to pursue its inquiries with due diligence: it was not employed as an inquiry agent. He held that in any event on the facts there was no breach of a duty, if there was one, to pursue inquiries with due diligence, and that no loss had been occasioned by the bank's breach of duty in failing to pass on the information in the further report.[2]

1 [1955] 2 Lloyd's Rep 147.
2 See [1955] 2 Lloyd's Rep 147 at 155–160.

4.22 The complaint in *Commercial Banking Co v Jalsard*[1] was that the bank had failed to advise the buyer's representative that the certificate of inspection should cover the checking of the quality or condition of the goods, not simply that the certifier had inspected them, ie had looked at them. In holding that the complaint failed, the Board of the Privy Council pointed out that there was no request by the representative for advice as to the nature of the certificate and that she had herself decided what form the certificate should take.

1 [1973] AC 279.

4.23 The position may thus be stated in general terms that a bank owes no duty to the applicant for the credit unless the particular facts show that the bank has undertaken a duty, and that the scope of any duty so undertaken will be determined and limited by the circumstances.

D. The Duty of the Buyer

4.24 It is the duty of the buyer to take up from the issuing bank documents which conform to his instructions and to pay the issuing bank in accordance with the arrangements between them, which may require a cash payment, or may entitle the bank to debit the buyer's account. Those arrangements may also provide for the release of the documents to the buyer upon terms, such as that he execute a trust receipt, as described in Chapter 11 below.

4.25 *The bank's security against the buyer* The question of security is considered in Chapter 11. The security of the bank was traditionally the documents against which it paid or undertook a payment obligation. Through them it should have the security of the goods themselves. If it does not, it has a doubtful security. When the transport document under a letter of credit was almost invariably a marine bill of lading, there was little difficulty because such a document is a document of title. With the increasing use today of other forms of transport document, the security of banks in documentary credit transactions has been greatly weakened. Such security has in the past been regarded as one of the essential elements of the transaction. The alternative form of security is security taken direct from the bank's customer such as general charges over the company's assets and guarantees from holding companies. It may well be that in the trading conditions of today banks often look to the latter for their security rather than to the documents coming through the credit.

4.26 *Charges and costs* The applicant for the credit is primarily liable for the costs incurred in connection with it.[1] He will have to pay the issuing bank its charges which are likely to be a small percentage on the amount available under the credit during the period that it is available and a full interest rate on sums advanced under it while not recouped from the applicant. He will also have to pay the bank its out-of-pocket expenses in communicating the credit. The charges of the advising bank are usually a matter of agreement. In default they are to be paid by the buyer as the initiator of the arrangement, which is confirmed by Article 18.a and .c quoted above. It should be made a term of the credit that the expenses of the advising bank will be payable by the seller. Then, in practice they will usually be deducted from the price otherwise payable to him.[2] This raises a problem where the credit is not utilised, or is not utilised through the advising bank. The ICC Banking Commission has expressed the view that, if the advising bank's expenses cannot be collected from the beneficiary, the advising bank should be able to collect them from the issuing bank (who will in turn collect them from the applicant for the credit).[3] This is now covered expressly by Article 18.c.

1 See Article 18. See also Ref 185 in the Opinions of the ICC Banking Commission 1989–91, Publication No 494, where American practice is considered and commented upon.
2 The advising fee and any amendments fees will have been charged at the time of the advice and amendments. But it very commonly happens that they remain unpaid until payment is made under the credit, when they are deducted with the payment fee.
3 See Opinions of the ICC Banking Commission, 1984–1986, Ref 141.

E. The Autonomy of the Credit: Restraining Payment

4.27 A documentary credit transaction is a transaction in the documents which are presented pursuant to the credit, and it is independent of the underlying transaction in goods or whatever the subject matter of the underlying contract may be. This, called the principle of the autonomy of the credit, has been introduced in Chapter 1.[1] Its consequence is that it is normally no ground for interfering with the operation of the credit, in particular by the grant of an injunction against a bank preventing it from paying, that the applicant, the buyer, alleges that the goods do not comply with the underlying contract. The one exception to this is where there is fraud on the part of the presenter of documents under the credit. The fraud exception and the question of injunctions is considered in Chapter 9.

1 Para 1.40 et seq.

Chapter 5

The Contracts of the Issuing Bank and the Confirming Bank with the Seller

A.   The Parallel between the Issuing Bank and the Confirming Bank

5.1 When a bank confirms a credit which has been issued by another bank, in effect it repeats as binding on itself the undertaking as to payment which has been given by the issuing bank. Therefore, as regards the beneficiary the position of an advising bank in its capacity of confirming bank is broadly the same as that of the issuing bank, and the two are thus considered together in this chapter. Otherwise the position of an advising or correspondent bank and the relations which it may have with the issuing bank and with the seller or beneficiary of the credit are considered in Chapter 6.

B.   The Contract or Contracts, and Consideration

5.2 *Irrevocable credits* The nature of an irrevocable credit has been described in Chapter 2.[1] An irrevocable credit constitutes a binding contract between the issuing bank and the beneficiary of the credit. Where a credit is confirmed by a second bank, a second and separate contract is established between the confirming bank and the beneficiary. A beneficiary does not obtain a contract with an advising bank unless it adds its confirmation of the credit. The requirement of English law that to be enforceable a contract must be supported by consideration moving from the promisee raises a question which is considered shortly.[2] It is, however, clear in English law that enforceable contracts come into being. Indeed this is recognised expressly or implicitly in every documentary credit case involving a bank as defendant and seller or other beneficiary as plaintiff. In *Donald H Scott & Co v Barclays Bank*[3] Scrutton LJ stated:[4]

> 'The appellants gave a confirmed credit to the respondents; that is to say that they entered into contractual relations with them from which they could not withdraw except with the consent of the other party, ...'

The most recent confirmation at the highest level is to be found in Lord Diplock's speech in *United City Merchants v Royal Bank of Canada*[5] where he referred to four contractual relationships which will be involved where there is a confirmed letter of credit.[6]

1 Para 2.10 et seq.
2 Para 5.6 et seq.
3 [1923] 2 KB 1.
4 Ibid at 14.
5 [1983] 1 AC 168 at 182, 3.
6 He omitted to refer to the contract between the issuing bank and the seller, but referred only to the contract between the confirming bank and the seller. The other three contracts referred to were the underlying contract of sale, the contract between the buyer and the issuing bank and that between the issuing bank and the confirming bank.

5.3 While the existence of the contracts is firmly established, it is not definitely established by case law when the contract comes into being. The point has been considered in paragraph 2.11, and Article 9 and the cases of *Urquhart, Lindsay & Co Ltd v Eastern Bank Ltd*[1] and *Dexters Ltd v Schenker & Co*[2] were cited. There can be little doubt that the credit becomes binding on the bank from the moment of receipt of advice of it by the beneficiary.[3] That does, however, give rise to one problem: what is the position where the beneficiary responds to its receipt by complaining that it does not accord with the underlying contract or otherwise asking for its amendment? If he does that, is the bank nonetheless bound by the credit which it has advised, should the beneficiary thereafter change his position and seek to hold the bank to it? The outcome of such a dispute would, no doubt, depend upon the detailed facts, in particular the terms in which the beneficiary had responded to the advice of the credit. It may be thought to be unlikely to arise before the courts. The alternative view, that the credit becomes binding when the beneficiary has done some act in reliance upon it would introduce an undesirable element of uncertainty.

1 [1922] 1 KB 318.
2 (1923) 14 Ll L Rep 586.
3 See also *Bunge-Corpn v Vegetable Vitamin Foods (Private) Ltd* [1985] 1 Lloyds Rep 613 at 617.

5.4 *Pre-advice or preliminary advice* Sometimes a bank is asked to notify the beneficiary of a forthcoming credit without awaiting its actual issue. The resulting notification may be called a pre-advice or a preliminary advice. If the bank gives such a notification, it is bound to issue a credit in terms not inconsistent with the pre-advice without delay. This may also occur with the notification of amendments. Article 11.c provides:

> ARTICLE 11.c[1] A preliminary advice of the issuance or amendment of an irrevocable Credit (pre-advice) shall only be given by an Issuing Bank if such bank is prepared to issue the operative Credit instrument or the operative amendment thereto. Unless otherwise stated in such preliminary advice by the Issuing Bank, an Issuing Bank having given such pre-advice shall be irrevocably committed to issue or amend the Credit, in terms not inconsistent with the pre-advice, without delay.

Where a confirming bank is involved, the pre-advice may almost certainly come through the confirming bank. Presumably the Article only refers to an issuing bank because of the complications which the involvement of a confirming bank as an obligated party at this stage would involve. A bank which has been asked to notify a pre-advice of a credit which it will in due course confirm will no doubt simply inform the beneficiary of the pre-advice without obligation on its part.

1 Article 11.c is a new provision.

5.5 *Revocable credits* Here no effective contract[1] comes into being until the beneficiary has presented documents which have been accepted. Although Article 8.b does not refer to the rights of the beneficiary, it is clear from the Article that once documents have been accepted the issuing bank can no longer revoke the credit, and the beneficiary is entitled to payment in accordance with the terms of the credit.[2]

1 For even if it is right to say that there is a contract, it is a contract which the bank can revoke or amend at any time prior to acceptance of documents.
2 See para 2.7 above.

5.6 *Consideration* It is a requirement of English law that for a contractual promise which is not under seal to be enforceable it must be supported by consideration moving from the promisee. As it is plainly established in English law that the opening of an irrevocable credit establishes a contract between the bank and the beneficiary, it is not important in practice whether there is consideration to be found for the bank's promise or whether the contract is an exception to the general rule as to consideration.

5.7 It is worth first looking at the matter without any preconceptions. How is the communication of the credit to the seller to be seen? It is suggested that can be described with some accuracy as an offer to the seller from the bank, that if he presents correct documents, payment will follow. This analysis is supported by the dictum of Donaldson J in *Elder Dempster Lines Ltd v Ionic Shipping Agency Inc*:[1]

> 'The best explanation of the legal phenomenon constituted by a banker's letter of credit is that it is an offer which is accepted by being drawn upon.'

But this does not explain as a matter of legal theory why the issuing bank and any confirming bank cannot withdraw the offer made by the opening of the credit at any time prior to the presentation of documents. Once the seller has acted upon the offer by presenting documents to the bank, there is no difficulty in finding consideration. The presentation of documents is a form of executed consideration, just as where a reward is offered and the claimant returns the lost article or provides information as to the crime, that act provides consideration and he has an enforceable right to the reward.[2] The difficulty is to find consideration moving from the beneficiary of the credit in order to establish a binding contract at the time that the credit is first advised to him.[3]

1 [1968] 1 Lloyd's Rep 529 at 535.
2 See generally, *Chitty on Contract* (26th edn) 'General Principles' paras 161 and 261.
3 Reference may also be made to the discussion of consideration in relation to performance bonds and guarantees in Chapter 12, para 12.54 et seq.

5.8 It is suggested that the true position is that irrevocable letters of credit which are governed by English law constitute an exception to the rule of English law as to consideration. The undertakings of the issuing and confirming banks are not supported by consideration moving from the seller, but are binding in law nonetheless.[1] The rationale may be given as 'mercantile usage', meaning that since the first development of irrevocable credits traders and banks have intended and accepted that banks should be bound. In *Hamzeh Malas & Sons v British Imex Industries Ltd*[2] Jenkins LJ stated:[3]

> 'We have been referred to a number of authorities, and it seems to be plain enough that the opening of a confirmed letter of credit constitutes a bargain between the banker and the vendor of the goods, which imposes upon the banker an absolute obligation to pay, irrespective of any dispute there may be between the parties as to whether the goods are up to contract or not. An elaborate commercial system has been built up on the footing that bankers' confirmed credits are of that character, and, in my judgment, it would be wrong for this court in the present case to interfere with that established practice.'

1 That an irrevocable credit is a clear exception to the doctrine of consideration is stated in *Chitty on Contract* (26th edn) 'General Principles' para 268.
2 [1958] 2 QB 127.
3 Ibid at 129.

5.9 Various arguments have been put forward from time to time in an attempt to find consideration to support the banker's promise, some of which are worth examination.

5.10 In *Dexters Ltd v Schenker & Co*[1] it was pleaded that the undertaking was not supported by consideration. But the plea was withdrawn by counsel at the trial. Greer J stated with reference to the plea 'Now it is clear that, until they got a form of banker's credit which would comply with the terms of the contract, the plaintiffs were not bound to send the goods forward at all; and therefore not having got the banker's credit until there was a substituted arrangement for another credit elsewhere, they were under no obligation to anybody to send forward the goods. Therefore it is quite clear there was full and ample consideration for this undertaking . . . .'. Where the underlying contract provides for payment by letter of credit the seller's obligation to the buyer to ship the goods and present documents is conditional on the letter of credit being provided.[2] When a credit conforming to the underlying contract is advised to the seller, his obligation towards the buyer becomes unconditional. However, these facts do not establish consideration moving from the seller in relation to the bank's undertaking to him. Consideration need not move towards the promisor: it is sufficient if the promisee suffers some detriment at the promisor's request although no corresponding benefit is conferred on the promisor. But here the promisee, the beneficiary, does nothing: all that happens is that one of the provisions of the contract which the beneficiary has previously made with the applicant for the credit takes effect in accordance with that contract.[3] If something which is relied on as consideration is not given or done in return for the promise in question, but was done before and independently of it, as is the case with the undertakings contained in the contract between the buyer and the seller, it cannot in law amount to consideration for the promise. It is what is called 'past consideration'. It has also to be borne in mind that there is no undertaking from the seller or beneficiary to the bank: the seller never becomes obliged to the bank to present documents conforming to the credit. This fact and the fact that the contract between the buyer and the seller precedes the opening of the credit and the banks are not involved at that stage, lie at the nub of the problem of consideration.

1 (1923) 14 Ll L Rep 586.
2 Para 3.24 above.
3 Cf *Benjamin's Sale of Goods* (4th edn) para 23–099.

5.11 The 'offer and acceptance' theory relies upon the seller's presentation of documents as an acceptance of the bank's offer made by notifying the credit. This cannot explain how the bank becomes bound prior to the presentation of documents as is the case save with revocable credits.

5.12 Another theory relies on the buyer being the seller's agent, on the ground that the buyer is to be taken to have the authority of the seller to arrange for the price to be paid by letter of credit as has been agreed between them. It is then apparently suggested that the consideration undoubtedly provided by the buyer to the bank can be taken as provided on behalf of the seller and used to support the contract between the bank and the seller. That suggestion has its own difficulties. But the theory collapses at the start. For the fact that it is the intention of the seller that the buyer should arrange the letter of credit does not make him the seller's agent to do so. It would come as a great surprise to any seller that, in applying to the issuing bank for the credit to be opened, the buyer was acting as his agent, and there is no justification for implying any such agency.

5.13 *The undertakings under the Uniform Customs*   The main ways in which a credit can be operated have been considered in Chapter 1,[1] and the undertakings which a bank may typically give have been generally described. Article 9 of the Uniform Customs sets out the undertakings of the banks in specific situations to which it refers. Article 9.a relates to those given by an issuing bank, and Article 9.b to those given by a confirming bank.

ARTICLE 9.a[2]   **Liability of Issuing and Confirming Banks**
An irrevocable Credit constitutes a definite undertaking of the Issuing Bank, provided that the stipulated documents are presented to the Nominated Bank or to the Issuing Bank and that the terms and conditions of the Credit are complied with:
i.   if the Credit provides for sight payment – to pay at sight;
ii. if the Credit provides for deferred payment – to pay on the maturity date(s) determinable in accordance with the stipulations of the Credit;
iii. if the Credit provides for acceptance:
    a. by the Issuing Bank – to accept Draft(s) drawn by the Beneficiary on the Issuing Bank and pay them at maturity,
    or
    b. by another drawee bank – to accept and pay at maturity Draft(s) drawn by the Beneficiary on the Issuing Bank in the event the drawee bank stipulated in the Credit does not accept Draft(s) drawn on it, or to pay Draft(s) accepted but not paid by such drawee bank at maturity;
iv. if the Credit provides for negotiation – to pay without recourse to drawers and/or bona fide holders, Draft(s) drawn by the Beneficiary and/or document(s) presented under the Credit. A Credit should not be issued available by Draft(s) on the Applicant. If the Credit nevertheless calls for Draft(s) on the Applicant, banks will consider such Draft(s) as an additional document(s).

ARTICLE 9.b[2]   A confirmation of an irrevocable Credit by another bank (the 'Confirming Bank') upon the authorisation or request of the Issuing Bank, constitutes a definite undertaking of the Confirming Bank, in addition to that of the Issuing Bank, provided that the stipulated documents are presented to the Confirming Bank or to any other Nominated Bank and that the terms and conditions of the Credit are complied with:
i.   if the Credit provides for sight payment – to pay at sight;
ii. if the Credit provides for deferred payment – to pay on the maturity date(s) determinable in accordance with the stipulations of the Credit;
iii. if the Credit provides for acceptance
    a. by the Confirming Bank – to accept Draft(s) drawn by the Beneficiary on the Confirming Bank and pay them at maturity;
    or

      b. by another drawee bank – to accept and pay at maturity Draft(s) drawn by the Beneficiary on the Confirming Bank, in the event the drawee bank stipulated in the Credit does not accept Draft(s) drawn on it, or to pay Draft(s) accepted but not paid by such drawee bank at maturity;

    iv. if the Credit provides for negotiation – to negotiate without recourse to drawers and/or bona fide holders, Draft(s) drawn by the Beneficiary and/or document(s) presented under the Credit. A Credit should not be issued available by Draft(s) on the Applicant. If the Credit nevertheless calls for Draft(s) on the Applicant, banks will consider such Draft(s) as an additional document(s).

The practical effect of these undertakings is considered below.

1 Para 1.34 et seq.
2 Articles 9.a and 9.b are based on Article 10.a and 10.b in the 1983 Revision.

5.14 In the simple case of a confirmed credit providing for sight payment, the credit will provide, or it is to be understood from it, that the documents are to be presented to the confirming bank. Assume that documents which do conform to the terms of the credit are presented within the time provided by the credit, but are wrongly rejected by the confirming bank. The seller can then sue the confirming bank.[1] Can he also sue the issuing bank even though no documents have been presented to, and none rejected by it? It is submitted that, should he need to do so, the seller can. He does not have to make a separate presentation of the documents to the issuing bank: the credit provides for a single presentation to the confirming bank, and as between the two banks the confirming bank is the agent of the issuing bank.[2] So the rejection of the documents by the former is to be attributed to the latter. Also, as a practical matter it may have become too late under the terms of the credit to present documents to the issuing bank. Under Article 10(a)(i) of the 1983 Revision the undertaking of the issuing bank where the credit provided for sight payment was 'to pay, or that payment will be made'. The latter words were looking to where payment was to be made by another, and that other would commonly be the confirming bank. The omission from Article 9.a.i of the words 'or that payment will be made' would seem an error. But it cannot be treated as one of consequence because any other position is unarguable. So the undertaking of the issuing bank where there is a confirming bank is that the confirming bank will pay. The issuing bank is thus in practical effect the guarantor of the confirming bank rather than the other way. The undertaking of a confirming bank to pay is stated in Article 9.b.i.

1 See among other cases *United City Merchants (Investments) Ltd v Royal Bank of Canada* [1983] 1 AC 168.
2 See para 6.13.

5.15 Where the credit provides for deferred payment the position is the same, and Articles 9.a.ii and 9.b.ii are to like effect. The seller is then entitled to payment from the banks after the interval provided by the deferred payment term of the credit. The same point arises as to the omission of 'or that payment will be made' as in the previous paragraph.

5.16 Where the credit calls for bills to be drawn by the beneficiary on the issuing bank, the 1984 Revision provided by Article 10.a.iii that the issuing bank should accept (and pay) drafts drawn on it, and by Article 10.b.iii that the confirming bank would be responsible for their acceptance and payment. Article 9.b.iii now provides that, if drafts are drawn on another bank (for example, the issuing bank), the confirming bank undertakes, first, to accept and pay at maturity drafts drawn on the confirming bank if the other bank fails to accept drafts drawn on it, and, second, to pay drafts accepted by the other bank but not paid at maturity. No point arises on the second obligation. But the idea of the beneficiary having to draw fresh drafts on the confirming bank if the issuing bank fails to accept drafts drawn on it, seems an unnecessary complication. The expression of the obligation in these terms can be argued to mean that the beneficiary must draw a further draft to render the confirming bank liable. The wording is not well chosen if the aim is to give the beneficiary an opportunity to draw fresh drafts for the purpose of having them discounted. But, it is suggested, such an argument must be wrong. As was provided by the 1983 Revision, the beneficiary must remain entitled simply to demand the money from the confirming bank at maturity. The position is the same under the 1993 Revision where the credit calls for drafts drawn on the confirming bank, but with the parties reversed: see Articles 9.a.iii.b and 9.b.iii.a. So it is suggested that the Article should not be read as requiring the beneficiary, as a pre-requisite of holding the issuing bank liable, to present a second draft to the issuing bank where the confirming bank has refused to accept a draft drawn on it as provided for by the credit. Nor should a second draft drawn on the confirming bank be required where it is the issuing bank which has failed to accept the draft drawn on it. That this is the correct reading of the Article and that the references to second drafts just give the beneficiary an option is confirmed by the commentary on the Article in the ICC's UCP 500 and 400 Compared.[1]

1 Publication No 4U.

5.17 *Drafts drawn on the applicant*   In the 1983 Revision Articles 10.a.iii and 10.b.iii referred to, and provided for, drafts drawn on the applicant. In some parts of the world, in India particularly, it is common for credits to involve such drafts. Their use can be argued to serve no practical purpose which cannot be better served by a draft drawn on a bank. Further, as credits involve undertakings by banks, it is undesirable to include as part of the operation of the credit a source of obligation between the beneficiary and the applicant by means of a draft drawn by one on the other. It is no doubt for such reasons that the 1993 Revision provides in Articles 9.a.iv and 9.b.iv[1] that credits shall not be issued available by drafts drawn on the applicant. The problem is what is to happen if nonetheless a credit is issued which does so provide. The Articles referred to state that, if it does, banks are to consider such documents as 'additional documents'. What does that mean? It is suggested that it must mean that the banks shall consider the draft as a document to be presented with the other documents called for by the credit, but not as playing any part in the mechanism of payment or involving any obligation on the part of the banks. In some circumstances it may be necessary for the banks to take further account of the term of the credit providing for drafts on the applicant. Suppose that the credit states that it is 'available by your drafts drawn on the applicant payable 30 days after sight'. Depending on other terms as to the availability the credit, that would probably mean that the credit would provide payment 30 days after the applicant had sight of the draft. In a situation involving a time draft to be drawn on an applicant, the credit cannot be treated as available by immediate payment, because that would defeat the clear intention of the parties. It is probably to be treated as providing for deferred payment 30 days after the documents are presented to the bank where the credit is available. This is a practical but not wholly logical solution to a problem which the Articles create but do not address. *Forestal Mimosa Ltd v Oriental Credit Ltd*[2] is an example of the application of Article 10(b)(iii) in the 1983 Revision. The defendant bank was held liable because bills drawn on the buyers pursuant to the credit had not been accepted by them.

1 Although these begin by referring to credits available by negotiation it is clear from the omission of drafts drawn on applicants from the remainder of Article 9 that the ban on drafts drawn on applicants is intended to be general.
2 [1986] 1 WLR 631.

5.18 Where the credit provides for negotiation, the issuing bank is obliged by Article 9.a.iv 'to pay' the drafts. The confirming bank is obliged by Article 9.b.iv 'to negotiate' them. It is suggested that there is no difference between payment and negotiation here: in this respect they follow Article 10 and Article 10's predecessor in the 1974 Revision, Article 3, had provided that the banks should 'purchase/negotiate' drafts in each case. In 1979 the ICC Banking Commission was asked to define 'purchase' and 'negotiation' in the context of Article 3 and responded that there was no difference between them.[1] It appears that in the preparation of the 1983 Revision it was decided to use a single word. 'To pay' was found appropriate for an issuing bank because the bank undertakes payment responsibility, whereas 'to negotiate' was appropriate for a confirming bank.[2] It is suggested that the thought processes may not yet be wholly clear. Negotiation will provide immediate payment in contrast with the situations referred to in (c) and (d) above, where payment should come from the acceptor of the bill at its maturity. Unless the credit provides that the beneficiary is entitled to the full amount of the draft, he will only receive its discounted value, ie its face value less interest over its period and charges. The last part of Article 10.a.iv in the 1983 Revision provided that where the credit provided for negotiation by another bank, the issuing bank undertook to pay if negotiation was not effected. This possibility is not covered in the 1993 Revision expressly.

1 See Decisions (1975–1979) of the ICC Banking Commission, Reference 2.
2 See UCP 1974/1983 Revisions Compared and Explained, ICC Publication No 411, pp 22, 23.

5.19 Where in accordance with the above principles the seller is entitled to receive payment on the presentation of the documents, if payment is refused he will be able to proceed against the confirming and issuing banks. If he is not entitled to immediate payment but, for example, payment is to be made 80 days after the bill of lading date available by drafts drawn on a bank, if the documents are not accepted by the confirming bank, the seller may proceed against the banks. If the documents are accepted by the banks but the bill is not accepted by the buyers, again the seller may proceed against the banks. Finally, if the bill is accepted but not paid, following the dishonour by non-payment the seller may then proceed against the banks.[1]

1 The right to proceed against a bank where another bank has failed to accept a draft drawn on it gives rise to the problem raised in paragraph 5.16 as to the need to present a new draft to the bank sought to be held liable. It is there suggested that despite the changes in the relevant Article, this is not necessary.

C. Amendment

5.20 The question of amendment of a credit has been considered in Chapter 3.[1] The essential point is that once a credit has been advised to its beneficiary it cannot be amended without his consent. For the advice of the credit brings into being a contract between the beneficiary and the bank or banks and contracts cannot be unilaterally amended.

1 Para 3.33 et seq. 3.38

D. Time for Presentation of Documents

5.21 There are three periods or dates to be considered. Firstly, the documents must be presented within the period of validity of the credit. Secondly, where a transport document is required, the documents must be presented within a period calculated from the date of shipment. Thirdly, it is likely that shipment itself must be made within a defined period or by a particular date.[1]

1 These must, of course, be considered separately: Case 279 in the ICC's More Case Studies on Documentary Credits, Publication No 489. The beneficiary has only to present the documents by the date: it is, of course, not necessary for him to do so in time to enable the documents to be processed by the bank by the date: Case 275 in More Case Studies.

5.22 *(a) Expiry date*   It is obvious that a credit should stipulate a latest date for presentation of documents. Article 42 provides:

ARTICLE 42[1]   **Expiry Date and Place for Presentation of Documents**
a. All Credits must stipulate an expiry date and a place for presentation of documents for payment, acceptance, or with the exception of freely negotiable Credits, a place for presentation of documents for negotiation. An expiry date stipulated for payment, acceptance or negotiation will be construed to express an expiry date for presentation of documents.
b. Except as provided in sub-Article 44(a), documents must be presented on or before such expiry date.
c. If an Issuing Bank states that the Credit is to be available 'for one month', 'for six months', or the like, but does not specify the date from which the time is to run, the date of issuance of the Credit by the Issuing Bank will be deemed to be the first day from which such time is to run. Banks should discourage indication of the expiry date of the Credit in this manner.

Documents cannot be presented once the expiry date has passed,[2] subject only to the possibility of an extension under Article 44.a.[3] For a beneficiary to be able to apply Article 42.c it is necessary for him to know the date on which the credit was issued – which will usually be different to the date of the advice of the credit to him as the advice will commonly come from an advising bank.

1 Article 42 is taken from Article 48 in the 1983 Revision. The reference to 'place' in Article 42.a is new, as is the second sentence.
2 This includes documents which are presented to 'repair discrepancies' as is confirmed by Case 276 in the ICC's More Case Studies on Documentary Credits, Publication No 489.
3 See para 5.25 below.

5.23 The place where the documents are to be by the date has also to be ascertained; and Article 42.a now provides that this must be stated in the credit. This will often be obvious as, for example, where the documents are to be presented direct to the confirming bank. But it may be less clear where the documents are to be negotiated through a second bank, as was the case in *European Asian Bank AG v Punjab and Sind Bank (No 2)*.[1] There the credit provided that it was valid for negotiation in Singapore until 15 September 1979, which in the context meant negotiation at the Algemene Bank to which negotiation was restricted under the terms of the credit. The second sentence of Article 42.a makes clear that with a negotiation credit it is the negotiation which must take place by the expiry date and not the presentation by the negotiating bank to the correspondent bank or issuing bank as it may be. This is reinforced by Article 10, which provides that with a freely negotiable credit any bank is a nominated bank. It is also confirmed by the commentary on Article 42 in the ICC's UCP 500 and 400 compared. This, of course, must be subject to any contrary indication in the credit itself.

1 [1983] 1 WLR 642, [1983] 1 Lloyd's Rep 611.

5.24 *(b) Time from date of issuance of transport documents*
Under a CIF contract it is the duty of the seller to make every reasonable effort to send the documents forward as soon as possible after he has despatched the goods to the buyer.[1] This may have been a source of the practice of banks in connection with letters of credit to reject bills of lading which were 'stale'. But that expression was not normally used to mean that the bills had not been presented as soon as they might have been: it usually meant that they had not been presented in time for the applicant for the credit to deal with the goods on the arrival of the ship, whereby he might have been put to extra expense, for example, by way of storage charges.[2] The practice was unsatisfactory in that certainty as to what was stale and what was not might often be impossible. Article 43 of the Uniform Customs avoids the difficulty. It provides:

ARTICLE 43[3] **Limitation on the Expiry Date**
    a. In addition to stipulating an expiry date for presentation of documents, every Credit which calls for a transport document(s) should also stipulate a specified period of time after the date of shipment during which presentation must be made in compliance with the terms and conditions of the Credit. If no such period of time is stipulated, banks will not accept documents presented to them later than 21 days after the date of shipment. In any event, documents must be presented not later than the expiry date of the Credit.
    b. In cases in which sub-Article 40.b applies, the date of shipment will be considered to be the latest shipment date on any of the transport documents presented.

Although Article 43.a refers to banks generally, it is clearly to be read as referring to the bank to whom documents are first to be presented under the credit, as Article 42 shows. There can be no question of an issuing bank declining documents presented to it by the advising bank, which were duly presented to the advising bank by the beneficiary by the required date. Where a standby credit is payable against written notification of non-payment for goods shipped, accompanied by a copy invoice and a copy bill of lading, Article 43.a does not apply to the copy bill of lading because it is not (and is not being presented as) a transport document.[4,5] Article 40.b (referred to in Article 43.b) relates to the position where one shipment is covered by more than one transport document. Shipment dates are otherwise to be determined in accordance with the provisions of the Articles relating to the different types of transport document considered in Part C of Chapter 8.

1 See *Sanders Bros v Maclean & Co* (1883) 11 QBD 327 and *Sassoon's CIF and FOB Contracts* (3rd edn) (British Shipping Laws Vol 5), para 242 and the cases there cited.
2 See *Schmitthoff's Export Trade* (9th edn) p 582, and Gutteridge & Megrah *The Law of Bankers' Commercial Credits* (7th edn) pp 122 and 153.
3 Article 43.a is based on Article 47.a in the 1983 Revision, Article 43.b is new.
4 Opinions of the ICC Banking Commission 1987–1988 at R 168.
5 The question of stale or out-of-date documents is also considered in Chapter 8, para 8.38.

5.25 *(c) Extension of time under Article 44*   The Article extends the time for presentation of documents to the next following business day on which the bank is open where the last day (either the expiry date or the last day for presentation of transport documents, whichever is first) falls on a day on which the bank is closed. Article 44.a states:

> ARTICLE 44.a[1]   **Extension of Expiry Date**
> If the expiry date of the Credit and/or the last day of the period of time for presentation of documents stipulated by the Credit or applicable by virtue of Article 43 falls on a day on which the bank to which presentation has to be made is closed for reasons other than those referred to in Article 17, the stipulated expiry date and/or the last day of the period of time after the date of shipment for presentation of documents, as the case may be, shall be extended to the first following day on which such bank is open.

The reasons referred to in Article 17 are 'Acts of God, riots, civil commotions, insurrections, wars or any other causes beyond their control, or by any strikes or lockouts'. The reason for these to be excluded may be that they are likely to be long-lasting as opposed to the effect of a weekend or public holiday, and it may be undesirable to have credits extended for long and uncertain periods. Where Article 44.a is operated, the bank to whom presentation is made on the first following business day must 'provide a statement that the documents were presented with the time limits extended in accordance with sub-Article 44.a of the Uniform Customs and Practice for Documentary Credits, 1993 revision, ICC Publication 500'. Where the credit provides a latest date for loading goods on board, or dispatch, or taking in charge, Article 44.b provides that that date is not to be extended by reason of Article 44.a. If no such latest date for shipment is stipulated in the credit, the bank will reject transport documents indicating a date of issuance later than the original expiry date. This is presumably on the basis that the original expiry date was necessarily the last day on which shipment could be made, and there is no reason for that to change because the bank cannot deal with the documents.

ARTICLE 44.b[1]   The latest date for shipment shall not be extended by reason of the extension of the expiry date and/or the period of time after the date of shipment for presentation of documents in accordance with sub-Article .a above. If no such latest date for shipment is stipulated in the Credit or amendments thereto, banks will not accept transport documents indicating a date of shipment later than the expiry date stipulated in the Credit or amendments thereto.

ARTICLE 44.c[1]   The bank to which presentation is made on such first following business day must provide a statement that the documents were presented within the time limits extended in accordance with sub-Article 44.a of the Uniform Customs and Practice for Documentary Credits, 1993 Revision, ICC Publication No. 500.

1 Article 44 follows Article 48 in the 1983 Revision.

5.26 (d) Shipment period   It is likely that the underlying contract of sale will contain a provision as to when shipment should be made. This should be repeated in the credit so that transport documents bearing inappropriate dates will be rejected. Here Article 46 of the Uniform Customs is relevant as to the meaning of shipment. It provides:

ARTICLE 46[1]   **General Expressions as to Dates for Shipment**
a. Unless otherwise stipulated in the Credit, the expression 'shipment' used in stipulating an earliest and/or a latest date for shipment will be understood to include expressions such as, 'loading on board', 'dispatch', 'accepted for carriage', 'date of post receipt', 'date of pick-up', and the like, and in the case of a Credit calling for a multimodal transport document the expression 'taking in charge'.
b. Expressions such as 'prompt', 'immediately', 'as soon as possible', and the like should not be used. If they are used banks will disregard them.
c. If the expression 'on or about' or similar expressions are used, banks will interpret them as a stipulation that shipment is to be made during the period from five days before to five days after the specified date, both end days included.

It has already been noted that no extension of shipping date is obtainable under Article 44, and that, where a credit contains no latest date for shipment, transport documents indicating a date of issue after the expiry date contained in the credit will be rejected even though an extension under the Article is otherwise available.

1 Derived from Article 50 in the 1983 Revision.

5.27 (e) Banking hours   Article 45 provides:

ARTICLE 45[1]   **Hours of Presentation**
Banks are under no obligation to accept presentation of documents outside their banking hours.

This leaves it free to a beneficiary in difficulties to make his own arrangements with a bank to accept documents out of hours, if he can. It is suggested in the ICC's UCP 500 and 400 Compared[2] that if a bank wishes to restrict the hours within which presentations may be made to a lesser period than its ordinary banking hours this may be stated in the credit.

1 As Article 49 in the 1983 Revision.
2 Publication No 511.

5.28 **(f) Instalments**   A credit may provide for drawings or shipments by instalments within given periods. If it does so, Article 41 of the Uniform Customs applies. It states:

> ARTICLE 41[1]   **Instalment Shipments/Drawings**
> If drawings and/or shipments by instalments within given periods are stipulated in the Credit and any instalment is not drawn and/or shipped within the period allowed for that instalment, the Credit ceases to be available for that and any subsequent instalments, unless otherwise stipulated in the Credit.

So the failure to ship or present documents in time will lose the benefit of the credit for subsequent instalments. The position will be the same where documents are presented in time but fail to comply with the credit. For the presentation of non-complying documents is the equivalent of no presentation. The Article may provide a trap where a standby credit is intended to act as a guarantee of more than one payment or obligation. If it is unnecessary to call it on the first occasion, the Article will prevent any further calls thereby defeating the object of the standby credit. Where a standby credit is of this nature, the Article should be excluded from the Credit.[2]

1 As Article 45 in the 1983 Revision.
2 See further para 12.19 below.

5.29 **(g) Where no time for presentation is stipulated**   Very occasionally and contrary to Article 42.a there is no statement of the time in which the documents must be presented. It is inconceivable that the parties should intend that the credit should remain open for an unlimited period, ie forever. So it is to be implied that presentation must take place within a reasonable time of the opening of the credit. There is no English authority supporting this implication, although it is clear as a matter of principle. There is some American authority.[1] What such time is will be determined by all the circumstances of the case, in particular the nature of the transaction. They will include the actual circumstances as they arise after the opening of the credit, and not caused or contributed to by the beneficiary.[2] If a bank becomes concerned that a credit with no express time limit remains open, it is open to it to serve a notice on the beneficiary giving the beneficiary a final further period, which must be a reasonable one, in which to present documents, stating that the bank will thereafter treat the credit as expired.[3] Reference may here be made to credits which have what is known as an 'evergreen clause'. This is usually to be found in American performance-related standby credits. The credit has an expiry date but is automatically reinstated unless the issuing bank gives notice that it is to expire.

1 See *Lamborn v National Park Bank of New York* 148 NE 664 at 666; affg 208 NYS 428 (1925).
2 See *Hick v Raymond and Reid* [1893] AC 22 at 29.
3 See *British and Commonwealth Holdings plc v Quadrex Holdings Inc* [1989] QB 842.

E. Partial Drawings

5.30 The underlying contract may provide for shipment to be made in instalments, in which case this will be reflected in the credit. The seller should then present documents separately in relation to each instalment. The effect of Article 41 of the Uniform Customs has been already described.[1] It is common also for credits expressly to permit the seller to make partial shipments. He may then present separately documents in respect of each shipment. If the credit is silent, partial drawings and shipments are allowed: Article 40.a provides:

> ARTICLE 40.a Partial drawings and/or shipments are allowed, unless the Credit stipulates otherwise.[2]

1 Para 5.28.
2 Article 40 is considered in Chapter 8, para 8.108.

F. The Examination and Acceptance or Rejection of Documents

5.31 *Outline* When documents are presented to a bank under a credit, it is the duty of the bank to examine them to see whether they accord with the credit. The first bank to do so will commonly be the advising bank which in the majority of cases will also have confirmed the credit. If it is satisfied that they conform, it will pay the beneficiary – if payment is what the credit provides, and will forward the documents to the issuing bank. The issuing bank in its turn will then examine the documents. If the advising bank considers that the documents do not conform to the credit, it may seek the instructions of the issuing bank (who will seek the instructions of the applicant) whether they may be accepted nonetheless.[1] Subject to that it is its duty to reject the documents and either to return them to the beneficiary or to hold them to his order. The duty of a bank in examining the documents, general requirements as to documents and requirements as to specific documents are considered in Chapter 8 so that the whole subject matter of documents is taken together. This section considers the procedural steps which banks should follow towards the beneficiary, in particular the course to be followed in rejecting documents.

1 As to this practice, see para 5.37 et seq. Note that Article 14.c refers only to the issuing bank and to its right to approach the applicant.

5.32 *Article 14* The bank to which documents are first presented under a credit has the duty of examining them for compliance with the credit, of deciding whether they should be accepted or refused, and, in the event of refusal, notifying that refusal to the party presenting the documents. The examination of the documents must be carried out with reasonable care in accordance with the provisions of Article 13.a, which is considered in paragraph 8.2 below. The procedure to be followed by the bank in the three tasks of examination, decision and notification is otherwise laid down by Article 14.b to 14.e. These provide:

ARTICLE 14   b. Upon receipt of the documents the Issuing Bank and/or Confirming Bank, if any, or a Nominated Bank acting on their behalf, must determine on the basis of the documents alone whether or not they appear on their face to be in compliance with the terms and conditions of the Credit. If the documents appear on their face not to be in compliance with the terms and conditions of the Credit, such banks may refuse to take up the documents.

c. If the Issuing Bank determines that the documents appear on their face not to be in compliance with the terms and conditions of the Credit, it may in its sole judgment approach the Applicant for a waiver of the discrepancy(ies). This does not, however, extend the period mentioned in sub-Article 13.b.

d.i. If the Issuing Bank and/or Confirming Bank, if any, or a Nominated Bank acting on their behalf, decides to refuse the documents, it must give notice to that effect by telecommunication or, if that is not possible, by other expeditious means, without delay but no later than the close of the seventh banking day following the day of receipt of the documents. Such notice shall be given to the bank from which it received the documents, or to the Beneficiary, if it received the documents directly from him.

ii. Such notice must state all discrepancies in respect of which the bank refuses the documents and must also state whether it is holding the documents at the disposal of, or is returning them to, the presenter.

iii. The Issuing Bank and/or Confirming Bank, if any, shall then be entitled to claim from the remitting bank refund, with interest, of any reimbursement which has been made to that bank.

e. If the Issuing Bank and/or Confirming Bank, if any, fails to act in accordance with the provisions of this Article and/or fails to hold the documents at the disposal of, or return them to the presenter, the Issuing Bank and/or Confirming Bank, if any, shall be precluded from claiming that the documents are not in compliance with the terms and conditions of the Credit.

In addition to the reference to a seven day period in Article 14.d.i the time permitted is provided for by Article 13.b, which states:

ARTICLE 13.b   The Issuing Bank, the Confirming Bank, if any, or a Nominated Bank acting on their behalf, shall each have a reasonable time, not to exceed seven banking days following the day of receipt of the documents, to examine the documents and determine whether to take up or refuse the documents and to inform the party from which it received the documents accordingly.

Articles 13.b to .e and 14 had their predecessors in Article 16 of the 1983 Revision. There are important changes which will be mentioned in commenting on the provisions.

5.33 The matters provided for by Articles 14.b to 14.e and 13.b are:
— The examination of the documents for discrepancies
— Approach to applicant for waiver of discrepancies
— Decision to refuse (in event of discrepancies)

— Notification to presenter of documents:
    (i)   of refusal
    (ii) of all discrepancies
    (iii) whether documents held at presenter's disposal or being
          returned
— All within the time limit provided by Article 13.b
— Documents to be held at presenter's disposal or to be returned to
   him.

Failure to comply precludes the bank from claiming that the documents
do not comply with the credit. So, if a bank fails to comply with any aspect
of these requirements, it may be left with documents on its hands for
which it must pay and which it cannot oblige the issuing bank or the
applicant (as it may be) to accept and pay for. So consequences which are
most serious for a bank can follow from even a minor non-compliance.

5.34 In considering the application of Articles 14.b to 14.e a point must be
remembered which the Article only spells out with regard to a nominated
bank. This is that, in English law at least, an advising bank which is given
the duty under the credit of checking and accepting the documents and
commonly also the function of paying, does so as the agent of the issuing
bank as is set out in Chapter 6.[1] Where the advising bank also confirms
the credit it will act in a dual capacity in performing those functions,
namely, so far as the issuing bank is concerned it acts as that bank's agent;
and with regard to its own obligations to the seller as the confirming
banker it acts as principal. So when an advising bank comes to examine
the documents presented to it, as it is the agent of the issuing bank it must
comply with Article 14 to secure compliance by the issuing bank with the
Article. If it fails to do so, the effect may be to bar the issuing bank from
contending against the beneficiary that the documents do not comply.
This will not arise where the beneficiary has been paid. For in that
situation the outcome will be that the issuing bank will refuse to pay the
advising bank (or, if the advising bank has been reimbursed prior to the
issuing bank's receipt and checking of the documents, it will be obliged to
repay the issuing bank). Where it will matter is if, under the terms of the
credit, the beneficiary has not been paid following presentation of documents (either because payment has been refused or is deferred under the
terms of the credit) and is looking to the issuing bank for payment. Then
non-compliance with Article 14 by the advising bank would bar the
issuing bank from alleging that the documents were not in order. Should
the buyer refuse to waive the discrepancy, the issuing bank could recover
its ultimate loss from the advising bank as damages for breach by the
advising bank of its duty as the issuing bank's agent.[2]

1 Para 6.11.
2 Reference should also be made to the argument arising from Article 18.a that all acts of
   the correspondent bank are at the risk of the applicant for the credit, which is considered
   in Chapter 4, para 4.18. The matters considered here are a further reason for rejecting
   that argument.

5.35 *The banks referred to in Article 14*   In Article 16 of the 1983
Revision the provisions equivalent to Article 14.b, 14.d, 14.e and 13.b[1]
referred only to the issuing bank. So where, as is very commonly the case,
the first bank to receive the documents for examination under the credit
was a correspondent bank (which would often have also confirmed the

credit), the provisions did not expressly apply but could only be applied by analogy.[2] This omission is now corrected. The agency position of a correspondent bank considered in the previous paragraph is probably the reason why it has been thought inappropriate to refer in Articles 14.d.iii and 14.e to a nominated bank. It may also have been thought that, if a nominated bank pays out in advance of its examination of the documents, it will be entitled to be reimbursed by its principal: the principal will have the claim to recover the money paid from the recipient of it – Article 14.d.iii. Likewise it is the principal for which the nominated bank acts, which is precluded as provided by Article 14.e. Whereas Article 14.d.ii requires notification to be given to the bank from which the documents are received or to the beneficiary if they were received from him, Article 14.d.iii refers only to reimbursement of monies paid to a remitting bank. The position of a beneficiary who has received payment in advance of the examination of his documents is not covered. But he will be similarly liable to refund what he has received, as a matter of law.

1 Article 16.b, 16.d, 16.e and 16.c respectively.
2 The position was considered in the recent case of *Seaconsar Far East Ltd v Bank Markazi* [1993] 1 Lloyd's Rep 236 at 241.2 and 255.1 but only so far as necessary to resolve a dispute as to jurisdiction.

5.36 *Examination of documents*   Article 14.b provides that the bank must determine on the basis of the documents alone whether to take them up or to refuse them and claim that they appear on their face not to be in accordance with the terms and conditions of the credit. This is fundamental. As is provided by Article 4 'In credit operations all parties concerned deal in documents and not in goods, services and/or other performances to which the documents may relate.' The bank is not entitled to take account of any information apart from the documents themselves. In particular it may not take account of information relating to the quality of the goods not shown by the documents. This principle, sometimes referred to as the principle of autonomy, has been discussed in Chapter 1[1] and is the foundation-stone of the discussion of fraud in Chapter 9.

1 Para 1.40 et seq.

5.37 *Consulting the applicant*   Article 14.c is a new provision. It spells out that, where an issuing bank finds discrepancies, it may approach its client, the applicant, for instructions whether they may be waived and the documents accepted. The purpose of the approach must be limited to waiver and may not be to enable a joint decision to be made as to possible discrepancies. This practice is very common and has the result that a large number of credit transactions go through which would otherwise fail.[1] Where documents are not initially presented to the issuing bank but to a confirming or other correspondent bank which is to examine the documents, it will be that bank which will have to decide whether to refuse the documents if discrepancies are found. It would be that bank which would have to seek the instructions of its principal, the issuing bank, which would in turn seek the instructions of the applicant whether the documents may nonetheless be accepted. This would be a time-consuming process and is therefore not one to be adopted save possibly at the request of the presenter of the documents. It is more important for the presenter to be speedily informed of the discrepancies in a notice rejecting the documents, so he may have an opportunity to put them right within the period of the credit. Article 14.c therefore makes no reference to a confirming bank seeking waivers of discrepancies.

1 It has been suggested that in England and America over half of the documents presented fail to comply on first presentation, and a witness in the *Bankers Trust* Case [1991] 2 Lloyd's Rep 443 stated that in 90% of the cases where the applicant's instructions were sought the instructions were to accept the documents.

5.38 It should be made clear that there can never be any occasion for the bank to permit the applicant itself to examine the documents for discrepancies. That is the job of the bank alone. The fact that Bankers Trust had permitted its client to double-check its examination of the documents (which took another three days) was fatal to its claim.[1] In the Court of Appeal it was stated 'In particular we are agreed that on no view should a bank be allowed time to enable the buyers to examine the documents for the purpose of discovering further discrepancies'.[2] It may on rare occasions be permissible for the bank to permit the applicant to examine the documents for the purpose of determining its correct course in the light of discrepancies already found.[3] This can only be where the discrepancies are of such a nature to require this for the applicant to assess their significance.

1 *Bankers Trust Co v State Bank of India* [1991] 2 Lloyd's Rep 443.
2 At 452.1, per Lloyd LJ.
3 At 455.1 per Farquharson LJ.

5.39 It is to be noted that Article 14.c gives a discretion to the bank: 'it may in its sole discretion approach the Applicant'. The Article is no doubt so worded to avoid placing any obligation on the bank to do so. It is suggested that the applicant will commonly expect to be consulted before the documents (and hence the goods) are rejected. Further, an applicant may well assert that it is his bank's duty to take his instructions before rejecting documents. Such a duty might be based on his express instructions to the bank, or, in default of that, on the course of their dealing and the nature of their relationship. On this basis an applicant might have a contractual claim for damages against a bank which rejected documents without consultation, which the applicant would have wished to accept. The discretion given by Article 14.c could be argued to give the bank a defence against such a claim. It is likely that the Article is worded as it is, not with that intention but simply to avoid by itself creating any duty on a bank to approach the applicant.

5.40 *The time for examination, determination and notification*   In the 1983 Revision Article 16.c provided for an issuing bank to have a reasonable time to examine documents and to determine whether to take up or to refuse them. The provision of a reasonable time is now found in Article 13.b. It also covers the notification of refusal. There is also now a limit of seven banking days. This is measured 'following the day of receipt of the documents', which will make the first day the day after the receipt thus giving a minimum of seven whole days.

5.41 It must be emphasised that Article 13.b does not allow seven banking days: it allows a reasonable time up to seven banking days. A reasonable time will in very many circumstances be less. Where a contract provides that something is to be done within a reasonable time, in English law this means such time as is reasonable in the circumstances of the particular case. In *Hick v Raymond and Reid*[1] Lord Herschell stated[2] '. . . there is of course no such thing as a reasonable time in the abstract. It must always depend upon circumstances . . . the only sound principle is that "reasonable time" should depend on the circumstances which actually exist.' Those which actually exist are to be contrasted with those that ordinarily exist. But those actually existing are to be excluded in so far as they have been caused or contributed to by the party having the duty to perform within the time. In the same case Lord Watson stated[3] '. . . the condition of reasonable time has been frequently interpreted; and has invariably been held to mean that the party upon whom it is incumbent duly fulfils his obligation, notwithstanding protracted delay, so long as such delay is attributable to causes beyond his control, and he has neither acted negligently nor unreasonably.' Matters which are obviously to be taken into account will include the numbers of documents to be examined and their complexity, language, and the problems posed in considering any possible discrepancies. It may also be relevant to consider the amount involved and any urgency, for example, caused by the period of time between the tender of the documents to the bank and the arrival of the vessel carrying the goods. A large and experienced bank operating in one of the world's financial centres may be expected to act more quickly than a small bank in an out of the way place.[4] It would be relevant that a bank's checking staff had been severely reduced by an epidemic or that the bank had a sudden and unexpected flood of credit work.

1 [1893] AC 22.
2 Ibid at 29.
3 Ibid at 32.
4 See the *Bankers Trust* case [1991] 2 Lloyd's Rep 443 at 455.1 per Farquharson LJ.

5.42 In *Bankers Trust Co v State Bank of India*[1] evidence was given of the practice of the United Kingdom clearing banks to set a three day time limit, which in general permitted two days for checking and one for taking instructions on any discrepancies found. In that case the bank had checked some 900 pages of documents in three days, but it fell down over the time wrongly allowed to its applicant to check them again.[2] In *Hing Yip Hing Fat Co Ltd v Daiwa Bank*[3] three banking days following receipt of documents was found reasonable to check 19 pages of documents against a four page credit. Kaplan J referred to the smaller size of the Daiwa Bank, to the fact that checkers in Hong Kong did not have English as their mother tongue and to the business of the particular month. In *Ozalid Group (Export) Ltd v African Continental Bank*[4] it was common ground that five days should be sufficient. In *Seaconsar Far East Ltd v Bank Marhazi*[5] it was conceded that the bank was entitled to five working days. It is suggested that a bank which goes about its task conscientiously should have nothing to fear provided, of course, that exceptional circumstances do not take it out of the seven day limit.[6] It may properly be hoped that the courts will not listen to criticisms made with hindsight taking an hour here and an hour or two there. The *Bankers Trust* and *Hing Yip* cases suggest that indeed they will not. The court will have in mind that the success of such an argument will mean that a beneficiary is paid for documents which do not comply with the credit, and the bank may find itself carrying a loss which is quite out of proportion to the fault on its part.

1 [1991] 2 Lloyd's Rep 443.
2 See para 5.39 above.
3 [1991] 2 HKLR 35.
4 [1979] 2 Lloyd's Rep 231.
5 [1993] 1 Lloyd's Rep 236 at 241.2.
6 In some exceptional circumstances a bank may be able to rely on Article 17, Force
  Majeure: see para 4.16 above.

5.43 *Time used in approaching the applicant*   Article 14.c provides that approaching the applicant for a waiver of discrepancies 'does not, however, extend the period mentioned in sub-Article 13.b.' In the *Bankers Trust* case[1] the Court of Appeal had to decide whether the reasonable time provided by the then Article 16.c for examination and determination of taking up or refusal should take account of any time required to consult the applicant.[2] The majority of the court (Farquharson LJ and Sir John Megaw) held that the time should be assessed taking account of that. The minority (Lloyd LJ) held that it should not. As has been noted there was no equivalent of Article 14.c. What is 'the period mentioned in Article 13.b' to which Article 14.c refers? Is it the period of seven banking days, leaving what is a reasonable time for the whole process to be assessed taking account of any consultation and subject to that limit? Or does Article 14.c mean that the reasonable time shall be assessed without regard to time which may properly be taken up with consultation? The wording itself is not clear. Nor does the further reference to the seven day period in Article 14.d.i assist. It is suggested that there is a powerful reason for concluding that the intention must be to include any time required for an approach to the applicant as a part of the reasonable time allowed by Article 13.b (but not so as to extend it beyond seven banking days). If it is reasonable to take a period of X to examine the documents within the bank and to assess any discrepancies found, and a period of Y to approach the applicant for a waiver of such actual discrepancies as the bank considers to exist, then the total period reasonably taken for the combined process is X plus Y. But if Y is not to be counted, then the bank can only achieve the desired aim of consulting the applicant, its client, if it has made time in which to do so by examining the documents in less time than a 'reasonable time' would allow. As Sir John Megaw put it in the context of the evidence in the *Bankers Trust* case:[3]

> 'The defendants' evidence . . . was that, in relation to import credits . . . the practice of the bank was to allow a maximum of three days before sending notice of a determination to refuse the documents. In many cases the examination of the documents took less than three days, in some cases much less. It might be less than one day. But the established practice . . . was on the basis that 48 hours should be allowed for the examination of the documents. Twenty-four hours were then added, "time to consult the applicant". . . . If, as the defendants contend, "time to consult the applicant", while such consultation is permissible, is not time which may be added to what otherwise would be a reasonable time, the practice spoken to . . . is not, as a matter of logic, time which may be added. If that practice is followed, a notice of the rejection of the documents, sent after the 48 hours (or lesser time, reasonably required for the examination of the documents in the particular case) has elapsed, is not within a reasonable time for the purpose of art 16(c). The three days maximum cannot be invoked to save it from being an invalid, out of time, notice: because . . . that maximum of three days has been brought into existence in order to include 24 hours for the very thing (consultation with the applicant) which, on the defendants' construction, is not a permissible element of the reasonable time specified under art 16(c).'

A second argument to the same end runs as follows. If a bank finds discrepancies, unless the applicant is consulted and is prepared to waive them the bank is bound to reject the documents: there is no process of determination whether to accept or reject to be undertaken. Therefore the determination referred to in Article 13.b must include the process of consulting the applicant. So that process is included within the reasonable time. This argument was adopted by Farquharson LJ in the *Bankers Trust* case.[4] It is therefore suggested that the purpose of the last sentence of Article 14.c is to make clear that consultation is not to be used to extend the seven day period, and that the time for carrying out the process of examination and decision including any consultation and then notification is a reasonable time subject to that maximum.

1 [1991] 2 Lloyd's Rep 443.
2 Consultation with the applicant is considered in para 5.38 et seq.
3 [1991] 2 Lloyd's Rep at 457.2.
4 [1991] Lloyd's Rep at 454.2, 455.1.

5.44 *Time to inform the remitting party*   The informing of the refusal of documents to the party who has remitted them to the bank is included in the time provided by Article 13.c. This is a change from its predecessor, Article 16.c. Article 14.d provides what is to be done, and repeats that it is to be done no later than the close of the seventh banking day. Does this mean that it must be sent before then, or that it must arrive with the other party before then? There should be no difference where telecommunication is used. The question may be material where telecommunication is not used and there is a delay between the sending and the receipt of the notice. It may well be said that A has not given notice to B until B has received the notice. Nonetheless it is suggested that in the context of Article 14 it is sufficient that the bank refusing the documents should complete the acts which it has itself to carry out to give notice within a reasonable time, without delay,[1] and in any event not later than the close of its seventh banking day following the receipt of the documents.

1 Article 14.d requires the notice to be given 'without delay'. This was held to mean 'without unreasonable delay' in *Rafsanjan Pistachio Producers v Bank Leumi Co-operative (UK) plc* [1992] 1 Lloyd's Rep 513 at 531.2.

5.45 *Means of informing the remitting party*   Article 14.d.i requires the use of 'telecommunication or, if that is not possible, by other expeditious means . . .'. Telecommunication includes telephone, telex, and fax. The ICC Commentary on the 1983 Revision refers to 'the practice of sometimes advising refusal by a properly authenticated telephone call'.[1] Where authentication is a problem it can be ensured by a follow-up communication. In *Rafsanjan Pistachio Producers Co-operative v Bank Leumi (UK) plc*[2] Hirst J stated 'Moreover in my judgment it would be most undesirable to construe Article 16(d) [now as amended, 14.d] in a manner which obliged a bank to use a particular form of telecommunication. A telephone call might sometimes be the best mode. But I think that a bank might justifiably consider that a rejection message, which is an extremely important step, . . . should normally be sent in writing by telex; this will also ensure that the message is timed and that the answerback records receipt, and will thus avoid any subsequent dispute . . .' In *Hing Yip Hing Fat Co Ltd v Daiwa Bank*[3] evidence was given that in Hong Kong fax and telex were not used to give notice of refusal because of problems with authentication and verification: advice was sent by mail, courier or messenger, which was found satisfactory given the size of Hong Kong and the propinquity of its banks. Kaplan J held that, if communication by phone, fax or telex was possible, it ought to be used so the beneficiary could know his position as soon as possible, in particular so he could, if he was able, correct the discrepancies before the credit's expiry or consider offering an indemnity. Had this been the only point in the case the bank would have lost by the difference between an afternoon and a morning. The case emphasises the need for banks to follow the requirements of Article 14 precisely.

1 It is suggested that it means instantaneous transmission (τηλε, from afar), and will cover all forms of electronic transmission.
2 [1992] 1 Lloyd's Rep 513 at 531.
3 [1991] 2 HKLR 35.

5.46 *The contents of the Article 14.d notice*   Article 14.d.i requires that the notice should state that the documents are being refused. Article 14.d.ii requires first that the notice must state all discrepancies in respect of which the bank refuses the documents, and second whether it is holding the documents at the disposal of, or is returning them to, the presenter.

5.47 *All discrepancies*   Article 14.d.ii had as its predecessor the second sentence of Article 16.d in the 1983 Revision. This referred to 'the discrepancies' as opposed to 'all discrepancies'. Articles 14.d.ii and 14.e do not expressly state that the bank cannot afterwards rely on any discrepancy not included in its notice. A bank will wish to do this if it finds that the discrepancies alleged in its notice are not valid discrepancies but discovers other matters on which it might rely as discrepancies to justify rejection. It is suggested that the clear intention of the Article is that it should not be able to do so. The question was considered in relation to Article 16 in Cases 52 and 53 of the ICC's Case Studies on Documentary Credits where it is stated first that a bank cannot by a second notice add to the discrepancies listed in a first notice, and second that a bank can never raise other discrepancies. Case 209 in the ICC's More Case Studies on Documentary Credits confirms this position. The point on Article 16.d came before Kaplan J in *Hip Hing Hip Fat Co Ltd v Daiwa Bank*.[1] He held that a bank was bound by the discrepancies in its notice of refusal and could not later add to them. There are good practical reasons for construing Article 14 in this way. One object of a speedy notification with grounds of refusal is to enable the beneficiary to rectify the discrepancies within the time limit of the credit: it would be unfair if he were then to be faced with further discrepancies.

1 [1991] 2 HKLR 35. The judgment considers a number of texts, none of which state a clear view on Article 16 or its predecessors.

5.48   The position in England at common law apart from the Uniform Customs is that a bank would be able to rely on discrepancies which it had not included in its notice of refusal unless the beneficiary was able to show that he had relied on a specific representation or promise made to him by the bank that, if the discrepancies listed were corrected, the bank would accept the documents.[1] The rule in the United States is that 'by formally placing its refusal to pay on one ground, the defendant must be held to have waived all others'.[2]

1 *Kydon Compania Naviera SA v National Westminster Bank Ltd, 'The Lena'* [1981] 1 Lloyd's Rep 68; also *Skandinaviska Akt v Barclays Bank* (1925) 22 Ll L Rep 523.
2 *Barclays Bank DCO v Mercantile National Bank* [1973] 2 Lloyd's Rep 541 at 549.1.

5.49 *Holding the documents at the disposal of the presenter*
Article 14.d.ii requires the notice of refusal to state whether the bank is holding the documents at the disposal of the presenter or is returning them to the presenter. Article 14.e refers to actual failure so to hold or return. Article 14.d.ii must be strictly complied with. In the *Bankers Trust* case[1] Bankers Trust's telex refusing the documents concluded 'Documents held at your risk and will be at your disposal after payment to us'. The bank had paid some US$10 million to the State Bank of India against the State Bank's telex that the documents complied with the credit: it wished to hold the documents (which had rightly been found not to comply) as security for repayment. The Court of Appeal unanimously held that this was a non-compliance with Article 16.d of the 1983 Revision. It might have been felt that a bank should be entitled to hold rejected documents as security against repayment. But the new Article 14.d is unchanged in this respect: so the decision continues to govern the position. In *The Royan*[2] the telex of refusal stated 'Please consider these documents at your disposal until we receive our principal's instructions concerning the discrepancies mentioned in your schedules'. In the Court of Appeal it was held that the telex complied with Article 16: 'The effect of that telex . . . was that the documents were being held unconditionally at the disposal of the sellers. The reference to 'until we receive our principal's instructions' was no doubt reflecting the hope that the buyers and sellers might come to some agreement. . . . I cannot read that expression of hope as meaning that the documents were not at the disposal of the sellers'.[3] In the *Bankers Trust* case[1] the narrow but critical difference was pointed to between documents being at the disposal of the sellers *until* something happens, and their being at their disposal *when* (ie after) something happens. It may be wondered how the documents in *The Royan* could be truly at the seller's disposal when, if the bank received instructions from their principal, the buyer, to take up the documents, the documents would cease to be at the seller's disposal. Wording as used in *The Royan* may be better avoided.

1 [1991] 2 Lloyd's Rep 443.
2 *Co-operative Centrale v Sumitomo Bank Ltd, 'The Royan'* [1987] 1 Lloyd's Rep 345; on appeal sub nom *Sumitomo Bank Ltd v Co-operative Centrale* [1988] 2 Lloyd's Rep 250.
3 At 254.1.

5.50 *Refusal irreversible*   Once a refusal has been notified to a presenter of documents, it can only be withdrawn with the agreement of the presenter.[1] For the documents are then at his disposal and he has the right to them. If the applicant gives authority that discrepancies may be waived after notice of refusal has been given, this may be too late. The presenter's authority is then required for them to be passed to the applicant. That authority will usually be readily forthcoming; but if, for instance, the market has risen, it may not.

1 See Case R12, Decisions of the ICC Banking Commission 1975–1979, ICC Publication No 371; also Case 54 in Case Studies on Documentary Credits, ICC Publication No 459.

5.51 *Subsequent presentations* The fact that a presentation has been made of documents which do not comply with the credit does not prevent the beneficiary presenting fresh sets of documents or documents to replace discrepant documents provided of course that the documents are presented in time. Presentation in time does not simply mean before the expiry of the credit: terms as to date of transport documents and any other terms as to time must be complied with. For this purpose the relevant date must be the date of the presentation of the last document required to complete the set of compliant documents. The process of correcting discrepancies by further presentations is commonplace.[1]

1 For an example taken from a well-known case see the facts set out in the judgment of Mocatta J in *United City Merchants v Royal Bank of Canada*, '*The American Accord*'. [1979] 1 Lloyd's Rep 267 at 272.

5.52 *Waiver by the bank of discrepancies* It is clear that a bank can waive discrepancies, or become estopped from relying on them, quite apart from the effect of a bank's failure to state them in a notice of refusal given under Article 14.d. This is made clear by the judgment in the *Lena*,[1] where the elements required, namely a representation by the bank coupled with reliance on it by the beneficiary, are considered. It may arise in two contexts. One is where documents have been delivered to a bank and having examined them the bank represents that the discrepancies which it had referred to are the only ones, or the only ones to which it will take objection, the effect being that, if they are corrected the bank will accept the documents. The other is where it makes a representation as to a discrepancy or possible discrepancy before any documents have been delivered to it. An example of the latter is provided by *Floating Dock Ltd v Hong Kong and Shanghai Banking Corpn*.[2] It was there held that the bank was not able to rely upon non-compliance with one term of the credit because the fact of the certain breach of the term was known to the bank at a time when it reached agreement to amend other terms of the credit so the transaction might go forward. The matter was dealt with on the basis of estoppel.[3] The combined effect of Articles 13 and 14 confirms the position at common law that failure to reject documents within a reasonable time will amount to an acceptance of them.[4]

1 [1981] 1 Lloyd's Rep 68.
2 [1986] 1 Lloyd's Rep 65.
3 See ibid at 78.1 and also *Astro Exito Navegacion SA v Chase Manhattan Bank NA, The Messiniaki Tolmi* [1986] 1 Lloyd's Rep 455 at 458, 9, Leggatt J.
4 *Westminster Bank Ltd v Banca Nazionale di Credito* (1928) 31 Ll L Rep 306 at 312.2.

5.53 *Bad faith by the bank* An exceptional situation arose in *Mannesman Handel AG v Kaunlaren Shipping Corpn*,[1] an action heard in the London Commercial Court but where Swiss law governed the points at issue. A Swiss bank opened a credit in favour of a German company at the request of a Bermudan company. The bank's position was secured by the assignment of the proceeds of a second credit opened by a Hong Kong bank in favour of an associate company of the Bermudan company. The same goods were intended to be used to perform the contracts underlying each credit. It appears that the overall purpose was to achieve the transfer of pig iron from Russia to China, countries between whom there were difficulties in direct trade. The goods were shipped by the German company. What should have happened was that the documents would have been presented under the credit opened by the Swiss bank and the German company would have been paid. The documents would then have been 'recut' to enable operation of the second credit and presented under it. However the Bermudan company did not wait for this. It presented documents under the second credit which were accepted. The goods were delivered to the buyers. Meanwhile the German company was pressing for amendments to the first credit which would have shown the Swiss bank that it was unable to present documents conforming to the credit as unamended. In that knowledge and in the knowledge that the Bermudan company had acted dishonestly in connection with the second credit, the Swiss bank claimed and received the proceeds under the second credit as due to it under the assignment. The Bermudan company had become insolvent and the Swiss bank wished to offset the proceeds of the second credit against the debt owed to it by the Bermudan company. Saville J held that in these circumstances, applying Swiss law, the refusal of the Swiss bank to accept and pay for the discrepant documents in due course presented by the German company was contrary to the principle of good faith (les regles de la bonne foi) established by Article 2 of the Swiss Civil Code. So the Swiss bank was not entitled to return the documents and had to pay the German company. Justice requires that the case should have the same outcome under English law: the likely route is by a species of estoppel.

1 [1993] 1 Lloyd's Rep 89.

5.54 ***The return of documents***   A credit sometimes provides that one original bill of lading should be sent direct to the buyer or be handed to the captain of the vessel, so the buyer may obtain possession of the goods on the vessel's arrival. If the documents are rejected by the bank as non-conforming, the bank will only be obliged to hold to the presenter's disposal, or to return to him, the documents which it received. They are the documents to which Article 16 relates. If the buyer has taken possession of the goods, he can reject them provided that when he took possession of them he was unaware of the documentary discrepancies and so there is no question of waiver. Alternatively it would seem he can waive the discrepancies and keep the goods: he must then pay for them at the contract price but he is not obliged to do so through the banks involved with the letter of credit provided that machinery has proved inoperative through no fault of his. It is obviously dangerous for a seller to send forward documents of title as this discussion envisages.

G.   Payment under a Reserve or against an Indemnity

5.55 It often happens that there is a disagreement between the party presenting documents and the bank receiving them, most often a confirming bank, as to whether the documents comply with the credit. The evidence in the *Banque de l'Indochine* case[1] was that as many as two-thirds of the presentations of documents against confirmed credits in London were thought to deviate from the terms of the credits in some respects; but in the great majority of cases this was outcome by agreement.[2] If there is goodwill between the presenting party and the bank, a solution may be obtained by the bank making payment 'under reserve', or against an indemnity. This will often provide for a satisfactory outcome because the buyer is prepared to accept the documents as tendered. But if he does not, the bank which has paid out will be looking to recover its money. In these circumstances, unless it is clear what the effect of the 'under reserve' arrangement or of the indemnity is, there may be a dispute. If it is simply agreed that the payment shall be 'under reserve', the effect is a matter of construing the term in the circumstances of the particular case. Subject to what is said in the next paragraph no universal answer can be given as to the term's meaning. If there is to be no room for dispute, the intended effect of any 'under reserve' arrangement should be agreed between the parties and recorded in writing. Likewise care must be taken to see that any indemnity agreed to be given is sufficiently and accurately spelt out.

1 See next paragraph.
2 See [1983] QB 711 at 733F.

5.56 In *Banque de l'Indochine et de Suez SA v J H Rayner (Mincing Lane) Ltd*,[1] a typical payment 'under reserve' situation was considered at first instance and in the Court of Appeal. The judgment of the Court of Appeal will provide guidance in cases where there are no distinguishing circumstances. The facts were that a Djibouti bank opened a credit in favour of the defendant sugar merchants, which was confirmed by the plaintiff bank. Documents were presented and were considered defective by the bank. Following a discussion it was agreed that payment should be made by the bank 'under reserve' owing to specified discrepancies. No consideration was given to the consequences of payment being so made. The Djibouti bank declined the documents as their clients, the buyers, would not lift the reserve. The plaintiff bank claimed that as the documents had been rejected for the specified discrepancies they were entitled to repayment from the sellers. The sellers argued that the documents conformed to the contract and so they were entitled to retain the money. Parker J found that the sellers were entitled to retain the money unless the documents were bad, which he held that they were. He held that the banking evidence established that there was no uniform practice as to the consequence of a payment being under reserve. He posed two alternatives: did the parties intend that the bank should be entitled to repayment by reason of the rejection of the documents by the Djibouti bank even if the bank were obliged to pay; or did they intend that the bank should only be entitled to repayment if the alleged discrepancies were valid, ie the purpose of the payment being 'under reserve' was solely to prevent the sellers alleging that they had received an unconditional payment. He rejected the former, and held that second meaning accorded with the reality of the situation.[2]

1 [1983] QB 711.
2 See ibid at 716.

5.57 The Court of Appeal reached the opposite conclusion, Sir John Donaldson MR holding that the judge had reached a 'lawyer's view' rather than a 'commercial view'. He imputed to the parties an imaginary dialogue as follows:

'*Merchant:*   "These documents are sufficient to satisfy the terms of the letter of credit and certainly will be accepted by my buyer. I am entitled to the money and need it."

Bank: "If we thought that the documents satisfied the terms of the letter of credit, we would pay you at once. However, we do not think that they do and we cannot risk paying you and not being paid ourselves. We are not sure that your buyer will authorise payment, but we can of course ask."

Merchant: "But that will take time and meanwhile we shall have a cash flow problem."

Bank: "Well the alternative is for you to sue us and that will also take time."

Merchant: "What about your paying us without prejudice to whether we are entitled to payment and then your seeing what is the reaction of your correspondent bank and our buyer?"

Bank: "That is all right, but if we are told that we should not have paid, how do we get our money back?"

Merchant: "You sue us."

Bank: "Oh no, that would leave us out of our money for a substantial time. Furthermore, it would involve us in facing in two directions. We should not only have to sue you, but also to sue the issuing bank in order to cover the possibility that you may be right. We cannot afford to pay on those terms."

Merchant: "All right. I am quite confident that the issuing bank and my buyer will be content that you should pay, particularly since the documents are in fact in order. You pay me and if the issuing bank refuses to reimburse you for the same reason that you are unwilling to pay, we will repay you on demand and then sue you. But we do not think that this will happen."

Bank: "We agree. Here is the money 'under reserve'."'[1]

Kerr LJ, agreeing, also pointed out that the bank could not have intended to be out of pocket and obliged to sue the seller and the issuing bank to resolve the dispute.[2]

1 See [1983] QB 711 at 727, 8.
2 Ibid at 733, 4.

5.58 Although the reasoning of Parker J does at first appear convincing, it is suggested that that of the Court of Appeal is ultimately the more forceful as well as being that of the superior court. The seller should, however, be watchful. By agreeing to such a payment under reserve he is putting himself into the hands of his buyer. For the buyer can refuse the goods regardless of whether the discrepancies alleged are in fact valid and the seller will have to reimburse the bank, leaving him with the by-now stale documents on his hands and a right to sue the bank to determine the validity of the alleged discrepancies. If the seller refuses to repay the bank contrary to the arrangement between them, the position under English procedure would be that the bank could obtain summary judgment against the seller under Order 14 of the Rules of the Supreme Court leaving the seller's claim against the bank to be determined at a trial in due course. In his judgment in the *Banque de l'Indochine* case Sir John Donaldson MR suggested that the ICC should turn their minds to the meaning of 'payment under reserve' when undertaking the next revision of the Uniform Customs.[1] This was done but without success, because of the difficulty created by the use of the phrase 'under reserve' in other banking contexts.[2]

1 [1983] QB 711 at 727.
2 See ICC Publication No 411, UCP 1974/1983 Revisions Compared and Explained, page 33.

5.59 Article 14.f refers to the possibility of payment under reserve in these terms:

> ARTICLE 14.f[1] If the remitting bank draws the attention of the Issuing Bank and/or Confirming Bank, if any, to any discrepancy(ies) in the document(s) or advises such banks that it has paid, incurred a deferred payment undertaking, accepted Draft(s) or negotiated under reserve or against an indemnity in respect of such discrepancy(ies), the Issuing Bank and/or Confirming Bank, if any, shall not be thereby relieved from any of their obligations under any provision of this Article. Such reserve or indemnity concerns only the relations between the remitting bank and the party towards whom the reserve was made, or from whom, or on whose behalf, the indemnity was obtained.

In other words any special arrangements bind only the parties to them. Where the remitting bank has accepted documents under such terms, the duty of the issuing bank to examine the documents and to accept or reject them in accordance with the terms of the credit remains unchanged. It is, however, particularly likely that in such situations it will take the instructions of the applicant if it is of the view that there are grounds for rejecting the documents.

1 This follows the wording of Article 16.f in the 1983 Revision with the substitution of 'issuing bank or confirming bank' for 'issuing bank'.

H. Documents Presented for Collection[1]

5.60 Documents which are known not to conform to the credit are sometimes sent to the issuing bank (or, perhaps, to the confirming bank) 'on a collection basis' or 'for collection'. Such phrases are themselves ambiguous, and their meaning must be obtained from the context.[2] The meaning may be that the documents are sent on the basis that they are being presented under the credit with what is in effect a request for the waiver of the discrepancies, such as that they be accepted out of time. In such a case the Uniform Customs will apply, and if the documents are accepted all the obligations of the issuing bank and any confirming bank arising under Article 9 of the Uniform Customs will become effective.[3] Or it may be that the documents are being sent on a basis independent of the credit (or, it may be said, outside it), namely for simple collection, the bank probably being made the agent of the party sending them to collect on them from the buyer if the buyer is prepared to take them. In such a case the ICC's Uniform Rules for Collections are likely to apply.[4] It appears that, if the correspondence shows that the presentation is being made under the credit, it will fall into the former category. This was the conclusion reached by Gatehouse J on the facts of the case in *Harlow & Jones Ltd v American Express Bank Ltd*.[5]

1 As to a bank collecting as a beneficiary's agent, see para 6.16 below, and Chapter 7.
2 See *Harlow & Jones Ltd v American Express Bank Ltd* [1990] 2 Lloyd's Rep 343 at 348.1.
3 See ibid at 347.2.
4 ICC Publication No 322.
5 See above.

I. The Seller's Rights against a Defaulting Bank

5.61 Where a bank wrongly refuses to accept documents under a credit, the seller may sue the bank which has given a payment undertaking claiming the price, provided that the seller remains able to tender the documents to the bank against the bank's payment. Where payment under a credit is to be made through a bill of exchange, the claim will be framed in damages, but will reflect the amount of the bill. It was argued in *Stein v Hambro's Bank of Northern Commerce*[1] that the position was analogous to that where documents were wrongly rejected by a buyer under a CIF contract and the seller is entitled only to damages for loss of his bargain and not to the price because the property has not passed.[2] This argument was rejected, the court stating 'It seems to me that this is clearly a case of a simple contract to pay money upon the fulfilment of conditions which have been fulfilled.'[3] The court gave judgment for the amount of the bill drawn under the credit with interest from the date the bill would have become due. The case went to appeal, but the Court of Appeal did not need to consider this point as it held that the bank was entitled to reject the documents. The seller's right to claim the price does not appear to have been questioned since and is now clearly accepted.[4] It was suggested in *Dexters Ltd v Schenker & Co*[5] that strictly the claim may be for damages for non-payment of money, which would usually be the sum unpaid. This has been held to be the position under Swiss law in an action in the London Commercial Court.[6] The relevance of the point was that the party standing in the position of the buyer might not have suffered damage in the full amount of the price because part had been recovered by the sellers from the carriers who had given up the goods without production of a bill of lading.

1 (1921) 9 Ll L Rep 433 and 507.
2 See *Benjamin's Sale of Goods* (4th edn) paras 19–184, 5.
3 (1929) 9 Ll L Rep 507.
4 See, inter alia, *British Imex Industries Ltd v Midland Bank Ltd* [1958] 1 QB 542; *United City Merchants (Investments) Ltd v Royal Bank of Canada* [1983] 1 AC 168; *Forestal Mimosa Ltd v Oriental Credit Ltd* [1986] 1 WLR 631 and *Floating Dock Ltd v Hongkong and Shanghai Banking Corpn* [1986] 1 Lloyd's Rep 65.
5 (1923) 14 Ll L Rep 586 at 588.
6 *Mannesman Handel AG v Kaunlaren Shipping Corpn* [1993] 1 Lloyd's Rep 89 at 94.1.

5.62 A problem may, however, arise because the goods have been shipped and will arrive in the buyer's country; but the seller retains the documents. Thus in *Belgian Grain and Produce Co Ltd v Cox & Co (France) Ltd*[1] (where the claim against the bank was for the purchase price of a shipment of peas) at the conclusion of the delivery of the Court of Appeal's judgments in favour of the seller the following exchange took place:

> '*Lord Justice Bankes:* What about judgment?
> *Mr Claughton Scott* said the amount asked in the writ was £9,495.14s, being the equivalent of 246,888f.
> *Mr Mackinnon:* What about my peas? I expect they have been sold.
> *Mr Claughton Scott:* I understand they have not been sold. I think they are in the custody of some French authority.
> *Lord Justice Bankes:* Then it will be judgment for plaintiffs (appellants) for £9,495.14s in exchange for the documents, with the costs of the appeal and the action. There will be liberty to apply to either party if any trouble arises.'

Had the peas been sold by the plaintiffs and had they been unable to tender the documents, they would not have been able to recover the price but would have had to sue for their loss by way of damages. Where the bank rejects the documents on the ground that they do not conform to the contract, unless the dispute can be quickly resolved the goods will sit in a warehouse collecting substantial charges and possibly deteriorating and at risk to market movement. An interim solution is for them to be sold for the joint account of the parties pending resolution of the dispute. This is easier where the goods are a commodity such as grain than where they are machinery intended for the buyer's use such as a printing press. In *British Imex Industries v Midland Bank Ltd*[2] the difficulty was avoided by the following litigation timetable: 10 December 1957 – documents presented to bank and rejected; 11 December, action commenced; 19 and 20 December, action heard concluding in judgment for plaintiff sellers. The goods were steel bars. In *Floating Dock Ltd v Hongkong and Shanghai Banking Corpn*[3] the documents were presented on 8 February 1985 and judgment was given on 3 May 1985. The goods were sections of a floating dock. It was ordered that payment be made within seven days in exchange for the documents tendered. In *Forestal Mimosa Ltd v Oriental Credit Ltd*[4] the credit was available by acceptance of the sellers' draft drawn on the buyers at 90 days' sight. It appears that there was some delay before the buyers declined to accept the bills and before it was alleged that the documents did not conform to the credit. The sellers claimed a declaration that the confirming bank was responsible for the acceptance and payment of the bills, and damages. The goods were mimosa extract: it does not appear from the report what had happened to them, nor who held the documents. Judgment was given for damages to be assessed. Such damages would appear primarily to have been the amount of the bills, with interest. The sellers also claimed their travel and other costs incurred in trying to overcome the unwarranted objections to the bills. These claims were not considered by the Court of Appeal, but were left over for the assessment of damages.[5] Where under the terms of the credit payment is not due immediately and the documents have been accepted by the bank and there is later a default in payment, either simply because payment is not made or a bill is dishonoured, the seller will have parted with the documents and his claim against the bank will be for the amount due and interest: no problem as to the goods arises. An example of such a claim is *Power Curber International Ltd v National Bank of Kuwait SAK*[6] where the bank failed to pay the balance due a year after shipment because of an injunction granted by its national court obtained by the buyer.

1 (1919) 1 Ll L Rep 256.
2 [1958] 1 QB 542.
3 [1986] 1 Lloyd's Rep 65.
4 [1986] 1 WLR 631.
5 Outcome unknown.
6 [1981] 1 WLR 1233.

5.63 If the bank has refused to pay on a bill as acceptor, section 57(1) of the Bills of Exchange Act 1882 will be directly applicable, providing for the recovery by way of damages of the amount of the bill together with interest.

5.64 It may happen that the bank rejects the documents on the ground that they do not conform to the credit and the seller does not want to run the risk of suing for the price and backing his own judgment of the documents against that of the bank, leaving the goods to accumulate charges in a foreign warehouse in the meanwhile. It is clear as a matter of principle and common sense that the seller can adopt an alternative course. He can accept the bank's refusal of the documents as a repudiation of its obligation to accept conforming documents and to pay as the credit provides, and such acceptance will terminate any on-going contractual obligations on either side. The seller can then use his continuing possession of the documents to resell the goods, thus hopefully recouping at least a substantial part of his money. If the market has risen, he could even make a better profit than under his original bargain. But if he is not so fortunate, his claim against the bank will be for the difference between the resale price and the price due under the credit to which could be added the costs of arranging the resale. It would be open to the bank to argue that the seller had failed to take reasonable steps to mitigate his loss and should have obtained a better resale price. Such an argument becomes unattractive once it is established that the bank should not have rejected the documents, and so it is the bank which is the author of the seller's problems. *Urquhart, Lindsay & Co Ltd v Eastern Bank Ltd*[1] illustrates the above principle in part and applies it to a credit providing for payment in instalments. The underlying contract was to manufacture machinery and ship it in instalments. The bank rejected the documents relating to one instalment. The sellers treated this as a repudiation of the whole contract constituting the credit. They claimed and were awarded damages calculated as the difference between the price which they would have received under the credit and the value of the materials left on their hands together with, it appears, the cost of completing the work.

1 [1922] 1 KB 318. The facts are set out in para 8.12 below.

5.65 *Delayed payment* Where a seller has suffered loss through delay in payment, he may recover that loss subject to his satisfying the court that it is recoverable applying the ordinary rules of causation and remoteness of damages. In *Ozalid Group (Export) Ltd v African Continental Bank Ltd*[1] the defendant bank delayed payment of US$125,939 to an English company for some two months, during which the dollar fell against the pound. Under the then existing exchange control requirements the company was obliged to sell its dollars for sterling. It was held that the bank should have been aware of this. The plaintiff sellers recovered the difference between the sterling value of the dollars when they should have been received and when they were in fact received, with interest on the total sum over the period of non-payment, and also their reasonable costs of attempting to collect payment. The correct approach in law to these facts in the light of subsequent authority is now shown by *International Minerals and Chemical Corpn v Karl O Helm AG*.[2] Had the exchange regulations not existed, it would nonetheless have been open to the English company to have proved, if it had been the case, that they would have sold the dollars for sterling on or shortly after their receipt, for reasons, for example, of company financial policy, and to justify their loss in that way. This would be likely to satisfy the tests as to remoteness (or likelihood) of damage variously recited in the speeches of the House of Lords in *Koufos v C Czarnikow Ltd*.[3] The position as to claiming interest where the bank pays prior to the commencement of any proceedings but pays late, is now governed by the House of Lords' decision in *President of India v La*

Pintada Cia Navegacion SA,[4] approving the Court of Appeal's decision in *Wadsworth v Lydall*.[5] The position appears to be this. An actual loss of interest must be shown thus constituting the claim one for special damage rather than general damage, and it must be shown that the circumstances giving rise to the loss were known to the bank when the credit was notified. If the bank has had no other contact with the beneficiary, the second requirement will be difficult to satisfy.

1 [1979] 2 Lloyd's Rep 231.
2 [1986] 1 Lloyd's Rep 81 at 105.
3 [1969] 1 AC 350.
4 [1985] AC 104.
5 [1981] 1 WLR 598.

5.66 ***Paying an incorrect party***   The bank must ensure that it makes payment to the party entitled to receive it. If it pays another person, its obligation to the party entitled will remain and it will have to pay a second time. This may arise where the bank believes that it is paying an agent of the beneficiary authorised to receive the money on the beneficiary's behalf and is mistaken. An example of such circumstances is provided by *Cleveland Manufacturing Co Ltd v Muslim Commercial Bank Ltd*.[1] There the documents were prepared and presented to the defendant bank by shipping agents instructed by the plaintiffs. The bank paid the shipping agents who did not account to the plaintiffs because they went into liquidation. The shipping agents were not authorised to receive payment, and so the plaintiffs succeeded against the bank.

1 [1981] 2 Lloyd's Rep 646.

J. Recourse by an Issuing or Confirming Bank against the Beneficiary

5.67 Circumstances may arise in which an issuing or confirming bank pays a beneficiary and then seeks to recover its payment. Perhaps the most likely situation is where the bank has examined documents and found them acceptable and so it pays, and it is subsequently found that they do not comply with the terms and conditions of the credit so the bank is not entitled to reimbursement from the applicant or the issuing bank as the case may be. Another situation is where the applicant becomes insolvent causing the bank to be unable to recover what it has paid out, and another is where the bank has negotiated documents including a draft drawn on the buyer or some other party, and the draft is later dishonoured. Perhaps the general answer is that an issuing or confirming bank has no such rights of recovery: it is contrary to the intention of documentary credits to provide a certain and secure means of payment that such rights should exist. Particular cases are considered below.

5.68 *(a) Rights arising in connection with bills of exchange*   As most credits are governed by the Uniform Customs, the relevant Articles are considered first. Article 9.a.iv specifically excludes a right of recourse where the issuing bank negotiates a bill, thus negating any right which the bank as holder or indorser of a bill dishonoured by non-acceptance or non-payment might have against the drawer. Unless negated such rights would otherwise be given by sections 43(2) and 47(2) of the Bills of

Exchange Act 1882. Article 9.b.iv does the same in respect of a confirming bank. Articles 9.a.iii and 9.b.iii make the banks responsible for acceptance and payment where bills are to be accepted by another bank, which is again inconsistent with any right of recourse on the bills. These are the only situations in which a right of recourse on bills could arise between an issuing or a confirming bank and a beneficiary.

5.69 The position here is to be contrasted with that between a bank which negotiates documents from the beneficiary under a negotiation credit but has no contract with the beneficiary by way of confirmation of the credit. Such a bank will have a right of recourse on a bill against the beneficiary.[1] The position of an advising bank which does not negotiate the credit but takes possession of documents to present them to the issuing bank on behalf of the beneficiary, and thus acts as the beneficiary's agent, will usually be that it has not paid the beneficiary and so it will not have become a party to the bill, nor will it have need of recourse. But, if it has paid, it will have a right to recourse.

1 See para 7.10 below.

5.70 The position is also to be contrasted with that where transactions take place involving bills where the transactions are outside the letter of credit. In *M A Sassoon & Sons Ltd v International Banking Corpn*[1] Sassoon were sellers in Calcutta of goods to buyers in London. The buyers opened a letter of credit with a London bank which was advised to the sellers through the London bank's Calcutta branch which confirmed the credit. Bills drawn on the buyers to which bills of lading were attached were discounted by the sellers with the plaintiff bank. The sellers' memorandum covering the documents to the bank referred to the letter of credit but it stated at its commencement that the drafts were D/A drafts. This was held by the Board of the Privy Council to be an instruction to the plaintiff bank to present the bills to the buyers for acceptance against delivery of the bills of lading (D/A = delivery against acceptance). This having been done, the letter of credit was in effect an irrelevance between the plaintiff bank and the sellers. The bank did not utilise the credit. The sellers were not able to say that, because the bank had not done so, the bank was barred from recourse against the sellers when the bills were dishonoured by non-payment. The sellers were therefore liable.[2] Had the agreement for the discounting of the bills between the bank and the sellers included an instruction to present the documents under the credit and thus designated the letter of credit as the security for the bills, and had the sellers ignored the credit in those circumstances, it appears that they could not have complained thereafter that the bills were dishonoured.[3] Had they in like circumstances attempted to obtain payment through the credit and had they failed through no fault of theirs to do so, it appears that the bank could have recovered its advance from the sellers.

1 [1927] AC 711.
2 See ibid at 730.
3 See ibid at 729–731.

5.71 If the Uniform Customs are not incorporated into a credit, may an issuing or confirming bank be entitled to recourse on a bill? It is suggested that the answer must clearly be no. For it is contrary to the whole object of the transaction, namely to provide a certain source of payment by a bank by means of an obligation undertaken by the bank, that there should be any such right of recourse. It was pointed out in the *Sassoon* case[1] that the sellers could not show that, when they discounted the bills, they had bargained that the transaction should be without recourse. This was in the context first that the discounting agreement had not designated the letter of credit as the source of repayment to the discounting bank, and secondly that the bank was not a party to the letter of credit. Where the bank is a party to the letter of credit as the issuing or confirming bank, the circumstances require that it be implied that there shall be no right of recourse where otherwise a right of recourse might arise. The acceptance of the Uniform Customs by British banks has simply confirmed this position.

1 [1927] AC 711 at 731.

5.72 (b) Mistake as to the documents   If an issuing or a confirming bank pays against documents presented under the credit which are later found not to conform with the requirements of the credit and are rejected by the buyer, can the bank allege against the beneficiary that the payment was made under a mistake of fact and so is recoverable? Such a claim may be met by the defence that the mistake was one of law where the bank's error was in substance the misconstruction of what the terms of the credit required. But it is otherwise a more difficult question. Gutteridge & Megrah[1] state that, where the lack of conformity of the documents with the credit is not obvious at the time of payment or negotiation, recourse is available if the seller has not changed his position and the claim is made within a reasonable time. No authority is cited. In *Benjamin on Sale of Goods*[2] it is doubted whether such a claim should be permissible, suggesting change of position or estoppel as barring the bank. But the similar position as between correspondent bank and issuing bank is stated to be open.[3]

1 (7th edn) p 87.
2 (4th edn) para 23–123.
3 Op cit para 23–138.

5.73   Where the Uniform Customs apply, Article 14.e[1] will bar any claim that the documents do not comply with the credit by an issuing bank which has not given notice of rejection of the documents and otherwise followed the requirements of the Article. Such a bank would be unable therefore to put forward a claim based on mistake of fact. The Article now places a confirming bank under the same duty in its handling of the documents and it will also be barred by the Article.[2]

1 Para 5.32.
2 Para 5.35.

5.74   It is suggested that the answer where the Uniform Customs do not apply may be found as follows. Where the buyer of goods under a contract receives them against payment, if he has a remedy in respect of a defect in the goods it is a remedy for breach of a term of the contract – fitness for purpose, compliance with description, an express warranty, as it may be. He may also have a claim for misrepresentation. But except in the most exceptional circumstances he cannot say that when he paid, he paid under a mistake of fact as to the quality of the goods, and that he would like his money back on that ground. The bank is not a purchaser of goods but of documents. The position however must be analogous. It is clear that, at least in the absence of fraud, a party presenting documents to a bank does not make any implied representations as to the documents – in particular that they comply with the terms of the credit. Nor does he give any warranty. So the bank has no remedy. Secondly, it is suggested that once the bank has decided not to reject the documents, it becomes under an obligation to pay for them. That is so whether or not they comply with the terms of the credit. The payment by the bank therefore discharges the bank's obligation to pay which has become effective on its acceptance of the documents. Where money is paid to discharge a genuine legal obligation it cannot be recovered as money paid under a mistake of fact.[1]

1 See, inter alia, *Chitty on Contract* (25th edn) para 1953.

5.75 (c) Failure of the applicant   The failure of the applicant to reimburse the issuing bank, or the failure of the issuing bank to reimburse the confirming bank, does not of itself give the bank which finds itself out of pocket, any rights against the beneficiary of the credit. This is so whether or not the failure arises by reason of insolvency.

5.76 (d) Fraud[1]   Where documents are presented to a bank by or on behalf of a party which knows that the documents are not what they purport to be because they are forged or for some other reason, the bank can refuse payment, or, if it has paid before discovering the position, it can recover any loss which it has made. In *Bank Russo-Iran v Gordon Woodroffe & Co Ltd*[2] the defendants presented documents which they knew included invoices in a sum which was massively in excess of the real value of the goods. It was held by Browne J that if a beneficiary presented forged or fraudulent documents a bank was entitled to refuse payment, and to recoup money paid as paid under a mistake of fact: see the citation of the *Bank Russo-Iran Case* in *Edward Owen Engineering Ltd v Barclays Bank*.[3] But the bank there failed to recover because it was held to have agreed to release the defendant. The reference to recovery as money paid under a mistake of fact is not explained in the reports cited. The Solicitors Journal report states that the claim was made alternatively for damages for fraudulent misrepresentation, and that this cause of action was held to have been established. This is the more obvious claim, the false representation being that the defendants believed at the time they presented the documents that they were not forged and were what they purported to be. For discussion of fraud in a wider context the reader is referred to Chapter 9 below.

1 As to the effect of the bank's involvement in fraud, see para 5.53 above.
2 (1972) 116 Sol Jo 921, (1972) Times, 4 October (but nowhere adequately reported).
3 [1978] QB 159 at 169.

K.   Set-off by a Bank against Claims under a Credit

5.77   It will very rarely happen that the factual situation between a paying bank and the beneficiary will be such as to enable the bank to raise a set-off against the beneficiary. This occurred in *Hongkong and Shanghai Banking Corpn v Kloeckner & Co AG*[1] where there were complicated arrangements between the bank and Kloeckner for the financing of oil trading. These included a standby letter of credit opened by the bank in Kloeckner's favour. Kloeckner made demands under the credit against which the bank sought to set off sums due under related transactions. Hirst J held that the bank was entitled to do so, because the set-off arose from the very transactions in connection with which the credit was opened and the set-off was for a liquidated amount. He held that the bank's obligation to pay, established by the Uniform Customs, had no bearing on the validity of a set-off against that obligation.[2] In *Etablissement Esefka International Anstalt v Central Bank of Nigeria*[3] it was suggested by Lord Denning MR[4] in the Court of Appeal on applications by the plaintiff beneficiary for a Mareva injunction and by the defendant bank for security for costs, that a bank might set off a claim to recover payments made under a credit in respect of fraudulent shipments against a claim by the beneficiary for payment under the credit in respect of demurrage incurred in relation to other shipments.

1 [1990] 3 All ER 513, [1989] 2 Lloyd's Rep 323.
2 See ibid at 330, 1.
3 [1979] 1 Lloyd's Rep 445.
4 Ibid at 448.1 and 449.2.

Chapter 6

The Correspondent Bank

6.1 *The correspondent bank* Because documentary credits are commonly used to finance international transactions, the issuing bank is normally in a different country to the beneficiary. While the issuing bank may deal directly with the beneficiary abroad, it is more usual for the issuing bank to utilise the services of a bank in the country of the beneficiary, which may be referred to as 'the correspondent bank'. Although the bank may be designated by the applicant pursuant to his arrangements with the intended beneficiary, it is more commonly left to the issuing bank to decide which bank it will use. There will normally be a particular bank (or perhaps more than one) in the country in question, with which it has arrangements under which that bank is prepared to act on the instructions of the issuing bank in connection with documentary credits. Depending on its instructions in the individual matter, such a bank may act in various capacities. Thus, the term 'correspondent bank' is used to refer to a bank, usually in the country of the seller or beneficiary, which deals with the beneficiary concerning the credit in accordance with instructions accepted by it from the issuing bank. The various forms which these relations may take are considered below.

A. The Functions which may be assumed by a Correspondent Bank

6.2 The function or functions which a correspondent bank performs and consequently its legal position are mainly dependent on the instructions which it receives. As will be seen there are some functions which it may take upon itself independently of its relationship with the issuing bank.

(1) As advising bank
6.3 *(a) No undertaking without confirmation* Unless the correspondent bank is asked to, and does, add its confirmation[1] to the credit, it will not undertake any obligation itself to the beneficiary in respect of payment: the sole undertaking in that regard remains that of the issuing bank.[2] It is usual for an advising bank in this situation to make its position clear by expressly stating when advising the credit that no undertaking on its part is included.

1 As to silent confirmations, see para 6.14 below.
2 See Article 10.c relating to the 'Nominated Bank'.

6.4 *(b) Agency* Unless the correspondent bank is instructed to issue the credit itself,[1] it will be asked to advise the seller/beneficiary of the opening of the credit by the issuing bank and of its terms. In doing so the correspondent bank acts as the agent of the issuing bank. In *Bank Melli Iran v Barclays Bank*[2] it was argued for Bank Melli that their relationship with Barclays was that of banker and customer and not that of principal and agent. In rejecting the plea McNair J stated:[3]

'In my judgment, both on the constructions of the documents under which the credit was established and in principle, the relationship between Bank Melli, the instructing bank, and Barclays Bank, the confirming bank, was that of principal and agent. This relationship was held to exist in substantially similar circumstances in *Equitable Trust Co of New York v Dawson Partners Ltd* (1927) 27 Ll L Rep 49 (see per Viscount Cave LC, at p 52, Lord Sumner at p 53, and Lord Shaw of Dunfermline at p 57), and the existence of this relationship is implicit in the judgments of the Court of Appeal in *J H Rayner & Co Ltd v Hambro's Bank Ltd* [1943] KB 37. I accept as accurate the statement of Professor Gutteridge KC, in his book on *Bankers' Commercial Credits*, at p 51, that "as between the issuing banker" (in this case Bank Melli) "and the correspondent" (in this case Barclays Bank) "the relationship is, unless otherwise agreed, that of principal and agent . . ." On the facts of this case I find no agreement to the contrary.'

The facts of the *Equitable Trust* case[4] have been set out in paragraph 4.11. It was held that the correspondent and confirming bank, the Hongkong and Shanghai Bank, were the agents of the Equitable Trust Co for the purpose of advising the credit.

1 See para 6.19 below.
2 [1951] 2 Lloyd's Rep 367.
3 Ibid at 376.
4 Supra.

6.5 *(c) Binding the issuing bank as to the terms of the credit*   As the advising bank is authorised to hold itself out to the seller/beneficiary as authorised on behalf of the issuing bank to pass the terms of the credit to the seller, the advising bank will bind the issuing bank even though it deviates from its instructions by, for example, failing to include in the terms of the credit a document called for by the instructions from the issuing bank. For the terms of the credit as so advised by the advising bank will fall within the ostensible authority of the advising bank.[1] The consequence is that, as regards the beneficiary, the issuing bank will be obliged to honour the credit as so advised. So, in the example taken, it will be obliged to pay against documents which do not include that omitted from the advice of the credit. But it may not have to do so where it is the advising bank which is to pay the beneficiary. The likely scenario will then be that the advising bank will pay in accordance with the credit which it has advised. It will forward the documents to the issuing bank, which will decline to accept them and to reimburse the advising bank on the ground that the documents do not comply with its instructions. This assumes that the advising bank has no defence by reason of Article 16 of the Uniform Customs.[2] It is suggested that in such circumstances Article 18 would assist neither the advising nor the issuing bank.[3] The position is more difficult where it is another bank, the issuing bank or a third bank, which is to pay the beneficiary. The bank will be obliged to pay in accordance with the credit as advised. Can the issuing bank then oblige the applicant to accept and pay for documents which do not accord with his instructions on the ground that the utilisation of the advising bank was at his risk, pursuant to Article 18? It is suggested in Chapter 4[4] that the issuing bank cannot: it must pay and recoup its payment from the party at fault, the advising bank, for breach of the contract between them.

1 See *Bowstead on Agency* (15th edn) pp 299–302.
2 See para 4.15 above.
3 See para 4.18 above.
4 Para 4.18.

6.6 *(d) Can a beneficiary claim against the advising bank where the latter wrongly advises the credit?*   If the credit provides that payment to the beneficiary is to be made by the issuing bank and the issuing bank declines to accept documents complying with credit as advised by the advising bank on the ground that the advising bank did not advise the credit correctly, can the beneficiary proceed against the advising bank in his own country rather than suing the foreign issuing bank? Because the advising bank's advice of the credit will have bound the issuing bank, it is difficult to see how the beneficiary can do so. For the beneficiary received a valid credit. But if, contrary to what is stated above, the issuing bank was in some way not bound by the credit as advised, under English law the advising bank would be liable to the beneficiary for damages for breach of warranty of authority, that is, for breach of the warranty which English law implies that every agent gives that he has the authority of his principal to act as he does. It is suggested that a statement that the credit is advised without engagement on the part of the advising bank would not avoid this liability: for the intention of that statement is simply to make clear that the advising bank is not joining with the issuing bank in the obligation undertaken by the credit. In neither situation does it appear necessary to consider whether there could be a cause of action in negligence.

6.7 *(e) The authenticity of the credit*   Article 7 of the Uniform Customs provides:

> ARTICLE 7[1]   **Advising Bank's Liability**
>
> a. A credit may be advised to a Beneficiary through another bank (the 'Advising Bank') without engagement on the part of the Advising Bank, but that bank, if it elects to advise the Credit, shall take reasonable care to check the apparent authenticity of the Credit which it advises. If the bank elects not to advise the Credit, it must so inform the Issuing Bank without delay.
>
> b. If the Advising Bank cannot establish such apparent authenticity it must inform, without delay, the bank from which the instructions appear to have been received that it has been unable to establish the authenticity of the Credit and if it elects nonetheless to advise the Credit it must inform the Beneficiary that it has not been able to establish the authenticity of the Credit.

The Article introduces the concept of the advising bank acting without engagement on its part, which means, in practical terms, without confirming the credit. The Article indicates that a bank may or may not choose to advise a credit. If it does so, it must take reasonable care to check the apparent authenticity of the credit, that is, whether or not it appears to be genuine, namely instructed by the issuing bank which appears to have instructed it and in the terms in which it appears that that has occurred. In most situations, under English law, a bank which advised a credit which it has not in fact been instructed to advise, would be liable for its breach of warranty of authority mentioned in the previous paragraph: for it would be purporting to act with the authority of a principal which it did not have. The two paragraphs of the Article make it reasonably clear that an advising bank is not to be under any such absolute liability: it will only be liable in respect of a credit which it has advised in respect of which it later turns out that its instructions were not genuine, if it was negligent in checking the authenticity of its instructions.[2] Where the check does not establish the authenticity of the instructions, the advising bank must without delay inform the bank from which they have purported to come, and it may advise the credit nonetheless provided that it informs the beneficiary that it has not been able to establish its authenticity.[3] If it does so, then of course the beneficiary will not be able to rely upon it as authentic until the authenticity is later assured.

1 The first sentence of Article 7.a follows Article 8 in the 1983 Revision: the remainder of Article 7 is new.

2 An intention first introduced in the 1983 Revision: see UCP 1074/1983 Revision Compared and Explained, ICC Publication No 411, page 19.

3 Cf Article 12, para 4.5 above.

6.8   Where a credit is advised by post, the advising bank should check the signature on behalf of the issuing bank against specimen signatures held by it. In the case of teletransmissions, individual test keys may be used, or the mechanism of SWIFT utilised.

6.9 *(2) As the bank to which documents are to be presented – As the bank 'nominated' under Article 10 of the Uniform Customs*   The credit should make clear to which bank the beneficiary is to present documents, that is, the bank which is to operate the credit so far as he is concerned. In many cases this will be to the bank which has advised the credit. Thus, with a credit which provides for immediate payment against documents, the credit will usually provide for the documents to be presented to the advising bank and for that bank to make payment to the beneficiary. Where this is the case it will be the duty of the advising bank to examine the documents for compliance with the credit and to accept or reject them accordingly. This may be the situation whether or not the advising bank has confirmed the credit. The credit may provide for payment to be made after a period, either because it utilises time drafts, or because it is a deferred payment credit.[1] Where a draft is called for, it may be drawn on the advising bank or on the issuing bank or other party[2] as the credit provides. Where the draft is not drawn on the advising bank, the beneficiary may still utilise the advising bank to forward the documents to the issuing bank. If it does so and the credit has not provided for the documents to be presented to the advising bank, the advising bank will simply act as a forwarder. It will not be its duty to examine the documents for compliance with the credit and to accept or refuse them. Nor would it be remunerated for doing so by the issuing bank. What it may do if it is the beneficiary's own bank is to check them to see if they are in order as part of the service which it provides to the beneficiary. This has now to be considered in conjunction with the position intended to be accorded to the 'nominated bank' under the Uniform Customs scheme.

1 Para 2.28.
2 But not on the applicant: see Article 9 and para 5.17 above.

6.10 Article 10 of the Uniform Customs largely relates to 'the Nominated Bank'. It provides:

ARTICLE 10[1]   **Types of Credit**
   a. All Credits must clearly indicate whether they are available by sight payment, by deferred payment, by acceptance or by negotiation.
   b.i. Unless the Credit stipulates that it is available only with the Issuing Bank, all Credits must nominate the bank (the 'Nominated Bank') which is authorised to pay, to incur a deferred payment undertaking, to accept Draft(s) or to negotiate. In a freely negotiable Credit, any bank is a Nominated Bank.
      Presentation of documents must be made to the Issuing Bank or the Confirming Bank, if any, or any other Nominated Bank.
   ii. Negotiation means the giving of value for Draft(s) and/or document(s) by the bank authorised to negotiate. Mere examination of the documents without giving of value does not constitute a negotiation.
   c. Unless the Nominated Bank is the Confirming Bank, nomination by the Issuing Bank does not constitute any undertaking by the Nominated Bank to pay, to incur a deferred payment undertaking, to accept Draft(s), or to negotiate. Except where expressly agreed to by the Nominated Bank and so communicated to the Beneficiary, the Nominated Bank's receipt of and/or examination and/or forwarding of the documents does not make that bank liable to pay, to incur a deferred payment undertaking, to accept Draft(s), or to negotiate.

    d. By nominating another bank, or by allowing for negotiation by any bank, or by authorising or requesting another bank to add its confirmation, the Issuing Bank authorises such bank to pay, accept Draft(s) or negotiate as the case may be, against documents which appear on their face to be in compliance with the terms and conditions of the Credit and undertakes to reimburse such bank in accordance with the provisions of these Articles.

These provisions regarding the nominated bank have also to be read with Article 42 in so far as it relates to place of presentation. It provides:

ARTICLE 42.a[2] All Credits must stipulate an expiry date and a place for presentation of documents for payment, acceptance, or with the exception of freely negotiable Credits, a place for presentation of documents for negotiation. An expiry date stipulated for payment, acceptance or negotiation will be construed to express an expiry date for presentation of documents.

The advising or correspondent bank will be the nominated bank where it is authorised to pay. That will cover the common position where the credit provides for immediate payment against documents, and also the less common one where the credit provides for deferred payment and nominates the correspondent bank as the bank to pay the beneficiary. Where the credit provides for negotiation as the means of providing the beneficiary with money and authorises the correspondent bank to negotiate the documents, it will be the nominated bank. In these cases the documents will be presented to the correspondent bank, and the nominated bank and the bank to which presentation should be made are one and the same. Where the credit utilises a draft and the draft is to be accepted by the issuing bank, that bank will be the nominated bank. If the documents are nonetheless to be presented by the beneficiary to the correspondent bank for acceptance or rejection as documents under the credit, the nominated bank and the bank to which documents are to be presented will not coincide. The second paragraph of Article 10.b.i is perhaps not very clearly worded. It must be read in the sense that 'presentation of documents must be made to the Nominated Bank, whether it be the Issuing Bank, or the Confirming Bank, if any, or any other bank'. It does not mean, for example, that the documents can be presented to the issuing bank as an alternative to the bank to which the credit provides that they are to be presented.

1 Article 10 is taken from Article 11 in the 1983 Revision. 'The Nominated Bank' did not appear in the 1983 Revision.
2 Article 42 is considered further in para 5.22.

6.11 Where the correspondent bank is the bank to which documents are to be presented for examination and acceptance or rejection under the credit, it will be its duty to examine them to see whether they appear on their face to be in accordance with the terms and conditions of the credit.[1] The bank has then to accept or to refuse the documents. The duties of a bank in carrying out such an examination and in connection with acceptance or refusal are considered in Chapter 8. The bank's right to reimbursement and to the payment of commission and other charges will be dependent on the proper performance of its duty under the terms of the credit. Article 14.a provides:

ARTICLE 14.a   When the Issuing Bank authorises another bank to pay, incur a deferred payment undertaking, accept Draft(s), or negotiate against documents which appear on their face to be in compliance with the terms and conditions of the Credit, the Issuing Bank and the Confirming Bank, if any, are bound:

    i. to reimburse the Nominated Bank which has paid, incurred a deferred payment undertaking, accepted Draft(s), or negotiated,

    ii. to take up the documents.

So if it pays or incurs other liabilities to the beneficiary in respect of documents which it should not have accepted, it will have no right to reimbursement unless the applicant is prepared to waive the discrepancies. In such a case, subject to any right of recourse against the beneficiary,[2] it will be left with the documents, and hence the goods, on its hands. Article 18 has also to be considered in this context. The position will be no different from that where the advising bank accepts documents which do not comply with the applicant's instructions because it has made an error in advising the credit rather than in examining the documents. It is suggested that Article 18 should not assist the banks in such a context.[3] In performing its task of examining and accepting or refusing the documents the correspondent bank acts so far as the issuing bank is concerned as its agent. In *Gian Singh & Co Ltd v Banque de l'Indochine*[4] Lord Diplock stated[5] '. . . the customer did not succeed in making out any case of negligence against the issuing bank or the notifying bank which acted as its agent, in failing to detect the forgery'. It is suggested that this is so whether or not the correspondent bank has confirmed the credit.[6] If the correspondent bank accepts the documents, as between the issuing bank and the beneficiary, its acceptance will bind the issuing bank, its principal.[7]

1 Where the correspondent bank does not confirm the credit and the credit does not provide for immediate payment, the correspondent bank may well undertake no duty under the credit to examine the documents, and the first examination will be by the issuing bank.
2 See para 6.28 et seq below.
3 See para 6.5 above, and also 4.18.
4 [1974] 1 WLR 1234, [1974] 2 Lloyd's Rep 1.
5 Ibid at 1239 and 11, 12.
6 See para 6.13 below.
7 See also para 6.27 below.

6.12 *(3) As the paying bank*   The credit may provide that the correspondent bank is the bank by which payment pursuant to the credit is to be made. This will usually be the case where the credit provides for immediate payment.[1] As regards the issuing bank it pays as the agent of the issuing bank which has undertaken that payment be made. This is so regardless of whether the correspondent bank has confirmed the credit and has an obligation to pay in its own right.

1 See para 6.9 above.

6.13 *(4) As the confirming bank*   The correspondent bank may be asked by the issuing bank to confirm the credit. If it is not prepared to do so, Article 9.c provides:

ARTICLE 9.c[1]   c.i. If another bank is authorised or requested by the Issuing Bank to add its confirmation to a Credit but is not prepared to do so, it must so inform the Issuing Bank without delay.

ii. Unless the Issuing Bank specifies otherwise in its authorisation or request to add confirmation, the Advising Bank may advise the Credit to the Beneficiary without adding its confirmation.

If it is willing, the correspondent bank then adds its own undertaking to that of the issuing bank as has been described in Chapter 2.[2] Article 9.b of the Uniform Customs sets out the undertakings given by a confirming bank in different situations.[3] The obligations of the confirming bank towards the beneficiary have been considered with those of the issuing bank in Chapter 5. The obligation of a confirming bank to pay, or to be responsible for payment if it is not itself to pay, is an obligation which it gives as a principal. This does not prevent it from acting in other respects as the agent of the issuing bank. The credit in the *Equitable Trust* case[4] was a confirmed credit.[5] The position is that in carrying out its functions, where appropriate, it will act in a dual capacity. In so far as its interests as a confirming bank are concerned, it acts as a principal: at the same time as regards the issuing bank it acts as agent. Thus in accepting documents and paying against documents it acts as a principal in relation to its obligations as confirming bank, and it acts as agent for the issuing bank with regard to the obligations of the issuing bank.

1 Article 9.c follows closely Article 10.c in the 1983 Revision.
2 Para 2.16.
3 Article 9.b is set out and its practical effect considered in paras 5.13 to 5.19.
4 (1927) 27 Ll L Rep 49.
5 See para 6.4 above.

6.14 *'Silent' confirmations*   Even where a beneficiary is prepared to pay the bank charges involved, some foreign banks will refuse requests by applicants to procure that credits opened by them should be confirmed. This may be because they see such a request as an insult to their credit worthiness or to the prestige of their country: in their view their own undertaking should be sufficient. A different and more acceptable reason is that national policy may direct the banks of a country not to request the confirmation of their credits because it utilises valuable and limited lines of credit. In view of the value and utility of a confirmation to the beneficiary, exporters have sought a way round this problem by themselves requesting the confirmation of a credit by the advising bank without the authorisation of the issuing bank. This is referred to as a 'silent' confirmation. Such a confirmation will fall outside the ambit of the Uniform Customs in that Article 9.b applies to confirmations authorised or requested by the issuing bank. Nonetheless the undertakings to be given by a 'silent' confirmer must follow those set out in the Article. For confirmation of a credit means that the confirmer binds itself that the undertakings constituted by the credit will be met: it guarantees the credit. So, as those obligations which it confirms will be those set out in Article 9.a, the expression of the silent confirmer's obligations will be found in Article 9.b even though the Article does not apply directly.[1] The confirming bank will have no rights against the issuing bank arising from its confirmation. Thus, unless it is entitled to be reimbursed because it is nominated by the credit as the paying bank, if its confirmation leads it to have to pay on the credit, it will not have a right of reimbursement. It will not have a right to object to amendments, and it may be dependent on the beneficiary for knowledge of their terms. It could be argued that a silent confirmation was contrary to Article 10.c in the 1983 Revision.[2] But Article 9.c is now phrased so that the point does not arise.

1 The practice of silent confirmations is discussed without disapproval in Cases 176 and 177 in the ICC's More Case Studies on Documentary Credits, Publication No 489.
2 See *Benjamin's Sale of Goods*, 4th edition, para 23–024.

6.15 *Permission to confirm on request* Sometimes the instruction to the advising bank will expressly permit it to confirm the credit at the beneficiary's request and expense. Article 9.b begins 'A confirmation . . . by another bank . . . upon the authorisation or request of the issuing bank . . .'. It is suggested that such an instruction will bring the confirmation within the express terms of Article 9 as a confirmation which has been authorised (though not requested) by the issuing bank.

6.16 *(5) As a collecting bank*[1] The position of a collecting bank is considered generally in Chapter 7. If the correspondent bank's sole duty under the credit is to advise the credit, this having been done it may happen that the beneficiary later presents documents to the advising bank and asks the bank to collect on them on its behalf. The advising bank then reverses roles and becomes the agent of the beneficiary to present the documents to the issuing bank and to receive payment on the beneficiary's behalf. If the documents are fraudulent to the beneficiary's knowledge, the issuing bank will be entitled to reject them.[2] This position is to be contrasted with that where a bank presents documents to the issuing bank in its own right having acquired them by negotiation, ie purchase, from the beneficiary, where fraud by the beneficiary is irrelevant if it is unknown to the negotiating bank.[3]

1 See also para 5.60 above.
2 See among other cases, *United City Merchants (Investments) Ltd v Royal Bank of Canada* [1983] 1 AC 168 and *European Asian Bank AG v Punjab Bank (No 2)* [1983] 1 WLR 642 at 652A, [1983] 1 Lloyd's Rep 611 at 615.1.
3 *European Asian Bank AG v Punjab Bank (No 2)* [1983] 1 WLR 642 at 657, [1983] 1 Lloyd's Rep 611 at 619. See also para 6.17.

6.17 *(6) As a negotiation bank* The position of a negotiation (or negotiating) bank is considered generally in Chapter 7.[1] A correspondent bank may come to negotiate documents in two situations. The first is where it is nominated in the credit to negotiate them. If it has confirmed the credit, it is obliged to do so. But if it has not, it is not so obliged although its refusal will put the issuing bank in breach of its agreement with the beneficiary. The second situation is where its instructions cover only the advice of the credit but the credit is a negotiation credit and the correspondent bank is approached by the beneficiary to negotiate and agrees to do so. In each case it will then purchase the documents from the beneficiary and present them to the issuing bank in its own right. In these instances the correspondent bank deals with the documents solely as principal in its own right, and does so neither as the agent of the issuing bank nor of the beneficiary.[2] The bank is unaffected by the fraud of the beneficiary provided that it has no knowledge of it.[3]

1 See also para 2.22 et seq.
2 See *Maran Road Saw Mill v Austin Taylor & Co Ltd* [1975] 1 Lloyd's Rep 156 at 161.1 and para 6.35 below.
3 The *European Asian Bank* case supra.

6.18 ***(7) As a discounter of time drafts***   Where the credit provides for drafts payable at a future date, the correspondent bank may be prepared to discount the drafts, that is to say, to make an immediate payment in purchase of them, the price being reduced by an amount of interest calculated as accruing over the period to the date when the draft becomes due for payment by the beneficiary or the issuing bank or other party as it may be. The situations in which it will do this are:

(a) where the credit provides that it is available by negotiation by the correspondent or advising bank. Having done so it is likely that the terms of its instructions from the issuing bank will entitle it to be reimbursed immediately by the issuing bank. Otherwise it must wait until the draft becomes due.

(b) where the credit is a negotiation credit and the correspondent bank's instructions from the issuing bank are limited to advising the credit, and it subsequently negotiates the documents as described in paragraph 6.17. It will then obtain payment itself when the draft becomes due.

(c) where the credit does not provide for negotiation in either of the above two ways, but involves time drafts. If documents are presented to it, the correspondent bank may of its own accord at the request of the beneficiary purchase the draft providing the beneficiary with immediate payment. The bank has then to forward the documents to the issuing bank and will receive payment when the draft becomes due.

In the first of these situations the correspondent bank is either acting simply as the agent of the issuing bank or as a confirming bank, depending on whether or not it has confirmed the credit. In either case, should the bank not itself receive reimbursement it cannot seek recourse against the beneficiary to recover its money: Article 9.a.iv or Article 9.b.iv deny such a right of recourse. In the second and third situations the correspondent bank will have such a right.[1]

---

1 There is no bar to it: for the position of a negotiating bank which is not obliged to negotiate, see para 7.9 below.

6.19 ***(8) As a correspondent issuer***   The correspondent bank may be asked to issue the credit in its own name, that is, so that it rather than the bank from which it receives its instructions will appear as the issuing bank. In such circumstances, even if the credit states that it is issued on the instructions of the bank instructing the correspondent bank, no relationship will come into being between the beneficiary and the instructing bank. As 'correspondent issuer' the correspondent bank is therefore the sole party undertaking liability to the beneficiary. Its position as regards the bank from which it receives its instructions (which cannot in this instance accurately be called 'the issuing banker') is similar to that between an applicant for a credit and an issuing banker.[1] Two early examples are contained in *National Bank of Egypt v Hannevig's Bank Ltd*[2] and *Skandinaviska Akt v Barclays Bank*.[3]

---

1 See Chapter 4.
2 (1919) 1 Ll L Rep 69.
3 (1925) 22 Ll L Rep 523.

B.   Advice of the Credit to the Correspondent Bank, Amendments

6.20   Article 11.a and .b[1,2] makes provisions mainly relating to the identification of the operative instrument where teletransmission[3] is used. It provides:

> ARTICLE 11   **Teletransmitted and Pre-Advised Credits**
> a.i.   When an Issuing Bank instructs an Advising Bank by an authenticated teletransmission to advise a Credit or an amendment to a Credit, the teletransmission will be deemed to be the operative Credit instrument or the operative amendment, and no mail confirmation should be sent. Should a mail confirmation nevertheless be sent, it will have no effect and the Advising Bank will have no obligation to check such mail confirmation against the operative Credit instrument or the operative amendment received by teletransmission.
> ii.   If the teletransmission states 'full details to follow' (or words of similar effect) or states that the mail confirmation is to be the operative Credit instrument or the operative amendment, then the teletransmission will not be deemed to be the operative Credit instrument or the operative amendment. The Issuing Bank must forward the operative Credit instrument or the operative amendment to such Advising Bank without delay.
> b.   If a bank uses the services of an Advising Bank to have the Credit advised to the Beneficiary, it must also use the services of the same bank for advising an amendment(s).

Many credits are now advised through SWIFT[4] which is an independent network run by banks to secure, inter alia, security and accuracy of communication.[5]

1 Article 11.a and .b is derived from Article 12 in the 1983 Revision.
2 Article 11.c relates to pre-advices and is considered in para 5.4 above.
3 It is suggested that teletransmission means instantaneous transmission (τηλε, from afar) and covers forms of electronic transmission.
4 Society for Interbank Financial Telecommunications.
5 An example is given by Form 5 in Appendix 5, below.

6.21   The question of amendments has been considered generally in Chapter 3.[1] Where the correspondent bank confirms the credit, the general position is as there stated, namely that it is bound by the credit as first advised unless amendments to it are agreed by it, the issuing bank and the beneficiary. Paragraph 3.38 discusses the possibility that a confirming bank may advise an amendment and withhold its confirmation of it, as provided for by Article 9.d.ii. Where the correspondent bank does not confirm the credit, its sole position is as agent for the issuing bank. What should it do if the issuing bank instructs it to advise an amendment to the beneficiary, which the beneficiary rejects but the issuing bank nonetheless then instructs the correspondent bank only to accept documents which conform to the credit as it would have been amended? The duty of the correspondent bank to its principal and its position as a responsible bank may then appear in conflict. Their relations, however, are governed by the Uniform Customs and the issuing bank is obliged to act in accordance with them in its instructions. It is suggested that the correspondent bank would be entitled to reject the instructions of the issuing bank as instructions which the issuing bank was not entitled to give. If that is right, it could pay the beneficiary against documents complying with the credit as unamended and would be entitled to be reimbursed by the issuing bank. The alternative argument is that it is bound to follow the instructions of its principal whatever they may be: therefore, as it owes no obligation to the beneficiary, it can and should reject documents not complying with the amendment and leave the beneficiary to his remedy against the issuing bank for breach of the credit. The former course carries the higher risk for the correspondent bank because it involves the bank in paying and seeking reimbursement from a bank whose instructions it has declined to follow. In practice it is unlikely that a correspondent bank would pay in these circumstances particularly if it was not in funds.[2]

1 Para 3.33 et seq.
2 For a different discussion of this problem arriving at the same conclusion by a majority, namely that the correspondent bank should accept documents complying with the credit as unamended, see Opinions of the ICC Banking Commission 1987–1988, Ref 149.

C. Effect of Under Reserve and Indemnity Arrangements

6.22 The effect as between a correspondent bank and a beneficiary of arrangements whereby the bank accepts documents which it considers to be non-conforming has been considered in Chapter 5.[1] Such arrangements have no effect as between the correspondent bank and the issuing bank. Article 14.f so provides. So the special arrangement means that there is no acceptance or rejection by the correspondent bank equivalent to that provided for by Article 14.d. The capacity in which the correspondent bank sends forward the documents to the issuing bank is uncertain. It may send them for acceptance or rejection by the issuing bank in a capacity of agent for the beneficiary similar to that of a collecting bank, or it may do so as principal in its own right. When documents are sent forward on such a basis, the sender may not be entitled to compliance with the machinery provided by Article 14 in connection with the rejection of documents.[2]

1 Para 5.55 et seq.
2 See the American decision, *Alaska Textile Co Inc v Lloyd Williams Fashions Inc* [1992] 1 Bank LR 408.

D. Reimbursement of the Correspondent Bank from Another Source

6.23 Article 19 of the Uniform Customs provides:

ARTICLE 19[1]   **Bank-to-Bank Reimbursement Arrangements**
    a. If an Issuing Bank intends that the reimbursement to which a paying, accepting or negotiating bank is entitled, shall be obtained by such bank (the 'Claiming Bank'), claiming on another party (the 'Reimbursing Bank'), it shall provide such Reimbursing Bank in good time with the proper instructions or authorisation to honour such reimbursement claims.
    b. Issuing Banks shall not require a Claiming Bank to supply a certificate of compliance with the terms and conditions of the Credit to the Reimbursing Bank.

    c. An Issuing Bank shall not be relieved from any of its obliga-
      tions to provide reimbursement if and when reimbursement
      is not received by the Claiming Bank from the Reimbursing
      Bank.
    d. The Issuing Bank shall be responsible to the Claiming Bank
      for any loss of interest if reimbursement is not provided by
      the Reimbursing Bank on first demand, or as otherwise
      specified in the Credit, or mutually agreed, as the case may
      be.
    e. The Reimbursing Bank's charges should be for the account
      of the Issuing Bank. However, in cases where the charges are
      for the account of another party, it is the responsibility of the
      Issuing Bank to so indicate in the original Credit and in the
      reimbursement authorisation. In cases where the Reimbur-
      sing Bank's charges are for the account of another party they
      shall be collected from the Claiming Bank when the Credit is
      drawn under. In cases where the Credit is not drawn under,
      the Reimbursing Bank's charges remain the obligation of the
      Issuing Bank.

Article 14.a obliges an issuing bank to reimburse a bank which it has
authorised to pay or to incur a payment undertaking pursuant to a credit.
The reimbursement will usually be effected by the issuing bank direct to
the correspondent bank. But it may be that under the issuing bank's
international arrangements funds for the country in question are provided via a third bank in another country or by a branch of the issuing
bank in another country. Thus a confirming bank in Singapore might be
instructed to reimburse itself from a New York bank in respect of a credit
issued by an Indian bank: compare the facts in *European Asian Bank AG
v Punjab Bank (No 2)*,[2] set out in Chapter 2.[3] Article 19 covers this
situation. The Court of Appeal had to consider the predecessor of Article
19, Article 21 in the 1983 Revision, in *Royal Bank of Scotland plc v Casa
di Risparmio*.[4] The Royal Bank of Scotland wished to sue Italian banks in
London for reimbursement under a credit which provided for reimbursement in New York, and relied on what is now Article 19.c to found an
alleged obligation to pay in London if repayment was not affected in New
York. It was held that for jurisdictional purposes the obligation to
reimburse was an obligation to reimburse in New York. The proceedings
in England were therefore set aside.

1 Article 19.a–.d closely follows Article 21 of the 1983 Revision. Article 19.e is new.
2 [1983] 1 WLR 642, [1983] 1 Lloyd's Rep 611.
3 Para 2.26.
4 [1992] 1 Bank LR 251.

6.24 In such a situation the reimbursing bank will not see the documents
because they will go to the issuing bank and so, if the credit provides for
immediate payment, the correspondent bank will be in a position to
demand payment from the reimbursing bank before the issuing bank will
have received the documents or checked them. So inevitably payment has
to be made by the reimbursing bank simply against the demand of the
correspondent bank. In order to try and exercise some control, some
issuing banks, particularly in India, required that the correspondent bank
certify to the reimbursing bank that the terms and conditions of the credit
had been complied with. This is now prohibited by Article 19.b of the
Uniform Customs. The reason is that the reimbursing bank's role should

be kept to that of paying against demand, and any disputes as to whether the documents comply with the credit should be resolved between the issuing and the paying bank. The provision of a certificate to the reimbursing bank is seen as suggesting that it should be the reimbursing bank which should seek to recover its payment if it turns out that the documents do not comply with the credit, whereas it should be for the issuing bank to effect recovery.[1] It appears that some banks still require the provision of such a certificate. As this will be an express term of the credit itself, it will override Article 19.b which is a term of the credit which is incorporated into the contract only by reference, and a certificate must be provided. The correspondent bank is of course entitled to object to the requirement and to ask for its removal referring to Article 19.b, and there is no reason why it should not decline to advise the credit unless it is removed.[2] A paying bank which considers that the documents which it has examined do comply with the credit, may well feel that it has nothing to lose by giving a certificate. It should however be pointed out that a bank's duty to inspect documents is to see that they 'appear on their face to be in accordance with the terms and conditions of the credit'. A certificate that they do comply with the terms and conditions of the credit could be argued to be in more absolute terms, although it may be seldom that the distinction will be of importance in practice. So such a certificate is not one which a bank should be required to give even without regard to Article 19.b.

1 See item R 19 in Decisions (1975–1979) of the ICC Banking Commission, ICC Publication No 371, commenting on the predecessor of Article 19.b and ICC Publication No 411 UCP, 1974/1983 Revisions Compared and Explained, pp 36, 37.
2 See ICC Publication No 459, Case Studies on Documentary Credits, Case 63.

6.25 As the reimbursing bank's role is to pay against demand, it is not relevant whether the documents which give rise to the demand do or do not comply with the credit. So, whether or not there are complying documents, the reimbursing bank is entitled to reimbursement either by retaining funds previously provided by the issuing bank or by payment by the issuing bank. If the documents do not comply, the issuing bank in its turn is entitled to recover the payment from the correspondent bank provided the issuing bank rejects the documents when they are received by it, and provided that it complies with Article 14 of the Uniform Customs. There is no privity of contract between the correspondent bank and the reimbursing bank. So, if the reimbursing bank fails to pay – probably because it has not been put in funds by the issuing bank – the correspondent bank has no rights against it: the correspondent bank's rights are against the issuing bank, namely, to recover the principal sum which it has paid out and interest accruing during the delay in payment. Article 19 not only covers the position of a correspondent bank which incurs a payment obligation, but also that of any bank which is entitled to and does negotiate the documents. The Article does not refer to the position where the party required to claim payment from the third bank is not a bank but is the beneficiary of the credit. The principles, however, will be the same as those underlying the Article.

E. Recourse between an Issuing Bank and its Correspondent

6.26 Article 14.a of the Uniform Customs sets out the principle that, where a bank effects payment or undertakes a payment obligation against documents which appear on their face to accord with the terms and conditions of the credit, it is entitled to reimbursement from the bank from which it received its instructions. An issuing bank is entitled to reimbursement from its customer, the applicant. If the documents conform, recourse on a draft being contrary to Article 9.a of the Uniform Customs,[1] no question of recourse appears possible. Where the documents do not in fact conform, the question could arise between the two banks if both of them fail to observe the discrepancy and the documents are then refused by the applicant. It is suggested that the issuing bank is not entitled to recourse against the correspondent bank in that situation. Reference is made to Chapter 5 where the question of recourse against the beneficiary on the ground that the documents do not conform is considered as between an issuing or confirming bank and the beneficiary.[2] The further argument has to be met here, that it is the duty of the advising bank as agent of the issuing bank to check the documents. Can the issuing bank claim against the advising bank as damages for breach of duty the sum which it has paid to the advising bank? Three main reasons are suggested as to why it cannot. First, it is also the duty of the issuing bank to check the documents itself: if it had correctly performed that duty, the loss would not have occurred: so the proximate cause of the loss is its own negligence. Second, because of the same duty on the part of the issuing bank to check the documents itself, by accepting the documents it is to be taken to have ratified the unauthorised act of the advising bank in accepting non-conforming documents. Third, if the issuing bank has accepted the documents, Article 14.e will preclude it from claiming subsequently that the documents are not in accordance with the terms and conditions of the credit. This will be the short answer in most cases, and the legal and practical rationale for it is to be found in the first two reasons.[3]

1 Para 5.68.
2 Para 5.72 et seq.
3 *Benjamin's Sale of Goods* (4th edn) para 21–138 states that the question of recourse where the issuing banker takes up a faulty set of documents tendered by the correspondent banker has to be regarded as open.

6.27 The position just considered must be distinguished from that where the correspondent bank fails to observe a discrepancy between the documents presented and the terms of the credit and the discrepancy is observed by the issuing bank. If payment has been made by the correspondent bank it will not be entitled to reimbursement from the issuing bank. The documents will be returned to it under Article 14.d of the Uniform Customs. If the credit provides for payment to be deferred, either because it utilises a time draft or because it is a deferred payment credit, the acceptance of the documents by the correspondent bank[1] will bind the issuing bank because the correspondent bank has acted as its agent to examine and accept or reject the documents.[2] If the applicant refuses the documents because of the discrepancy, the issuing bank will have to pay the beneficiary without a right of reimbursement by the applicant. It will then be entitled to recover its loss from the correspondent bank for breach of its duty to examine the documents with reasonable care. If it has returned the documents to the correspondent bank, its loss will be the amount of its payment to the beneficiary. Otherwise its loss will be the amount of the payment less what it may have been able to recoup as a result of having the security of the documents. The position may be complicated by the correspondent bank having been nominated under the credit as the paying bank.

1 This assumes that the correspondent bank has accepted a duty under the credit to examine the documents. Where it has not confirmed the credit and where the credit does not provide for immediate payment, it may well not do so, and the first examination of the documents will be by the issuing bank.
2 Para 6.11.

F. Recourse between the Correspondent Bank and the Beneficiary

6.28 The position where the correspondent bank confirms the credit has already been considered in Chapter 5.[1] It is suggested that in the absence of fraud there can be no right of recourse.

1 Para 5.67 et seq.

6.29 The question of recourse where the correspondent bank does not confirm the credit is one on which there is very limited authority. It may arise in a number of situations, some of which are complicated. It is not something which is covered in the Uniform Customs. It may be suggested that, because the Uniform Customs provide in Article 9 for there to be no recourse by issuing and confirming banks on drafts drawn in connection with a credit, there should otherwise be recourse on drafts. But two points must be borne in mind. First, the Uniform Customs do not purport to cover all situations. Second, the rights and obligations in connection with credits were to be found in the common law and banking practice without reference to the Uniform Customs before the situation arose where they are incorporated into, it is believed, all credits coming before the English courts save some standby credits. The common law and banking practice are still the source where the Uniform Customs do not cover a situation. The Uniform Customs do not deal with the position of an advising bank as to recourse, nor that of a negotiation bank.

6.30 Where the credit provides for immediate payment by a non-confirming correspondent bank and documents are accepted and, contrary to the usual case, payment is made without the bank having been first put in funds, the question of recourse by the correspondent bank against the beneficiary will arise if the issuing bank fails and is unable to reimburse the correspondent bank.[1] It is suggested that these facts would not give the correspondent bank any cause of action against the beneficiary. Would it affect the position if the documents included a sight draft drawn on the issuing bank, which was dishonoured by non-acceptance? The correspondent bank as holder would prima facie have a right of recourse against the beneficiary, the drawer, unless the draft was marked 'without recourse'. It seems unfair to the beneficiary that the probably casual inclusion of the sight draft among the documents should reverse his position. It will have that effect unless an absence of recourse is to be derived from the circumstances of the negotiation as would be the case in respect of an issuing or confirming bank in the absence of the Uniform Customs. Where the credit does not provide for immediate payment but utilises a time draft, the failure of the issuing bank will not result in the correspondent bank being out of pocket because it will not have paid.

1 The problem will be avoided if the timing is such that the correspondent bank can treat its contract with the issuing bank as terminated and arrange with the buyer for the buyer to take up the documents against payment.

6.31 Where immediate payment against documents is made by a non-confirming advising bank, the question of recourse will also arise where it is found that the documents do not conform to the credit and so the advising bank is not reimbursed by the issuing bank. Can it be asserted against the beneficiary that the payment was made under a mistake of fact that the documents were conforming? The bank would first have to establish that the error which it made was properly to be categorised as a mistake of fact. Because the bank has no contractual relationship with the beneficiary the analysis must be to some extent different to that in Chapter 5 relating to the position of issuing and confirming banks.[1] The position of the bank is that it has purported to pay and has paid as agent for its principal even though as between it and the principal, the issuing bank, the payment was in breach of the terms of the agency. It is suggested that an agent in such a situation can have no better right of recovery than his principal. The view has been previously expressed that the issuing bank has no right of recovery.[2] But it should not be thought that by reason only of the bank's position as agent it would be barred from suing. In *Colonial Bank v Exchange Bank of Yarmouth*[3] it was stated[4] in respect of the plaintiff bank which had paid by mistake 'It seems a perfectly untenable position to say that an agent in that position has not got an interest to recall the money, so that it may be put into the right channel.'[5] It is suggested that in the absence of fraud by the beneficiary or other party presenting the documents, a correspondent bank would have no right of recourse against that party on the ground that it had accepted the documents in the mistaken belief that they complied with the credit whereas in fact they did not. This conclusion may be considered consistent with the commercial function of documentary credits, and with the scheme of Article 14 of the Uniform Customs, namely that the buyer/beneficiary should know that once the documents which he has tendered under a credit have been accepted, his right to payment has become absolute.

1 Para 5.67 et seq.
2 Paras 5.73, 74.
3 (1885) 11 App Cas 84.
4 Ibid at 91.
5 See generally *Bowstead on Agency* (15th edn) Article 117.

6.32 The situation considered in the last paragraph may also be complicated by the inclusion of a sight draft among the documents as has been discussed in paragraph 6.30. The considerations will be similar.

6.33 Where the credit provides for payment to be deferred but does not utilise a time draft, ie it is a deferred payment credit, and the correspondent bank accepts documents presented to it pursuant to the credit which do not conform to the credit,[1] it is suggested that the position is as follows. The acceptance of the documents by the correspondent bank binds the issuing bank so far as the beneficiary is concerned and the beneficiary becomes entitled against the issuing bank to receive payment when the appointed time comes.[2] If the applicant declines to accept the documents the issuing bank then has a claim against the correspondent bank.[3] Can it pass on this claim to the beneficiary? It is suggested that it cannot. The claim is not even to recover money paid under a mistake of fact but to recover a sum for which the bank has become liable in damages. The beneficiary does not warrant that the documents which it presents comply with the terms of the credit. It is suggested that no such claim will lie.

1 This makes the assumption, made in para 6.27, that the correspondent bank has accepted a duty under the credit to examine the documents. In the circumstances posed it may well not do so. The first examination of the documents will be by the issuing bank.
2 Paras 6.11 and 6.27.
3 Para 6.27.

6.34 Where the credit provides for deferment of payment by utilising a time draft among the documents to be presented, if the documents do not conform to the credit but are accepted by the correspondent bank and then rejected by the buyer or applicant, as between the issuing bank and the beneficiary the documents have been accepted under the credit and the issuing bank is bound to make payment. If the correspondent bank comes to have a claim as the holder of a dishonoured draft, because it has had to pay the issuing bank on the draft, then the question of recourse on the draft will arise. It is to be questioned whether there is any logical reason for distinguishing the position where payment is deferred but no bill is involved.

6.35 The last position to be considered is that where the credit provides that it is available by negotiation by the advising bank. So the correspondent bank will purchase at a discount for interest the documents which will include a time draft. Here there is authority. In *Maran Road Saw Mill v Austin Taylor & Co Ltd*[1] a credit was opened by Sale & Co available by 90-day drafts drawn on them together with shipping documents as specified, which were to be negotiable by the Bangkok Bank in Kuala Lumpur. It appears that the credit was advised through the latter.[2] Sale & Co failed after the Bangkok Bank had paid on drafts and documents presented to them. The drafts having been dishonoured, the bank claimed repayment from the sellers. The sellers felt obliged to pay and sought to recover the price of the goods from their agents, Austin Taylor, who had arranged the credit as the means of transferring the price to them.[3] Austin Taylor raised the question whether the sellers had been obliged to repay the bank. Ackner J held that they had. After referring to Article 3 of the 1962 Revision of the Uniform Customs he stated:[4]

'This article makes it clear that a confirming bank may not have recourse. It is otherwise in the case of a non-confirming bank. The reason is that whereas the latter is the agent of the issuing bank for the purpose of advising the credit, it acts as principal vis-à-vis the beneficiary. He is under no duty to negotiate and if it does so, it may make whatever conditions it likes as to a pre-requisite to doing so. It follows that if the credit is available by "time" draft, the negotiating bank may have recourse on the draft if this is ultimately unpaid. The fact of *advising* places no responsibility on the negotiating bank, no greater responsibility than if it were not the advising bank; and it makes no difference that negotiations may be restricted to that bank.' (See Gutteridge and Megrah: The Law of Bankers' Commercial Credits, 4th ed., p 73.)[5]

The statement '. . . whereas the latter[6] is the agent of the issuing bank for the purpose of advising the credit, it acts as principal vis-à-vis the beneficiary' is somewhat compressed. The meaning appears to be that in negotiating the documents and draft the advising bank acts as principal. If so, an advising bank nominated to negotiate documents is in the same position as a third party bank which negotiates documents under a negotiation credit, and there is a contrast with the position where the bank receives documents under credits containing other forms of undertaking. Having negotiated the draft and documents as principal, it then presents them to the issuing bank and provided they conform it is entitled to payment as the credit may provide. Therefore, like a negotiation bank[7] it is entitled to recourse against the beneficiary on the bill should it not be honoured. The ICC Banking Commission has concluded in two decisions[8] that an advising bank which has not confirmed a credit but negotiates documents under it, has a right of recourse, basing its decisions on Article 3 of the Uniform Customs, 1974 Revision, now Article 9.[9]

1 [1975] 1 Lloyd's Rep 156.
2 See [1975] 1 Lloyd's Rep at 161.1 line 21.
3 See para 3.49 above.
4 [1975] 1 Lloyd's Rep 156 at 161.1.
5 Page 87 in the 7th edition.
6 The non-confirming bank.
7 Para 7.10.
8 Decisions of the ICC Banking Commission 1975–1979, References 6 and 7.
9 The same view is taken in the *ICC's Guide to Documentary Credit Operations* p 31.

G.   The Correspondent Bank and the Applicant or Buyer

6.36 Whatever functions the correspondent bank fulfils there is no contract between it and the applicant for the credit. It was accepted by the Court of Appeal in *United Trading Corpn SA v Allied Arab Bank Ltd*[1] that it was arguable that a bank at one end of a performance bond chain owed a duty of care to the account party at the other end not to pay a fraudulent demand made by the beneficiary. This was questioned by the Court of Appeal in *GKN Contractors Ltd v Lloyds Bank plc*.[2] It is at least as difficult to see how a correspondent bank might owe such a duty. Where a tender of documents is made to the correspondent bank and discrepancies are found which are advised to the buyer through the issuing bank, the buyer may give instructions to take up the documents. If it is later found that there are other discrepancies in addition, the buyer will not be obliged to take up the documents unless he is willing to waive them also. They will be left on the hands of the bank.

1 [1985] 2 Lloyd's Rep 554n at 560.
2 (1985) 30 BLR 48 at 62 and see paras 9.34 and 12.60 below.

H.   Charges of the Correspondent Bank

6.37 Article 18.a provides that the utilisation by one bank of another to give effect to the instructions of the applicant is done for the account of the applicant. It may of course be arranged between the applicant and the issuing bank that the charges of the advising bank shall be for the account of the beneficiary, this being a provision of the underlying contract of sale. The credit will then include a term that the charges of the correspondent bank are for the account of the beneficiary, and the charges will be deducted from the payment due to the beneficiary when conforming documents are presented.[1] If they are not presented, depending on the term of its arrangement with the issuing bank, the correspondent bank may be entitled to recover its charges for advising the credit from the issuing bank, which, in its turn, will seek to recover them from the applicant in reliance on Article 18.c.ii.[2]

1 The advising fee and any amendments fees will have been charged at the time of the advice and amendments. But it very commonly happens that they remain unpaid until payment is made under the credit, when they are deducted with the payment fee.
2 For discussion of problems which may arise in connection with reimbursing banks' commission, see Opinions of the ICC Banking Commission 1984–1986, R 141, and 1987–1988, R 155. The reliance there upon Article 21 of the Uniform Customs is not understood.

6.38 Where the correspondent bank's sole initial role is that of advising bank and it subsequently acts as a collecting bank for the beneficiary, or negotiates the documents from the beneficiary and presents them in its own right, it will deduct its charges from what it would otherwise pay the beneficiary. It is the general rule of agency law that an agent is accountable to his principal for any profits above his entitled remuneration from his principal. It is suggested that an attempt to use this rule to require a correspondent bank to pay over these charges to its principal, the issuing bank, would be doomed to failure. For there is nothing improper in a correspondent bank acting in this way; nor are the charges to be attributed to its employment as agent. So also where the correspondent bank makes a profit from discounting a time draft drawn under the credit.[1]

1 Cf *Benjamin's Sale of Goods* (4th edn) para 23–139.

Chapter 7

The Collecting Bank and the Negotiation Bank

7.1 *(Advising banks)* An advising bank whose instructions are limited to the advice of the credit may on occasion act as a collecting bank or as a negotiation bank. Its functions in such a situation have been considered in the previous chapter.

A. Collecting Banks

7.2 *(1) General* A collecting bank is a bank which is requested by the beneficiary to present the documents under the credit on the beneficiary's behalf. It may come to act as collecting bank for two rather different reasons. First, the beneficiary may find it convenient to use its services in this way. For example, the beneficiary may prefer to use its own bank to forward the documents where they have to be presented abroad rather than forwarding them itself. It may also want to have the documents checked by the bank for compliance with the credit. If there are discrepancies, a bank may be in a better position to request their waiver than the beneficiary itself. Second, the beneficiary may have been financed by the bank to obtain the goods which are the object of the transaction underlying the credit, either by way of a general overdraft arrangement or by a specific advance. In either case the bank may well require that the documents be presented through it, so that it has control of the documents in the event that the transaction goes wrong. Where a credit is a straight credit, that is to say, is not a negotiation credit, the only way in which the beneficiary's bank can involve itself with the documents to be presented under the credit is to act as agent for collection unless, of course, the credit has been advised through it.

7.3 *(2) The collecting bank as agent* A collecting bank acts as the agent of the beneficiary for the purposes of presentation and receiving payment. This has the consequence that, if the documents are fraudulent to the beneficiary's knowledge, the paying bank, ie the issuing or the confirming bank, will not be obliged to pay the collecting bank.[1] So if the collecting bank makes an advance to the beneficiary in anticipation of the collection, it will be at risk. In cases of fraud it will be important to determine whether the bank is collecting in its own right having negotiated, ie purchased, the documents from the beneficiary, or whether it is collecting as the beneficiary's agent. This may involve a careful examination of the relations between the bank and the beneficiary and of the relevant documents, particularly as to at what stage, if it did, the bank credited the beneficiary with the sum in question.[2]

1 See among other cases, *United City Merchants (Investments) Ltd v Royal Bank of Canada* [1983] 1 AC 168 and *European Asian Bank AG v Punjab Bank (No 2)* [1983] 1 WLR 642 at 652A, [1983] 1 Lloyd's Rep 611 at 615.1.
2 See *European Asian Bank AG v Punjab Bank (No 2)* [1983] 1 WLR 642 at 657, [1983] 1 Lloyd's Rep 611 at 618, 619. For reference to the cases relating specifically to discount and collection of bills of exchange see *Benjamin's Sale of Goods* (4th edn) paras 22–063 et seq.

7.4 *(3) Recourse and fraud* If, contrary to the view of this book,[1] it is open to a paying bank to bring an action to recover its payment on the ground of mistake, the action would not lie against a collecting bank which had accounted to its principal, the beneficiary, for the payment which it had received.[2] If the amount of the payment had been credited to the beneficiary's account so that he could draw on it, it is suggested that this would bar such a right of recovery, if any. Unless the collecting bank was itself party to the beneficiary's fraud, any action to recover a payment on the ground of fraud could be brought by the paying bank only against the beneficiary.

1 Paras 5.72 et seq and 6.31.
2 See *Bowstead on Agency* (15th edn) Article 118(2)(c).

B. Negotiation Banks

7.5 *(1) General* The term is here used to refer to a bank which acquires documents in its own right to be presented by it as a principal under a letter of credit which is a negotiation credit. Straight and negotiation credits have been considered in Chapter 2.[1] In short, a negotiation credit in this sense is one where the undertaking given by the credit is addressed to all *bona fide* holders of the documents, or to banks generally or to banks of a particular description. It is open to such parties to negotiate, that is, to buy, the documents and to present them under the credit in their own right. In contrast, the undertaking contained in a straight credit is directed only to the beneficiary, and no other party can obtain rights under the credit save by transfer (if it is transferable) or by assignment. A bank which purchases the documents under a negotiation credit may be called a negotiation bank. The essential distinction from a collecting bank is that a negotiation bank holds the documents in its own right, whereas a collecting bank holds them as agent for the beneficiary.

1 Para 2.22.

7.6 *(2) The contract* A negotiation bank becomes a contracting party to the credit, and, if the undertaking contained in the credit is not honoured, it may sue the issuing bank and any confirming bank. The contract probably comes into being when the bank acquires the documents in reliance on the credit. The alternative is that it comes into being when the documents are presented by it. The former appears more consistent with the likely position between the issuing bank and the beneficiary, which is that the contract comes into being on the advice of the credit to the beneficiary.[1] A bank may acquire documents without reliance on, and without intending to utilise, the letter of credit.[2] If it does so, it may be that it cannot then operate the credit. This appears to be the position in the United States.[3] If it is the case that the contract between a negotiation bank and the issuing bank comes into being when the negotiation bank acquires the documents, it would follow that no contract would then come into being if the negotiation bank acquires the documents with a different intention. But this need not prevent a contract coming into being subsequently if the intention changes, at any rate by the time documents are actually presented. It is to be pointed out that the paying bank (ie the issuing or confirming bank) will not know in what circumstances and with what intention the negotiation bank acquired the documents and so, if that were relevant, it would not know whether or not it was bound to accept them. It is therefore suggested that the more practical view is that a bank which acquires documents without the intention of presenting them under the credit, may later change its intention and do so. There is, however, no authority in English law.

1 Para 5.3.
2 See the facts in *MA Sassoon & Sons v International Banking Corpn* [1927] AC 711 set out in Chapter 5, para 5.70.
3 See *Banco Nacional Ultramarino v First National Bank of Boston* 289 F 169 (1923).

7.7 *(3) Recourse against a negotiation bank*   A negotiation bank is in the same position as the beneficiary of a credit so far as any question of recourse by an issuing or confirming bank is concerned. It is suggested that there is, therefore, no right of recourse for the reasons discussed in Chapters 5 and 6.[1]

1 Paras 5.67 et seq and 6.28 et seq.

7.8 *(4) Fraud*   The right of a negotiation bank to operate the credit is not defeated by the fact that the beneficiary or a third party has been fraudulent, provided that it takes the documents in good faith. The negotiation bank is not responsible for the genuineness of the documents.[1] It will be able to rely on Article 14.a of the Uniform Customs, for it will be a Nominated Bank under Article 10.b.i.

1 See *Guaranty Trust Co of New York v Hannay & Co* [1918] 2 KB 623, and more generally *United City Merchants (Investments) Ltd v Royal Bank of Canada* [1983] 1 AC 168 and Chapter 9 below.

7.9 *(5) Recourse by negotiation bank*   The bank will undertake to negotiate the documents upon terms which may be found in the bank's form completed by the beneficiary requesting the bank to negotiate the documents, or the terms may be found in other documents. It is essential to examine the relevant documents to see what the terms are. Generally the position may be stated as follows. Whereas an issuing bank can look only to the applicant for reimbursement and if the documents which it has accepted do not conform to the credit it is at risk, and a confirming bank can only look to the issuing bank and is similarly at risk, a negotiation bank stands on the other side of the fence, that is to say, it stands on the beneficiary's side. The negotiation bank's position is closely allied to that of the beneficiary and unlike an issuing and a confirming bank, will ordinarily have recourse against the beneficiary if the credit fails to provide payment, as is discussed in the next two paragraphs. The reason for the credit failing to provide payment may be the fault of the negotiation bank. The most likely instance is the failure by the bank to present documents under the credit within the time stipulated by the credit. The beneficiary can assert that it was a term of the contract between it and the negotiation bank relating to the negotiation that the bank should present the documents in due time as a condition of any potential right of recourse against the beneficiary. It is suggested that it will usually be correct to imply such a term as a necessary incident of the contract. Otherwise the bank could forget or ignore the need to present, which would be unacceptable. But the facts and circumstances of any individual case will require consideration.

7.10 *(a) Bills of exchange* Where, as is usually the case, a negotiation bank buys documents which include drafts, if these are dishonoured the bank has the right of recourse of a holder against the beneficiary as the drawer of the draft.[1] The negotiation bank will only not have this right on the bill if it is expressly agreed that it shall not, either as part of the terms on which the bill is discounted, or by the beneficiary marking the bill when he draws it 'without recourse' or with some other wording so as to exclude his liability under it to a holder.[2] Such a wording, however, would not exclude recourse where the beneficiary was fraudulent, although, as the negotiation bank if *bona fide* would take the documents free of the fraud and be able to present under the credit, recourse should not then be necessary.[3] Even where the bill is drawn without recourse, the negotiation bank may perhaps have a right of recourse arising not on the bill but separately from the negotiation transaction itself.[4] But it is more likely that the drawing of the bill 'without recourse' negates any such right. In short, the negotiation bank will normally be entitled to recover from the beneficiary what it has paid with interest in the event that the bill is dishonoured because the documents are rejected as not complying with the credit, or for any other reason not the fault of the negotiation bank. For authority reference may be made to the decisions considered in paragraph 6.35 above.

1 Bills of Exchange Act 1882, s 55(1).
2 See Bills of Exchange Act 1882, s 16(1).
3 See also s 58(3) of the Bills of Exchange Act 1882.
4 See Case 11 in Case Studies on Documentary Credits, ICC Publication No 459.

7.11 *(b) Without bills* It is thought that in the past it was unusual for a negotiation bank to purchase documents which did not include a bill of exchange. The position is changing with the growth of deferred payment credits (which do not utilise a time draft but achieve the same effect). Drafts may also not be used to avoid the heavy stamp duty payable on them in some countries. In the event that this occurs the negotiation bank should agree as one of the terms whereby it undertakes the negotiation that, in the event of the failure of the letter of credit to provide payment, the negotiation bank should be entitled to return the documents to the beneficiary against reimbursement. In the absence of any express term it is suggested that the position would be uncertain. It would as always depend on the facts and circumstances of the particular case. As the beneficiary provides the documents to the negotiation bank on the basis that the credit provides a secure means of payment and that the documents will enable that payment to be obtained, it is suggested that the tendency should be to provide the bank with recourse against the beneficiary in the event that, through no fault of the bank, payment is not available by means of the credit.

Chapter 8

The Documents and their Examination

8.1 *Introduction* When a bank examines documents presented to it under a credit, questions may arise as to the extent of the bank's duty in conducting the examination, that is, as to the degree of skill and care which it is required to bring to the task and as to the ambit of its examination. Secondly, questions may arise as to what the credit requires in the documents themselves, which is what the bank should be checking in its examination. Those requirements may be requirements which apply to all types of documents, or they may be peculiar to particular types, such as bills of lading or the insurance documents. This chapter therefore divides into three sections: the bank's duty, general requirements as to documents and requirements as to particular documents.

A.   A Bank's Duty in the Examination of Documents

8.2 *The duty*   The purpose of a bank's examination of documents is to see whether the documents presented meet the requirements of the credit. The bank's duty, however, is not to be expressed in absolute terms: it does not in effect guarantee that documents accepted by it as a result of its examination comply with the credit. The duty of the bank is to examine them with reasonable care to ascertain that they appear on their face to be in accordance with the terms and conditions of the credit. In *Gian Singh & Co Ltd v Banque de l'Indochine*[1] Lord Diplock stated[2] that the relevant provision of the Uniform Customs (there the 1962 Revision, but unchanged in the 1983 Revision and substantially reproduced by Article 13.a of the 1993 Revision) did no more than state the duty of a bank at common law. Article 15 of the Uniform Customs provides:

> ARTICLE 13.a[3]   **Standard for Examination of Documents**
> a. Banks must examine all documents stipulated in the Credit with reasonable care, to ascertain whether or not they appear, on their face, to be in compliance with the terms and conditions of the Credit. Compliance of the stipulated documents on their face with the terms and conditions of the Credit, shall be determined by international standard banking practice as reflected in these Articles. Documents which appear on their face to be inconsistent with one another will be considered as not appearing on their face to be in compliance with the terms and conditions of the Credit.
> Documents not stipulated in the Credit will not be examined by banks. If they receive such documents, they shall return them to the presenter or pass them on without responsibility.

The first paragraph of the Article establishes three principles:

(a) that the duty is to examine with reasonable care to ascertain whether the documents appear on their face to be in compliance;
(b) that compliance is to be determined by international standard banking practice as reflected in the Articles of the Uniform Customs;
(c) that documents appearing inconsistent with each other will be considered not to comply.

The first and second are considered in this Part of this Chapter,[4] while the third is considered in Part B.[5] The second paragraph of the Article is a new provision. While it may seem to state the obvious, it is directed at avoiding any problem arising from a discrepancy in a document not called for by the credit, such as an inconsistency in the description of the goods. Because such a document is not to be examined, such a discrepancy is of no relevance and must be ignored.

1 [1974] 1 WLR 1234, [1974] 2 Lloyd's Rep 1.
2 Ibid at 1238 and 11 respectively.
3 The first and last sentences of the first paragraph repeat Article 15 in the 1983 Revision with some changes.
4 Paras 8.4 et seq and 8.8 below.
5 Para 8.25 below.

8.3   The following other Articles are also relevant to the appreciation of a bank's duty:

ARTICLE 3.a **Credits v Contracts**

a. Credits, by their nature, are separate transactions from the sales or other contract(s) on which they may be based and banks are in no way concerned with or bound by such contract(s), even if any reference whatsoever to such contract(s) is included in the Credit. Consequently, the undertaking of a bank to pay, accept and pay Draft(s) or negotiate and/or to fulfil any other obligation under the Credit, is not subject to claims or defences by the Applicant resulting from his relationships with the Issuing Bank or the Beneficiary.

ARTICLE 4 **Documents v Goods/Services/Performances**

In Credit operations all parties concerned deal with documents, and not with goods, services and/or other performances to which the documents may relate.

Article 4 may be seen as restating Article 3 in terms of documents and goods rather than transactions and contracts.

ARTICLE 15 **Disclaimer on Effectiveness of Documents**

Banks assume no liability or responsibility for the form, sufficiency, accuracy, genuineness, falsification or legal effect of any document(s), or for the general and/or particular conditions stipulated in the document(s) or superimposed thereon; nor do they assume any liability or responsibility for the description, quantity, weight, quality, condition, packing, delivery, value or existence of the goods represented by any document(s), or for the good faith or acts and/or omissions, solvency, performance or standing of the consignors, the carriers, the forwarders, the consignees or the insurers of the goods, or any other person whomsoever.

Article 15 may be seen as setting out some of the particular consequences of Articles 3.a and 4.

8.4 It would seem to follow from Article 13.a that a bank which has examined documents with reasonable care as the Article provides should be entitled to pass on the documents to the applicant for the credit, or down the banking chain as the case may be, against indemnity, and that it should not prevent the bank from doing so that there was something about a document or documents, which an examination with reasonable care had not revealed and which meant that the documents did not in fact comply with the credit. Article 14.a, however, makes no reference to reasonable care when it provides for the right of a bank to be reimbursed:

ARTICLE 14.a **Discrepant Documents and Notice**

a. When the Issuing Bank authorises another bank to pay, incur a deferred payment undertaking, accept Draft(s), or negotiate against documents which appear on their face to be in compliance with the terms and conditions of the Credit, the Issuing Bank and the Confirming Bank, if any, are bound:

i. to reimburse the Nominated Bank which has paid, incurred a deferred payment undertaking, accepted Draft(s), or negotiated,

ii. to take up the documents.

The assumption must be that the exercise of reasonable care will detect all discrepancies in the documents 'which appear on their face'. If the assumption is justified, it follows that any bank exercising reasonable care will be entitled to be reimbursed. If it is not and there is an exceptional case where a failure to accord with the credit appears on the face of the documents but is not discovered despite the exercise of reasonable care, is the bank entitled to be reimbursed? There must be a strong argument that it is, on the ground that Articles 13 and 14 must be read together.

8.5 *'On their face'*   It may be questioned what is meant by 'appear on their face'. Do the last three words refer to the face of the documents as opposed to the reverse or back (on which the small print may appear in the case of bills of lading and other transport documents)? Or are they there as a reference to the principle of Articles 3 and 4, that the bank should look only at the documents? The French edition reads as follows:

> ARTICLE 13.a   Les banques doivent examiner avec un soin raisonnable tous les documents stipulés dans le crédit pour vérifier s'ils présentent ou non l'apparence de conformité avec les termes et conditions du crédit.

Likewise Article 14 refers to 'paiement . . . contre des documents présentant l'apparence de conformité avec les termes et conditions du crédit . . .'. As it has no words equivalent to 'on their face', the French makes clear that 'on their face' is to be read in terms of Articles 3 and 4, and not as a reference to the front of the documents. That this is the correct reading is also confirmed by the commentary on the Article in the ICC's UCP 500 and 400 Compared.[1]

1 Publication No 511.

8.6 *The principle in practice: the facts in the* **Gian Singh** *case*[1]   although unusual are worth consideration as an illustration of the principle in practice. The underlying contract was for the sale of a fishing vessel. One of the documents required was a certificate signed by Balwant Singh, holder of Malaysian Passport E-13276, certifying that the vessel had been correctly built and was in a condition to sail. The certificate which was presented was forged and was not the certificate of Balwant Singh. Lord Diplock stated:[2]

> 'The instant case differs from the ordinary case in that there was a special requirement that the signature on the certificate should be that of a person called Balwant Singh, and that that person should also be the holder of Malaysian passport no. E.13276. This requirement imposed upon the bank the additional duty to take reasonable care to see that the signature on the certificate appeared to correspond with the signature on an additional document presented by the beneficiary which, on the face of it appeared to be a Malaysian passport no. E.13276 issued in the name of Balwant Singh. The evidence is that that is what the notifying bank had done when the certificate was presented. The onus of proving lack of reasonable care in failing to detect the forgery of the certificate lies upon the customer. In their Lordships' view, in agreement with all the members of the Court of Appeal, the customer did not succeed in making out any case of negligence against the issuing bank or the notifying bank which acted as its agent, in failing to detect the forgery.'

Here, unusually, the bank had to examine not only the documents which were presented to it to be transferred against payment, but also the document which purported to be the relevant passport, in order to check the consistency of the signatures.[3]

1 [1974] 1 WLR 1234, [1974] 2 Lloyd's Rep 1.
2 Ibid at 1239 and 11.
3 See para 8.15 below.

8.7 *What is reasonable care?*   Where it is alleged that a bank's examination of documents should have uncovered a discrepancy and it is denied by the bank that it was negligent in failing to do so, the question of negligence is to be determined by examining the facts of the particular case together with such expert evidence as may be appropriate as to what would be correct banking practice in those circumstances. Thus reasonable care is simply the care that would be exercised in the particular circumstances by a bank competent to handle documentary credit transactions. The question of a bank's duty in the examination of 'small print' clauses is examined in the next paragraph.

8.8 *Compliance by 'international standard banking practice as reflected in these Articles'*   The commentary on a preliminary draft of this provision stated that relevant banking practices were not hard to locate, and that many were already to be found in the provisions of the Uniform Customs. An example was given of the provision in the Uniform Customs as to the degree of correspondence required between the description of goods in the credit and in the documents presented, namely Article 37.c, which was stated to reflect standard banking practice. If 'international standard banking practice as reflected in these Articles' were to mean no more than the banking practice which is already reflected in the Articles (and it can be read in this way) the provision means little. It is, however, clearly the intention of the provision that there are other standard practices which should be complied with. The same commentary referred to practices which may find their way into training manuals and educational and trade publications including those of the ICC. As was pointed out in the Preface to the First Edition of this book there are difficulties in looking to the practices of banks as a source of documentary credit obligation. To quote one sentence 'A number of Opinions of the ICC Banking Commission show the differences that can exist on important questions'. It may be difficult for a checker in one bank in one country to know whether a practice of which he is aware is indeed 'standard international banking practice'. As has been pointed out in chapter 1,[1] in disputed cases expert evidence is often called on both sides to support rival contentions as to suggested established banking practice. The outcome may be difficult to predict: it is sometimes that there is no established practice.[1] The provision should nonetheless be welcome in the long term, because it will encourage the development of standard practice. It has also to be stated that it does no more than reflect the previous position under English law.

1 Para 1.19.

8.9 *'Small print' clauses*   Bills of lading and other transport documents frequently contain numerous detailed provisions, usually on their reverse. How far is a bank obliged to study such terms and their effect to see if they may contain something that would make the document objectionable? This has been touched on in two dicta in English cases, but there has been no specific determination of such a question in a reported case. In *National Bank of Egypt v Hannevig's Bank*[1] Scrutton LJ stated:

'In some cases, the obligation of a banker, under such a credit, may need very careful examination. I only say at present that to assume that for one-sixteenth per cent of the amount he advances, a bank is bound carefully to read through all bills of lading presented to it in ridiculously minute type and full of exceptions, to read through the policies and to exercise a judgment as to whether the legal effect of the bill of lading and the policy is, on the whole, favourable to their clients, is an obligation which I should require to investigate considerably before I accepted it in that unhesitating form.'

In *British Imex Industries Ltd v Midland Bank Ltd*[2] Salmon J expressed the same sentiments:[3]

'The defendant bank contends that inasmuch as the bills of lading do not contain on their face an express acknowledgement that the goods have been marked in accordance with the provisions of Additional Clause B, then either they are not clean bills of lading – I have dealt with that point – or that they are so seriously defective that the bank is entitled to refuse payment. It is to be observed that the letter of credit did not call for bills of lading to be indorsed with any acknowledgement that the provisions of Additional Clause B had been complied with. I do not consider that the bank has any right to insist on such an acknowledgement before payment. According to their case, it was their duty, for the remuneration of £18, to read through the multifarious clauses in minute print on the back of these bills of lading, and, having observed Additional Clause B, to consider its legal effect, and then to call for an acknowledgement that it had been complied with. I respectfully share the doubt that Lord Justice Scrutton expressed in *National Bank of Egypt v Hannevig's Bank* as to whether any such duty is cast upon the Bank. I doubt whether they are under any greater duty to their correspondents than to satisfy themselves that the correct documents are presented to them, and that the bills of lading bear no indorsement or clausing by the shipowners or shippers which could reasonably mean that there was or might be some defect in the goods, or in their packing.'

This can be read as suggesting that a bank may wholly ignore the small print. That may seem a somewhat bold view. However, if the bank is not bound to study it in detail, can it be that, if its duty is only to look at it cursorily, its cursory examination may be held to have been negligent? That would invite a contradiction in terms. The practice of banks is generally not to examine such provisions. This practice is now confirmed in the transport document provisions of the Uniform Customs. For example in Article 23.a.v it is stated that 'banks will not examine the contents of such terms and conditions'. 'Such' refers to 'the terms and conditions of carriage'.[4]

1 [(1919) 3 Legal Decisions Affecting Bankers (the case is also reported in 1 Ll L Rep 69 but Scrutton LJ is simply reported as having given a judgment concurring with that of Bankes LJ).
2 [1958] 1 QB 542.
3 Ibid at 551.
4 See also the commentary on Article 23.a.v in UCP 500 and 400 Compared, ICC Publication No 511.

8.10 *The burden of proof*   It will be noted that the passage quoted in paragraph 8.6 above placed the burden of proof on the bank's customer with regard to lack of reasonable care in failing to detect the forgery. That must be correct. It does not follow, however, that it is not for the bank which seeks reimbursement to establish at least a prima facie case that the documents which it has examined and accepted do conform to the credit.

If it fails in that, it will of course lose the case. But it will otherwise win unless the defendant applicant, or issuing bank, succeeds in establishing a discrepancy or discrepancies and that the bank seeking reimbursement should have discovered them. In practical terms the burden will therefore be on the party alleging the discrepancy to establish first the discrepancy and second a lack of care on the part of the examining bank.

8.11 *The autonomy of the credit; extraneous matters*   The bank should not take account of any matters other than the terms of the credit and the documents which are presented to it. This is subject to the possible exception considered under the next heading[1] and to the exception of established fraud which is covered in the next chapter. This principle, referred to as the principle of autonomy of the credit has been introduced in Chapter 1.[2] Its observation is essential to the viability of documentary credits as a means of secured payment under international contracts. The principle is implanted in Articles 3 and 4 of the Uniform Customs. The leading English authority is now *United City Merchants v Royal Bank of Canada*[3] where Lord Diplock stated:[4]

> 'If, on their face, the documents presented to the confirming bank by the seller conform with the requirements of the credit as notified to him by the confirming bank, the bank is under a contractual obligation to the seller to honour the credit, notwithstanding that the bank has knowledge that the seller at the time of presentation of the conforming documents is alleged by the buyer to have, and in fact has already, committed a breach of his contract with the buyer for the sale of the goods to which the documents appear on their face to relate, that would have entitled the buyer to treat the contract of sale as rescinded and to reject the goods and refuse to pay the seller the purchase price. The whole commercial purpose for which the system of confirmed irrevocable documentary credits has been developed in international trade is to give to the seller an assured right to be paid before he parts with control of the goods that does not permit of any dispute with the buyer as to the performance of the contract of sale being used as a ground for non-payment or reduction or deferment of payment.'

1 Para 8.14.
2 Para 1.40.
3 [1983] 1 AC 168.
4 Ibid at 183.

8.12   An early illustration is the case of *Urquhart, Lindsay & Co Ltd v Eastern Bank Ltd*.[1] The plaintiff sellers had entered a contract with buyers in Calcutta to ship machinery in instalments at agreed prices subject to a term that if the cost of labour increased, the price should be correspondingly increased. A confirmed irrevocable credit was opened by the defendant bank with a limit of £70,000, the documents to include 'signed invoices in duplicate'. Two shipments were made and paid for. The buyers then found that the invoices had included an element on account of increased costs and directed the bank to decline to pay more than the original prices. The bank accepted, and acted on, the buyer's direction. So the plaintiffs refused to part with their documents. They cancelled the contract and sued the bank for damages, being the loss of material thrown on their hands and loss of profit. It was argued for the defendants that the letter of credit should be taken to incorporate the contract between the parties and that under it any price increases were to be dealt with outside the letter of credit. Rowlatt J stated[2] 'The answer to this is that the defendants [the bank] undertook to pay the amount of invoices for machinery without qualification, the basis of this form of banking facility being that the buyer is taken for the purposes of all questions between himself and his banker or between his banker and the seller to be content to accept the invoices of the seller as correct.' The plaintiffs succeeded against the bank, and it is to be hoped that the bank was able to obtain an indemnity from its clients whose instructions it had accepted, but should have refused.

1 [1922] 1 KB 318.
2 Ibid at 322, 323.

8.13 In *Westpac Banking Corpn v South Carolina National Bank*[1] the Privy Council held that the court below had erred in speculating how a bill of lading came to be issued rather than considering only the documents. Lord Goff of Chieveley stated:[2]

> 'Their Lordships approach the matter as follows. First, they are unable to accept the proposition that the words "Shipped on Board" make the bill internally inconsistent. True it is that the bill is on a "received for shipment" form and for that reason refers to *Columbus America* as the intended vessel; but there is nothing inconsistent in a document which states that the specified goods have been received for shipment on board a named vessel and have in fact been shipped on board that vessel. Their Lordships feel bound to say, with all respect, that the majority of the Court of Appeal fell into error in their approach to the construction of the bill of lading. For, as appears from the judgment of Mr Justice Priestly, he went beyond the terms of the document itself and sought to draw inferences of fact as to what had occurred at the time when the document was issued. In particular, he inferred that the bill of lading was in fact the receipt which was issued for the goods received at Sydney, and that it was in fact so issued at the time when those goods were so received. In their Lordships' view there was no sufficient basis for either inference. Some other more informal receipt may have been provided by the agents at Sydney at the time when the goods were received there, to be replaced later by the bill of lading issued at Newcastle; and in any event the bill of lading may have been signed and issued at Newcastle at some date after the date of the receipt of the goods at Sydney. Be that as it may, it is well settled that a bank which issues a letter of credit is concerned with the form of the documents presented to it, and not with the underlying facts. It forms no part of the bank's function, when considering whether to pay against the documents presented to it, to speculate about the underlying facts. For that reason, the Court of Appeal erred in approaching the problem by seeking to draw the inferences of fact to which their Lordships have referred.'[3]

In short a bank should not speculate as to facts which may lie behind the documents.

1 [1986] 1 Lloyd's Rep 311.
2 Ibid at 315.
3 See further para 8.65 below.

8.14 In *J H Rayner & Co Ltd v Hambro's Bank Ltd*[1] the judge at first instance had heard evidence that there was a trade usage that 'coromandel groundnuts' were the same as 'machine-shelled groundnut kernels', these being respectively the terms employed in the credit itself, and in the bills of lading, and he held that the bank was not obliged to reject the documents in the light of this. The Court of Appeal dismissed the usage as irrelevant. The terms of the bank's mandate were to pay against documents relating to coromandel groundnuts, and it paid against any other documents at its peril.[2]

1 [1943] KB 37.
2 As to trade usage, see also para 8.33 below.

8.15 ***Non-documentary conditions: the inclusion of 'facts' among the requirements of the credit***   It sometimes happens that the credit requires that the bank shall be satisfied of a fact before it accepts documents, or it contains a provision which has that effect. Two examples may be given. In the *Gian Singh* case[1] as set out in paragraph 8.6 above, one of the documents required was a certificate signed by Balwant Singh, holder of a passport of a particular number. This meant that the passport had to be presented with the documents so the bank could compare the signatures to see if that on the passport corresponded with that on the certificate. The passport was not a document which would be retained by the bank after payment and passed with the other documents to the applicant. After checking it would be returned to the person who presented the documents. It appears that in this case by their agreement that the credit should take this form the buyer and seller had imposed on the bank a duty which fell outside its duty as foreseen by the Uniform Customs. The bank's duty was still a documentary one and by agreeing to open a credit in such terms it was indicating that it was prepared to undertake the duty. In *Banque de l'Indochine v J H Rayner (Mincing Lane) Ltd*[2] under the heading 'Special Conditions' the credit stated 'Shipment to be effected on vessel belonging to shipping company that member of an International Shipping Conference'. Parker J held[3] that, although no specific documentary proof was called for, as parties to credits deal only in documents, the beneficiaries were obliged to provide reasonable documentary proof. Thus the absence of a certificate to the required effect would have given the bank reason to refuse payment. In the Court of Appeal Sir John Donaldson MR stated:[4]

> 'This is an unfortunate condition to include in a documentary credit because it breaks the first rule of such a transaction, namely, that the parties are dealing in documents, not facts. The condition required a state of fact to exist. What the letter of credit should have done was to call for a specific document which was acceptable to the buyer and his bank evidencing the fact that the vessel was owned by a member of a conference. It did not do so and as, accordingly, the confirming bank had to be satisfied of the fact, it was entitled to call for any evidence establishing that fact. All sorts of interesting questions could have arisen as to what evidence could have been called for and what would have been the position if, contrary to that evidence, the vessel was not owned by a conference member. In fact it was so owned and merchants produced the evidence required by the bank before the expiry of the credit. Accordingly no such questions arise.'[5]

1 [1974] 1 WLR 1234, [1974] 2 Lloyd's Rep 1.
2 [1983] QB 711.
3 Ibid at 719 B/C.
4 Ibid at 728 G-H.
5 See also *Astro Exito Navegacion S.A. v Chase Manhattan Bank NA, The Messiniaki Tolmi* [1986] 1 Lloyd's Rep 455 at 461–4, and see also Opinions of the ICC Banking Commission 1984–1986, R 111.

8.16   The problem of non-documentary conditions is now covered expressly by Article 13.c. This is a new provision.[1] It provides:

ARTICLE 13.c   If a Credit contains conditions without stating the document(s) to be presented in compliance therewith, banks will deem such conditions as not stated and will disregard them.

The alternative which was considered and rejected was that a bank might accept any documentary proof which it deemed sufficient where there was a non-documentary condition. The problem of non-documentary conditions is a real one, to which the Article may provide a solution. The only satisfactory solution, however, is that banks should not accept instructions to issue or to confirm credits containing non-documentary conditions. Article 13.c may give rise to two difficulties. The first can be illustrated on the facts of the *Banque de l'Indochine* case and of the *Gian Singh* case, which have been considered already.[2] In the *Banque de l'Indochine* case, if Article 13.c had been applied, there would have been no need for any confirmation that the vessel belonged to an International Shipping Conference. In the *Gian Singh* case, if applied, it would probably have had the result that the bank could have ignored the requirement to compare the signatures. The former confirmation as to the vessel may not have been of fundamental importance: but the latter verification of signature was intended as an essential step to prevent fraud. Is it right that a bank can accept such instructions and then by reliance on the Uniform Customs be entitled to disregard them? It could well be argued that a bank was in breach of its duty to the applicant/customer in accepting such instructions without pointing out that, once incorporated in the credit, they would have to be ignored. If a bank accepts instructions in relation to a credit which contains a condition which is not meant to be complied with by means of a document, Article 13.c should be excluded. If the condition can be complied with in documentary form, it should be expressed in a documentary form.

1 For further discussion of the position in the absence of the Article, see paras 8.15 and 8.16 of the First Edition.
2 Paras 8.6 and 8.15.

8.17 The second problem arises in connection with the construction of a credit which contains a non-documentary condition and incorporates Article 13.c.[1] It arises because the parties to a contract are free to make their own bargain within the limits of the law, and the Uniform Customs do not have the force of law. It is clear that, if a credit expressly provided that Article 13.c should not apply, it would not. It can be strongly argued that the same result can be achieved by implication in appropriate circumstances. For the inclusion of a term in the credit that payment is only to be made if a non-documentary condition is satisfied is an expression of the parties' intention which is specific to that credit and to which it may be assumed from the circumstances that the parties have directed their attention. It is a principle of English law relating to the construction of contracts that, where there is a conflict between an express term of the contract and a standard incorporated term, the express term should be given preference on the ground that it is a term to which the parties have given their attention.[2] Where a credit is issued containing a non-documentary condition among those to be satisfied before payment, it can certainly be argued that it is Article 13.c which must give way. The strength of the argument will be increased the greater the importance of the condition to the working of the credit. Nonetheless it is suggested that in many situations which are likely to arise an English court will seek to uphold the intention of the Uniform Customs. For the desirability of upholding the internationally chosen solution is plain.

1 The exclusion of Article 13.c from the credit would make plain the parties' intention that the credit should be operated in accordance with its terms.
2 See generally *Chitty on Contract* (26th edn), General Principles, paras 826 and 833.

8.18 *The bank is not concerned with 'why?'* It is a bank's duty to construe its instructions which have become the terms of the credit, and to consider the documents presented to it, without speculating on what may have been in its customer's mind. In *Commercial Banking Co of Sydney Ltd v Jalsard Pty Ltd*,[1] Lord Diplock stated:[2]

'The banker is not concerned as to whether the documents for which the buyer has stipulated serve any useful commercial purpose or as to why the customer called for tender of a document of a particular description.'

But this must not be taken too far. The commercial purpose of most documents is clear, and, should it need to, a bank is entitled to have that purpose in mind in considering whether a tendered document satisfies the credit. What the bank is not entitled to do is to say 'I do not see the point of this, so I will not bother about it'. It is not for a bank to reason why.[3]

1 [1973] AC 279, PC.
2 Ibid at 286.
3 See per Devlin J in *Midland Bank Ltd v Seymour* [1955] 2 Lloyd's Rep 147 at 151.2.

8.19 *Ambiguity* Where the terms of the credit are ambiguous in the sense that it is unclear what is called for, or unclear whether A or B is called for, a bank may be entitled to act on its own interpretation of the terms provided that it is reasonable. This and the opposing concept that in this time of often almost instantaneous communications a bank should seek instructions to clarify the ambiguity have been considered in Chapter 4.[1]

1 Paras 4.5 to 4.7.

B.   General Requirements as to Documents

8.20 *Strict compliance* The documents must comply strictly with the requirements of the credit. As stated by Viscount Sumner in *Equitable Trust Co of New York v Dawson Partners Ltd*:[1]

'It is both common ground and common sense that in such a transaction the accepting bank can only claim indemnity if the conditions on which it is authorised to accept are in the matter of the accompanying documents strictly observed. There is no room for documents which are almost the same, or which will do just as well. Business could not proceed securely on any other lines. The bank's branch abroad, which knows nothing officially of the details of the transaction thus financed, cannot take upon itself to decide what will do well enough and what will not. If it does as it is told, it is safe; if it declines to do anything else, it is safe; if it departs from the conditions laid down, it acts at its own risk.'

Quoting this passage in the *Gian Singh* case[2] Lord Diplock stated:[3] 'This oft-cited[4] passage has never been questioned or improved upon.' The issue in the *Equitable Trust* case was whether a requirement of 'a certificate of quality to be issued by experts who are sworn brokers' was satisfied by a certificate signed by one such broker. It was held by the House of Lords that it was not. Reference may also be made to the dictum of Bailhache J in *English, Scottish and Australian Bank Ltd v Bank of South Africa*[5] which has also often been referred to:

> 'It is elementary to say that a person who ships in reliance on a letter of credit must do so in exact compliance with its terms. It is also elementary to say that a bank is not bound or indeed entitled to honour drafts presented to it under a letter of credit unless those drafts with the accompanying documents are in strict accord with the credit as opened.'

The principle has a number of obvious applications some of which are considered with examples in the following paragraphs.

1 (1926) 27 Ll L Rep 49 at 52.
2 [1974] 1 WLR 1234.
3 Ibid at 1239, 1240.
4 See, for instance, *JH Rayner & Co Ltd v Hambros Bank Ltd* [1943] KB 37 at 40; *Bank Melli Iran v Barclays Bank* [1951] 2 Lloyd's Rep 367 at 374; *Moralice (London) Ltd v ED and F Man* [1954] 2 Lloyd's Rep 526 at 532; *Banque de l'Indochine v JH Rayner Ltd* [1983] QB 711 at 730.
5 (1922) 13 Ll L Rep 21 at 24.

8.21 **(a) *Technicalities*** A discrepancy may not affect the value or merchantability of the goods, and may thus appear merely technical. A bank is nonetheless obliged to take the point unless it is instructed by its customer, the buyer, that the documents are acceptable. The buyer may not do so thus if the market has moved against him or if he has other extraneous reasons for not wanting to take up the documents and pay for them. Because so many sets of documents are presented which do not comply with the terms and conditions of the credit,[1] this may be the buyer's best chance of avoiding taking up documents where he suspects that the goods do not comply with the contract.

1 See *Banque de l'Indochine v J H Rayner Ltd* [1983] QB 711 at 733F.

8.22 **(b) *All documents*** All documents must be tendered. In *Donald H Scott & Co v Barclays Bank Ltd*[1] Bankes LJ stated:[2] 'A tender of two bills of lading and understanding to produce the third, or of two bills of lading and an indemnity, is not a compliance with a condition requiring production of a full set.' That much is straightforward. A credit may call for a certificate as to quality and a certificate of weight. What if the two certificates are combined in one? Or if the certificate of weight is written on the face of the invoice? It can be argued that there is a document which is a certificate of weight, although it is also a certificate of quality or an invoice as the facts may be. The credit, however, is likely to contain a list of documents from which it can reasonably be deduced that a specific number of documents is required. The combination of the document into one would be inconsistent with that.[3] There may also be good practical reasons why a buyer would not want combined documents. Thus if he was selling on the documents he would not want to include the invoice addressed to him as a certificate of weight to his own buyer and indeed his buyer might be able to refuse such a certificate. In the Hong Kong case of *Netherlands Trading Society v Wayne and Haylitt*[4] it was held combined certificates of weight and certificates by the jute mill were acceptable. Evidence was called that it was usual to combine the two certificates. Neither does there appear to have been any commercial objection to the combination on the facts of the case. Article 38 of the Uniform Customs[5] provides that an attestation or certification of weight may be superimposed on the transport document (other than one by sea) unless the credit specifically stipulates a separate document.

1 [1923] 2 KB 1.
2 Ibid at 11.
3 This view is supported by Case 227 in the ICC's More Case Studies on Documentary Credits, Publication No 489.
4 (1952) 36 HKLR 109.
5 Para 8.129 below.

8.23 *(c) No application of the de minimis rule*   In *Moralice (London) Ltd v E D and F Man*[1] the documents were required to evidence the shipment of 500 metric tons of sugar in bags of 100 kgs net weight each. The shipment was three bags short (0.06%). It was held that because it was a letter of credit transaction the maxim *de minimis non curat lex*, or the rule of insignificance, could not be relied upon, and the bank was entitled to reject the documents. This case would today be decided differently by reason of Article 39.b of the Uniform Customs, which allows a tolerance of 5% 'unless a credit stipulates that the quantity of the goods specified must not be exceeded or reduced'.[2] Among the several points taken in *Soproma SpA v Marine and Animal By-Products Corpn*[3] it was argued that the bills of lading did not comply with the credit because they stated that at the moment of loading the temperature of the fish meal did not exceed 100° F, whereas the credit referred to 37½° C. The difference was a matter of 0.5° F. McNair J who had also decided the *Moralice* case[4] stated[5]: 'Seeing that the de minimis rule does not apply to the tender of documents under a letter of credit (see the [*Moralice* case]) I suppose that in strict law I should give effect to this objection, but I confess I should be reluctant to do so if it stood alone.' There were other valid objections to the documents and so the point was unimportant. The case indicates the proper reluctance of judges to take the principle of strict compliance to absurd lengths. It may well be that had the temperature point been the sole point in the case the court would have found a way round it, perhaps by concluding that to the nearest degree 100° F was the Fahrenheit equivalent of 37½° Centigrade. The point also illustrates the desirability of following the terms of the credit precisely: if the document had been expressed in Centigrade, no point should have arisen. This aspect of the strict compliance principle is relevant where there are very small numerical discrepancies. Because Article 39.b gives a tolerance of 5% save where the credit stipulates that the quantity of goods is not to be exceeded or reduced, the principle will seldom apply where the quantity shipped is in question. It will be relevant in the case of other such divergences. When it can be plainly seen that the divergence is of no possible importance, the court may look for a way round, or ignore it where it is almost imperceptible.[6] But otherwise, a set of documents which does not precisely meet the terms of the credit must be rejected.

1 [1954] 2 Lloyd's Rep 526.
2 See paras 8.42 et seq.
3 [1966] 1 Lloyd's Rep 367.
4 Supra.
5 Ibid at 390.
6 See *Astro Exito Navegacion SA v Chase Manhattan Bank NA* [1986] 1 Lloyd's Rep 455 at 461, Leggatt J.

8.24 ***Errors in names and such like***   What is the position where there is a small error in a name on an invoice or bill of lading? This was one of the points raised in the *Hip Hing* case[1] in Hong Kong. The credit was applied for by Cheergoal Industries Limited, and this name appeared on the credit. But the presenting bank 'presented the letter of credit on a document which showed the drawee as Cheergoal Industrial Limited'.[2] Kaplan J referred to a passage from *Gutteridge and Megrah*[3] to the effect that strict compliance did not extend to the dotting of i's and the crossing of t's or obvious typographical errors, concluding that it was impossible to generalise: each case had to be considered on its own merits. He held that the reference to 'Industrial' was an obvious typographical error, had caused no confusion and could not be relied upon as a discrepancy. It is suggested that an English court will not treat as discrepancies mistakes which are of no significance and which may be due to carelessness or are of a typographical nature. Although this type of problem arises every day and the answer will often be obvious, each case turns upon its particular facts and there will be borderline cases of real difficulty. Decisions from other jurisdictions show the problems of predicting an outcome.[4]

1 *Hip Hing Fat Co Ltd v Daiwa Bank Ltd* [1991] 2 HKLR 35.
2 So it is not clear which document or documents required by the credit was discrepant.
3 *The Law of Bankers' Commercial Credits* (7th edn), p 120.
4 See the authorities listed in *Benjamin's Sale of Goods* (4th edn) para 23–155 et seq.

8.25 ***Consistency***   The third sentence of Article 13.a provides 'Documents which appear on their face to be inconsistent[1] with one another will be considered as not appearing on their face to be in compliance with the terms and conditions of the Credit.' Prima facie this is simply to be taken as meaning that documents which are inconsistent in that they contain contradictions are unacceptable. An example which is sometimes given is found in the *Soproma* case.[2] The credit stated that the documents were to cover 'Chilean Fish Fullmeal 70% Protein . . .'. An invoice from the shippers included in error among the documents presented referred to 'minimum 67% protein'. The certificate of quality gave the analysis as 'Protein 67 per cent minimum'. The analysis certificate stated 'Protein 69.7 per cent'. The last two documents were held to be a bad tender. This could be justified on the straightforward basis that neither showed protein of 70%. The two documents are probably also inconsistent in that one suggests protein at 69.7%, and the other a lower percentage going down to not less than 67%. An example of inconsistency between documents which did not involve an inconsistency between the documents and the term of the credit would be where goods were sold ex-warehouse in Singapore and the documents showed two warehouse addresses for the goods in relation to the same day.

1 Consistent—agreeing or according in substance or form: *Shorter Oxford English Dictionary*.
2 [1966] 1 Lloyd's Rep 367.

8.26   Consistency has been given a somewhat different meaning by the ICC Banking Commission.[1] The Commission was asked which of two meanings it had, the two being:

   '(a) that the whole of the documents must obviously relate to the transaction covered by the credit and not be inconsistent with one another, ie that each should bear a link with the others;

or
(b) that all the documents should be *exactly* consistent in their wording of the description of the goods in the commercial invoice and/or the shipping document.'

In its answer the Commission drew attention to the purpose of the Article (then, in the 1973 Revision, Article 7) 'to ensure that the documents provided were not contradictory with one another', which reflects the meaning already considered. It 'decided that the notion of "consistency" referred to in Article 7[2] should be understood as meaning that the whole of the documents must obviously relate to the same transaction, that is to say, that each should bear a relation (link) with the others on its face, and the documents should not be inconsistent with one another.' This leads to the questions of how far the documents must each precisely describe the goods, and how far they should each identify the particular goods being sold, which will provide a link between them.

1 See Decisions, 1975–79, Ref 11, ICC Publication No 371.
2 Now Article 13.

8.27 *Description of goods* Article 37.c of the Uniform Customs provides:

> ARTICLE 37.c[1] The description of the goods in the commercial invoice must correspond with the description in the Credit. In all other documents, the goods may be described in general terms not inconsistent with the description of the goods in the Credit.

The principle of the Article may be illustrated with the facts relating to one aspect of *Banque de l'Indochine v J H Rayner Ltd.*[2] The description of the goods given in the credit was '200 (two hundred) metric tons up to 5% more or less EEC white crystal sugar category no 2 minimum polarisation 99.8 degrees, Moisture Maximum 0.08 per cent'. It appears that this was set out on the invoice. It was sufficient if the other documents such as the bills of lading or certificates of origin gave a simpler description such as 'sugar' provided that it was not inconsistent. If they had referred to a type of sugar other than 'white crystal' or stated a polarisation of less than 99.8 degrees, there would have been an inconsistency between the document and the term of the credit. Such an inconsistency was among the problems which arose in *Bank Melli Iran v Barclays Bank*,[3] a case which did not involve the Uniform Customs. The description of the goods in the credit was 'sixty new Chevrolet trucks'. The delivery order described the trucks as 'new-good'. McNair J stated[4] 'In my judgment this description, like the description "new, good" or "in new condition" is not the same as "new".' *J H Rayner & Co Ltd v Hambro's Bank Ltd*[5] is an earlier illustration of the difficulties with description. It likewise was not a Uniform Customs case. The credit referred to a cargo of 'Coromandel groundnuts'. The documents presented included a bill of lading for 'machine-shelled groundnut kernels' and an invoice for 'Coromandel groundnuts'. The Court of Appeal held that the bill of lading was objectionable and that it was nothing to the point that there was evidence that machine-shelled groundnut kernels meant Coromandels in the trade. The court probably considered that the bill of lading had to refer to precisely the description of the goods given in the credit. The case would be likely to be decided with the same outcome today on the ground that the two descriptions were inconsistent as a matter of words and any special meaning in the trade was something which the bank was neither bound nor entitled to take into account. Issues as to description must be distinguished from those relating to identification.

1 Unchanged from Article 41 in the 1983 Revision.
2 [1983] QB 711.
3 [1951] 2 Lloyd's Rep 367.
4 Ibid at 375.
5 [1943] KB 37.

8.28 Without the clarification provided by the Uniform Customs the position was less certain. In *London and Foreign Trading Corpn v British and Northern European Bank*[1] the invoice was to be for 500 tons South African maize meal CIF Liverpool. The bill of lading stated that what was shipped was 5895 bags of maize meal. The invoice gave the weight of bags as 190 lbs. The bill of lading was held to be deficient in that it did not obtain the responsibility of the ship for the particular tonnage or any specific tonnage. The case has been cited for the proposition that at common law the invoice and the bill of lading must refer to the same description of goods precisely. But the reasoning of the judgment does not go so far. In *Midland Bank Ltd v Seymour*[2] the question arose how far the particulars of the goods were required to be repeated on all documents. Devlin J stated:[3]

'The set of documents must contain all the particulars and, of course, they must be consistent between themselves, otherwise they would not be a good set of shipping documents. But here you have a set of documents which is not only consistent with itself, but also incorporates to some extent the particulars that are given in the other – the shipping mark on the bill of lading leading to the invoice that bears the same shipping mark and which would be tendered at the same time, which sets out the full description of the goods.'[4]

1 (1921) 9 Ll L Rep 116.
2 [1955] 2 Lloyd's Rep 147.
3 Ibid at 153.
4 See also page 155.1.

8.29 ***Identification of the goods: linkage*** To what extent must documents identify the goods to which they relate? The inclusion of a transport document among the documents to be presented will identify the goods in respect of which payment is being sought as the goods shipped under that document. Where the goods are shipped on a vessel named in the transport document the invoice should identify the goods as shipped on that vessel, although in the circumstances this adds nothing to the buyer's security and could be said to be immaterial. There must of course be no inconsistencies between the two. But it is also important that other documents which are required should be capable of being related to the goods shipped. An insurance document must show that it covers the goods shipped under the transport document. A certificate relating to the quality of the goods is of no value unless it is clear that its subject matter is the goods for which payment is sought, namely those covered by the transport document.

8.30 In order to assess the present position under the Uniform Customs it is helpful to see how it has developed historically.

(a) The bar on inconsistent documents appears in the same terms in Article 7 of the 1974 Revision, in Article 15 of the 1983 Revision and in Article 13 of the 1993 Revision.

(b) Article 33 in the 1974 Revision was as follows:

> 'When other documents are required, such as Warehouse Receipts, Delivery Orders, Consular Invoices, Certificates of Origin, of Weight, of Quality or of Analysis etc and when no further definition is given, banks will accept such documents as tendered.'

Thus it was silent about the identification of the goods and 'linkage'.

(c) In 1982 in *Banque de l'Indochine v JH Rayner Ltd*[1] the Court of Appeal had to consider the question of identification of the goods and linkage between documents. Sir John Donaldson MR stated 'However general the description, the identification must, in my judgment, be unequivocal. Linkage between the documents is not, as such, necessary, provided that each directly or indirectly refers unequivocally to "the goods". This seems to me to be the proper and inevitable construction to place upon Article 32(c) if the specified documents are to have any value at all.'[2] The reference was to Article 32(c) in the 1974 Revision, which is now repeated as Article 37.c[3] in the 1993 Revision. The court rejected an argument based on Articles 33 and 7 (Article 7 is now incorporated in Article 13.a) that the documents need not be linked through identification of the goods, provided that they were not inconsistent with each other. In the *Banque de l'Indochine* case,[1] the bill of lading showed that the goods had been loaded on the *Markhor* at Antwerp bound for Djibouti in transit for the Yemen. One quality certificate related to sugar loaded on the 'MV Markhor or substitute'. That could have been a different vessel and so a different parcel of sugar. One certificate of origin was similarly worded. The other referred to 'Transport mixtes à destination Djibouti Port in Transit Yemen'. Each could have referred to different parcels of sugar. The three EUR1 certificates gave no means of relating the sugar to which they referred to the sugar shipped on the *Markhor*. It seems that, had the documents referred to the correct quantities and named the *Markhor*, that would have been sufficient. It may be that some other means of identification would also have been adequate, such as references to the markings on the bags. For the difficulty arose at least in part because the certificates were prepared prior to loading on the vessel. At the end of the relevant passage in his judgment Sir John Donaldson MR stated 'Clearly these certificates could relate to the goods, but they do not necessarily do so. This will not do.' The judgment does not refer to the commercial invoice save to note that no complaint was made by the bank about it.[4] The thought process in the judgment was clearly to identify the goods sold as the shipment of sugar on the *Markhor* and to require the sugar referred to in the certificates to be related to that. It is unclear how far the necessity of relationship referred to by Sir John Donaldson is to be taken. It is possible, for example, that sugar described in a certificate as loaded on the *Markhor* could have been loaded on a voyage subsequent to that covered by the bill of lading and so be a different parcel of sugar. If that may seem fanciful, it is less so where the connecting factor is the marking on the bags, particularly if that is a simple one, such as a single letter. Perhaps 'necessarily' in the passage quoted from the judgment of the Master of the Rolls should have been 'with reasonable certainty'.

(d) The 1983 Revision replaced Article 33 with Article 23 which read:

ARTICLE 23   When documents other than transport documents, insurance documents and commercial invoices are called for, the credit should stipulate by whom such documents are to be issued and their wording or data content. If the credit does not so stipulate, banks will accept such documents as presented, provided that their data content makes it possible to relate the goods and/or services referred to therein to those referred to in the commercial invoice(s) presented, or to those referred to in the credit if the credit does not stipulate presentation of a commercial invoice.

In the ICC's Case Studies on Documentary Credits[5] it is stated that the passage containing the words 'make it possible to relate' were added 'as a result of a law case which established that the documents must show a link one with the other'. The case is not identified. If it is the *Banque de l'Indochine* case, it is doubtful if the chosen words fully reflect the court's reasoning. This is because unless the commercial invoice identifies the goods to which it relates as the goods covered by the transport document, an ability to relate the goods covered by a certificate to the goods covered by the invoice does not equate with an ability to relate them to the goods being shipped.

(e) Article 23 is now represented by Article 21 in the 1993 Revision. The change is to the important proviso at the end, which is now omitted:

ARTICLE 21   **Unspecified Issuers or Contents of Documents**
When documents other than transport documents, insurance documents and commercial invoices are called for, the Credit should stipulate by whom such documents are to be issued and their wording or data content. If the Credit does not so stipulate, banks will accept such documents as presented, provided that their data content is not inconsistent with any other stipulated document presented.

The drafting history is that initially no change was proposed. The change was introduced under cover of a comment simply noting minor changes. The commentary on the Article in the ICC's UCP 500 and 400 Compared merely states 'There are minor changes made to UCP 400 Article 23 for clarity and concision'. So it appears that no change of significance was intended. Nonetheless the change can be argued to be of considerable significance. For it can be said that it is no longer necessary that goods referred to in a certificate should be referrable to those in the invoice, only that there be no inconsistency. If so, certificates etc need not be capable of being positively related to, or identified with, the goods for which payment is sought. That would be an invitation to fraud and would greatly detract from the security which the inclusion of such documents is aimed to provide. It is to be hoped that banks will continue the practice in accordance with the position as it was held to be at the time of the *Banque de l'Indochine* case[1] of requiring that documents sufficiently identify the goods to which they relate. This would be an international standard banking practice as referred to in Article 13.a, not spelt out in the Uniform Customs themselves. But the change of wording does not make this straightforward. A second approach to the same end is to treat the concept of linkage as incorporated in the requirement for consistency between documents which is stated in Article 13. It is suggested that this is to stretch the ordinary meaning of consistent and inconsistent. But the view taken by the ICC Banking Commission cited in paragraph 8.26

above supports this.[6] The safe course is for the applicant to ensure that the position is covered by the express wording of the credit: issuing banks need to be alive to the point.

1 [1983] QB 711.
2 Ibid at 732D.
3 Set out at para 8.27 above.
4 [1983] QB 711 at 731B.
5 Case 75, ICC Publication 459: see note 6 below.
6 Case 75 in the ICC's Case Studies on Documentary Credits is also relevant though not of assistance. It reads:
    'QUERY   The phrase "makes it possible to relate" appears to clash with the provision in Article 15 [1983 Revision] which states that the documents must appear on their face to be consistent with each other.
    ANSWER   The phrase was added as a result of a law case which established that the documents must show a link, one with the other. This is in no way a contradiction of Article 15 which refers to documents "inconsistent" with each other.'

8.31 ***Regular on their face, not inviting further enquiry, current in the trade*** There are dicta in various cases which support the propositions that the documents must be regular on their face, should not be such as to invite further enquiry, and should be such as are current in the trade in question. But examination of the cases suggests that a bank would do well to avoid reliance on such general principles and seek to identify specific defects in the documents, which defects entitle rejection.

8.32 A famous passage is contained in the speech of Lord Sumner in *Hanson v Hamel and Horley Ltd*.[1]

> 'When documents are to be taken up the buyer is entitled to documents which substantially confer protective rights throughout. He is not buying a litigation, as Lord Trevethin (then AT Lawrence J) says in the *General Trading Co's Case* (1911) 16 Com Cas 95 at 101. These documents have to be handled by banks, they have to be taken up or rejected promptly and without any opportunity for prolonged inquiry, they have to be such as can be re-tendered to sub-purchasers, and it is essential that they should so conform to the accustomed shipping documents as to be reasonably and readily fit to pass current in commerce. I am quite sure that, under the circumstances of this case, this ocean bill of lading does not satisfy these conditions. It bears notice of its insufficiency and ambiguity on its face: for, though called a through bill of lading, it is not really so. It is the contract of the subsequent carrier only, without any complementary promises to bind the prior carriers in the through transit.'

The contract in question was a sale c. and f. Norway to Japan and did not involve a letter of credit. The goods were first shipped in several shipments to Hamburg where bills of lading were issued. It was held that the Hamburg bills were not through bills as they gave no protection to the buyers on the voyage from Norway to Hamburg and so did not satisfy the conditions of the contract. Secondly, the contract of carriage had not been procured, as was necessary, on shipment, and the bills issued 13 days later in another country were also defective for that reason.

1 [1922] 2 AC 36 at 46.

8.33 The central passage from the above extract was quoted by both Donaldson J and the Court of Appeal in *M Golodetz & Co Inc v*

Czarnikow-Rionda Co Inc.[1] The problem in that case was that when the sugar, the subject of the c. and f. contract, was partly loaded fire broke out on the vessel and 200 tons were damaged by the fire and by water used to extinguish it. The 200 tons had to be unloaded and became subject to general average. A separate bill of lading was issued in respect of it which bore a typed notation to the effect that the cargo it covered had been discharged at port of loading due to fire and/or water damage. The question was whether the sellers were entitled to tender this bill to the buyers and be paid the price. Donaldson J and the Court of Appeal held that they were. The arbitrators (who first heard the case and determined the facts) had not found that the bills of lading were not acceptable in the trade in this form, and it was held that they were clean bills in the sense they contained nothing to qualify the ship's admission that the goods were in apparent good order and condition at the time of shipment. While this is not a letter of credit case, it is sometimes cited as if it were.

1 [1980] 1 WLR 495.

8.34 Suppose that a bank were to find such a bill of lading among the documents when it came to check them against the terms and conditions of a letter of credit. The checker might say 'Well, the goods were shipped in good order and that is the sellers' duty, so we must take up the documents and leave it to the buyer to claim on the insurance which he should have taken out.' He would be right. But one may wonder whether a bank is obliged to take such a bold line where there is a bill of lading with such an unusual notation, and whether the bank might not say, 'This bill reeks of trouble; it is not our job to be legal experts, and we are not going to accept.'

8.35 Where the point at issue is one of what is acceptable in a particular trade, if the bill is claused in a way to raise doubt about its acceptability, there is a distinction between a merchant who has to determine whether to pay against documents and a bank. For it is reasonable to assume that a merchant is familiar with his particular trade, and there is no reason to attribute the same knowledge to a bank. In *J H Rayner & Co Ltd v Hambro's Bank Ltd*[1] it was held that trade usage was irrelevant. Admittedly this was in part on the ground that the contract there involved shipment from India to Denmark, and the evidence of usage was as to the business usages of Mincing Lane. But Mackinnon LJ continued[2] 'Moreover, quite apart from these considerations, it is quite impossible to suggest that a banker is to be affected with knowledge of customs and customary terms of every one of the thousands of trades for whose dealings he may issue letters of credit.' Goddard LJ likewise stated that trade practice is irrelevant. There may be a distinction to be drawn between the customs of a particular trade of which a bank is not required to have knowledge and which it should ignore, and matters of general commercial custom such as those pertaining to bills of lading, of which a bank should take notice. The latter, however, will often come to points which a judge will feel competent to decide as matters of law. In the *Golodetz* case,[3] not a letter of credit case, the court relied on the fact that the arbitrators had not found the claused bill of lading to be unusual in the trade. But a bank has no time to seek the views of trade arbitrators. It must act on what it sees before it, and, if what it sees raises problems which cannot be answered readily, it should be entitled and obliged to reject the documents. The proposition which is here advanced may be said not to give sufficient weight to the early decision of the Court of Appeal in *National Bank of Egypt v Hannevig's Bank*.[4] Here the plaintiff bank paid out against documents as the bank which had opened the credit on the instructions of the defendant bank. The latter bank refused to pay because the bills of lading were marked 'several bags torn and re-sewn' and so were not 'clean'. The case was actually decided on the basis that the defendants had authorised the plaintiffs to pay against claused bills. But the court queried whether clean bills were in fact required in view of the difficult conditions affecting the Egyptian onion trade in wartime, and attributed knowledge of this to the paying bank. In view of the actual decision that is to be treated as obiter dicta, and was advanced as a matter of uncertainty rather than the concluded view of the court.

1 [1943] KB 37.
2 Ibid at 41.
3 Supra.
4 (1919) 1 Ll L Rep 69 and see 3 Legal Decisions Affecting Bankers 69.

8.36 A letter of credit was at issue in *National Bank of South Africa v Banca Italiana di Sconto*[1] and it was alleged and held that the bills of lading presented were not in usual form.[2] The bill was in a form which left it unclear whether it was to shipper's order or to the order of the consignee – who had not endorsed it. It was held to be a bad tender. This case shows that where a document raises on its face some uncertainty, which cannot readily be resolved by the bank, the bank is entitled to reject the documents. The statement of Lord Sumner quoted above[3] and contained in a judgment delivered on the same day (16 March 1922) is directly applicable.

1 (1922) 10 Ll L Rep 531.
2 Ibid at 535.1 and 536.2.
3 Para 8.32.

8.37 A document which is or has become ineffective and illegal at the time of presentation to the bank is a bad tender. In *Arnhold Karberg & Co v Blythe Green Jourdain & Co*[1] sellers under a CIF contract tendered a bill of lading evidencing shipment on an enemy vessel. As, on the outbreak of war, the bill had become void and unenforceable as regards any obligations, this was held to have been a bad tender.

1 [1916] 1 KB 495.

8.38 *Stale or out-of-date documents*   The position in respect of transport documents, in particular the requirement of Article 43.a of the Uniform Customs that they be presented within 21 days of date of issue in the absence of any other period having been prescribed by the credit, is considered in Chapter 5[1] as part of the discussion of when documents must be presented. The reason for requiring transport documents to be presented within a period is to ensure that they are available to enable the applicant for the credit to take possession of the goods. Other classes of document may become out-of-date in a different manner. Thus inspection certificates which pre-dated the bill of lading by any substantial amount might be thought unacceptable. To take two examples, this would be true of a certificate which covered the presence of weevils or other pests; it would be true of a certificate covering the polarisation and moisture content of samples from a cargo of sugar. This problem should be avoided by the credit prescribing when and perhaps where the inspection is to take place. If it is not, in most cases a bank is likely to rely upon Articles 21 and 22 as entitling it to accept the documents regardless of their date. Article 21 has been considered in another context in paragraph 8.30 at (c) where it is set out. Article 22 is considered in the next paragraph. It is suggested that in all but clear cases a bank should take the position that it is for the applicant to include an appropriate provision in the credit and, if he fails to do so, the bank will accept documents as presented. But in a case where it is clear that a document such as a certificate is out of date in the sense that it cannot be relied upon as informative of the condition of the goods at date of shipment, it should be rejected.[2]

1 Para 5.24 et seq.
2 This view is supported by Case 230 in the ICC's More Case Studies on Documentary Credits, Publication 489.

8.39 Article 22 provides:

ARTICLE 22[1]   **Issuance Date of Documents v Credit Date**
Unless otherwise stipulated in the Credit, banks will accept a document bearing a date of issuance prior to that of the Credit, subject to such document being presented within the time limits set out in the Credit and in these Articles.

This Article was introduced as a new Article in the 1983 Revision. It was introduced to reflect the view of the ICC Banking Commission that 'shipping documents bearing a date of issuance prior to that of the documentary credit should be accepted.'[2] The scope of the Article was widened to include all documents. As has previously been stated,[3] Article 43 requires credits to provide a period from the date of shipment[4] within which they must be presented, failing which they must be presented within 21 days from the date of shipment.[4] There is no equivalent provision relating to other types of documents, nor is it usual for credits in practice to provide such a period. It is to be noted that Article 22 states '. . . banks will accept . . .'. It is suggested that this is not to be read as meaning that banks 'must accept' documents bearing date of issuance prior to that of the credit however old they are by the time of presentation, just as it is not to be read as obliging banks to accept documents so dated which contain other defects. That surely cannot be the intention behind the Article. The problem would be avoided if the Article provided that the dating of a document prior to the date of issuance of the credit should not be a bar to acceptance.

1 Unchanged from Article 24 in the 1983 Revision.
2 See UCP 1974/1983 Revisions Compared and Explained, ICC Publication No 411, page 44, and Opinions of the ICC Banking Commission 1975–1979, R 50.
3 Chapter 5, para 5.24.
4 As to date of shipment, see para 8.70 (bills of lading).

8.40 *Original documents and copy documents: signatures* The basic rule is and has always been that original documents are required. The use of carbon copy bills of lading might appear to be an exception.

But these are original copies as much as the top copy is an original. They would be signed, and would be marked as 'original'. In order to bring the Uniform Customs into line with modern practices and technology Article 22(c) was introduced in the 1983 Revision. Article 22(c) now finds itself in amended form as Article 20.b together with new Articles 20.c and 20.d. These provisions reflect the difficulties which face banks as the technology of communication and documentation advances.

ARTICLE 20.b   Unless otherwise stipulated in the Credit, banks will also accept as an original document(s), a document(s) produced or appearing to have been produced:
i.   by reprographic, automated or computerized systems;
ii. as carbon copies;
provided that it is marked as original and, where necessary, appears to be signed.
A document may be signed by handwriting, by facsimile signature, by perforated signature, by stamp, by symbol, or by any other mechanical or electronic method of authentication.

ARTICLE 20.c   i. Unless otherwise stipulated in the Credit, banks will accept as a copy(ies), a document(s) either labelled copy or not marked as an original—copy(ies) need not be signed.
ii. Credits that require multiple documents(s) such as 'duplicate', 'two fold', 'two copies' and the like, will be satisfied by the presentation of one original and the remaining number in copies except where the document itself indicates otherwise.

ARTICLE 20.d   Unless otherwise stipulated in the Credit, a condition under a Credit calling for a document to be authenticated, validated, legalised, visaed, certified or indicating a similar requirement, will be satisfied by any signature, mark, stamp or label on such document that on its face appears to satisfy the above condition.

8.41 The following points arise on Article 20.b. A reprographic system must mean a system for reproducing writing. So it would include photocopying. The view of the ICC Banking Commission in 1985[1] was that the then Article 22(c) did not authorise presentation of simple photocopies of original documents, but that original documents produced by photocopying systems were acceptable. In any event the document must be marked as an original. This must be done in original writing on the document: it would be pointless if it were sufficient for a photocopy document to have the word 'original' photocopied onto it. Original documents must appear to be signed 'where necessary'. Earlier drafts had provided 'where the credit so stipulates' they must be signed. 'Where necessary' must be taken as meaning where stipulated in the credit or required under the Articles of the Uniform Customs or by law or commercial custom. There is no need, however, for documents to be signed simply because they are not produced by traditional techniques.[2] Problems may well arise as to the need for signature, and an example can be taken from the Case Studies on Documentary Credits[3] where there appears the following:

'QUERY If a credit stipulates a signed invoice in several copies, some banks will accept carbon copies, of which one is manually signed whereas the other copies are carbon signed. Other banks are of the opinion that all copies must be manually signed. What is correct?

ANSWER There are conflicting views on this. Some banks insist upon each copy being a manually signed one. Other banks are content to accept the top copy signed with the carbon copies "carbon signed". Under particular circumstances and in order to be on the safe side, it may be advisable to require that all copies be originally signed.'

This suggested an undesirable variation of practice and an uncertainty which was likely to spread wider than the particular point raised in the query here. Such difficulties should now be resolved by the wide terms of Article 20.b, particularly the paragraph relating to signature, and by Article 20.c which provides that, unless the credit stipulates otherwise copies need not be signed: so it will need an express provision to require a copy to be signed, and a 'carbon' signature would in any event be permitted by Article 20.b.

1 This is confirmed by Opinions of the ICC Banking Commission 1984–1986, R 107.
2 Opinions of the ICC Banking Commission 1984–1986, ICC Publication No 434, at R 110.
3 ICC Publication No 459, Case 69.

8.42 *The amount of the credit, the quantity, the unit price*   Article 39 of the Uniform Customs provides:

ARTICLE 39.a[1]   **Allowances in Credit Amount, Quantity and Unit Price**
The words 'about', 'approximately', 'circa' or similar expressions used in connection with the amount of the Credit or the quantity or the unit price stated in the Credit are to be construed as allowing a difference not to exceed 10% more or 10% less than the amount or the quantity or the unit price to which they refer.

ARTICLE 39.b[2]   Unless a Credit stipulates that the quantity of the goods specified must not be exceeded or reduced, a tolerance of 5% more or 5% less will be permissible, always provided that the amount of the drawings does not exceed the amount of the Credit. This tolerance does not apply when the Credit stipulates the quantity in terms of a stated number of packing units or individual items.

ARTICLE 39.c[3]   Unless a Credit which prohibits partial shipments stipulates otherwise, or unless sub-Article (b) above is applicable, a tolerance of 5% less in the amount of the drawing will be permissible, provided that if the Credit stipulates the quantity of the goods, such quantity of goods is shipped in full, and if the Credit stipulates a unit price, such price is not reduced. This provision does not apply when expressions referred to in sub-Article (a) above are used in the Credit.

Article 39.a permits a variation of up to 10% in the amount of the credit or the quantity to be supplied, or the unit price, where in the credit the relevant amount is preceded by the word 'about', 'circa' or a similar expression (ie one indicating an approximation to the amount stated rather than precision). The amount of the credit means the sum of money available under the credit. This cannot be exceeded by reason, for example, of the quantity being exceeded within the 10% margin unless the amount too is preceded by a word such as 'about' entitling the beneficiary to a 10% margin in respect of it.

1 Article 39.a follows Article 43.a in the 1983 Revision very closely.
2 Article 39.b follows Article 43.b in the 1983 Revision with the omission of 'even if partial shipments are not permitted'.
3 Article 39.c is a new provision.

8.43 In contrast Article 39.b does not need words such as 'about' for it to apply. It relates only to the quantity of the goods. If the quantity is intended to be precisely adhered to, the credit must say so. Otherwise a tolerance of 5% will be permitted, provided, of course, that the amount of the proposed drawing does not exceed the amount of the credit. This was previously 3% in the 1974 Revision of the Uniform Customs. The tolerance does not apply where the credit stipulates the quantity in terms of a number of packing units or individual items. The sphere of its application therefore appears to be where the quantity is given by weight or by volume. Thus a credit which gave the quantity as 1000 metric tons would permit a 5% tolerance, whereas one which gave it as 10,000 bags of 100 kilos each would not. So the decision in *Moralice (London) Ltd v ED and F Man*[1] would today have been in favour of the shipper had the Uniform Customs applied because the documents were to evidence 'shipment of the following goods: . . . 500 metric tons Tate & Lyle granulated sugar of UK manufacture, packed in heavy single bags, each bag of 100 kgs nett weight . . .'. To take another example from a decided case, it does not apply to the tonnage of a vessel being sold, because the tonnage is part of the description of the vessel, and is not a quantity, just as with the phrase 'about 100 planks of sawn timber about 30 foot long and about 18 inches wide', the quantity is about 100 and the measurements are part of the description of the planks.[2] Where a credit covers '116 mt net (six isotanks)', the 5% tolerance may be applied to the tonnage.[3] Where a credit provides for 'up to 3400 long tons', there is no limitation on the minimum amount of 5 per cent as provided by Article 39.b.[4] The Article is of particular relevance in considering the application of the de minimis rule to quantities, which is discussed in paragraph 8.23 above.

1 [1954] 2 Lloyd's Rep 526. See para 8.23 above.
2 See *Kydon Compania Naviera SA v National Westminster Bank* [1981] 1 Lloyd's Rep 68 at 76.1.
3 See Case 272 in the ICC's More Case Studies on Documentary Credits, Publication No 489.
4 See Case 270 in More Case Studies (note 3 above).

8.44 The tolerance permitted by Article 39.b cannot be used as a means of increasing the amount of the credit. So if the amount of the credit is stated as the multiple of the stated quantity and the stated unit price and is not preceded by any word such as 'about', the 5% tolerance cannot be used to recover the price in respect of a shipment over the stated quantity but within 5% of it. The position would then be governed by Article 37.b.[1] Unless the credit otherwise provides, the bank is given an option to accept a commercial invoice issued for an amount in excess of the amount permitted by the credit. But the bank may not pay an amount in excess of that amount. So the seller would not be paid through the credit for the extra amount that he had shipped. He would need to proceed against the buyer for the balance, and in that he might face some difficulty if they did not have good relations.

1 See para 8.56 below.

8.45 Where it applies, Article 39.c allows a tolerance of 5% less in the amount drawn (ie money value) whereas, where Article 39.b applies, it allows a tolerance of 5% more or less in quantity (eg tonnage). Article 39.c requires that if the credit states a quantity it is shipped in full and that any unit price is not to be reduced. Its practical sphere of operation would appear to be credits where the unit price underlying the transaction may turn out to be less than allowed for because insurance or freight charges turn out to be less than anticipated, or where the credit amount results from a rounding up of unit price and quantity.[1]

1 See commentary in the ICC's UCP 500 and 400 Compared, Publication No 511.

8.46 Subject to these points it is of course essential that the correct quantity should be evidenced by the documents as the *Moralice* case[1] demonstrates. And it is also obvious that the documents must evidence that quantity and not a quantity in some other unit which cannot be related to it. Thus in *London and Foreign Trading Corpn v British and Northern European Bank*[2] the credit described the goods as 500 tons South African maize meal CIF Liverpool. The bill of lading simply stated a quantity of 5895 bags of maize meal. The invoice gave the same number of bags and the weight of the bags as 190 lbs, which gave 500 tons. The bank was held not to have been entitled to pay against such a bill because it gave the buyer no rights against the ship in respect of any particular tonnage without establishing the weight of the bags, which the buyer might or might not be able to do. In fact the number of bags was found to be correct, but there was a shortfall in weight.

1 Supra para 8.23.
2 (1921) 9 Ll L Rep 116.

8.47 *Terms as to dates* Article 47 of the Uniform Customs contains provisions as to the application of a number of terms which may be used in connection with dates. It provides:

ARTICLE 47 **Date Terminology for Periods of Shipment**
    a. The words 'to', 'until', 'till', 'from' and words of similar import applying to any date or period in the Credit referring to shipment will be understood to include the date mentioned.
    b. The word 'after' will be understood to exclude the date mentioned.
    c. The terms 'first half', 'second half' of a month shall be construed respectively as the 1st to the 15th, and the 16th to the last day of such month, all dates inclusive.
    d. The terms 'beginning', 'middle', or 'end' of a month shall be construed respectively as the 1st to the 10th, the 11th to the 20th, and the 21st to the last day of such month, all dates inclusive.

These provisions apply only to dates referring to shipment. The provisions in the 1983 Revision which they replace, Articles 51, 52 and 53 were of general application, which had led to opposing views in the ICC Banking Commission.[1] Article 47.c will provide a trap where the month is February.

1 See the discussion on Case 149 in the Case Studies on Documentary Credits, ICC Publication No 459: it is not understood how given the plain terms of Article 51 it was possible for some members of the Banking Commission to consider that the Article was of limited application. Perhaps their view was not as to the effect of the Article as worded, but as to the effect which it was desirable for it to have. See also Case 151.

8.48 *Terms as to issuers of documents* There is a temptation for an applicant for a credit to seek to strengthen his position by requiring documents to be issued by parties who are described with adjectives which sound well but are incapable of any precise application, such as 'first class' or 'official' to take two examples. Article 20.a provides that such terms should not be used, and that if, nonetheless, they are, they are to be ignored and the document accepted provided that it otherwise appears to meet the credit and is not issued by the beneficiary. The Article states:

ARTICLE 20.a[1] **Ambiguity as to the Issuers of Documents**
a. Terms such as 'first class', 'well known', 'qualified', 'independent', 'official', 'competent', 'local' and the like, shall not be used to describe the issuers of any document(s) to be presented under a Credit. If such terms are incorporated in the Credit, banks will accept the relative document(s) as presented, provided that it appears on its face to be in compliance with the other terms and conditions of the Credit and not to have been issued by the Beneficiary.

1 Article 20.a is derived from Article 22.b in the 1983 Revision.

8.49 The following Articles of the Uniform Customs have been considered in Chapter 5 – Article 42 (expiry date for presentation),[1] Article 43 (time for presentation from date of issuance of transport documents),[2] Article 44 (extension of expiry date)[3] and Article 45 (no obligation to accept outside banking hours),[4] Article 46 (general expressions as to dates for shipment).[5]

1 Para 5.22.
2 Para 5.24.
3 Para 5.25.
4 Para 5.27.
5 Para 5.26.

C. Requirements as to Particular Documents

1. The Commercial Invoice

8.50 Although the importance of the commercial invoice is outshone by that of the transport document which evidences the shipment of the goods and possession of which will often enable the buyer to obtain possession of the goods, it is the commercial invoice which is the primary document in the sense that it sets out what the goods are in respect of which presentation is being made and it states the price which is being claimed in respect of them.

8.51 *Name of applicant* Article 37.a of the Uniform Customs provides:

ARTICLE 37.a[1] **Commercial Invoices**
Unless otherwise stipulated in the Credit, commercial invoices;
i. must appear on their face to be issued by the Beneficiary named in the Credit (except as provided in Article 48), and
ii. must be made out in the name of the Applicant (except as provided in sub-Article 48(h)), and
iii. need not be signed.

This is simply to say that, where the underlying contract is one of sale, the invoice must be made out in the name of the seller[2] and must be addressed to the buyer. The exception to this is where the credit has been transferred, and there is a second beneficiary in relation to whom the first (or original) beneficiary stands as applicant. Article 48 covers transfer and is considered in Chapter 10.

1 Paragraphs i. and iii. are new. Paragraph ii. is taken from Article 41.a.
2 Compare Article 31.iii which permits the naming of the consignor as a party other than the beneficiary.

8.52 *Description*   The invoice should set out a description of the goods which fully and accurately follows the description in the credit. As has been noted above[1] Article 37.c provides:

> ARTICLE 37.c[2]   The description of the goods in the commercial invoice must correspond with the description in the Credit. In all other documents, the goods may be described in general terms not inconsistent with the description of the goods in the Credit.

The words 'must correspond' do not mean that they must be precisely the same. But there should be no differences in the descriptive words themselves. The safe course is to follow the wording of the credit precisely. This may be illustrated by one aspect of *Kydon Compania Naviera SA v National Westminster Bank Ltd, The Lena*.[3] The underlying contract was for the sale of a vessel described in the credit as 'one Greek flag motor vessel "LENA", built January 1951 of about 11250 tons gross register 6857 tons net register and about 5790 long tons light displacement "as built", with all equipment outfit and gear belonging to her on board, as per M.O.A.[4] dated 2nd July 1974'. It may be thought that this was not a well-considered wording. The wording of the invoices (three were required, signed, with a certificate that the vessel was as per the Memorandum of Agreement) stated:

> 'To net sale price of "LENA" . . . (US$953,771.00). We hereby certify that the mt "LENA" registered under the Greek Flag under official number 3723 of 11,123.89 tons gross and 6,297.41 tons net is as per Memorandum of Agreement dated 2nd July 1974 . . .'

It will be seen that:

(i)   Both gross[5] and net register tonnages were different.[6]
(ii)   The year of construction was not mentioned.
(iii)   The light displacement tonnage 'as built' was not mentioned.
(iv)   It was not stated that all equipment and gear belonging to her was on board.

In an attempt to avoid these great difficulties it was argued that all that was required was a certificate that the vessel complied with the agreement, and that it would have been sufficient 'description' merely to refer to the vessel '*Lena*'. It was held that the certification requirement was an additional requirement and did not obviate the need that the description in the invoice should correspond with that in the credit. Parker J stated:[7]

> 'Unless otherwise specified in the credit, the beneficiary must follow the words of the credit and this is so even where he uses an expression which, although different from the words of the credit, has, as between buyers and sellers, the same meaning as such words. It is important that this principle should be

strictly adhered to. An example of its operation is to be found in *J H Rayner & Co Ltd v Hambro's Bank Ltd* (1943) 74 Ll L Rep 10, [1943] KB 37. Departure from the principle would involve banks in just those sort of uncertainties which it is essential for the proper operation of the credit system should be avoided. Mr Tugendhat's overall answer to the discrepancies that the specific provisions as to invoices on the continuation sheet of the credit calls merely for –

> . . . Signed invoices . . . certifying the vessel is as per Memorandum of Agreement dated the 2nd July 1974 . . .

and the invoices in fact provided did so certify and that they were therefore sufficient cannot in my judgment succeed. The specific requirement for certification was an additional requirement. The obligation was still to provide an invoice in accordance with the terms of UCP. The description of the vessel in the invoice must therefore correspond with the description in the credit. On the face of it, it does not. It may be that the year of building, light displacement tonnage "as built" and so on as set out in the letter of credit do appear in the memorandum of agreement so that the certificate incorporates them, but this is not a matter which is of any concern to the bank. For all it knows the year of building, et cetera, may have been contained in some separate documents. If specific items of description are included in the credit they must also be included in the invoice. The certification may no doubt incorporate this and a lot more detail besides, but all of these are nothing to do with the bank.'

1 Para 8.27.
2 Unchanged from Article 41.c in the 1983 Revision.
3 [1981] 1 Lloyd's Rep 68.
4 Memorandum of Agreement.
5 It may be suggested that 11,123.89 tons gross corresponds with 'about 11,250 tons gross'.
6 As to the inapplicability of Article 39, see para 8.43 above.
7 [1981] 1 Lloyd's Rep 68 at 76.

8.53 The problem as to the invoice which faced Leggatt J in *Astro Exito Navegacion SA v Chase Manhattan Bank NA*[1] involved considering first the precision with which the description had to be followed and second what constituted the description. The credit was not well drawn in this respect. The underlying contract was for the sale of a vessel, and the credit required among the documents a copy of the notice of readiness covering:

> '. . . a Greek flag motor tanker, Messiniaki Tolmi ex Berger Pilot of about 20,150 long tonnes displacement with one bronze working propeller, one spare tail end shaft to arrive under own power at Kaohsiung, Taiwan, on or before September 30th 1980 as is and always safely afloat and substantially intact as per memorandum of agreement dated July 2nd 1980.'

Having referred to Article 32(c) of the 1974 Revision, the predecessor of Article 37.c, the judge continued:[2]

> 'The reference in the article itself to a "description in general terms not inconsistent with the description in the credit" suggests that correspondence in description requires all the elements in the description to be present, although the article does not say that the description in the invoice must be the same as that in the credit. As to the expressions "ex Berger Pilot" and "previous name Berger Pilot", between which a distinction has been sought to be drawn, I hold that in this context "ex" means "previous" name. There therefore was correspondence in that respect. The remaining question is whether "as is and always safely afloat and substantially intact" is part of the description. It does not seem to matter whether the words "as per MOA" governs those words or the words "to arrive" (with or without some part of what follows), since the "as is"

clause is already reproduced verbatim from the memorandum of agreement. The clause is obviously a vital element in the condition of the vessel, but is it part of the description, even if not part of the particulars required by par. 2 of the letter of credit? I have come to the conclusion that it is not. The words from "to arrive" to the end of the paragraph relate merely to the condition of the vessel when the notice of readiness is issued. They do not form part of the description of the particular vesssel being sold.'

These cases demonstrate the importance of the description of the goods being clearly identifiable as the description in the credit, and of keeping it simple.

1 [1986] 1 Lloyd's Rep 455.
2 Ibid at 458.

8.54 A problem of a different nature is considered in an Opinion of the ICC Banking Commission.[1] The credit was transmitted by SWIFT MT 700 and the description of the physical goods was followed by 'FOB Keelung as per Incoterms 1980 Edition'. The invoice presented stated 'FOB Keelung' only. The Commission considered that the reference to Incoterms was part of the description. This was reinforced by the fact that it had been transmitted in field 45 of MT 700, which was set aside for the description of the goods.

1 Decisions of the ICC Banking Commission, 1987–1988, R 166.

8.55 Amount The total amount of the invoice will include the cost of freight and insurance if these are to be borne by the buyer, and should state them as separate items if the credit provides for separate sums to be attributed to them rather than including them as part of an all-in figure.[1] If the freight has not been prepaid, the transport document is likely to be marked 'freight collect'. Such a document is acceptable under Article 33.a[2] provided, first, that it is not otherwise stipulated in the credit, and, second, that it is not inconsistent with any of the other documents presented under the credit. There would be such an inconsistency if a price was used on the invoice which included freight and the freight was not deducted from it.

1 Cf *Ireland v Livingston* (1872) LR 5 HL 395 at 406 per Blackburn J.
2 See para 8.107 below.

8.56 The total amount of the invoice should not exceed the amount of the credit. If it does, so long as the credit does not otherwise provide, if it chooses to, the bank may accept the documents, against payment of the maximum amount of the credit. This is the effect of Article 37.b, which states:

ARTICLE 37.b[1] Unless otherwise stipulated in the Credit, banks may refuse commercial invoices issued for amounts in excess of the amount permitted by the Credit. Nevertheless, if a bank authorised to pay, incur a deferred payment undertaking, accept Draft(s), or negotiate under a Credit accepts such invoices, its decision will be binding upon all parties, provided that such bank has not paid, incurred a deferred payment undertaking, accepted Draft(s) or negotiated for an amount in excess of that permitted by the Credit.

This article is also considered in connection with the 'tolerance' provision of Article 39 of the Uniform Customs in paragraph 8.44.

1 Taken with immaterial changes from Article 41(b) in the 1983 Revision.

2. Transport Documents

8.57 *Introduction*   A transport document has two basic functions. The first to evidence receipt of the goods by the carrier. The second is to evidence the terms of the contract of carriage. In the case of a negotiable bill of lading it also acts as a document of title. The last is most important where a bank intends to look to its possession of documents for security.[1] Until the spread of container transportation, the usual form of transport document was a marine bill of lading, and this is the form with which most of the reported decisions of the courts have been concerned. The growth of container transportation has involved the appearance of container freight stations, which are often inland, where containers are assembled and may be filled (or stuffed) with the goods of different consignors (or shippers), and of container ports specialising in the handling of containers and of container vessels. Thus container transport typically involves more than one mode of carriage, for example, carriage by road and carriage by sea. It is to be contrasted with the classical CIF contract (whether or not involving a letter of credit) where the seller or his agent delivers the goods to a vessel at the port of loading and receives bills of lading which are transferred to the buyer and the buyer or his agent presents the bills to the ship at the port of discharge and receives the goods. A similar comparison can be made for FOB contracts. Container transport has led to the creation of new forms of transport document. This situation has led to major changes in the Uniform Customs, first in the 1974 Revision and then in the 1983 Revision and again in the 1993 Revision. The changes in both the 1983 and 1993 Revisions involved a complete re-organisation and re-drafting of the section covering transport documents.

1 Chapter 11 post, para 11.1 in particular.

8.58 *The scheme of the Revisions compared*   In the *1974 Revision* Articles 15 to 18 covered respectively date of shipment, freight, shipper's load and count, and clean shipping documents. Articles 19 to 22 covered marine bills of lading. Article 23 covered combined documents, and Article 24 covered all other types of transport document from railway bills and postal receipts to air waybills.

In the *1983 Revision* Article 25 covered all types of transport document save marine bills of lading and post documents. Articles 26 covered marine bills of lading, and Article 30 post documents. Article 27 covered taking in charge and loading on board including date; Article 28 covered freight; Article 32 shipper's load and count; Article 33 consignor/ beneficiary; and Article 35 clean transport documents.

The *1993 Revision* takes a different approach. It has no Article attempting a general coverage equivalent to the previous Article 26 but addresses itself to specific types of transport document (which largely it does not attempt to describe or define). The scheme is:

      Article 23 – marine or ocean bills of lading
           24 – non-negotiable sea waybills
           25 – charterparty bills of lading
           26 – multimodal transport documents

Article 27 – air transport documents
      28 – road, rail, inland waterway transport documents
      29 – courier and post receipts
      30 – transport documents issued by freight forwarders
      31 – on deck, shipper's load and count, name of consignor
      32 – clean documents
      33 – freight

Provisions as to date of shipment are contained within the Articles relating to specific forms of document. It follows from the scheme adopted that if the credit calls for or permits a transport document which manages not to fall within any of Articles 23 to 29 it will not be covered, there being no catch-all Article.

Marine Bills of Lading

8.59 Article 23 of the Uniform Customs sets out provisions which relate specifically to marine (or ocean) bills of lading. It provides:

ARTICLE 23   **Marine/Ocean Bill of Lading**

a. If a Credit calls for a bill of lading covering a port-to-port shipment, banks will, unless otherwise stipulated in the Credit, accept a document, however named, which:

i. appears on its face to indicate the name of the carrier and to have been signed or otherwise authenticated by:

(*a*) the carrier or a named agent for or on behalf of the carrier, or

(*b*) the master or a named agent for or on behalf of the master.

Any signature or authentication of the carrier or master must be identified as carrier or master, as the case may be. An agent signing or authenticating for the carrier or master must also indicate the name and the capacity of the party, ie carrier or master, on whose behalf that agent is acting, and

ii. indicates that the goods have been loaded on board, or shipped on a named vessel.

Loading on board or shipment on a named vessel may be indicated by pre-printed wording on the bill of lading that the goods have been loaded on board a named vessel or shipped on a named vessel, in which case the date of issuance of the bill of lading will be deemed to be the date of loading on board and the date of shipment.

In all other cases loading on board a named vessel must be evidenced by a notation on the bill of lading which gives the date on which the goods have been loaded on board, in which case the date of the on board notation will be deemed to be the date of shipment.

If the bill of lading contains the indication 'intended vessel', or similar qualification in relation to the vessel, loading on board a named vessel must be evidenced by an on board notation on the bill of lading which, in addition to the date on which the goods have been loaded on board, also includes the name of the vessel on which the goods have been loaded, even if they have been loaded on the vessel named as the 'intended vessel'.

If the bill of lading indicates a place of receipt or taking in charge different from the port of loading, the on board notation must also include the port of loading stipulated

in the Credit and the name of the vessel on which the goods have been loaded, even if they have been loaded on the vessel named in the bill of lading. This provision also applies whenever loading on board the vessel is indicated by pre-printed wording of the bill of lading.
and

iii. indicates the port of loading and the port of discharge stipulated in the Credit, notwithstanding that it:

(*a*) indicates a place of taking in charge different from the port of loading, and/or a place of final destination different from the port of discharge,
and/or

(*b*) contains the indication 'intended' or similar qualification in relation to the port of loading and/or port of discharge, as long as the document also states the ports of loading and/or discharge stipulated in the Credit,
and

iv. consists of a sole original bill of lading or, if issued in more than one original, the full set as so issued,
and

v. appears to contain all of the terms and conditions of carriage, or some of such terms and conditions by reference to a source or document other than the bill of lading (short form/blank back bill of lading); banks will not examine the contents of such terms and conditions,
and

vi. contains no indication that it is subject to a charter party and/or no indication that the carrying vessel is propelled by sail only,
and

vii. in all other respects meets the stipulations of the Credit.

b. For the purpose of this Article, transhipment means unloading and reloading from one vessel to another vessel during the course of ocean carriage from the port of loading to the port of discharge stipulated in the Credit.

c. Unless transhipment is prohibited by the terms of the Credit, banks will accept a bill of lading which indicates that the goods will be transhipped, provided that the entire ocean carriage is covered by one and the same bill of lading.

d. Even if the Credit prohibits transhipment, banks will accept a bill of lading which:

i. indicates that transhipment will take place as long as the relevant cargo is shipped in Container(s), Trailer(s) and/or 'LASH' barge(s) as evidenced by the bill of lading, provided that the entire ocean carriage is covered by one and the same bill of lading,
and/or

ii. incorporates clauses stating that the carrier reserves the right to tranship.

Matters arising on Article 23

8.60 *Marine bill of lading* The Article is entitled Marine/Ocean Bill of Lading and applies where 'a bill of lading covering a port-to-port' shipment is called for. That may be spelt out further as a bill of lading covering carriage by sea from one port to another. The use of marine or ocean is to distinguish inland waterway bills.[1] If the transport document does not refer exclusively to a carriage by sea but combines it with other carriage such as a carriage by land, it will be a form of multimodal or combined transport document which will fall within Article 26 and not Article 23. This is confirmed by an Opinion of the ICC Banking Commission, should confirmation be necessary.[2] The document may nonetheless show places of taking in charge and final destination different to the ports of loading and discharge respectively, as is permitted by Article 26.a.iii. A document which is in the form of a standard form combined transport bill will nonetheless meet the requirements of Article 23 if it is completed so that it relates exclusively to sea carriage and otherwise meets the requirements of Article 23, in particular is notated to show receipt on board a named vessel. The ICC Banking Commission has had to consider the FIATA Combined Transport Bill of Lading in this context, and has confirmed that it may be so completed that it is a marine bill of lading complying with the requirements of Article 23.[3] In a later Opinion the Commission confirmed the view that other appropriately worded and completed forms of combined transport document could comply with Article 23, but denigrated any proliferation of such forms.[4] It appears that at the time of these decisions there was uncertainty among banks and their practice varied. This was undesirable, particularly with regard to the FIATA Combined Transport Bill, which is in very common use. The need for the transport document to provide cover in respect of the whole of the voyage in the form of an undertaking of liability by the signatory carrier in respect of the whole voyage is discussed in paragraph 8.77 below.

1 Case 85, Case Studies on Documentary Credits, ICC Publication No 459.
2 Opinions of the ICC Banking Commission 1984–1986 at R 120.
3 Opinions of the ICC Banking Commission 1987–1988 at R 159; see also R 160.
4 These Opinions consider the 1983 Revision but remain applicable even though the FIATA bill is no longer mentioned in Article 23 as it was in Article 26 of the 1983 Revision.

8.61 A brief consideration of what is a bill of lading is appropriate. *Sassoon on CIF and FOB Contracts*[1] states:

'A bill of lading is a document which is signed by the carrier or his agent acknowledging that goods have been shipped on board a particular vessel bound for a particular destination and stating the terms on which the goods so received are to be carried.'

Scrutton on Charterparties[2] gives an expanded statement and refers to the uncertain position of some 'through' bills of lading:

'After goods are shipped, a document called a bill of lading is issued, which serves as a receipt by the shipowner, acknowledging that the goods have been delivered to him for carriage.

Besides acting as a receipt for the goods, the bill of lading serves also as:

(1) Evidence of the contract of affreightment between the shipper and the carrier.

(2) A document of title, by the indorsement of which the property in the goods for which it is a receipt may be transferred, or the goods pledged or mortgaged as security for an advance.

By statute, the rights and liabilities of the shipper under the contract of affreightment as set out in the bill of lading may be transferred with the full property in the goods to the consignee of the goods or the indorsee of the bill of lading.

It is becoming increasingly common for liner companies and others to issue documents called *through bills of lading*, which may evidence a contract for carriage by land or air as well as by water. Such documents present special problems, and it is doubtful to what extent they share the characteristics of the conventional bill of lading.'

The three characteristics of a bill of lading are therefore (1) as a receipt, (2) as a contract of carriage, and (3) as a document of title. The Bills of Lading Act 1855 was passed to enable endorsees of bills to sue on the contract of carriage. In modern times the Act was found deficient in important respects. It was repealed by the Carriage of Goods by Sea Act 1992 which came into effect on 16 September 1992. The new Act provides for the ability of the holder of a bill of lading to sue on the contract of carriage, and makes equivalent provisions in respect of sea waybills and ship's delivery orders.

1 (3rd edn) British Shipping Laws Vol 5, para 132.
2 (19th edn) p 2, cited by its earlier edition by Sassoon.

8.62 *Name of carrier* A bill of lading is acceptable which 'appears on its face to indicate the name of the carrier' who is undertaking the carriage.[1] As a bill of lading evidences a contract of carriage it is fundamental that it should indicate who the carrier is. The carrier named need not be the vessel owner nor have the right to the vessel whether by charter or otherwise. He may be a non-vessel owning carrier who has taken space on a vessel and issues his own bills of lading which enable the goods to be collected by presentation of a bill to the carrier's agent and not to the ship or its agent: but he must identify himself in the document as carrier.[2,3] Article 30 provides that bills issued by freight forwards are not acceptable unless the name of the forwarder appears as carrier or as agent for the carrier.[4] This exclusion of freight forwarder bills is in accordance with banking practice as it was found by Diplock J in *Enrico Furst & Co v W E Fischer Ltd*.[5]

1 Illustrated in Case 236 in More Case Studies on Documentary Credits, ICC Publication No 489.
2 See R121, Opinions of the ICC Banking Commission 1984–86, ICC Publication No 434. The introduction to the Opinion refers to a definition of 'carrier' which appeared in a draft for the 1983 Revision [Document 470/391] which probably did not cover non-vessel-owning operators. See also Case 87 in Case Studies on Documentary Credits, ICC Publication No 459.
3 The position in the United States regarding NVOCCs is outlined at R187 in Opinions of the ICC Banking Commission 1989–1991. The term (NVOCC) is defined in the Shipping Act 1984 as '. . . a common carrier that does not operate the vessel by which the ocean transportation is provided, and is a shipper in its relationship with an ocean common carriage'. The operation of NVOCCs is controlled by law including a requirement to obtain a bond to ensure financial responsibility for damage etc. It is ultimately what an NVOCC does which determines its status, rather than what it calls itself.
4 See further para 8.98 below.
5 [1960] 2 Lloyd's Rep 340 at 345, 346.

8.63 *Signature or authentication* The bills of lading must be signed or authenticated by the carrier or the master, or by an agent of one of them. The Article does not require that when the master signs he signs on behalf of the carrier: it is enough if the carrier is named on the bills and they are signed by the master.[1] This may be presumed to be because it is within the ordinary authority of a master to issue bills of lading on behalf of the party who has the right to the use of the vessel. The carrier will almost always be a company and so cannot provide a handwritten signature save by an agent, whether that agent be an employee of the carrier or of another company which is acting as the agent of the carrier. It is helpful here to set out part of Article 20.b and also Article 20.d:

ARTICLE 20.b . . .
A document may be signed by handwriting, by facsimile signature, by perforated signature, by stamp, by symbol, or by any other mechanical or electronic method of authentication.

ARTICLE 20.d   Unless otherwise stipulated in the Credit, a condition under a
Credit calling for a document to be authenticated, validated . . .
will be satisfied by any signature, mark, stamp or label on such
document that on its face appears to satisfy the above condition.

The requirement of Article 23.a.i for signature or authentication is a
condition of a credit to which Article 20 applies and so may be satisfied in
the wide-ranging ways that Article 20 permits.[2] Although Article 20 gives
considerable latitude in this respect, where the signature or authentication is by an agent, the agent must nonetheless indicate the name and
capacity of the party (carrier or master) on whose behalf he is acting. A
freight forwarder must sign as carrier or as agent for a named carrier.[3]

1 As background see R189 in Opinions of the ICC Banking Commission, 1989–91, ICC
  Publication No 494, and Cases 235 and 237 in the ICC's More Case Studies on Documentary Credits, Publication No 489.
2 The provisions quoted are new, and as well as providing clarification may provide a
  relaxation. In Cases 218 and 224 in the ICC's More Case Studies on Documentary Credits
  the position was taken that it was for banks examining bills of lading issued in their own
  country to ensure that they were signed in a manner valid under that law. But, to take the
  example from Case 224, a national law may not yet have got to grips with laser printed
  signatures: it is as well for the Uniform Customs to cover the position.
3 Article 30, considered in para 8.98 below.

8.64 *Loaded on board or shipped on a named vessel*   The bills of
lading must indicate that the goods have been loaded on board (or
shipped) on a named vessel. It is not enough that the goods have been
received for shipment; the buyer is entitled to the carrier's assurance that
the goods have actually been taken on board. This is in accordance with
the decisions of the English courts that received-for-shipment bills are not
a good tender under a CIF contract.[1] Article 23.a.ii provides for this to be
done in two ways.

1 See *Diamond Alkali Export Corpn v Bourgeois* [1921] 3 K.B. 443 and *Yelo v Machado &
  Co Ltd* [1952] 1 Lloyd's Rep 183 at 192.

8.65 *Pre-printed loaded-on-board bills*   The first is where the bills have
pre-printed wording showing that the goods have been loaded or shipped
on a named vessel. This does not require the name of the vessel to be
printed: but the printed bills must be in a loaded-on-board form rather
than in a received-for-shipment form. Even though it may have been on
the bill when issued, an annotation to that effect, that is, anything which
does not form part of the orginal printed bill, makes the bills of the
received-for-shipment type and must be completed in the second way.[1] If
the bills indicate a place of receipt different from the port of loading, a
notation is required as described in paragraph 8.67 below even if the bills
are printed in a loaded-on-board form.

1 Compare *Westpac Banking Corpn and Commonwealth Steel Co Ltd v South Carolina
  National Bank* [1986] 1 Lloyd's Rep 311, Privy Council, which would now be decided
  differently: see Case 106 in the ICC's Case Studies on Documentary Credits, Publication
  No 459. Banks should not be, and now are not, required to try to ascertain when a
  notation was placed on a bill.

8.66 *Notations*   In all other cases loading or shipment on board a named
vessel must be established by a notation on the bills of lading, that is, by
something that does not form part of the printed part of the bills. So bills
which are printed in a received-for-shipment form may be stamped
'Loaded on board'. The date of the notation must be added. The Article

does not require, as its predecessor, Article 27.b, did, that the notation should be signed or initialled by the carrier or his agent. The change is intentional: it was felt that such signing or initialling provided no additional protection to the parties and caused problems to banks.

8.67 **Intended vessels**   Where the bills as originally drawn name the vessel as an intended vessel or use words to like effect, the on-board notation must include the name of the vessel on which they are loaded even where it is the same as the intended vessel. Where the bills as originally drawn name a vessel without qualification but are in the received-for-shipment form, need the notation repeat the vessel's name? The relevant part of Article 23.a.ii refers only to bills using the indication 'intended vessel' or a similar qualification, and so would not apply in this case. There may be a change here from Article 27.b in the 1983 Revision which has been construed as requiring the name of the vessel to be mentioned even where the bills name a vessel without qualification.[1]

1 Case 90 in the ICC's Case Studies on Documentary Credits, argued to be wrong in para 8.61 of the 1st Edn.

8.68   Where a credit permits transhipment and the bill of lading indicates that carriage will be effected in two journeys, the bills should acknowledge loading on board the first vessel. This is so even if the division of the voyages indicates that the first ship is of the nature of a feeder vessel.[1]

1 Opinions of the ICC Banking Commission 1984–1986, at R 118.

8.69 *Notation where place of receipt different to port of loading*   The last paragraph of Article 23.a.ii provides that, where the bills of lading indicate a place of receipt different from the port of loading, even if the bills are printed in the loaded-on-board form,[1] there must be a loaded-on-board notation including the port of loading and the name of the vessel (even if the vessel is that named without qualification in the bills). It is only sensible that the notation should be dated in all cases. In the case of a pre-printed bill of the loaded-on-board type which nonetheless names a place of receipt different from the port of loading,[2] the need for a date can be derived from the word 'also' in the penultimate sentence of Article 23.a.ii.

1 This must be the effect of the last sentence of Article 23.a.ii.
2 Which may be thought unlikely.

8.70 *Date of shipment*   Where the bills are pre-printed in the loaded-on-board form, the date of issue of the bills is deemed to be the date of shipment. Where there is an on-board notation, the date of the notation is deemed to be the date of shipment. Where the bills are pre-printed in the loaded-on-board form but indicate a place of receipt different to the port of loading, a notation is required: see the last paragraph above. The date of the notation must be deemed to be the date of shipment even though Article 23 does not spell this out.

8.71 *Port of loading and of discharge*   Article 27.a.iii provides that the bills of lading must indicate the port of loading[1] and the port of discharge required by the credit. But it does not matter that they show a place of taking in charge (or receipt) different to the port of loading, nor a place of final destination different to the port of discharge. This covers the possibility that, if the goods are containerised, they are likely to be taken in charge prior to arrival at the port of loading and delivered up beyond the port of discharge. Nor does it matter that the ports required by the credit are prefixed in the bills by qualification such as 'intended'. But where the place of receipt is different from the place of loading there must be a notation as set out in paragraph 8.67 above.

1 The credit may not mention a port of loading. Thus, if the underlying contract is for sale of wheat CIF Antwerp, the port of loading is likely to be at the choice of the seller and will not be referred to in the credit.

8.72 *Full set of original bills* Article 23.a.iv requires the full set of original bills of lading as issued or the sole original bill if only one was issued. The origin of the practice of issuing bills of lading in sets (usually of three) lies in the earlier difficulties of transport when bills were dispatched separately by different routes to the buyer for safety. Each bill is effective to pass the property, and any one may be presented to the vessel to obtain delivery of the goods. So under the old wording bills were often expressed to be 'of even tenor, the one being accomplished, the others to stand void.' Such a system presents opportunities for fraud. Thus it was usual for credits to require that the full set of bills of lading should be presented to obtain payment, as was the case in *Donald H Scott & Co v Barclays Bank Ltd*[1] where it was held that two out of three bills would not do. The Uniform Customs now make this the requirement unless it is otherwise stipulated in the credit. The bills presented must be originals (unless otherwise stipulated). As the bank has to be satisfied that it has the full set, the bills of lading must indicate how many the set consists of. The consignor need not be the beneficiary unless the credit so provides: see Article 31.iii.[2]

1 [1923] 2 KB 1.
2 Para 8.100 below.

8.73 *Short form bills* Article 23.a.v requires either the bills of lading to contain all the terms and conditions of carriage, or to do so by incorporating them from another document. When the latter is done, the bills are called short form or blank-back bills (because the back is devoid of all the usual small print). Banks are not required to examine terms which are incorporated but not set out in the bills, which they will not have before them.

8.74 *Subject to a charterparty* Article 23.a.vi requires that the bills of lading should not be subject to a charterparty. This may of course be allowed by a term of the credit. Charterparty bills are considered under Article 25 in paragraph 8.85.

8.75 *Sail only* Article 23.a.vi also provides that bills of lading must not indicate that the carrying vessel is propelled by sail only.

8.76 *Transhipment* Articles 23.b–d relate to transhipment. Article 23.b defines transhipment as 'unloading and reloading from one vessel to another during the course of ocean carriage from the port of loading to the port of discharge as[1] stipulated in the credit'.[2] The Article is intended to reflect the realities of container transport and also to take account of the fact that a prohibition on transhipment will often be inserted into a credit even though it is unrealistic. Article 23.c provides that, unless the credit prohibits transhipment, bills of lading are acceptable which indicate that the goods will be transhipped provided that the entire ocean carriage is covered by one bill of lading.[3] But, even if transhipment is prohibited by the credit, Article 23.d.i provides that, where the goods are shown by the bills of lading to be shipped in containers, trailers or lash barges, the bills may show that transhipment will take place, again provided that the entire ocean carriage is covered by one bill of lading. Lastly Article 23.d.ii ensures that a bill of lading which only reserves a right to tranship is acceptable. The position at common law is that a bill of lading which permits transhipment is permissible provided, first, that the bill of lading does give rights in respect of the entire carriage[3] and, second, that transhipment is not prohibited by the terms of the credit.[4]

1 The 'as' appears superfluous.
2 Compare the previous wider definition in Article 29.a of the 1983 Revision.
3 See para 8.77 below.
4 See the *Marlborough Hill* [1921] 1 AC 444 at 452; *Holland Colombo Trading Society Ltd v Alawdeen* [1954] 2 Lloyd's Rep 45 at 53.2.

8.77 *Through bills: to cover the whole carriage* The commencement of Article 23.a refers to bills of lading covering port-to-port shipment, and the transhipment provisions emphasise the need for one bill (or set of bills), that is one contract of carriage, to cover the entire ocean carriage. The underlying rule is that the bills of lading must evidence a contract of carriage covering the whole of the journey from the port of shipment to the port of discharge. This is the general common law rule subject to the proof of custom to the contrary: see *Hansson v Hamel and Horley Ltd*[1] and *Arnold Otto Meyer NV v Aune.*[2] The credit may specify the port of shipment as well as the port of discharge, in which case the bill must cover the whole voyage to comply with that express provision. If the credit is silent as to the port of shipment, the reason for requiring a bill of lading which covers the whole of the sea journey from the actual port of shipment is that the buyer is entitled to have a document giving him rights covering all the journey so that he is properly covered in the event of loss or damage to the goods. It must be emphasised that a liberty to tranship, whether arising from the express terms of the credit or by reason of Article 23, does not affect the principle that the transport document must cover the whole voyage. Thus a document issued by a carrier which covers transport by more than one carrier, is acceptable only if the issuing carrier undertakes liability in respect of the whole voyage. If he accepts liability only in respect of that part carried out by him and acts as agent in respect of carriage by vessels owned by other carriers, the document is unacceptable unless the credit expressly permits this. It is particularly important here not to be guided by the title of the document: it is necessary to examine its terms and conditions to see what liability the issuing carrier is undertaking.

1 [1922] 2 AC 36; see the quotation in para 8.32 above.
2 [1939] 3 All ER 168.

8.78 Where a bill of lading gives a liberty to tranship in its small print which may, if exercised, mean that the carrier will no longer be contractually responsible for part of the voyage, the position at common law is more uncertain: the answer may be that at least if the liberty is unexercised, the bill is not objectionable. In *Soproma SpA v Marine and Animal By-Products Corpn*[1] McNair J stated:[2]

'As at present advised I should not be disposed to hold that a bill of lading otherwise unobjectionable in form which did in fact cover the whole transit actually performed would be a bad tender merely because it contained a liberty not in fact exercised, but which, if exercised, would not have given the buyers continuing cover for the portion of the voyage not performed by the vessel named in the bill of lading.'

If that is the correct approach, it would appear to involve the bank possibly taking account of a fact which would not be apparent from the face of the documents presented to it, namely that there had been transhipment if there had. This would breach the rule as to the autonomy of the credit. If the terms of the credit prohibit transhipment, a bill with such a clause can nonetheless be argued to be permitted by Article 23.d despite the fact the bills will give no cover if transhipment occurs, because the Article makes no reference to this situation. The contrary argument would rely on the underlying principle that the bills must give complete cover. But a bank is not obliged to look at the terms and conditions at the back of a transport document to see whether there is such a right to tranship: see paragraph 8.9 above.

1 [1966] 1 Lloyd's Rep 367.
2 Ibid at 388.2.

8.79 Issued on shipment   The bill of lading should be issued 'on shipment'. In *Hansson v Hamel and Horley Ltd*[1] Lord Sumner stated:[2]

'I do not understand this proposition as meaning that the bill of lading would be bad, unless it was signed contemporaneously with the actual placing of the goods on board. "On shipment" is an expression of some latitude. Bills of lading are constantly signed after the loading is complete and, in some cases, after the ship has sailed. I do not think that they thereby necessarily cease to be procured "on shipment", nor do I suppose that the learned judge so intended his words. It may also be that the expression would be satisfied, even though some local carriage on inland waters, or by canal, or in an estuary or barge or otherwise preceded the shipment on the ocean steamer, provided that the steamer's bill of lading covered that prior carriage by effectual words of contract. "On shipment" is referable both to time and place. . . . I am quite sure that a bill of lading only issued thirteen days after the original shipment, at another port in another country many hundreds of miles away, is not duly procured "on shipment".'

In *M Golodetz & Co v Czarnikow-Rionda*[3] it was argued before Donaldson J but not before the Court of Appeal that the bill of lading was stale in this particular sense because it was issued on 6 April when loading was complete on 24 March. This was probably caused by the fact that the parcel in question was loaded early in the vessel's loading which continued over a period and it was intended to issue one bill covering all the cargo covered by the contract, not only the cargo which became fire damaged. The judge stated 'it was issued as soon as reasonably practicable after the completion of the loading of the whole parcel and at or about the time when the ship sailed'. The objection failed.

1 [1922] 2 AC 36.
2 Ibid at 47.
3 [1980] 1 WLR 495.

8.80 To order blank endorsed   This means that the bill of lading must provide for delivery 'to order', that is, that there is no named consignee, and 'to order' is written in the space for the name of the consignee. It means to order of the shipper. The buyer or his bank may be nominated as the 'notify' party. 'Blank endorsed' means that the shipper is, as it were, to give his order by endorsing the bills in blank, that is to say they are simply to be endorsed with his signature[1] on the bill. The bill can then be transferred without further endorsement by mere delivery. A bill which is not made out to order but is made out to a named consignee is not negotiable unless it contains words indicating transferability and has been endorsed by the consignee. In *Skandinaviska Akt v Barclays Bank*[2] blank endorsed bills were called for by the credit. The 'to order' bills did not name a shipper and so it was unclear who was entitled to endorse them: they were a bad tender. In *Soproma SpA v Marine and Animal By-Products Corpn*[3] the bills of lading were bad because, inter alia, they were straight bills made out to the consignees instead of being issued to order and blank endorsed.[4] Where it is uncertain whether a bill of lading is to be construed as a bill to shipper's order or to the order of the consignee the bill is to be rejected: *National Bank of South Africa v Banca Italiana di Sconto.*[5]

1 Ie the company name with the signature of an authorised person in the case of a company.
2 (1925) 22 Ll L Rep 523.
3 [1966] 1 Lloyd's Rep 367.
4 See [1966] 1 Lloyd's Rep at 388.1.
5 (1922) 10 Ll L Rep 531.

8.81 ***Other stipulations of the credit***   Article 23.a.vii requires bills of lading to meet the stipulations of the credit. So it may not be enough for a marine bill simply to comply with Article 23: there may be provisions in the credit with which it must also comply. The opening words of the Article should also be borne in mind here: Article 23.a applies 'unless otherwise stipulated in the credit'. So its provisions may be modified by the terms of the credit itself.

8.82 ***Other matters affecting marine bills of lading***   The following topics which are relevant to transport documents generally are considered subsequently:

Documents issued by freight forwarders	para 8.96
'On deck', 'shipper's load and count'	8.97, 98
Name of consignor	8.99
Clean documents	8.100
Freight	8.104
Partial shipments	8.106
Date of shipment and presentation	8.107
Description and identification of goods	8.110

Non-negotiable sea waybills
8.83   The waybill concept has been long established in rail transport and later in air transport. It has more recently been applied to sea carriage, partly to overcome the problem that, while goods now arrive more rapidly, the postal services relied on to convey bills of lading have deteriorated. It achieves this by providing that the goods shall be delivered to the consignee named in the waybill upon proof of identity, rather than to the holder of the document. It shares the characteristics of bills of lading in that it is

both a receipt for goods and a contract of carriage. It is not however a document of title nor is it negotiable: its transfer cannot be used to transfer the ownership of the goods to which it relates. This may make it unsuitable where it is intended to resell goods afloat.[1] The use of waybills in paperless electronic trading (by EDI[2]) does not present the same problems as the use of bills of lading. As electronic trading becomes more general, the use of waybills is likely to increase. Important provisions relating to waybills are made by the Carriage of Goods by Sea Act 1992 (which likewise apply to bills of lading[3]). The nature of a waybill has two consequences which are important in documentary credits:

(a) Unless the seller/consignor gives up the right, he will have the right to vary his instruction to the carrier at any time up to the consignor's identification of himself and request for the goods. It is important that the consignor should not be able in this way to direct delivery to a third party while the documents are going through the credit. This may be done by the inclusion of a *non-disposal clause* in the waybill (often called a NODISP clause), whereby the consignor irrevocably gives up the right to vary the identity of the consignee during transit. But while such a clause protects the buyer, it leaves the seller in an impossible position if the documents are rejected under the credit. A solution (whose success may depend upon the timing of events) is for the clause to provide for the seller to give up his right to vary the identity of the consignee upon the acceptance of the waybill under a documentary credit and the confirmation of that acceptance by the accepting bank to the carrier.

(b) As the consignee is entitled to the delivery of the goods without the production of the waybill, he will be able to obtain delivery of them without the documents having come to him through the credit. He may do this with the result of defrauding the seller who has not been paid under the credit, or with the result of defrauding the bank which has paid under the credit but which has not been reimbursed by him. The seller can prevent the former, if time allows and if he is aware of the need to do so, by changing his delivery instructions to the carrier. If he does so and the carrier nonetheless delivers to the buyer, the carrier will be liable for misdelivery. The carrier would not be liable in the absence of a change of instructions. Whereas, with a bill of lading, if the seller remained entitled to the bills and hence to the possession of the goods, the carrier would be liable for misdelivery because he had delivered up the goods without production of a bill of lading even though there had been no change of instructions. A bank can prevent a buyer taking possession of the goods without having settled with the bank, by requiring itself to be named in the waybill as the consignee and the buyer as the notify party. It can then assign its rights as consignee to the buyer on receipt of settlement from the buyer, and will then notify the carrier enabling the buyer to obtain delivery. If the bank takes this course it will become a party to the contract of carriage, and so liable under it. Nonetheless many third world countries insist on this procedure to seek to control their foreign exchange position. An alternative is for the bank to require that the waybill be endorsed with a clause to the effect that the bank has a lien on the goods and that delivery was only to be made against written authority from the bank.

1 The end result may be achieved by the consignee taking a delivery order from the carrier and endorsing the order to the subpurchaser, who can then present the delivery order to claim the goods from the carrier.
2 EDI – Electronic Data Interchange.
3 See para 8.61 above.

8.84 Article 24 governs the position where the credit calls for a non-negotiable sea waybill covering port-to-port shipment. It begins:

> ARTICLE 24   If a Credit calls for a non-negotiable sea waybill covering a port-to-port shipment, banks will, unless otherwise stipulated in the Credit, accept a document, however named, which:
> . . .

The Article then follows precisely[1] the wording of Article 23 with the substitution of 'non-negotiable sea waybill' for 'bill of lading'. The comments on Article 23 will apply.

1 Save that an 'also' is omitted from the penultimate paragraph of Article 24.a.ii. This is immaterial.

Charterparty bills of lading

8.85 Charterparty[1] bills of lading are marine bills of lading which are issued subject to the terms of a charterparty. These are not acceptable unless the credit expressly so provides. This is the effect of Article 23.a.vi and Article 25. This follows the practice of banks as established in the case of *Enrico Furst & Co v W E Fischer Ltd*.[2] Charterparty bills are provided for by Article 25:

> ARTICLE 25   **Charter Party Bill of Lading**
> a. If a Credit calls for or permits a charter party bill of lading, banks will, unless otherwise stipulated in the Credit, accept a document, however named, which:
>   i.   contains any indication that it is subject to a charter party, and
>   ii. appears on its face to have been signed or otherwise authenticated by:
>   (a) the master or a named agent for or on behalf of the master, or
>   (b) the owner or a named agent for or on behalf of the owner.
>   Any signature or authentication of the master or owner must be identified as master or owner as the case may be. An agent signing or authenticating for the master or owner must also indicate the name and the capacity of the party, ie master or owner, on whose behalf that agent is acting, and
>   iii. does or does not indicate the name of the carrier, and
>   iv. indicates that the goods have been loaded on board or shipped on a named vessel.
>   Loading on board or shipment on a named vessel may be indicated by pre-printed wording on the bill of lading that the goods have been loaded on board a named vessel or shipped on a named vessel, in which case the date of issuance of the bill of lading will be deemed to be the date of loading on board and the date of shipment.

In all other cases loading on board a named vessel must be evidenced by a notation on the bill of lading which gives the date on which the goods have been loaded on board, in which case the date of the on board notation will be deemed to be the date of shipment,

and

v. indicates the port of loading and the port of discharge stipulated in the Credit,

and

vi. consists of a sole original bill of lading or, if issued in more than one original, the full set as so issued,

and

vii. contains no indication that the carrying vessel is propelled by sail only,

and

viii. in all other respects meets the stipulations of the Credit.

b. Even if the Credit requires the presentation of a charter party contract in connection with a charter party bill of lading, banks will not examine such charter party contract, but will pass it on without responsibility on their part.

1 Usually one word in England, eg *Scrutton on Charterparties*.
2 [1960] 2 Lloyd's Rep 340 at 345,6.

8.86 The Uniform Customs might have dealt with charterparty bills of lading by modification of Article 23. Article 25 takes the longer but probably clearer route of starting afresh. The Article follows Article 23 with these exceptions:

(a) Bills subject to charterparty are permitted.

(b) The bills need not name the carrier. It is common for charterparty bills not to do so. This gave rise to a question whether, if charterparty bills were permitted, it followed that the carrier need not be named. The ICC Banking Commission concluded that it was not necessary.[1] The point is now expressly covered in the Uniform Customs themselves.

(c) Signature or authentication of the bills must be by or on behalf of the master or owner (the owner does not appear in Article 23[2]).

(d) The 'intended vessel' provisions in Article 23.a.ii are omitted, presumably on the basis that if the bills are subject to a charterparty it follows that the vessel must have been identified.

(e) The bills must indicate the port of loading and the port of discharge stipulated in the credit. The passages in Article 23.a.ii and iii relating to places of receipt and final destination different from ports of loading and of discharge are omitted. Again this must be because in the circumstances in which charterparty bills are issued these passages would be inappropriate. Likewise the provision in Article 23.a.iii covering 'intended' ports is omitted.

(f) The reference to short form/blank back bills is omitted: for a charterparty bill is by definition just such a bill.

(g) The provisions relating to transhipment are omitted: for a bill which is subject to a charterparty supposes the one vessel.

(h) Article 25.b excuses banks from examining the charterparty even if it is a document which the credit requires to be presented.

Although it is not indicated in the Article, just as with bills of lading which are not subject to a charterparty, charterparty bills must cover the whole of the carriage. Paragraph 8.77 above therefore applies. But in the context in which charterparty bills are issued this should not be a problem.

1 Case R119, 1984–86.
2 This may be an accident in the drafting. At one stage the owner appeared in the draft for Article 23 but was later removed.

Multimodal transport documents

8.87 Multimodal transport documents are documents which cover at least two different modes of transport, for example, rail and sea, or road and air. Article 26 applies when the credit calls for such a document:

ARTICLE 26 **Multimodal Transport Document**
a. If a Credit calls for a transport document covering at least two different modes of transport (multimodal transport), banks will, unless otherwise stipulated in the Credit, accept a document, however named, which:
i. appears on its face to indicate the name of the carrier or multimodal transport operator and to have been signed or otherwise authenticated by:
(*a*) the carrier or multimodal transport operator or a named agent for or on behalf of the carrier or multimodal transport operator, or
(*b*) the master or a named agent for or on behalf of the master.
Any signature or authentication of the carrier, multimodal transport operator or master must be identified as carrier, multimodal transport operator or master, as the case may be. An agent signing or authenticating for the carrier, multimodal transport operator or master must also indicate the name and the capacity of the party, ie carrier, multimodal transport operator or master, on whose behalf that agent is acting,
and
ii. indicates that the goods have been dispatched, taken in charge or loaded on board.
Dispatch, taking in charge or loading on board may be indicated by wording to that effect on the multimodal transport document and the date of issuance will be deemed to be the date of dispatch, taking in charge or loading on board and the date of shipment. However, if the document indicates, by stamp or otherwise, a date of dispatch, taking in charge or loading on board, such date will be deemed to be the date of shipment,
and
iii. (*a*) indicates the place of taking in charge stipulated in the Credit which may be different from the port, airport or place of loading, and the place of final destination stipulated in the Credit which may be different from the port, airport or place of discharge, and/or
(*b*) contains the indication "intended" or similar qualification in relation to the vessel and/or port of loading and/or port of discharge,
and

iv. consists of a sole original multimodal transport document or, if issued in more than one original, the full set as so issued,
and

v. appears to contain all of the terms and conditions of carriage, or some of such terms and conditions by reference to a source or document other than the multimodal transport document (short form/blank back multimodal transport document); banks will not examine the contents of such terms and conditions,
and

vi. contains no indication that it is subject to a charter party and/or no indication that the carrying vessel is propelled by sail only,
and

vii. in all other respects meets the stipulations of the Credit.

b. Even if the Credit prohibits transhipment, banks will accept a multimodal transport document which indicates that transhipment will or may take place, provided that the entire carriage is covered by one and the same multimodal transport document.

8.88 Article 26 follows the same form as Article 23, and so having commented fully on Article 23 it is again convenient to compare the two:

(a) Article 26 applies where the credit calls for a transport document covering at least two different modes of transport.

(b) The document must indicate the name of the carrier or multimodal transport operator. They must sign or authenticate it. Alternatively it may be signed by the master, or a named agent for them or the master. The agent must indicate the name and capacity of the party he is acting for, in the same way, mutatis mutandis, as is provided by Article 23 – Article 26.a.i.

(c) The documents must indicate that the goods have been dispatched, taken in charge or loaded on board. Where the document shows a date of dispatch etc by a stamp or otherwise, that date is to be taken as the date of shipment: otherwise the date of issue of the document is to be taken as the date of shipment (Article 26.a.ii, cf Article 23.a.ii).

(d) It must indicate the place of taking in charge and the place of final destination stipulated in the credit. These may be different from the ports, airports or places of loading and unloading respectively (Article 26.a.iii.a, cf Article 23.a.iii.a).

(e) Any vessel and the port of loading and of discharge may be qualified as 'intended' or similarly (Article 26.a.iii.b, cf Article 23.a.iii.b).

(f) It must not indicate that it is subject to a charterparty (Article 26.a.vi – as Article 23.a.vi).

(g) Even where the credit prohibits transhipment, the document may show that transhipment will or may take place, provided that the entire carriage is covered by the one document[1] (Article 26.b – cf Article 23.d).

1 See para 8.77 above.

Air transport documents

8.89 Air transport documents usually take the form of an air waybill. International carriage by air is covered by international Conventions, in particular by the Hague-Warsaw Convention.[1] An air waybill is a document made out in three original parts by the consignor. One part is designated for the carrier and is signed by the consignor. One part is designated for the consignee: it is signed by the consignor and the carrier and accompanies the cargo. The third is designated for the consignor: it is signed by the carrier and is handed to the consignor after the acceptance of the cargo. On the arrival of the cargo at destination the consignee is entitled to have the second original handed to him. It will be seen that the only original available to the consignor and therefore which the consignor/beneficiary can present under a credit is the third original signed by the carrier.

1 Made part of English law by the Carriage by Air Act 1961 which sets out the Convention as the First Schedule. The Montreal amendments to the Hague-Warsaw Convention giving rise to the Hague-Warsaw-Montreal Convention which is set out as Schedule 1 to the Carriage by Air and Road Act 1979, have not yet been brought into force.

8.90 Air transport documents did not previously have their own Article in the Uniform Customs, but were covered by the portmanteau Article 25 in the 1983 Revision. Article 27 now provides:

ARTICLE 27 **Air Transport Document**

a. If a Credit calls for an air transport document, banks will, unless otherwise stipulated in the Credit, accept a document, however named, which:

i. appears on its face to indicate the name of the carrier and to have been signed or otherwise authenticated by:
    (*a*) the carrier, or
    (*b*) a named agent for or on behalf of the carrier.
    Any signature or authentication of the carrier must be identified as carrier. An agent signing or authenticating for the carrier must also indicate the name and the capacity of the party, ie carrier, on whose behalf that agent is acting,
    and

ii. indicates that the goods have been accepted for carriage,
    and

iii. where the Credit calls for an actual date of dispatch, indicates a specific notation of such date, the date of dispatch so indicated on the air transport document will be deemed to be the date of shipment.
    For the purposes of this Article, the information appearing in the box on the air transport document (marked 'For Carrier Use Only' or similar expression) relative to the flight number and date will not be considered as a specific notation of such date of dispatch.
    In all other cases, the date of issuance of the air transport document will be deemed to be the date of shipment,
    and

iv. indicates the airport of departure and the airport of destination stipulated in the Credit,
    and

v. appears to be the original for consignor/shipper even if the Credit stipulates a full set of originals, or similar expressions,
    and

vi. appears to contain all of the terms and conditions of carriage, or some of such terms and conditions, by reference to a source or document other than the air transport document; banks will not examine the contents of such terms and conditions,
and
vii. in all other respects meets the stipulations of the Credit.
b. For the purposes of this Article, transhipment means unloading and reloading from one aircraft to another aircraft during the course of carriage from the airport of departure to the airport of destination stipulated in the Credit.
c. Even if the Credit prohibits transhipment, banks will accept an air transport document which indicates that transhipment will or may take place, provided that the entire carriage is covered by one and the same air transport document.

8.91 It will be seen that:

(a) Article 27.a.i requires the name of the carrier to appear and the document to be signed or authenticated by the carrier or on his behalf. These provisions broadly follow those of Article 23.a.i, which have been considered in paragraph 8.62 above.

(b) Article 27.a.v requires the document to be the original for the consignor/shipper, thus identifying it as the third original referred to in paragraph 8.88 above. Any reference in the credit to a full set of originals may be ignored: it is inappropriate – air waybills are not issued in sets to the consignor like bills of lading but as has been described.

(c) It must show that the goods have been accepted for carriage – Article 27.a.ii.

(d) Where the credit requires an actual date of despatch to be shown, there must be a specific notification of the date of despatch (Article 27.a.iii). That is then the date of shipment. Such a requirement is not satisfied by the appearance of a flight number and date in the box on the document marked 'For carrier use only' or with a similar expression: a separate notification is required.

(e) Where the credit does not call for an actual date of despatch, the date of issue is to be taken as the date of shipment (Article 23.a.iii).

(f) It must show the airport of departure and of destination (Article 23.a.iv).

(g) It must either show all the terms and conditions of carriage itself or show them by reference to another source: but banks will not examine them (Article 27.a.vi).

(h) Transhipment as defined by Article 27.b is permissible even though the credit prohibits it, provided that the entire carriage is covered by the one document. This takes account of the realities of air transport and the non-availability of direct flights between many airports.[1]

1 As indicated in Case R.124 in Opinions of the ICC Banking Commission 1984–86, Publication No 434.

8.92 Difficulties have arisen in the past concerning house air waybills, that is, air waybills issued not by an airline but by freight forwarders or consolidators. Cases 78 to 82 in the ICC's Case Studies on Documentary Credits and Case 232 in the ICC's More Case Studies concern these problems.

The position is the same as for the issue of marine documents by non-vessel-owning carriers considered in paragraph 8.62 above. Thus the waybill must either be signed by the freight forwarder as carrier, or as agent for the actual carrier. Further, that it is so signed must appear on the face of the waybill. So a house air waybill is acceptable where the issuer/signatory puts his name to it as carrier. A house air waybill issued by a forwarder as forwarder but countersigned by the carrier airline appears acceptable.[1]

1 Case 81 in Case Studies on Documentary Credits, ICC Publication No 459.

Road, rail or inland waterway transport documents

8.93 A provision in a credit for a road, rail or inland waterway transport document will be governed by Article 28, which therefore covers some disparate transport forms. The Article provides:

ARTICLE 28   **Road, Rail or Inland Waterway Transport Documents**

a. If a Credit calls for a road, rail, or inland waterway transport document, banks will, unless otherwise stipulated in the Credit, accept a document of the type called for, however named, which:

  i.   appears on its face to indicate the name of the carrier and to have been signed or otherwise authenticated by the carrier or a named agent for or on behalf of the carrier and/or to bear a reception stamp or other indication of receipt by the carrier or a named agent for or on behalf of the carrier.

      Any signature, authentication, reception stamp or other indication of receipt of the carrier, must be identified on its face as that of the carrier. An agent signing or authenticating for the carrier, must also indicate the name and the capacity of the party, ie carrier, on whose behalf that agent is acting, and

  ii. indicates that the goods have been received for shipment, dispatch or carriage or wording to this effect. The date of issuance will be deemed to be the date of shipment unless the transport document contains a reception stamp, in which case the date of the reception stamp will be deemed to be the date of shipment, and

  iii. indicates the place of shipment and the place of destination stipulated in the Credit, and

  iv. in all other respects meets the stipulations of the Credit.

b. In the absence of any indication on the transport document as to the numbers issued, banks will accept the transport document(s) presented as constituting a full set. Banks will accept as original(s) the transport document(s) whether marked as original(s) or not.

c. For the purpose of this Article, transhipment means unloading and reloading from one means of conveyance to another means of conveyance, in different modes of transport, during the course of carriage from the place of shipment to the place of destination stipulated in the Credit.

d. Even if the Credit prohibits transhipment, banks will accept a road, rail, or inland waterway transport document which indicates that transhipment will or may take place, provided that the entire carriage is covered by one and the same transport document and within the same mode of transport.

8.94 The features provided for by the Article are:

(a) It must give the name of the carrier and be signed or authenticated by or on behalf of the carrier, as is required also by Article 23.[1]

(b) It must show that the goods[2] have been received for shipment etc. The date of issue is deemed the date of shipment unless there is a reception stamp (whose date is then deemed the date of shipment).

(c) It must show the places of shipment and destination stipulated in the credit.

(d) A full set of documents must be presented: but unless the numbers on the documents presented indicate otherwise the documents presented will be accepted as a full set. The documents need not be marked as original.

(e) Even if prohibited by the credit transhipment is acceptable provided that the entire carriage is covered by the one document and is within the same mode of transport. So, if more than one mode of transport is to be utilised, the credit should provide for a multimodal transport document as set out in Article 26.

1 See paras 8.62 and 8.63 above.
2 As to the non-acceptability of a groupage rail waybill, see para 8.112, note 4.

Courier and post receipts

8.95 It is curious that before the establishment of a postal system couriers were much in use and now they return to the fore. Article 28.a covers post receipts and certificates of posting: Article 29.b deals with couriers and expedited delivery services. They provide:

ARTICLE 29.a **Courier and Post Receipts**
a. If a Credit calls for a post receipt or certificate of posting, banks will, unless otherwise stipulated in the Credit, accept a post receipt or certificate of posting which:
i. appears on its face to have been stamped or otherwise authenticated and dated in the place from which the Credit stipulates the goods are to be shipped or dispatched and such date will be deemed to be the date of shipment or dispatch,
and
ii. in all other respects meets the stipulations of the Credit.

ARTICLE 29.b b. If a Credit calls for a document issued by a courier or expedited delivery service evidencing receipt of the goods for delivery, banks will, unless otherwise stipulated in the Credit, accept a document, however named, which:
i. appears on its face to indicate the name of the courier/service, and to have been stamped, signed or otherwise authenticated by such named courier/service (unless the Credit specifically calls for a document issued by a named Courier/Service, banks will accept a document issued by any Courier/Service),
and
ii. indicates a date of pick-up or of receipt or wording to this effect, such date being deemed to be the date of shipment or dispatch,
and
iii. in all other respects meets the stipulations of the Credit.

8.96 Article 29.a simply requires that unless the credit requires more, where a post receipt or certificate of posting is called for, the document must appear to have been stamped or authenticated and dated in the place of shipment or despatch given by the credit. That date is deemed to be the date of shipment or despatch.

8.97 Article 29.b requires that the document should indicate the name of the courier or expedited delivery service and have been stamped, signed or otherwise authenticated by it. Any courier or service will be accepted unless one is named in the credit. The document must also show a date of pick up or receipt (or similar): that date is deemed to be the date of shipment or dispatch.

Provisions relating to transport documents generally

8.98 *Transport documents issued by freight forwarders* Unless the credit authorises otherwise, a freight forwarder's name may only[1] appear on a transport document if the freight forwarder is and is stated to be the carrier, or if the freight forwarder signs or authenticates the document as agent for the carrier.[2] Article 30 provides:

> ARTICLE 30 **Transport Documents issued by Freight Forwarders**
> Unless otherwise authorised in the Credit, banks will only accept a transport document issued by a freight forwarder if it appears on its face to indicate:
> i. the name of the freight forwarder as a carrier or multimodal transport operator and to have been signed or otherwise authenticated by the freight forwarder as carrier or multimodal transport operator,
> or
> ii. the name of the carrier or multimodal transport operator and to have been signed or otherwise authenticated by the freight forwarder as a named agent for or on behalf of the carrier or multimodal transport operator.

Paragraph 8.62 deals with the requirement to name the carrier and with the exclusion[3] of freight forwarder bills unless Article 30 is complied with.

1 The 1974 Revision had rejected freight forwarder bills completely. The 1983 Revision permitted them in similar terms to the 1993 Revision.
2 For an example of how this may be done, see Case 83 in the ICC's Case Studies on Documentary Credits, Publication No 459.
3 Subject to the credit authorising otherwise.

8.99 *Carriage on deck* Unless the credit provides otherwise, where the credit includes carriage by sea, a positive statement in a transport document that goods will be carried on deck makes the document unacceptable. One which refers to the possibility only is acceptable. Article 31.i provides:

> ARTICLE 31.i[1] Unless otherwise stipulated in the Credit, banks will accept a transport document which:
> i. does not indicate, in the case of carriage by sea or by more than one means of conveyance including carriage by sea, that the goods are or will be loaded on deck. Nevertheless, banks will accept a transport document which contains a provision that the goods may be carried on deck, provided that it does not specifically state that they are or will be loaded on deck.

It has always been the practice of banks to refuse bills showing stowage on deck because of the additional likelihood of damage to goods so stowed. In view of the construction of many container vessels whereby the containers are stacked several high on a low deck, the situation is today rather altered. Article 31.i does not state what the position is if the credit specifically prohibits loading on deck, or calls for under-deck loading. In Gutteridge & Megrah[2] it is stated that where a credit calls for shipment under deck, a bill of lading will not be accepted unless it states categorically that the goods are shipped under deck, even if the goods are such as would normally be so carried and the bills do not show to the contrary. It is suggested that this is right. The documents to be presented must show on their face that the terms of the credit have been complied with. Article 31.i is not relevant to the solution of this problem.

1 Article 31.i is taken from Article 28 in the 1983 Revision.
2 *The Law of Bankers' Commercial Credits* (7th edn) p 156.

8.100 ***'Shipper's load and count'*** A transport document which is claused 'shipper's load and count' or 'said by shipper to contain' or such like is acceptable unless the credit provides otherwise. Article 31.ii provides:

> ARTICLE 31.ii[1] Unless otherwise stipulated in the Credit, banks will accept a transport document which:
>
> . . .
>
> ii. bears a clause on the face thereof such as 'shipper's load and count' or 'said by shipper to contain' or words of similar effect.

The effect of such a clausing is that the carrier is not bound by the quantity or weight declared to him by the consignor and which he would otherwise acknowledge by the bill of lading. The need to be able to clause bills in this way is greatly increased by the use of containers: unless the carrier has put the goods into the container himself it is only in exceptional circumstances that he will check the contents. Bills of lading frequently contain a printed clause stating 'weight, measure, quantity, contents and value unknown'. This does not render the bill unclean. Nor does it qualify an acknowledgement of apparent condition.[2]

1 Article 31.ii follows Article 32 in the 1983 Revision.
2 See *M Golodetz & Co Inc v Czarnikow-Rionda Co Inc* [1980] 1 WLR 495 at 512 per Donaldson J whose decision was not taken to appeal on this point.

8.101 ***Name of consignor*** The credit may stipulate who should be the consignor or shipper of the goods named in the transport document. If it does not, the consignor so named need not be the beneficiary under the credit, ie the seller. This takes account of the possibility that the beneficiary may well be a purchaser in a string or otherwise from a third party who has shipped the goods. Article 31.iii of the Uniform Customs thus provides:

> ARTICLE 31.iii[1] Unless otherwise stipulated in the Credit, banks will accept a transport document which:
>
> . . .
>
> iii. indicates as the consignor of the goods a party other than the Beneficiary of the Credit.

1 Article 31.iii follows Article 33 in the 1983 Revision.

8.102 ***Clean transport documents*[1]** It is usual for credits to state expressly that bills of lading or other transport documents must be clean. Under the Uniform Customs, clean transport documents are required unless the credit expressly stipulates the clauses or notations which may be accepted.[2] At common law, in nearly all circumstances clean bills would be required even if the credit was silent on the point. In *British Imex Industries Ltd v Midland Bank Ltd*[3] Salmon J stated:[4]

'The letter of credit stipulated that payment would be made against bills of lading without qualification. The plaintiffs suggest that this does not necessarily mean clean bills of lading. In my judgment, when a credit calls for bills of lading, in normal circumstances it means clean bills of lading. I think that in normal circumstances the ordinary business man who undertakes to pay against the presentation of bills of lading means clean bills of lading: and he would probably consider that that was so obvious to any other business man that it was hardly necessary to state it. That seems to have been the view taken by Bailhache J in *National Bank of Egypt v Hannevig's Bank*. I entirely agree with it. No doubt, as was pointed out by the Court of Appeal in that case, (1919) 1 Ll L Rep 69 and 3 Legal Decisions Affecting Bankers 213 there may be circumstances where, for instance, business has been disorganized by war, in which a credit against bills of lading is not necessarily a credit against clean bills of lading. That is a point which it is unnecessary to decide in this case, for here there are no special circumstances, and I read "bills of lading" in the letter of credit as meaning clean bills of lading. A "clean bill of lading" has never been exhaustively defined, and I certainly do not propose to attempt that task now. I incline to the view, however, that a clean bill of lading is one that does not contain any reservation as to the apparent good order or condition of the goods or the packing. In my judgment, the bills of lading in this case are plainly clean bills of lading. They contain no reservation by way of endorsement, clausing or otherwise, to suggest that the goods or the packing are or may be defective in any respect.'

Reference may also be made to *Hannevig's* case (where the Court of Appeal's doubt that in the particular circumstances clean bills would have been required even in the absence of a direction to accept claused bills was no doubt influenced by the need to encourage trade in wartime and the very fact of that direction) and to *Westminster Bank v Banca Nazionale di Credito*[5] where Roche J commented on the conflict in *Hannevig's* case between the view of Bailhache J and that of the Court of Appeal arising on the particular facts of the case.[6] In *M Golodetz & Co v Czarnikow-Rionda, the Galatria*[7] Donaldson J held and it was accepted in the Court of Appeal that in the context of a CIF contract a 'clean bill' is one in which there is nothing to qualify the admission by the carrier that the goods were in apparent good order and condition at the time of shipment. It was accepted by the buyers in the Court of Appeal that the bill (which was claused to the effect that the goods had been damaged by fire after shipment and had had to be discharged) was clean in that sense. A wider argument was advanced that the bill was not 'clean' in the sense that it was not a document that would ordinarily and properly have been accepted in the trade as being an appropriate document, citing the dictum of Lord Sumner from *Hansson v Hamel and Horley Ltd*.[8] The Court of Appeal held that as the arbitrators had not found that the bill was not reasonably and readily fit to pass current in commerce, the bill was 'clean' in the wider sense.[9] (It may be helpful to point out that the loss of the goods subsequent to loading does not entitle the buyer under a CIF contract not to take up the documents: he must take up the documents and pay for them, and his remedy is against the carrier or on the insurance. Thus in *Manbre Saccharine Co v Corn Products Co*[10] the vessel was sunk on 12 March 1917 and the sellers were held entitled to make a good tender on 14 March despite their knowledge of the loss. The argument in *Golodetz* was not based on the loss of the cargo but on the clausing of the bill.)

1 The ICC publishes a pamphlet entitled 'Clean Transport Documents', ICC Publication No 473.
2 Article 32, which is considered in para 8.103 below.
3 [1958] 1 QB 542.
4 Ibid at 551.
5 (1928) 31 Ll L Rep 306.
6 Ibid at 311.
7 [1980] 1 WLR 495; see para 8.32.
8 [1922] 2 AC 36 at 46.
9 For a discussion of this conclusion, see paras 8.33 and 8.34 above.
10 [1919] 1 KB 198.

8.103 The Uniform Customs define a clean transport document in Article 32, which states:

ARTICLE 32 **Clean Transport Documents**
  a. A clean transport document is one which bears no clause or notation which expressly declares a defective condition of the goods and/or the packaging.
  b. Banks will not accept transport documents bearing such clauses or notations unless the Credit expressly stipulates the clauses or notations which may be accepted.
  c. Banks will regard a requirement in a Credit for a transport document to bear the clause 'clean on board' as complied with if such transport document meets the requirements of this Article and of Articles 23, 24, 25, 26, 27, 28 or 30.

Article 32 closely follows Article 34 of the 1983 Revision. Article 34 referred to a 'superimposed clause or notation'. 'Superimposed' has gone, presumably because it was unnecessary. It will be seen that:

(i) Even where a credit expressly calls for 'clean on board' bills of lading, or bills marked 'clean on board', it is not necessary for the words 'clean on board' to appear: Article 32.c covers this situation and the requirement is deemed to be complied with if the bills bear no clause or notation declaring a defective condition of the goods.[1] A notation declaring a defect need not be signed, initialled or authenticated.[2]

(ii) The definition is confined to the narrow sense of 'clean' (see the discussion of *Golodetz* in para 8.102 above) and follows the common law view as expressed in the *British Imex* and *Golodetz* cases. It is suggested that the wider objection to a bill which was sought to be advanced in *Golodetz* that, because of a clausing or notation, it would not be fit to pass current in the trade, is unaffected by the Article, which is not seeking to deal with that situation.

(iii) The Article does not refer to the time to which any clause or notation should relate. As Donaldson J remarked in *Golodetz*[3] the crucial time as between the shipowner and shipper including those who claim through the shipper as holders of the bill of lading is the time of shipment. It is to this time that the clause or notation must relate. It is perhaps surprising that after the problems in *Golodetz* the Uniform Customs still do not make this clear.

(iv) Paragraph (b) makes clear that the ordinary position is that the bills must be clean, even if the credit is silent on the point. For documents which are claused are to be rejected 'unless the credit expressly stipulates the clauses or notation which may be accepted'.

1 Case R 130, Opinions of the ICC Banking Commission 1984–86, Publication No 434.
2 There is no requirement in the Article: see also Case 242 in the ICC's More Case Studies on Documentary Credits, Publication No 489.
3 [1980] 1 WLR 495 at 510.

8.104 *Reservations not rendering a bill of lading unclean*   Article 31.ii of the Uniform Customs has been set out in paragraph 100 and reservations on a bill as to quantity etc are considered there.

8.105 *Clean bills of lading given against indemnity*   Where a carrier is minded to clause a transport document with a notation which would render it unclean, the shipper may attempt to avoid this by offering the carrier, in return for the issue of a clean transport document, an indemnity against liability asserted against him on the ground that the bill was clean. This is a dangerous and highly undesirable practice. The document so produced may well be considered to be a fraud on the transferee of the bill who will take delivery of the goods. As the indemnity is a part of the fraud and is against the consequences of fraud, it will be unenforceable.[1] A bank which gives the indemnity, or which is involved in its preparation, may be held party to the fraud.

1 *Brown, Jenkinson & Co Ltd v Percy Dalton (London) Ltd* [1957] 2 QB 621.

8.106 *Freight*   Under a CIF contract the general rule is that a seller has an option: he can pay the freight and provide pre-paid bills of lading, or he can provide what are called freight collect bills and invoice the CIF price less freight (freight collect bills are bills under which the freight is payable by the receiver of the goods).[1] This is, of course, subject to any relevant provision of the particular contract. The position under a letter of credit is the same. The seller has a choice unless the credit provides that the freight must be prepaid. In *Soproma SpA v Marine and Animal By-Products Corpn*[2] the credit required 'Full set clean on board ocean B/L issued to the order and blank endorsed; destination Sarona, marked "freight prepaid".' The bills of lading rendered were marked 'freight collect'. McNair J referred to the arbitrators' finding that freight collect bills were commonly regarded as a good tender provided freight was either deducted from the invoice or shown to have been paid by the freight receipt. He continued:

'If this finding means more than that it commonly happens that buyers do not take the objection that a bill of lading in this form is not a valid tender if either the freight is deducted from the price in the invoice or a receipt for freight is tendered, it would, as it seems to me, be a finding which could not be sustainable in law since on the hypothesis stated the documents would be mutually inconsistent.'

It is not clear what documents he was referring to as being inconsistent. If freight was deducted from the invoice, this would not be inconsistent with the bill of lading being marked 'freight collect'. Nor would it be clear that a freight collect bill was inconsistent with a receipt. He must have meant that the marking on the bill of lading was inconsistent with the express provision of the credit, which is surely the point.

1 See *Sassoon on C.I.F. and F.O.B. Contracts* British Shipping Laws, Volume 5, para 104–107 and *The Pantanassa* [1970] 1 All ER 848 at 855.
2 [1966] 1 Lloyd's Rep 367.

8.107 Article 33 of the Uniform Customs now provides:

ARTICLE 33[1]   **Freight Payable/Prepaid Transport Documents**
a. Unless otherwise stipulated in the Credit, or inconsistent with any of the documents presented under the Credit, banks will accept transport documents stating that freight or transportation charges (hereafter referred to as 'freight') have still to be paid.
b. If a Credit stipulates that the transport document has to indicate that freight has been paid or prepaid, banks will accept a transport document on which words clearly indicating payment or prepayment of freight appear by stamp or otherwise, or on which payment or prepayment of freight is indicated by other means. If the Credit requires courier charges to be paid or prepaid banks will also accept a transport document issued by a courier or expedited delivery service evidencing that courier charges are for the account of a party other than the consignee.
c. The words 'freight prepayable' or 'freight to be prepaid' or words of similar effect, if appearing on transport documents, will not be accepted as constituting evidence of the payment of freight.
d. Banks will accept transport documents bearing reference by stamp or otherwise to costs additional to the freight, such as costs of, or disbursements incurred in connection with, loading, unloading or similar operations, unless the conditions of the Credit specifically prohibit such reference.

The reference in paragraph (a) to inconsistency with any other documents presented under the credit is likely to be mainly directed at the need for the invoice to show the deduction of freight where the bills are freight collect.[2] A point arose on the predecessor of paragraph (d) in *Banque de l'Indochine v J H Rayner Ltd.*[3] The credit called for documents covering shipment of sugar at a specified price 'Cost and freight liner out of Djibouti'. It was agreed that this meant that freight covered all costs up to and including discharge at Djibouti. The Court of Appeal, differing from the judge on this point, held that this was a prohibition in terms of the then Article 16(d), and that, as the bill of lading contained a clause 'not portmarked, vessel not responsible for incorrect delivery. Any extra expense incurred in consequence to be borne by consignee', the bill contemplated additional charges for getting the sugar to Djibouti and was to be rejected. Where a credit indicates that the goods are to be delivered on FOB terms, bills of lading which are marked freight pre-paid are acceptable provided that first the credit terms do not provide to the contrary and second that the price on the commercial invoice is the FOB price and does not include freight.[4]

1 This closely follows Article 31 of the 1983 Revision save that the second sentence of Article 33.b is new.
2 See also para 8.55 above.

3 [1983] QB 711.
4 See Reference 126, Opinions of the ICC Banking Commission, ICC Publication No 434.

8.108 *Partial shipments*   The credit may prohibit partial shipments. If it does not, they are allowed. Article 40 of the Uniform Customs provides for this and also provides that certain shipments are not to be regarded as partial shipments and therefore as caught by a prohibition. It states:

> ARTICLE 40[1]   **Partial Shipments/Drawings**
> a. Partial drawings and/or shipments are allowed, unless the Credit stipulates otherwise.
> b. Transport documents which appear on their face to indicate that shipment has been made on the same means of conveyance and for the same journey, provided they indicate the same destination, will not be regarded as covering partial shipments, even if the transport documents indicate different dates of shipment and/or different ports of loading, places of taking in charge, or despatch.
> c. Shipments made by post or by courier will not be regarded as partial shipments if the post receipts or certificates of posting or courier's receipts or dispatch notes appear to have been stamped, signed or otherwise authenticated in the place from which the Credit stipulates the goods are to be dispatched, and on the same date.

The reference in Article 40.b to 'made on the same means of conveyance and for the same journey' is comparable with 'made on the same vessel and for the same voyage' in Article 44.b in the 1983 Revision. Drafting documents show that no change of meaning is intended and that the change results from the modification of Article 44.b to cover all forms of transport (save post and courier) in Article 40.b.

Where partial shipments are made, the documents should nonetheless be presented to the bank in a single presentation unless the credit permits drawings by instalments or shipments by instalments. For unless that liberty is given, the documents are bound to be rejected: for they will not be for the correct quantity if they are presented in part. Where the credit provides for drawings and/or shipments within given periods, failure to ship or draw within one period means that the credit ceases to be available for that and any subsequent instalments unless the credit otherwise provides: see Article 41.[2]

1 Although redrafted, Article 40 is to the same effect as Article 44 in the 1983 Revision.
2 Considered at paras 5.28 above.

8.109 *Date of shipment and presentation*   The Articles relating to specific types of transport document contain provisions to identify the date of shipment or of despatch. The date may be relevant in three respects.

(a) The credit may well provide a period for shipment or a latest date for shipment. Bills of lading or other transport documents not adhering to the provision will be rejected: see Chapter 5,[1] where Article 46 of the Uniform Customs is referred to and set out.

1 Para 5.26.

8.110 (b) Bills of lading and other transport documents must be issued on shipment. This is considered in paragraph 8.79 above.

8.111 (c) The credit should provide a period after the date of issue of the bills of lading or other transport documents within which the documents must be presented to the bank: Article 43.a. The concept of 'stale' transport documents and Article 43 are considered in Chapter 5 under the heading 'Time for Presentation of Documents'.[1] Article 22[2] should also be noted. It provides that it is no bar to the acceptance of a document that it bears a date of issue prior to the date of the credit.

1 Para 5.24.
2 See para 8.39 above.

8.112 ***Description and identification of goods in transport documents*** Transport documents other than courier and post receipts (ie those falling within Articles 23 to 28, but not Article 29) must indicate that 'the goods have been loaded on board or shipped' to take the wording of Article 23. So they must show that there is a contract of carriage relating to 'the goods' and that 'the goods' have been placed with the carrier. 'The goods' must be the goods for which the applicant is being invoiced. Whereas the description may be in terms which are not inconsistent with the terms of the invoice and the credit,[1] the quantity must of course state the quantity in the same terms as the invoice or in a manner which can be directly related to the invoice quantity as being the same: see, for an example of where this could not be done, *London and Foreign Trading Corpn v British and Northern European Bank*.[2] Another example is given in Case 250 in the ICC's More Case Studies on Documentary Credits.[3] There the bill of lading referred to 25 containers with their numbers. The invoice referred to 25 containers but did not give their numbers. The majority view of the group of experts was that because the documents were consistent in a number of respects (same letter of credit reference, same description of goods, number of containers and net weight) they complied with the requirements of the credit: it was unnecessary for the container numbers to be shown on the invoice. It is suggested that this is indeed correct. On the other hand the transport document must not cover additional goods: if it does it is unacceptable.[4] This may well happen in situations where there has been 'groupage' of the relevant goods with other goods.

1 See Article 37.c and para 8.25 et seq above.
2 (1921) 9 Ll L Rep 116, considered more fully in para 8.45 above.
3 ICC Publication No 489.
4 Bills of lading, see Case R.65 in Decisions (1975–79) of the ICC Banking Commission, Publication No 371; groupage rail waybill, see Case 233 in the ICC's More Case Studies on Documentary Credits, Publication No 489.

3. Insurance Documents

8.113 ***Instructions and the risks to be covered*** The importance of compliance with Article 5.b – all instructions for the issue of credits should state precisely the documents against which payment is to be made, is emphasised by the provisions of Article 35.a and .b. They provide:

ARTICLE 35.a[1] **Type of Insurance Cover**
Credits should stipulate the type of insurance required and, if any, the additional risks which are to be covered. Imprecise terms such as 'usual risks' or 'customary risks' shall not be used; if they are used, banks will accept insurance documents as presented, without responsibility for any risks not being covered.

ARTICLE 35.b[1]   Failing specific stipulations in the Credit, banks will accept insurance documents as presented, without responsibility for any risks not being covered.

In most cases, the trade being one in which the buyer is experienced, the buyer will have no difficulty in specifying the cover that he requires. In other cases it is important that he should give appropriate consideration and seek advice as necessary. For the terms to be used in specifying terms of insurance cover can be highly technical. Then the requirement should be stated in the credit with precision but without undue complexity.

1 Articles 35.a and .b repeat Articles 38.a and .b in the 1983 Revision.

8.114   It is suggested that Article 35 will not entitle a bank to accept an insurance document without any examination of its content. The insurance document must comply with the other Articles of the Uniform Customs relating to insurance and it must provide at least basic cover in respect of the relevant goods for the relevant carriage. The Article should be regarded more as a protection for banks where inadequate instructions have been incorporated into the credit and where particular risks which have not been referred to in the credit are not covered by the policy. An example may be taken from a case prior to the Uniform Customs. In *Borthwick v Bank of New Zealand*[1] the issuing bank negotiated documents including a draft which it passed to the buyer for acceptance. A partial loss of the goods took place which could not be recovered under the policy included with the tender because the policy contained a clause 'to pay a total loss by total loss of vessel only'. The credit referred simply to 'shipping documents, (ie bills of lading invoice and insurance policy)'. Evidence was given that in the particular trade it was usual to include with the shipping documents an 'all risks' policy. As the bank was in breach of its duty in checking the documents to see if they were acceptable, it was held liable to reimburse its customer, the buyer. It is improbable that today the bank would be held liable on the basis of a customer in the particular trade. Nonetheless a policy which will only pay as per the clause quoted may be thought to provide cover which is clearly defective. It is suggested that in such an extreme case the result should be the same today and Article 35 would not protect a bank where a policy was tendered which was so obviously defective. 'All risks' cover is considered separately below.[2]

1 (1900) 17 TLR 2, 6 Com Cas 1.
2 Para 8.115.

8.115   *All risks*   The expression 'all risks' is often used and its meaning has been the subject of a number of decisions.[1] The difficulties which it poses are substantially avoided by Article 36, which provides:

ARTICLE 36[2]   **All Risks Insurance Cover**
Where a Credit stipulates 'insurance against all risks', banks will accept an insurance document which contains any 'all risks' notation or clause, whether or not bearing the heading 'all risks', even if the insurance document indicates that certain risks are excluded, without responsibility for any risk(s) not being covered.

The insurance document need not have an 'all risks' heading and it does not matter that certain risks are excluded, provided that the document contains an 'all risks' notation or clause. The Article does not contain words to make its effect subject to any provisions of the credit. But obviously this must be so. There must also be some limit to the risks that can be excluded. It is suggested that this is a matter for the bank to consider. If the cover provided is so cut down by the exclusions that it would clearly fall short of the cover to be reasonably expected for the transaction in question, it should be rejected.

1 See *Sassoon on CIF & FOB Contracts* (3rd edn) paras 190–193.
2 Article 36 is taken without material change from Article 39 in the 1983 Revision.

8.116 *The document to be issued* Article 34.a to .c provides:

ARTICLE 34[1] **Insurance Documents**
   a. Insurance documents must appear on their face to be issued and signed by insurance companies or underwriters or their agents.
   b. If the insurance document indicates that it has been issued in more than one original, all the originals must be presented unless otherwise authorised in the Credit.
   c. Cover notes issued by brokers will not be accepted, unless specifically authorised in the Credit.

There appears strictly to be a conflict between paragraph (a) and paragraph (c). For the latter part of (a) beginning 'and must be issued . . .' would prohibit a cover note issued by a broker even if the credit permitted it. That cannot be the intention: the two paragraphs must be read together. A cover note issued by a broker is commonly issued by the broker as his own indication that he has arranged cover. It is not issued with the authority of the insurer. Where a broker has that authority and so acts as agent of the insurer, the position is different. The unacceptability of a broker's cover note was considered, probably obiter, in the early case of *Wilson, Holgate & Co v Belgian Grain and Produce Co Ltd*.[2]

1 Article 34.a is derived from Article 35.a in the 1983 Revision, Article 34.b is new. Article 34.c follows Article 35.b in the 1983 Revision.
2 1920 2 KB 1.

8.117 Article 34.d is a new provision and deals with *open covers*. An open cover is a policy issued by an insurer which enables a named party, perhaps a broker or an underwriting agent or, less often, a party through whose hands goods pass, to make declarations under it of risks which fall within the risks permitted by the cover. Article 34.d provides:

ARTICLE 34.d Unless otherwise stipulated in the Credit, banks will accept an insurance certificate or a declaration under an open cover pre-signed by insurance companies or underwriters or their agents. If a Credit specifically calls for an insurance certificate or a declaration under an open cover, banks will accept, in lieu thereof, an insurance policy.

So, unless the credit provides otherwise, an open cover can be used. Where the credit calls for a policy, is this to be taken as a contrary stipulation in the credit, so Article 34.d will not apply? It is suggested that it is. The Article does not permit the use of open cover documents where a policy is called for.

8.118 The Article provides that the certificate or declaration must be 'pre-signed' by the insurance company, an underwriter, or an agent for either. Underwriter is simply the appropriate expression for the insurer where there are individuals as on Lloyds. The requirement for pre-signing is curious. Does it mean that the issuer of the certificate or declaration must have been supplied in advance with pre-signed forms? It is suggested that the issuer will often have the authority of the insurer to sign the document on the insurer's behalf and so he will fall within the wording of the Article as 'agent'. It seems ridiculous to suggest that he must pre-sign. In any event how is the bank examining the documents to tell whether a certificate has been pre-signed or not? It is suggested that the requirement for pre-signing may have little significance in practice.

8.119 A problem arising with certificates or declarations issued under open covers is that they do not usually set out the full terms of the insurance. It is suggested that where by reason of the Article an open cover document is acceptable, it will not be defective simply because it refers to the terms of the policy itself which will be unknown to the bank and which cannot be examined by the bank. Nonetheless it must contain sufficient information to show that the terms of the credit as to insurance have been complied with. It is suggested that the position is different in this respect to that without the Article. In the early case of *Donald H Scott & Co Ltd v Barclays Bank Ltd*[1] the document tendered was a certificate of insurance that the goods were insured under a policy having a particular number. As Bankes LJ stated[2] 'That only indicates that a policy has been issued by this company; but the terms of that policy, the risks insured against, and the conditions imposed by the policy respecting shipment can only be ascertained by reference to some document which did not accompany the certificate and of which [the bank] could know nothing.'[3]

1 [1923] 2 KB 1.
2 Ibid at 12.
3 See also *Diamond Alkali Export Corpn v Bourgeois* [1921] 3 KB 443 and *Malmberg v Evans & Co* (1924) 41 TLR 38.

8.120 Article 34.d also provides that where the credit calls for a certificate or declaration under an open cover, a policy will be acceptable, presumably on the basis that a policy is the better option.

8.121 *Period of cover* By the transport document the carrier usually acknowledges the acceptance of the goods in apparent good order and condition. The insurance should cover the goods from the moment of taking in charge by the carrier to that of delivery at destination. This is reflected in Article 34.e which relates to insurance documents bearing a date later than the date of loading on board, etc as indicated by the transport document. It provides:

> ARTICLE 34.e[1] Unless otherwise stipulated in the Credit, or unless it appears from the insurance document that the cover is effective at the latest from the date of loading on board or dispatch or taking in charge of the goods, banks will not accept an insurance document which bears a date of issuance later than the date of loading on board or dispatch or taking in charge as indicated in such transport document.

1 Taken with slight changes from Article 36 in the 1983 Revision.

8.122 *Currency* If a policy is expressed in a currency different to that of the credit there may be a problem in evaluating the cover provided, and, more importantly, fluctuations in exchange rate could cause the devaluation of the policy. In *Scott & Co Ltd v Barclays Bank Ltd*[1] it was left undecided whether a policy in a foreign currency was acceptable. It is suggested in *Benjamin's Sale of Goods*[2] that the tender of a foreign currency policy under a CIF contract would be good. However, in respect of documentary credits Article 34.f.i of the Uniform Customs states that it must be in the same currency as the credit unless the credit provides otherwise, which avoids these difficulties:

> ARTICLE 34.f.i[3] Unless otherwise stipulated in the Credit, the insurance document must be expressed in the same currency as the Credit.

The fact that the policy is issued abroad should not make it objectionable.

1 [1923] 2 KB 1.
2 (4th edn) para 19–43.
3 Article 34.f.i repeals Article 37.a in the 1983 Revision.

8.123 *Amount* The purpose of the insurance is to cover the goods for their full value under the contract, which is in effect their arrived value and so freight and the cost of insurance during the carriage are to be added. Article 34.f.ii provides for this in the following terms:

> ARTICLE 34.f.ii Unless otherwise stipulated in the Credit, the minimum amount for which the insurance document must indicate the insurance cover to have been effected is the CIF (cost, insurance and freight (. . . 'named port of destination')) or CIP (carriage and insurance paid to (. . . 'named place of destination')) value of the goods, as the case may be, plus 10%, but only when the CIF or CIP value can be determined from the documents on their face. Otherwise, banks will accept as such minimum amount 110% of the amount for which payment, acceptance or negotiation is requested under the Credit, or 110% of the gross amount of the invoice, whichever is the greater.

The CIF and CIP definitions in brackets have been inserted to be in line with the relevant CIF and CIP provisions in Incoterms 1990.[1] The first sentence follows the previous Article 37.b closely. But the second sentence is new and corrects a deficiency in the 1983 Revision, namely that where the CIF or CIP value could not be determined from the documents, the minimum amount of insurance was the greater of the amount for which payment was requested and the amount of the invoice. These amounts might not cover freight and they would not cover the applicant's profit on the goods. The 110% at the end of the new Article now mirrors the 10% referred to earlier in it.

1 The ICC definitions of international commercial terms, Publication No 460.

8.124 Article 35.c provides:

> ARTICLE 35.c[1] Unless otherwise stipulated in the Credit, banks will accept an insurance document which indicates that the cover is subject to a franchise or an excess (deductible).

A franchise is an amount or percentage stated in a policy which must be reached before any claim is payable. If it is reached, then the claim is payable in full. The words which are customarily used to indicate that there is to be no franchise provision are 'irrespective of percentage'. In foreign insurances 'franchise' may be used to mean what in English insurances is termed an 'excess' or a 'deductible'. An excess or deductible is similar to a franchise save that after the amount or percentage is reached only the amount in excess of it is recoverable.[2] The extent to which a deductible or franchise may be acceptable to the buyer obviously depends upon its amount. There is a world of difference between a 2% excess and one of 30%. It is suggested that if an insurance document indicates a franchise or excess which is exceptionally large, it might be rejected despite the terms of Article 40.

1 To the same effect as Article 40 in the 1983 Revision.
2 See the *Dictionary of Marine Insurance Terms* (4th edn).

4. Certificates etc

8.125   The buyer may require the inclusion of other documents in addition to the ordinary CIF documents (invoice, bills of lading, insurance document) with the object of obtaining greater control as to what is shipped, and documents included with that aim will usually fall under the general description of certificate. Certificates of weight, certificates of origin, certificates of quality and certificates of analysis fall into this category.

8.126   *Instructions*   There are four points to be borne in mind by the seller in instructing the bank as to the requirements of the credit in this respect: who is to be the certifier;[1] what is he to do prior to issuing his certificate; what is he to cover in his certificate (which should include setting out that he has done what he was intended to do); the need to relate the goods certified to the goods shipped. The instructions to the bank will not cover the second as the bank will not be concerned with the second. The problem of relating the goods certified to those shipped is considered in paragraph 8.127 below. If these matters are not covered the bank will accept what the seller provides subject otherwise to compliance with Article 21:[2]

> ARTICLE 21   **Unspecified Issuers or Contents of Documents**
> When documents other than transport documents, insurance documents and commercial invoices are called for, the Credit should stipulate by whom such documents are to be issued and their wording or data content. If the Credit does not so stipulate, banks will accept such documents as presented, provided that their data content is not inconsistent with any other stipulated document presented.

The phrase 'banks will accept such documents as presented' does not mean that a seller can provide a document which is not a certificate of analysis or which does not appear to provide an analysis of the goods where a certificate of analysis, for example, is called for. An example of a case where the buyer wanted protection but failed to give adequate thought to these matters is *Commercial Banking Co of Sydney Ltd v Jalsard Pty Ltd*.[3] All the credit required in accordance with the buyer's instructions was 'Certificate of Inspection'. The goods were battery-operated Christmas lights to be shipped from Taiwan to Sydney. Two certificates were provided from surveying companies in Taipei in substantially the same form and they certified that the surveyor had checked the quantity and condition of the goods. It was apparent from the certificates, although they did not expressly so state, that the surveyors had found no defects in their goods or their packing. The buyers argued that the certificates were required to state that the goods were of acceptable standard and condition (which would have involved electrical testing as opposed to a merely visual inspection). This argument was rejected. The Board of the Privy Council stated:[4]

> ' "Certificate of Inspection" is a term capable of covering documents which contain a wide variety of information as to the nature and the results of the inspection which had been undertaken. The minimum requirement implicit in the ordinary meaning of the words is that the goods the subject-matter of the inspection have been inspected, at any rate visually, by the person issuing the certificate. If it is intended that a particular method of inspection should be adopted or that particular information as to the result of the inspection should be recorded, this, in their Lordships' view, would not be implicit in the words "Certificate of Inspection" by themselves, but would need to be expressly stated.'

The credit in the *Jalsard* case was not apparently subject to the Uniform Customs. If it had been, Article 21 would have made the buyer's position even more difficult. Had the buyer named the inspection agency to be used, and specified that the certificate should certify that the goods had been inspected visually and that samples chosen in a particular manner had been tested electrically, the shipment of defective goods might have been avoided.[5] It may be important to provide for the inclusion in the credit as to how samples are to be drawn. Thus in *Basse and Selve v Bank of Australasia*[6] the analysis was genuine but the certificate was not required to cover the drawing of the sample and it was here that the fraud by the seller arose. The use of terms such as 'exporting country' and 'local chamber of commerce' require care because they may often be capable of referring either to the seller's country or to the country of ultimate origin of the goods. In such cases further definition is required.[7]

1 Care must be taken not to use general adjectives which cannot be precisely applied in describing the certifier, such as 'first class', independent etc. These add nothing and will be ignored by a bank; see para 8.48 above and Article 20.a.
2 As to the derivation of the Article, see para 8.30 above.
3 [1973] AC 279, PC.
4 Ibid at 285.
5 The failure of the buyer's alternative case against the bank for alleged negligence in advising as to the terms of the credit is discussed at para 4.22 above.
6 (1904) 90 LT 618.
7 See Opinion of the ICC Banking Commission 1984–1986, at R 112 and R 113.

8.127 *Compliance*   Strict compliance with the terms of the credit relating to the certificate is required. Thus in *Equitable Trust Co of New York v Dawson Partners Ltd*[1] (in which Lord Sumner made his celebrated comment that 'There is no room for documents which are almost the same or will do just as well') the certificate was signed by an expert and not by experts, and should have been rejected.[2] It must certify in the terms required, and so in *Bank Melli Iran v Barclays Bank*[3] a certificate was to be rejected which certified that 100 surplus US army trucks were 'new, good' instead of simply 'new': 'The description of the trucks as "new comma good" may clearly connote something different from the description "new". It may have a special trade meaning in relation to motor vehicles. It is sufficient to say that it is not the same'.[4] The effect of Articles 20.a and 21 has already been described in paragraphs 8.48 and 8.126.

1 (1927) 27 Ll L Rep 49.
2 Whether the sellers could have produced a certificate signed by two or more 'experts who were sworn brokers' to cover what was said to be 'a quantity of sticks, stones and old iron' instead of '3000 kilos Java vanilla beans, sound, sweet and of prime quality' is unknown.
3 [1951] 2 Lloyd's Rep 367.
4 Ibid at 375.2.

8.128 *Relation to the goods*   Article 21's predecessor in the 1983 Revision, Article 23, required that the data content of documents should make it possible to relate the goods to those referred to in the commercial invoice, whereas Article 21 has dropped this requirement from the wording of the Article and expressly requires only that there should be no inconsistency in data content. The change has been considered in paragraph 8.29 and following paragraphs under the heading of 'identification of goods'. It is essential that any certificate or other document of like nature should indeed relate to the goods which have been shipped and not to some other goods of acceptable quality which have been examined and certified but not shipped. The possibility of fraud is obvious. It is suggested in paragraph 8.30 above that banks should still require documents to be capable of being related to the goods invoiced and shipped, despite the change in the Article. But in view of the change, it is important that buyers ensure that the terms of credits expressly require that any certificates should be sufficiently linked to the goods shown to have been shipped. Cases preceding the Uniform Customs but illustrating the previous need for certificates to be capable of being related to the goods shown to have been shipped include the *Bank Melli Case*[1] where the certificate failed on this count among others, and the old case of *Re Reinhold & Co and Hansloh's Arbitration*[2] where the certificate might have applied to any 1000 tons of the maize on the vessel rather than to all of it: so it was unclear whether the buyer would get maize that had been examined and certified. The decision of the Court of Appeal on this point in *Banque de l'Indochine v J H Rayner Ltd*[3] has been considered above.[4]

1 [1951] 2 Lloyd's Rep 367 at 375.2.
2 (1896) 12 TLR 422.
3 [1983] QB 711.
4 Para 8.30(c).

8.129 *Certificate of weight*   Article 38 provides:

ARTICLE 38[1]   **Other Documents**
If a Credit calls for an attestation or certification of weight in the case of transport other than by sea, banks will accept a weight stamp or declaration of weight which appears to have been superimposed on the transport document by the carrier or his agent unless the Credit specifically stipulates that the attestation or certification of weight must be by means of a separate document.

Note that this does not apply where transport is by sea nor when the credit calls for a separate document. The stamp or declaration must appear to have been superimposed by the carrier or his agent.

1 Article 38 follows Article 42 in the 1983 Revision.

8.130 *Several certificates*   It is suggested that generally fractional certificates can be used, that is to say, certificates each covering part of the shipment and together covering the whole, and a single global certificate is not usually required. No objection was taken on this ground in the *Banque de l'Indochine* case, and with large quantity commodity contracts it is common practice.

8.131 *Certificates requiring the buyer's co-operation*   Perhaps the strongest protection that the buyer can seek is that the documents to be presented should include a certificate signed by the buyer or his agent that he has inspected the goods on or prior to shipment and found them to comply with the contract. Sometimes the certifier is named as the holder of a particular passport number, which appears to require the bank to verify the signature on the certificate against that on the passport: see *Gian Singh Ltd v Banque de l'Indochine.*[1] But as that case shows, even these expedients can be defeated by the seller bent on fraud. They can also be abused by the buyer. For if the transaction becomes unattractive to him, he can refuse to co-operate. Swift action may find a way round this in section 39 of the Supreme Court Act 1981, as is considered in the next chapter.[2]

1 [1974] 1 WLR 1234, see para 8.6 above.
2 Para 9.42.

5.   Drafts – Bills of Exchange

8.132 In some transactions where the credit called for a draft, the draft may seem of little importance as, for example, where a sight draft drawn on the issuing or the confirming bank is required. Even in these instances the principle of strict compliance should be adhered to. It is considered in Chapter 4[1] whether a bank may waive provisions inserted for its benefit, and it is doubted whether today it may do so. An argument that a draft was unnecessary because it was of no importance was advanced in *Kydon Compania Naviera SA v National Westminster Bank Ltd, The Lena,*[2] in relation to a requirement for a sight draft drawn on the purchasers and was rejected.[3] This was followed in *The Messiniaki Tolmi*[4] where the sight draft was to be drawn on the confirming bank. The draft presented must comply with the terms of the credit. Thus it must be drawn by the correct party or parties – see *Elder Dempster Lines Ltd v Ionic Shipping Agency Inc.*[5] It must be drawn on the correct party: *The Lena.*[6]

1 Para 4.19.
2 [1981] 1 Lloyd's Rep 68.
3 [1981] 1 Lloyd's Rep at 75.1.
4 [1986] 1 Lloyd's Rep 455 at 457.2.
5 [1968] 1 Lloyd's Rep 529.
6 Supra.

8.133 The draft must have the correct time for payment, ie at sight, a period after sight, or after bill of lading date, etc. There was here a problem of interpretation arising on Article 51 of the 1983 Revision. Article 51 has now been replaced by Article 47.a[1] which applies only to dates or periods referring to shipment and is inapplicable to datse relating to drafts. The problem was that, applying Article 51, '30 days after bill of lading date' where the bill of lading was dated 10 May, would give 9 June, and '30 days from bill of lading date' would give 8 June. It is suggested that, Article 51 apart, the two would ordinarily be construed as meaning the same in the context of a bill of exchange, and the correct date for payment is 9 June. Section 14(2) and (3) of the Bills of Exchange Act 1882 provides:

> '14(2) Where a bill is payable at a fixed period after date, after sight or after the happening of a specified event, the time of payment is determined by excluding the day from which the time is to begin to run and by including the date of payment.
> (3) Where a bill is payable at a fixed period after sight, the time begins to run from the date of the acceptance if the bill be accepted, and from the date of noting or protest if the bill be noted or protested for non-acceptance, or for non-delivery.'

The use of 'after' and 'from' will be noted: 'from' is plainly used to have the same meaning as 'after'. 'After' is the word which is more commonly found on bills of exchange and is the only word used in Article 33 of the Uniform Law on Bills of Exchange and Promissory Notes annexed to the Geneva Convention on Bills of Exchange of 1932.

1 See para 8.47 above.

8.134 It is common although not essential for credits to require that drafts should be noted as drawn under the credit and marked with the number and date of the credit and the name of the issuing bank.

Chapter 9

Fraud and Injunctions

9.1 ***A developing area of law***   The law and practice relating to the effect of fraud in the field of documentary credits has been developed by a number of modern decisions, some of which have related to credits and others to demand guarantees (or performance bonds as they are often called). Whereas the law based on the existing authorities can be stated with reasonable certainty, it is an area in which further developments can be expected, particularly if a growth in fraud is perceived by the courts to require a shift in the balance as it is presently established.[1]

1 See para 9.36 below.

9.2 ***Two related topics***   This chapter deals with two topics: fraud, which is a matter of substantive law, and the question of injunctions, which is largely a matter of procedure once the underlying rights have been determined. Fraud in relation to documentary credits mainly arises in the following situations:

(1)   Where documents have been presented but the paying bank has refused to pay, and is being sued by the beneficiary/seller and is resisting payment on the ground of fraud.

(2)   Where the paying bank has not yet paid and the applicant for the credit desires to prevent it paying because the applicant believes that the beneficiary/seller is fraudulent, or that payment should not be made on some other ground.

(3)   Where the paying bank has paid and recovery of the payment is sought by it on the ground that the presentation of documents to it involved fraud.

In the second situation the applicant will seek an injunction to prevent the bank from paying and this is the reason why the topic of injunctions is included in this chapter. For fraud is certainly the main, and probably the only, ground on which such an injunction might be sought. Even then a claim for an injunction faces great difficulties.

A.   Fraud

9.3   *The fraud exception to the autonomy of the credit*   By the autonomy of the credit is meant the principle that documents presented under a credit are to be considered in the context of the credit alone and without reference to the underlying contract between the applicant for the credit and the beneficiary, or to other facts.[1] Thus, in the Uniform Customs, Article 3 emphasises the separateness of credits from the sales or other contracts on which they are based; Article 4 emphasises that in credits parties deal in documents and not in goods, and Article 14.a entitles payment against the acceptance of documents which appear on their face to be in accordance with the terms and conditions of the credit. There is an established exception to this in the case of fraud, the ambit of which will be considered. It is an exception in this sense, that the court will take into account evidence, that is, evidence apart from the terms of the credit and the documents themselves, which is put before it with the intention of establishing fraud. Such evidence may relate to the goods themselves; for example, that which has been shipped is not bottles of gin as per contract but bottles of water, or it may relate to a document, for example, that an inspection certificate purporting to be made out by the inspection authority named in the credit was not made out by it. Such evidence should cover the knowledge of the party presenting the documents of these matters.

1 See paras 1.40 et seq and 8.11 et seq above.

9.4   *Fraud and the Uniform Customs*   The Uniform Customs do not attempt to set out the position where documents which are presented under a letter of credit are forged or otherwise fraudulent. This may be because of the uncertainty of the position in municipal laws or differences in municipal laws. Under the Uniform Customs the duty of a bank in respect of all documents is to examine them with reasonable care: Article 13.a. Then, if they appear on their face to be in accordance with the terms and conditions of the credit a bank which pays against them is entitled to reimbursement from the party giving it its authority: Article 14.a. Article 15 begins:

> ARTICLE 15   Banks assume no liability or responsibility for the form, sufficiency, accuracy, genuineness, falsification or legal effect of any document(s) . . .

It goes on to emphasise the absence of responsibility of banks for the satisfaction of conditions contained in documents or superimposed on them, and lastly for a wide variety of matters which might arise in connection with the goods including their existence. Thus the Uniform Customs emphasise the autonomy of credits, and that banks are concerned with documents alone. There is no reference in the Uniform Customs to the existence of any exception to the autonomy principle where there is fraud. Such exception has to be found in the relevant municipal law, which is English law where the law governing the relationship between the party presenting the documents and the paying bank is English law. That it is the intention of the Uniform Customs to leave questions of fraud to the relevant municipal law and not to deny the existence of a fraud exception is confirmed by an Opinion of the ICC Banking Commission.[1] The Commission was asked whether a negotiating bank which had paid and been paid on documents which included a bill of lading found on receipt of the documents by the opening bank to be forged, was obliged to refund the money it had received. The Commission's Opinion was that the negotiating bank was protected by Article 9 – the 1974 Revision equivalent of Article 15, 'unless it was itself a party to the fraud, or it had knowledge of the fraud prior to presentation of the documents, or unless it had failed to exercise reasonable care, eg if the forgery were apparent "on the face" of the document'. The Opinion concludes 'The Commission noted that this was in line with various court rulings.' As will be seen, as a statement of the position under English law this would require some refinement, in particular as to the knowledge of the fraud of the party presenting the documents to the negotiating bank. But broadly it is consistent with the position under English law.

1 Opinions (1980–1981) of the ICC Banking Commission, ICC Publication No 399 at R 76, page 27.

9.5 *The* Sztejn *case* The foundation stone of English law in this area is an American case, *Sztejn v J Henry Schroder Banking Corpn*.[1] In this action the applicant for a credit claimed an injunction against the issuing bank to prevent the issuing bank paying on the documents which had been presented. The credit had been advised to the seller in India by the issuing bank's correspondent in India. The correspondent had not confirmed the credit. The applicant alleged that what had been shipped was rubbish rather than any resemblance of the goods contracted for. The bank applied to dismiss the claim for an injunction on the ground that there was no cause of action. For the purpose of hearing that motion the court assumed the facts alleged by the buyer to be true, and thus the buyer did not face the difficulty (which has caused great problems for buyers in subsequent English cases) of establishing the fraud which he alleged with sufficient certainty to satisfy the court. Having set out the principle that normally complaints about the goods are no ground for a court demanding or even permitting a bank to delay payment, Shientag J stated:

'However, I believe that a different situation is presented in the instant action. This is not a controversy between the buyer and seller concerning a mere breach of warranty regarding the quality of the merchandise; on the present motion, it must be assumed that the seller has intentionally failed to ship any goods ordered by the buyer. In such a situation, where the seller's fraud has been called to the bank's attention before the drafts and documents have been presented for payment, the principle of the independence of the bank's obligation under the letter of credit should not be extended to protect the unscrupulous seller. It is true that even though the documents are forged or fraudulent, if the issuing bank has already paid the draft before receiving notice of the seller's fraud, it will be protected if it exercised reasonable diligence before making such payment. (Citations.) However, in the instant action Schroder has received notice of Transea's active fraud before it accepted or paid the draft. The Chartered Bank, which under the allegations of the complaint stands in no better position than Transea, should not be heard to complain because Schroder is not forced to pay the draft accompanied by documents covering a transaction which it has reason to believe is fraudulent.

Although our courts have used broad language to the effect that a letter of credit is independent of the primary contract between the buyer and seller, that language was used in cases concerning alleged breaches of warranty; no case has been brought to my attention on this point involving an intentional fraud on the part of the seller which was brought to the bank's notice with the request that it withhold payment of the draft on this account. The distinction between a breach of warranty and active fraud on the part of the seller is supported by authority and reason. As one court has stated: "Obviously, when the issuer of a letter of credit knows that a document, although correct in form, is, in point of fact, false or illegal, he cannot be called upon to recognise such a document as complying with the terms of a letter of credit." (Citations.)

No hardship will be caused by permitting the bank to refuse payment where fraud is claimed, where the merchandise is not merely inferior in quality but consists of worthless rubbish, where the draft and the accompanying documents are in the hands of one who stands in the same position as the fraudulent seller, where the bank has been given notice of the fraud before being presented with the drafts and documents for payment, and where the bank itself does not wish to pay pending an adjudication of the rights and obligations of the other parties. While the primary factor in the issuance of the letter of credit is the credit standing of the buyer, the security afforded by the merchandise is also taken into account. In fact, the letter of credit requires a bill of lading made out to the order of the bank and not the buyer. Although the bank is not interested in the exact detailed performance of the sales contract, it is vitally interested in assuring itself that there are some goods represented by the documents. (Citations.)

On this motion only the complaint is before me and I am bound by its allegation that the Chartered Bank is not a holder in due course but is a mere agent for collection for the account of the seller charged with fraud. Therefore, the Chartered Bank's motion to dismiss the complaint must be denied. If it had appeared from the face of the complaint that the bank presenting the draft for payment was a holder in due course, its claim against the bank issuing the letter of credit would not be defeated even though the primary transaction was tainted with fraud.'

So the case is authority that the court may interfere to prevent a bank with whom the party applying to the court is in contractual relations paying against documents which have been presented by, or on behalf of, a party whose fraud has been called to the bank's attention. It must follow that the same fraud would entitle the bank of its own motion to refuse to pay, and provide it also with a defence to any action subsequently brought against it to enforce payment.

1 31 NYS 2d 631 (1941). See *Discount Records Ltd v Barclays Bank Ltd* [1975] 1 WLR 315 at 318; *Edward Owen Engineering Ltd v Barclays Bank International Ltd* [1978] QB 159 at 169; *United City Merchants (Investments) Ltd v Royal Bank of Canada* [1983] 1 AC 168 at 183.

9.6 *United City Merchants v Royal Bank of Canada*[1]   This is the leading English case on fraud and also on illegality.

1 [1983] 1 AC 168, HL; [1982] QB 208, CA; [1979] 1 Lloyd's Rep 267 and [1979] 2 Lloyd's Rep 498 Mocatta J.

9.7 *(1) The facts* The facts which were relevant to fraud were as follows. The documents were presented for payment to the defendants, the confirming bank, who refused to pay and were sued by the assignees of the beneficiary/sellers. The ground on which the bank supported its refusal to pay was that the documents contained a material misstatement, namely that the bill of lading showed that shipment had been made on 15 December 1976, when it had in fact been made on 16 December 1976, the last date for shipment provided by the credit being 15 December. The date was inserted by an employee of the loading brokers to the carriers. He acted fraudulently in that he knew that the date he inserted was a false one. The judge held that neither the sellers nor their merchant bankers (to whom they had assigned their interest under the credit) were privy to the brokers' employee's fraud: they believed that the statement that the goods had been loaded on 15 December was true. The goods which had been shipped were a glass-fibre forming plant, and the fact that it was shipped a day late would seem to have made very little difference in practical terms. But had the true date been shown on the bill of lading, the sellers could not have obtained payment under the credit unless the buyers were prepared to waive the discrepancy. Although the goods arrived in Peru, the buyers did not take delivery of them.[1]

1 See [1982] QB 208 at 218A/B.

9.8 *(2) The decision of the judge*[1]   Mocatta J held:[2]

'The question remains of the effect, if any, upon the plaintiffs' claim of what I have found to be the fraudulent misrepresentations of Mr Baker in relation to the date the goods were shown on the bills of lading to have been on board. I have found that Mr Baker was not the plaintiffs' agent for making out the bills of lading and that there was no fraud on the part of the plaintiffs in presenting them. The case is, therefore, vitally different from the *Sztejn v Schroder* case[3] approved by the Court of Appeal in the recent *Edward Owen v Barclays Bank* case.[4] Where there has been personal fraud or unscrupulous conduct by the seller presenting the documents under the letter of credit, it is right that a bank should be entitled to refuse payment against apparently conforming documents on the principle *ex turpi causa non oritur actio*. But here I have held that there was no fraud on the part of the plaintiffs, nor can I, as a matter of fact, find that they knew the date on the bills of lading to be false when they presented the documents. Further, there is no plea either by way of an implied term or by way of a warranty imposed by the law that the presenter of documents under a letter of credit warrants their accuracy. Accordingly, I take the view, on the principle so recently affirmed by the Court of Appeal, that the plaintiffs are, on the matters which have so far been argued before the Court, entitled to succeed.'

1 [1979] 1 Lloyd's Rep 267.
2 Ibid at 278.
3 Above.
4 [1978] QB 159.

9.9 *(3) The decision of the Court of Appeal*[1]   The Court of Appeal held that because the bill of lading had been fraudulently completed (in the sense that the employee had misstated the date with intention to deceive), even though the sellers were not party to this fraud, the bank was entitled to refuse to pay. This made it unnecessary for the court to consider the main argument which had been addressed to it, that any inaccurate and material statement in a document was a ground for a bank to refuse to pay. The main strand of the court's reasoning was that a document which was a nullity because it was forged could be rejected by a bank, even though it was forged other than by the beneficiary, and there was no reason for distinguishing from a document which was a nullity, one which was in any way false to the knowledge of a third person.[2]

1 [1982] QB 208.
2 See [1982] QB 208 at 239D, 247F/H and 255B/C.

9.10 *(4) The decision of the House of Lords*[1]   The leading judgment was given by Lord Diplock. He had delivered the judgment of the Privy Council in *Gian Singh & Co Ltd v Banque de l'Indochine*,[2] which affirmed that a bank was entitled to be reimbursed by its customer against documents which included a forged certificate, the documents having been examined with due care and the forgery not having been detected. Lord Diplock began with a description of the autonomous contracts which may arise in connection with letters of credit, and emphasised that disputes as to the goods are irrelevant to the seller's rights to payment. He continued:[3]

'To this general statement of principle as to the contractual obligations of the confirming bank to the seller, there is one established exception: that is, where the seller, for the purpose of drawing on the credit, fraudulently presents to the confirming bank documents that contain, expressly or by implication, material representations of fact that to his knowledge are untrue.'

After referring to the *Sztejn* case[4] he went on:

'The exception for fraud on the part of the beneficiary seeking to avail himself of the credit is a clear application of the maxim ex turpi causa non oritur actio or, if plain English is to be preferred, "fraud unravels all". The courts will not allow their process to be used by a dishonest person to carry out a fraud.'

The argument against the sellers had been 'that a confirming bank is not under any obligation legally enforceable against it by the seller/ beneficiary of a documentary credit, to pay to him the sum stipulated in the credit against presentation of documents, if the documents presented, although conforming on their face with the terms of the credit, nevertheless contain some statement of material fact that is not accurate'.[5] As Lord Diplock pointed out[6] this would render the fraud exception to the autonomy rule superfluous. He held that such a rule would undermine the whole system of credits by destroying their autonomy. He then came to the proposition of the Court of Appeal, categorised as a 'half-way house' because it was half-way between the fraud exception as stated by Lord Diplock and the main argument on behalf of the bank. Lord Diplock held that his rejection of the main argument also entitled the rejection of the argument relating to material representation of fact false to the knowledge of the person issuing (in contrast with presenting) the document; for if documents containing a material misrepresentation of fact were not to be rejected, what difference could it make if unknown to the seller the misstatement was made fraudulently rather than by mistake? Lord Diplock referred to the Court of Appeal's reliance upon the position as stated by it in relation to forged documents. He stated:[7]

'I would not wish to be taken as accepting that the premiss as to forged documents is correct, even where the fact that the document is forged deprives it of all legal effect and makes it a nullity, and so worthless to the confirming bank as security for its advances to the buyer. This is certainly not so under the Uniform Commercial Code as against a person who has taken a draft drawn under the credit in circumstances that would make him a holder in due course, and I see no reason why, and there is nothing in the Uniform Commercial Code to suggest that, a seller/beneficiary who is ignorant of the forgery should be in any worse position because he has not negotiated the draft before presentation. I would prefer to leave open the question of the rights of an innocent seller/beneficiary against the confirming bank when a document presented by him is a nullity because unknown to him it was forged by some third party; for that question does not arise in the instant case. The bill of lading with the wrong date of loading placed on it by the carrier's agent was far from being a nullity. It was a valid transferable receipt for the goods giving the holder a right to claim them at their destination, Callao, and was evidence of the terms of the contract under which they were being carried.'

1 [1983] 1 AC 168.
2 [1974] 1 WLR 1234.
3 [1983] 1 AC 168 at 183G.
4 Supra, para 9.5.
5 See [1983] 1 AC 168 at 184.
6 Ibid.
7 Ibid at 187H.

9.11 *The fraud exception as established in English law*   The fraud exception is an exception to the rule that the contracts made in connection with credits are autonomous. It enables a bank when presented with documents which appear on their face to accord with the credit to take account of something external to the documents, namely the fraud of which the presenting party has knowledge, and to refuse to pay on that ground. The main cases by which the exception may be said to be established in English law apart from the *United City Merchants* case[1] are as follows:

Hamzeh Malas & Sons v British Imex Industries Ltd[2]
Discount Records Ltd v Barclays Bank Ltd[3]
Edward Owen Engineering Ltd v Barclays Bank Ltd[4]
Etablissement Esefka International Anstalt v Central Bank of Nigeria[5]

For the purposes of the fraud exception, cases relating to performance bonds or guarantees have been treated by the English courts as involving the same principles as documentary credits, and, on the examples which have arisen to date, this is clearly correct. The distinction which could be relevant lies in the nature of the documents to be presented under a documentary credit and the 'demand' which usually triggers payment under a performance bond or standby credit. Other cases which may be referred to are as follows:

Harbottle Mercantile Ltd v National Westminster Bank Ltd[6]
United Trading Corpn SA v Allied Arab Bank Ltd[7]
European Asian Bank v Punjab and Sind Bank[8]
GKN Contractors Ltd v Lloyds Bank[9]
Tukan Timber Ltd v Barclays Bank plc[10]
Rafsanjan Pistachio Producers v Bank Leumi[11]

1 Supra.
2 [1958] 2 QB 127 at 130 per Sellers LJ.
3 [1975] 1 WLR 315.
4 [1978] QB 159.
5 [1979] 1 Lloyd's Rep 445 per Lord Denning MR.
6 [1978] QB 146.
7 [1985] 2 Lloyd's Rep 554n.
8 [1983] 1 Lloyd's Rep 611.
9 (1985) 30 BLR 48.
10 [1987] 1 Lloyd's Rep 171.
11 [1992] 1 Lloyd's Rep 513.

Points arising in connection with the fraud exception:

9.12 (1) The exception arises as a part of the common law. It does not derive from the Uniform Customs.

9.13 (2) The effect of the exception is to provide banks with a ground for refusing to pay and with a defence should they be sued by the beneficiary or other party presenting the documents whom the bank alleges to be party to the fraud. The bank has to decide on the documents and the facts which it knows or suspects whether to allege fraud and to refuse to pay. If it does refuse, it will then have to establish the fraud at a trial if it is sued. The civil burden of proof is generally proof on the balance of probabilities. But 'the degree depends on the subject matter. A civil court when considering a charge of fraud will naturally require for itself a higher degree of probability than that which it would require when asking if negligence is established.'[1] So if a bank refuses to pay on the ground of fraud, it takes upon itself the burden of establishing the fraud. It is likely that the alleged facts relating to the fraud will have been supplied to it by the buyer, and the bank will effectively be looking to the buyer to provide the necessary evidence. A bank will be well-advised to take an indemnity from the buyer against the consequences before it refuses to pay on the ground of fraud.

1 Per Denning LJ in *Bater v Bater* [1951] P 35 at 37 cited with other cases in *Phipson on Evidence* (13th edn) para 4.35. In *Rafsanjan Pistachio Producers v Bank Leumi* [1992] 1 Lloyd's Rep 513, a documentary credit case, Hirst J referred to the need to establish the case 'to the highest level of probability', citing *Hornal v Newburger Products Ltd* [1957] 1 QB 247, CA, though the phrase is not there used.

9.14 (3) On occasions, which it is suggested will be very rare, the effect of the exception may also be to enable an applicant/buyer to prevent by injunction a bank from paying on fraudulent documents. This is considered below.[1]

1 Para 9.28 et seq.

9.15 (4) What is 'fraud': what misrepresentation? In stating the exception[1] Lord Diplock referred to 'documents that contain, expressly or by implication, material representations of fact that to his knowledge are untrue'. This is very close to a statement of the elements of fraudulent misrepresentation which constitute the tort of deceit and of fraudulent misrepresentation in relation to the performance of a contract. But there are crucial distinctions. For the bank has not been induced into making any contract by fraud, nor has it acted on any misrepresentation. It made the contract with the beneficiary by advising the credit.[2] It is refusing to perform that contract because of the fraud, rather than being duped by the fraud.[3] Nonetheless the heart of the exception is a misrepresentation of fact known to be untrue by the party putting the document forward.[4] 'Fraud' can be used in a wider sense, to refer to any dishonest conduct whereby financial advantage is obtained involving a degree of deception. But it is suggested that it is right in this context to define it as Lord Diplock defined it. Thus, although the judge did not, and did not need to, analyse the facts in this manner, in the *Sztejn* case[5] the bills of lading presumably stated that the goods on board were bristles which was what the contract of sale provided, and, as the buyer alleged, was false to the knowledge of the seller. In the performance bond or guarantee cases such as *Edward Owen Ltd v Barclays Bank*[6] the maker of the demand represents by making it that he honestly believes that the event on which the bond becomes payable has occurred.[7]

1 [1983] 1 AC 168 at 183G.
2 Chapter 5.
3 See *Rafsanjan Pistachio Producers v Bank Leumi* [1992] 1 Lloyd's Rep 513 at 542.1.
4 See the *Rafsanjan* case (above) at 540.1 and 2.
5 Supra, para 9.5.
6 [1978] QB 159.
7 See *United Trading Corpn SA v Allied Arab Bank Ltd* [1985] 2 Lloyd's Rep 554n at 559.1 where Ackner LJ cited the dictum of Lord Denning MR from *State Trading Corpn of India Ltd v E D and F Man (Sugar) Ltd* [1981] Com LR 235 and *GKN Contractors v Lloyd's Bank* (1985) 30 BLR 48 at 63.

9.16 (5) The representation must be 'material'. It is suggested that this must mean material to the bank's duty to pay, so that if the document stated the truth the bank would be obliged to reject the documents. For example, if the bill of lading and invoice in the *Sztejn* case[1] had stated that the shipment consisted of 'cowhair and rubbish purporting to be bristles', they would not have conformed. And, in the *UCM* case[2] itself, if the bill of lading had had the correct date of shipment, it would have been outside the credit period. It does not mean 'material' in the sense of being of concern to the bank.[3]

1 Supra, para 9.5.
2 Supra, para 9.6.
3 *Rafsanjan Pistachio Producers v Bank Leumi* [1992] 1 Lloyd's Rep 513 at 541.2.

9.17 (6) The representation must be untrue to the knowledge of the presenter of the documents. What may be covered by 'knowledge'? Actual knowledge is the state of mind that is primarily to be considered. But it may be that something less will do. In the tort of deceit the following states of mind are sufficient: (i) knowing the representation to be false; (ii) without belief in its truth; or (iii) recklessly, careless whether it be true or false.[1] It may well be that where the party presenting the documents has some serious ground for suspicion of a document so that if he gave proper consideration to it he would realise that it most likely contained a false statement but shuts his eyes to that, this would be sufficient. Proof, however, might be very difficult. A bank is not under any duty to investigate any allegation.

1 See generally *Clerk & Lindsell on Tort* (16th edn) para 18–21.

9.18 (7) Lord Diplock refers simply to the seller. If the party presenting the documents is a collecting bank and is therefore the seller's agent, the bank will be in no better position than the seller. It is also possible but unlikely that a bank collecting on its own behalf such as a negotiation bank could have knowledge of the fraud. If so, it would be unable to collect. In *GKN Contractors v Lloyd's Bank*[1] Parker LJ postulated the case of a bank receiving a demand which it appreciated was mistaken, then passing it on as genuine, which could be resisted on the ground of fraud.[2]

1 (1985) 30 BLR 48.
2 Ibid at 63.

9.19 (8) Lord Diplock stated that the basis for the exception is that the courts will not allow their process to be used by a dishonest person to carry out a fraud.[1] For the obtaining of payment through the credit by means of dishonest documents is the essence of the fraud, which the court would be assisting if they did not permit the exception. The law of misrepresentation cannot be relied upon to provide a basis, because as pointed out, the bank has never been deceived.[2] Any alternative basis for the exception must be found in the terms of the contract made with the beneficiary by the advising of the credit. A possible alternative is that it is an implied term of that contract that the documents to be presented under the credit shall not, to the presenter's knowledge, make, either expressly or impliedly, any statements of fact which are false. Breach of the term would entitle the bank to reject the documents for non-compliance with it. Such a term could be implied as necessary for the proper working of the contract.[3] There is, however, no authority for it in English law.

1 He quoted the maxim *ex turpi causa non oritur actio*.
2 See para 9.15.
3 As to the basis on which a term will be implied into a contract governed by English law, see *Liverpool City Council v Irwin* [1977] AC 239.

9.20 (9) Fraud of the applicant. The credit may be tainted with fraud from the start in that it has been opened by the bank in reliance upon a fraudulent misrepresentation made by the applicant in the application to open the credit, for example, as to the facts concerning the goods which it is intended should form the subject matter of the credit. If at the start the beneficiary is party to this fraud, it will bar him from any entitlement to payment.[1] If the beneficiary discovers the applicant's fraud subsequently, he will be barred from operating the credit unless he has given consideration (or acted to his detriment) prior to his discovery.[2] In any situation where the beneficiary is party to a fraud by the applicant, it seems factually unlikely that the beneficiary will not also be guilty of fraud by presenting documents which he knows are in some way false.

1 *Rafsanjan Pistachio Producers v Bank Leumi* [1992] 1 Lloyd's Rep 513 at 535–9.
2 This appears to be the reasoning in the *Rafsanjan* case (above) at 539.1,2.

9.21 ***Documents which are a 'nullity'*** Lord Diplock referred in the *United City Merchants* case[1] to the fraud exception as he there defined it, as the 'one established exception'. Subsequently he referred to the position regarding forged documents which are so forged as to deprive the document of all legal effect so that such document is a 'nullity'.[2] In the passage quoted at the end of paragraph 9.10 he reserved the position as to such documents, perhaps doubting that the position adopted by the Court of Appeal – that the bank was entitled to refuse them – was correct. A document will be a nullity if it is forged or fraudulent in such a way as to destroy its essence. Thus a bill of lading evidences a contract of affreightment and is utilised to enable the holder to obtain possession of the goods shipped. If a bill is purportedly made out on behalf of the shipping line whose name appears on it by some third party having no authority to do so, or is made out on behalf of a line which does not exist, it will evidence nothing nor will it give any rights to the holder. It will mean that a bank which has paid out against it and is unable to obtain reimbursement through the credit chain will be in possession of a valueless security and will have lost its money (if it cannot recover it from the party to whom it paid it). A buyer who has paid the issuing bank will receive documents of no value. Such a bill is to be contrasted with the bill of lading in the *United City Merchants* case.[3] The bill there was not a nullity: all that was false was the date, and there were valuable goods which had been shipped and to which the bill could give the right of possession.[4] A second example of a document which would be a nullity is a certificate of inspection which is required to be made out by a named certification agency and is made out by someone who has no connection with the agency. As a certificate it is wholly without effect, and the fact that it has been brought into existence and tendered is likely to mean that the goods are far from what they are meant to be. Is the right of a bank to reject such a document dependent on it establishing that the party presenting the documents has knowledge of the fraud? Does it make any difference whether the presenter is the beneficiary or is a negotiation bank who has purchased the documents in good faith from the beneficiary? It is to be remembered that the beneficiary himself may be a purchaser of the documents if he is in a string of contracts, and may be acting in good faith.

1 Supra at [1983] 1 AC 168 at 183G, quoted at para 9.10 above.
2 Ibid at 187H.
3 Supra.
4 See also *Kwei Tek Chao v British Traders and Shippers* [1954] 2 QB 459 at 475, 6.

9.22 The basis on which a bank might reject a document as a nullity where the party presenting it has no knowledge of any fraud, cannot be the *ex turpi causa* rule.[1] If such documents can be rejected, it must surely be on the basis that a document which is forged so as to be a nullity and wastepaper is simply not a 'bill of lading' or a 'certificate of inspection', namely one of the documents which the credit requires, even though on its face it appears to be.

1 See para 9.19 above. See per Ackner LJ in the *United City Merchants* case at [1982] QB 208 at 246.

9.23 It is suggested that a bank should not be entitled to reject such documents unless it can bring itself within the fraud exception as already considered. If the party presenting the documents to the bank is a negotiation bank,[1] it will be covered by Articles 14.a and 10.d of the Uniform Customs and will be entitled to be reimbursed pursuant to these Articles: see per Lord Diplock in the *United City Merchants* case[2] quoted above in paragraph 9.10. In the *Sztejn* case Shientag J stated at the conclusion of the passage quoted in paragraph 9.5 above, that the claim of a holder in due course of a draft would not be defeated even though the primary transaction was tainted with fraud. There seems no reason to distinguish between such a party and the beneficiary unless it is that the beneficiary is likely to be the innocent party who puts the person responsible for the document into a position to do as he has done, and so the innocent beneficiary should bear the loss rather than the bank.[3] However, it appears more likely in a case where a document is a nullity and the beneficiary is not party to the fraud, that the beneficiary will have had nothing at all to do with the creation of the document. This will be the case where he is himself the purchaser in a string. It may seem startling that a bank can be compelled to purchase worthless paper which passes down the credit chain to the buyer who is left to sue the seller on the contract of sale if he can. But it is suggested that it is the better rule that a party innocent of any fraud should be entitled to reimbursement against documents which appear on their face to accord with the terms and conditions of the credit. Such a rule will assist the integrity of the system of documentary credit as a means of financing international transactions, whereas any widening of the fraud exception will detract from it.

1 Para 2.21.
2 [1983] 1 AC 168 at 187H.
3 Compare per Stephenson LJ in the *United City Merchants* case [1982] QB at 239H–240A.

9.24 *Forged documents* A document may be fraudulent without being forged, and a document may contain a forgery without being a nullity. It is suggested that whether or not a document is correctly described as being forged is a question which is irrelevant to the application of the fraud exception as established by the *United City Merchants* case.[1] A document is unlikely to be a nullity unless it is forged, but forgery is not determinative of that question.

1 Supra, para 9.10.

9.25 *The bank's right of reimbursement when it pays against documents in the face of evidence of fraud* It is suggested above[1] that a bank which is provided by a buyer with evidence of fraud should seek an indemnity from the buyer before it determines to refuse payment on the ground of fraud. But the bank might well be unhappy with such a course because the evidence of fraud may not seem so strong to the bank as it does to the buyer, and because of that, or independently, the bank may consider that to refuse to pay will injure its reputation as a reliable principal in international transactions. One course which is open to it is to invite the buyer to seek an injunction against it to prevent it from paying. If the court grants the injunction, the bank may well feel that this will protect its reputation when it does not pay. If the injunction is refused, the bank will pay and it will be entitled to be reimbursed by the buyer. If no such application is made and the bank pays, will it put at risk its right to reimbursement? As will appear from the consideration of the cases relating to injunctions,[2] it has been held that in the absence of clear evidence of fraud and of the bank's knowledge of it the bank will not be injuncted. The balance of convenience is most likely also to be against the grant of an injunction.[3] It follows that in the absence of clear evidence the bank should pay and can do so without putting at risk its right to reimbursement. It is suggested that, unless the fraud is clearly established so that the bank is satisfied of it and is not able to give any reason of substance for remaining doubtful of the position, the court will uphold the bank's right to be reimbursed if the bank determines to accept the documents and pay against them.

1 Para 9.13.
2 Para 9.28 et seq.
3 Para 9.35.

9.26 *Recovery by a bank which has paid on fraudulent documents* If a bank pays on documents which are fraudulent but which appear on their face to accord with the terms and conditions of the credit, it is entitled to be reimbursed by the party from whom its authority under the credit derives, unless it was clearly established to the bank at the time of payment that the documents were fraudulent to the knowledge of the party presenting them to the bank.[1] It will usually be reimbursed from that source. If, however, the fraud is a fraud by both buyer and seller on the banks so that the object of the credit is simply to be a means of extracting money from a bank, and the 'seller' has not disappeared with the money, the bank may choose to seek recovery from the fraudulent seller who presented the documents or on whose behalf they were presented. This occurred in *Bank Russo-Iran v Gordon Woodroffe & Co Ltd*.[2] The bank issued in Teheran a letter of credit payable in London in favour of the defendant company, which acquired goods worth some £9,000 which it invoiced for some £229,000. There was no real sale at all. The bank was held to have had a cause of action to recover the amount paid on the ground of fraudulent misrepresentation, in that the invoices were fraudulent to the knowledge of the defendant. It was also held that money was recoverable as money paid under a mistake of fact. The outcome, however, was that the bank failed to recover because it was held to have released the defendant. Although the judgment was 249 pages, unfortunately the available reports do not contain any examination of the cause of action. The conclusion of the judge is quoted by Lord Denning MR in *Edward Owen Ltd v Barclays Bank Ltd*[3] as follows 'In my judgment, if the documents are presented by the beneficiary himself, and are forged or fraudulent, the bank is entitled to refuse payment if it finds out before payment, and is entitled to recover the money as paid under a mistake of fact if it finds out after payment.' This has now to be read in the light of the *United City Merchants* case. It does not mention the right of recovery for fraudulent misrepresentation which is referred to in the reports cited. Lord Denning affirmed the right of recovery in *Etablissement Esefka International Anstalt v Central Bank of Nigeria*.[4] But the other members of the Court of Appeal were more guarded in their reasons for refusing a Mareva injunction against the bank and for granting it an order for security against the plaintiff.

1 See Uniform Customs, Articles 14.a and 10.d; *Edward Owen Engineering Ltd v Barclays Bank International Ltd* [1978] QB 159, and generally the cases cited at para 9.11 above.
2 (1972) 116 Sol Jo 921, (1972) Times, 4 October (but nowhere adequately reported).
3 [1978] QB 159 at 169.
4 [1979] 1 Lloyd's Rep 445 at 447.2, 448.1.

9.27 If a bank is entitled to refuse to pay on the ground of fraud it seems plainly right that it should be entitled to recover a payment where there is fraud to the knowledge of the party presenting documents. But the cause of action has to be precisely identified. Fraudulent misrepresentation is the obvious candidate. What is the misrepresentation which the presenter makes? It cannot be that the documents contain no material misstatements: it must be that to his knowledge they do not contain any express or implied misstatements of fact. This may be compared with Lord Diplock's formulation of the fraud exception in the *United City Merchants* case[1] quoted at paragraph 9.10 above. It is not easy to see how the cause of action for recovery as money paid under a mistake of fact suggested in the *Bank Russo-Iran* case is to be formulated. It must be formulated to exclude recovery where the documents contain a material misstatement but this is unknown to the presenter. So the mistake to be pleaded would have not only to be as to the existence of the misstatement. This seems somewhat artificial, and it is suggested that the formulation as a cause of action for fraudulent misrepresentation is to be preferred.

1 Supra, para 9.10.

B. Injunctions

9.28 Introduction Where the applicant for a documentary credit or a performance bond considers that the beneficiary is going to make or has made a presentation under the credit or bond which he should not make and which should not be met with payment by the paying bank, he may seek to prevent the presentation or payment or both by applying for injunctions against relevant parties. Such an application will meet a number of difficulties. Although applications have sometimes been successful at the *ex parte* stage, this is less likely now that the principles have been stated by the Court of Appeal in a number of cases. In no reported case has an injunction ultimately been granted by the court. A plaintiff faces two difficulties in particular. Firstly, he must show that he has a good arguable claim against the party he is seeking to injunct. This will involve him establishing a case of fraud to the knowledge of the party to be injuncted (otherwise the court will not interfere with the operation of the credit), and he must establish a duty owed to him by that party, either in contract or in tort. Secondly, it must appear that the grant of an injunction is the correct exercise of the court's discretion after considering the balance of convenience. So, even if a case as to fraud is sufficiently established, the case is likely to fail where the party sought to be injuncted is a bank because damages will be a sufficient remedy for any breach of duty by the bank. These principles as developed in connection with documentary credit and performance bond or guarantee cases are considered below. The general principles to be applied in applications for interlocutory injunctions were set out in the speech of Lord Diplock in *American Cyanamid Co v Ethicon Ltd.*[1]

1 [1975] AC 396.

9.29 The basic rule – the autonomy of the credit The basic rule is that the court will not interfere to prevent the operation of a credit on the ground of matters which are extraneous to the credit itself. This is but one aspect of the autonomy principle. In *Hamzeh Malas & Sons v British Imex Industries Ltd*[1] the plaintiff buyers considered that the goods supplied as the first instalment under a two-instalment contract were seriously defective and sought to prevent the defendant sellers from presenting documents in respect of the second instalment under the confirmed credit which the buyers had arranged to be opened as the means of payment. The injunction was refused. In giving the leading judgment[3] in the Court of Appeal Jenkins LJ stated:[2]

'We have been referred to a number of authorities, and it seems to be plain enough that the opening of a confirmed letter of credit constitutes a bargain between the banker and the vendor of the goods, which imposes upon the banker an absolute obligation to pay, irrespective of any dispute there may be between the parties as to whether the goods are up to contract or not. An elaborate commercial system has been built up on the footing that bankers' confirmed credits are of that character, and, in my judgment, it would be wrong for this court in the present case to interfere with that established practice.

There is this to be remembered, too. A vendor of goods selling against a confirmed letter of credit is selling under the assurance that nothing will prevent him from receiving the price. That is of no mean advantage when goods manufactured in one country are being sold in another. It is, furthermore, to be observed that vendors are often reselling goods bought from third parties. When they are doing that, and when they are being paid by a confirmed letter of credit, their practice is – and I think it was followed by the defendants in this case – to finance the payments necessary to be made to their suppliers against the letter of credit. That system of financing these operations, as I see it, would break down completely if a dispute as between the vendor and the purchaser was to have the effect of "freezing", if I may use that expression, the sum in respect of which the letter of credit was opened.'

1 [1958] 2 QB 127.
2 See [1958] 2 QB at 129.

9.30 In *Howe Richardson Scale Co Ltd v Polimex-Cekop*[1] the plaintiff sellers had arranged for a performance bond or guarantee to be given by the second defendant bank in respect of the deposit paid to them by the buyers (who were the first defendants), the deposit to be repaid by the bank on the buyer's first demand if the goods were not delivered by a date. Problems arose in the performance of the contract, in particular as to the opening by the buyers of a letter of credit. The sellers contended that in any event the goods were delivered to warehouse by the date. The buyers made a demand on the bond and the bank informed the sellers that it felt bound to pay. The sellers initially sought injunctions against the buyers and the bank, but did not pursue the latter on appeal. The buyers did not take part in resisting the application, the case being argued by the bank. The Court of Appeal declined to follow *Elian and Rabbath v Matsas*[2] where an injunction restraining a party from calling a guarantee was granted, stating that that decision should be regarded as very special.[3] Roskill LJ stated:[4]

'The bank, in principle, is in a position not identical with but very similar to the position of a bank which has opened a confirmed irrevocable letter of credit. Whether the obligation arises under a letter of credit or under a guarantee, the obligation of the bank is to perform that which it is required to perform by that particular contract, and that obligation does not in the ordinary way depend on the correct resolution of a dispute as to the sufficiency of performance by the seller to the buyer or by the buyer to the seller as the case may be under the sale and purchase contract; the bank here is simply concerned to see whether the event has happened upon which its obligation to pay has arisen. The bank takes the view that that time has come and that it is compelled to pay; and in my view it would be quite wrong for the Court to interfere with Polimex's apparent right under this guarantee to seek payment from the bank, because to do so would involve putting upon the bank an obligation to inquire whether or not there had been timeous performance of the sellers' obligations under the sale contract.'

1 [1978] 1 Lloyd's Rep 161.
2 [1966] 2 Lloyd's Rep 495.
3 See [1978] 1 Lloyd's Rep at 165.1.
4 [1978] 1 Lloyd's Rep at 165.2.

9.31 Lastly, it is worth quoting an often-referred-to passage from the judgment of Kerr J in *R D Harbottle (Mercantile) Ltd v National Westminster Bank Ltd.*[1] He stated:

'It is only in exceptional cases that the courts will interfere with the machinery of irrevocable obligations assumed by banks. They are the life-blood of international commerce. Such obligations are regarded as collateral to the underlying rights and obligations between the merchants at either end of the banking chain. Except possibly in clear cases of fraud of which the banks have notice, the courts will leave the merchants to settle their disputes under the contracts by litigation or arbitration . . . The courts are not concerned with their difficulties to enforce such claims; these are risks which the merchants take. In this case the plaintiffs took the risk of the unconditional wording of the guarantees. The machinery and commitments of banks are on a different level. They must be allowed to be honoured, free from interference by the courts. Otherwise, trust in international commerce could be irreparably damaged.'

1 [1978] QB 146 at 155H/156A.

9.32 *The fraud exception and proof* As indicated in the passage quoted above from the judgment of Kerr J the only exception is where there is fraud of which a bank has notice. The exception has been considered specifically in relation to injunctions in a number of cases.[1] It has been emphasised in all of them that the fraud and the knowledge of the bank must be clearly established. Thus in the *Edward Owen* case[2] Lord Denning MR stated[3] 'The only exception is where there is a clear fraud of which the bank had notice' and Browne LJ stated[4] 'But it is certainly not enough to allege fraud: it must be "established" and in such circumstances I should say very clearly established.' Geoffrey Lane LJ referred[5] to 'if it had been clear and obvious to the bank that the buyers had been guilty of fraud'. With this in mind, at the termination of the judgment of the Court of Appeal in *Bolivinter Oil SA v Chase Manhattan Bank*[6] the court gave general guidance as to the granting of *ex parte* injunctions in relation to credits and bonds. The court stated:[7]

'Before leaving this appeal, we should like to add a word about the circumstances in which an *ex parte* injunction should be issued which prohibits a bank from paying under an irrevocable letter of credit or a purchase bond or guarantee. The unique value of such a letter, bond or guarantee is that the beneficiary can be completely satisfied that whatever disputes may thereafter arise between him and the bank's customer in relation to the performance or indeed existence of the underlying contract, the bank is personally undertaking to pay him provided that the specified conditions are met. In requesting his bank to issue such a letter, bond or guarantee, the customer is seeking to take advantage of this unique characteristic. If, save in the most exceptional cases, he is to be allowed to derogate from the bank's personal and irrevocable undertaking, given be it again noted at his request, by obtaining an injunction restraining the bank from honouring that undertaking, he will undermine what is the bank's greatest asset, however large and rich it may be, namely its reputation for financial and contractual probity. Furthermore, if this happens at all frequently, the value of all irrevocable letters of credit and performance bonds and guarantees will be undermined.

Judges who are asked, often at short notice and *ex parte*, to issue an injunction restraining payment by a bank under an irrevocable letter of credit or performance bond or guarantee should ask whether there is any challenge to the validity of the letter, bond or guarantee itself. If there is not or if the challenge is not substantial, *prima facie* no injunction should be granted and the bank should be left free to honour its contractual obligation, although restrictions may well be imposed upon the freedom of the beneficiary to deal with the money after he has received it. The wholly exceptional case where an injunction may be granted is where it is proved that the bank knows that any demand for payment already made or which may thereafter be made will clearly be fraudulent. But the evidence must be clear, both as to the fact of fraud and as to the bank's knowledge. It would certainly not normally be sufficient that this rests upon the uncorroborated statement of the customer, for irreparable damage can be done to a bank's credit in the relatively brief time which must elapse between the granting of such an injunction and an application by the bank to have it discharged. The appeal will be dismissed.'

1   *Discount Records Ltd v Barclays Bank Ltd* [1975] 1 WLR 315; *R D Harbottle (Mercantile) Ltd v National Westminster Bank Ltd* [1978] QB 146; *Edward Owen Engineering Ltd v Barclays Bank International Ltd* [1978] QB 159; *Bolivinter Oil SA v Chase Manhattan Bank* [1984] 1 Lloyd's Rep 251, also reported in part at [1984] 1 All ER 351n, [1984] 1 WLR 392; *United Trading Corpn SA v Allied Arab Bank* [1985] 2 Lloyd's Rep 554n; *Tukan Timber Ltd v Barclays Bank plc* [1987] 1 Lloyd's Rep 171.
2   Supra.
3   [1978] QB at 171C.
4   [1978] QB at 173A.
5   [1978] QB at 175.
6   Supra.
7   [1984] 1 Lloyd's Rep at 251, [1984] 1 WLR at 393, [1984] 1 All ER at 352.

9.33   In *United Trading Corpn SA v Allied Arab Bank*[1] the Court of Appeal had to consider an argument that every possibility of an innocent explanation had to be excluded by the applicant for the injunction. In rejecting this as an over-statement of the burden of proof the court entered upon a detailed examination of what must be shown and concluded that it was sufficient that it established as seriously arguable that, on the material available, the only realistic inference was that the beneficiary was guilty of fraud. It stated:[2]

'The evidence of fraud must be clear, both as to the fact of fraud and as to the bank's knowledge. The mere assertion of allegation of fraud would not be sufficient (see *Bolivinter Oil SA v Chase Manhattan Bank* [1984] 1 Lloyd's Rep 251 per Sir John Donaldson MR at p 257). We would expect the Court to require strong corroborative evidence of the allegation, usually in the form of contemporary documents, particularly those emanating from the buyer. In general, for the evidence of fraud to be clear, we would also expect the buyer to have been given an opportunity to answer the allegation and to have failed to provide any, or any adequate answer in circumstances where one could properly be expected. If the Court considers that on the material before it the only realistic inference to draw is that of fraud, then the seller would have made out a sufficient case of fraud.

While accepting that letters of credit and performance bonds are part of the essential machinery of international commerce (and to delay payment under such documents strikes not only at the proper working of international commerce but also at the reputation and standing of the international banking community), the strength of this proposition can be over-emphasised. As Mr Justice Neill observed in the judgment under appeal, it cannot be in the interests of international commerce or of the banking community as a whole that this important machinery that is provided for traders should be misused for the purposes of fraud. It is interesting to observe that in America, where concern to avoid irreparable damage to international commerce is hardly likely to be lacking, interlocutory relief appears to be more easily obtainable. A temporary restraining order is made essentially on the basis of suspicion of fraud, followed some months later by a further hearing, during which time the applicant has an opportunity of adding to the material which he first put before the Court. Moreover, their conception of fraud is far wider than ours and would appear to include ordinary breach of contract. (See *Dynamics Corpn of America v Citizens and Southern National Bank* 356 F Supp 991 (1973); *Harris Corpn v NIRT* 691 F 2d 1344 (1982); and *Itek Corpn v F N Bank of Boston* 566 F Supp 1210 (1983)). These cases appear to indicate that, for the purpose of obtaining relief in such cases, it is not necessary for an American plaintiff to demonstrate a cause of action against a bank, whereas it is as previously stated, common ground that a plaintiff must in this country show a cause of action. There is no suggestion that this more liberal approach has resulted in the commercial dislocation which has, by implication at least, been suggested would result from rejecting the respondent's submissions as to the standard of proof required from the plaintiffs. Moreover, we would find it an unsatisfactory position if, having established an important exception to what had previously been thought an absolute rule, the Courts in practice were to adopt so restrictive an approach to the evidence required as to prevent themselves from intervening. Were this to be the case, impressive and high-sounding phrases such as "fraud unravels all" would become meaningless.

The learned Judge concluded that the test to be applied by the Courts is the standard of the hypothetical reasonable banker in possession of all the relevant facts. Unless he can say "this is plainly fraudulent; there cannot be any other explanation", the Courts cannot intervene. We respectfully disagree. The corroborated evidence of a plaintiff and the unexplained failure of a beneficiary to respond to the attack, although given a fair and proper opportunity, may well make the only realistic inference that of fraud, although the possibility that he may ultimately come forward with an explanation cannot be ruled out. The claim before us is a claim for an interlocutory judgment. The first question is therefore – following the principles laid down in *American Cyanamid Co v Ethicon Ltd* [1975] AC 396 – Have the plaintiffs established that it is seriously arguable that, on the material available, the only realistic inference is that Agromark could not honestly have believed in the validity of its demands on the performance bonds?'

It was held that on the evidence before the court the plaintiff had not met that test. An important point was that the failure of Agromark, the beneficiary, to explain its defence to the charge of fraud was explicable by the fact that Agromark was contesting the jurisdiction of the English court and so would be wary of taking any steps which might be said to be a submission to the jurisdiction. The court also considered the relevant time at which the bank's knowledge as to the alleged fraud is to be considered, which is at any time prior to actual payment.[3] So if the bank has not paid, its education as to the fraud may be continued by means of the evidence in the case itself. In none of the cases cited did the plaintiff succeed in establishing fraud to the satisfaction of the court, save in the *Tukan Timber* case.[4] The fraud in the latter case involved the forgery of signatures, which in the particular circumstances was capable of clear proof, and indeed the bank did not argue otherwise. The injunction was refused on the ground that the bank had already declined to pay against the documents presented under the credit to date, and in the circumstances an injunction against it was unnecessary.

1 [1985] 2 Lloyd's Rep 554.
2 [1985] 2 Lloyd's Rep at 861.
3 See [1985] 2 Lloyd's Rep at 560.
4 [1987] 1 Lloyd's Rep 171.

9.34 *Parties and cause of action* Where the applicant in respect of a credit or performance bond is contemplating applying for an injunction he has to consider whom to attempt to injunct, and he has to find a basis on which he can found his action against the defendant. If the beneficiary has already presented documents or made his claim, so far as he is concerned it is too late. But if not, he is a contracting party with the applicant to the underlying contract, and so there should be no difficulty in finding a cause of action against him, whether actual or on a *quia timet* (threatened) basis. The underlying contract may be governed by a foreign law, and may contain an arbitration or foreign jurisdiction clause. But these may be no bar to interlocutory relief by way of injunction in England. With regard to banks, the bank which must be prevented from paying is the first bank to pay because, once it has paid, its right to be indemnified will arise, with which the court is even less likely to interfere. Where the first bank to pay is the issuing bank (that is, there is no correspondent bank who pays), the applicant has a contract with that bank and no problem as to finding a legal right on which to found the claim arises. Likewise where the paying bank is the advising bank and has not confirmed the credit, the paying bank will act simply as the agent of the issuing bank[1] and an injunction against the issuing bank from paying by itself or by its agents should prevent payment. A confirming bank has in addition given its own undertaking to pay, and so an injunction directly against it is likely to be necessary as it is entitled to make up its own mind how to perform its obligation. The applicant has no contract with it, and so any legal right has to be based in tort on a duty of care. It was recognised as arguable that such a duty existed in a similar situation involving a performance bond in the *United Trading* case.[2] The situation with a performance bond is usually that the original bond is given by a bank in the beneficiary's country which is backed by a counter-guarantee from the applicant's bank which is in turn backed by a counter-guarantee from the applicant; and there may be further intermediary banks and counter-guarantees. So there is no possibility of any relationship as the agent of a party contracting with the applicant's own bank. In the *United Trading* case it was accepted by the banks as arguable that a bank contemplating payment against an allegedly fraudulent demand by the beneficiary under a performance bond owed a duty of care to the party ultimately liable at the end of the chain. That was in 1984 since when the tendency has been to restrict the ambit of claims in negligence after some years of unpruned growth. In *GKN Contractors v Lloyd's Bank*[3] Parker LJ felt bound to follow *United Trading* in this but in terms which suggest that if the point were fully argued no duty would be found.[4] Lastly, with regard to foreign parties, it is necessary for the applicant, as always where foreign entities are involved, to find a basis for the jurisdiction of the English court over them, a matter which having been mentioned can be stated as beyond the ambit of this book.[5]

1 See Chapter 6, para 6.14.
2 See [1985] 2 Lloyd's Rep 554n at 560.1.
3 (1985) 30 BLR 48 at 62.
4 See para 12.60 below where it is suggested that no duty of care arises.
5 See the *Supreme Court Practice*, and Dicey & Morris *The Conflict of Laws*, among other works.

9.35 *The balance of convenience* This is likely to raise a further considerable difficulty in the way of a plaintiff. A question which arises on every application for an interlocutory injunction (that is an injunction pending the full trial of the action) is whether the balance of convenience favours the grant or refusal of the injunction. If damages would be a sufficient remedy no injunction will ordinarily be granted. That apart, it will be considered whether more harm will be done by granting or refusing the injunction.[1] Thus in *Harbottle (Mercantile) Ltd v National Westminster Bank* Kerr J stated:[2]

> 'The plaintiffs then still face what seems to me to be an insuperable difficulty. They are seeking to prevent the bank from paying and debiting their account. It must then follow that if the bank pays and debits the plaintiffs' account, it is either entitled to do so or not entitled to do so. To do so would either be in accordance with the bank's contract with the plaintiffs or a breach of it. If it is in accordance with the contract, then the plaintiffs have no cause of action against the bank and, as it seems to me, no possible basis for an injunction against it. Alternatively, if the threatened payment is in breach of contract, which the plaintiffs' writs do not even allege and as to which they claim no declaratory relief, then the plaintiffs would have good claims for damages against the bank. In that event the injunctions would be inappropriate, because they interfere with the bank's obligations to the Egyptian banks, because they might cause greater damage to the bank than the plaintiffs could pay on their undertaking as to damages, and because the plaintiffs would then have an adequate remedy in damages. The balance of convenience would in that event be hopelessly weighted against the plaintiffs.'

This was also seen to be an insuperable difficulty in the way of the grant of an injunction in *GKN Contractors v Lloyds Bank*[3] where the plaintiff's dilemma was emphasised: if there is no breach by the bank, there is no case for an injunction; if there is or may be a breach, the bank will be well able to pay such damage as may be suffered, so there is no need for the injunction. In the *Harbottle* case the claim was for declarations against the English and Egyptian banks that the beneficiaries were not entitled to claim under the guarantee, and for injunctions restraining the banks from paying under it. The position in the *United Trading* case[4] was similar. In each the beneficiary had made its claim under the guarantee, and the question therefore was whether the banks should be permitted to pay against it. The position may be more favourable to the grant of an injunction where the issue is whether the beneficiary should be permitted to claim. It must be remembered, however, that if the beneficiary is not permitted to claim (or to present documents in the case of a credit) he will lose his opportunity to do so when the expiry date passes. So the effect of an injunction will be to deprive the beneficiary wholly and finally of the benefit for which he contracted. In a clear case of fraud this may be thought immaterial.

1 For the origin of the modern law, see *American Cyanamid Co v Ethicon Ltd* [1975] AC 396.
2 [1978] QB 146 at 155, cited with approval by the Court of Appeal in *United Trading Corpn SA v Allied Arab Bank Ltd* [1985] 2 Lloyd's Rep 554n at 565.
3 (1985) 30 BLR 48 at 64, 5.
4 Supra.

9.36 *Future development* It may be thought that, with their emphasis on the individual contracts and on the high standard of proof which is required, the English courts have taken a course which is unduly favourable to the beneficiary whose good faith is in dispute. This may be particularly the case where dubious demands are made under standby credits or demand guarantees (eg performance bonds) in situations where, once the money has been paid by the bank or banks within the jurisdiction of the English court, there is little realistic chance of its recovery whatever the merits of the account party's position. The sums involved are often very large. If English law is to develop further in this area, the way forward must be towards establishing a process whereby, in appropriate cases, rights under credits and guarantees can be held in abeyance while the underlying dispute is investigated. This, of course, would be directly contrary to the principle of autonomy and great care would be needed. But the principle should not be allowed to become a cause of injustice. In the *United Trading* case[1] Ackner LJ referred to the position in United States law, which has in part been developed in cases involving calls made against American parties following the Islamic Revolution in Iran.[2] It is likely that guidance for future development will be found among those cases.

1 [1985] 2 Lloyd's Rep 554n at 561 and set out in para 9.33 above.
2 For a consideration of the American position, see *Benjamin's Sale of Goods* (4th edn), para 23–109 et seq.

9.37 *Mareva injunctions* A Mareva injunction[1] restrains a defendant from removing his monies or other assets out of the jurisdiction, or otherwise dealing with them within the jurisdiction subject to a limitation in amount, which is usually the amount of the plaintiff's claim together with an allowance for his likely costs. It is available only where the plaintiff can establish that there is a risk of the assets being removed or otherwise dissipated. Ordinarily those assets must be in England.[2] Because a Mareva order is of the nature that it is and is not a preservation order it is an imperfect weapon, though it is often effective to achieve what a plaintiff requires. In *Z Ltd v A-Z and AA-LL*[3] Lord Denning MR stated of a Mareva injunction:

'The injunction does not prevent payment under a letter of credit or under a bank guarantee (. . . [citations] . . .); but it may apply to the proceeds as and when received by or for the defendant.'

Similarly, in the passage quoted from *Bolvinter*[4] the court made the caveat 'although restrictions may well be imposed on the freedom of the beneficiary to deal with the money after he has received it'.

1 So-called from case of *Mareva Cia Naviera SA v International Bulkcarriers SA* [1980] 1 All ER 213n, [1975] 2 Lloyd's Rep 509.
2 See para 9.38 at note 2.
3 [1982] QB 558 at 574.
4 Supra, para 9.32.

9.38 A buyer who suspects his seller of fraud or simply of providing goods which do not fully accord with the contract of sale, may not fancy his chances of enforcing his claim against the seller if the credit is operated and the seller receives the price and is free to do what he likes with it. For the seller may be in a jurisdiction where proceedings against him will be difficult, or he may become insolvent, or disappear. Instead of trying to prevent the bank paying, which even in the case of fraud will face the great difficulties already discussed, the buyer may consider an application for a Mareva injunction. Because the order does not interfere with the operation of the credit, but restrains the use of the proceeds of its operation, the buyer does not have to bring himself within the fraud exception to the autonomy rule to claim a Mareva order. The claim for a Mareva order may be supported by a simple claim by the buyer against the seller for breach of contract. A Mareva order is ordinarily drafted to affect only assets within the jurisdiction of the English court. Where it is served upon a bank the order should be confined by its terms to the defendant's bank accounts themselves and should not extend to the defendant's assets as may be comprised by a documentary credit itself. The bank must be free to honour such credit in accordance with its terms.[1] Although worldwide Mareva orders may be made in exceptional circumstances[2] it is thought unlikely that circumstances will arise in which an English court would make an order affecting money paid under a letter of credit by a bank abroad. So an order will only be of use where a credit is payable within the jurisdiction. Then, if the other requirements for an order are satisfied, the beneficiary can be restrained from disposing of money within the jurisdiction (this assumes, of course, that the only asset within the jurisdiction will be the proceeds of sale received from the credit: if there are other assets, these will introduce fresh considerations and ease the buyer's situation).

1 *Z Ltd v A-Z and AA-LL* [1982] QB 558 at 591.
2 See *Derby & Co Ltd v Weldon (No 3 and 4)* [1990] Ch 65.

9.39 The position is illustrated by the case of *Intraco Ltd v Notis Shipping Corpn, The Bhoja Trader*.[1] The defendants sold their vessel, the *Bhoja Trader*, to the plaintiffs who provided a bank guarantee for part of the price. The vessel was delivered but shortly afterwards it was arrested and the plaintiffs had to pay money to secure its release and suffered losses due to cargo cancellations. The sellers had no assets in England other than their rights under the guarantee. An *ex parte* injunction was granted restraining them from calling on the guarantee. This was discharged on the basis that such an injunction should not be granted unless there was fraud. But an injunction was granted in its place restraining the sellers from removing from the jurisdiction or otherwise disposing of their assets, in particular the proceeds of the guarantee, save in so far as they exceeded a nominated sum. In the Court of Appeal it was established that the guarantee was payable in Greece and not in London and so the court discharged the injunction, stating 'If this guarantee is to be treated as cash it must be treated as cash in Greece.' In its judgment the court referred to the rule that in the absence of fraud an injunction would not be granted to interfere with a seller's right to call on a bank to make payment under a letter of credit or a bank guarantee. It continued:[2]

> 'The learned Judge went on to say that this did not prevent the Court, in an appropriate case, from imposing a *Mareva* injunction upon the fruits of the letter of credit or guarantee. Again we agree. It is the natural corollary of the proposition that a letter of credit or bank guarantee is to be treated as cash that when the bank pays and cash is received by the beneficiary, it should be subject to the same restraints as any other of his cash assets. Enjoining the beneficiary

from removing the cash asset from the jurisdiction is not the same as taking action, whether by injunction or an order staying execution, which will prevent him obtaining the cash (see *Montecchi v Shimco (UK) Ltd* [1980] 1 Lloyd's Rep 50, [1979] 1 WLR 1180).

　　If therefore this bank guarantee had provided for payment in London, we should have agreed wholly with the learned Judge's judgment, . . .'

The court reserved the position where the beneficiary of a guarantee could, at his option, call for payment within or without the jurisdiction. It is suggested that in those circumstances he could not be forced to exercise his option by calling for payment in England. For there would be no grounds on which to do so, and it is established by the cases referred to that the court will not prevent a beneficiary calling a bank guarantee. If the beneficiary then called for payment abroad, the situation would be covered by the decision in the *Intraco* case.

1　[1981] 2 Lloyd's Rep 256.
2　[1981] 2 Lloyd's Rep 256 at 258.

9.40 *Potton Homes Ltd v Coleman Contractors Ltd*[1]　Here both parties were English companies. The plaintiffs agreed to supply prefabricated homes to the defendants in Libya. The defendants were in arrears with their payments but alleged defects in the houses delivered. The plaintiffs had given a performance bond. The judge at first instance gave judgment for the plaintiffs for £89,621 but stayed execution on the ground that the defendants had a counterclaim which they were entitled to set off against it. A call had been made by the defendants on the bond for £68,816. The judge held that following authority he was not able to prevent the call. Nor, he held, were the facts such that in reliance on *The Bhoja Trader*,[2] he was justified in granting a Mareva order restraining dealing with the proceeds of the call. Nonetheless he considered that the proceeds should be frozen and that he had power to do so under Order 29 rule 2(1) of the Rules of the Supreme Court (which relates to the preservation of property involved in an action). This was set aside by the Court of Appeal. Eveleigh LJ took the view that documentary credits and performance bonds were not necessarily to be treated in the same way, particularly so far as the buyer and seller were concerned. He stated:

'As between buyer and seller the underlying contract cannot be disregarded so readily. If the seller has lawfully avoided the contract *prima facie*, it seems to me he should be entitled to restrain the buyer from making use of the performance bond. Moreover, in principle I do not think it possible to say that in no circumstances whatsoever, apart from fraud, will the court restrain the buyer. The facts of each case must be considered. If the contract is avoided or if there is a failure of consideration between buyer and seller for which the seller undertook to procure the issue of the performance bond, I do not see why, as between seller and buyer, the seller should not [?] be unable to prevent a call upon the bond by the mere assertion that the bond is to be treated as cash in hand. It is true that in *Edward Owen Ltd v Barclays Bank* it was unsuccessfully submitted that the failure of the buyer to procure a letter of credit in accordance with the contract terms should entitle the plaintiffs to an injunction against the bank. That case, however, was not concerned with the position as between buyer and seller, . . .

For a large construction project the employer may agree to provide finance (perhaps by way of advance payments) to enable the contractor to undertake the works. The contractor will almost certainly be asked to provide a performance bond. If the contractor were unable to perform because the employer failed to provide the finance, it would seem wrong to me if the court was not entitled to have regard to the terms of the underlying contract and could be prevented from considering the question whether or not to restrain the employer by the mere assertion that a performance bond is like a letter of credit.

There are differences between a performance bond and a letter of credit. They operate from different directions. When a bank pays under a letter of credit upon receipt of the documents, those documents provide some security, namely, title to the goods themselves. There is no such security in the case of the performance bond.

I have made these observations in order to sound a note of caution. I would not wish in these interlocutory proceedings to say more than is necessary for the purpose of deciding the matter with which we have to deal. I particularly would not wish to add to the entrenched status of the bond beyond the limits set in the decided cases. I would wish at least to leave it open for consideration how far the bond is to be treated as cash in hand as between buyer and seller.'

He went on to hold that as the judge had found that there were no grounds for a Mareva injunction the court should not interfere with the bargain which the parties had made by restraining the ability of the defendants to obtain the money which the bond provided on call. The other member of the court, May LJ, held that, as the judge had found that the facts did not justify a Mareva order, he had been wrong to make any order freezing the proceeds of the call. Both Lords Justice held that the court had no power under Order 29 rule 2(1) in the circumstances. This was not a case where the demand was alleged to be fraudulent. The remarks of Eveleigh LJ relating to the position of the buyer and seller are, it is suggested, in conflict with the statement of Donaldson LJ in *The Bhoja Trader*[3] 'In refusing to interfere with the sellers' right to call upon the bank to make payment under its guarantee, the learned judge acted in conformity with the well-established principle that the Court will not grant such an injunction unless fraud is involved.' The Court of Appeal of Hong Kong declined in *Guangdong Transport Ltd v Ancora Transport NV*[4] to apply the dictum of Eveleigh LJ and declined to hold that the position between buyer and seller was any different.

1 (1984) 28 BLR 19.
2 Supra.
3 [1981] 2 Lloyd's Rep 256 at 257.2.
4 [1987] HKLR 923.

9.41 *The appointment of a receiver* Where a credit is payable in England, there may be a possibility for a buyer who suspects his seller of fraud or simply of providing goods which do not accord with the contract of sale, of applying to the court for the appointment of a receiver and for an order that the payment under the credit be made not to the seller, but to the receiver pending the resolution of the dispute between the buyer and the seller.[1] This would have the advantage of putting the money into the hands of an independent third party whereas the effect of a Mareva order is only to prevent the seller dissipating it. It is understood that one such application has been successfully made.[2] So the jurisdiction and practice in relation to the appointment of receivers and payments under letters of credit have yet to be established. The appointment of a receiver has much the same effect as the sequestration effected by order of the Swiss courts in *Camilla Cotton Oil Co v Granadex SA*,[3] where the buyers paid through the letter of credit and then, on the ground of claims against the sellers on other contracts, sequestrated the payment before it could be transferred to the sellers. The difficulty with the jurisdiction may be that although an order can be framed so that the receiver takes the payment on behalf of the sellers, his intervention does in reality prevent the seller taking possession of the money due under the credit, which is at least contrary to the spirit of the *Edward Owen* line of cases, and is probably contrary to the ratio of the decision of the Court of Appeal in the *Potton Homes* case.[4] A Mareva order, on the other hand, permits the seller to have possession, but seeks to tie his hands thereafter.

1 The jurisdiction to appoint a receiver is given in wide terms by section 37 of the Supreme Court Act 1981: see, generally, Gee *Mareva Injunctions & Anton Pillar Relief* (2nd edn) Ch 12.
2 The judgment was given in Chambers and is therefore not public.
3 [1976] 2 Lloyd's Rep 10, HL; revsd [1975] 1 Lloyd's Rep 470, CA, see the facts at 472.2.
4 Supra, para 9.40.

9.42 *Where the operation of the credit requires the co-operation of the buyer: orders under section 39 of Supreme Court Act 1981* Some credits include among the documents which are to be presented to obtain payment a document which is to be executed by the buyer or his agent. Such a provision is inserted by the buyer to obtain protection for himself, for example, by enabling him to certify that he has inspected the goods to be shipped. But it also enables him to frustrate the credit by refusing to provide the document when he should. In appropriate circumstances the court will order the buyer to execute the document so that it can be presented to the bank and payment obtained, and on default it can order a third party (who is likely to be an officer of the court) to execute the document on the buyer's behalf. This course was followed in *Astro Exito Navegacion SA v Southland Enterprise Co Ltd (No 2) (Chase Manhattan Bank NA intervening)*.[1] The underlying contract was for the sale of a ship. Payment was by letter of credit confirmed by a London bank. By an amendment to the credit accepted by the seller under protest it was provided that the notice of readiness was to be signed and accepted by the buyers' agents. The buyers refused to accept the notice of readiness. The letter of credit would expire on 30 October. The judge made an order that the buyers by their agents sign the notice of readiness by noon on 28 October, failing which a master of the Supreme Court was to sign the order on behalf of the buyers under section 47 of the Supreme Court of Judicature (Consolidation) Act 1925 (now section 39 of the Supreme Court Act 1981). He also ordered the buyers to instruct the issuing bank in Taiwan to instruct the confirming bank in London to release the full amount of the letter of credit. The proceeds were to be paid into an interest-bearing account in the joint names of the buyers' and the sellers' solicitors. The sellers presented the documents to the bank including the notice of readiness signed by a master of the Supreme Court. But the bank refused to pay. The House of Lords held that the order of the judge was within the ambit of section 47 and was properly made.[2] The facts in this case may be compared with those in *Elder Dempster Lines Ltd v Ionic Shipping Agency Inc and Midland Bank*.[3] There the plaintiffs agreed to sell a vessel to the first defendants. The deposit was guaranteed by a letter of credit issued by the second defendants payable against a bill drawn by the plaintiffs and first defendants jointly. The plaintiffs obtained an order that the first defendants join with

them in drawing a bill. But the first defendants did not comply with the
order and the credit expired, no order having been obtained under
section 47 of the 1925 Act. The plaintiffs' claim against the bank failed.
The power under section 39 of the 1981 Act may be a useful power where
documents are to be presented under a credit in England and one of the
documents requires the co-operation of the buyer.

1 [1983] 2 AC 787.
2 When the sellers' action against the bank for non-payment came to trial their claim failed
  because it was held that the documents did not appear on their face to accord with the
  credit: in particular there was nothing to show that the gas free certificate had the
  approval of the Harbour Bureau of Kaohsiung: *Astro Exito Navegacion SA v Chase
  Manhattan Bank NA, The Messiniaki Tolmi* [1986] 1 Lloyd's Rep 455 discussed at para
  8.53 in relation to the description of the vessel on the invoice.
3 [1968] 1 Lloyd's Rep 529.

Chapter 10

Transfer and Assignment

A. Transfer

10.1 *Introduction* The transfer of credits is a well-established practice which is now regulated by Article 48 of the Uniform Customs. Article 48 is reasonably comprehensive in its practical scope although some important matters are dealt with indirectly rather than directly and it is not set out in the form of a logical and comprehensive code. The transfer of a credit adds complications to the contractual relationships embodied by a credit by introducing fresh parties and relationships. Article 48 does not attempt to define these or the obligations undertaken: compare Article 9. There is only one reported English decision on the transfer of credits.[1]

1 *Bank Negara Indonesia 1946 v Lariza (Singapore) Pte Ltd* [1988] AC 583, Privy Council, considered below.

10.2 *Function* Where the seller in a transaction in respect of which payment is to be provided through a credit is buying the goods from a third party, he may use the transfer of the credit to pay the party selling to him. When the credit has been transferred to the third party (who is called the second beneficiary), the third party can present documents under the credit including his own invoice and will receive payment. Where the seller is buying from more than one third party he may transfer an appropriate part of the credit to each of his sellers. Assuming of course that the price the second beneficiary receives is lower than that provided for by the credit as between the buyer and the original seller, the seller (called the first beneficiary) can present his own invoice to the bank and receive in payment the difference in price between his invoice and what has already been invoiced by the second beneficiary. In this way he receives his profit on the transaction. The bank then substitutes his invoice for that of the second beneficiary and the documents are passed on and will reach the buyer. The buyer will know from the fact that the party selling to him has asked for the credit to be transferable that the seller is acting as a middleman (if that was not already known to him) but he will not know who the third party is unless this is revealed by other documents such as the transport documents which might name the third party seller as the consignor.[1] The importance of the first beneficiary's ability to conceal the name of the party selling to him lies in the fact that otherwise the buyer might cut him out on future transactions dealing directly and more cheaply with the third party seller. Concealment may be difficult to achieve where the transfer of a credit is used. An alternative means to this end is to use a back-to-back credit as considered in Chapter 2.[2]

1 Article 31.iii of the Uniform Customs permits acceptance of transport documents which indicate as the consignor of the goods a party other than the beneficiary of the credit. The Article is made subject to the terms of the credit: but a prohibition of transport documents in any name other than that of the beneficiary named in the credit would make transfer difficult.
2 Para 2.31.

10.3 *Transferability – a trap* Where a seller wishes to transfer a credit to provide the means of payment to his own seller, he will agree with his buyer that the credit shall be transferable, and the credit will be designated as transferable when it is issued. This will not, however, give him a right to require transfer. It will only give him a right to request transfer, at least where the Uniform Customs apply. The bank to which the request is made may refuse it outright or it may only agree to it to such extent and in such manner as it will accept. The Privy Council so held in respect of Article 46 of the 1974 Revision of the Uniform Customs in *Bank Negara Indonesia 1946 v Lariza (Singapore) Pte Ltd*,[1] and Article 54 of the 1983 Revision and now Article 48 of the 1993 Revision are in clearer terms. The first three paragraphs of Article 48 provide:

ARTICLE 48 **Transferable Credit**
　　　　a.[2] A transferable Credit is a Credit under which the Beneficiary (First Beneficiary) may request the bank authorised to pay, incur a deferred payment undertaking, accept or negotiate (the 'Transferring Bank'), or in the case of a freely negotiable Credit, the bank specifically authorised in the Credit as a Transferring Bank, to make the Credit available in whole or in part to one or more other Beneficiary(ies) (Second Beneficiary(ies)).
　　　　b.[3] A Credit can be transferred only if it is expressly designated as 'transferable' by the Issuing Bank. Terms such as 'divisible', 'fractionable', 'assignable', and 'transmissible' do not render the Credit transferable. If such terms are used they shall be disregarded.

c.[4] The Transferring Bank shall be under no obligation to effect such transfer except to the extent and in the manner expressly consented to by such bank.

1 [1988] AC 583.
2 Article 48.a is a restatement of Article 54.a in the 1983 Revision.
3 Article 48.b is a restatement of Article 54.b in the 1983 Revision.
4 Article 48.c is a restatement of Article 54.c in the 1983 Revision.

10.4 The unhappy story in the *Bank Negara* case[1] was as follows. Lariza were commodity dealers and agreed to sell palm oil to Bakrie, and they contracted to purchase the oil from Ban Lee. On Bakrie's application, a credit which was designated as transferable was issued by Bank Negara and advised th ough the Bank of Canton, Lariza's own bankers. Lariza requested the Bank of Canton and then Bank Negara to transfer the credit to Ban Lee. Both refused, the Bank of Canton on the grounds that the credit was badly drafted and that in any event they were only the advising bank. So no credit was opened in favour of Ban Lee who sued Lariza and obtained judgment. Bakrie had become insolvent and had gone into liquidation. Lariza tried to recover its loss from Bank Negara for breach of its alleged undertaking to transfer the credit. The Privy Council held that before a bank was obliged to effect a transfer under the terms of Article 46 of the 1974 Revision the bank must have consented to the particular transfer requested. In over-ruling the Court of Appeal of Singapore the Board held that the consent of a bank requested to transfer a credit was not to be found in its agreement to designate the credit as transferable: a separate consent to the particular transfer was required. The Board also stated:

'The Court of Appeal was concerned that, unless the beneficiary had not only a right to instruct the issuing bank to effect a transfer, but also a right to have his instructions complied with, the whole purpose of his having a transferable letter of credit could readily be defeated. That may be so, although, without expert evidence on the relevant banking practice, it is not possible to estimate the likelihood of this happening at all frequently.'[2]

1 [1988] AC 583.
2 Ibid at 599H.

10.5 What Lariza might have done was to open a new credit through the Bank of Canton on a back-to-back basis but avoiding the unsatisfactory drafting of the first credit. This would not have been possible if the Bank of Canton were not prepared to open a new credit because they would only do so on the strength of a satisfactory and workable credit which would back the new one: they presumably felt that the first credit's operation was likely to give rise to problems and the documents might be refused. It may well be that the issuing bank was at fault in not securing compliance with Article 14 (incomplete or unclear instructions) and with Article 22 (precision as to the documents against which payment is to be made).

10.6 It might be thought desirable that, if banks are to have the right to refuse to transfer transferable credits, there should at least be some limit on the exercise of that right. It is suggested in *Benjamin's Sale of Goods*[1] that a bank should only be entitled to refuse to transfer a transferable credit on reasonable grounds, drawing an analogy with the limited right of a landlord to refuse to grant his consent to the transfer of a lease (although it is noted that the basis of the limitation there is statutory). If this were the case, it would cause uncertainty which would be undesirable, in particular as the beneficiary might not know the reasons for the refusal. But in any event there seems no basis on which to imply such a limitation, particularly as the Uniform Customs are subject to revision and refinement and, if it were intended, it could easily have been stated.

1 (4th edn) para 23–040.

10.7 The fact that a transferable credit can only be transferred if the bank to whom request is made agrees to it is something of a contradiction in terms. If the arrangements resulting from transfer were always simple, there would be a strong argument for saying that it was undesirable that there should be such a right of refusal. But they are not always simple, and it is understandable that banks should wish to keep the right to say no where they anticipate that a transfer may lead to difficulties for them and the parties with whom they deal. If they are to have that right, it is probably correct that they should have an unfettered right leaving it to their good sense in each case (they are hardly likely to act out of spite) to determine whether there are objections to a transfer, rather than attempting to impose limitations which might lead to uncertainties and disputes.

10.8 **Which bank should effect transfer?** The predecessor of Article 48, Article 54, gave rise to a problem of identification of the bank which might be requested to effect the transfer.[1] Article 48.a intends to avoid this by providing for a 'Transferring Bank'. It makes a distinction between credits which are freely negotiable[2] and those which are not.

1 See 1st Edn, paras 10.8–10.13.
2 See para 2.22 above.

10.9 Where the credit is not a freely negotiable credit, the Transferring Bank is the bank authorised to pay, incur a deferred payment undertaking or to accept drafts or negotiate. Where the correspondent bank is so authorised, it is suggested that the Transferring Bank will be the correspondent bank. The issuing bank will also be so authorised (by the beneficiary). But by its reference to 'the bank authorised to . . .' the Article foresees only one such bank as the Transferring Bank. The tenor of the Article and practicality suggest that this should be the correspondent bank and not the issuing bank. Where there is no correspondent bank, or where the correspondent bank is not authorised to pay or . . . , the issuing bank will be the Transferring Bank.

10.10 Where the credit is a freely negotiable credit, request may be made to 'the bank specifically authorised in the credit as a Transferring Bank'. So, although the Article does not say so in terms, the credit must itself nominate the Transferring Bank. No guidance is given as to which bank should be chosen. Article 54 in the 1983 Revision provided that any bank entitled to effect negotiation might be requested to transfer the credit. The terms of Article 48 leave it open for a freely negotiable credit to authorise any bank party to the credit or which could be asked to negotiate the documents (which is any bank) to be the Transferring Bank.[1] If a bank is nominated which is not by reason of its position towards the credit bound to receive advice of proposed amendments, this will give rise to problems. This is considered further below in relation to amendments.[2] What if no bank is authorised? The choice is between saying that the credit cannot then be transferred, or treating it as if it were a non-negotiable credit. The latter must be the preferable choice.

1 The consequences of this freedom have not been followed through in Article 48.i, which assumes that the Transferring Bank will be presenting documents to the issuing bank. If it is a negotiating bank, it may well be presenting documents to a correspondent bank.
2 Para 10.28 et seq.

10.11 ***Mechanics: substitution of invoice and drafts*** The procedure of transfer has already been outlined in the preceding paragraphs. Article 48.i refers to the First Beneficiary's right to substitute his own invoices and drafts (if called for by the credit) for those of the second beneficiary. This enables him to provide the documents which the credit as issued requires and thus to make effective his own right to be paid. Article 48.i is in these terms:

> ARTICLE 48.i[1] The First Beneficiary has the right to substitute his own invoice(s) (and Draft(s)) for those of the Second Beneficiary(ies), for amounts not in excess of the original amount stipulated in the Credit and for the original unit prices if stipulated in the Credit, and upon such substitution of invoice(s) (and Draft(s)) the First Beneficiary can draw under the Credit for the difference, if any, between his invoice(s) and the Second Beneficiary's(ies') invoice(s).
>
> When a Credit has been transferred and the First Beneficiary is to supply his own invoice(s) (and Draft(s)) in exchange for the Second Beneficiary's(ies') invoice(s) (and Draft(s)) but fails to do so on first demand, the Transferring Bank has the right to deliver to the Issuing Bank the documents received under the transferred Credit, including the Second Beneficiary's(ies') invoice(s) (and Draft(s)) without further responsibility to the First Beneficiary.

1 Article 48.i follows closely Article 54.f in the 1983 Revision.

10.12 ***An example of transfer with a freely negotiable credit*** Let it be supposed that the Alpha Bank issues a transferable credit which is advised and confirmed by the Beta Bank to Export Ltd, the beneficiary. The credit provides for deferred payment 60 days after bill of lading date, and is 'freely negotiable by any bank'. The credit names Beta Bank as the transferring bank. Export Ltd is buying the goods from Sources SA, which banks with Nego Bank. Export will request Beta Bank to transfer to Sources so much of the credit as will pay to Sources the price payable to Sources by Export. Beta Bank will then advise Sources of the credit as transferred. Sources can then approach its bank, Nego Bank, to ask if it will negotiate documents under the transferred credit. If it agrees, on receipt of documents Nego Bank will check them against the credit, and if they comply will buy them from Sources, crediting Sources with the discounted value, that is, less a discount to take account of the delay in payment under the credit. Nego Bank will pass the documents to Beta Bank which will check them in its turn. It will substitute for the invoice of Sources the invoice which Export will supply to it and pass the documents to Alpha Bank. Alpha Bank will check them again and will then deal with them in accordance with its arrangements with its customer, the buyer/

applicant. Sixty days after bill of lading date Alpha Bank is bound to pay Beta Bank the full amount of the invoice of Export.[1] Beta Bank will pay to Nego Bank the amount of Sources' invoice, and the difference to Export.

1 This is subject to the reimbursement arrangements between them. In practice these may well allow the earlier reimbursement of the banks.

10.13 *Transfer of parts of a credit: no second transfer* As has been indicated a beneficiary will usually only wish to transfer such part of the credit as will enable him to pay his supplier, leaving a portion to himself representing his profit. He may also be using more than one supplier. He will then want to transfer part of the credit to one and part to another, while still retaining a balance for himself. In the past credits frequently stated that they were 'transferable and divisible' or used a similar wording. This concept should now be incorporated by the use of the single word 'transferable'. This is the effect of Article 48.b and 48.g. Article 48.g also provides that, subject to the terms of the credit, a credit can only be transferred once: it cannot be transferred and retain its transferability. A second transfer would involve such complications that there would be a high risk of something going wrong. Second transfers are sometimes called vertical transfers and have been considered inadvisable by the ICC Banking Commission.[1] Article 48.g provides:

> ARTICLE 48.g   Unless otherwise stated in the Credit, a transferable Credit can be transferred once only. Consequently, the Credit cannot be transferred at the request of the Second Beneficiary to any subsequent Third Beneficiary. For the purpose of this Article, a retransfer to the First Beneficiary does not constitute a prohibited transfer.
> Fractions of a transferable Credit (not exceeding in the aggregate the amount of the Credit) can be transferred separately, provided partial shipments/drawings are not prohibited, and the aggregate of such transfers will be considered as constituting only one transfer of the Credit.

1 See Decisions 1975–79, ICC Publication 371.

10.14 *Terms of the credit as transferred* Article 48.h provides:

> ARTICLE 48.h   The Credit can be transferred only on the terms and conditions specified in the original Credit, with the exception of:
>   (i)   the amount of the Credit,
>   (ii) any unit price stated therein,
>   (iii) the expiry date,
>   (iv) the last date for presentation of documents in accordance with Article 43,
>   (v)   the period for shipment,
> any or all of which may be reduced or curtailed.
> The percentage for which insurance cover must be effected may be increased in such a way as to provide the amount of cover stipulated in the original Credit, or these Articles.
> In addition, the name of the First Beneficiary can be substituted for that of the Applicant, but if the name of the Applicant is specifically required by the original Credit to appear in any document(s) other than the invoice, such requirement must be fulfilled.

The matters that can be varied are:

1 *The amount of the credit, and any unit prices.* This enables the first beneficiary to receive his profit on the transaction and to pay to the second beneficiary or beneficiaries what is due to them.

2 *The expiry date and the last date for presentation of documents in accordance with Article 43.* It might be thought that the purpose of this was to enable the first beneficiary to shorten the periods so he could be sure of being able to present his own invoice within the periods limited by the credit. However, it appears from Article 48.i and .j[1] that he need not do so. Article 48.i institutes a procedure whereby the paying, accepting or negotiating bank may demand the invoice (and draft) from the first beneficiary and if he fails to supply them 'on first demand' the bank can deliver the documents to the issuing bank with the second beneficiary's invoice and drafts. This suggests that the time limits are irrelevant to the first beneficiary's performance of the contract. Secondly the wording of Article 48.j shows that the second beneficiary may have the full period of the credit in which to present documents. These provisions are considered further under 'Date for Presentation' below.[2] Although it might be expected that it would be more prominently stated, this makes it clear that the time limits which would apply to presentation under the original credit do not apply to the first beneficiary once the credit has been transferred. The only purpose in curtailing the periods as permitted by Article 48.h would appear to be to enable the credit as transferred to match the contract of sale between the first and second beneficiaries where this sets a stricter time-table.

3 *The last date for presentation in accordance with Article 43.* Article 43[3] relates to the period after shipment within which presentation must be made. The points are to be made as in the previous paragraph.

4 *The period for shipment.* This is of a different nature because it does not directly affect the time for presentation of documents. But the purpose for which it is permitted appears to be the same.

5 *The percentage for which insurance cover must be effected.* This enables the first beneficiary to ensure that the cover provided by the second beneficiary will be sufficient to enable the first beneficiary to be paid under the credit as he will have to provide a certificate which fully covers the value of the cargo to the applicant. Thus, if the credit requires insurance to the CIF value of the goods which is £110,000, and the CIF price payable to the second beneficiary is £98,000, the credit as transferred should be amended to require insurance for 112.25% of CIF value as per the documents to be presented by the second beneficiary. This will mean that the first beneficiary's level of profit is disclosed, which is a disadvantage of transfer.

6 *The name of the first beneficiary* can be substituted for that of the original applicant but if the applicant's name is to appear in any document other than the invoice it must appear. The invoice will of course be substituted. If the name of the applicant does have to appear, this will destroy part of the confidentiality which the system of transfer is designed to maintain.

7 *Drafts.* Drafts are not referred to in Article 48.h and it would appear from this provision by itself that any term of the credit relating to drafts cannot be varied. As considered in the next paragraph Article 48.i and j show otherwise.

1 Article 48.i: para 10.11 above; Article 48.j: para 10.17 below.
2 Para 10.16.
3 Para 5.24.

10.15 *Drafts* If the credit requires drafts, they will almost certainly be the drafts of the first beneficiary. Article 48.h does not include any provision as to drafts among the terms which exceptionally may be varied. However Article 48.i refers to the right of the first beneficiary 'to substitute his own invoice(s) (and Draft(s)) for those of the Second Beneficiary(ies)'. So if the credit as originally drawn requires sight drafts drawn on the issuing bank it would appear that the credit as transferred should require drafts so drawn by the second beneficiary. The first beneficiary will in due course substitute his draft for the full amount to be drawn under the credit.

10.16 *Date for presentation of substituted documents by first beneficiary* It has been observed that the terms of the credit as transferred relating to the expiry date, the last date for presentation of documents in accordance with Article 43 and the period of shipment may be reduced.[1] In connection with this it was pointed out that it follows from Article 48.i and .j, particularly the latter, that the first beneficiary need not provide his invoices (and drafts) for substitution within the period limited by the credit either originally or as transferred.[2] He may provide them to the transferring bank[3] in advance of the presentation of documents by the second beneficiary to await their arrival. That is the prudent course. Or he may wait until the bank demands them from him, when he must provide them 'on first demand'. 'On demand' means that the party shall have a reasonable time to respond to the demand according to the nature of the thing to be done.[4] The addition of the word 'first' simply emphasises that the bank need not give the first beneficiary a reminder, though no doubt it would be courteous and perhaps avoid a dispute if the bank did check with the first beneficiary what the position was. Thus there is to be permitted a reasonable time for the provision of the documents to the bank, after which the bank may send the documents received by it from the second beneficiary to the issuing bank. This is a drastic step because the first beneficiary then loses his right to payment. Although the Uniform Customs do not expressly say so, it is to be inferred that the issuing bank is entitled to be paid in its turn by the applicant against the second beneficiary's documents.

1 Para 10.14.
2 This is confirmed by an Opinion of the ICC Banking Commission, Reference 83, Opinions 1980–1981, ICC Publication No 399. See also Case 286 in More Case Studies on Documentary Credits, ICC Publication No 489.
3 Where the transferring bank is the issuing bank because it is the accepting bank – see above, he will provide them through the advising bank.
4 See *Toms v Wilson* (1862) 32 LJQB 33 at 37, per Blackburn J (affd at 32 LJQB 382).

10.17 *Transfer to another place (bank)* Article 48.j makes it clear that the credit can be transferred so that the second beneficiary can receive payment at a bank to which the credit is transferred as the paying or negotiating bank. It provides:

> ARTICLE 48.j[1] The First Beneficiary may request that payment or negotiation be effected to the Second Beneficiary(ies) at the place to which the Credit has been transferred up to and including the expiry date of the Credit, unless the original Credit expressly states that it may not be made available for payment or negotiation at a place other than that stipulated in the Credit. This is without prejudice to the First Beneficiary's right to substitute subsequently his own invoice(s) (and Draft(s)) for those of the Second Beneficiary(ies) and to claim any difference due to him.

The reference to 'payment or negotiation be effected to the Second Beneficiary(ies) at the place to which the credit has been transferred' can only be taken as referring to a branch of a bank, although it is odd that it is not made more clear. This bank is then likely to become the advising bank for advising the credit to the second beneficiary. If requested by the transferring bank it could, it is thought, add its confirmation, or it could do so without engagement on its part. Transferable credits may sometimes indicate to which countries transfer may be effected rather than leaving it to the discretion of the bank to whom the request for transfer is to be made.

1 Article 48.j is based upon Article 54.g in the 1983 Revision.

10.18 A credit which is stated to be transferable may also state that it is available at a stated banker's counters. It is the view of the ICC Banking Commission that this does not prevent transfer to another bank in the country of the second beneficiary.[1]

1 See Opinions of the ICC Banking Commission 1984–1986 at R 139, and 1987–1988 at R 172.

10.19 *The legal analysis* Article 48 does not indicate the legal nature of the transactions for which it provides, and there have been no reported decisions in English law touching on it. It is suggested that the matter must be approached on the basis of ordinary contractual principles, and that there are two situations which must be treated separately. The first is that where the transfer is effected by a bank involved with the original credit such as the confirming bank, and the second is that where it is effected by a third party bank under a negotiation credit.

10.20 (a) Take first the case where the transferring bank is the correspondent or advising bank which is also the paying bank (and which may or may not also confirm the credit), and take the simple case where the terms of the credit as transferred are advised to the second beneficiary by that bank and the transferred credit is not made payable at another bank as provided for in Article 48.j. It is suggested that the relationships of the banks with the second beneficiary are exactly the same as those between them and the first beneficiary save that the terms of the credit as transferred, in particular as to amount, are likely to be different as permitted under Article 48.h. The undertakings provided for by Article 9 of the Uniform Customs will apply to the credit as transferred, and thus the second beneficiary has the issuing bank's undertaking that payment will be made (if the credit provides for payment) and it has a confirming bank's undertaking to pay.[1]

1 A different analysis is suggested in Gutteridge & Megrah *The Law of Bankers' Commercial Credits* (7th edn) p 103. Having referred to the contract between the issuing bank and the first beneficiary it is then stated: 'When a transferee is introduced a fresh contract is set up between the primary beneficiary and the transferee and probably with an intermediary bank also, that contract depending first, on the terms on which the transfer is made, but second on the appropriate Article 46 [now 48] of the Uniform Customs. The issuing bank is not in privity with the transferee.' This analysis is not accepted.

10.21 (b) Take next the case which is the same as that considered at (a) but assume that the transferred credit is advised to the second beneficiary by, and is made available at, a third bank which may or may not be in the same country as the original correspondent bank. It is suggested that with regard to the relationships of the second beneficiary with the issuing bank and with the correspondent bank, the position is unchanged: the second beneficiary will have the Article 9 undertakings as appropriate. The third bank is in the position of an advising bank and acts as the agent of the bank from which it received its instructions, namely, the transferring bank. Its position as regards advising the credit, examining documents, payment and its right to reimbursement following payment is the same as any other advising bank. If it is asked to confirm the credit and is prepared to do so, it will give the appropriate undertaking to the second beneficiary as provided for by Article 9.b. It should be stated that it is not known whether it is the practice that in appropriate circumstances a bank to whom a credit is transferred should confirm the credit: if it is, it considerably increases the value of transfer to the transferee.

10.22 (c) In the situations considered it is suggested that the contracts between the issuing bank and the confirming bank (if any) and the first beneficiary remain unchanged in their nature. But their performance is affected by the transfer. For by asking for the transfer the first beneficiary accepts that he will only be able to collect the difference between the value of his invoice and the second beneficiary's invoice. Even where there will be no balance for him to draw, he will retain an interest in the performance of the contract and will need to substitute his own invoice: he does not drop out. When his request for transfer is accepted by the bank, this acts as a variation of the contracts with him in that respect. It is uncertain whether the issuing and confirming banks undertake to him that documents will be accepted from the second beneficiary, and the second beneficiary will be paid, in accordance with the transferred credit. But it is suggested that this should be the case. An analogy may be drawn with the situation where A agrees to buy goods from B for £100 and then agrees to accept goods from C in performance paying £80 to C and £20 to B. A is contractually bound to B to accept the goods from C and to pay C. A is in the position of a bank which has given an undertaking under a credit and later agreed to its transfer.

10.23 (d) Where the credit transferred is a negotiation credit and the request for transfer is made to a bank which is simply a bank entitled to negotiate the credit, by acceding to the request for transfer the negotiating bank must be taken also to have agreed with the first beneficiary to negotiate documents which conform to the credit when they are presented in due course. For although prior to its agreement to the request the bank had no obligations in relation to the credit, it would be nonsensical if an agreement to transfer did not also carry with it agreement to negotiate the documents in due course. If this were not so, it would mean that the negotiating bank could subsequently decline to negotiate documents from the second beneficiary and decline to pay the first beneficiary on substitution of its invoice and draft. It follows that, by its agreement to transfer the credit, unless it specifies the terms on which it is acting, the negotiating bank may put itself into a position similar to that of an issuing bank, and broadly its position as regards the first and second beneficiaries and any bank through which the transferred credit is advised to the second beneficiary would be as discussed at (a) to (c) above. But the fee that a negotiation bank usually takes is a small one. It is therefore very likely to make it a term of the transfer that it does so without engagement on its part: it will negotiate with recourse.

10.24 (e) Where the transfer is effected by a negotiating bank the first beneficiary retains his remedies against the issuing bank and any confirming bank, as discussed at (c) above. The second beneficiary's position against them is as discussed at (a), namely, in relation to the transferred credit it has the benefit of the undertakings provided by Article 9.

10.25 The position may be summarised as follows. A transferable credit embodies a contract or contracts with the first beneficiary which the credit foresees may be varied on transfer. On transfer variation of the contract or contracts with the first beneficiary takes place, and contracts also then come into being between the issuing bank and any confirming bank with the second beneficiary.

10.26 *Other views* Other views have been expressed as to the legal nature of a transfer. One is that it is an equitable assignment of the benefit of the credit. It is doubtful whether the transaction can properly be described as an assignment, particularly as the second beneficiary can only obtain the benefits by performance on his part, that is, by presenting conforming documents. It certainly does not appear to assist in understanding the transaction to consider it in this way. It has secondly been suggested that there is a novation. A 'novation takes place where the two contracting parties agree that a third shall stand in the relation to either of them to the other. There is a new contract and it is therefore essential that the consent of all parties shall be obtained.'[1] As in nearly all cases the first beneficiary will remain entitled to claim the balance due to him after payment of the second beneficiary and in any event retains an interest in the performance of the contract and will need to insert his own invoice; this analysis is unsatisfactory. Neither does it throw light on the nature of the transaction.[2]

1 *Chitty On Contracts* (26th edn) 'General Principles' para 1436.
2 The views (and their difficulties) are also considered in *Benjamin's Sale of Goods* (4th edn) para 23–041.

10.27 *Amendments* The amendment of a transferred credit gives rise to serious practical and theoretical difficulties. Article 9.d.i provides 'Except as otherwise provided by Article 48[1] an Irrevocable Credit can neither be amended nor cancelled without the agreement of the Issuing Bank, the Confirming Bank, if any, and the Beneficiary'. This simply reflects the legal position that when a contract has been made it can only be amended with the agreement of the parties to it.[2] Where a credit has been transferred there are two parallel contracts or sets of contracts, namely those between the first beneficiary and the issuing and any confirming bank, and those between the second beneficiary and the banks.[3] Prior to the 1993 Revision the Uniform Customs did not deal with the question of the amendment of transferred credits. It was suggested in the First Edition of this book[4] that it would be impracticable to have amendments which were valid as between the banks and one beneficiary but not between the banks and another beneficiary. It was suggested that,

if any beneficiary objected to an amendment, it should not become
effective. An Opinion of the ICC Banking Commission was cited in
support.[5]

1 Article 48 relates to transfer.
2 See para 3.34 et seq above.
3 If the analysis put forward in para 10.20 et seq is correct.
4 Para 10.31.
5 Case 156 in the ICC's Case Studies on Documentary Credits. See also now Case R. 193 in
  the Opinion of the ICC Banking Commission 1989–91 as to disagreement on the then
  position.

10.28 The Uniform Customs now deal with the amendment of transferred
credits in these terms:

> ARTICLE 48.d At the time of making a request for transfer and prior to
> transfer of the Credit, the First Beneficiary must irrevocably
> instruct the Transferring Bank whether or not he retains the
> right to refuse to allow the Transferring Bank to advise amend-
> ments to the Second Beneficiary(ies). If the Transferring Bank
> consents to the transfer under these conditions, it must, at the
> time of transfer, advise the Second Beneficiary(ies) of the First
> Beneficiary's instructions regarding amendments.
>
> ARTICLE 48.e If a Credit is transferred to more than one Second Benefici-
> ary(ies), refusal of an amendment by one or more Second
> Beneficiary(ies) does not invalidate the acceptance(s) by the
> other Second Beneficiary(ies) with respect to whom the Credit
> will be amended accordingly. With respect to the Second
> Beneficiary(ies) who rejected the amendment, the Credit will
> remain unamended.

10.29 Article 48.d provides either expressly or by implication that:

(i)   The first beneficiary has a right to refuse to allow the transferring
    bank to pass amendments on to the second beneficiary.
(ii) He may only exercise this right if he instructs the transferring bank,
    when he requests the transfer, that he is retaining the right to
    refuse.
(iii) The transferring bank may take his retention or non-retention of the
    right into account in deciding whether to consent to the transfer.
(iv) The second beneficiary must be informed by the transferring bank
    whether the first beneficiary has retained his right to refuse the
    advice of amendments.
(v)   When a credit has been transferred to a second beneficiary and the
    right to refuse advice of amendments to him has been retained by the
    first beneficiary, the first beneficiary may, or may not, exercise that
    right in respect of any particular amendment.
(vi) When, in a case where the first beneficiary has retained his right to
    refuse, an amendment is advised to the transferring bank, the bank
    must advise the first beneficiary of it and give the first beneficiary a
    reasonable time to instruct the bank whether it is to be advised to the
    second beneficiary. If the first beneficiary does not exercise his right
    of refusal within a reasonable time, it appears that the amendment
    should be advised to the second beneficiary.

If the first beneficiary retains his right to refuse advice of amendments
to the second beneficiary, what is then the position as to the acceptance of

amendments? Although the Article does not deal with this, which is both strange and unfortunate, the position must be that the exercise or non-exercise of the right determines which beneficiary is to have the right to accept or refuse amendments. If the first beneficiary refuses to allow an amendment to be advised to the second beneficiary, then it is the first beneficiary's acceptance or refusal of the amendment which will determine whether or not the credit is amended for both of them. If the first beneficiary consents to the advice of the amendment to the second beneficiary, it must then be for the second beneficiary to accept or to refuse it. Likewise, if the first beneficiary does not retain the right to refuse advice of amendments to the second beneficiary, he should be taken to have given up any right to accept or reject amendments himself: he has consented to the decision being made by the second beneficiary. Because the Article does not set out these consequences there must be an element of uncertainty about them. But if the advice or non-advice of amendments to the second beneficiary does not determine whether the first or second beneficiary is to have the right to accept or reject an amendment, there seems little real purpose in giving the first beneficiary a right to refuse to allow the advice of amendments to second beneficiaries. The commentary on Article 48.d in the ICC's UCP 500 and 400 Compared begins 'Sub-Article 48(d) addresses whose consent is required to amend the transferred credit'. This confirms the interpretation suggested, although it makes it the more remarkable that the Article fails to refer directly to the question of whose consent is to be determinative. Support is also obtained from Article 48.e which suggests that where an amendment is advised to second beneficiaries the first beneficiary has no part to play in its acceptance or refusal.

Where an amendment is accepted, the amendment of the credit becomes effective and the beneficiaries have to meet its amended terms. They will be unable to do this if they do not know of the amendment or that it has been accepted. They will only know if the transferring bank (assuming that it is the bank which is effectively dealing with amendments) informs them. So the continuing workability of the credit may depend on the bank informing the beneficiary who has not taken the decision to accept or refuse the amendment, of the amendment once it has come into effect. Again this is not a matter addressed by the Article. Indeed it is at first sight a contradiction of the express terms of Article 48.d.

Where there is more than one second beneficiary, Article 48.e provides that one may accept an amendment and another reject it. If that occurs, the term of the credit will then be different in respect of the amounts transferred to each. The position of the first beneficiary will be that the two parts of the credit have different terms so far as he is concerned. He is entitled to whatever payment is due to him against documents which take account of the differing terms and, if the difference affects the invoice which he is to substitute, his invoice must take account of it.

10.30 The amendment of transferred credits is necessarily complex. Because of the need to keep credit operations as simple as possible, there may be no wholly satisfactory solution. How the scheme apparently intended by Article 48.d will work in practice is uncertain. Much will depend on the common sense and clear thinking of the first beneficiary. If he wishes to retain any control over amendments, he must retain his right to refuse to allow the advice of amendments to the second beneficiary. When, having retained that right, an amendment is advised to him, if it is acceptable to him he has a choice. He can accept it and refuse to allow its advice to the second beneficiary (for acceptance or refusal by the second beneficiary). The credit will then become amended as regards both beneficiaries, and, as stated, the second beneficiary will need to be informed. Or the first beneficiary may give his consent for the amendment to be advised to the second beneficiary who will then decide whether it is acceptable and so whether the credit becomes amended. If the amendment is unacceptable to the first beneficiary, he will refuse it and will refuse his consent for its advice to the second beneficiary. The correct course for the first beneficiary to follow must be considered by him in the context of the particular amendment and the circumstances which have led up to it.

10.31 *Notification of transfer to issuing bank*   There is no requirement for the transferring bank to notify the issuing bank of a transfer unless the credit itself provides for it. It is suggested that it is generally undesirable if the notification consists of more than the fact of transfer because it may lead to breach of confidentiality as to the first beneficiary's supplier and the price between them.[1]

1 See Decisions (1975–1979) of the ICC Banking Commission, Reference 57, ICC Publication No 371 and the Case Studies on Documentary Credits, Case 154, ICC Publication No 459.

10.32 *Charges*   Unless there is agreement otherwise, the costs of transfer are payable by the first beneficiary. Article 48.f provides:

> ARTICLE 48.f[1]   Transferring Bank charges in respect of transfers including commissions, fees, costs or expenses are payable by the First Beneficiary, unless otherwise agreed. If the Transferring Bank agrees to transfer the Credit it shall be under no obligation to effect the transfer until such charges are paid.

1 Based on Article 54.d in the 1983 Revision.

B.   Assignment

10.33 *Function*   Assignment as it is considered here performs a wholly different function to transfer, and is quite different to transfer. The assignment referred to is an assignment of either the right to monies which may become payable under a credit following the future presentation of documents by the beneficiary, or of the right to monies which will become payable in accordance with the terms of the credit, documents having already been presented. It is concerned with the transfer of a future debt from the one creditor, the beneficiary, to another, the assignee. It enables the assignee instead of the beneficiary to receive payment following the beneficiary's performance of the credit contract. In contrast the transfer of a credit provides for a second beneficiary to present documents pursuant to the credit and so to be paid for them, and by transfer the first beneficiary hopes largely to avoid the presentation of documents himself.

10.34 *Article 49* of the Uniform Customs provides:

> ARTICLE 49 **Assignment of Proceeds**
> The fact that a Credit is not stated to be transferable shall not affect the Beneficiary's right to assign any proceeds to which he may be, or may become, entitled under such Credit, in accordance with the provisions of the applicable law. This Article relates only to the assignment of proceeds and not to the assignment of the right to perform under the Credit itself.

The first sentence of the Article follows Article 55 in the 1983 Revision: the second sentence is new.

10.35 *Assignment under English law* The law to be applied must be the law governing the various aspects of the assignment.[1] In English law assignments are divided into legal assignments and equitable assignments. Where an assignment is governed by English law, an assignee should aim to achieve a legal assignment complying with the terms of section 136 of the Law of Property Act 1925. But this may not always be possible. Two situations have to be considered. One is the assignment by the beneficiary of the proceeds of the credit which he intends will become payable following his successful presentation of documents. The other is the assignment by the beneficiary of the proceeds where he has already presented conforming documents but the credit does not provide for immediate payment. It will be understood that questions as to assignments under section 136 and in equity can be complicated and this is not the place for a general treatment of them.[2]

1 See Article 12 of the Rome Convention.
2 Reference may be made to Marshall *The Assignment of Choses in Action* (1950); *Chitty on Contracts* (20th edn) 'General Principles' ch 19; *Snell's Principles of Equity* (25th edn) ch 5; 6 Halsbury's Laws (4th edn).

10.36 *Assignment before presentation of documents* Before documents have been presented there is nothing owed to the beneficiary, and, because he may fail to present documents in time or at all or to present conforming documents, nothing may become due. So the coming into being of an actual debt is contingent on the presentation of conforming documents. It is not wholly certain whether such a future and contingent debt can be assigned under section 136, although the cases suggest that it can because it arises out of an existing contract.[1] The assignment should be in writing and signed by or on behalf of the assignor and it should be absolute, that is, not by way of charge only, nor for part of the debt only. Notice of the assignment should be given by the assignee to the paying bank (and preferably also to any other bank which has given an undertaking in respect of payment). Section 136 will then be complied with and the assignee can sue the bank in his own name if the bank fails to pay him when payment is due. The assignee will take subject to any set-off arising between the bank and the assignor/beneficiary (but only if the set-off arises prior to the date of the assignment in the case of a set-off arising out of a separate transaction).[2] If, because the debt is only future and contingent at the date of the assignment, section 136 is inapplicable, the assignment will be treated in equity as an agreement to assign taking effect as soon as the debt becomes payable. When the debt becomes payable an equitable interest will at once pass to the assignee.[3] In the context that is likely where a credit is concerned, the main advantage of establishing that section 136 applies is that the assignee need not join the assignor/beneficiary in his action against the bank.

1 See, inter alia, *Walker v Bradford Old Bank* (1884) 12 QBD 511; *Hughes v Pump House Hotel Co* [1902] 2 KB 190; *Torkington v Magee* [1902] 2 KB 427 and *Earle Ltd v Hemsworth RDC* (1928) 140 LT 69. It is suggested that there is no fully satisfactory discussion of the problem in the authorities.
2 As to such set-off, see Chapter 5 para 5.78.
3 *Tailby v Official Receiver* (1888) 13 App Cas 523.

10.37 *Assignment after presentation of documents*   Here the difficulties as to the debt being contingent which are considered in the previous paragraph do not arise. The assignment will certainly be effective under section 136 provided that it is in writing signed by the assignor, that it is 'absolute' (not by way of charge or of part of the debt), and written notice is given to the paying bank (and preferably also to any other bank giving an undertaking as to payment). The position as to any set-off will be as previously stated. If these conditions are not satisfied, it may nonetheless be valid as an equitable assignment.

10.38 *Assignment to support a second credit*   Where a buyer in a string wishes to use a credit opened in his favour by one bank to support a credit opened on his instructions with a second bank, this can be achieved by the assignment of the proceeds of the first credit to the second bank. An example of this (and of the disastrous consequences brought upon itself by the second or assignee bank) is provided by *Mannesman Handel AG v Kaunlaren Shipping Corpn.*[1]

1 [1993] 1 Lloyd's List Rep 89. See also para 2.31 above.

10.39 *Irrevocable mandates or instructions*   It appears that where a credit is not transferable and a solution is not found by opening a back-to-back credit, beneficiaries under credits sometimes seek to secure payment to their own suppliers by giving the paying bank an irrevocable mandate or instruction to pay to the supplier a sum from the proceeds of the credit, and the bank then confirms to the supplier its receipt of the instruction. According to the authority of *Brice v Bannister*,[1] this would be a good assignment in equity under English law. In that case Gough agreed to build a vessel for Bannister and later directed Bannister to pay £100 to Brice out of money due or to become due from Bannister to Gough. The majority of the court held that this was a good equitable assignment. It would strengthen the third party supplier's position if in addition to the instruction from the beneficiary to the bank, the beneficiary made a written assignment of the sum in question due or to become due from the bank under the credit, which it enclosed to the bank with its instruction.

1 (1878) 3 QBD 569, CA.

10.40 *Credits payable to the order of the beneficiary*   Where the beneficiary foresees that he will or may wish to instruct the paying bank in the manner which has just been considered, he may feel that it will ease his way if the credit is made payable to his order rather than to him. The advising bank could not then object to acting on his instructions. This appears to be foreseen by Article 2 of the Uniform Customs where it refers to:

> 'whereby a bank . . . acting at the request . . . of a customer . . ., (i) is to make a payment to *or to the order*[1] of a third party (the 'Beneficiary') . . .'

1 Author's italics.

10.41 *'Assignment of the credit'* It is sometimes considered whether the credit itself, that is the right to present documents under it and to receive payment, can be assigned.[1] It is suggested that transfer is the only appropriate mechanism because, first, the credit is addressed specifically to the beneficiary and it is with him and not some other party that the applicant and the banks wish to deal and, second, because the mechanism provided for transfer by Article 48 (if the credit is designated as transferable) taken with Article 49 shows that what would amount to a transfer by assignment is not intended. So if a credit is not designated as transferable, the only and limited mechanism which can be used to enable another party to receive the payment which the credit should provide, is an assignment of the proceeds as envisaged by Article 49, and the validity and effect of that assignment will depend upon its governing law.

1 See Gutteridge & Megrah *The Law of Bankers' Commercial Credits* (7th edn) p 105.

Chapter 11

The Banks' Security

11.1 *Introduction* When a bank pays on a letter of credit it looks for reimbursement to the next in the chain, namely to the issuing bank if it is a confirming bank and to the applicant if it is an issuing bank. It is only when that payment is not made that the question of security arises. A confirming bank and an issuing bank may not receive payment as they intend in two quite different situations. One is where the paying party has become insolvent. The other is where the bank has erred and paid on documents which are found not to comply with the credit and so it has no right of indemnity. In the former case any security arrangements which the bank has in relation to the paying party may be relied upon, and the bank will have the security of the documents provided it retains them and they are such as to provide security. Where the bank has paid in error, it will have only the latter, namely such security as the documents may provide. The security provided to banks by the documents was regarded historically as an important aspect of the letter of credit arrangement. Thus in *Guaranty Trust Co of New York v Hannay*[1] Scrutton LJ included in his description of a credit using time drafts the following:[2] 'The vendor thus gets his money before the purchaser would, in the ordinary course, pay; the exchange house duly presents the bill for acceptance, and has, until the bill is accepted, the security of a pledge of the documents attached and the goods they represent.' When the transport document was almost invariably a negotiable bill of lading and therefore a document of title, there was little difficulty. But today the use of other forms of transport document[3] which are not documents of title has greatly weakened the banks' security. Today banks are more likely to look to the creditworthiness of the parties with whom they deal, and to their security arrangements with them, than to the security provided by the documents to be presented under the credit. Thus, where a bank has made an error and so can look only to the security of the documents, it may find it is of little value. This would seem to be an important trend in the development of credits as this century draws to its close. After a hundred and fifty years of having the goods as an alternative security at least, banks today must look to their arrangements with their clients as their source of security. If a bank cannot do that, either because it has no rights because it has erred in the operation of the credit, or because its clients are not good for the money, as a result of the development of new forms of transport document the bank may simply be left facing a loss.

1 [1918] 2 KB 623.
2 Ibid at 659.
3 In relation to the sea waybill, see the discussion at 8.83 above.

11.2 *Securities provided by the paying party* Depending on the arrangements which it has made, an issuing bank may have various securities which it can rely on in the event of the insolvency of the applicant. It may have taken a debenture over the assets of the applicant, or a charge over particular properties. It may hold guarantees from its holding companies or from its directors. These are only mentioned for the sake of completeness, and their legal attributes are not within the scope of this book. A confirming bank which finds itself to have confirmed a credit issued by a bank which then becomes insolvent may be holding deposits from the issuing bank under the terms of the arrangements whereby it agreed to act as the issuing bank's correspondent. If it holds those deposits on appropriate terms it may be able to reimburse itself from them rather than having to refund them to the liquidator and to prove in the liquidation for its entitlement and, as is then likely, to receive only a dividend.

11.3 *Security provided by the documents – pledge* A pledge may be described as the transfer of the possession of goods by way of security whereby the ownership of the goods remains in the pledgor and the pledgee obtains a right to possession only. He has a 'special interest' in the goods, which includes a right to sell.[1] The goods must be transferred to the possession of the pledgee and actual possession is normally required. One of the exceptions to actual possession is the case where a bill of lading is transferred with the intention of pledging the goods to which the bill is title. Then the pledge is effective on the transfer of the bill alone. The special position of a bill of lading is emphasised in the judgment of the Privy Council in *Official Assignee of Madras v Mercantile Bank of India*[2] where Lord Wright stated:[3]

'But where goods were represented by documents the transfer of the documents did not transfer the possession of the goods, save one exception, unless the custodier (carrier, warehouseman or such) was notified of the transfer and agreed to hold in future as bailee for the pledgee. The one exception was the case of bills of lading, the transfer of which by the law merchant operated a transfer of the possession of, as well as the property in, the goods.'

The limited interest passed by the pledge of a bill of lading was considered by the House of Lords in *Sewell v Burdick*,[4] in holding on the particular facts that bankers to whom bills of lading had been delivered as security for a loan were not liable for freight.[5] Where the goods are in a warehouse at the time of the transaction and are intended to remain there, as is indicated in the passage quoted, a bank may seek to protect its interest and to obtain a pledge by getting the warehouseman to attorn to the bank. This can be achieved by the bank requiring the inclusion among the documents to be presented under the credit of warehouse receipts made out of its own order.[6]

1 *The Odessa* [1916] 1 AC 145.

2 [1935] AC 53.
3 Ibid at 59.
4 (1884) 10 App Cas 74.
5 See per Lord Blackburn, ibid at 92, 93.
6 See as an intended example of this, *Rafsanjan Pistachio Producers v Bank Leumi* [1992] 1
Lloyd's Rep 513.

11.4 The position of a bank as pledgee which receives documents under a
documentary credit has been touched on in the reported cases rather than
forming the nub of the case or part of the *ratio decidendi*. But it is clear that
in the classic situation where the bank receives bills of lading made out to
the order of the shipper and blank endorsed it becomes a pledgee of
them. The position is that, when the documents are accepted by the bank
as conforming to the credit, the property in the goods which has previously been retained by the seller will pass to the buyer, the intention
being that the seller no longer looks to the documents for his security (or
the goods) but looks to the promise of the bank. As Paull J stated in *Sale
Continuation Ltd v Austin Taylor & Co Ltd*:[1]

> 'The ownership of the goods passes to the buyer but the bank has the posses-
> sory title of a pledgee as against the buyer. He has that title until the buyer puts
> the bank in funds and discharges his liability for interest payable in respect of
> the draft. If the pledgor does not do so the bank has the usual right of a pledgee
> to sell as if he were the owner.'[2]

Where the bills of lading are drawn to the order of the bank or are
endorsed to the order of the bank, the bank will obtain a pledge in the
same way as where the bills are drawn to order and blank endorsed.
Where they are drawn in favour of the buyer or other consignee, the
bank, it is suggested, still obtains its pledge (for by setting up the credit
the buyer has consented to the bank doing so). But, unless the bank can
obtain the endorsement of the bills to itself, its power of sale will be
ineffective because the bills themselves will not evidence any right on the
part of the bank to the goods. So, if a bank finds itself holding such
documents on which it has paid but in respect of which it has no right of
reimbursement from the applicant (or if it is a confirming bank from the
issuing bank) because in fact the documents do not comply with the
credit, it will have to approach the appropriate party to obtain the
endorsement of the bills of lading to itself (probably only to be obtained
against an indemnity).

1 [1968] 2 QB 849 at 861.
2 See also the judgments of Scrutton LJ in *Guaranty Trust Co of New York v Hannay & Co*
[1918] 2 KB 623 at 659, 660; *Rosenberg v International Banking Corpn* (1923) 14 Ll L Rep
344 at 347; and *Guaranty Trust Co of New York v Van Den Berghs Ltd* (1925) 22 Ll L Rep
447 at 452.2; and per Devlin J in *Kwei Tek Chao v British Traders and Shippers Ltd* [1954]
2 QB 459 at 487. As to the retention by the seller of the property in the goods prior to the
operation of the credit, see *The Glenroy (No 2)* [1945] AC 124.

11.5 It is worth briefly considering what happens to the property in the goods
in these circumstances. On acceptance of the documents presented by the
seller to the bank, the property in the goods will have passed to the buyer.
The seller has either been paid by the bank or has acquired a right to be
paid. When the buyer declines the documents on the ground that they do
not comply with the credit, either himself or by declining to authorise the
issuing bank to take them up from the errant confirming bank, the
property must pass from him. Where a buyer rejects goods because they

are found on arrival not to conform to the contract, the property in the goods – which has been described as vesting in the buyer conditionally – revests in the seller.[1] But that would be inappropriate here. For the seller has been paid, or has his right to be paid, by the bank and has no further interest in the goods. It is therefore tentatively suggested that the property should find a resting place with the bank, so that although the bank may not always have a complete documentary title it will become the owner of the goods.

1 See *Kwei Tek Chao v British Traders and Shippers Ltd* [1954] 2 QB 459 at 487.

11.6 In the preceding paragraphs the bank's position as pledgee is considered on the basis that the pledge arises, in effect by implication, from the circumstances. In the case of an issuing bank it may well be that the pledge is expressly provided for in the terms of the application made by the buyer to the bank for the opening of the credit. The terms of the pledge and of any specific remedies should then be referred to.

11.7 *Sale by pledgee* The right of sale has already been mentioned. Provided that the bank has the bills of lading and they are made out to the bank or to the seller's order and blank endorsed, the bank may take possession of the goods and sell them.[1] Where there is no time fixed for payment, before a pledgee can exercise his right of sale he must give notice to the pledgor.[2] The bank, however, will have informed its customer that the documents are available for collection and will have required to be put in funds, so this will not arise. Where the bank is a confirming bank which has had documents rejected by the issuing bank on the ground of non-compliance with the credit, the documents are returnable to the confirming bank.[3]

1 Provided, of course, that the goods have not already been discharged and become unavailable.
2 *Deverges v Sandeman, Clark & Co* [1902] 1 Ch 579.
3 Article 14.d of the Uniform Customs.

11.8 *Claim in conversion by pledgee* When the bank calls for the goods it may find that they have been released by the carrier against an indemnity and without production of the bill of lading to, for example, a sub-purchaser. Nor is it unknown for a dishonest buyer to refuse the documents on the ground of discrepancies and so avoid having to pay through the credit, while at the same time arranging to take up the goods against an indemnity so it can sell them on and itself receive payment. In such circumstances the bank will have a right to sue the carrier for misdelivery and the buyer and the party who has received the goods (and anyone else who has dealt in them) in conversion.[1]

1 *Glyn, Mills Currie & Co v East and West India Dock Co* (1882) 7 App Cas 591 at 606; *Bristol and West of England Bank v Midland Rly Co* [1891] 2 QB 653; and *Ernest Scragg & Sons Ltd v Perseverance Banking and Trust Co Ltd* [1973] 2 Lloyd's Rep 101. In *Mannesman Handel AG v Kaunlaran Shipping Corpn* [1993] 1 Lloyd's Rep 89 demise charterers had settled a claim made on this basis.

11.9 *Documents not including a bill of lading – lien* Where the credit calls for a transport document which is not a bill of lading, in some cases it may nonetheless be capable of argument that by modern mercantile usage the document is a negotiable document of title and so the bank has a pledge.[1] But otherwise the bank will be unable to put itself forward as a pledgee. Where the bank cannot assert a pledge, the best that it will be able to assert is a lien over the documents, namely the right of retaining the documents until its claims are satisfied. Where the problem is the insolvency of the applicant, this may enable the bank to negotiate with the liquidator or receiver of the applicant, and it can be agreed that the goods be sold on terms that the proceeds (or at least the greater part) go in reduction of the bank's claim against the applicant. Where the problem is that the bank has paid against documents which do not conform to the credit, it is in an unenviable position. Suppose – to take a clear example – that the transport document which it holds is an airway bill, being the consignor's copy, naming the buyer as the consignee.[2] In such a situation, which is now increasingly likely, one of the elements previously considered an essential part of the scheme of documentary credits is missing: the bank does not have the security of the goods by means of negotiable documents of title.[3] It may be, as suggested above,[4] that the ingenuity of the law will find a way of vesting the property in the goods in the bank in such situations, and possibly even of compelling the seller or buyer to do what may be necessary to complete the bank's documentary title where that is needed. But this is an area which has yet to be considered by the courts. No doubt where such situations have arisen, on becoming aware of the legal difficulties banks and traders have found ways of settling their differences without resort to law. The clausing of a sea waybill to provide security for a bank by way of a lien has been referred to in paragraph 8.83.

1 A candidate is the 'combined transport bill of lading'.
2 See Carriage by Air Act 1961, Sch 1, art 6(2).
3 See the cases cited above at para 11.4 and the emphasis on security by Lord Wright in *Ross T Smyth & Co Ltd v T D Bailey, Son & Co* [1940] 3 All ER 60 at 68 where Lord Wright appears to be considering a pledge of goods arising on a negotiation of documents prior to presentation of them under the credit.
4 Para 11.5.

11.10 *Where time drafts result in a delay in payment* Where the credit provides for immediate payment the banks involved need not lose possession of the documents, or the right to their possession, until they receive payment themselves. Thus an issuing bank is not obliged to release documents to its customer, the buyer, save against payment, and a confirming bank is entitled to have the documents returned to it where they are rejected by the issuing bank. But the position is different where time drafts are involved. Suppose that a draft is drawn on the issuing bank, or on the buyer, payable three months after sight. When the three months are up, the documents will have long since reached the buyer who will have taken possession of the goods and the bank's security will have been lost. In this situation an issuing bank can protect itself by ensuring that it has other securities from the buyer such as debentures, charges or guarantees. Or it may utilise the mechanism of a trust receipt.

11.11 *Trust receipts* It was held in *North Western Bank Ltd v Poynter, Son and Macdonalds*[1] that the transfer of possession of goods by means of the return of the bill of lading by a pledgee to the pledgor for the purpose of sale on the pledgee's behalf, the pledgor undertaking to account for the proceeds of sale towards satisfaction of the debt, did not destroy the pledgee's security: the pledgee was entitled to the proceeds against the general creditors of the pledgor.[2] The ability to transfer possession for such a purpose is the foundation of trust receipts. Under a trust receipt the bank releases the bills of lading to the applicant for the credit on the applicant's undertaking that on taking possession of the goods he will hold them in trust for the bank and will sell them on behalf of the bank. He likewise undertakes to hold on trust the proceeds of sale, which will be remitted to the bank, at least up to the amount due. The document will contain other terms to protect the bank's interest such as a requirement to keep the goods and monies separate from other goods and monies, and to insure the goods. The document is not registrable as a bill of sale (where the applicant is an individual) nor as a charge (in the case of a company) because, among other reasons, the rights of the bank arise from the pre-existing pledge. This was established in *Re David Allester*,[3] where it was held that trust receipts were effective against a liquidator. The case involved the pledge of bills of lading to a bank to secure an overdraft and the liquidator claimed the proceeds of sale against the bank. Such a situation is to be distinguished from that where there is no pledge in advance of the transaction, as was the case in *Ladenburg & Co v Goodwin, Ferreira & Co Ltd*.[4] There the defendant merchants sold goods to customers in South America and the property in the goods passed to the customers. The merchants sent to the plaintiff bankers for acceptance drafts drawn on the bankers, together with copies of the bills of lading and invoices. The bank accepted the drafts. The merchants' letter enclosing the drafts had stated that the goods and their proceeds were hypothecated to the bank. The merchants went into liquidation and the bank claimed the proceeds of sale against the liquidator. It has held that the merchants had created a charge on their book debts, which was void as it had not been registered. The bank never had the right to possession of the goods either prior to the transaction (as is the case with a trust receipt) or as the outcome of the transaction itself.

1 [1895] AC 56.
2 See also *Official Assignee of Madras v Mercantile Bank of India* [1935] AC 53 at 63, 64, PC, per Lord Wright.
3 [1922] 2 Ch 211.
4 [1912] 3 KB 275.

11.12 Where the applicants for a credit who have possession of goods under a trust receipt deal in the goods dishonestly by, for example, raising fresh monies on the security of them, their acts will bind the bank. For they are likely to be treated as mercantile agents, and the bank is the owner for the purposes of section 2(1) of the Factors Act 1889, as is shown by *Lloyds Bank Ltd v Bank of America National Trust*.[1] If the applicant for the credit after having entered into the trust receipt arrangement simply fails to account to the bank for the proceeds of sale, which are disposed of and cannot be identified, the bank will only have a claim in debt against the applicant.[2] A trust receipt is therefore efficacious where an honest applicant becomes insolvent, but it may fail to protect the bank's interest when the applicant is dishonest.

1 [1938] 2 KB 147, CA.
2 If they can be identified in the hands of a volunteer (one who did not give value) a tracing claim may be possible, and a claim could also be made against anyone who received the proceeds of sale with notice of the breach of trust: see generally *Goff & Jones on Restitution* (3rd edn).

11.13 *Pledge essential to trust receipt* If the documents which come
into the bank's hands through the credit are not such that the bank
becomes a pledgee of the goods, the release of them to the buyer under a
trust receipt will not protect the bank's interest. In *Official Assignee of
Madras v Mercantile Bank of India*[1] the railway receipts with which the
case was concerned were documents of title under the Indian Contract
Act 1872 and were to be treated in the same way as bills of lading.[2] So, if
the transport documents are not bills of lading, or are not other negotiable transport documents which are to be treated in the same way as bills
of lading, the device of a trust receipt cannot be used.

1 [1935] AC 53.
2 See ibid at 63.

11.14 *Trust receipts and the failure of the bank* If a bank which has
undertaken to pay on a time draft becomes insolvent or otherwise makes
it clear that it will not perform its obligation, the pledge is likely to be
released. This emerges from the complicated facts in *Sale Continuation
Ltd v Austin Taylor & Co Ltd*.[1] The application of the principles applied
in this case to the more usual situation is considered at the end of this
paragraph. Sale, the plaintiffs by their liquidator, were merchant bankers
who later became insolvent. They agreed with the defendants, Austin
Taylor, who were timber merchants and brokers, to open a letter of credit
in favour of foreign principals of Austin Taylor named Nenasi. The credit
was available by drafts drawn on the bank accompanied by usual documents. Austin Taylor undertook to the bank to indemnify it. The bank
accepted a draft and handed the documents to Austin Taylor under the
terms of a trust receipt so Austin Taylor could present the documents to
the buyers and receive payment for which they would be accountable to
the bank. After the documents had been delivered to the buyers but
before they had paid, the bank was put into receivership, and then went
into liquidation. The draft was returned dishonoured to Nenasi. When
Austin Taylor received payment from the buyers they remitted it to their
principals, Nenasi. The liquidator of the bank claimed from Austin
Taylor the amount of the draft, alternatively damages for breach of the
trust constituted by the receipt. It was held by Paull J that it was an
implied term of the contract between the bank and Austin Taylor that the
bank should honour drafts drawn on them by payment as well as by
acceptance, and that Austin Taylor's obligation to provide funds to the
bank only arose when it had done so. The appointment of the receiver
and the company's entering into liquidation had the effect of evincing an
intention by the bank not to pay on the draft even if put in funds. This
released Austin Taylor from the mutual obligation to put the bank in
funds. So far as the trust receipt was concerned Paull J found as follows:

'In this case by the terms of the contract with the buyers, entered into by their
agents (the defendants), Nenasi parted with their property in the goods for all
purposes when the goods were shipped except for their vendors' lien for the
unpaid purchase price and when Nenasi sent the documents to the plaintiffs
Nenasi retained that lien as against the buyers. Having that lien they pledged
the documents to the plaintiffs who took them as security against not receiving
the purchase price before they had to honour the draft, subject to the buyers'
right to demand them as soon as they paid for the goods. The application states
that the drafts are to be secured by the delivery of the documents of title as
collateral security.

Now the essence of a pledge is that it is security against either an immediate advance or against a present liability to make a future payment. The trust receipt contemplated that the defendants would part with the documents to the Belgian buyer and recover the purchase price. It was no breach of trust to do so. In my judgment the same principle applies to the money as applies to the obligation to put the plaintiffs in funds before the maturity date of the draft. Once the draft is dishonoured (or notice of intention not to honour given) Nenasi is entitled to cancel the contract of pledge by returning the draft for cancellation and claiming the purchase money from their agents, the defendants. It is as though a pawnbroker having received the pledge and given his pawn ticket to the pledgor refused to hand over the sum agreed to be lent. The pledgor can say: "Very well, here is your pawn ticket. Hand me back my goods." In this case "the goods" (being the documents of title, or rather the money received for them) were already in the hands of the pledgor.'[2]

In the more usual situation the trust receipt is entered into by the buyer rather than by an agent for the seller. Translating the reasoning of the decision to that situation provides for it to be an implied term of the buyer's or applicant's contract with the bank that the bank shall pay the seller in due course. When the bank becomes insolvent it repudiates that undertaking and releases the applicant buyer from the contract. The foundation of the trust receipt is the pledge to the bank to secure the bank's liability to pay. So, when that liability is repudiated, the foundation is gone. As the applicant already has possession of the goods pledged under the terms of the trust receipt, he is entitled to terminate the pledge (and the trust arrangement) and to retain the goods. He may then pay the seller direct as he will be liable to do when the credit fails to pay through the insolvency of the bank – unless the credit was provided as absolute rather than conditional payment (which is unlikely).[3]

1 [1968] 2 QB 849.
2 For a discussion of criticisms of the decision and their refutation, see *Benjamin's Sale of Goods* (4th edn) paras 23–062, 3.
3 Chapter 3, para 3.52 et seq.

11.15 *Bills of exchange drawn against goods*   Bills of exchange may sometimes state that they are drawn against particular goods or against a particular cargo. Unless the holder of the bill also has the bills of lading, the fact that a draft is so drawn will not give him any rights in the cargo. As was stated by Mellish LJ in *Robey & Co's Perseverance Ironworks v Ollier*:[1] 'A mercantile man who is intended to have a lien on a cargo expects to have the bill annexed; if there is no bill of lading annexed he only expects to get the security of the bill itself.' The position will be the same where the holder of such a bill of exchange delivers the bills of lading to a bank under a letter of credit against the bank's acceptance of the bill: he loses any right in the cargo which he had through the bills of lading. Thus in *Re Suse, ex p Dever*[2] a London bank opened a letter of credit in favour of a Shanghai tea merchant on terms that bills of exchange drawn on the bank should identify the parcels of tea in respect of which they were drawn. Bills drawn on the bank were discounted together with the bills of lading with a Chinese bank, the Hongkong & Shanghai bank, whose agent in London presented the bills for acceptance to the bank. The bank accepted the bills of exchange against delivery of the bills of lading. The bank then went into liquidation. It was held that the holders of the bills of exchange had no rights in the tea.[3] The function of such a statement on a bill of exchange appears simply to be to encourage its negotiation by indicating that the bill is part of transactions relating to specific goods: it does not add to the rights given by the bill.

1 (1872) 7 Ch App 695 at 699.
2 (1884) 13 QBD 766.
3 See also *Banner v Johnston* (1871) LR 5 HL 157 and *Brown, Shipley & Co v Kough* (1885) 29 Ch D 848.

Chapter 12

Standby Credits, and Demand Guarantees and Bonds

A. Introductory

12.1 ***This chapter***   The main function of this chapter is to consider standby credits and what may be called demand guarantees.[1] Standby credits come within the ambit of this book because they are a form of documentary credit, and the Uniform Customs apply to them 'to the extent to which they may be applicable.'[2] They have a different function to the traditional type of credit which has so far been considered. They have an American origin, and outside the United States the same function is often performed by demand guarantees. In a number of recent English decisions analogies have been drawn between the performance bonds or guarantees before the court and letters of credit, and some of the principles applicable to letters of credit have been applied to them. Further, authorities for some aspects of the English law relating to documentary credits are to be found among the cases on performance bonds and guarantees, and have already been referred to, in particular in Chapter 9 relating to fraud and injunctions. As standby credits and performance bonds and guarantees are similar in function, they are taken together in this chapter.

1 The nomenclature is discussed in paragraph 12.26. The term 'demand guarantee' is used
   to refer to those undertakings which are sometimes called 'guarantee' and sometimes
   'bond', as for instance in 'first demand performance bond'.
2 Article 1.

12.2 ***The function of the undertakings considered in this chapter***   The bank undertakings considered in this chapter have a fundamentally different function to that of letters of credit as developed in English law which are the primary subject matter of this book. The function of the latter is to provide payment for goods or services against documents. The most usual function of the bank undertakings considered in this chapter is to enable one party to a contract to obtain money from a bank when the other party has failed, or is alleged to have failed, to perform the contract or some aspect of it. Thus, under an ordinary credit the bank pays the beneficiary (the seller or, in the case of a construction contract for example, the contractor) when he performs his part of the contract with the buyer or employer. Whereas, with these other undertakings, the bank pays the beneficiary (the buyer or, in the case of a construction contract, the employer) in the event of the seller or contractor failing to perform his part of the contract.

12.3 ***Standby credits, demand guarantees and conditional guarantees***   Both standby credits and demand guarantees involve a payment against documents, even if the only document is the demand received from the beneficiary. They are autonomous contracts in just the same way as a traditional documentary credit is autonomous: the paying party is not concerned with the merits of the performance (or lack of it) in relation to the underlying contract – it is only concerned whether the document or documents presented to it entitle the presenter to payment or not. This is in contrast with what may be called a conditional guarantee or a suretyship guarantee. Where the guarantor is in the position of surety, his liability is conditional upon the non-performance of the party whom he is guaranteeing. Some features of conditional guarantees are considered in the following paragraphs so that the distinctions between their legal attributes and those of demand guarantees and standby credits may be clear. Then, for the same purpose, follows a brief description of traditional English performance bonds.

12.4 ***Conditional guarantees or contracts of guarantee strictly so called*** In English law a guarantee may be defined as 'an accessory contract by which the promisor undertakes to be answerable to the promisee for the debt, default or miscarriage of another person, whose primary liability to the promisee must exist or be contemplated'.[1] It is often called a collateral contract as it is collateral to the contract providing the primary liability which is guaranteed. There are four points which require specific mention.

1 70 Halsbury's Laws (4th edn) para 101.

12.5 (i) A guarantee falling within the Statute of Frauds, must be in writing and signed by the person sought to be made liable under it, or by his agent.[1]

1 The Statute of Frauds 1677. The rule is here stated in very short form, and reference should be made to another work if a fuller statement on this very technical topic is required.

12.6 (ii) Every guarantee not under seal must be supported by consideration moving from the beneficiary of the guarantee, ie the creditor. It need not benefit the guarantor directly but may consist of an advantage given to the principal debtor by the creditor at the surety's request, such as an advance of money, or a forbearance to seek to recover money due. A past or executed consideration is insufficient.[1]

1 See *Chitty on Contract* (26th edn) Vol 2, paras 5020 et seq, 20 Halsbury's Laws (4th edn) para 114 et seq; *Rowlatt on Principal & Surety* (4th edn) pp 9 et seq.

12.7 (iii) In an action on a guarantee the claimant must ordinarily prove the fact of the indebtedness of the party guaranteed and the amount, and the guarantor has all the defences available to the party guaranteed. So, for example, with a guarantee of a construction contract which took this form, the employer would have to prove against the guarantor of the contractor's performance the same probably detailed and complicated case which he would have to prove were he to sue the contractor himself for damages for default in the performance of the contract. As a modern example, see *General Surety and Guarantee Co Ltd v Francis Parker Ltd.*[1] A judgment or an arbitration award against the principal debtor will not avoid the need for this.[2] Thus a guarantee as described provides the party to whom it is addressed with a second, and in financial terms, hopefully more secure source of payment. But, subject to its terms, it does not otherwise improve his position. In particular he is in no better position against the guarantor in proving that the money is owed than he is against the main debtor. It is necessary to say 'subject to the terms of the guarantee' because it is not uncommon for guarantees, particularly bank guarantees, to provide that the certificate[3] of, for example, the bank, shall be conclusive evidence of the indebtedness of the party guaranteed. Such a term will be given effect to by an English court, and is likely to be construed as covering both the legal existence of the debt and its amount: see *Dobbs v National Bank of Australasia Ltd*[4] and *Bache & Co (London) Ltd v Banque Vernes*.[5] Thus it was stated in *Dobbs*:[6]

> 'It was contended, however, for the appellant that, upon its true construction, the clause did not make the certificate conclusive of the legal existence of the debt but only of the amount. It is not easy to see how the amount can be certified unless the certifier forms some conclusion as to what items ought to be taken into account, and such conclusion goes to the existence of the indebtedness. Perhaps such a clause should not be interpreted as covering all grounds which go to the validity of the debt; for instance, illegality, a matter considered in *Swan v Blair* (1836) 6 ER 1566. But the manifest object of the clause was to provide a ready means of establishing the existence and amount of the guaranteed debt and avoiding an inquiry upon legal evidence into the debits going to make up the indebtedness. The clause means what it says, that a certificate of the balance due to the bank by the customer shall be conclusive evidence of his indebtedness to the bank.'

1 (1977) 6 BLR 16.
2 *Bruns v Colocotronis* [1979] 2 Lloyd's Rep 412.
3 This enables an analogy to be drawn with standby credits and demand guarantees in that payment is in effect required to be made against a document, namely the certificate. But the form is different and the circumstances are different.
4 (1935) 53 CLR 643.
5 [1973] 2 Lloyd's Rep 437.
6 At 53 CLR 651.

12.8 (iv) As a surety a guarantor has a favoured position in English law. A number of events may result in his discharge, which the beneficiary of the guarantee would not ordinarily intend or perhaps expect.[1] Thus, if the principal debtor is discharged, the surety is usually discharged. Any variation of the terms of the contract with the principal debtor which might prejudice the surety and which occurs without the surety's consent will discharge the surety,[2] including an agreement to give time to the debtor. These serious inconveniences can be avoided by drawing the contract of guarantee appropriately.

1 See *Chitty on Contract* (26th edn), 'Specific Contracts', Vol 2, paras 5044–5064.
2 See the argument which prevailed at first instance in *Mercers v New Hampshire Insurance* [1992] 2 Lloyd's Rep 365.

12.9 *Traditional English performance bonds* A bond is simply a deed promising the payment of a sum of money. A practice of requiring contractors in building or construction contracts to provide a bond or guarantee from a bank or insurance company to secure the performance of their obligations is of long standing in England. It has usually taken the form of what is known as a double or conditional bond. A conditional bond has two parts. The first is a promise to pay a sum of money, namely the maximum to which the obligor is to be liable. The second part is phrased as a condition to the first part and sets out the real promise, which is to the following effect. If the contractor performs the contract or, if on his default the obligor satisfies the damages thereby sustained by the employer, the promise contained in the first part shall be void. To avoid problems of consideration such a bond is always under seal. The use of this form is traditional but it is not seen as having any advantage over a guarantee in conventional and unarchaic form. Apart from providing what should be a secure source of payment the provision of such a bond does not make the employer's task of recovering loss any easier than against the contractor. For in the absence of a specific provision in the bond to contrary effect he has to prove the contractor's default and what it has cost him. He may also face the special defences provided under English law to protect the position of sureties.[1]

1 A useful discussion of English law in relation to bonds and guarantees in connection with construction contracts and the problems which can arise is contained in *Wallace's Construction Contracts*, paras 19.01 to 19.20. For typical forms of bond, see Abrahamson *Engineering Law and the ICE Contracts* (4th edn) p 320 and 4 Forms & Precedents (5th edn) Form 20 et seq. For two recent cases, see *Nene Housing Society Ltd v National Westminster Bank Ltd* (1980) 16 BLR 22, and *Tins Industrial Co Ltd v Kono Insurance Ltd* (1987) 42 BLR 114, CA of Hong Kong and *Mercers v New Hampshire Insurance Co.* [1992] 2 Lloyd's Rep 365.

12.10 Lastly it is illustrative to set out a range of events or documents on which guarantee obligations may become payable, moving from those most favourable to the seller or contractor to those most favourable to the buyer or employer:

most favourable to seller/contractor	– proof of liability under a guarantee strictly so called, as set out at paragraph 12.4 above
	– a judgment or arbitration award in favour of the buyer or employer against the seller or contractor
	– the certificate of an (independent) third party, such as the engineer appointed pursuant to the conditions of an engineering or construction contract
	– a formal statement or certificate by the buyer or employer that there has been a default, and/or that the amount demanded is due
most favourable to buyer/employer	– the simple demand of the buyer or employer

B. Standby Letters of Credit

12.11 *Outline* Standby letters of credit originated in the United States, and came about because of prohibitions on national banking associations from issuing bonds by way of guarantees. Japanese banks have a similar legal disability to American banks in relation to the issuing of guarantees, and so standby credits are also used in Japan to overcome this. A standby credit performs the function of a guarantee in that it enables the beneficiary, in accordance with its terms, to obtain money from the issuing bank, or any confirming bank, in relation to the performance, or non-performance, of a contract between the beneficiary and the party who has arranged the opening of the credit. The credit will state the documents against which payment (or acceptance, etc in the case of a time draft) will be made. These may range from a simple statement of demand by the beneficiary, or a statement by the beneficiary that an amount is due, or a certificate signed by a third party, to an arbitration award or judgment, possibly accompanied by other documents. The important feature is that the bank gives an undertaking to pay against documents, which creates a primary obligation on the bank which is independent of the underlying transaction. Thus, although the function is different to ordinary credits, the form of the transaction and the substance of the undertakings are the same as with ordinary credits. Thus a correspondent bank may be used to advise the credit to the beneficiary and to effect payment when the credit is operated by presentation of documents, and this bank may confirm the credit.

12.12 It is probable that until recently standby letters of credit were used outside the United States mostly in transactions with an American or Japanese connection, in particular the involvement of an American or Japanese bank. In other cases a British bank will more often use a demand guarantee, unless the function of the standby credit is to guarantee payment as discussed later in this paragraph. Standby credits have featured in a very few English decisions such as *Offshore International SA v Banco Central SA*,[1] where the question for the court was the proper law of a credit opened by a Spanish bank through a New York bank at which documents were to be presented and by which payment was to be made. The credit secured the repayment of US$3m paid on the signing of a contract for the construction of an oil rig in the event of cancellation of the contract. It was therefore a standby credit although the term was not used in the judgment. But there are no English reported decisions where the matter before the court required consideration of the nature of a standby credit.[2] It appears that in the United States standby credits have been mainly used in domestic transactions of a very wide variety.[3] One function for which they are increasingly used in England and Europe is to guarantee payment as an alternative to a traditional letter of credit. They are particularly used in this way in the international oil trade. The bank undertakes that it will pay against, for example, the written certificate of the seller that documents complying with the underlying contract have been presented to the buyer but payment has not been made. Alternatively, copies of some or all of the documents presented to the buyer are also required. This has the advantage that the buyer and seller are able to deal with each other direct so far as the documents are concerned and to avoid the banking chain, while giving the seller the security of a bank's undertaking with regard to payment. This may be compared with the intended arrangements in the *Sinason-Teicher* case[4] cited in paragraph 3.19 above. There the buyers undertook to provide through their London bank a guarantee to the sellers that documents would be taken up under the CIF contract between them. It appears that the guarantee would have required the sellers to prove that documents had not been taken up in order to establish the bank's liability.[5]

1 [1977] 1 WLR 399.
2 A standby credit also featured in *Hongkong and Shanghai Banking Corpn v Kloeckner & Co AG* [1989] 2 Lloyd's Rep 323 and allegations concerning the opening of one were considered in *Paclantic Financing Co Inc v Moscow Narodny Bank Ltd* [1984] 1 WLR 930. Reference was also made to the origin and nature of standby credits in *Potton Homes Ltd v Coleman Contractors Ltd* (1984) 28 BLR 19 at 26 per Eveleigh LJ.

3 See *Benjamin's Sale of Goods* (4th edn) para 23–186.
4 [1954] 1 WLR 935 and 1394.
5 Ibid at 941.

12.13 It follows from the nature of standby credits that the risk to the account party – that is, the applicant – can be increased or diminished by choice of the document or documents against which the bank is to pay. Thus a credit which is payable against the beneficiary's draft accompanied by the beneficiary's demand with or without the beneficiary's statement that the sum has become due will afford the greatest security to the beneficiary and creates the greatest risk for the account party. On the other hand, one that requires a judgment or arbitration award against the account party to be included with the documents to be presented is difficult for the beneficiary to utilise and creates no undue risk for the account party. The one function which by its nature a standby credit cannot perform is that of a guarantee which is payable not when documents are presented to the bank but is payable upon the fact (which must be proved) of non-performance of an underlying contract by a third party – usually the account party – namely the function fulfilled by a conditional guarantee as described at paragraph 12.4 above. The nearest that a standby credit can obtain is to include among the documents to be presented a judgment or arbitration award or a signed admission by the account party that the amount called is due. Because of the certainty afforded by standby credits as opposed to traditional guarantees they are becoming more popular among banks.

12.14 *Legal nature* At the heart of standby letters of credit is the bank's undertaking to the beneficiary to pay as the credit provides if documents are presented in accordance with the terms and conditions of the credit. While the function is substantially the converse of that performed by an ordinary credit, the nature of the undertaking is the same. Subject to such minor distinctions as may follow from the difference in function and hence the differences mainly in the type of documents to be presented which follow, it is suggested that in law a standby credit is no different from any other type of credit. The same principles apply. In particular a standby credit is a transaction in documents, and it is an autonomous contract in that its performance is separate from and unaffected by the contract between the applicant or account party and the beneficiary which has given rise to it.[1] The means of making a standby credit available in the beneficiary's country is the use of an advising bank in that country which will usually handle the operation of the credit and which may confirm the credit to give the beneficiary a bank undertaking enforceable in his own country. In contrast, where a bond or guarantee is used the guarantee will usually be given by a bank in the beneficiary's own country, which will be secured by a line of counter-guarantees or indemnities going back down the banking chain to the account party.

1 See para 1.40 and Chapter 9.

12.15 *An American decision* The nature of a particular standby credit was examined by the United States Court of Appeals in *Barclays Bank DCO v Mercantile National Bank*.[1] From the fact that it reached this level of appeal it may be deduced that the case was atypical in at least one factor, namely, that the credit was not issued by a bank but was confirmed by a bank. But apart from that feature the case demonstrates one manner in which standby credits may commonly be used. The facts were as follows. BHC in Trinidad wished to borrow money from Barclays Bank in New York to finance a property development. AMI who were mortgage brokers in Atlanta, Georgia, issued to Barclays a letter of credit in the amount of the loan made to BHC by Barclays. The credit was sent to Barclays by AMI's bankers, Mercantile National Bank, under cover of a letter confirming that it was a valid letter of credit and giving the bank's confirmation of it and undertaking to honour drafts presented in accordance with it. Payment was to be made against a draft accompanied by 'This letter of credit. A signed statement to you[2] to the effect that the amount for which the draft is due and payable by [BHC] to you on account of loans from you to it, which matured . . . and are past due and unpaid . . .' It will be seen that another means of achieving the same effect under English law (but not under US law because of the prohibition on national banks giving guarantees) would have been for the Mercantile National Bank to have issued their guarantee to Barclays payable against Barclays' demand accompanied by their certification of the amount due. This guarantee would have been backed by a guarantee or indemnity in favour of the Mercantile National Bank from AMI, and AMI would in their turn have received a guarantee or indemnity from BHC, the property developers. Returning to the facts of the case, when AMI dishonoured a draft drawn by Barclays pursuant to the credit, Barclays presented it to the Mercantile National Bank who denied liability. The court held that the credit fell within section 5.102 of the Uniform Code, and that there was no reason why a bank should not confirm a non-bank's credit. In reaching this conclusion the court looked to the intent and purpose of the Code rather than to its precise wording – which probably favoured the opposite conclusion. In dealing with an argument that the credit was a guarantee and ultra vires the bank the court stated:[3]

> 'Mercantile's relationship to this transaction has been established as that of a confirming bank. "A confirming bank by confirming a credit *becomes directly obligated* on the credit to the extent of its confirmation as though it were its issuer and acquires the rights of an issuer." Section 5.107(2) (emphasis added). "It may seem that a letter of credit is in the nature of a guaranty. In fact, there is a vast difference between a guaranty and a letter of credit. The issuer of a credit assumes a primary obligation to the beneficiary as opposed to a secondary obligation under a guaranty." It is clear that Mercantile's obligation here is not a guaranty.'[4]

1 [1973] 2 Lloyd's Rep 541 and 481 F 2d 1224.
2 Sic: 'by you' was surely intended.
3 At [1973] 2 Lloyd's Rep 548.2.
4 The second quotation is from 50 Minn L Rev 454, J Halls. The court's own footnote to the final sentence is also worth quoting: 'A letter of credit always serves as a guaranty. This does not mean that it is a guaranty. A letter of credit is an identical twin to a guaranty, but the fact that the two things look alike and may be used for the same purpose and are difficult to distinguish one from the other, does not mean that they are the same thing, and does not mean that there are not differences, which, however subtle, are of major importance.' [H. Harfield, Uniform Commercial Code: Symposium – Code Treatment of Letters of Credit, 48 Corn LQ 92, 93 (1963).] The comparison with a guarantee is not, it is suggested, valid where the transaction underlying the credit is one of sale or the provision of services. It is appropriate only where the credit is a standby credit as discussed under this heading.

12.16 *The Uniform Customs*   In 1977 the ICC Banking Commission was asked by the Foreign Exchange Dealers Association of India whether a standby letter of credit was to be regarded as a documentary credit covered by the 1973 Revision of the Uniform Customs or as a guarantee. The explanation provided to the Commission and on which the Commission gave its opinion was that a standby credit had the function of guaranteeing the performance of a contract and was realisable on the presentation to the issuing bank of a declaration that the underlying contract had not been fulfilled, with any other specified documents. It was said that standby credits were frequently used by United States and Japanese banks which were not authorised by law to issue guarantees. The Banking Commission's view was that such a standby credit fell within the definition provided, and that it should bear the wording that it was issued subject to the Uniform Customs. As a result, when the 1983 Revision was being drafted, it was decided to refer expressly to standby credits in Article 1.[1] This position is confirmed in the 1993 Revision.

1 See the Decisions (1975–79) of the ICC Banking Commission, ICC Publication No 371, at RI, and UCP 1974/1983 Revisions Compared and Explained, ICC Publication No 411, page 10.

12.17 Article 1 of the Uniform Customs begins 'The Uniform Customs . . . shall apply to all Documentary Credits (including to the extent to which they may be applicable, Standby Letter(s) of Credit.' . . . Thus banks which adhere to the Uniform Customs should arrange to incorporate them in standby credits which they issue, as well as in other credits. But because many of the Articles in the Uniform Customs assume that the credit is one relating to sale of goods and involving transport documents and associated documents, Article 1 accepts that there is much in the Uniform Customs which is simply inapplicable to a standby credit. On the other hand, where an Article can be applied it should be. Article 2 first provides that both documentary credits and standby credits are thereafter referred to in the Uniform Customs as 'credits'. This may suggest a distinction between 'documentary credits' and 'standby credits'. But the intention of the two Articles is clear and both types of credit are documentary in that they involve a payment undertaking against documents as the single definition provided by Article 2 for both types of credit establishes. The full text of Article 2 is:

ARTICLE 2 **Meaning of Credit**

For the purposes of these Articles, the expressions 'Documentary Credit(s)' and 'Standby Letter(s) of Credit' (hereinafter referred to as 'Credit(s)'), mean any arrangement, however named or described, whereby a bank (the 'Issuing Bank') acting at the request and on the instructions of a customer (the 'Applicant') or on its own behalf,

i. is to make a payment to or to the order of a third party (the 'Beneficiary'), or is to accept and pay bills of exchange (Draft(s)) drawn by the Beneficiary,
or

ii. authorises another bank to effect such payment, or to accept and pay such bills of exchange (Draft(s)),
or

iii. authorises another bank to negotiate,

against stipulated document(s), provided that the terms and conditions of the Credit are complied with.

For the purposes of these Articles, branches of a bank in different countries are considered another bank.

Because this is phrased in terms of applicant, beneficiary and banks, payment undertakings and documents without any reference to function it covers both traditional (or sale-of-goods type) credits and standby credits and could cover any other arrangement which takes the form outlined. It is also to be noted that the name which is given to the arrangement is immaterial: 'however named or described'.

12.18 *Application* The Uniform Customs will only apply to a standby credit if the credit incorporates them. It appears that there is no uniformity of practice, and they may be incorporated in only approximately one-half of standby credits.[1] But it is suggested that the growing practice in Europe is usually for them to be incorporated. Provided that a credit incorporating the Uniform Customs conforms to the definition given by Article 2, in particular providing for payments etc against stipulated documents, there is no difficulty. A problem may arise where the credit provides for payment against the beneficiary's draft unaccompanied by any document, which is sometimes called a 'clean credit' – though in such a case it is hard to see how it is of the nature of a credit at all. In such a case there is a contradiction because the credit indicates that the Uniform Customs are to apply, whereas the Uniform Customs themselves have the effect that they are inapplicable because by Article 2 they apply only to transactions where payment, etc is made against documents. The aim in construing the credit to resolve the contradiction is to seek to give effect to the presumed intention of the parties, and not to defeat it. It is suggested that the Uniform Customs should be applied to the extent that they can be. But it is also suggested that very many of the provisions will not be capable of application. A similar problem arises where the party issuing the credit is not a bank, or it is uncertain whether it is a bank or not. 'Bank' is not defined by the Uniform Customs, and what may be a bank under one municipal law may not be one under another. Here there is every reason to give effect to the intention of the parties expressed by the incorporation of the Uniform Customs into the credit, and to treat the party whose status as a bank is uncertain, or which is not a bank, as if it were one. That is clearly what the parties intended or would have intended had they considered the specific difficulty. The approach is supported by the decision in *Barclays Bank DCO v Mercantile National Bank*[2] discussed in paragraph 12.15 above.

1 See *Benjamin's Sale of Goods* (4th edn) para 23–195.
2 [1973] 2 Lloyd's Rep 541 (United States Court of Appeal).

12.19 *Applicable Articles* The Articles which refer generally to the rights and obligations of the parties to a credit will normally apply to a standby credit. Thus, in particular, Article 9 setting out the undertakings of the issuing bank and any confirming bank will be applicable. Articles 3, 4 and 15 which reflect the principle of the autonomy of the credit will apply. Thus the credit is generally to be operated without regard to the terms or the performance of the underlying transaction. Articles 13 and 14 as to the duty of banks examining documents and as to the duty of an issuing bank in taking up or refusing documents are also important. Precision of instruction as to the document or documents which are to be presented is particularly important (Articles 20 and 21), because it may alter the nature of the undertaking. To take an example from a performance guarantee case, one document required was a certificate signed by 'registered quantity surveyor'. Did this mean any registered quantity surveyor, or the surveyor appointed under the underlying construction contract? One suspects that the parties may have meant the latter. But it was held that because the parties had failed to make it clear, the former construction must be applied.[1] The greater part of the Articles relating to documents will be inapplicable. Thus the proviso to Article 21's second sentence is inapplicable,[2] and Articles 23 to 38 are inapplicable. Articles 42 and 44 which cover expiry dates and date for presentation are applicable.[3] As has been mentioned in paragraph 5.28, Article 41 provides a trap for standby credits. It states that, if the credit provides for instalments within given periods and any instalment is not drawn or shipped within the period, then the credit ceases to be available for that and any later instalments. The Article could be read as having the effect that, where a standby credit permits instalment drawings and one is not drawn because of the performance of the underlying obligation to which the credit relates, then the credit cannot be drawn on for any later instalment. This is the view taken in the ICC's UCP 500 and 400 Compared. Where a standby credit permits instalment drawings, either Article 41 should be excluded, or there should be an express provision stipulating that failure to draw in one period is not to affect the beneficiary's ability to draw in subsequent periods.

1 *Gur Corpn v Trust Bank of Africa Ltd* (28 October 1986, unreported) Commercial Court, Leggatt J, Lexis.
2 'Provided that their data content makes it possible to relate the goods . . .'
3 As to the applicability of Article 43.a to a copy transport document, see para 5.24.

12.20 *Strict compliance*   Although the document or documents which the credit requires will often be such as to make the requirement of strict compliance one which is easily satisfied, perhaps even a formality, the bank should reject documents which do not comply strictly with the terms of the credit.[1] Documents 'which are almost the same, or which will do just as well' are to be rejected.[2] Of course, if the credit is not worded with precision, there may be little or nothing to which to apply the principle and, in the words of Article 23 'banks will accept such documents as are presented'. In short, the applicant for the credit should state clearly the terms in which the demand under the credit should be made, and also the terms of any accompanying certificate or other documents. Then, having incorporated the instructions in the credit, the bank must ensure that the beneficiary has precisely accorded with them before paying on the credit.[3]

1 See Case R184 in Opinions of the ICC Banking Commission 1988–91, which indicates that in the United States compliance is more strictly required with standby credits than with ordinary credits.
2 Lord Sumner's dictum from *Equitable Trust Co of New York v Dawson Partners Ltd* (1926) 27 Ll L Rep 49 at 52.
3 Reference may also be made to para 12.45 below, where the need for strict compliance is considered in connection with performance bonds and guarantees.

12.21 *Sharp practice and risk*   Where the document or documents against which the credit is payable lie within the power of the beneficiary alone as is the position where the document is the beneficiary's written demand or his demand accompanied by his own certificate or statement in terms provided by the credit, the credit is open to considerable abuse by the beneficiary. If he is without scruple, he may make a demand under the credit whether or not he has a genuine belief that the account party is at fault in the manner intended by the credit. He will nonetheless be assured of payment unless the bank is prepared to refuse payment on the ground that it can establish lack of genuine belief so the fraud exception is established.[1] As is made clear by the outcome of the cases on fraud considered in Chapter 9, it will be an exceptional case in which a beneficiary fails to obtain payment on this ground. Even in cases where the situation is that the applicant is only arguably at fault and there may be considerable doubt about it, unless the beneficiary wishes to preserve his relationship with the account party, he is very likely to present documents under the credit to utilise his advantage.

1 See Chapter 9 and para 12.24 below.

12.22 An account party who wishes to avoid being wholly at the mercy of the beneficiary may have two lines of action open to him depending on whether he is in a position to negotiate the terms of the credit or not. His best course is to arrange for the inclusion among the documents to be presented of one which depends upon a third party of integrity. Thus his position might be improved if, where the underlying contract was an engineering or construction contract, the certificate of the architect, engineer or quantity surveyor appointed under the contract was required. It has to be borne in mind that such persons are appointed by the employer under the contract, namely the beneficiary of the credit, and may tend to favour the employer. This may be particularly so in situations where the protection is most badly needed because the employer is seen as likely to behave in an unscrupulous manner. Where the underlying contract is one of sale of goods, the certificate of an independent inspection agency may be required. In other situations it may be possible to utilise the certificate of a company's auditors or that of an independent firm of accountants.

12.23 Another means of providing some limited protection is to ensure that the credit does not become operable until an appropriate event has occurred. This will probably be the opening of the credit by which payment pursuant to the underlying contract is to be made to the account party for the standby credit. Similarly the account party may try to arrange a cut-off point at the other end. Obviously the earlier the expiry date is, the more advantageous to him. It has to be remembered that it may well happen that, as the expiry date draws near, an unscrupulous beneficiary will ask for the credit to be extended, threatening that, if it is not, he will present documents under the credit. The applicant may try to include a cancellation clause, entitling him to require the cancellation of the credit by presenting a certificate that the underlying contract has been fully and satisfactorily performed on his part.

12.24 *Fraud* Fraud and the problems facing an applicant (or account party) for a credit where that party believes that the beneficiary is acting fraudulently, have been considered in Chapter 9. The same principles must apply to a standby credit as apply to an ordinary credit and which have also been applied by the English courts to first demand performance bonds and guarantees. It appears that the American courts have applied the fraud exception to the autonomy principle in a manner more favourable to credit applicants, as do many other European countries. It may be that in the case of standby credits and performance bonds the English courts will tend to the easing of the rule in order to check at least some of the apparently blatant abuses by beneficiaries which have gone unchecked so far.[1] It must be said, however, that if parties enter into transactions which may so easily be abused, there is only a very limited role which the courts can play in preventing that abuse if they are not to rewrite the bargains into which the parties have entered.

1 See *United Trading Corpn SA v Allied Arab Bank Ltd* [1985] 2 Lloyd's Rep 554n at 561 and para 9.36 above.

12.25 ***Comparison of standby credits with demand guarantees and performance bonds*** This is considered in Part C in paragraph 12.61 and following.

C. Demand Guarantees and Bonds

12.26 ***Nomenclature: demand and conditional guarantees*** In the absence of an authority to define terms it appears that 'bond' and 'guarantee' have often been used interchangeably, sometimes prefaced by 'performance', and sometimes also by 'demand' or by 'first demand'. Thus Lord Denning MR began his judgment in *Edward Owen Engineering Ltd v Barclays Bank International Ltd*[1] 'This case concerns a new business transaction called a performance guarantee or a performance bond.'[2]

1 [1978] QB 159 at 164.
2 In *Harbottle (Mercantile) Ltd v National Westminster Bank Ltd* [1978] QB 146 at 149 Kerr J stated 'All the contracts provided that the plaintiffs were to establish a guarantee confirmed by a bank of 5% of the price in favour of the buyers. These were in effect to be performance bonds. They were called guarantees simpliciter, but their purpose was to provide security to the buyers for the fulfilment by the plaintiffs of their obligations under the contracts.'

12.27 It is suggested that the nomenclature can be simplified if an essential distinction is remembered. This is the distinction between those guarantees which are payable against the presentation of the specified documents to the bank, and those which are not payable against documents but when the party whose performance is guaranteed fails to carry out that performance in accordance with his contract. The former can now be referred to as demand guarantees adopting the name used in the ICC Uniform Rules for Demand Guarantees.[1] This is an appropriate name because the bank pays against a written demand accompanied by such other documents as may be called for. The latter may be called conditional guarantees because they are conditional on the non-performance of the underlying obligation. Demand guarantees are 'unconditional' in that sense: they are autonomous contracts just as documentary credits including standby credits are autonomous.

1 See para 12.71 et seq below.

12.28 In *I E Contractors Ltd v Lloyds Bank plc*[1] Leggatt J summarised the position: 'Under what are sometimes called first demand bonds the obligation to pay arises without any evidence of the validity of the claim on a simple demand, or on a demand either in a specified form or accompanied by a specified document.' The same judge had also to consider the undertaking in *Gur Corpn v Trust Bank of Africa Ltd*,[2] where the guarantee was payable on receipt of a claim accompanied by a 'certificate from the Department approved and signed by registered quantity surveyor, that such amount is payable by GUR Corporation to the Department'. Having stated that counsel for the bank 'stresses the importance of the distinction between two classes of instrument: one group consisting of letters of credit, standby letters of credit, first demand guarantees and like instruments, and the second group consisting of forms of guarantee which require proof of an underlying default before they can be called upon', Leggatt J continued '[Counsel for the bank] submits that it is axiomatic that for the purposes of the first class of instrument there must be commercial certainty, and that what in practice is required is that the documents identified in the instrument should be presented and that they should be seen to conform to the requirements of the instrument before its expiry. I prefer the argument of [counsel for the bank]. It seems to me that in its nature the guarantee with which I am concerned is one which falls into [counsel's] first category rather than into his second, . . .'.

1 [1989] 2 Lloyd's Rep 205 at 207.1, for further proceedings see note 1 to para 12.42.
2 Leggatt J (28 October 1986, unreported) Lexis.

Common functions of demand guarantees and bonds

12.29 *(a) Performance bonds and guarantees* These are the most common, and can be used for straightforward contracts of sale as well as for construction and other complicated projects. Thus, in the case of sale, if a buyer is in a sufficiently strong commercial position to do so, he may require the seller to open a performance bond for a proportion, perhaps 5% or 10% of the purchase price, this to be payable on first demand in the event of the seller's failure correctly to perform the sale contract. For example, the underlying contracts in the *Harbottle* case[1] were for the sale of horse tic beans and for the sale of coal. If the seller is wise, he will, if he can, procure that his bond only becomes effective after the buyer has opened his letter of credit: this will avoid the risk that there will be disputes over the credit and the buyer will call the bond.[2] Sometimes a seller will simply add the amount of the bond, or a substantial proportion of it, to the contract price because he knows that there is a strong likelihood of the bond being called whether or not he correctly performs his part of the contract.

1 [1978] QB 146.
2 Cf *Edward Owen Engineering Ltd v Barclays Bank International Ltd* [1978] QB 159.

12.30 *(b) Bid or tender bonds or guarantees* Where bids or tenders are called for on large contracts the buyer (or employer) may want an assurance that the tenderers are wholly serious and capable of undertaking the work and will be able to enter a contract to do so supported by the appropriate performance bond if they are selected. The tender instructions will then require that the tenderers supply a bond which will be released either if the tenderer is not selected or following the entering into of the contract and the provision of the contract performance bond within a specified period. The tender bond must almost of necessity be a demand bond.

12.31 *(c) Advance payment bonds or guarantees* If an advance payment is to be made to a contractor or seller to provide him with some immediate finance, the employer or buyer can obtain security by means of a bond providing for repayment of the advance should the seller fail to perform the contract. An example is to be found in *Howe Richardson Scale Ltd v Polimex-Cekop*.[1] The guarantee covered an advance payment of £25,000 on the contract price of £500,000 for equipment to be manufactured by the plaintiffs. The guarantee was called by the making of a demand when the plaintiffs who had completed manufacture did not ship the equipment: the defendants had failed to open a letter of credit and to give shipping instructions.

1 [1978] 1 Lloyd's Rep 161.

12.32 *(d) Retention money bonds or guarantees* It is common practice for construction and engineering contracts to provide for monies otherwise certified as payable to be retained until completion of the work, partly by way of security, and partly because although work may have been certified for payment it is possible that maintenance work will be required in respect of it under the maintenance provisions of the contract. The employer may be prepared to release all or part of the retention monies against a bond provided by the contractor which will give the employer security of recovery should the contractor default.

12.33 *(e) Maintenance bonds or guarantees* These secure the performance of a contractor during the maintenance period of a construction contract and are commonly linked to the release of retention monies.

12.34 *Contractual relationships – the indemnity chain* Where there is only one bank involved the relationships are straightforward. The account party – the equivalent of the applicant for a letter of credit – approaches a bank, which is likely to be his own bank, and instructs it to provide a bond or guarantee in favour of the beneficiary in the terms in which he has contracted with the beneficiary to provide it. If it is agreeable, the bank will then issue its bond or guarantee to the beneficiary. Before doing so it will require the account party to sign an undertaking in favour of the bank agreeing to indemnify the bank in respect of any amount that it pays out under the bond to the beneficiary. The terms of the indemnity will be drafted by the bank, and will be favourable to the bank. If the account party were simply to undertake to reimburse the bank such amounts as the bank might be obliged to pay out pursuant to its undertaking to the beneficiary, this would enable the account party to question whether the bank was obliged to pay what it had in fact paid before the account party reimbursed the bank. That is not usually acceptable to banks. So the account party will usually be required to sign an indemnity which requires it to pay whatever the bank has in fact paid. Thus the form signed by Edward Owen Engineering in *Edward Owen Engineering v Barclays Bank International Ltd*[1] was in these terms:

'In consideration of your procuring the giving by Barclays Bank International Ltd of a . . . guarantee in the terms of the copy attached hereto . . . we . . .

agree to keep you indemnified . . . and . . . irrevocably authorise you to make any payments and comply with any demands which may be claimed or made under the said . . . guarantee . . . and agree that any payment which you shall make . . . shall be binding upon . . . us and shall be accepted by . . . us as conclusive evidence that you were liable to make such payment or comply with such demand.'

1 See [1978] QB 159 at 167.

12.35 It is more common for at least two banks to be involved, one the account party's bank in his own country and a second in the beneficiary's country which will be instructed by the first to issue the guarantee or bond to the beneficiary. The bank issuing the guarantee or bond to the beneficiary will be given an undertaking of indemnity from the account party's bank from which it receives its instructions. It may happen that a third bank is involved which acts as intermediary between the account party's bank and the bank issuing the guarantee to the beneficiary.[1] This will happen where the account party's bank does not have a correspondent in the country of the beneficiary. In such a case the bank issuing the guarantee will take an indemnity from this intermediary bank and the intermediary bank will take an indemnity in turn from the account party's bank. There is thus a chain of indemnities. The contrast with a letter of credit will be noted. A credit is usually issued by the applicant's bank and the problem of providing an undertaking which can be enforced in the beneficiary's own country is met by the device of a confirmation of the credit provided by the advising bank. Just as with the indemnity which the account party for the guarantee or bond has to provide to his own bank, the indemnities which the banks in the chain provide to one another are usually devised to ensure that, if the bank to be indemnified has paid, the indemnifying bank is bound to reimburse it without the possibility of argument that the former bank was not obliged to pay and should not have paid. One such provision was as follows:[2]

'In case of implementation, any claim or claims will be paid to us on first demand, despite any contestation between principals and the beneficiaries.'

1 See, for example, *Esal (Commodities) Ltd v Oriental Credit Ltd* [1985] 2 Lloyd's Rep 546, discussed in para 12.36 below.
2 See *United Trading Corpn v Allied Arab Bank* [1985] 2 Lloyd's Rep 554n.

12.36 *The chain in the Esal Commodities case: confirmation*[1] Reltor Ltd, an English company, made a successful bid to sell sugar to Estram, an Egyptian corporation, which was to be supported by a performance bond for 10% of the purchase price. Reltor approached their London bank, Oriental Credit, in connection with the bond. Oriental Credit instructed the London office of Wells Fargo Bank to establish the bond through their correspondents in Cairo, the Banque du Caire, and it appears that the Banque du Caire were asked to add their confirmation. The bond was therefore issued by Wells Fargo and advised through the Banque du Caire, who confirmed it. The bond as issued by Wells Fargo was made subject to the Uniform Customs, a matter which is discussed below.[2] This borrowing from the documentary credit scheme may have been due to the involvement of an American bank as the issuing bank. It demonstrates the closeness of first demand bonds to standby letters of credit. It also appears that the mechanism of confirmation may have been used in the *Harbottle* case.[3]

1 *Esal (Commodities) Ltd v Oriental Credit Ltd* [1985] 2 Lloyd's Rep 546.
2 Para 12.69.
3 [1978] QB 146: see the judgment at [1978] QB 149B/C.

12.37 ***The construction of guarantees and bonds: demand or conditional*** Where the bank's undertaking provides that documents in addition to a demand are to be provided to it, in most cases it will be clear that, if the documents are provided, nothing else is required and the bank must pay.[1] In other cases there may be more room for argument as to whether the bank must pay on a simple but appropriate demand, or whether proof of liability under the underlying contract is also required. The cases in which this difficulty has arisen are discussed in paragraphs 12.38 to 12.42 below.

1 It has to be said 'in most cases' because of the ingenuity with which it was argued in the *Gur* case (see para 12.41 below) that the guarantee was nonetheless conditional.

12.38 *(a) Howe Richardson Scale Co Ltd v Polimex-Cekop*[1] The relevant terms were '. . . guarantee for refund of the advance payment . . . in favour of Messrs Polimex on their first demand in case of non-delivery of the ordered goods until 31 March 1977 and when the delay is due to *force majeure* until 30 September 1977 at the latest'. This could be read as meaning that payment was required to be made against Polimex's first demand provided that delivery had not been made as set out. Or it might mean that payment was due against demand, the intention being that a demand should only be made if delivery had not been made as set out but this not being something which the bank was bound to verify or was entitled to have verified. Although an injunction against Polimex was refused, the court did not decide this question. Roskill LJ stated:

> 'For my part I express no view whether the obligation of the bank is what was called in argument an absolute obligation or a conditional obligation (by a conditional obligation I mean an obligation which arises only if it can be shown to the bank that delivery has not been given timeously); I rest my view that the injunction should not be granted on wider grounds.'

1 [1978] 1 Lloyd's Rep 161.

12.39 *(b) Esal Commodities Ltd v Oriental Credit Ltd*[1] The applicant for the bond, Reltor Ltd, an associate company of Esal, went into liquidation. The bond provided 'We, hereby issue this performance bond for a sum not exceeding US$487,300 . . . being 10 per cent of the tender value. . . . We undertake to pay the said amount of your written demand in the event that the supplier fails to ship the agreed quantity in accordance with the terms of their contract with you and subject to the receipt of irrevocable sight letter of credit confirmed and payable in London from you in their favour.' It was contended by Oriental Credit as the bank indemnifying Wells Fargo Bank who in their turn were indemnifying the Banque du Caire who had confirmed and paid on the bond, that there was no liability under the bond unless and until there had been a breach of the underlying contract of sale and that this had never been established. The court held that the bond was not conditional, because the parties could not have intended that it should be. If it was conditional, the bank would have had to decide the merits of the dispute under the contract of sale. '. . . if the performance bond was so conditional, then unless there was clear evidence that the seller admitted that he was in breach of the contract of sale, payment could never safely be made by the bank except on a judgment of a competent court of jurisdiction and this result would be wholly inconsistent with the entire object of the transaction, namely to enable the beneficiary to obtain prompt and certain payment'.[2] The court also referred to the nature of a performance bond as established in the *Edward Owen* case,[3] in particular that the bank is not concerned with relations between the supplier and the customer and the performance of the contractual obligations between them, subject to the fraud exception.[4] It may be said that the approach of the court was to categorise the bond as a first demand performance bond and to deduce from this that it was unconditional and the bank was not concerned with liability on the underlying contract. But banks do give conditional guarantees, whose function is the perfectly valid one of providing security against the insolvency of a seller or a contractor, and which are not intended to provide payment until the default has been established. The answer provided by the Court of Appeal was almost certainly correct. But the reasoning had surely to start with the wording of the undertaking. The reasoning might have been: it is called a performance bond; it relates to an international sale of a commodity, sugar; it refers to 'paying the amount of your written demand'; it then refers to the event in which demand may be made; but that is not expressed in a way which makes it clear, contrary to what is commonly to be expected in transactions such as this, that the demand can only be made if the event has in fact occurred; the bond is therefore to be construed as payable simply on an appropriate demand. In any event it is to be remembered that the bond was issued in Egypt and was probably subject to Egyptian law. The Banque du Caire had been held liable under the bond in proceedings before an Egyptian tribunal. So there is some unreality in discussing the nature of the undertaking as if English law applied to it.

1 [1985] 2 Lloyd's Rep 546.
2 Ibid at 549.2.
3 [1978] QB 159.
4 See [1985] 2 Lloyd's Rep at 549.2.

12.40 *(c) Siporex Trade SA v Banque Indosuez*[1]   The key words were '. . . we hereby engage and undertake to pay on your first written demand any sum or sums not exceeding US$1,071,000 in the event that, by latest 7 December 1984 no banker's irrevocable letter of credit has been issued in favour of Siporex. . . . Any claims hereunder must be supported by your declaration to that effect . . .'. Hirst J referred to the decision of the Court of Appeal in the *Esal* case[2] and commented on the similarity of the wording of the bond in that case. The judge accepted that every bond had to be construed according to its terms, but he held that he was bound by authority to construe it as an unconditional bond payable on demand without reference to the underlying events. He continued:

> 'I also consider it is extremely important that, for such a frequently adopted commercial transaction, there should be consistency of approach by the Courts, so all parties know clearly where they stand. The whole commercial purpose of a performance bond is to provide a security which is to be readily, promptly and assuredly realizable when the prescribed event occurs; a purpose

reflected in the provision here that it should be payable "on first demand". The defendants' approach in this part of the case would frustrate that essential purpose.'

It is suggested that the wording was in fact clearer than in the *Esal* case,[3] because of the need for a declaration to the effect that no credit had been issued. This showed that the bond was payable on a written demand accompanied by the declaration.[4]

1 [1986] 2 Lloyd's Rep 146.
2 Supra.
3 Supra.
4 For reports of the subsequent proceedings brought by the buyers, Comdel, in support of their attempts to recover by arbitration the amount paid under the bond and in respect of which they had had to indemnify Banque Indosuez, see *Comdel v Siporex* (No 2) [1988] 2 Lloyd's Rep 590 (Steyn J); on appeal [1989] 2 Lloyd's Rep 13, CA; affd [1990] 2 All ER 552, HL.

12.41 *(d) GUR Corpn v Trust Bank of Africa Ltd*[1] This has been referred to in connection with the distinction between conditional and unconditional bonds and guarantees in paragraph 12.28 above. The terms of the guarantee are not set out in full in the judgment. However, it does not appear that the words 'on demand' or their equivalent appeared. It provided that a claim must be received prior to the expiry of the guarantee, and it also provided for a certificate as has been described. It was argued for the beneficiary of the guarantee, the Government of the Republic of Ciskei, that, provided a claim was made within the period, the certificate could be provided subsequently. Not surprisingly this argument was rejected: the effect of the guarantee was that it was payable on receipt of a claim accompanied by a certificate not later than the time of expiry.

1 Leggatt J (28 October 1986, unreported) Lexis, earlier hearings at [1987] QB 599.

12.42 *(e) IE Contractors Ltd v Lloyds Bank plc*[1] These proceedings concerned three performance bonds which had been issued in favour of an Iraqi beneficiary by an Iraqi bank, Rafidain, in relation to the performance by the ultimate account party, *IE*,[2] of contracts to build three poultry slaughterhouses in Iraq. The bonds were issued by Rafidain at the request of IE's bank, Lloyds, against counter-indemnities from Lloyds who in turn received counter-indemnities from IE. The bonds were governed by the law of Iraq. In giving the leading judgment in the Court of Appeal Staughton LJ pointed out that the general nature of performance bonds had been often considered by the English courts over 12 years, and that the decisions, and the general practice of bankers, may be a guide as to what the parties are likely to have intended, and may be treated as part of the surrounding circumstances which are relevant to the construction of a bond. Nonetheless, as he emphasised, it was the task of the court to construe the particular documents. He continued:

'The first principle which the cases establish is that a performance bond, like a letter of credit, will generally be found to be conditioned upon the presentation of one or more documents, rather than upon the actual existence of facts which those documents assert. If the letter of credit or bond requires a document asserting that goods have been shipped or that a contract has been broken, and if such a document is presented, the bank must pay. It is nothing to the point that the document is untruthful, and that the goods have not been shipped or the contract not broken. The only exception is what is called established or obvious fraud. This doctrine had been laid down in recent years by cases too numerous to mention. The justification for it is said to be that bankers can check documents, but do not have the means or the inclination to check facts, at any rate for the modest commission which they charge on a letter of credit or performance bond. There has been no suggestion that the fraud exception applies in this case.

We were told, and I am quite prepared to accept, that some performance bonds are payable merely upon a demand being made, without requiring the presentation of any other document or the assertion of any fact (unless the demand itself contains an implied assertion that the money is due). It was suggested that even an oral demand would be sufficient; but I would hesitate long before construing a performance bond as having that effect.

On the other hand there is no reason why a performance bond should not depart from the usual pattern, and be conditioned upon the existence of facts rather than the production of a document asserting those facts. It might be inconvenient for the bank, but it is a perfectly lawful contract if the parties choose to make it.'

He then referred to the *Esal* case[3] and after quoting from the judgment of Ackner LJ[4] stated:

'I take this to show that there is a bias or presumption in favour of the construction which holds a performance bond to be conditioned upon documents rather than facts. But I would not hold the presumption to be irrebuttable, if the meaning is plain.'[5]

He held that on the wording of the bond it was payable on a demand being made stating that it was a claim for damages brought about by IE. It is suggested that this judgment, with which Purchas LJ agreed, correctly sets out the approach which will now be adopted by an English court.[6]

1 [1990] 2 Lloyd's Rep 496; on appeal from [1989] 2 Lloyd's Rep 205, injunction proceedings at (1985) 30 BLR 48.
2 Formerly called *GKN Contractors*.
3 Above, para 12.39.
4 At [1985] 2 Lloyd's Rep 546 at 549.
5 Later in his judgment he held that two of the three counter-indemnities given by Lloyds to Rafidain were payable on an occurrence and a demand, the occurrence being that Rafidain was obliged to pay under its guarantee to the Iraqi beneficiary: see para 12.48 below.
6 The short judgment of the third member of the court, Sir Denys Buckley, expressed neither agreement nor disagreement with these principles, but set out his reasoning for reaching a like conclusion to that of Staughton LJ on the particular wording of the Iraqi bonds.

12.43 ***Conclusion***   It is to be concluded from the above cases, in particular from the *IE Contractors* case, that, where a guarantee or bond is stated to be payable by a bank or other financial institution on demand, in the absence of clear words indicating that liability under it is conditional upon the existence of liability on the part of the account party in connection with the underlying transaction, the guarantee is to be construed as entitling its beneficiary to payment simply against an appropriately worded demand accompanied by such other documents as the guarantee may require. In particular, such a guarantee will not be construed as payable only if a particular event has occurred simply because the guarantee sets out, without more, the event or events following the happening of which it is intended that a demand may be made. It is probable that where the guarantee is part of an international transaction the tendency of the court to hold that all that is required is an appropriate demand together with any other documents as may be specified by the guarantee, will be stronger than in a purely domestic context.

12.44 ***Calling the guarantee or bond: strict compliance*** What has to be done by the beneficiary to entitle him to payment is a question of construing the wording of the guarantee. A well-worded guarantee will make clear what is required.[1] So, if it is intended that the beneficiary should state that the account party has defaulted in a particular way and that the beneficiary has thereby been caused loss in an amount not less than the amount of his demand, this should be set out in the guarantee with clarity and precision. But as appears from the cases which have been considered in paragraphs 12.38 to 12.42 above in connection with the question whether a guarantee is a demand bond or a conditional guarantee, it is common for this not to be done.

1 See Article 3 of the ICC Uniform Rules for Demand Guarantees, Appendix 4 post.

12.45 It is suggested that the principle of strict compliance can and should be applied to demand guarantees and bonds to the extent that the wording of the guarantee or bond makes it appropriate.[1] Thus in the *Siporex* case[2] the demand was required to be accompanied by a declaration 'to that effect'.[3] It was there argued for the bank that the principle of strict compliance as established in relation to letters of credit was applicable. It was submitted on behalf of Siporex that there was a substantial difference between letters of credit and performance bonds in that with letters of credit exact compliance with documentary requirements was imperative, whereas with performance bonds precise wording was not essential, particularly where the bond required a declaration 'to that effect'. The judge accepted the buyer's argument 'subject to the rider, on this point of principle, that of course it is quite essential that there should be no ambiguity, no risk of the bank being misled, and no risk of it being confused or otherwise prejudiced'. It is to be questioned whether any such distinction is to be drawn. The only valid distinction between traditional letters of credit and bonds and guarantees in this respect lies in the fact that the documentary requirements of the former are different to those of the latter and so the scope for application of the principle may be more limited with the latter. This was the view of Leggatt J in *IE Contractors Ltd v Lloyds Bank plc*.[4] He stated:

'The demand must conform strictly to the terms of the bond in the same way that documents tendered under a letter of credit must conform strictly to the terms of the credit. In particular, ..., it is important to determine whether the bond is on simple first demand, or on first demand in a specified form, or on first demand supported by a specified document. Where courts seem to have divagated from these simple principles they may have only been responding to the wording of the particular bonds under consideration.'

In the Court of Appeal, after referring to the *Siporex* case[5] Staughton LJ stated:

'I agree that there is less need for a doctrine of strict compliance in the case of performance bonds, since I imagine that they are used less frequently than letters of credit, and attract attention at a higher level in banks. They are not so much part of the day-to-day mechanism of ordinary trade. And as Hirst J pointed out, the kind of documents which they require is usually different from the kind required under a letter of credit. Nevertheless, the reasoning of Goddard LJ in *Rayner's* case (sic) at p 43 still applies:

"The question is 'What was the promise which the bank made to the beneficiary under the credit, and did the beneficiary avail himself of that promise?'"

The degree of compliance required by a performance bond may be strict, or not so strict. It is a question of construction of the bond. If that view of the law is unattractive to banks, the remedy lies in their own hands.'

It is true that performance bonds (or demand guarantees) are less common than traditional documentary credits, and it may be that, because of this, they attract attention at a higher level in issuing banks. It is suggested, however, that this is not a good reason for applying any different principle of construction. The degree of leeway to be made available to the beneficiary cannot depend upon the standing of the bank official examining the documents. As Staughton LJ concluded, the application of the principle of strict compliance will depend upon the construction of the guarantee or bond. If it is loosely worded, then the wording of the demand and the content of any other documents must comply with the wording, but to say that they must comply strictly is a contradiction in terms. If, on the other hand, the guarantee or bond is precise in its requirements, they must be followed with appropriate precision.

1 Cf Article 19 of the ICC Uniform Rules for Demand Guarantees.
2 [1986] 2 Lloyd's Rep 146.
3 See para 12.40 above.
4 [1989] 2 Lloyd's Rep 205 at 207.
5 Supra, para 12.42.

12.46 ***The demand: a need to state the basis of claim?*** The guarantee or bond may refer to the events on which it is intended that the demand may be made without making it clear whether the demand should refer to the satisfaction of them as its basis.[1] The form which the demand must take is to be determined by considering the particular words of the bond in question, and a decision on one wording may or may not be helpful on another depending on the similarities and differences. A question arose in the *Esal Commodities* case[2] which was of this nature. The relevant wording has been set out in paragraph 12.39 above. In the Court of Appeal Ackner LJ with whom Glidewell LJ agreed, held:[3]

'In addition to the beneficiary making the demand, he must also inform the bank that he does so on the basis provided in the performance bond itself. This interpretation not only gives meaning and effect to the words "in the event that the supplier fails . . ." which otherwise would be mere surplusage, but it in no way imposes an extravagant demand upon the bank. A beneficiary may seek, honestly or dishonestly, to apply a performance bond to the wrong contract, and the need to inform the bank of the true basis upon which he is making his demand may be very salutary. Moreover, the desire for an extension of the performance bond may, on occasions, be due to the fact that the performance, for one reason or another, might have been justifiably delayed and the beneficiary will not yet know whether or not there will in due course be full compliance with the contract. The requirement that he must, when making his demand for payment in order to support his request for an extension, also commit himself to claiming that the contract has not been complied with, may prevent some of the many abuses of the performance bond procedure that undoubtedly occur.'

The relevance of the reference to an extension was that Estram, the beneficiary, had asked the Banque du Caire either to extend the bond or to remit its amount. The reliance upon what may be salutary was criticised by Staughton LJ in the *IE Contractors* case[4] as an insufficient reason to adopt a particular construction of a commercial document. It may, however, be something which may be presumed to have been in the parties' minds when the bond was issued and is therefore a legitimate guide to their intentions if a bond is unclear in its wording. It is surely within the competence of the court to adopt a construction of a document of a kind which is frequently abused, which may lessen that abuse, provided of course that the document is indeed not clear in its wording. Neill LJ who otherwise agreed with the judgment of Ackner LJ preferred to leave open for decision on some future occasion the question whether it is necessary for a beneficiary to give express notice to the bank that the qualifying event has occurred. He indicated his reluctance to introduce a rule 'which provided scope for an argument that the qualifying event had not been sufficiently identified'.[5] The point did not in fact need to be decided by the court and so the view expressed by Ackner LJ was obiter, because there had been proceedings in Egypt between Estram and the Banque du Caire in which the Banque had been held liable. The Banque's submission that the demand was required to be accompanied by a statement that the supplier had failed to execute the contract had been rejected by the Egyptian tribunal. It was therefore held by the Court of Appeal that the Banque was entitled to be indemnified whether or not the Egyptian tribunal's holding was correct. It may be noted that the Court of Appeal did not consider what law was to be applied to determine the effect of the bond. This was probably Egyptian law, and, if so, the Egyptian tribunal's decision was entitled to respect for that reason.

1 Cf Article 20 of the ICC Uniform Rules for Demand Guarantees considered in paragraph 12.71 below. This specifically requires that the breach of the underlying contract be specified.
2 [1985] 2 Lloyd's Rep 546.
3 Ibid at 550.2.
4 Supra, [1990] 2 Lloyd's Rep 496.
5 [1985] 2 Lloyd's Rep at 554.1.

12.47 The views expressed in the *Esal* case were considered by Leggatt J in the *IE Contractors* case[1] and were also mentioned by the Court of Appeal.[2] Leggatt J defined the approach of the court in unexceptionable terms as follows: 'First it must construe the performance bond itself, in order to see what the beneficiary has to do for the purpose of making a valid demand under it; and secondly, it must construe the call and any associated document, in order to see whether the beneficiary has done that which for the purpose of making a valid demand is required of him.' In reliance upon the wording in the bonds 'covering damages which you claim are duly and properly owing to your organisation . . . under the terms of the contract . . .' he held that the beneficiary was required to assert a claim that the damages in respect of which a call was made were duly and properly owing to the beneficiary under the terms of the contract. In the Court of Appeal Staughton LJ held that the part of the bond from which the words quoted were taken was directed to Article 395 of the Iraqi Commercial Code, which requires a performance bond to state the purpose for which it is issued. He relied on another part, which read

'We undertake to pay you, unconditionally, the said amount on demand, being your claim for damages brought about by the above-named principle', and concluded that the demand was required to state that it was a claim for damages brought about by the contractor. The demands made asserted breaches of contract but did not in terms mention damages. He referred to question of the degree of strict compliance required and concluded that the precise words of the part of the bond quoted were not required. He held that the demand made did say in substance, although not in express words, that what it claimed was damages for breach of contract. He and the other members of the court found that the demands were valid demands under the bonds. Leggatt J had held that they were not. It is probably not possible to draw any general conclusions from this part of the Court of Appeal's judgments, save perhaps that, with foreign language bonds governed by foreign law the English court will avoid technicality unless the need for it is plainly established. On the wording of the particular bonds the approach of Ackner LJ in the *Esal* case was not followed.

1 [1989] 2 Lloyd's Rep 205.
2 [1990] 2 Lloyd's Rep 496.

12.48 *Calling the indemnity*   Just as the beneficiary must comply with the terms of the guarantee in formulating his demand, so must the issuing bank comply with the terms of its indemnity when it in its turn makes its demand. The demands of Rafidain in the *IE Contractors* case[1] were found by the Court of Appeal to comply in two instances, but not in the third, because the third counter-indemnity required Rafidain to state that they were obliged to pay the beneficiary, which the demand failed to do. Thus Rafidain succeeded in the two cases where they had to show an actual liability, but not in the third where they were entitled on their own say-so, which may be a curious outcome.

1 Supra, para 12.42.

12.49 *The legal nature of demand guarantees and bonds: autonomous contracts; fraud*   Most of the cases concerning demand guarantees or bonds which have been considered by the English courts have emphasised the autonomy of the contract between the bank issuing the guarantee or bond and the beneficiary. The analogy with documentary credits in this respect has also been strongly emphasised. As has been made clear in Chapter 9 dealing with the topics of fraud and the granting of injunctions, the cases relating to demand guarantees and fraud are equally applicable to the position in respect of documentary credits and vice versa. In *Edward Owen Engineering Ltd v Barclays Bank International Ltd*[1] Lord Denning MR stated:[2]

> 'All this leads to the conclusion that the performance guarantee stands on a similar footing to a letter of credit. A bank which gives a performance guarantee must honour that guarantee according to its terms. It is not concerned in the least with the relations between the supplier and the customer; nor with the question whether the supplier is in default or not. The bank must pay according to its guarantee, on demand, if so stipulated, without proof or conditions. The only exception is where there is a clear case of fraud of which the bank has notice.'

1 [1978] QB 159.
2 Ibid at 171.

12.50 In *GKN Contractors Ltd v Lloyds Bank plc*[1] Parker LJ stated with reference to the fraud that may be committed in relation to demand guarantees[2] 'In those cases the fraud considered was a fraud on the part of the beneficiary, and in my view plainly refers to what may be called common law fraud, that is to say, a case where the named beneficiary presents a claim which he knows at the time to be an invalid claim, representing to the bank that he believes it to be a valid claim.' See also per Lord Denning MR in *State Trading Corpn of India Ltd v Man (Sugar) Ltd*[3] cited in *United Trading Corpn SA v Allied Arab Bank*:[4] 'The only term which is to be imported is that the buyer when giving notice of default, must honestly believe that there has been a default on the part of the seller. Honest belief is enough. If there is no honest belief, it may be evidence of fraud.' The representation will be made expressly in a case where the guarantee requires a statement that there has been a default. It will be one made by implication from the making of the demand where a demand is all that the bond requires. Reference should be made to Chapter 9 for a detailed treatment of the fraud exception to the autonomy rule and the problems of obtaining an injunction to prevent payment under a guarantee or under an indemnity given by the account party's bank to the bank issuing the guarantee.

1 (1985) 30 BLR 48.
2 Ibid at 63.
3 [1981] ComLR 235.
4 [1985] 2 Lloyd's Rep 554n at 559.

12.51 The reported decisions relating to demand guarantees and bonds and fraud are the following:

Harbottle (Mercantile) Ltd v National Westminster Bank Ltd[1]
Howe Richardson Scale Co Ltd v Polimex-Cekop[2]
Edward Owen Engineering Ltd v Barclays Bank International Ltd[3]
State Trading Corpn of India Ltd v Man (Sugar) Ltd[4]
Bolivinter Oil SA v Chase Manhattan Bank[5]
Potton Homes Ltd v Coleman Contractors Ltd – not itself a fraud case[6]
United Trading Corpn SA v Allied Arab Bank Ltd[7]
GKN Contractors Ltd v Lloyds Bank plc[8]

1 Kerr J [1978] QB 146.
2 Court of Appeal [1978] 1 Lloyd's Rep 161.
3 Court of Appeal [1978] QB 159.
4 Court of Appeal [1981] Com LR 235.
5 Court of Appeal [1984] 1 WLR 392, fully reported at [1984] 1 Lloyd's Rep 251.
6 Court of Appeal (1984) 28 BLR 19.
7 Court of Appeal [1985] 2 Lloyd's Rep 554n.
8 Court of Appeal (1985) 30 BLR 48.

12.52 *Risk* The same danger of abuse which has been referred to in connection with standby credits exists in connection with demand guarantees and bonds. Reference may be made to paragraphs 12.21 to 12.23 above. In the *Edward Owen* case[1] Lord Denning referred to the possibility of a guarantee being called on account of a trivial breach or no breach at all. He stated[2] 'This possibility is so real that the English supplier, if he is wise, will take it into account when quoting his price for the contract.' In the *Harbottle* case[3] Kerr J stated[4] 'In effect, the sellers rely on the probity and reputation of their buyers and on their good relations with them. But this trust is inevitably sometimes abused, and I understand that such guarantees are sometimes drawn upon, partly or wholly, without any or any apparent justification, almost as though they represented a discount in favour of the buyers.'

1 [1978] QB 159.
2 Ibid at 170.
3 [1978] QB 146.
4 Ibid at 150.

12.53 If the intended beneficiary of the guarantee insists on a guarantee which is payable against his demand alone, the account party can only seek to diminish his risk by endeavouring to negotiate that the guarantee does not come into effect until the payment documentary credit is in place in his favour, and that the period during which the guarantee may be called is as short as possible.[1] The account party should give careful attention to the wording of the guarantee. Thus, even if it is to include the words 'first demand', he may be able to include words which make it clear that the demand should set out the basis of the claim.[2] The account party will improve his position if he provides for the guarantee to be subject to the ICC Uniform Rules for Demand Guarantees.[3] In particular, Article 20 of the Uniform Rules requires the demand to include or to be accompanied by a statement that the account party is in breach of his obligations, and the respect in which he is in breach. The problem which arose in the *Gur* case, due to a small drafting error, has been described in paragraph 12.19.

1 Paragraphs 12.22 and 12.23 above are equally applicable here.
2 See paras 12.46 and 12.47 above.
3 See para 12.71 post, and Appendix 4.

12.54 *The question of consideration as between the issuing bank and the beneficiary*   It may be thought that in a commercial situation where the parties intend that their undertakings shall be enforceable between them, the need for consideration as a condition of that enforceability is an outmoded concept. But while the court will take a practical approach and will find consideration in such situations wherever it may be found,[1] where no consideration exists for a promise it is ordinarily only enforceable in English law if it is made under seal. The need for consideration is well established in respect of traditional contracts of guarantee (here called conditional guarantees), and it is also well established in that field that past consideration will not save the contract.[2]

1 See per Lord Wilberforce in *New Zealand Shipping Co Ltd v Satterthwaite Ltd* [1975] AC 154 at 167, PC.
2 As to consideration generally, see *Chitty on Contract* (26th edn) Vol 1, ch 3; as to consideration in relation to guarantees, see *Chitty*, op cit, Vol 2, paras 5020–5022, and *Rowlatt on Principle and Surety* (4th edn) ch 2. For a view that consideration is required for first demand bonds and guarantees, see *Wood's Law & Practice of International Finance* para 13.6(3). See also *Wallace's Construction Contracts*, para 19.04. For two recent cases showing how the problem of past consideration can be avoided on appropriate facts relating to the entering into of the guarantee, see *Pao On v Lau Yiu Long* [1980] AC 614, PC and *Bruns v Colocotronis* [1979] 2 Lloyd's Rep 412.

12.55 There are two aspects to the problem:[1]
(a) The more difficult aspect is to find consideration to support the bank's promise from the moment of the issue of the guarantee. This is the difficulty which arises in connection with irrevocable documentary

credits.[2] If a demand guarantee is not under seal and consideration is required and cannot be found, the consequence is that it is open to the issuing bank at any time at least up to the presentation of a demand to repudiate its liability under the guarantee and in effect to withdraw the guarantee. The position in respect of irrevocable documentary credits is that it is established that they are binding in law from the moment of issue. The legal basis is unclear: it is suggested that mercantile custom has established an exception to the consideration rule.[3] The position at and after a presentation of a demand to the bank under a demand guarantee gives rise to the second aspect.

1 The problem will only arise where the relevant obligation is governed by English law or some other law which requires consideration.
2 See Chapter 5, para 5.7.
3 Chapter 5, para 5.8.

12.56 (b) The second aspect is the position when and after a demand is made pursuant to the terms of the guarantee. If a demand guarantee is enforceable from the moment of issue, this does not require separate examination. But, if it is assumed that it is not, the guarantee can be treated as an offer that, if a demand according with its terms is made, payment will be made by the bank in accordance with the guarantee. The presentation of the demand is then an acceptance of this offer. The preparation of the document or documents and the delivery of them to the bank by the beneficiary can be treated as a detriment suffered by him, which provides the consideration to support the contract made by the offer and acceptance as described. This will not be artificial where the beneficiary has had to obtain a third party document such as a certificate. Where all that is required is the beneficiary's demand, the criticism of artificiality has greater weight. Nonetheless, if a guarantee is not binding for lack of consideration prior to the making of a demand and given the great need to find consideration and achieve enforceability, it may be that it can be found in this way even where all that has to be presented is a demand. If that is right, the ambit of the problem, and the risk to a beneficiary, are reduced to whether it is open to a bank which has issued a demand guarantee or bond to repudiate its obligation at any time before the beneficiary has made his demand.

12.57 When a bank issues a demand guarantee, that will often be the first contact between the bank and the beneficiary. The reason for its issue is the previously concluded underlying contract made between the account party and the beneficiary. But it is unlikely that the issuing bank will have had any involvement in the negotiations at that stage. Further, where the issuing bank is a bank instructed and to be indemnified by the account party's bank, as is usually the case, it will have no contact at all with the account party. Consideration must move from the promisee, here the beneficiary. It need not move to the promisor, the bank giving the undertaking. Nonetheless, it is difficult to see what consideration the beneficiary of a bond provides in connection with the actual issue of the guarantee, whether by way of detriment to himself, or by way of benefit to another. The problem is that the underlying contract between the account party and the beneficiary precedes the issue of the guarantee and the bank will normally have no involvement with it. It was held in a Malaysian case, *Perbadanam Kemajuan Negeri Selangor v Public Bank*

Bhd,[1] that consideration was to be found in the fact that on the execution and presentation of the guarantee required under a construction contract the contractor was given the right and benefit of commencing work under the contract. But he was not given that right by the employer, the beneficiary of the guarantee, in consequence of the employer's receipt of the guarantee. It was a contractual right which he already had, and it did not lie in the hands of the employer to stop him. The position is the same as, or very similar to, that with a documentary credit. It has been suggested in Chapter 5 that documentary credits are best seen as an exception to the rule that, if a conctract is not made under seal, it must be supported by consideration to be enforceable. It may well be that first demand bonds and guarantees are to be treated in the same way. An argument which strongly supports this is that where the bond or guarantee is payable against stipulated documents it may fall within the definition of a documentary credit provided by Article 2 of the Uniform Customs.[2] That being so, the choice is either to separate standby credits from traditional credits and to hold that they are unenforceable under English law for want of consideration, or to hold that where a bond or guarantee is payable by a bank against stipulated documents (or a stipulated document) it stands in the same position as regards consideration and enforceability as a documentary credit. The latter must surely be the correct choice. If a bond which is payable simply on receipt of a written demand is not to be treated as payable against a stipulated document for the purposes of the Uniform Customs, there is nonetheless no reason for such a bond to be treated differently in respect of consideration from one which is payable against stipulated documents.

1 [1980] 1 MLJ 173.
2 This is developed in para 12.68 below.

12.58 There is, however, a difficulty which exists in relation to bonds and guarantees which does not exist in relation to credits. It is that it is clearly established in relation to guarantees strictly so called, namely conditional guarantees, that consideration is required, or they must be under seal, as a requirement of enforceability.[1] If consideration is not to be required in relation to international demand guarantees or bonds it may be difficult to draw the line between them and guarantees and bonds which do require either consideration or to be under seal to be enforceable under English law.

1 Para 12.6 above.

12.59 It would be surprising if a bank of any standing and reputation were to be prepared to repudiate its obligations under a demand guarantee on the ground that, despite the fact that the bank had happily taken its commission from the applicant (or account party), its undertaking was worth nothing because it was unsupported by consideration. It would be the more surprising if, having done so, it was prepared to face a trial and a certain place in banking journals and in the law reports. So the problems discussed under this heading may well remain unresolved. In the meantime it must be prudent for beneficiaries under bonds and guarantees which may be governed in English law, to ensure that they are made under seal. Where a bond or guarantee is not governed by English law, if

it is a valid contract under its proper law despite any absence of consideration, it is enforceable in England.[1]

1 *Re Bonacina* [1912] 2 Ch 394.

12.60 *The question of a relationship between the account party and the issuing bank* Where the guarantee is issued by the account
party's own bank, there is, of course, no problem: the relationship is one
of a direct contract between them. It is more difficult where the issuing
bank is one which is instructed by the account party's bank against an
indemnity from that bank. It cannot then be suggested that there is a
contractual relationship between the account party and the issuing bank.
The Court of Appeal so held in *United Trading Corpn SA v Allied Arab
Bank*.[1] It was submitted on behalf of United Trading in that case that the
issuing bank (and the other banks in the chain) would arguably be liable
to them in the tort of negligence if they complied with a demand made by
the beneficiary which, to the knowledge of the bank at the time of
payment, was fraudulent. This was based on ordinary negligence principles relying on the fact that United Trading would ultimately have to
bear the loss if payment was made against a fraudulent demand. This
submission as to arguability was accepted on behalf of the Allied Arab
Bank and the case therefore proceeded on that basis. The same argument
was raised in *GKN Contractors Ltd v Lloyds Bank plc*.[2] Parker LJ
remarked 'That cause of action is one which I have some difficulty in
appreciating.' But in view of the *United Trading* case he likewise proceeded on the basis that the cause of action was arguable. It is suggested
that, were the point to be decided, the decision would be that there was
no such duty of care on the ground that the bank and the account party
were not in such a relationship that a duty of care towards the account
party should be imposed on the bank in its operation of the bond.[4]

1 [1985] 2 Lloyd's Rep 554n at 559.2.
2 (1985) 30 BLR 48.
3 The point was not argued at the trial, perhaps because it was unnecessary: see *IE
   Contractors Ltd v Lloyds Bank plc* [1989] 2 Lloyd's Rep 205 (Leggatt J) and Court of
   Appeal [1990] 2 Lloyd's Rep 496.
4 There may also be the question of foreign law.

**12.61 *Comparison of demand guarantees and bonds with docu-
mentary credits*** The English cases have been content to draw the
analogy between letters of credit and what they have usually referred to as
performance bonds or guarantees and have not entered upon an analysis of
their similarities and differences. In their references to letters of credit the
courts have had in mind credits performing the traditional function of letters
of credit rather than standby credits. The following points may be made.

12.62 (a) Both documentary credits and demand guarantees involve payment
undertakings by banks which are autonomous in that the undertakings
must be honoured according to their terms irrespective of any dispute
between the applicant or account party and the beneficiary relating to the
underlying contract. The exception in each case is where there is fraud to
the knowledge of the party presenting documents or making the demand.

12.63 (b) The function of demand guarantees and bonds is the same or similar to
that of most standby credits and contrasts with that of traditional credits.

12.64 (c) All credits involve a payment undertaking by a bank which becomes effective on the presentation to the bank of the documents specified, or stipulated as the Uniform Customs put it, in the credit. Some guarantees and bonds have the same characteristic, namely that the bank must pay when it receives an appropriate written demand accompanied by other documents as specified in the bank's undertaking. If a written demand in the form required by a guarantee, in so far as the guarantee requires it to be in any particular form,[1] is to be treated for this purpose as a document (and it should be), then all demand guarantees and bonds share this documentary characteristic whether or not any document is required in addition to the written demand.

1 See paras 12.44 to 12.48 above.

12.65 (d) Guarantees and bonds which are payable upon a liability or upon any event other than the presentation of a document or documents are fundamentally different from documentary credits.

12.66 (e) Documentary credits are usually issued by the applicant's bank in the applicant's country and advised to the beneficiary by a bank in the beneficiary's country, which confirms the credit where this is required. In contrast it is usual for demand guarantees to be issued by a bank in the beneficiary's country, that bank being in receipt of an undertaking of indemnity from the account party's bank. This point was taken up by Parker LJ in *GKN Contractors Ltd v Lloyds Bank plc*.[1] He stated:

> 'Turning to the law, the cases clearly establish that transactions by way of performance guarantee are similar to, albeit not indentical with, transactions under confirmed letters of credit. The analogy cannot, however, be pressed too far, because in the case of performance guarantees there are, not merely one set of documents passing up the chain with one question arising namely, whether the documents tendered were or were not in accordance with the credit, but three different contracts. It is true that in the case of letters of credit there are also different contracts, but the difference in the case of performance guarantees is that there are differing documents between each case.'

Thus, with a demand guarantee supported by a chain of indemnities, the bank which receives the demand does not pass on it and any accompanying documents down the line as it would with a credit: it makes its own demand in accordance with the contract of indemnity which it holds from the bank next in the line.

1 (1985) 30 BLR 48 at 62.

12.67 (f) As has been mentioned in paragraph 12.36 above the mechanism of confirmation is sometimes used in connection with bonds and guarantees of the first demand type.

12.68 *The Uniform Customs* Now that the ICC has published its Uniform Rules for Demand Guarantees,[1] it should be clear that demand guarantees are not intended to be made subject to the Uniform Customs and Practice for Documentary Credits, and that it is inappropriate to do so.

Nonetheless guarantees which are correctly described as providing for payment 'against stipulated documents' may fall within the definition of credit given by Article 2 of the Uniform Customs. It will be remembered that Article 2 refers to any 'arrangement, however named or described'. It continues 'whereby a bank (the "Issuing Bank") acting at the request and on the instructions of a customer (the "Applicant") . . .'. This will be complied with where a guarantee is issued by the applicant's bank. But it will not be met in the more common case where the applicant's bank instructs another bank to issue the guarantee against the indemnity of the applicant's bank. It would then be unrealistic to treat the instructing bank as the 'customer' of the issuing bank. But Article 2.ii will be met because in such a situation the applicant's bank 'authorises another bank to effect such payment', being 'a payment to or to the order of a third party (the "Beneficiary")'.

1 See paras 12.71 et seq below.

12.69 The only English authority which in any way touches on the point is *Esal (Commodities) Ltd v Oriental Credit Ltd.*[1] It will be remembered[2] that this concerned a bond issued by the London office of Wells Fargo Bank advised to Estram in Egypt through the Banque du Caire and confirmed by that bank. One of Esal's complaints was that Wells Fargo Bank had incorporated the Uniform Customs in the bond without authority. They no doubt did so because as an American bank they treated the bond as a standby credit. It was held by the Court of Appeal that as the Uniform Customs had played no part in the reasoning of the Egyptian tribunal which had held the Banque du Caire liable, the point could not assist Esal.

1 [1985] 2 Lloyd's Rep 546.
2 See para 12.36.

The ICC Uniform Rules for Demand Guarantees

12.70 In 1978 the ICC published *Uniform Rules for Contract Guarantees.*[1] They remain available for incorporation into a guarantee, but it is thought unlikely that they will have any active life. They were published by the ICC in 1978 with the object of avoiding the abuses arising in connection with first demand bonds. They seek to do so mainly by providing that, if a guarantee does not specify the documentation to be produced or specifies only a statement of claim by the beneficiary, in the case of a performance guarantee or a repayment guarantee there must be provided 'either a court decision or an arbitral award justifying the claim, or the approval of the principal in writing to the claim and the amount to be paid.' Their application would therefore carry a guarantee payable on demand from one end of the scale set out in paragraph 12.11 to the other. They apply to guarantees and bonds which state that they are made subject to them.

1 ICC Publication No 325.

12.71 In April 1992 the ICC published *Uniform Rules for Demand Guarantees.*[1] These seek to provide a more even balance between the interests of the beneficiary and the party ultimately paying. The manner in which it is hoped to achieve this is as follows. Article 20 provides that any demand under the guarantee shall (in addition to any other document required) be supported by a written statement stating that (i) the Principal[2] is in breach of his obligations under the underlying contract or, in the case of a tender guarantee, the tender conditions, and (ii) the respect in which the Principal is in breach. Where a guarantee is made subject to the Rules, this Article applies unless it is specifically excluded.[3] So if a demand guarantee incorporating the Rules states that it is payable simply against a demand, the bank guarantor should not pay unless there is a demand complying with the express terms of the guarantee and also a statement which complies with Article 20. A dishonest beneficiary has therefore to be more brazenly dishonest if Article 20 applies. This is a psychological pressure which may curb some of the worst excesses. The Rules are generally to be welcomed as they provide a framework for the operation of demand guarantees, which will lead to greater uniformity and certainty. Many of the Articles have their parallels among the Uniform Customs, but obviously the problem of inapplicable Articles which arises when the Uniform Customs are applied to standby credits does not arise. It is unfortunate that provisions covering the situation where the guarantor bank is instructed not by the party to the underlying contract but by an intermediary bank, were not included until a late stage, and the necessary modifications have not been pursued throughout the Rules.

1 ICC Publication No 458, which is set out in Appendix 4 post. The ICC also publishes a Guide to the Rules by Professor Roy Goode, ICC Publication No 510.
2 This is the party who initiates the guarantee's issue and is ultimately liable in respect of it: Article 2.
3 Article 20.c.

12.72 In summary the more important Articles of the Rules provide:

1	Application is by incorporation.
2	Definitions, and autonomy of guarantee contract from underlying transaction.
3	Requirement of clarity and precision, setting out basics to be stated.
5	Irrevocable unless otherwise stated.
9	Guarantor to examine the documents presented with care for conformity on their face with the terms of the guarantee.
10(a)	Guarantor to have a reasonable time to examine and to decide to pay or refuse.
(b)	Immediate notice to beneficiary of refusal: documents to be held at disposal of beneficiary.
17	Parties down the line to be informed of any demand without delay.
19	Demand and all documents required including Article 20 statement to be presented on or before expiry date.
20	Demands to be supported by written statement as to breach: see 12.71 above.
22–26	Expiry provisions including in Article 26 covering the position where the beneficiary requests an extension of the expiry date as an alternative to payment.
27, 28	Proper law[1] and jurisdiction.

1 See paras 13.23 and 13.24 post.

12.73 It is too soon to say how general the application of the Rules will become. They may so far have found greater favour in Europe than in England. In England, at least where the beneficiary and its bank have influence, their incorporation may be seen as burdensome on the beneficiary. But whereas the unattractiveness of the 1978 Rules is immediately apparent,[1] these Rules may well in due course acquire an acceptance approaching that of the Uniform Customs. Only time will tell whether they should be moved to the head of this chapter.

1 See paragraph 12.70 above.

Chapter 13

Conflict of Laws, Illegality and Exchange Control, Sovereign Immunity

A. Conflict of Laws

13.1 *Introduction*   The preceding chapters have intended to set out the law of England relating to documentary credits. That law will be appropriate where English law is the law which governs the question at issue, and it will be of assistance where the governing law is the law of a country whose relevant law follows that of England. It must here be noted that in an English court it is for a party who relies on a foreign law as being the relevant law to prove what the provisions of that law are. In the absence of such proof the English court will assume that the foreign law is not different from English law. Documentary credits as much as or more than any other type of commercial transaction involve more than one country, and of course England may not be involved at all in the credit and its performance. The conflict of laws[1] is the curiously named branch of a country's law which determines which system of law is to be applied by the courts of that country to a question involving a foreign element. This chapter is concerned with the principles which will be applied by an English court in deciding what law, whether English law or a foreign law, should be applied to determine questions arising in a dispute involving a foreign element. Until recently these principles were those which had been developed by the courts on a case-by-case basis over the years and had become well-established, although their application to the factual situations arising in connection with credits had yet to be worked out fully. These common law rules have now been replaced by the provisions of the EEC Convention on the Law Applicable to Contractual Obligations 1980, which is known as the Rome Convention. This became part of English law on 1 April 1991 following the passing of the Contracts (Applicable Law) Act 1990. It applies to contracts made after that date.[2] The chapter also deals with the question of what may broadly be called illegality or unenforceability by reason of a foreign law, in particular by reason of foreign exchange control regulations or court orders.[3] Lastly the question of sovereign immunity is briefly referred to.

1 Sometimes also called private international law.
2 Article 17 of the Convention.
3 There is now no exchange control existing under English law itself.

13.2 *The Uniform Customs* The Uniform Customs contain no provisions relevant to the question of what national law is to be applied to determine any particular question which may arise in connection with a credit.[1] Because they now apply by incorporation to nearly all credits regardless of country, they provide for uniformity and should diminish the differences that might otherwise arise through the application of different national laws. It is, however, for the courts of each country to interpret the Uniform Customs in accordance with the principles of its own national law, and so differences of interpretation may arise. Nonetheless it is to be expected that the courts of one country should heed the decisions on similar points of the courts of other countries. Thus, whereas on general questions of contract law it may be of little interest to an English court what approach has been adopted in continental jurisdictions, decisions on particular questions involving the construction of provisions of the Uniform Customs would be given careful attention.

1 Compare Article 27 of the ICC Uniform Rules for Demand Guarantees; post para 13.23.

13.3 *The general principles* The relationships which arise in connection with documentary credits are primarily contractual. Choice of law questions arising in relation to credit contracts made after 1 April 1991 are therefore to be answered by the application of the Articles of the Rome Convention.[1] The rules contained in the Convention apply to contractual obligations in any situation involving a choice between the laws of different countries: there need be no EEC connection.[2] The position in relation to contracts made up to that date is determined by common law principles, and is considered in the First Edition to this book.[3] It is suggested that while the Convention may in some aspects require a different route, the governing law will usually be the same as that which would have been chosen by the common law rules.

1 See para 13.1 above, Introduction.
2 Article 1. For this purpose England, Scotland and Northern Ireland are different countries.
3 The common law authorities are reviewed in paragraphs 13.7 to 13.14 below as part of the discussion of the likely resolution to be achieved under the Convention.

13.4 In outline[1] the Articles of the Convention which are likely to be relevant to documentary credits are the following:

Article 3 provides that a contract shall be governed by the law chosen by the parties and states that the choice must be express or demonstrated with reasonable certainty by the terms of the contract or the circumstances of the case. If the choice is not express, the court is not permitted to infer a choice of law where the parties had no clear intention of making a choice: that situation is provided for by Article 4.[2]

Article 4.1 provides that where no choice of law is made under Article 3 the contract shall be governed by the law of the country with which it is most closely connected: a severable part of the contract more closely connected with the law of another country may by way of exception be governed by the law of that country. By *Article 4.2* and subject to Article 4.5 it is to be presumed that the contract is most closely connected with the country where the party 'who is to effect the performance which is characteristic of the contract' has, at the time of the conclusion of the contract, in the case of a company its central administration. But where the contract is entered into in the course of that party's trade, the country shall be that where the company's place of business through which the performance is to be effected is situated.[3]

Article 4.5 provides that Article 4.2 shall not apply if 'the characteristic performance' cannot be determined; and that Article 4.2 shall be disregarded if it appears from the circumstances as a whole that the contract is more closely connected with another country. Logic might suggest that the court must look to see if indeed it does so appear before the presumption in Article 4.2 is applied with finality. However the intention is more probably that the presumption should be applied in most situations without the need for that exercise, leaving Article 4.5 as an alternative route where greater flexibility is required to enable the appropriate law to be chosen.[4]

In determining the effect of the provisions of the Convention regard is to be had to the Report on the Convention known as the Giuliano-Lagarde Report.[5] This is particularly important in deciding what is meant by 'the performance which is characteristic of the contract'. The Report states that it is usually the performance for which payment is due, for example the delivery of goods.[6] Performance under a documentary credit contract involves the delivery of documents to a bank and the coming into being of a right to payment in consequence. The Report states that 'in a banking contract the law of the country of the banking establishment with which the transaction is made will normally govern the contract.'[7] While a documentary credit contract may be described as a banking contract, it is not, of course, among the most typical of banking contracts such as for the establishment of an account or for a loan.

1 The Articles are summarised only so far as appears relevant to documentary credits. For a fuller treatment, see Cheshire & North *Private International Law*, 12th Edition, Chapter 18; and Dicey & Morris, *The Conflict of Laws*, 12th Edition; also Plender, *The European Contracts Convention*.
2 See page 17 of the Report (for which see note 5 below).
3 This states the practical effect of the second sentence of Article 4.2.
4 Compare Cheshire & North, *Private International Law*, pp 494.5.
5 The Report on the Convention by Professors Mario Giuliano and Paul Lagarde, Official Journal of the European Communities, OJ 1980 No C 282/1, 31.10.80.
6 Report, p 21.
7 Report, p 21.

13.5 ***Contracts between bank and beneficiary*** It is unusual for a credit to specify a governing law, though there is no legal reason why it should not do so. An issuing bank might see an advantage in specifying the law of the country where it is situated as the governing law: but where the credit is payable in another country this would be undesirable from the beneficiary's point of view as in some circumstances it could undermine the security of payment which the credit is intended to provide.[1] As banking practice currently stands it is unlikely that Article 3 of the Convention will be applicable in a credit situation.

1 See the facts in *Power Curber International Ltd v National Bank of Kuwait* [1981] 1 WLR 1233 set out in para 13.8 below.

13.6 If Article 3 does not apply, the governing law must be found by the application of Article 4. The purpose of the Convention is to provide for uniformity in choice of law.[1] It must also be to provide certainty. It should be remembered that any factual situation may have its own unique characteristics which may distinguish it from the usual situation and require the choice of a law appropriate to those characteristics. But, subject to that possibility, it is suggested that the approach to the question of governing law in documentary credits should be to find a choice of law rule which can be easily and uniformly applied to the common situations which occur. With regard to contracts between bank and beneficiary there are three main situations:

(i)   Issuing bank advises credit direct to beneficiary; documents to be presented to issuing bank; no other bank involved; beneficiary has one contract only.

(ii) Issuing bank advises credit to beneficiary through an advising bank; documents to be presented to the advising bank which will accept or reject them on behalf of the issuing bank; beneficiary has one contract only.

(iii) As (ii), save advising bank confirms the credit; the beneficiary has two contracts.

It is sugggested that in each of these situations in the ordinary case the governing law should be that of the country in which the bank (or branch) is situated, which is to be the first to examine the documents and to determine acceptance or rejection. Where the credit is confirmed this should be so whether it is the contract between the beneficiary and the issuing bank or the contract between the beneficiary and the confirming bank which is under examination. The performance of the advising/confirming bank is central to both contracts: the application of different laws to the two contracts would create considerable difficulties.[2] It is suggested that the performance of that bank in examining the documents and in determining their acceptance or rejection is the performance characteristic of the contract. Where there is only one bank involved, namely the situation at (i) above, or where the contract under examination is that between the confirming bank and the beneficiary, the application of Article 4.2 of the Convention will provide as the governing law suggested. Where there are two banks involved and the contract under examination is that between the issuing bank and the beneficiary, the presumption in Article 4.2 can only be applied to give the suggested desired result if the advising/confirming bank can be treated as 'a place of business other than the principle place of business'[3] of the issuing bank.

Unless the one is a branch of the other this will not be the case. So Article 4.5 must be applied to give the outcome desired. In the Report on the Convention it is stated that it is 'quite natural' that the place of business shall prevail over the country of performance where they differ.[4] It is suggested that the circumstances of documentary credit contracts are significantly different to the two-party single contract situation which the Report may be presumed to have in mind here, and that this paragraph should not be applied to documentary credits. The choice of the law of the place where the bank to whom presentation of documents is to be made is situated, has the advantage that in examining the documents the bank is able to apply its own law and not a foreign law. Further, the bank is usually the advising bank which is often also a confirming bank and is usually in the same country as the beneficiary. The choice of law of the country where is situated the bank to which documents are to be presented by the beneficiary, as the law of the country with which the contract is most closely connected, can be derived from, and supported by, the reported English common law decisions concerning governing law.

1 See Report, p 4.
2 See *Offshore International SA v Banco Central SA* [1977] 1 WLR 399, per Ackner J, post para 13.7.
3 The relevant words from Article 4.2.
4 Report, pp 20, 21.

13.7 The first decision in point of time is that of Ackner J in *Offshore International SA v Banco Central SA*.[1] In order to provide for the repayment, in the event of the cancellation of the contract, of a substantial downpayment under a contract for the building of an oil rig made between a Spanish construction company and Panamanian oil rig operators based in Texas, a Spanish bank opened a letter of credit through a New York bank as correspondent bank. The New York bank did not confirm the credit.[2] The credit was payable in US dollars by the New York bank on production of documents including sight drafts drawn on the New York bank. After pointing out that the underlying contract for the construction of the rig was irrelevant, the judge turned to consider with what system of law the contract between the defendant Spanish bank and the plaintiff rig operators was governed. He stated:

'The contest here is between New York law and Spanish law. What are the relevant factors in favour of each? As regards New York law, the credit was opened through a New York bank; payment was to be made in US dollars. Further, such payment was only to be made against documents presented in New York. In favour of Spanish law being the proper law, is the fact that the letter of credit was opened by a Spanish bank, the first defendants.

Thus, on the side of New York law are all matters of performance, whereas, in relation to Spanish law, Spain and a Spanish bank was the source of the obligation.

In my judgement, it is with New York law that the transaction has its closest and most real connection. Moreover, despite Mr Alexander's characteristically persuasive submission, I am satisfied that Mr Yorke was correct in his contention that very great inconvenience would arise, if the law of the issuing bank were to be considered as the proper law. The advising bank would have constantly to be seeking to apply a whole variety of foreign laws. Indeed it is very difficult to follow exactly what would flow from Mr Alexander's submission, if the advising bank was (as was not this case) to confirm the letter of credit.'

The reference to the possibility of confirmation raises an important point. For there is a powerful argument that the confirming bank's obligation to the beneficiary should be governed by the law of the country where it, and probably also the beneficiary, are situated, and where documents are to be presented to it by the beneficiary. If the relations between the confirming bank and the beneficiary are to be governed by that law, can a different law govern those between the issuing bank and the beneficiary as would be the case if the law of the place where the issuing bank was was chosen to govern its relations? The alternative argument is that, if the law of the contract between the issuing bank and the beneficiary is the law of the place where the issuing bank is situated, as the confirming bank is 'confirming' that contract, the contract arising from the confirmation should be governed by the same law.

1 [1977] 1 WLR 399.
2 The credit was a standby credit, but that term was not used in the judgment.

13.8 Five years later a similar question came before the Court of Appeal in *Power Curber International Ltd v National Bank of Kuwait SAK*.[1] Unfortunately it appears that the court approached the problem before it without a sufficiently full analysis of the positions adopted by two of the banks involved. The plaintiffs, Power Curber, carried on business in North Carolina USA, and exported goods to a trading concern called Hammoudeh in Kuwait. Payment was by letter of credit; 25% was to be paid on presentation of documents and 75% one year after shipment. The credit was opened by the National Bank of Kuwait and was advised by the National Bank of Kuwait to the Bank of America in Miami, Florida. The National Bank's letter asked the Bank of America to advise the credit through the North Carolina National Bank in Charlotte, North Carolina (with whom Power Curber banked). The letter to the Bank of America stated 'In reimbursement of your negotiations under this credit, please draw on our account with Bank of America (International), New York, in respect of sight payment.' Drafts were to be drawn on the opener, namely, Hammoudeh. The goods were shipped and documents presented. The 25% was paid against presentation. Presumably the documents were presented by the North Carolina National Bank to the Bank of America in Miami, which reimbursed itself in respect of the 25% from the Bank of America (International) New York, the reimbursement being an example of the operation of Article 21 of the Uniform Customs. The North Carolina National Bank may have presented the documents as collecting agent for Power Curber or it may have negotiated the documents from Power Curber and collected on its own behalf – although strictly the bank's right to negotiate could have been questioned under the terms of the credit.[2] The National Bank of Kuwait wrote to the North Carolina National Bank to say that the draft for the 75% had been accepted by their principals and that 'We shall not fail to remit to you the above mentioned amount through Morgan Guaranty Trust Co New York at maturity on December 26, 1980.'[3] Before this could happen Hammoudeh began an action against Power Curber in the courts of Kuwait claiming an amount, which perhaps related to commissions, exceeding the amount of the draft, and applied for an order of provisional attachment of the sum payable by the National Bank of Kuwait to Power Curber under the credit. A provisional attachment was ordered, which prevented the bank from making any further payment under the credit and made the bank accountable to the court for the amount involved. The bank's application to have the order set aside was refused, and the refusal was confirmed on appeal. Power Curber first started proceedings against the National Bank of Kuwait in North Carolina. But it discontinued these and began proceedings in London where the National Bank had a branch.

1 [1981] 1 WLR 1233.
2 The fact that Power Curber was the plaintiff in respect of the 75% might suggest that it was the former: but the North Carolina National Bank could have renegotiated the bill to Power Curber following its dishonour, leaving it to Power Curber to collect on the bill on which they were in any event liable to the North Carolina National Bank as the drawers of a bill which had been negotiated with recourse and been dishonoured.
3 The statement by Lord Denning MR at [1981] 1 WLR 1238C that Hammoudeh drew a draft on the National Bank of Kuwait, which the bank accepted, is inconsistent both with the terms of the credit and with the letter just quoted: it must be wrong.

13.9 The Court of Appeal had to decide two questions. First, did the National Bank have any defence against Power Curber's claim, or should Power Curber have judgment against the bank for the amount of the unpaid draft? Second, if Power Curber was entitled to judgment, should execution on the judgment be stayed by reason of the order of the Kuwait court? On the first question it was argued for the bank that the proper law of the credit was Kuwaiti law and so, as payment was unlawful by that law, the bank had a defence. Alternatively it was argued that the situs of the debt was Kuwait and as Kuwaiti law governed the effect of the order of attachment all countries should give effect to it. Lord Denning MR stated:[1]

'The proper law of the contract is to be found by asking: With what law has the contract its closest and most real connection? In my opinion it was the law of North Carolina where payment was to be made (on behalf of the issuing bank) against presentation of documents.'

Griffiths LJ took a similar view:[2]

'In my view the proper law of the letter of credit was the law of the state of North Carolina. Under the letter of credit the bank accepted the obligation of paying or arranging the payment of sums due in American dollars against presentation of documents at the sellers' bank in North Carolina. The bank could not have discharged its obligation by offering payment in Kuwait. Furthermore the bank undertook to reimburse the advising bank if they paid on their behalf in dollars in America. In *Offshore International SA v Banco Central SA* [1977] 1 WLR 399 Ackner J held that the place at which the bank must perform its obligation under a letter of credit determines the proper law to be applied to the letter of credit. In my view that case was correctly decided.'

Both he and Lord Denning also agreed that the situs of the debt was North Carolina. Lord Denning stated:[3]

'Nor can I agree that the *lex situs* of the debt was Kuwait. It was in North Carolina. A debt under a letter of credit is different from ordinary debts. They may be situate where the debtor is resident. But a debt under a letter of credit is situate in the place where it is in fact payable against documents.'

The third member of the court, Waterhouse J, agreed that the proper law was the law of North Carolina. But he found the question of situs more difficult. He stated:[4]

'A debt is generally to be looked upon as situate in the country where it is properly recoverable or can be enforced and it is noteworthy that the sellers here submitted voluntarily to the dismissal of their earlier proceedings against the bank in North Carolina. We have been told that they did so because of doubts about the jurisdiction of the North Carolina court, which was alleged in the pleadings to be based on the transaction of business by the bank there, acting by itself or through another named bank as its agent. As for the question of residence, the bank has been silent about any residence it may have within the United States of America. In the absence of previous binding authority, I have not been persuaded that this debt due under an unconfirmed letter of credit can be regarded as situate in North Carolina merely because there was provision for payment at a branch of a bank used by the sellers in Charlotte: and I do not regard the analogy of a bill of exchange or a security transferable by delivery as helpful.'

1 At [1981] 1 WLR 1240E.
2 Ibid at 1242F.
3 Ibid at 1240F.
4 Ibid at 1244C.

13.10 It is suggested that the role of the North Carolina National Bank is not as clear as may appear from the judgments of Lord Denning and Griffiths LJ. Certainly the Bank of America was to advise the credit to the bank and it was to advise Power Curber in its turn. But the credit did not provide for it to pay Power Curber on presentation of documents to it. The fact that a letter was written to the North Carolina National Bank by the National Bank of Kuwait stating that the draft had been accepted suggests that the documents were presented through it; but the correct analysis may well be that in presenting the documents to the Bank of America it was acting as collecting agent of Power Curber. The letter was probably written as the most direct means of informing Power Curber, the drawer of the bill and the party entitled to be paid on it, that it had been accepted. The bank which was to pay against documents in respect of the 25% was the Bank of America, which was to be reimbursed in its turn from New York. The Bank of America was to examine the documents for compliance with the credit, and it was a term of their right to reimbursement that they certify to the National Bank of Kuwait that the credit had been complied with. That would take place in Florida. The 75% was to be paid to the North Carolina National Bank through the Morgan Guaranty Trust of New York. It is also clear that the 75% was intended to be paid to the North Carolina National Bank because Power Curber had an account with that bank. So the North Carolina National Bank would receive the money as Power Curber's bankers and there would be no question of further payment of the sum to Power Curber save by crediting their account. So the Court of Appeal's analysis of the arrangements between the particular banks may be faulty. The decision is nonetheless clear authority that, where a credit provides for documents to be presented to a bank and for payment to be made by that bank, the proper law of the credit will be the law of the place where that bank is situated.

13.11 The second question which the Court of Appeal had to consider was whether execution on the judgment should be stayed. The court held that it should not, because the order of the Kuwaiti court struck at the essence of a credit, namely that disputes between buyer and seller should not prevent payment being made under the credit. In such circumstances the principle of international comity did not require the order of the Kuwaiti court to be recognised and given effect to by the English court.

13.12 In *European Asian Bank AG v Punjab and Sind Bank*[1] the court had to decide whether the action which had been commenced in England should be allowed to continue or whether there was another more appropriate venue. The facts have been set out in Chapter 2.[2] Robert Goff J stated:[3]

> 'Second, reference was made to the letter of credit contract, and it was submitted by the Punjab Bank that that contract was governed by Indian law. That submission I am unable to accept. True, the letter of credit was issued by an Indian bank; but it was notified through a correspondent bank in Singapore, which later confirmed the credit, and was issued in favour of sellers in Singapore, who were advised of it through another bank in Singapore. The letter of credit was payable against documents; it contemplated negotiation of documents through certainly one bank in Singapore (ABN), in which event payment to the beneficiary would have been made in Singapore, though it was provided that "in negotiation please claim reimbursement from Irving Trust Co, 1 Wall Street" – no doubt as a matter of convenience because this was a dollar credit. In all events, payment would not have been made in India. In these circumstances, I do not consider that the governing law of the letter of credit was Indian law; most probably it was the law of Singapore – cf *Offshore International SA v Banco Central SA*.[4] I should add that the evidence before the court is that the law concerning letters of credit in Singapore is identical to the law concerning letters of credit in this country. I should add that since, under the letter of credit, the European Asian Bank, if entitled to payment, was entitled to be paid in New York, the breach occurred and so the cause of action arose in New York; but neither party has contended that New York has more than an incidental connection with this case.'

He decided that the action should continue in England. His decision was upheld by the Court of Appeal. Only Ackner LJ referred to the question of proper law. He stated:[5]

> 'I do not accept that the contract was governed by Indian law, although the letter of credit was issued by an Indian Bank. It was notified through a correspondent bank in Singapore, which confirmed the credit, and it was issued in favour of sellers in Singapore, who were advised of it through another bank in Singapore. Negotiation was contemplated in Singapore, as was payment. In these circumstances the proper law was probably that of Singapore – see *Offshore International SA v Banco Central SA* [1976] 2 Lloyd's Rep 402, [1977] 1 WLR 399 approved in *Power Curber v National Bank of Kuwait*.'

The reference to payment in Singapore contrasts with the judgment below.

1 [1981] 2 Lloyd's Rep 651; affd [1982] 2 Lloyd's Rep 356, CA.
2 Para 2.26.
3 At [1981] 2 Lloyd's Rep 656.2.
4 Supra para 13.7.
5 At [1982] 2 Lloyd's Rep 368.

13.13 The contract before the Court of Appeal in *Attock Cement Co v Romanian Bank for Foreign Trade*[1] was a performance bond issued in connection with a contract to build a cement plant, which contract was expressly governed by English law. It was argued that the bond which was issued by the Romanian Bank for Foreign Trade directly to the plaintiff's employers was also governed by English law by reason of a collateral agreement. But this argument was rejected by the court. In considering what the proper law was, the court first emphasised the separateness of the construction contract and the bond. Staughton LJ giving the judgment of the court stated:[2]

> 'Almost every letter of credit or performance bond is issued pursuant to some underlying commercial transaction. Yet we were referred to no case where it had even been argued that one was affected by the proper law of the other. Seeing that the letter of credit or performance bond is intended to be a separate transaction, I would hold that it is not so affected, and is ordinarily to be governed by the law of the place where payment is to be made under it. That is in general accord with the rule applicable to the banker-customer relationship arising from a current or deposit account, which is ordinarily governed by the law of the place where the account is kept: *Libyan Arab Foreign Bank v Manufacturers Hanover Trust Co* [1988] 2 Lloyd's Rep 494. The *Broken Hill* case is in my opinion readily distinguishable: a guarantee is often intended to be governed by the same law as the principal obligation, but it is of the essence of performance bonds and letters of credit that they are not, in law, guarantees.'

Having failed to establish English law as the proper law of the bond, the plaintiffs failed to establish the jurisdiction of the English court.

1 [1989] 1 WLR 1147.
2 Ibid at 1159.

13.14 Most recently in *Turkiye Is Bankasi A/S v Bank of China*[1] Phillips J held that the governing law of counter-guarantees given by the Bank of China to the Turkiye Is Bankasi to support performance bonds given by the latter to a Turkish company and relating to the performance of a Chinese sub-contractor to that company was Turkish law. The first ground of the decision was that it could be inferred from the terms of the documents that Turkish law was to apply. It was secondly held that the guarantees were most closely connected with Turkish law because of their close relationship to the performance bonds which they supported, which bonds were issued in Turkey to a Turkish beneficiary by a Turkish bank and were governed by Turkish law. In doing so the judge rightly rejected an argument that the relationship between the two was irrelevant and should be disregarded on the ground of autonomy. Credit and performance bond contracts stand independently of the underlying sales or construction contracts: but for governing law purposes they do not stand independently of other related bank contracts.

1 [1993] 1 Lloyd's Rep 132.

13.15 The choice of the law of the country where the documents are first examined and accepted or refused follows the decision in *Offshore International SA v Banco Central SA*[1] and accords with the ratio of the decision in the *Power Curber* case.[2] (It is suggested that a strong case can be made on the facts of *Power Curber* for the law of Florida as the proper law on the ground that the documents were to be presented for examination and acceptance to the Bank of America in Miami.) It accords with the tentative conclusion in the *European Asian Bank* case.[3] It does not follow the wording of the decision in *Attock*.[4] But it is suggested that, had the Court of Appeal there had in mind the situations where the place of payment is different from the place of first presentation of documents, different wording would have been chosen. The use of the word 'ordina-rily' in the judgment is to be noted. It is also consistent with the actual outcome in the *Turkiye Is Bankasi* Case,[5] although the second ratio of that decision shows that contracts in a performance bond chain may require an approach different to that appropriate to credit contracts.

1 [1977] 1 WLR 399.   2 [1981] 1 WLR 1233.
3 [1981] 2 Lloyd's Rep 651 and [1982] 2 Lloyd's Rep 356.
4 [1989] 1 WLR 1147.   5 [1993] 1 Lloyd's Rep 132.

13.16 *Contracts between applicant and issuing bank*   The applicant and issuing bank will normally be in the same country. It is suggested that on any analysis the contract between them must ordinarily be governed by the law of the country in which the issuing bank is situated. It is the issuing bank which effects 'the performance which is characteristic of the contract'.[1] The statement in the Report that 'in a banking contract the law of the country of the banking establishment with which the transaction is made will normally govern the contract'[2] is directly applicable. The applicant will usually have an account with the issuing bank. In *Libyan Arab Foreign Bank v Bankers Trust*[3] Staughton J stated[4] 'As a general rule the contract between a bank and its customer is governed by the law of the place where the account is kept, in the absence of agreement to the contrary.' The applicant will usually have an account with the issuing bank, and the one law will govern their relations both in respect of the account and such credits as the bank is requested to open.

1 Article 4.2 of the Rome Convention.
2 Report, p 21: see note 5 to para 13.4 above.
3 [1988] 1 Lloyd's Rep 259. See also Dicey & Morris, *The Conflict of Laws* (12th edn) p 1336, note 47 and authorities there cited.
4 Ibid at 270.

13.17 *Relations between banks*   If a correspondent bank is employed, it will almost certainly be in a different country to the issuing bank. The functions which it performs are carried out vis-à-vis the issuing bank as the agent of the issuing bank.[1] Those functions, namely the advising of the credit, the examination of documents and payment functions, are all carried out by it in the country in which it is situated. It is suggested that the 'performance which is characteristic of the contract'[2] is effected by the correspondent bank. It is suggested that these factors point to the law of the place where the correspondent bank is as the appropriate law to govern their contract.[3] This is likely to be the same law as that which governs the credit itself.

1 See Chapter 6, paras 6.4, 6.11, 6.12.
2 Article 4.2 of the Rome Convention.
3 Support for this is obtained by analogy from the situations referred to in Dicey & Morris, *The Conflict of Laws* (12th edn) pp 1453, 4.

13.18 *Negotiation credits*   The credit may enable any bank to negotiate documents and to present them under the credit to the advising bank or as the credit provides, or negotiation may be restricted to a class of banks (probably defined by situation) or just one bank. In each of these situations two relationships have to be considered: first, that between the negotiation bank and the banks giving undertakings under the credit; second, that between the beneficiary and the negotiation bank.

13.19 (a) With regard to the negotiation bank and the banks giving under-takings in respect of the credit, it is suggested that a negotiating bank is in the same position as the beneficiary himself, whom it has effectively become. Thus the same governing law must apply between the negotia-tion bank and the issuing and any confirming bank, and it will be the law of the place where the bank is situated to which presentation of docu-ments is to be made by the negotiating bank, in accordance with para-graph 13.6 above. It cannot make any difference that the negotiating bank is situated in another country: among other reasons, if that could affect the choice of proper law, it would mean that the proper law of the credit varied with whether negotiation occurred and where the negotiat-ing bank was. If the negotiation takes place in the same country as the bank to which presentation of documents is to be made under the credit, the same law will apply between the beneficiary and the negotiating bank as governs the credit.[1] But it might take place in another country. For example, an issuing bank might advise a negotiable credit direct to a beneficiary in another country in which negotiation then takes place. Where the credit is available by negotiation in the sense that the credit provides for the advising bank to negotiate the documents, the governing law of the credit will be the law of the place where the advising bank is situated in accordance with paragraph 13.6 above. It is suggested in paragraph 13.17 above that the law governing relations between an issuing bank and an advising bank which has to handle the documents is likely to be the law of the place where the advising bank is situate. It is suggested that this will be the case where the credit is available by negotiation by the advising bank. If that is right, it follows in this respect an advising bank nominated by the credit to negotiate is in a different position to that of a bank which negotiates under a freely negotiable credit: the former's relations with the issuing bank to which it must present the documents which it has negotiated are governed by the law of the place where it is situate; the latter's relations with the bank to which it must present the documents are governed by the law of the place where that bank is situate. This is not illogical because of the special position of a bank nominated by the credit to handle the documents.

1 See para 13.20 below.

13.20 (b) The law governing relations between the beneficiary and the bank to which it negotiates the documents need not be, and is perhaps unlikely to be, the same law as that governing the credit itself. Although that law is one factor in determining the governing law between the negotiation bank and the beneficiary, each case has to be examined on its own facts to see with which system of law the contract between them relating to the negotiation has its closest and most real connection. The law of the country where the negotiation takes place is likely to be a strong contender.

13.21 ***Transferable credits*** Where a credit is transferred to a second bene-ficiary, new relationships come into being with the banks giving under-takings under the credit in that those undertakings are extended to the new beneficiary as well as remaining extended to the old.[1] Where the place of presentation of documents remains unchanged by the transfer, it is clear that the proper law should govern the undertakings given to the second beneficiary as governs those given to the first. The credit may be transferred to another place in another country pursuant to Article 48.j of the Uniform Customs, with the object that the second beneficiary can present documents in his own country. Does this then mean that the undertakings given to him by the issuing and any confirming bank will be governed by a different law, namely the law of that country? It is suggested that it does not, that there should remain one law governing the whole operation of the credit as between the undertaking banks and both beneficiaries, which should be determined, as has been discussed, as the law of the place where the bank is situated to which documents are to be presented by the first beneficiary. Anything else means that transfer of the credit to another country has the effect of partially changing its governing law.[2] If there is the one governing law, it may mean that the bank to which the credit is transferred and the second beneficiary will be obliged to operate the credit in accordance with a foreign law.[3] If the bank to whom the credit is transferred confirms it to the second beneficiary, it is suggested in this instance that the contract between it and the second beneficiary should have as its governing law the same governing law as the contract which is being confirmed, namely the contract between the issuing bank and the second beneficiary arising from the transfer.

1 Para 10.20 above.
2 It can be suggested that, in accordance with the reasoning previously adopted, the governing law must be the law of the place where the bank to which the documents are to be presented is situate, that is, of the country of the bank at which the documents are to be presented under the transferred credit. There are here, however, other important elements to consider, which make preferable the solution proposed.
3 A possibility to be borne in mind is that provisions of the law of the country where presentation of documents is to take place, may require to be applied to questions specifically concerning presentation.

13.22 *Bills of exchange*   Where a question of what law is applicable arises in connection with the right of a claimant to be paid in reliance upon rights given by a bill of exchange rather than by the undertakings arising in connection with the credit pursuant to which the bill has come into being, in England the applicable law is determined by section 72 of the Bills of Exchange Act 1882. Questions arising under bills of exchange and other negotiable instruments are excluded from the ambit of the Rome Convention by Article 12.c. A claimant may be relying on the bill rather than on the credit when he is the holder of an accepted bill either as the drawer or as a party to whom it has been negotiated, and he is claiming against the acceptor. Likewise where the claim is against the drawer of the bill (the beneficiary of the credit) and the claim is made by one to whom the bill has been negotiated with recourse. Section 72 provides:

'72. Where a bill drawn in one country is negotiated, accepted, or payable in another, the rights, duties, and liabilities of the parties thereto are determined as follows:
(1) The validity of a bill as regards requisites in form is determined by the law of the place of issue, and the validity as regards requisites in form of the supervening contracts, such as acceptance, or indorsement, or acceptance supra protest, is determined by the law of the place where such contract was made.
Provided that –
(a) Where a bill is issued out of the United Kingdom it is not invalid by reason only that it is not stamped in accordance with the law of the place of issue.

(b) Where a bill, issued out of the United Kingdom, conforms, as regards requisites in form, to the law of the United Kingdom, it may, for the purpose of enforcing payment thereof, be treated as valid as between all persons who negotiate, hold, or become parties to it in the United Kingdom.

(2) Subject to the provisions of this Act, the interpretation of the drawing, indorsement, acceptance, or acceptance supra protest of a bill, is determined by the law of the place where such contract is made.

Provided that where an inland bill is indorsed in a foreign country the indorsement shall as regards the payer be interpreted according to the law of the United Kingdom.

(3) The duties of the holder with respect to presentment for acceptance or payment and the necessity for or sufficiency of a protest or notice of dishonour, or otherwise, are determined by the law of the place where the act is done or the bill is dishonoured.

(4) (Repealed by Administration of Justice Act 1977, Section 4(2)).

(5) Where a bill is drawn in one country and is payable in another, the due date thereof is determined according to the law of the place where it is payable.'

Demand guarantees and performance bonds

13.23 It is intended here to refer to unconditional performance bonds and guarantees of the first demand type.[1] Demand guarantees are commonly issued by a bank in the country of the beneficiary. So once it is appreciated that the underlying contract between the beneficiary and his contractor is of no relevance to the question of governing law of the guarantee,[2] there will commonly be no difficulty in deciding the governing law. Where bank and beneficiary are in different countries, the governing law will usually be that of the country in which the bank is situated: for it is the bank which effects the performance characteristic of the contract.[3] This choice is also consistent with the decision in the *Attock Cement* case.[4] Where the Uniform Rules for Demand Guarantees[5] are incorporated, the Rules make an express choice of law, which is again the law of the place of business of the branch issuing the guarantee.[6]

1 For these terms, see Chapter 12, Part C, para 12.26 et seq.
2 See the *Attock Cement* case [1989] 1 WLR 1147 considered in para 13.13 above.
3 Article 4.2 of the Rome Convention.
4 See note 2 above.
5 See para 12.71 above.
6 Article 27 of the Rules, given effect as the parties' choice by Article 3.1 of the Convention.

13.24 The guarantee will often be backed by an indemnity (or counter-guarantee) in favour of the issuing bank given by a second bank which will usually be in another country. In the *Turkiye Is Bankasi* case[1] it was held that the indemnities or counter-guarantees were governed by the law of the country of the bank to be indemnified on the alternative grounds first that an intention was to be inferred from the documents that Turkish law should apply, and second that the indemnity was closely related to the bond itself which was governed by that law. The second ground tentatively suggests that, in the absence of other factors, at common law an English court would choose as the law to govern the indemnity that of the country of the bank issuing the bond and to be indemnified, on the ground that that is the country with which the indemnity is most closely connected. A similar approach is possible via Article 4.5 of the Convention.

But Article 4.2 suggests a different law, namely that of the country where the bank providing the indemnity is situated, on the ground that it is that bank which will effect the characteristic performance. Important factors are likely to be whether the form of the counter-guarantee or indemnity is that of the grantor or grantee, and language. Where the Uniform Rules for Demand Guarantees[2] are incorporated, the Rules make an express choice, namely the law of the place where the branch issuing the counter-guarantee is situated.[3] It is stated in the Guide to the Rules[4] that it is a logical consequence of the fact that the guarantee and counter-guarantee are independent contracts that they should be governed by different laws: it is also pointed out that it is open to the parties, if they can agree, to choose one law.[5]

1 [1993] 1 Lloyd's Rep 132.
2 See para 12.71 above.
3 Article 27 of the Rules.
4 By Professor Goode, ICC Publication 510, page 35.
5 Note also the similar jurisdictional split provided for by Article 28.

B.   Illegality and Unenforceability (Exchange Control)

13.25 *Introduction*   The performance of a contract may be contrary to law and unenforceable, or simply unenforceable, on a variety of grounds. As the function of the contracts which arise in connection with documentary credits is the payment of money, the ground on which illegality or unenforceability is likely to arise is by reason of a prohibition on the movement of money, and that will most often take the form of exchange control legislation. Prohibition or restriction can also occur where the effect of an order of the courts of a country is to prohibit a party from performing its obligations under a credit. The question which is to be considered in connection with proceedings before an English court is whether, and sometimes to what extent, foreign exchange control legislation or a foreign court's orders will be treated as relevant to the obligations sought to be enforced before the English court. Problems may arise in two different contexts. First, where it is alleged that a party is excused from procuring the opening of a letter of credit; second, where it is alleged that payment under a credit previously set up is prevented.

13.26 *Three principles*   Three principles may be stated at the outset, the first two of which are of general application and the third of which is specifically related to exchange control:
(1) Where the prohibition or restriction which is relied upon is part of the governing law of the contract it will be given effect to by an English court.[1]
(2) Where the prohibition is part of the law of the place where the contract is to be performed it will be given effect to by an English court.[2]
(3) Exchange contracts involving the currency of any member of the International Monetary Fund and contrary to that member's exchange control regulations are unenforceable in England by reason of the Bretton Woods Agreement and related legislation.
These are considered in turn.[3]

1 See Dicey & Morris *The Conflict of Laws* (12th edn) Rules 178 and 210(a); *De Beéche v South American Stores Ltd* [1935] AC 148; *St Pierre v South American Stores Ltd* [1937] 3 All ER 349, and the commentary on these cases in Mann *The Legal Aspects of Money* (4th edn) p 413, text and note 58.

2 See *Dicey & Morris*, op cit, Exception 1 to Rule 178 and Rule 210(b); *Ralli Bros v Cia Naviera Sota y Aznor* [1920] 2 KB 287; cf *Kleinwort, Sons & Co v Ungarische Baumwolle Industrie Akt* [1939] 2 KB 678, 694.
3 In *Congimex Companhia Geral de Comercio v Tradax Export SA* [1981] 2 Lloyd's Rep 687 at 691.1 Staughton J at first instance stated concisely '. . . supervening illegality is only a defence if (1) it arises by the proper law of the contract or (2) it arises by the law of the place of performance. In the case of exchange contracts, there is a third category by virtue of the Bretton Woods Order in Council.' CA – [1983] 1 Lloyd's Rep 250.

Illegality by governing law

13.27 *(1) Opening of credit* Suppose that a buyer in Ruritania contracts with a seller to buy goods and to open a letter of credit, and that this contract of sale is governed by Ruritanian law. Suppose that Ruritania has in force at the time the contract is made exchange control regulations which require the buyer to obtain permission of the Ruritanian central bank to open the credit, and that the central bank refuses permission. The opening of it without permission would then be illegal under Ruritanian law. It has to be remembered that the contract of sale is governed by Ruritanian law, and so the effect on the performance of the contract of the failure to obtain permission has to be considered under that law. If Ruritanian law were the same as English law the approach would be as follows. First, does the contract refer to exchange control? For example, it might make it a condition of the contract that exchange control permission could be obtained. In that event the failure to obtain permission will excuse the parties from further performance. That is subject to the implied proviso that permission has been applied for by the buyer and due diligence used to obtain it.[1] Alternatively there might be a term of the contract making it the duty, the absolute duty, of the buyer to obtain permission. Then any failure would render him liable in damages for non-performance of the contract. If the contract is silent, a term is to be implied that the buyer shall apply for permission and at least use reasonable diligence to obtain it. Or it may be implied that the duty on the buyer is absolute. It may be possible to infer from the express terms of the contract whether it is a duty to use due diligence or an absolute duty.[2] Where the contract does not assist, under English law the position is uncertain.[3] Where the exchange control law is imposed after the contract is made the position may be different as the parties may well not have had the need to obtain any permission in mind at the time of making the contract, and it is suggested that it will be easier for the buyer to establish that an inability on his part to obtain the required permission excuses his failure to open the credit. Where the governing law of the contract between buyer and seller is not the law under which the exchange control regulations are imposed, obviously it cannot be relied upon under this head. Thus in *Toprak Mahsulleri Ofisi v Finagrain Cie Commerciale*[4] the buyers and the regulations which they alleged prevented them from opening the credit were Turkish. But the contract was governed by English law and so the buyers had to base their argument on the law of the place of performance. They were unsuccessful.

1 It is suggested that such implication is necessary to give efficacy to the contract: compare *Re Anglo-Russian Merchant Traders and John Batt & Co (London) Ltd* [1917] 2 KB 679 at 685, 689.
2 Cf *Congimex Companhia Geral de Comercio v Tradax Export SA* [1981] 2 Lloyd's Rep 687 at 692,3; affd [1983] 1 Lloyd's Rep 250 at 253, CA.

3 See the cases cited (above) which relate to import or export licences; compare the view expressed in Sassoon *CIF and FOB Contracts* (3rd edn) para 624: 'In fact the formalities which the buyer may have to go through to obtain funds (including any foreign exchange permits) are normally regarded as entirely at the buyer's risk and responsibility, and absent an express stipulation which may protect him against default in the event of his failure to obtain the necessary permits, he will normally be liable for breach if payment is unaffected by his inability to obtain the necessary exchange authorisation.'
4 [1979] 2 Lloyd's Rep 98.

13.28 *(2) Operation of credit*   Here it is the governing law of the credit which is relevant and not the governing law of the underlying contract between the applicant and the beneficiary. It is to be remembered that the governing law is, as is suggested above,[1] the law of the place where the bank to which documents are to be presented is situated. It is likely also to be this bank which is to make payment. So there is a probability that the law of the place of performance and the governing law of the credit will coincide. If the bank is prevented from paying by the law which governs its undertaking to the beneficiary, then an English court will not enforce payment. If the credit has been opened, the bank is unlikely to be prevented by reason of exchange control regulations: that difficulty will have been surmounted by the obtaining of permission prior to it being opened. But it can happen that a court of the country providing the governing law of the contract makes an order restraining payment. Thus, if the governing law of the credit in the *Power Curber* case[2] had been Kuwaiti, the English court would have given effect to the Kuwaiti court's order on the ground that the bank had a good defence under Kuwaiti law.[3] The credit may provide for presentation of documents in one country but for payment to be provided in another, as was the case in *European Asian Bank v Punjab and Sind Bank*.[4] If payment under the credit in that other country is illegal by the governing law of the credit, namely the law of the country of presentation, the bank will be excused payment. But the regulations in question, or the court order in question, are to be examined to see if they do in fact have extra-territorial effect.[5] It may well be that a court would be reluctant to construe them in that way.[6] Where, as will usually be the case, a credit is provided as conditional payment rather than in absolute payment[7] the failure of the credit to provide payment will enable the seller to sue the buyer. But he is likely to have to do so in the buyer's own country and so is likely to meet the same problems as have defeated the credit.

1 Para 13.6.
2 [1981] 1 WLR 1233 (see above).
3 See *Kahler v Midland Bank Ltd* [1950] AC 24.
4 [1981] 2 Lloyd's Rep 651; affd [1982] 2 Lloyd's Rep 356.
5 See *Rossano v Manufacturers Life Insurance Co* [1963] 2 QB 352 at 374.
6 See Mann *The Legal Aspect of Money* (4th edn) p 416.
7 See Chapter 3, para 3.44.

Illegality by law of place of performance

13.29 *(1) Opening of credit*   A buyer who is in practical difficulties in opening a credit because of exchange control restrictions but cannot rely on the governing law of his contract with the seller may seek to rely on the restrictions as to the law of the place of performance. His difficulties are illustrated by the situation of the buyers in *Toprak Mahsulleri Ofisi v Finagrain Cie Commerciale*.[1] The buyers, a Turkish state organisation, agreed to buy a large tonnage of wheat c. and f. named Turkish ports, payment by 'irrevocable, divisible, transferable letter of credit to be opened in Sellers' favour with and confirmed by a first class US or West European Bank covering 100% payments against presentation of shipping documents'. The contract provided that it was governed by English law and that disputes should be determined by arbitration in London. The buyers were unable to obtain foreign currency from the Turkish Ministry of Finance, no credit was opened and the sellers cancelled the contract and claimed damages by arbitration. Lord Denning MR with whom the other members of the Court of Appeal agreed stated:[2]

> 'I will read the particular paragraph in the case stated[3] on which the Turkish state enterprise rely. It is para 23:
>
> "At all times in 1974 and 1975 it would have been illegal for the Buyers to have procured the opening of a Letter of Credit to pay a foreign seller of wheat in foreign currency without first obtaining exchange control permission from the Ministry of Finance. Furthermore, because of the tight control exercised over foreign exchange, and the number of checks and safeguards built into the routine established for the opening of Letters of Credit by Turkish companies it would in practice have been impossible for the Buyers to have opened such a Letter of Credit without such permission."
>
> In those circumstances, the Turkish state enterprise say that in view of that illegality by Turkish law they have a defence to this claim. They rely particularly on the well-known case *Ralli Bros v Cia Naviera Sota y Aznar*.[4] In that case under the law of Spain it was illegal to pay more than a certain price. And by the very terms of the contract the payment had to be made in Spain. It was an English contract, but it was to be performed by its very terms in Spain: and it was illegal by the law of the place of performance. It was held that this illegality was an answer.
>
> In this particular case the place of performance was not Turkey. Illegality by the law of Turkey is no answer whatever to this claim. The letter of credit had to be a confirmed letter of credit, confirmed by a first-class West European or US bank. The sellers were not concerned with the machinery by which the Turkish state enterprise provided that letter of credit at all. The place of performance was not Turkey.'

Had it been a term of the contract that the credit should be issued in Turkey as well as providing that it be confirmed by a US or West European bank as the contract in fact provided, the defence would have succeeded.

1 [1979] 2 Lloyd's Rep 98.
2 Ibid at 113, 4.
3 By the arbitrators for the decision of the court.
4 [1920] 2 KB 287, 2 Ll L Rep 550.

13.30 *(2) Operation of credit*   As considered in paragraph 13.6 the law of the place of payment under the credit will often be the same as the governing law of the credit. It is suggested that this will not be so where payment is not to be made by the bank to which documents are to be presented (the situation of which, it is suggested, determines the governing law).[1] If documents are to be presented in a country where exchange control will prevent payment pursuant to the credit, this will provide the bank with a defence.[2] If, for example, documents are to be presented in Turkey where exchange control will prevent the bank from paying, but payment is to be made by a bank in New York following the presentation of documents in Turkey which are found to conform with the credit, the position in Turkey is irrelevant to payments so far as the law of the place of performance (payment) is concerned. It may, however, provide a defence under the governing law: this will depend upon whether the exchange control regulations or the court order applying in the country where the documents are to be presented have effect to make it illegal under the proper law for payment to be made in New York, which must be examined closely.[3] Where, as will usually be the case, a credit is provided as conditional payment rather than in absolute payment[4] the failure of the credit to provide payment will enable the seller to sue the buyer. But he is likely to have to do so in the buyer's own country and so is likely to meet the same problems as have defeated the credit.

1 See para 13.6 above.
2 Compare the *Power Curber* case, had payment been due in Kuwait.
3 See *Rossano v Manufacturers Life Insurance Co* [1963] 2 QB 352 and para 13.28 above.
4 See Chapter 3, para 3.44 et seq.

13.31 *The Bretton Woods Agreement* The International Monetary Fund Agreement, commonly known as the Bretton Woods Agreement, is made part of English law by the Bretton Woods Agreements Order in Council 1946,[1] and of course England is a member of the Fund.[2] Article VIII(2)(b) of the Agreement provides:

> 'Exchange contracts which involve the currency of any member and which are contrary to the exchange control regulations of any member maintained or imposed consistently with this agreement shall be unenforceable in the territories of any member.'

Pursuant to powers given by Article XVIII of the Agreement, in 1949 the Executive Directors published an interpretation of the provision, which is as follows:

> '1 Parties entering into exchange contracts involving the currency of any member of the Fund and contrary to exchange control regulations of that member which are maintained or imposed consistently with the Fund Agreement will not receive the assistance of the judicial or administrative authorities of other members in obtaining the performances of such contracts. That is to say, the obligations of such contracts will not be implemented by the judicial or administrative authorities of member countries, for example, by decreeing performance of the contracts or by awarding damages for their non-performance.
> 2 By accepting the Fund Agreement members have undertaken to make the principle mentioned above effectively part of their national law. This applies to all members, whether or not they have availed themselves of the transitional arrangements of Article XIV, section 2.
> An obvious result of the foregoing undertaking is that if a party to an exchange contract of the kind referred to in Article VIII, section 2(b) seeks to enforce such a contract, the tribunal of the member country before which the proceedings are brought will not, on the ground that they are contrary to the public policy (ordre public) of the forum, refuse recognition of the exchange control regulations of the other member which are maintained or imposed consistently with the Fund Agreement. It also follows that such contracts will be treated as unenforceable notwithstanding that under the private international law of the forum, the law under which the foreign exchange control regulations are maintained or imposed is not the law which governs the exchange contract or its performance.

The Fund will be pleased to lend its assistance in connection with any problem which may arise in relation to the foregoing interpretation or any other aspect of Article VIII, section 2(b). In addition, the Fund is prepared to advise whether particular exchange control regulations are maintained or imposed consistently with the Fund Agreement.'

This is not binding on an English court but will be treated as what is called 'persuasive authority'. The major problem to which Article VIII(2)(b) gives rise – and the above does nothing to resolve it – is the interpretation of the expression 'exchange contract'.

1 SR & O 1946 No 36 made under the Bretton Woods Agreements Act 1945.
2 As to something of the manner in which the agreement came about, see *Wilson Smithett and Cope Ltd v Terruzzi* [1976] QB 683 at 711D et seq per Lord Denning MR.

13.32 ***Exchange contracts*** Although at one point there was uncertainty in English law as to the meaning of exchange contract[1] this has now been clarified. In *Wilson, Smithett and Cope Ltd v Terruzzi*[2] the plaintiffs were brokers on the London Metal Exchange and they dealt with the defendant, a dealer and the speculator, who lived in Italy. He made various contracts with them for the purchase and sale of metals in respect of which he was in breach of Italian exchange control as he had not obtained ministerial authorisation. He ended up owing the brokers substantial sums on his account. He argued that the contracts were exchange contracts within the meaning of the Article and so were unenforceable in the English courts. This defence was rejected. Lord Denning MR stated:[3]

'The mischief being thus exposed, it seems to me that the participants at Bretton Woods inserted article VIII section 2(b) so as to stop it. They determined to make exchange contracts of that kind – for the exchange of currencies – unenforceable in the territories of any member. I do not know of any similar mischief in regard to other contracts, that is contracts for the sale or purchase of merchandise or commodities. Businessmen have to encounter fluctuations in the price of goods, but this is altogether different from the fluctuations in exchange rates. So far from there being any mischief, it seems to me that it is in the interest of international trade that there should be no restrictions on contracts for the sale and purchase of merchandise and commodities: and that they should be enforceable in the territories of the members.
   The Bretton Woods Agreement itself makes provision to that end. Thus . . .
   In conformity with those provisions, I would hold that the Bretton Woods Agreement should not do anything to hinder legitimate contracts for the sale or purchase of merchandise or commodities. The words "exchange contracts" in article VIII, section 2(b), refer only to contracts to exchange the currency of one country for the currency of another.'

He concluded that the contracts in question were legitimate contracts for the sale and purchase of metals and were not contracts for the exchange of currencies. This narrow definition of 'exchange contracts' may be contrasted with the wider definition which had been argued for, and also proposed elsewhere, as any contract which in any way affected a country's exchange resources. The definition given by the Court of Appeal was approved by the House of Lords in *United City Merchants (Investments) Ltd v Royal Bank of Canada*[4] to which reference may now be made for a number of points in relation to the effect of exchange control and the Bretton Woods Agreement on documentary credits.

1 See *Kahler v Midland Bank* [1948] 1 All ER 811 at 819, CA and *Sharif v Azad* [1967] 1 QB
   605.
2 [1986] QB 683.
3 Ibid at 713.
4 [1983] 1 AC 168.

13.33 *United City Merchants (Investments) Ltd v Royal Bank of
Canada*[1] The facts which are relevant for present purposes are as
follows.[2] The Peruvian buyers wished to utilise the opportunity presented
by their purchase of a glass-fibre forming plant from England to transfer
money from Peru to the United States, or, put in terms of currencies, to
exchange Peruvian currency for US dollars to be available to them in
Florida. They therefore arranged for the sellers to invoice them for
double the price which they had quoted and to remit one-half of each of
the amounts which they would draw under the credit to the dollar account
in Miami of an American corporation controlled by the buyers. The
transfer of Peruvian currency into US dollars was contrary to the
exchange control regulations of Peru, a member of the IMF. The following points emerge from the speech of Lord Diplock, with which the
remainder of the House agreed.

1 Supra.
2 The facts relevant to the question of the fraudulent bills of lading are set out in Chapter 9,
   para 9.7.

13.34 (1) The narrow interpretation of the expression 'exchange contracts' in
Article VIII(2)(b) of the Bretton Woods Agreement is correct. 'It is confined to contracts to exchange the currency of one country for the currency
of another; it does not include contracts entered into in connection with sales
of goods which require the conversion by the buyer of one currency into
another in order to enable him to pay the purchase price.'[1]

1 See [1983] 1 AC at 188G.

13.35 (2) In considering the application of the Article the court should look at
the substance of the contract and not the form. 'It should not enforce a
contract that is a "mere monetary transaction in disguise".'[1]

1 See [1983] 1 AC at 188H.

13.36 (3) The effect of breach of the Article is to render the contract
unenforceable rather than illegal. This has two consequences. On becoming aware of a point concerning the Article the court must take the point
itself even if the party to whose advantage it might work has not done so,
and the court must refuse to lend its aid to enforce the contract. Second, it
does not make the contract 'illegal' under English law, nor does it make it
unlawful under the law of England for a party to do acts in performance of
the contract. So a party may do so if it wishes, but it cannot be obliged to
do so by legal action.[1]

1 See [1983] 1 AC at 189 A-C citing *Batra v Ebrahim* noted at [1982] 2 Lloyd's Rep 11n and
   referred to at [1982] QB 208 at 241F–242B. As to proof, see para 13.40 below.

13.37 (4)

'The question whether and to what extent a contract is unenforceable under
the Bretton Wood Agreement Order in Council 1946 because it is monetary

transaction in disguise is *not* a question of construction of the contract, but a question of the substance of the transaction to which enforcement of the contract will give effect.' Thus it is not a matter which is to be determined on the basis whether the contract can as a matter of construction be severed into parts which are unenforceable by reason of the Order, and parts which are not. The task of the court is 'to penetrate any disguise presented by the actual words the parties have used, to identify any monetary transaction (in the narrow sense of that expression as used in the *Terruzzi* case[1] which those words were intended to conceal and to refuse to enforce the contract to the extent that to do so would give effect to the monetary transaction.'[2]

1 [1976] QB 683 and para 13.32 above.
2 See [1983] 1 AC at 189G–190B.

13.38 (5) On the facts of the case:

(a)   The transaction was, as a matter of construction, simply a contract to pay currency against documents including documents of title to goods. That concealed the monetary transaction to exchange Peruvian currency for dollars.

(b)   Payment of that part of the money payable under the credit which the sellers would receive on trust for the buyers to remit to Florida, was unenforceable as an essential part of the monetary transaction or exchange contract.

(c)   Payment of that part payable under the credit which the sellers would retain as the genuine purchase price of the goods payable by the buyers was enforceable.

(d)   As to the first instalment of 20%, this had been paid in full and no enforcement was needed. The bank could have resisted paying one-half of it had it known of the monetary transaction at the time it came to pay, but, even if it knew, there was nothing in English law to prevent it paying in full.[1]

1 See [1983] 1 AC at 190 B to F.

13.39 It follows from the *UCM* case that, where the English court can identify a monetary transaction which is an exchange contract within Article VIII(2)(b), it will refuse to enforce the transaction even though the refusal may involve the court in declining to give effect in whole or in part to an autonomous contract constituted by a letter of credit.[1]

1 See *Mansouri v Singh* [1986] 1 WLR 1393 at 1401 per Neill LJ.

13.40 *Proof* It was stated in *Mansouri v Singh*[1] that the burden of proving the exchange control regulations (and presumably also the breach of them if payment were made) is on a defendant, that is on the party relying on them as a reason for not paying. How does this relate to the duty of the court to take a point arising under the Bretton Woods Agreements Order for itself? In the *UCM* case[2] Lord Diplock referred to the court becoming aware of the unenforceability.[3] In *Mansouri*[4] the case was remitted to the trial judge for further hearing on the ground that he had decided in favour of the defendant on inadequate evidence. The outcome is that an English court will only treat a payment obligation as unenforceable when it is proved that to enforce it would be to enforce an exchange contract contrary to the exchange control regulations of an IMF member. Proof will be proof at least on the balance of probabilities. It need not be proof by a party in the sense that a party has set out to prove it: it may simply become clear during the course of the case, perhaps despite the parties' efforts to conceal it. It does not appear that once the possibility is raised by the evidence it is for the court to conduct its own enquiry.

1 [1986] 1 WLR 1393 at 1404.
2 Supra.
3 See [1983] AC at 189B.
4 Supra.

C. Sovereign Immunity

13.41 *At common law*   At common law an independent sovereign state could not be sued in an English court without its consent. It was argued on behalf of the Central Bank of Nigeria in *Trendtex Trading Corpn v Central Bank of Nigeria*[1] that it could not be ordered to retain within the jurisdiction $13,968,190 pending the trial of a claim against it on a letter of credit opened in London through the Midland Bank Ltd (which did not confirm the credit) as its agents, because it was a department of the State of Nigeria and therefore immune from suit. It was held by the Court of Appeal that the bank was not an emanation, arm, alter ego or department of the State of Nigeria and so was not entitled to immunity from suit. Two of the three member court also held that, even if it had been a part of the Government of Nigeria, it was not immune from suit in respect of ordinary commercial transactions as distinct from acts of a governmental nature. The injunction was therefore continued. This emphasises the two points which were relevant at common law; first, the nature of the entity claiming immunity – is it sufficiently a part of the foreign sovereign state to be accorded the immunity accorded to the state; second, if the entity is entitled to immunity, as to the nature of the transaction – is it a commercial transaction not attracting immunity, or a governmental transaction attracting immunity?

1 [1977] QB 529, CA.

13.42 *The State Immunity Act 1978*   The position in respect of claims to immunity on the ground of foreign sovereignty is now governed by the State Immunity Act of 1978. Because of section 3 of the Act it seems impossible that a bank could now achieve immunity in respect of a documentary credit transaction even if it established that it fell within section 14(1) or (2) of the Act and so was of a nature to attract immunity in respect of appropriate subject matter. Section 3 provides:

'3 (1)   A State is not immune as respects proceedings relating to –
(a) a commercial transaction entered into by the State; or
(b) an obligation of the State which by virtue of a contract (whether a commercial transaction or not) falls to be performed wholly or partly in the United Kingdom.
(2)   This section does not apply if the parties to the dispute are States or have otherwise agreed in writing; and subsection (1)(b) above does not apply if the contract (not being a commercial transaction) was made in the territory of the State concerned and the obligation in question is governed by its administrative law.
(3)   In this section "commercial transaction" means –
(a) any contract for the supply of goods or services;

(b) any loan or other transaction for the provision of finance and any guarantee or indemnity in respect of any such transaction or of any other financial obligation; and

(c) any other transaction or activity (whether of a commercial, industrial, financial, professional or other similar character) into which a State enters or in which it engages otherwise than in the exercise of sovereign authority;

but neither paragraph of subsection (1) above applies to a contract of employment between a State and an individual.'

As to the property of a state's central bank or other monetary authority which might otherwise be taken in execution, reference should be made to section 14(4) of the Act.

Appendices

The Uniform Customs and Practice for Documentary Credits (1993 Revision) ICC Publication No 500

An index will be found in
Appendix 2 of the primary
references to each Article in
the text.

A. General Provisions and Definitions

Article 1

Application of UCP

The Uniform Customs and Practice for Documentary Credits, 1993 Revision, ICC Publication No 500, shall apply to all Documentary Credits (including to the extent to which they may be applicable, Standby Letter(s) of Credit) where they are incorporated into the text of the Credit. They are binding on all parties thereto, unless otherwise expressly stipulated in the Credit.

Article 2

Meaning of Credit

For the purposes of these Articles, the expressions 'Documentary Credit(s)' and 'Standby Letter(s) of Credit' (hereinafter referred to as 'Credit(s)'), mean any arrangement, however named or described, whereby a bank (the 'Issuing Bank') acting at the request and on the instructions of a customer (the 'Applicant') or on its own behalf,
i. is to make a payment to or to the order of a third party (the 'Beneficiary'), or is to accept and pay bills of exchange (Draft(s)) drawn by the Beneficiary,
or
ii. authorises another bank to effect such payment, or to accept and pay such bills of exchange (Draft(s)),
or
iii. authorises another bank to negotiate,
against stipulated document(s), provided that the terms and conditions of the Credit are complied with.
For the purposes of these Articles, branches of a bank in different countries are considered another bank.

Article 3

Credits v contracts

a. Credits, by their nature, are separate transactions from the sales or other contract(s) on which they may be based and banks are in no way concerned with or bound by such contract(s), even if any reference whatsoever to such contract(s) is included in the Credit. Consequently, the undertaking of a bank to pay, accept and pay Draft(s) or negotiate and/or to fulfil any other obligation under the Credit, is not subject to claims or defences by the Applicant resulting from his relationships with the Issuing Bank or the Beneficiary.

b. A Beneficiary can in no case avail himself of the contractual relationships existing between the banks or between the Applicant and the Issuing Bank.

Article 4

Documents v goods/services/performances

In Credit operations all parties concerned deal with documents, and not with goods, services and/or other performances to which the documents may relate.

Article 5

Instructions to issue/amend Credits

a. Instructions for the issuance of a Credit, the Credit itself, instructions for an amendment thereto, and the amendment itself, must be complete and precise.
In order to guard against confusion and misunderstanding, banks should discourage any attempt:
i. to include excessive detail in the Credit or in any amendment thereto;
ii. to give instructions to issue, advise or confirm a Credit by reference to a Credit previously issued (similar Credit) where such previous Credit has been subject to accepted amendment(s), and/or unaccepted amendment(s).

b. All instructions for the issuance of a Credit and the Credit itself and, where applicable, all instructions for an amendment thereto and the amendment itself, must state precisely the document(s) against which payment, acceptance or negotiation is to be made.

B. Form and Notification of Credits

Article 6

Revocable v irrevocable Credits

a. A Credit may be either
i. revocable,
or
ii. irrevocable.

b. The Credit, therefore, should clearly indicate whether it is revocable or irrevocable.

c. In the absence of such indication the Credit shall be deemed to be irrevocable.

Article 7

Advising Bank's Liability

a. A Credit may be advised to a Beneficiary through another bank (the 'Advising Bank') without engagement on the part of the Advising Bank, but that bank, if it elects to advise the Credit, shall take reasonable care to check the apparent authenticity of the Credit which it advises. If the bank elects not to advise the Credit, it must so inform the Issuing Bank without delay.

b. If the Advising Bank cannot establish such apparent authenticity it must inform, without delay, the bank from which the instructions appear to have been received that it has been unable to establish the authenticity of the Credit and if it elects nonetheless to advise the Credit it must inform the Beneficiary that it has not been able to establish the authenticity of the Credit.

Article 8

Revocation of a Credit

a. A revocable Credit may be amended or cancelled by the Issuing Bank at any moment and without prior notice to the Beneficiary.

b. However, the Issuing Bank must:
i. reimburse another bank with which a revocable Credit has been made available for sight payment, acceptance or negotiation – for any payment, acceptance or negotiation made by such bank – prior to receipt by it of notice of amendment or cancellation, against documents which appear on their face to be in compliance with the terms and conditions of the Credit;
ii. reimburse another bank with which a revocable Credit has been made available for deferred payment, if such a bank has, prior to receipt by it of notice of amendment or cancellation, taken up documents which appear on their face to be in compliance with the terms and conditions of the Credit.

Article 9

Liability of Issuing and Confirming Banks

a. An irrevocable Credit constitutes a definite undertaking of the Issuing Bank, provided that the stipulated documents are presented to the Nominated Bank or to the Issuing Bank and that the terms and conditions of the Credit are complied with:
i. if the Credit provides for sight payment – to pay at sight;

ii. if the Credit provides for deferred payment – to pay on the maturity date(s) determinable in accordance with the stipulations of the Credit;

iii. if the Credit provides for acceptance:

a. by the Issuing Bank – to accept Draft(s) drawn by the Beneficiary on the Issuing Bank and pay them at maturity, or

b. by another drawee bank – to accept and pay at maturity Draft(s) drawn by the Beneficiary on the Issuing Bank in the event the drawee bank stipulated in the Credit does not accept Draft(s) drawn on it, or to pay Draft(s) accepted but not paid by such drawee bank at maturity;

iv. if the Credit provides for negotiation – to pay without recourse to drawers and/or bona fide holders, Draft(s) drawn by the Beneficiary and/or document(s) presented under the Credit. A Credit should not be issued available by Draft(s) on the Applicant. If the Credit nevertheless calls for Draft(s) on the Applicant, banks will consider such Draft(s) as an additional document(s).

b. A confirmation of an irrevocable Credit by another bank (the 'Confirming Bank') upon the authorisation or request of the Issuing Bank, constitutes a definite undertaking of the Confirming Bank, in addition to that of the Issuing Bank, provided that the stipulated documents are presented to the Confirming Bank or to any other Nominated Bank and that the terms and conditions of the Credit are complied with:

i. if the Credit provides for sight payment – to pay at sight;

ii. if the Credit provides for deferred payment – to pay on the maturity date(s) determinable in accordance with the stipulations of the Credit;

iii. if the Credit provides for acceptance:

a. by the Confirming Bank – to accept Draft(s) drawn by the Beneficiary on the Confirming Bank and pay them at maturity, or

b. by another drawee bank – to accept and pay at maturity Draft(s) drawn by the Beneficiary on the Confirming Bank, in the event the drawee bank stipulated in the Credit does not accept Draft(s) drawn on it, or to pay Draft(s) accepted but not paid by such drawee bank at maturity;

iv. if the Credit provides for negotiation – to negotiate without recourse to drawers and/or bona fide holders, Draft(s) drawn by the Beneficiary and/or document(s) presented under the Credit. A Credit should not be issued available by Draft(s) on the Applicant. If the Credit nevertheless calls for Draft(s) on the Applicant, banks will consider such Draft(s) as an additional document(s).

c. **i.** If another bank is authorised or requested by the Issuing Bank to add its confirmation to a Credit but is not prepared to do so, it must so inform the Issuing Bank without delay.

ii. Unless the Issuing Bank specifies otherwise in its authorisation or request to add confirmation, the Advising Bank may advise the Credit to the Beneficiary without adding its confirmation.

d. **i.** Except as otherwise provided by Article 48, an irrevocable Credit can neither be amended nor cancelled without the agreement of the Issuing Bank, the Confirming Bank, if any, and the Beneficiary.

ii. The Issuing Bank shall be irrevocably bound by an amendment(s) issued by it from the time of the issuance of such amendment(s). A Confirming Bank may extend its confirmation to an amendment and shall be irrevocably bound as of the time of its advice of the amendment. A Confirming Bank may, however, choose to advise an amendment to the Beneficiary without extending its confirmation and if so, must inform the Issuing Bank and the Beneficiary without delay.

iii. The terms of the original Credit (or a Credit incorporating previously accepted amendment(s)) will remain in force for the Beneficiary until the Beneficiary communicates his acceptance of the amendment to the bank that advised such amendment. The Beneficiary should give notification of acceptance or rejection of amendment(s). If the Beneficiary fails to give such notification, the tender of documents to the Nominated Bank or Issuing Bank, that conform to the Credit and to not yet accepted amendment(s), will be deemed to be notification of acceptance by the Beneficiary of such amendment(s) and as of that moment the Credit will be amended.

iv. Partial acceptance of amendments contained in one and the same advice of amendment is not allowed and consequently will not be given any effect.

Article 10

Types of Credit

a. All Credits must clearly indicate whether they are available by sight payment, by deferred payment, by acceptance or by negotiation.

b. **i.** Unless the Credit stipulates that it is available only with the Issuing Bank, all Credits must nominate the bank (the 'Nominated Bank') which is authorised to pay, to incur a deferred payment undertaking, to accept Draft(s) or to negotiate. In a freely negotiable Credit, any bank is a Nominated Bank.

Presentation of documents must be made to the Issuing Bank or the Confirming Bank, if any, or any other Nominated Bank.

ii. Negotiation means the giving of value for Draft(s) and/or document(s) by the bank authorised to negotiate. Mere examination of the documents without giving of value does not constitute a negotiation.

c. Unless the Nominated Bank is the Confirming Bank, nomination by the Issuing Bank does not constitute any undertaking by the Nominated Bank to pay, to incur a deferred payment undertaking, to accept Draft(s), or to negotiate. Except where expressly agreed to by the Nominated Bank and so communicated to the Beneficiary, the Nominated Bank's receipt of and/or examination and/or forwarding of the documents does not make that bank liable to pay, to incur a deferred payment undertaking, to accept Draft(s), or to negotiate.

d. By nominating another bank, or by allowing for negotiation by any bank, or by authorising or requesting another bank to add its confirmation, the Issuing Bank authorises such bank to pay, accept Draft(s) or negotiate as the case may be, against documents which appear on their face to be in compliance with the terms and conditions of the Credit and undertakes to reimburse such bank in accordance with the provisions of these Articles.

Article 11

Teletransmitted and pre-advised Credits

a. **i.** When an Issuing Bank instructs an Advising Bank by an authenticated teletransmission to advise a Credit or an amendment to a Credit, the teletransmission will be deemed to be the operative Credit instrument or the operative amendment, and no mail confirmation should be sent. Should a mail confirmation nevertheless be sent, it will have no effect and the Advising Bank will have no obligation to check such mail confirmation against the operative Credit instrument or the operative amendment received by teletransmission.

ii. If the teletransmission states 'full details to follow' (or words of similar effect) or states that the mail confirmation is to be the operative Credit instrument or the operative amendment, then the teletransmission will not be deemed to be the operative Credit instrument or the operative amendment. The Issuing Bank must forward the operative Credit instrument or the operative amendment to such Advising Bank without delay.

b. If a bank uses the services of an Advising Bank to have the Credit advised to the Beneficiary, it must also use the services of the same bank for advising an amendment(s).

c. A preliminary advice of the issuance or amendment of an irrevocable Credit (pre-advice), shall only be given by an Issuing Bank if such bank is prepared to issue the operative Credit instrument or the operative amendment thereto. Unless otherwise stated in such preliminary advice by the Issuing Bank, an Issuing Bank having given such pre-advice shall be irrevocably committed to issue or amend the Credit, in terms not inconsistent with the pre-advice, without delay.

Article 12

Incomplete or unclear instructions

If incomplete or unclear instructions are received to advise, confirm or amend a Credit, the bank requested to act on such instructions may give preliminary notification to the Beneficiary for information only and without responsibility. This preliminary notification should state clearly that the notification is provided for information only and without the responsibility of the Advising Bank. In any event, the Advising Bank must inform the Issuing Bank of the action taken and request it to provide the necessary information.

The Issuing Bank must provide the necessary information without delay. The Credit will be advised, confirmed or amended, only when complete and clear instructions have been received and if the Advising Bank is then prepared to act on the instructions.

C. Liabilities and Responsibilities

Article 13

Standard for examination of documents

a. Banks must examine all documents stipulated in the Credit with reasonable care, to ascertain whether or not they appear, on their face, to be in compliance with the terms and conditions of the Credit. Compliance of the stipulated documents on their face with the terms and conditions of the Credit, shall be determined by international standard banking practice as reflected in these Articles. Documents which appear on their face to be inconsistent with one another will be considered as not appearing on their face to be in compliance with the terms and conditions of the Credit.
Documents not stipulated in the Credit will not be examined by banks. If they receive such documents, they shall return them to the presenter or pass them on without responsibility.

b. The Issuing Bank, the Confirming Bank, if any, or a Nominated Bank acting on their behalf, shall each have a reasonable time, not to exceed seven banking days following the day of receipt of the documents, to examine the documents and determine whether to take up or refuse the documents and to inform the party from which it received the documents accordingly.

c. If a Credit contains conditions without stating the document(s) to be presented in compliance therewith, banks will deem such conditions as not stated and will disregard them.

Article 14

Discrepant documents and notice

a. When the Issuing Bank authorises another bank to pay, incur a deferred payment undertaking, accept Draft(s), or negotiate against documents which appear on their face to be in compliance with the terms and conditions of the Credit, the Issuing Bank and the Confirming Bank, if any, are bound:
i. to reimburse the Nominated Bank which has paid, incurred a deferred payment undertaking, accepted Draft(s), or negotiated,
ii. to take up the documents.

b. Upon receipt of the documents the Issuing Bank and/or Confirming Bank, if any, or a Nominated Bank acting on their behalf, must determine on the basis of the documents alone whether or not they appear on their face to be in compliance with the terms and conditions of the Credit. If the documents appear on their face not to be in compliance with the terms and conditions of the Credit, such banks may refuse to take up the documents.

c. If the Issuing Bank determines that the documents appear on their face not to be in compliance with the terms and conditions of the Credit, it may in its sole judgment approach the Applicant for a waiver of the discrepancy(ies). This does not, however, extend the period mentioned in sub-Article 13(b).

d. **i.** If the Issuing Bank and/or Confirming Bank, if any, or a Nominated Bank acting on their behalf, decides to refuse the documents, it must give notice to that effect by telecommunication or, if that is not possible, by other expeditious means, without delay but no later than the close of the seventh banking day following the day of receipt of the documents. Such notice shall be given to the bank from which it received the documents, or to the Beneficiary, if it received the documents directly from him.

ii. Such notice must state all discrepancies in respect of which the bank refuses the documents and must also state whether it is holding the documents at the disposal of, or is returning them to, the presenter.

iii. The Issuing Bank and/or Confirming Bank, if any, shall then be entitled to claim from the remitting bank refund, with interest, of any reimbursement which has been made to that bank.

e. If the Issuing Bank and/or Confirming Bank, if any, fails to act in accordance with the provisions of this Article and/or fails to hold the documents at the disposal of, or return them to the presenter, the Issuing Bank and/or Confirming Bank, if any, shall be precluded from claiming that the documents are not in compliance with the terms and conditions of the Credit.

f. If the remitting bank draws the attention of the Issuing Bank and/or Confirming Bank, if any, to any discrepancy(ies) in the document(s) or advises such banks that it has paid, incurred a deferred payment undertaking, accepted Draft(s) or negotiated under reserve or against an indemnity in respect of such discrepancy(ies), the Issuing Bank and/or Confirming Bank, if any, shall not be thereby relieved from any of their obligations under any provision of this Article. Such reserve or indemnity concerns only the relations between the remitting bank and the party towards whom the reserve was made, or from whom, or on whose behalf, the indemnity was obtained.

Article 15

Disclaimer on effectiveness of documents

Banks assume no liability or responsibility for the form, sufficiency, accuracy, genuineness, falsification or legal effect of any document(s), or for the general and/or particular conditions stipulated in the document(s) or superimposed thereon; nor do they assume any liability or responsibility for the description, quantity, weight, quality, condition, packing, delivery, value or existence of the goods represented by any document(s), or for the good faith or acts and/or omissions, solvency, performance or standing of the consignors, the carriers, the forwarders, the consignees or the insurers of the goods, or any other person whomsoever.

Article 16

Disclaimer on the transmission of messages

Banks assume no liability or responsibility for the consequences arising out of delay and/or loss in transit of any message(s), letter(s) or document(s), or for delay, mutilation or other error(s) arising in the transmission of any telecommunication. Banks assume no liability or responsibility for errors in translation and/or interpretation of technical terms, and reserve the right to transmit Credit terms without translating them.

Article 17

Force majeure

Banks assume no liability or responsibility for the consequences arising out of the interruption of their business by Acts of God, riots, civil commotions, insurrections, wars or any other causes beyond their control, or by any strikes or lockouts. Unless specifically authorised, banks will not, upon resumption of their business, pay, incur a deferred payment undertaking, accept Draft(s) or negotiate under Credits which expired during such interruption of their business.

Article 18

Disclaimer for acts of an instructed party

a.   Banks utilizing the services of another bank or other banks for the purpose of giving effect to the instructions of the Applicant do so for the account and at the risk of such Applicant.

b.   Banks assume no liability or responsibility should the instructions they transmit not be carried out, even if they have themselves taken the initiative in the choice of such other bank(s).

c.   **i.**   A party instructing another party to perform services is liable for any charges, including commissions, fees, costs or expenses incurred by the instructed party in connection with its instructions.
ii.   Where a Credit stipulates that such charges are for the account of a party other than the instructing party, and charges cannot be collected, the instructing party remains ultimately liable for the payment thereof.

d.   The Applicant shall be bound by and liable to indemnify the banks against all obligations and responsibilities imposed by foreign laws and usages.

Article 19

Bank-to-bank reimbursement arrangements

a.   If an Issuing Bank intends that the reimbursement to which a paying, accepting or negotiating bank is entitled, shall be obtained by such bank (the 'Claiming Bank'), claiming on another party (the 'Reimbursing Bank'), it shall provide such Reimbursing Bank in good time with the proper instructions or authorisation to honour such reimbursement claims.

b. Issuing Banks shall not require a Claiming Bank to supply a certificate of compliance with the terms and conditions of the Credit to the Reimbursing Bank.

c. An Issuing Bank shall not be relieved from any of its obligations to provide reimbursement if and when reimbursement is not received by the Claiming Bank from the Reimbursing Bank.

d. The Issuing Bank shall be responsible to the Claiming Bank for any loss of interest if reimbursement is not provided by the Reimbursing Bank on first demand, or as otherwise specified in the Credit, or mutually agreed, as the case may be.

e. The Reimbursing Bank's charges should be for the account of the Issuing Bank. However, in cases where the charges are for the account of another party, it is the responsibility of the Issuing Bank to so indicate in the original Credit and in the reimbursement authorisation. In cases where the Reimbursing Bank's charges are for the account of another party they shall be collected from the Claiming Bank when the Credit is drawn under. In cases where the Credit is not drawn under, the Reimbursing Bank's charges remain the obligation of the Issuing Bank.

D. Documents

Article 20

Ambiguity as to the issuers of documents

a. Terms such as 'first class', 'well known', 'qualified', 'independent', 'official', 'competent', 'local' and the like, shall not be used to describe the issuers of any document(s) to be presented under a Credit. If such terms are incorporated in the Credit, banks will accept the relative document(s) as presented, provided that it appears on its face to be in compliance with the other terms and conditions of the Credit and not to have been issued by the Beneficiary.

b. Unless otherwise stipulated in the Credit, banks will also accept as an original document(s), a document(s) produced or appearing to have been produced:
i. by reprographic, automated or computerized systems;
ii. as carbon copies;
provided that it is marked as original and, where necessary, appears to be signed.
A document may be signed by handwriting, by facsimile signature, by perforated signature, by stamp, by symbol, or by any other mechanical or electronic method of authentication.

c. **i.** Unless otherwise stipulated in the Credit, banks will accept as a copy(ies), a document(s) either labelled copy or not marked as an original – a copy(ies) need not be signed.

ii. Credits that require multiple document(s) such as 'duplicate', 'two fold', 'two copies' and the like, will be satisfied by the present-ation of one original and the remaining number in copies except where the document itself indicates otherwise.

d. Unless otherwise stipulated in the Credit, a condition under a Credit calling for a document to be authenticated, validated, legalised, visaed, certified or indicating a similar requirement, will be satisfied by any signature, mark, stamp or label on such document that on its face appears to satisfy the above condition.

Article 21

Unspecified issuers or contents of documents

When documents other than transport documents, insurance documents and commercial invoices are called for, the Credit should stipulate by whom such documents are to be issued and their wording or data content. If the Credit does not so stipulate, banks will accept such documents as presented, provided that their data content is not inconsistent with any other stipulated document presented.

Article 22

Issuance date of documents v Credit date

Unless otherwise stipulated in the Credit, banks will accept a document bearing a date of issuance prior to that of Credit, subject to such docu-ment being presented within the time limits set out in the Credit and in these Articles.

Article 23

Marine/ocean bill of lading

a. If a Credit calls for a bill of lading covering a port-to-port shipment, banks will, unless otherwise stipulated in the Credit, accept a docu-ment, however named, which:
i. appears on its face to indicate the name of the carrier and to have been signed or otherwise authenticated by:
– the carrier or a named agent for or on behalf of the carrier, or
– the master or a named agent for or on behalf of the master.
Any signature or authentication of the carrier or master must be identified as carrier or master, as the case may be. An agent signing or authenticating for the carrier or master must also indicate the name and the capacity of the party, ie carrier or master, on whose behalf that agent is acting,
and
ii. indicates that the goods have been loaded on board, or shipped on a named vessel.
Loading on board or shipment on a named vessel may be indicated by pre-printed wording on the bill of lading that the goods have been loaded on board a named vessel or shipped on a named vessel, in

which case the date of issuance of the bill of lading will be deemed to be the date of loading on board and the date of shipment.

In all other cases loading on board a named vessel must be evidenced by a notation on the bill of lading which gives the date on which the goods have been loaded on board, in which case the date of the on board notation will be deemed to be the date of shipment.

If the bill of lading contains the indication 'intended vessel', or similar qualification in relation to the vessel, loading on board a named vessel must be evidenced by an on board notation on the bill of lading which, in addition to the date on which the goods have been loaded on board, also includes the name of the vessel on which the goods have been loaded, even if they have been loaded on the vessel named as the 'intended vessel'.

If the bill of lading indicates a place of receipt or taking in charge different from the port of loading, the on board notation must also include the port of loading stipulated in the Credit and the name of the vessel on which the goods have been loaded, even if they have been loaded on the vessel named in the bill of lading. This provision also applies whenever loading on board the vessel is indicated by pre-printed wording on the bill of lading,
and

iii. indicates the port of loading and the port of discharge stipulated in the Credit, notwithstanding that it:

a. indicates a place of taking in charge different from the port of loading, and/or a place of final destination different from the port of discharge,
and/or

b. contains the indication 'intended' or similar qualification in relation to the port of loading and/or port of discharge, as long as the document also states the ports of loading and/or discharge stipulated in the Credit,
and

iv. consists of a sole original bill of lading or, if issued in more than one original, the full set as so issued,
and

v. appears to contain all of the terms and conditions of carriage, or some of such terms and conditions by reference to a source or document other than the bill of lading (short form/blank back bill of lading); banks will not examine the contents of such terms and conditions,
and

vi. contains no indication that it is subject to a charter party and/or no indication that the carrying vessel is propelled by sail only,
and

vii. in all other respects meets the stipulations of the Credit.

b. For the purpose of this Article, transhipment means unloading and reloading from one vessel to another vessel during the course of ocean carriage from the port of loading to the port of discharge stipulated in the Credit.

c. Unless transhipment is prohibited by the terms of the Credit, banks will accept a bill of lading which indicates that the goods will be transhipped, provided that the entire ocean carriage is covered by one and the same bill of lading.

d. Even if the Credit prohibits transhipment, banks will accept a bill of lading which:
i. indicates that transhipment will take place as long as the relevant cargo is shipped in Container(s), Trailer(s) and/or 'LASH' barge(s) as evidenced by the bill of lading, provided that the entire ocean carriage is covered by one and the same bill of lading,
and/or
ii. incorporates clauses stating that the carrier reserves the right to tranship.

Article 24

Non-negotiable sea waybill

a. If a Credit calls for a non-negotiable sea waybill covering a port-to-port shipment, banks will, unless otherwise stipulated in the Credit, accept a document, however named, which:
i. appears on its face to indicate the name of the carrier and to have been signed or otherwise authenticated by:
– the carrier or a named agent for or on behalf of the carrier, or
– the master or a named agent for or on behalf of the master,
Any signature or authentication of the carrier or master must be identified as carrier or master, as the case may be. An agent signing or authenticating for the carrier or master must also indicate the name and the capacity of the party, i.e. carrier or master, on whose behalf that agent is acting,
and
ii. indicates that the goods have been loaded on board, or shipped on a named vessel.
Loading on board or shipment on a named vessel may be indicated by pre-printed wording on the non-negotiable sea waybill that the goods have been loaded on board a named vessel or shipped on a named vessel, in which case the date of issuance of the non-negotiable sea waybill will be deemed to be the date of loading on board and the date of shipment.
In all other cases loading on board a named vessel must be evidenced by a notation on the non-negotiable sea waybill which gives the date on which the goods have been loaded on board, in which case the date of the on board notation will be deemed to be the date of shipment.
If the non-negotiable sea waybill contains the indication 'intended vessel', or similar qualification in relation to the vessel, loading on board a named vessel must be evidenced by an on board notation on the non-negotiable sea waybill which, in addition to the date on which the goods have been loaded on board, includes the name of the vessel on which the goods have been loaded, even if they have been loaded on the vessel named as the 'intended vessel'.
If the non-negotiable sea waybill indicates a place of receipt or taking in charge different from the port of loading, the on board notation

must also include the port of loading stipulated in the Credit and the name of the vessel on which the goods have been loaded, even if they have been loaded on a vessel named in the non-negotiable sea waybill. This provision also applies whenever loading on board the vessel is indicated by pre-printed wording on the non-negotiable sea waybill,
and

iii. indicates the port of loading and the port of discharge stipulated in the Credit, notwithstanding that it:

a. indicates a place of taking in charge different from the port of loading, and/or a place of final destination different from the port of discharge,
and/or

b. contains the indication 'intended' or similar qualification in relation to the port of loading and/or port of discharge, as long as the document also states the ports of loading and/or discharge stipulated in the Credit,
and

iv. consists of a sole original non-negotiable sea waybill, or if issued in more than one original, the full set as so issued,
and

v. appears to contain all of the terms and conditions of carriage, or some of such terms and conditions by reference to a source or document other than the non-negotiable sea waybill (short form/ blank back non-negotiable sea waybill); banks will not examine the contents of such terms and conditions,
and

vi. contains no indication that it is subject to a charter party and/or no indication that the carrying vessel is propelled by sail only,
and

vii. in all other respects meets the stipulations of the Credit.

b. For the purpose of this Article, transhipment means unloading and reloading from one vessel to another vessel during the course of ocean carriage from the port of loading to the port of discharge stipulated in the Credit.

c. Unless transhipment is prohibited by the terms of the Credit, banks will accept a non-negotiable sea waybill which indicates that the goods will be transhipped, provided that the entire ocean carriage is covered by one and the same non-negotiable sea waybill.

d. Even if the Credit prohibits transhipment, banks will accept a non-negotiable sea waybill which:

i. indicates that transhipment will take place as long as the relevant cargo is shipped in Container(s), Trailer(s) and/or 'LASH' barge(s) as evidenced by the non-negotiable sea waybill, provided that the entire ocean carriage is covered by one and the same non-negotiable sea waybill,
and/or

ii. incorporates clauses stating that the carrier reserves the right to tranship.

Article 25

Charter party bill of lading

a.   If a Credit calls for or permits a charter party bill of lading, banks
will, unless otherwise stipulated in the Credit, accept a document,
however named, which:
i.   contains any indication that it is subject to a charter party,
and
ii.   appears on its face to have been signed or otherwise authenticated by:
– the master or a named agent for or on behalf of the master, or
– the owner or a named agent for or on behalf of the owner.
Any signature or authentication of the master or owner must be
identified as master or owner as the case may be. An agent signing or
authenticating for the master or owner must also indicate the name
and the capacity of the party, ie master or owner, on whose behalf
that agent is acting,
and
iii.   does or does not indicate the name of the carrier, and
iv.   indicates that the goods have been loaded on board or shipped
on a named vessel.
Loading on board or shipment on a named vessel may be indicated by
pre-printed wording on the bill of lading that the goods have been
loaded on board a named vessel or shipped on a named vessel, in
which case the date of issuance of the bill of lading will be deemed to
be the date of loading on board and the date of shipment.
In all other cases loading on board a named vessel must be evidenced
by a notation on the bill of lading which gives the date on which the
goods have been loaded on board, in which case the date of the on
board notation will be deemed to be the date of shipment,
and
v.   indicates the port of loading and the port of discharge stipulated
in the Credit,
and
vi.   consists of a sole original bill of lading or, if issued in more than
one original, the full set as so issued,
and
vii.   contains no indication that the carrying vessel is propelled by sail
only,
and
viii. in all other respects meets the stipulations of the Credit.

b.   Even if the Credit requires the presentation of a charter party contract in connection with a charter party bill of lading, banks will not
examine such charter party contract, but will pass it on without
responsibility on their part.

Article 26

Multimodal transport document

a.   If a Credit calls for a transport document covering at least two
different modes of transport (multimodal transport), banks will,

unless otherwise stipulated in the Credit, accept a document, however named, which:

i. appears on its face to indicate the name of the carrier or multimodal transport operator and to have been signed or otherwise authenticated by:
- the carrier or multimodal transport operator or a named agent for or on behalf of the carrier or multimodal transport operator, or
- the master or a named agent for or on behalf of the master.

Any signature or authentication of the carrier, multimodal transport operator or master must be identified as carrier, multimodal transport operator or master, as the case may be. An agent signing or authenticating for the carrier, multimodal transport operator or master must also indicate the name and the capacity of the party, ie carrier, multimodal transport operator or master, on whose behalf that agent is acting,
and

ii. indicates that the goods have been dispatched, taken in charge or loaded on board.

Dispatch, taking in charge or loading on board may be indicated by wording to that effect on the multimodal transport document and the date of issuance will be deemed to be the date of dispatch, taking in charge or loading on board and the date of shipment. However, if the document indicates, by stamp or otherwise, a date of dispatch, taking in charge or loading on board, such date will be deemed to be the date of shipment,
and

iii. *a.* indicates the place of taking in charge stipulated in the Credit which may be different from the port, airport or place of loading, and the place of final destination stipulated in the Credit which may be different from the port, airport or place of discharge,
and/or

 b. contains the indication 'intended' or similar qualification in relation to the vessel and/or port of loading and/or port of discharge,
and

iv. consists of a sole original multimodal transport document or, if issued in more than one original, the full set as so issued,
and

v. appears to contain all of the terms and conditions of carriage, or some of such terms and conditions by reference to a source or document other than the multimodal transport document (short form/blank back multimodal transport document); banks will not examine the contents of such terms and conditions,
and

vi. contains no indication that it is subject to a charter party and/or no indication that the carrying vessel is propelled by sail only,
and

vii. in all other respects meets the stipulations of the Credit.

b. Even if the Credit prohibits transhipment, banks will accept a multimodal transport document which indicates that transhipment will or may take place, provided that the entire carriage is covered by one and the same multimodal transport document.

Article 27

Air transport document

a. If a Credit calls for an air transport document, banks will, unless otherwise stipulated in the Credit, accept a document, however named, which:

i. appears on its face to indicate the name of the carrier and to have been signed or otherwise authenticated by:

– the carrier, or

– a named agent for or on behalf of the carrier.

Any signature or authentication of the carrier must be identified as carrier. An agent signing or authenticating for the carrier must also indicate the name and the capacity of the party, ie carrier, on whose behalf that agent is acting,

and

ii. indicates that the goods have been accepted for carriage,

and

iii. where the Credit calls for an actual date of dispatch, indicates a specific notation of such date, the date of dispatch so indicated on the air transport document will be deemed to be the date of shipment.

For the purpose of this Article, the information appearing in the box on the air transport document (marked 'For Carrier Use Only' or similar expression) relative to the flight number and date will not be considered as a specific notation of such date of dispatch.

In all other cases, the date of issuance of the air transport document will be deemed to be the date of shipment,

and

iv. indicates the airport of departure and the airport of destination stipulated in the Credit,

and

v. appears to be the original for consignor/shipper even if the Credit stipulates a full set of originals, or similar expressions,

and

vi. appears to contain all of the terms and conditions of carriage, or some of such terms and conditions, by reference to a source or document other than the air transport document; banks will not examine the contents of such terms and conditions,

and

vii. in all other respects meets the stipulations of the Credit.

b. For the purpose of this Article, transhipment means unloading and reloading from one aircraft to another aircraft during the course of carriage from the airport of departure to the airport of destination stipulated in the Credit.

c. Even if the Credit prohibits transhipment, banks will accept an air transport document which indicates that transhipment will or may take place, provided that the entire carriage is covered by one and the same air transport document.

Article 28

Road, rail or inland waterway transport document

a. If a Credit calls for a road, rail, or inland waterway transport document, banks will, unless otherwise stipulated in the Credit, accept a document of the type called for, however named, which:
i. appears on its face to indicate the name of the carrier and to have been signed or otherwise authenticated by the carrier or a named agent for or on behalf of the carrier and/or to bear a reception stamp or other indication of receipt by the carrier or a named agent for or on behalf of the carrier.
Any signature, authentication, reception stamp or other indication of receipt of the carrier, must be identified on its face as that of the carrier. An agent signing or authenticating for the carrier, must also indicate the name and the capacity of the party, ie carrier, on whose behalf that agent is acting,
and
ii. indicates that the goods have been received for shipment, dispatch or carriage or wording to this effect. The date of issuance will be deemed to be the date of shipment unless the transport document contains a reception stamp, in which case the date of the reception stamp will be deemed to be the date of shipment,
and
iii. indicates the place of shipment and the place of destination stipulated in the Credit,
and
iv. in all other respects meets the stipulations of the Credit.

b. In the absence of any indication on the transport document as to the numbers issued, banks will accept the transport document(s) presented as constituting a full set. Banks will accept as original(s) the transport document(s) whether marked as original(s) or not.

c. For the purpose of this Article, transhipment means unloading and reloading from one means of conveyance to another means of conveyance, in different modes of transport, during the course of carriage from the place of shipment to the place of destination stipulated in the Credit.

d. Even if the Credit prohibits transhipment, banks will accept a road, rail, or inland waterway transport document which indicates that transhipment will or may take place, provided that the entire carriage is covered by one and the same transport document and within the same mode of transport.

Article 29

Courier and post receipts

a. If a Credit calls for a post receipt or certificate of posting, banks will, unless otherwise stipulated in the Credit, accept a post receipt or certificate of posting which:

i. appears on its face to have been stamped or otherwise authenticated and dated in the place from which the Credit stipulates the goods are to be shipped or dispatched and such date will be deemed to be the date of shipment or dispatch,
and
ii. in all other respects meets the stipulations of the Credit.

b. If a Credit calls for a document issued by a courier or expedited delivery service evidencing receipt of the goods for delivery, banks will, unless otherwise stipulated in the Credit, accept a document, however named, which:
i. appears on its face to indicate the name of the courier/service, and to have been stamped, signed or otherwise authenticated by such named courier/service (unless the Credit specifically calls for a document issued by a named Courier/Service, banks will accept a document issued by any Courier/Service),
and
ii. indicates a date of pick-up or of receipt or wording to this effect, such date being deemed to be the date of shipment or dispatch,
and
iii. in all other respects meets the stipulations of the Credit.

Article 30

Transport documents issued by freight forwarders

Unless otherwise authorised in the Credit, banks will only accept a transport document issued by a freight forwarder if it appears on its face to indicate:
i. the name of the freight forwarder as a carrier or multimodal transport operator and to have been signed or otherwise authenticated by the freight forwarder as carrier or multimodal transport operator,
or
ii. the name of the carrier or multimodal transport operator and to have been signed or otherwise authenticated by the freight forwarder as a named agent for or on behalf of the carrier or multimodal transport operator.

Article 31

'On deck', 'shipper's load and count', name of consignor

Unless otherwise stipulated in the Credit, banks will accept a transport document which:
i. does not indicate, in the case of carriage by sea or by more than one means of conveyance including carriage by sea, that the goods are or will be loaded on deck. Nevertheless, banks will accept a transport document which contains a provision that the goods may be carried on deck, provided that it does not specifically state that they are or will be loaded on deck,
and/or

ii. bears a clause on the face thereof such as 'shipper's load and count' or 'said by shipper to contain' or words of similar effect, and/or

iii. indicates as the consignor of the goods a party other than the Beneficiary of the Credit.

Article 32

Clean transport documents

a. A clean transport document is one which bears no clause or notation which expressly declares a defective condition of the goods and/or the packaging.

b. Banks will not accept transport documents bearing such clauses or notations unless the Credit expressly stipulates the clauses or notations which may be accepted.

c. Banks will regard a requirement in a Credit for a transport document to bear the clause 'clean on board' as complied with if such transport document meets the requirements of this Article and of Articles 23, 24, 25, 26, 27, 28 or 30.

Article 33

Freight payable/prepaid transport documents

a. Unless otherwise stipulated in the Credit, or inconsistent with any of the documents presented under the Credit, banks will accept transport documents stating that freight or transportation charges (hereafter referred to as 'freight') have still to be paid.

b. If a Credit stipulates that the transport document has to indicate that freight has been paid or prepaid, banks will accept a transport document on which words clearly indicating payment or pre-payment of freight appear by stamp or otherwise, or on which payment or prepayment of freight is indicated by other means. If the Credit requires courier charges to be paid or prepaid banks will also accept a transport document issued by a courier or expedited delivery service evidencing that courier charges are for the account of a party other than the consignee.

c. The words 'freight prepayable' or 'freight to be prepaid' or words of similar effect, if appearing on transport documents, will not be accepted as constituting evidence of the payment of freight.

d. Banks will accept transport documents bearing reference by stamp or otherwise to costs additional to the freight, such as costs of, or disbursements incurred in connection with, loading, unloading or similar operations, unless the conditions of the Credit specifically prohibit such reference.

Article 34

Insurance documents

a. Insurance documents must appear on their face to be issued and signed by insurance companies or underwriters or their agents.

b. If the insurance document indicates that it has been issued in more than one original, all the originals must be presented unless otherwise authorised in the Credit.

c. Cover notes issued by brokers will not be accepted, unless specifically authorised in the Credit.

d. Unless otherwise stipulated in the Credit, banks will accept an insurance certificate or a declaration under an open cover pre-signed by insurance companies or underwriters or their agents. If a Credit specifically calls for an insurance certificate or a declaration under an open cover, banks will accept, in lieu thereof, an insurance policy.

e. Unless otherwise stipulated in the Credit, or unless it appears from the insurance document that the cover is effective at the latest from the date of loading on board or dispatch or taking in charge of the goods, banks will not accept an insurance document which bears a date of issuance later than the date of loading on board or dispatch or taking in charge as indicated in such transport document.

f. **i.** Unless otherwise stipulated in the Credit, the insurance document must be expressed in the same currency as the Credit.
ii. Unless otherwise stipulated in the Credit, the minimum amount for which the insurance document must indicate the insurance cover to have been effected is the CIF (cost, insurance and freight (. . . 'named port of destination')) or CIP (carriage and insurance paid to (. . . 'named place of destination')) value of the goods, as the case may be, plus 10%, but only when the CIF or CIP value can be determined from the documents on their face. Otherwise, banks will accept as such minimum amount 110% of the amount for which payment, acceptance or negotiation is requested under the Credit, or 110% of the gross amount of the invoice, whichever is the greater.

Article 35

Type of insurance cover

a. Credits should stipulate the type of insurance required and, if any, the additional risks which are to be covered. Imprecise terms such as 'usual risks' or 'customary risks' shall not be used; if they are used, banks will accept insurance documents as presented, without responsibility for any risks not being covered.

b. Failing specific stipulations in the Credit, banks will accept insurance documents as presented, without responsibility for any risks not being covered.

c. Unless otherwise stipulated in the Credit, banks will accept an insurance document which indicates that the cover is subject to a franchise or an excess (deductible).

Article 36

All risks insurance cover

Where a Credit stipulates 'insurance against all risks', banks will accept an insurance document which contains any 'all risks' notation or clause, whether or not bearing the heading 'all risks', even if the insurance document indicates that certain risks are excluded, without responsibility for any risk(s) not being covered.

Article 37

Commercial invoices

a. Unless otherwise stipulated in the Credit, commercial invoices;
i. must appear on their face to be issued by the Beneficiary named in the Credit (except as provided in Article 48), and
ii. must be made out in the name of the Applicant (except as provided in sub-Article 48(h)), and
iii. need not be signed.

b. Unless otherwise stipulated in the Credit, banks may refuse commercial invoices issued for amounts in excess of the amount permitted by the Credit. Nevertheless, if a bank authorised to pay, incur a deferred payment undertaking, accept Draft(s), or negotiate under a Credit accepts such invoices, its decision will be binding upon all parties, provided that such bank has not paid, incurred a deferred payment undertaking, accepted Draft(s) or negotiated for an amount in excess of that permitted by the Credit.

c. The description of the goods in the commercial invoice must correspond with the description in the Credit. In all other documents, the goods may be described in general terms not inconsistent with the description of the goods in the Credit.

Article 38

Other documents

If a Credit calls for an attestation or certification of weight in the case of transport other than by sea, banks will accept a weight stamp or declaration of weight which appears to have been superimposed on the transport document by the carrier or his agent unless the Credit specifically stipulates that the attestation or certification of weight must be by means of a separate document.

E. Miscellaneous Provisions

Article 39

Allowances in Credit amount, quantity and unit price

a. The words 'about', 'approximately', 'circa' or similar expressions used in connection with the amount of the Credit or the quantity or the unit price stated in the Credit are to be construed as allowing a difference not to exceed 10% more or 10% less than the amount or the quantity or the unit price to which they refer.

b. Unless a Credit stipulates that the quantity of the goods specified must not be exceeded or reduced, a tolerance of 5% more or 5% less will be permissible, always provided that the amount of the drawings does not exceed the amount of the Credit. This tolerance does not apply when the Credit stipulates the quantity in terms of a stated number of packing units or individual items.

c. Unless a Credit which prohibits partial shipments stipulates otherwise, or unless sub-Article (b) above is applicable, a tolerance of 5% less in the amount of the drawing will be permissible, provided that if the Credit stipulates the quantity of the goods, such quantity of goods is shipped in full, and if the Credit stipulates a unit price, such price is not reduced. This provision does not apply when expressions referred to in sub-Article (a) above are used in the Credit.

Article 40

Partial shipments/drawings

a. Partial drawings and/or shipments are allowed, unless the Credit stipulates otherwise.

b. Transport documents which appear on their face to indicate that shipment has been made on the same means of conveyance and for the same journey, provided they indicate the same destination, will not be regarded as covering partial shipments, even if the transport documents indicate different dates of shipment and/or different ports of loading, places of taking in charge, or despatch.

c. Shipments made by post or by courier will not be regarded as partial shipments if the post receipts or certificates of posting or courier's receipts or dispatch notes appear to have been stamped, signed or otherwise authenticated in the place from which the Credit stipulates the goods are to be dispatched, and on the same date.

Article 41

Instalment shipments/drawings

If drawings and/or shipments by instalments within given periods are stipulated in the Credit and any instalment is not drawn and/or shipped within the period allowed for that instalment, the Credit ceases to be available for that and any subsequent instalments, unless otherwise stipulated in the Credit.

Article 42

Expiry date and place for presentation of documents

a. All Credits must stipulate an expiry date and a place for presentation of documents for payment, acceptance, or with the exception of freely negotiable Credits, a place for presentation of documents for negotiation. An expiry date stipulated for payment, acceptance or negotiation will be construed to express an expiry date for presentation of documents.

b. Except as provided in sub-Article 44(a), documents must be presented on or before such expiry date.

c. If an Issuing Bank states that the Credit is to be available 'for one month', 'for six months', or the like, but does not specify the date from which the time is to run, the date of issuance of the Credit by the Issuing Bank will be deemed to be the first day from which such time is to run. Banks should discourage indication of the expiry date of the Credit in this manner.

Article 43

Limitation on the expiry date

a. In addition to stipulating an expiry date for presentation of documents, every Credit which calls for a transport document(s) should also stipulate a specified period of time after the date of shipment during which presentation must be made in compliance with the terms and conditions of the Credit. If no such period of time is stipulated, banks will not accept documents presented to them later than 21 days after the date of shipment. In any event, documents must be presented not later than the expiry date of the Credit.

b. In cases in which sub-Article 40(b) applies, the date of shipment will be considered to be the latest shipment date on any of the transport documents presented.

Article 44

Extension of expiry date

a. If the expiry date of the Credit and/or the last day of the period of time for presentation of documents stipulated by the Credit or applicable by virtue of Article 43 falls on a day on which the bank to which presentation has to be made is closed for reasons other than those referred to in Article 17, the stipulated expiry date and/or the last day of the period of time after the date of shipment for presentation of documents, as the case may be, shall be extended to the first following day on which such bank is open.

b.   The latest date for shipment shall not be extended by reason of the extension of the expiry date and/or the period of time after the date of shipment for presentation of documents in accordance with sub-Article (a) above. If no such latest date for shipment is stipulated in the Credit or amendments thereto, banks will not accept transport documents indicating a date of shipment later than the expiry date stipulated in the Credit or amendments thereto.

c.   The bank to which presentation is made on such first following business day must provide a statement that the documents were presented within the time limits extended in accordance with sub-Article 44(a) of the Uniform Customs and Practice for Documentary Credits, 1993 Revision, ICC Publication No 500.

Article 45

Hours of presentation

Banks are under no obligation to accept presentation of documents outside their banking hours.

Article 46

General expressions as to dates for shipment

a.   Unless otherwise stipulated in the Credit, the expression 'shipment' used in stipulating an earliest and/or a latest date for shipment will be understood to include expressions such as, 'loading on board', 'dispatch', 'accepting for carriage', 'date of post receipt', 'date of pick-up', and the like, and in the case of a Credit calling for a multimodal transport document the expression 'taking in charge'.

b.   Expressions such as 'prompt', 'immediately', 'as soon as possible', and the like should not be used. If they are used banks will disregard them.

c.   If the expression 'on or about' or similar expressions are used, banks will interpret them as a stipulation that shipment is to be made during the period from five days before to five days after the specified date, both end days included.

Article 47

Date terminology for periods of shipment

a.   The words 'to', 'until', 'till', 'from' and words of similar import applying to any date or period in the Credit referring to shipment will be understood to include the date mentioned.

b.   The word 'after' will be understood to exclude the date mentioned.

c.   The terms 'first half', 'second half' of a month shall be construed respectively as the 1st to the 15th, and the 16th to the last day of such month, all dates inclusive.

d. The terms 'beginning', 'middle', or 'end' of a month shall be construed respectively as the 1st to the 10th, the 11th to the 20th, and the 21st to the last day of such month, all dates inclusive.

F. Transferable Credit

Article 48

Transferable Credit

a. A transferable Credit is a Credit under which the Beneficiary (First Beneficiary) may request the bank authorised to pay, incur a deferred payment undertaking, accept or negotiate (the 'Transferring Bank'), or in the case of a freely negotiable Credit, the bank specifically authorised in the Credit as a Transferring Bank, to make the Credit available in whole or in part to one or more other Beneficiary(ies) (Second Beneficiary(ies)).

b. A Credit can be transferred only if it is expressly designated as 'transferable' by the Issuing Bank. Terms such as 'divisible', 'fractionable', 'assignable', and 'transmissible' do not render the Credit transferable. If such terms are used they shall be disregarded.

c. The Transferring Bank shall be under no obligation to effect such transfer except to the extent and in the manner expressly consented to by such bank.

d. At the time of making a request for transfer and prior to transfer of the Credit, the First Beneficiary must irrevocably instruct the Transferring Bank whether or not he retains the right to refuse to allow the Transferring Bank to advise amendments to the Second Beneficiary(ies). If the Transferring Bank consents to the transfer under these conditions, it must, at the time of transfer, advise the Second Beneficiary(ies) of the First Beneficiary's instructions regarding amendments.

e. If a Credit is transferred to more than one Second Beneficiary(ies), refusal of an amendment by one or more Second Beneficiary(ies) does not invalidate the acceptance(s) by the other Second Beneficiary(ies) with respect to whom the Credit will be amended accordingly. With respect to the Second Beneficiary(ies) who rejected the amendment, the Credit will remain unamended.

f. Transferring Bank charges in respect of transfers including commissions, fees, costs or expenses are payable by the First Beneficiary, unless otherwise agreed. If the Transferring Bank agrees to transfer the Credit it shall be under no obligation to effect the transfer until such charges are paid.

g. Unless otherwise stated in the Credit, a transferable Credit can be transferred once only. Consequently, the Credit cannot be transferred at the request of the Second Beneficiary to any Subsequent Third Beneficiary. For the purpose of this Article, a retransfer to the First Beneficiary does not constitute a prohibited transfer.
Fractions of a transferable Credit (not exceeding in the aggregate the amount of the Credit) can be transferred separately, provided partial

shipments/drawings are not prohibited, and the aggregate of such transfers will be considered as constituting only one transfer of the Credit.

h. The Credit can be transferred only on the terms and conditions specified in the original Credit, with the exception of:
– the amount of the Credit,
– any unit price stated therein,
– the expiry date,
– the last date for presentation of documents in accordance with Article 43,
– the period for shipment,
any or all of which may be reduced or curtailed.
The percentage for which insurance cover must be effected may be increased in such a way as to provide the amount of cover stipulated in the original Credit, or these Articles.
In addition, the name of the First Beneficiary can be substituted for that of the Applicant, but if the name of the Applicant is specifically required by the original Credit to appear in any document(s) other than the invoice, such requirement must be fulfilled.

i. The First Beneficiary has the right to substitute his own invoice(s) (and Draft(s)) for those of the Second Beneficiary(ies), for amounts not in excess of the original amount stipulated in the Credit and for the original unit prices if stipulated in the Credit, and upon such substitution of invoice(s) (and Draft(s)) the First Beneficiary can draw under the Credit for the difference, if any, between his invoice(s) and the Second Beneficiary's(ies') invoice(s).
When a Credit has been transferred and the First Beneficiary is to supply his own invoice(s) (and Draft(s)) in exchange for the Second Beneficiary's(ies') invoice(s) (and Draft(s)) but fails to do so on first demand, the Transferring Bank has the right to deliver to the Issuing Bank the documents received under the transferred Credit, including the Second Beneficiary's(ies') invoice(s) (and Draft(s)) without further responsibility to the First Beneficiary.

j. The First Beneficiary may request that payment or negotiation be effected to the Second Beneficiary(ies) at the place to which the Credit has been transferred up to and including the expiry date of the Credit, unless the original Credit expressly states that it may not be made available for payment or negotiation at a place other than that stipulated in the Credit. This is without prejudice to the First Beneficiary's right to substitute subsequently his own invoice(s) (and Draft(s)) for those of the Second Beneficiary(ies) and to claim any difference due to him.

G.   Assignment of Proceeds

Article 49

Assignment of proceeds

The fact that a Credit is not stated to be transferable shall not affect the Beneficiary's right to assign any proceeds to which he may be, or may become, entitled under such Credit, in accordance with the provisions of the applicable law. This Article relates only to the assignment of proceeds and not to the assignment of the right to perform under the Credit itself.

Appendix 2

Index to Articles of 1993 Revision and Cross-References to Articles of 1983 Revision

Article in 1993 Revision	Subject matter of 1993 Revision Article[1]	Main reference in text: paragraph no	Article in 1983 Revision
1	application	1.25	1
2	meaning of credit	1.32	2
3.a	autonomy of credits	1.42, 8.3	3
.b			6
4	credits concern documents	1.42, 8.3	4
5.a	instructions	4.3	5
.b			22.a
6	revocable/irrevocable	2.2	7
7	advising bank's liability	6.7	8
8	revocation	2.6	9
9.a	liability of issuing bank	5.13	10.a
.b	liability of confirming bank	5.13	10.b
.c	refusal to confirm	6.13	10.c
.d	amendments	3.35	10.d
10	types of payment provision	6.10, 2.17, 2.21	11
11.a	teletransmission	6.20	12.a, b
.b	use of same bank	3.35, 6.20	12.d
.c	preliminary advice	5.4	none
12	incomplete/unclear instructions	4.5	14
13.a	examination of documents	8.2	15
.b	time for examination etc	5.32	16.c
.c	non-documentary conditions	8.16	none
14.a	reimbursement of authorised bank	6.11, 8.4	16.a
.b	determination of refusal/ acceptance	5.32	16.b
.c	approach to applicant	5.32, 5.37	new
.d	notice of refusal	5.32, 5.45–49	16.d
.e	effect of failure to comply	5.32, 5.33	16.e
.f	negotiation under reserve	5.59	16.f
15	disclaimer beyond face of documents	1.42, 8.3	17
16	disclaimer on transmission	4.15	18
17	force majeure	4.16	19
18.a, b	disclaimer re acts of banks instructed	4.18	20.a, b
.c	charges	4.18, 4.26	new
.d	foreign laws and usages	4.18	20.c
19	reimbursement	6.23	21
20.a	terms as to issuers	8.48	22.b

1 This does not always follow the headings in the Uniform Customs.

Appendix 3

The Uniform Customs and Practice for Documentary Credits (1983 Revision) ICC Publication No 400

A. General Provisions and Definitions

Article 1

These articles apply to all documentary credits, including, to the extent to which they may be applicable, standby letters of credit, and are binding on all parties thereto unless otherwise expressly agreed. They shall be incorporated into each documentary credit by wording in the credit indicating that such credit is issued subject to Uniform Customs and Practice for Documentary Credits, 1983 revision, ICC Publication No 400.

Article 2

For the purposes of these articles, the expressions 'documentary credit(s)' and 'standby letter(s) of credit' used herein (hereinafter referred to as 'credit(s)', mean any arrangement, however named or described, where a bank (the issuing bank), acting at the request and on the instructions of a customer (the applicant for the credit),

i is to make a payment to or to the order of a third party (the beneficiary), or is to pay or accept bills of exchange (drafts) drawn by the beneficiary, or

ii authorizes another bank to effect such payment, or to pay, accept or negotiate such bills of exchange (drafts),

against stipulated documents, provided that the terms and conditions of the credit are complied with.

Article 3

Credits, by their nature, are separate transactions from the sales or other contract(s) on which they may be based and banks are in no way concerned with or bound by such contract(s), even if any reference whatsoever to such contract(s) is included in the credit.

Article 4

In credit operations all parties concerned deal in documents, and not in goods, services and/or other performances to which the documents may relate.

Article 5

Instructions for the issuance of credits, the credits themselves, instructions for any amendments thereto and the amendments themselves must be complete and precise.

In order to guard against confusion and misunderstanding, banks should discourage any attempt to include excessive detail in the credit or in any amendment thereto.

Article 6

A beneficiary can in no case avail himself of the contractual relationships existing between the banks or between the applicant for the credit and the issuing bank.

B.   Form and Notification of Credits

Article 7

a.   Credits may be either
i revocable, or
ii irrevocable.

b.   All credits, therefore, should clearly indicate whether they are revocable or irrevocable.

c.   In the absence of such indication the credit shall be deemed to be revocable.

Article 8

A credit may be advised to a beneficiary through another bank (the advising bank) without engagement on the part of the advising bank, but that bank shall take reasonable care to check the apparent authenticity of the credit which it advises.

Article 9

a.   A revocable credit may be amended or cancelled by the issuing bank at any moment and without prior notice to the beneficiary.

b.   However, the issuing bank is bound to:
i reimburse a branch or bank with which a revocable credit has been made available for sight payment, acceptance or negotiation, for any payment, acceptance or negotiation made by such branch or bank prior to receipt by it of notice of amendment or cancellation, against documents which appear on their face to be in accordance with the terms and conditions of the credit.
ii reimburse a branch or bank with which a revocable credit has been made available for deferred payment, if such branch or bank has, prior to receipt by it of notice of amendment or cancellation, taken up documents which appear on their face to be in accordance with the terms and conditions of the credit.

Article 10

a. An irrevocable credit constitutes a definite undertaking of the issuing bank, provided that the stipulated documents are presented and that the terms and conditions of the credit are complied with:
i if the credit provides for sight payment – to pay, or that payment will be made;
ii if the credit provides for deferred payment – to pay, or that payment will be made, on the date(s) determinable in accordance with the stipulations of the credit;
iii if the credit provides for acceptance – to accept drafts drawn by the beneficiary if the credit stipulates that they are to be drawn on the issuing bank, or to be responsible for their acceptance and payment at maturity if the credit stipulates that they are to be drawn on the applicant for the credit or any other drawee stipulated in the credit;
iv if the credit provides for negotiation – to pay without recourse to drawers and/or bona fide holders, draft(s) drawn by the beneficiary, at sight or at a tenor, on the applicant for the credit or on any other drawee stipulated in the credit other than the issuing bank itself, or to provide for negotiation by another bank and to pay, as above, if such negotiation is not effected.

b. When an issuing bank authorizes or requests another bank to confirm its irrevocable credit and the latter has added its confirmation, such confirmation constitutes a definite undertaking of such bank (the confirming bank), in addition to that of the issuing bank, provided that the stipulated documents are presented and that the terms and conditions of the credit are complied with:
i if the credit provides for sight payment – to pay, or that payment will be made;
ii if the credit provides for deferred payment – to pay, or that payment will be made, on the date(s) determinable in accordance with the stipulations of the credit;
iii if the credit provides for acceptance – to accept drafts drawn by the beneficiary if the credit stipulates that they are to be drawn on the confirming bank, or to be responsible for their acceptance and payment at maturity if the credit stipulates that they are to be drawn on the applicant for the credit or any other drawee stipulated in the credit;
iv if the credit provides for negotiation – to negotiate without recourse to drawers and/or bona fide holders, draft(s) drawn by the beneficiary, at sight or at a tenor, on the issuing bank or on the applicant for the credit or on any other drawee stipulated in the credit other than the confirming bank itself.

c. If a bank is authorized or requested by the issuing bank to add its confirmation to a credit but is not prepared to do so, it must so inform the issuing bank without delay. Unless the issuing bank specifies otherwise in its confirmation authorization or request, the advising bank will advise the credit to the beneficiary without adding its confirmation.

d. Such undertakings can neither be amended nor cancelled without the agreement of the issuing bank, the confirming bank (if any), and the beneficiary. Partial acceptance of amendments contained in one and the same advice of amendment is not effective without the agreement of all the above named parties.

Article 11

a. All credits must clearly indicate whether they are available by sight payment, by deferred payment, by acceptance or by negotiation.

b. All credits must nominate the bank (nominated bank) which is authorized to pay (paying bank), or to accept drafts (accepting bank), or to negotiate (negotiating bank), unless the credit allows negotiation by any bank (negotiating bank).

c. Unless the nominated bank is the issuing bank or the confirming bank, its nomination by the issuing bank does not constitute any undertaking by the nominated bank to pay, to accept, or to negotiate.

d. By nominating a bank other than itself, or by allowing for negotiation by any bank, or by authorizing or requesting a bank to add its confirmation, the issuing bank authorizes such bank to pay, accept or negotiate, as the case may be, against documents which appear on their face to be in accordance with the terms and conditions of the credit, and undertakes to reimburse such bank in accordance with the provisions of these articles.

Article 12

a. When an issuing bank instructs a bank (advising bank) by any tele-transmission to advise a credit or an amendment to a credit, and intends the mail confirmation to be the operative credit instrument, or the operative amendment, the teletransmission must state 'full details to follow' (or words of similar effect), or that the mail confirmation will be the operative credit instrument or the operative amendment. The issuing bank must forward the operative credit instrument or the operative amendment to such advising bank without delay.

b. The teletransmission will be deemed to be the operative credit instrument or the operative amendment, and no mail confirmation should be sent, unless the teletransmission states 'full details to follow' (or words of similar effect), or states that the mail confirmation is to be the operative credit instrument or the operative amendment.

c. A teletransmission intended by the issuing bank to be the operative credit instrument should clearly indicate that the credit is issued subject to Uniform Customs and Practice for Documentary Credits 1983 revision, ICC Publication No 400.

d. If a bank uses the services of another bank or banks (the advising bank) to have the credit advised to the beneficiary, it must also use the services of the same bank(s) for advising any amendments.

e. Banks shall be responsible for any consequences arising from their failure to follow the procedures set out in the preceding paragraphs.

Article 13

When a bank is instructed to issue, confirm or advise a credit similar in terms to one previously issued, confirmed or advised (similar credit) and the previous credit has been the subject of amendment(s), it shall be understood that the similar credit will not include any such amendment(s) unless the instructions specify clearly the amendment(s) which is/are to apply to the similar credit. Banks should discourage instructions to issue, confirm or advise a credit in this manner.

Article 14

If incomplete or unclear instructions are received to issue, confirm, advise or amend a credit, the bank requested to act on such instructions may give preliminary notification to the beneficiary for information only and without responsibility. The credit will be issued, confirmed, advised or amended only when the necessary information has been received and if the bank is then prepared to act on the instructions. Banks should provide the necessary information without delay.

C. Liabilities and Responsibilities

Article 15

Banks must examine all documents with reasonable care to ascertain that they appear on their face to be in accordance with the terms and conditions of the credit. Documents which appear on their face to be inconsistent with one another will be considered as not appearing on their face to be in accordance with the terms and conditions of the credit.

Article 16

a. If a bank so authorised effects payment, or incurs a deferred payment undertaking, or accepts, or negotiates against documents which appear on their face to be in accordance with the terms and conditions of a credit, the party giving such authority shall be bound to reimburse the bank which has effected payment, or incurred a deferred payment undertaking, or has accepted, or negotiated, and to take up the documents.

b. If, upon receipt of the documents, the issuing bank considers that they appear on their face not to be in accordance with the terms and conditions of the credit, it must determine, on the basis of the documents alone, whether to take up such documents, or to refuse them and claim that they appear on their face not to be in accordance with the terms and conditions of the credit.

c. The issuing bank shall have a reasonable time in which to examine the documents and to determine as above whether to take up or to refuse the documents.

d. If the issuing bank decides to refuse the documents, it must give notice to that effect without delay by telecommunication or, if that is not possible, by other expeditious means, to the bank from which it received the documents (the remitting bank), or to the beneficiary, if it received the documents directly from him. Such notice must state the discrepancies in respect of which the issuing bank refuses the documents and must also state whether it is holding the documents at the disposal of, or is returning them to, the presentor (remitting bank or the beneficiary, as the case may be). The issuing bank shall then be entitled to claim from the remitting bank refund of any reimbursement which may have been made to that bank.

e. If the issuing bank fails to act in accordance with the provisions of paragraphs (c) and (d) of this article and/or fails to hold the documents at the disposal of, or to return them to, the presentor, the issuing bank shall be precluded from claiming that the documents are not in accordance with the terms and conditions of the credit.

f. If the remitting bank draws the attention of the issuing bank to any discrepancies in the documents or advises the issuing bank that it has paid, incurred a deferred payment undertaking, accepted or negotiated under reserve or against an indemnity in respect of such discrepancies, the issuing bank shall not be thereby relieved from any of its obligations under any provision of this article. Such reserve or indemnity concerns only the relations between the remitting bank and the party towards whom the reserve was made, or from whom, or on whose behalf, the indemnity was obtained.

Article 17

Banks assume no liability or responsibility for the form, sufficiency, accuracy, genuineness, falsification or legal effect of any documents, or for the general and/or particular conditions stipulated in the documents or superimposed thereon; nor do they assume any liability or responsibility for the description, quantity, weight, quality, condition, packing, delivery, value or existence of the goods represented by any documents, or for the good faith or acts and/or omissions, solvency, performance or standing of the consignor, the carriers, or the insurers of the goods, or any other person whomsoever.

Article 18

Banks assume no liability or responsibility for the consequences arising out of delay and/or loss in transit of any messages, letters or documents, or for delay, mutilation or other errors arising in the transmission of any telecommunication. Banks assume no liability or responsibility for errors in translation or interpretation of technical terms, and reserve the right to transmit credit terms without translating them.

Article 19

Banks assume no liability or responsibility for consequences arising out of the interruption of their business by Acts of God, riots, civil commotions, insurrections, wars or any other causes beyond their control, or by any strikes or lockouts. Unless specifically authorised, banks will not, upon resumption of their business, incur a deferred payment undertaking, or effect payment, acceptance or negotiation under credits which expired during such interruption of their business.

Article 20

a. Banks utilising the services of another bank or other banks for the purpose of giving effect to the instructions of the applicant for the credit do so for the account and at the risk of such applicant.

b. Banks assume no liability or responsibility should the instructions they transmit not be carried out, even if they have themselves taken the initiative in the choice of such other bank(s).

c. The applicant for the credit shall be bound by and liable to indemnify the banks against all obligations and responsibilities imposed by foreign laws and usages.

Article 21

a. If an issuing bank intends that the reimbursement to which a paying, accepting or negotiating bank is entitled shall be obtained by such bank claiming on another branch or office of the issuing bank or on a third bank (all hereinafter referred to as the reimbursing bank) it shall provide such reimbursing bank in good time with the proper instructions or authorisation to honour such reimbursement claims and without making it a condition that the bank entitled to claim reimbursement must certify compliance with the terms and conditions of the credit to the reimbursing bank.

b. An issuing bank will not be relieved from any of its obligations to provide reimbursement itself if and when reimbursement is not effected by the reimbursing bank.

c. The issuing bank will be responsible to the paying, accepting or negotiating bank for any loss of interest if reimbursement is not provided on first demand made to the reimbursing bank, or as otherwise specified in the credit, or mutually agreed, as the case may be.

D. Documents

Article 22

a. All instructions for the issuance of credits and the credits themselves and, where applicable, all instructions for amendments thereto and the amendments themselves, must state precisely the document(s) against which payment, acceptance or negotiation is to be made.

b. Terms such as 'first class', 'well known', 'qualified', 'independent', 'official', and the like shall not be used to describe the issuers of any documents to be presented under a credit. If such terms are incorporated in the credit terms, banks will accept the relative documents as presented, provided that they appear on their face to be in accordance with the other terms and conditions of the credit.

c. Unless otherwise stipulated in the credit, banks will accept as originals documents produced or appearing to have been produced:

i by reprographic systems;
ii by, or as the result of, automated or computerised systems;
iii as carbon copies,
if marked as originals, always provided that, where necessary, such documents appear to have been authenticated.

Article 23

When documents other than transport documents, insurance documents and commercial invoices are called for, the credit should stipulate by whom such documents are to be issued and their wording or data content. If the credit does not so stipulate, banks will accept such documents as presented, provided that their data content makes it possible to relate the goods and/or services referred to therein to those referred to in the commercial invoice(s) presented, or to those referred to in the credit if the credit does not stipulate presentation of a commercial invoice.

Article 24

Unless otherwise stipulated in the credit, banks will accept a document bearing a date of issuance prior to that of the credit, subject to such document being presented within the time limits set out in the credit and in these articles.

D1. *Transport documents (documents indicating loading on board or dispatch or taking in charge)*

Article 25

Unless a credit calling for a transport document stipulates as such document a marine bill of lading (ocean bill of lading or a bill of lading covering carriage by sea), or a post receipt or certificate of posting:

a. banks will, unless otherwise stipulated in the credit, accept a transport document which:
i appears on its face to have been issued by a named carrier, or his agent, and
ii indicates dispatch or taking in charge of the goods, or loading on board, as the case may be, and
iii consists of the full set of originals issued to the consignor if issued in more than one original, and
iv meets all other stipulations of the credit.

b. Subject to the above, and unless otherwise stipulated in the credit, banks will not reject a transport document which:
i bears a title such as 'Combined transport bill of lading', 'Combined transport document', 'Combined transport bill of lading or port-to-port bill of lading', or a title or a combination of titles of similar intent and effect, and/or
ii indicates some or all of the conditions of carriage by reference to a source or document other than the transport document itself (short form/blank back transport document), and/or

iii indicates a place of taking in charge different from the port of loading and/or a place of final destination different from the port of discharge, and/or
iv relates to cargoes such as those in Containers or on pallets, and the like, and/or
v contains the indication 'intended', or similar qualification, in relation to the vessel or other means of transport, and/or the port of loading and/or the port of discharge.

c. Unless otherwise stipulated in the credit in the case of carriage by sea or by more than one mode of transport but including carriage by sea, banks will reject a transport document which:
i indicates that it is subject to a charter party, and/or
ii indicates that the carrying vessel is propelled by sail only.

d. Unless otherwise stipulated in the credit, banks will reject a transport document issued by a freight forwarder unless it is the FIATA Combined Transport Bill of Lading approved by the International Chamber of Commerce or otherwise indicates that it is issued by a freight forwarder acting as a carrier or agent of a named carrier.

Article 26

If a credit calling for a transport document stipulates as such document a marine bill of lading:
a. banks will, unless otherwise stipulated in the credit, accept a document which:
i appears on its face to have been issued by a named carrier, or his agent, and
ii indicates that the goods have been loaded on board or shipped on a named vessel, and
iii consists of the full set of originals issued to the consignor if issued in more than one original, and
iv meets all other stipulations of the credit.

b. Subject to the above, and unless otherwise stipulated in the credit, banks will not reject a document which:
i bears a title such as 'Combined transport bill of lading', 'Combined transport document', 'Combined transport bill of lading or port-to-port bill of lading', or a title or a combination of titles of similar intent and effect, and/or
ii indicates some or all of the conditions of carriage by reference to a source or document other than the transport document itself (short form/blank back transport document), and/or
iii indicates a place of taking in charge different from the port of loading, and/or a place of final destination different from the port of discharge, and/or
iv relates to cargoes such as those in Containers or on pallets, and the like.

c. Unless otherwise stipulated in the credit, banks will reject a document which:
i indicates that it is subject to a charter party, and/or
ii indicates that the carrying vessel is propelled by sail only, and/or

iii contains the indication 'intended', or similar qualification in relation to

● the vessel and/or the port of loading – unless such document bears an on board notation in accordance with article 27(b) and also indicates the actual port of loading, and/or

● the port of discharge – unless the place of final destination indicated on the document is other than the port of discharge, and/or

iv is issued by a freight forwarder, unless it indicates that it is issued by such freight forwarder acting as a carrier, or as the agent of a named carrier.

Article 27

a. Unless a credit specifically calls for an on board transport document, or unless inconsistent with other stipulation(s) in the credit, or with Article 26, banks will accept a transport document which indicates that the goods have been taken in charge or received for shipment.

b. Loading on board or shipment on a vessel may be evidenced either by a transport document bearing wording indicating loading on board a named vessel or shipment on a named vessel, or, in the case of a transport document stating 'received for shipment', by means of a notation of loading on board on the transport document signed or initialled and dated by the carrier or his agent, and the date of this notation shall be regarded as the date of loading on board the named vessel or shipment on the named vessel.

Article 28

a. In the case of carriage by sea or by more than one mode of transport but including carriage by sea, banks will refuse a transport document stating that the goods are or will be loaded on deck, unless specifically authorized in the credit.

b. Banks will not refuse a transport document which contains a provision that the goods may be carried on deck, provided it does not specifically state that they are or will be loaded on deck.

Article 29

a. For the purpose of this article transhipment means a transfer and reloading during the course of carriage from the port of loading or place of dispatch or taking in charge to the port of discharge or place of destination either from one conveyance or vessel to another conveyance or vessel within the same mode of transport or from one mode of transport to another mode of transport.

b. Unless transhipment is prohibited by the terms of the credit, banks will accept transport documents which indicate that the goods will be transhipped, provided the entire carriage is covered by one and the same transport document.

c. Even if transhipment is prohibited by the terms of the credit, banks will accept transport documents which:

i incorporate printed clauses stating that the carrier has the right to tranship, or

ii state or indicate that transhipment will or may take place, when the credit stipulates a combined transport document, or indicates carriage from a place of taking in charge to a place of final destination by different modes of transport including a carriage by sea, provided that the entire carriage is covered by one and the same transport document, or

iii state or indicate that the goods are in a Container(s), trailer(s), 'LASH' barge(s), and the like and will be carried from the place of taking in charge to the place of final destination in the same Container(s), trailer(s), 'LASH' barge(s), and the like under one and the same transport document.

iv state or indicate the place of receipt and/or of final destination as 'C.F.S.' (container freight station) or 'C.Y.' (container yard) at, or associated with, the port of loading and/or the port of destination.

Article 30

If the credit stipulates dispatch of goods by post and calls for a post receipt or certificate of posting, banks will accept such post receipt or certificate of posting if it appears to have been stamped or otherwise authenticated and dated in the place from which the credit stipulates the goods are to be dispatched.

Article 31

a. Unless otherwise stipulated in the credit, or inconsistent with any of the documents presented under the credit, banks will accept transport documents stating that freight or transportation charges (hereinafter referred to as 'freight') have still to be paid.

b. If a credit stipulates that the transport document has to indicate that freight has been paid or prepaid, banks will accept a transport document on which words clearly indicating payment or prepayment of freight appear by stamp or otherwise, or on which payment of freight is indicated by other means.

c. The words 'freight prepayable' or 'freight to be prepaid' or words of similar effect, if appearing on transport documents, will not be accepted as constituting evidence of the payment of freight.

d. Banks will accept transport documents bearing reference by stamp or otherwise to costs additional to the freight charges, such as costs of, or disbursements incurred in connection with, loading, unloading or similar operations, unless the conditions of the credit specifically prohibit such reference.

Article 32

Unless otherwise stipulated in the credit, banks will accept transport documents which bear a clause on the face thereof such as 'shipper's load and count' or 'said by shipper to contain' or words of similar effect.

Article 33

Unless otherwise stipulated in the credit, banks will accept transport documents indicating as the consignor of the goods a party other than the beneficiary of the credit.

Article 34

a. A clean transport document is one which bears no superimposed clause or notation which expressly declares a defective condition of the goods and/or the packaging.

b. Banks will refuse transport documents bearing such clauses or notations unless the credit expressly stipulates the clauses or notations which may be accepted.

c. Banks will regard a requirement in a credit for a transport document to bear the clause 'clean on board' as complied with if such transport document meets the requirements of this article and of article 27(b).

D2. *Insurance documents*

Article 35

a. Insurance documents must be as stipulated in the credit, and must be issued and/or signed by insurance companies or underwriters, or their agents.

b. Cover notes issued by brokers will not be accepted, unless specifically authorised by the credit.

Article 36

Unless otherwise stipulated in the credit, or unless it appears from the insurance document(s) that the cover is effective at the latest from the date of loading on board or dispatch or taking in charge of the goods, banks will refuse insurance documents presented which bear a date later than the date of loading on board or dispatch or taking in charge of the goods as indicated by the transport document(s).

Article 37

a. Unless otherwise stipulated in the credit, the insurance document must be expressed in the same currency as the credit.

b. Unless otherwise stipulated in the credit, the minimum amount for which the insurance document must indicate the insurance cover to have been effected is the CIF (cost, insurance and freight . . . 'named port of destination') or CIP (freight/carriage and insurance paid to 'named point of destination') value of the goods, as the case may be, plus 10%. However, if banks cannot determine the CIF or

CIP value, as the case may be, from the documents on their face, they will accept as such minimum amount the amount for which payment, acceptance or negotiation is requested under the credit, or the amount of the commercial invoice, whichever is the greater.

Article 38

a.   Credits should stipulate the type of insurance required and, if any, the additional risks which are to be covered. Imprecise terms such as 'usual risks' or 'customary risks' should not be used; if they are used, banks will accept insurance documents as presented, without responsibility for any risks not being covered.

b.   Failing specific stipulations in the credit, banks will accept insurance documents as presented, without responsibility for any risks not being covered.

Article 39

Where a credit stipulates 'insurance against all risks', banks will accept an insurance document which contains any 'all risks' notation or clause, whether or not bearing the heading 'all risks', even if indicating that certain risks are excluded, without responsibility for any risk(s) not being covered.

Article 40

Banks will accept an insurance document which indicates that the cover is subject to a franchise or an excess (deductible), unless it is specifically stipulated in the credit that the insurance must be issued irrespective of percentage.

D3.   *Commercial invoice*

Article 41

a.   Unless otherwise stipulated in the credit, commercial invoices must be made out in the name of the applicant for the credit.

b.   Unless otherwise stipulated in the credit, banks may refuse commercial invoices issued for amounts in excess of the amount permitted by the credit. Nevertheless, if a bank authorised to pay, incur a deferred payment undertaking, accept, or negotiate under a credit accepts such invoices, its decision will be binding upon all parties, provided such bank has not paid, incurred a deferred payment undertaking, accepted or effected negotiation for an amount in excess of that permitted by the credit.

c.   The description of the goods in the commercial invoice must correspond with the description in the credit. In all other documents, the goods may be described in general terms not inconsistent with the description of the goods in the credit.

D4. *Other documents*

Article 42

If a credit calls for an attestation or certification of weight in the case of transport other than by sea, banks will accept a weight stamp or declaration of weight which appears to have been superimposed on the transport document by the carrier or his agent unless the credit specifically stipulates that the attestation or certification of weight must be by means of a separate document.

E. Miscellaneous Provisions

Quantity and amount

Article 43

a. The words 'about', 'circa' or similar expressions used in connection with the amount of the credit or the quantity or the unit price stated in the credit are to be construed as allowing a difference not to exceed 10% more or 10% less than the amount or the quantity or the unit price to which they refer.

b. Unless a credit stipulates that the quantity of the goods specified must not be exceeded or reduced, a tolerance of 5% more or 5% less will be permissible, even if partial shipments are not permitted, always provided that the amount of the drawings does not exceed the amount of the credit. This tolerance does not apply when the credit stipulates the quantity in terms of a stated number of packing units or individual items.

Partial drawings and/or shipments

Article 44

a. Partial drawings and/or shipments are allowed, unless the credit stipulates otherwise.

b. Shipments by sea, or by more than one mode of transport but including carriage by sea, made on the same vessel and for the same voyage, will not be regarded as partial shipments, even if the transport documents indicating loading on board bear different dates of issuance and/or indicate different ports of loading on board.

c. Shipments made by post will not be regarded as partial shipments if the post receipts or certificates of posting appear to have been stamped or otherwise authenticated in the place from which the credit stipulates the goods are to be dispatched, and on the same date.

d. Shipments made by modes of transport other than those referred to in paragraphs (b) and (c) of this article will not be regarded as partial shipments, provided the transport documents are issued by one and the same carrier or his agent and indicate the same date of issuance, the same place of dispatch or taking in charge of the goods, and the same destination.

Drawings and/or shipments by instalments

Article 45

If drawings and/or shipments by instalments within given periods are stipulated in the credit and any instalment is not drawn and/or shipped within the period allowed for that instalment, the credit ceases to be available for that and any subsequent instalments, unless otherwise stipulated in the credit.

Expiry date and presentation

Article 46

a. All credits must stipulate an expiry date for presentation of documents for payment, acceptance or negotiation.

b. Except as provided in Article 48(a), documents must be presented on or before such expiry date.

c. If an issuing bank states that the credit is to be available 'for one month', 'for six months' or the like, but does not specify the date from which the time is to run, the date of issuance of the credit by the issuing bank will be deemed to be the first day from which such time is to run. Banks should discourage indication of the expiry date of the credit in this manner.

Article 47

a. In addition to stipulating an expiry date for presentation of documents, every credit which calls for a transport document(s) should also stipulate a specified period of time after the date of issuance of the transport document(s) during which presentation of documents for payment, acceptance or negotiation must be made. If no such period of time is stipulated, banks will refuse documents presented to them later than 21 days after the date of issuance of the transport document(s). In every case, however, documents must be presented not later than the expiry date of the credit.

b. For the purpose of these articles, the date of issuance of a transport document(s) will be deemed to be:
i   in the case of a transport document evidencing dispatch, or taking in charge, or receipt of goods for shipment by a mode of transport other than by air – the date of issuance indicated on the transport document or the date of the reception stamp thereon whichever is the later.
ii in the case of a transport document evidencing carriage by air – the date of issuance indicated on the transport document or, if the

credit stipulates that the transport document shall indicate an actual flight date, the actual flight date as indicated on the transport document.

iii in the case of a transport document evidencing loading on board a named vessel – the date of issuance of the transport document or, in the case of an on board notation in accordance with Article 27(b), the date of such notation.

iv in cases to which Article 44(b) applies, the date determined as above of the latest transport document issued.

Article 48

a. If the expiry date of the credit and/or the last day of the period of time after the date of issuance of the transport document(s) for presentation of documents stipulated by the credit or applicable by virtue of Article 47 falls on a day on which the bank to which presentation has to be made is closed for reasons other than those referred to in Article 19, the stipulated expiry date and/or the last day of the period of time after the date of issuance of the transport document(s) for presentation of documents, as the case may be, shall be extended to the first following business day on which such bank is open.

b. The latest date for loading on board, or dispatch, or taking in charge shall not be extended by reason of the extension of the expiry date and/or the period of time after the date of issuance of the transport document(s) for presentation of document(s) in accordance with this article. If no such latest date for shipment is stipulated in the credit or amendments thereto, banks will reject transport documents indicating a date of issuance later than the expiry date stipulated in the credit or amendments thereto.

c. The bank to which presentation is made on such first following business day must add to the documents its certificate that the documents were presented within the time limits extended in accordance with Article 48(a) of the Uniform Customs and Practice for Documentary Credits, 1983 revision, ICC Publication No 400.

Article 49

Banks are under no obligation to accept presentation of documents outside their banking hours.

Loading on board, dispatch and taking in charge (shipment)

Article 50

a. Unless otherwise stipulated in the credit, the expression 'shipment' used in stipulating an earliest and/or a latest shipment date will be understood to include the expressions 'loading on board', 'dispatch' and 'taking in charge'.

b.   The date of issuance of the transport document determined in accordance with Article 47(b) will be taken to be the date of shipment.

c.   Expressions such as 'prompt', 'immediately', 'as soon as possible', and the like should not be used. If they are used, banks will interpret them as a stipulation that shipment is to be made within thirty days from the date of issuance of the credit by the issuing bank.

d.   If the expression 'on or about' and similar expressions are used, banks will interpret them as a stipulation that shipment is to be made during the period from five days before to five days after the specified date, both end days included.

Date terms

Article 51

The words 'to', 'until', 'till', 'from', and words of similar import applying to any date term in the credit will be understood to include the date mentioned. The word 'after' will be understood to exclude the date mentioned.

Article 52

The terms 'first half', 'second half' of a month shall be construed respectively as from the 1st to the 15th, and the 16th to the last day of each month, inclusive.

Article 53

The terms 'beginning', 'middle', or 'end' of a month shall be construed respectively as from the 1st to the 10th, the 11th to the 20th, and the 21st to the last day of each month, inclusive.

F.   Transfer

Article 54

a.   A transferable credit is a credit under which the beneficiary has the right to request the bank called upon to effect payment or acceptance or any bank entitled to effect negotiation to make the credit available in whole or in part to one or more other parties (second beneficiaries).

b.   A credit can be transferred only if it is expressly designated as 'transferable' by the issuing bank. Terms such as 'divisible', 'fractionable', 'assignable', and 'transmissible' add nothing to the meaning of the term 'transferable' and shall not be used.

c. The bank requested to effect the transfer (transferring bank), whether it has confirmed the credit or not, shall be under no obligation to effect such transfer except to the extent and in the manner expressly consented to by such bank.

d. Bank charges in respect of transfers are payable by the first beneficiary unless otherwise specified. The transferring bank shall be under no obligation to effect the transfer until such charges are paid.

e. A transferable credit can be transferred once only. Fractions of a transferable credit (not exceeding in the aggregate the amount of the credit) can be transferred separately, provided partial shipments are not prohibited, and the aggregate of such transfers will be considered as constituting only one transfer of the credit. The credit can be transferred only on the terms and conditions specified in the original credit, with the exception of the amount of the credit, of any unit prices stated therein, of the period of validity, of the last date for presentation of documents in accordance with Article 47 and the period for shipment, any or all of which may be reduced or curtailed, or the percentage for which insurance cover must be effected, which may be increased in such a way as to provide the amount of cover stipulated in the orginal credit, or these articles. Additionally, the name of the first beneficiary can be substituted for that of the applicant for the credit, but if the name of the applicant for the credit is specifically required by the original credit to appear in any document other than the invoice, such requirement must be fulfilled.

f. The first beneficiary has the right to substitute his own invoices (and drafts if the credit stipulates that drafts are to be drawn on the applicant for the credit) in exchange for those of the second beneficiary, for amounts not in excess of the original amount stipulated in the credit and for the original unit prices if stipulated in the credit, and upon such substitution of invoices (and drafts) the first beneficiary can draw under the credit for the difference, if any, between his invoices and the second beneficiary's invoices. When a credit has been transferred and the first beneficiary is to supply his own invoices (and drafts) in exchange for the second beneficiary's invoices (and drafts) but fails to do so on first demand, the paying, accepting or negotiating bank has the right to deliver to the issuing bank the documents received under the credit, including the second beneficiary's invoices (and drafts) without further responsibility to the first beneficiary.

g. Unless otherwise stipulated in the credit, the first beneficiary of a transferable credit may request that the credit be transferred to a second beneficiary in the same country, or in another country. Further, unless otherwise stipulated in the credit, the first beneficiary shall have the right to request that payment or negotiation be effected to the second beneficiary at the place to which the credit has been transferred, up to and including the expiry date of the original credit, and without prejudice to the first beneficiary's right subsequently to substitute his own invoices and drafts (if any) for those of the second beneficiary and to claim any difference due to him.

Assignment of proceeds

Article 55

The fact that a credit is not stated to be transferable shall not affect the beneficiary's right to assign any proceeds to which he may be, or may become, entitled under such credit, in accordance with the provisions of the applicable law.

Appendix 4

The ICC Uniform Rules for Demand Guarantees ICC Publication No 458

A. Scope and Application of the Rules

Article 1

These Rules apply to any demand guarantee and amendment thereto which a Guarantor (as hereinafter described) has been instructed to issue and which states that it is subject to the Uniform Rules for Demand Guarantees of the International Chamber of Commerce (Publication No 458) and are binding on all parties thereto except as otherwise expressly stated in the Guarantee or any amendment thereto.

B. Definitions and General Provisions

Article 2

a. For the purpose of these Rules, a demand guarantee (hereinafter referred to as 'Guarantee') means any guarantee, bond or other payment undertaking, however named or described, by a bank, insurance company or other body or person (hereinafter called 'the Guarantor') given in writing for the payment of money on presentation in conformity with the terms of the undertaking of a written demand for payment and such other document(s) (for example, a certificate by an architect or engineer, a judgment or an arbitral award) as may be specified in the Guarantee, such undertaking being given
i. at the request or on the instructions and under the liability of a party (hereinafter called 'the Principal'); or
ii. at the request or on the instructions and under the liability of a bank, insurance company or any other body or person (hereinafter 'the Instructing Party') acting on the instructions of a Principal
to another party (hereinafter the 'Beneficiary').

b. Guarantees by their nature are separate transactions from the contract(s) or tender conditions on which they may be based, and Guarantors are in no way concerned with or bound by such contract(s), or tender conditions, despite the inclusion of a reference to them in the Guarantee. The duty of a Guarantor under a Guarantee is to pay the sum or sums therein stated on the presentation of a written demand for payment and other documents specified in the Guarantee which appear on their face to be in accordance with the terms of the Guarantee.

c. For the purpose of these Rules, 'Counter-Guarantee' means any guarantee, bond or other payment undertaking of the Instructing Party, however named or described, given in writing for the payment of money to the Guarantor on presentation in conformity with the terms of the undertaking of a written demand for payment and other documents specified in the Counter-Guarantee which appear on their face to be in accordance with the terms of the Counter-Guarantee. Counter-Guarantees are by their nature separate trans-actions from the Guarantees to which they relate and from any underlying contract(s) or tender conditions, and Instructing Parties are in no way concerned with or bound by such Guarantees, con-tract(s) or tender conditions, despite the inclusion of a reference to them in the Counter-Guarantee.

d. The expressions 'writing' and 'written' shall include an authenticated teletransmission or tested electronic data interchange ('EDI') mes-sage equivalent thereto.

Article 3

All instructions for the issue of Guarantees and amendments thereto and Guarantees and amendments themselves should be clear and precise and should avoid excessive detail. Accordingly, all Guarantees should stipulate:

a. the Principal;

b. the Beneficiary;

c. the Guarantor;

d. the underlying transaction requiring the issue of the Guarantee;

e. the maximum amount payable and the currency in which it is payable;

f. the Expiry Date and/or Expiry Event of the Guarantee;

g. the terms for demanding payment;

h. any provision for reduction of the guarantee amount.

Article 4

The Beneficiary's right to make a demand under a Guarantee is not assignable unless expressly stated in the Guarantee or in an amendment thereto.
This Article shall not, however, affect the Beneficiary's right to assign any proceeds to which he may be, or may become, entitled under the Guarantee.

Article 5

All Guarantees and Counter-Guarantees are irrevocable unless other-wise indicated.

Article 6

A Guarantee enters into effect as from the date of its issue unless its terms expressly provide that such entry into effect is to be at a later date or is to be subject to conditions specified in the Guarantee and determinable by the Guarantor on the basis of any documents therein specified.

Article 7

a. Where a Guarantor has been given instructions for the issue of a Guarantee but the instructions are such that, if they were to be carried out, the Guarantor would by reason of law or regulation in the country of issue be unable to fulfil the terms of the Guarantee, the instructions shall not be executed and the Guarantor shall immediately inform the party who gave the Guarantor his instructions by telecommunication, or, if that is not possible, by other expeditious means, of the reasons for such inability and request appropriate instructions from that party.

b. Nothing in this Article shall oblige the Guarantor to issue a Guarantee where the Guarantor has not agreed to do so.

Article 8

A Guarantee may contain express provision for reduction by a specified or determinable amount or amounts on a specified date or dates or upon presentation to the Guarantor of the document(s) specified for this purpose in the Guarantee.

C. Liabilities and Responsibilities

Article 9

All documents specified and presented under a Guarantee, including the demand, shall be examined by the Guarantor with reasonable care to ascertain whether or not they appear on their face to conform with the terms of the Guarantee. Where such documents do not appear so to conform or appear on their face to be inconsistent with one another, they shall be refused.

Article 10

a. A Guarantor shall have a reasonable time within which to examine a demand under a Guarantee and to decide whether to pay or to refuse the demand.

b. If the Guarantor decides to refuse a demand, he shall immediately give notice thereof to the Beneficiary by teletransmission, or, if that is not possible, by other expeditious means. Any documents presented under the Guarantee shall be held at the disposal of the Beneficiary.

Article 11

Guarantors and Instructing Parties assume no liability or responsibility for the form, sufficiency, accuracy, genuineness, falsification, or legal effect of any document presented to them or for the general and/or particular statements made therein, nor for the good faith or acts or omissions of any person whomsoever.

Article 12

Guarantors and Instructing Parties assume no liability or responsibility for the consequences arising out of delay and/or loss in transit of any messages, letters, demands or documents, or for delay, mutilation or other errors arising in the transmission of any telecommunication. Guarantors and Instructing Parties assume no liability for errors in translation or interpretation of technical terms and reserve the right to transmit Guarantee texts or any parts thereof without translating them.

Article 13

Guarantors and Instructing Parties assume no liability or responsibility for consequences arising out of the interruption of their business by acts of God, riots, civil commotions, insurrections, wars or any other causes beyond their control or by strikes, lock-outs or industrial actions of whatever nature.

Article 14

a. Guarantors and Instructing Parties utilising the services of another party for the purpose of giving effect to the instructions of a Principal do so for the account and at the risk of that Principal.

b. Guarantors and Instructing Parties assume no liability or responsibility should the instructions they transmit not be carried out even if they have themselves taken the initiative in the choice of such other party.

c. The Principal shall be liable to indemnify the Guarantor or the Instructing Party, as the case may be, against all obligations and responsibilities imposed by foreign laws and usages.

Article 15

Guarantors and Instructing Parties shall not be excluded from liability or responsibility under the terms of Articles 11, 12, and 14 above for their failure to act in good faith and with reasonable care.

Article 16

A Guarantor is liable to the Beneficiary only in accordance with the terms specified in the Guarantee and any amendment(s) thereto and in these Rules, and up to an amount not exceeding that stated in the Guarantee and any amendment(s) thereto.

D. Demands

Article 17

Without prejudice to the terms of Article 10, in the event of a demand the Guarantor shall without delay so inform the Principal or, where applicable, his Instructing Party, and in that case the Instructing Party shall so inform the Principal.

Article 18

The amount payable under a Guarantee shall be reduced by the amount of any payment made by the Guarantor in satisfaction of a demand in respect thereof and, where the maximum amount payable under a Guarantee has been satisfied by payment and/or reduction, the Guarantee shall thereupon terminate whether or not the Guarantee and any amendment(s) thereto are returned.

Article 19

A demand shall be made in accordance with the terms of the Guarantee before its expiry, that is, on or before its Expiry Date and before any Expiry Event as defined an Article 22. In particular, all documents specified in the Guarantee for the purpose of the demand, and any statement required by Article 20, shall be presented to the Guarantor before its expiry at its place of issue; otherwise the demand shall be refused by the Guarantor.

Article 20

a. Any demand for payment under the Guarantee shall be in writing and shall (in addition to such other documents as may be specified in the Guarantee) be supported by a written statement (whether in the demand itself or in a separate document or documents accompanying the demand and referred to in it) stating:
i. that the Principal is in breach of his obligation(s) under the underlying contract(s) or, in the case of a tender guarantee, the tender conditions; and
ii. the respect in which the Principal is in breach.

b. Any demand under the Counter-Guarantee shall be supported by a written statement that the Guarantor has received a demand for payment under the Guarantee in accordance with its terms and with this Article.

c. Paragraph (a) of this Article applies except to the extent that it is expressly excluded by the terms of the Guarantee. Paragraph (b) of this Article applies except to the extent that it is expressly excluded by the terms of the Counter-Guarantee.

d. Nothing in this Article affects the application of Articles 2(b) and 2(c), 9 and 11.

Article 21

The Guarantor shall without delay transmit the Beneficiary's demand and any related documents to the Principal or, where applicable, to the Instructing Party for transmission to the Principal.

E.   Expiry Provisions

Article 22

Expiry of the time specified in a Guarantee for the presentation of demands shall be upon a specified calendar date ('Expiry Date') or upon presentation to the Guarantor of the document(s) specified for the purpose of expiry ('Expiry Event'). If both an Expiry Date and an Expiry Event are specified in a Guarantee, the Guarantee shall expire on whichever of the Expiry Date or Expiry Event occurs first, whether or not the Guarantee and any amendment(s) thereto are returned.

Article 23

Irrespective of any expiry provision contained therein, a Guarantee shall be cancelled on presentation to the Guarantor of the Guarantee itself or the Beneficiary's written statement of release from liability under the Guarantee, whether or not, in the latter case, the Guarantee or any amendments thereto are returned.

Article 24

Where a Guarantee has terminated by payment, expiry, cancellation or otherwise, retention of the Guarantee or of any amendments thereto shall not preserve any rights of the Beneficiary under the Guarantee.

Article 25

Where to the knowledge of the Guarantor the Guarantee has terminated by payment, expiry, cancellation or otherwise, or there has been a reduction of the total amount payable thereunder, the Guarantor shall without delay so notify the Principal or, where applicable, the Instructing Party and, in that case, the Instructing Party shall so notify the Principal.

Article 26

If the Beneficiary requests an extension of the validity of the Guarantee as an alternative to a demand for payment submitted in accordance with the terms and conditions of the Guarantee and these Rules, the Guarantor shall without delay so inform the party who gave the Guarantor his instructions. The Guarantor shall then suspend payment of the demand for such time as is reasonable to permit the Principal and the Beneficiary to reach agreement on the granting of such extension and for the Principal to arrange for such extension to be issued.

Unless an extension is granted within the time provided by the preceding paragraph, the Guarantor is obliged to pay the Beneficiary's conforming demand without requiring any further action on the Beneficiary's part. The Guarantor shall incur no liability (for interest or otherwise) should any payment to the Beneficiary be delayed as a result of the above-mentioned procedure.

Even if the Principal agrees to or requests such extension, it shall not be granted unless the Guarantor and the Instructing Party or Parties also agree thereto.

F. Governing Law and Jurisdiction

Article 27

Unless otherwise provided in the Guarantee or Counter-Guarantee, its governing law shall be that of the place of business of the Guarantor or Instructing Party (as the case may be), or, if the Guarantor or Instructing Party has more than one place of business, that of the branch that issued the Guarantee or Counter-Guarantee.

Article 28

Unless otherwise provided in the Guarantee or Counter-Guarantee, any dispute between the Guarantor and the Beneficiary relating to the Guarantee or between the Instructing Party and the Guarantor relating to the Counter-Guarantee shall be settled exclusively by the competent court of the country of the place of business of the Guarantor or Instructing Party (as the case may be), or, if the Guarantor or Instructing Party has more than one place of business, by the competent court of the country of the branch which issued the Guarantee or Counter-Guarantee.

Copyright © 1992 – International Chamber of Commerce (ICC)
Published in its official English version by
the International Chamber of Commerce, Paris
Available from ICC PUBLISHING SA, 38 Cours Albert 1er, 75008
Paris, France and from ICC UNITED KINGDOM,
14/15 Belgrave Square, London SW1X 8PS

Appendix 5

Standard Forms used by the Midland Bank plc in Connection with Documentary Credits

1. Request to open documentary credit – in blank.

2. Request to open, using Form 1, completed to request a negotiable credit to be advised through a foreign bank.

3. Advice of credit requested at 2 to advising bank, by mail, computer generated.

4. Advice as in Form 3, but by SWIFT, computer generated.

5. Advice to beneficiary of in-coming confirmed credit, computer generated. Details of the credit itself are provided by means of a photocopy of the credit as issued to the bank.

6. Advice of amendment to advising bank, computer generated.

7. Advice of amendment as advising bank, computer generated.

8. Advice to beneficiary of transferable credit.

9. Request for transfer of 8.

10. Advice of credit as transferred to second beneficiary.

Form 1: Request to open documentary credit – in blank

REQUEST TO OPEN AN IRREVOCABLE DOCUMENTARY CREDIT

MIDLAND
TRADE & INTERNATIONAL
BANKING SERVICES

TO : **Midland Bank plc** .... Branch / IBC

Date : ....

For Bank Use :
L/C No. .... D/T No. .... CID No. ....

| INDICATE CHOICE WITH | ☒ | REMAINDER TO BE TYPED OR COMPLETED IN BLACK INK IN BLOCK CAPITALS |

APPLICANT'S NAME

& ADDRESS

Applicant's reference (Not transmitted)

BENEFICIARY'S NAME

& ADDRESS

METHOD OF ADVICE ☐ TELETRANSMISSION (SWIFT OR TELEX) ☐ MAIL ☐ COURIER

TRANSFERABILITY THIS CREDIT IS TRANSFERABLE ☐ TO .... ONLY

EXPIRY DATE .... **PLACE** ....

LATEST DATE FOR SHIPMENT ....

PERIOD FOR PRESENTATION Documents to be presented within .... days of the date of the transport document but in any event within the credit validity.

AMOUNT CURRENCY .... **FIGURES** ....

WORDS ....

AMOUNT VARIATION + / – .... %

AVAILABLE BY ☐ PAYMENT ☐ ACCEPTANCE ☐ NEGOTIATION ☐ DEFERRED PAYMENT

WITH DRAFTS (if applicable) **DRAWN AT** ....

PARTSHIPMENTS ☐ ALLOWED ☐ PROHIBITED

TRANSHIPMENTS ☐ ALLOWED ☐ PROHIBITED

SHIPMENT / DESPATCH / TAKING IN CHARGE

FROM .... TO ....

INCOTERMS .... (ie EXW / FCA / FAS / FOB / CFR / CIF / CPT / CIP / DAF / DES / DEQ / DDU / DDP)

PLACE ....

QUANTITY & DESCRIPTION OF GOODS (avoiding excessive detail)

member HSBC **X** *group*

DOCUMENTS REQUIRED	☒ Invoice in .... copies

TRANSPORT DOCUMENT
EITHER :

☐ Full set "on board" Marine Bills of Lading

    ☐ to order & blank endorsed   ☐ to order of Applicant

OR :   ☐ Non- Negotiable Sea Waybill evidencing goods consigned to Applicant

OR :   ☐ Full set Multimodal Transport Document

    ☐ to order & blank endorsed   ☐ to order of Applicant

OR :   ☐ Air Waybill evidencing goods consigned to Applicant

    ☐ Air Waybill to show actual flight number & date

OR :   ☐ CMR (Road Transport)   }

    } evidencing goods consigned to Applicant

OR: ☐ Rail Consignment Note   }

OTHER: (specify) ☐ ....

TRANSPORT DOCUMENT TO BE MARKED ☐ Freight paid ☐ Freight payable at destination

NOTIFY PARTY (if any)

INSURANCE DOCUMENT
EITHER : ☐ Insurance Certificate ☐ Insurance Policy ☐ Insurance document not required

RISKS TO BE COVERED

☐ Institute Marine Cargo Clauses (A) ☐ Institute Air Cargo Clauses (A) ☒ War Risks

☐ Other Risks (specify) ....

INSURED AMOUNT

☐ Gross Invoice Amount Plus 10 % ☐ Other Amount (specify) ....

☐ Packing List in .... copies ☐ Certificate of .... Origin in .... copies

☐ Weight List in .... copies ☐ GSP Certificate of Origin Form 'A' in .... copies

OTHER DOCUMENTS (if any)

ADDITIONAL CONDITIONS (if any)

CHARGES
Unless otherwise stipulated all charges will be for the account of the applicant and will be taken in Sterling

Midland charges payable by : ☐ Applicant ☐ Beneficiary

Other charges payable by : ☐ Applicant ☐ Beneficiary

DRAWINGS under this credit are to be debited to our ☐ Sterling ☐ .... Currency Account No. ....

Please convert currency drawings utilising ☐ Spot rate ☐ Forward Contract ☐ Currency Option No. ....

Please open for our account a documentary credit in accordance with the abovementioned particulars and, except so far as otherwise expressly stated, subject to the Uniform Customs & Practice for Documentary Credits in operation at the time of issuance.

SIGNED For and on behalf of the Company .... as Applicant

Guidance Notes for Documentary Credit Applicants

MIDLAND
TRADE & INTERNATIONAL
BANKING SERVICES

General

All Documentary Credits (D/Cs) will be issued subject to the Uniform Customs and Practice for Documentary Credits (UCP) applicable at the time of issuance as published by the International Chamber of Commerce (ICC). The issuance of any credit will be at the discretion of the bank and subject to availability of a banking facility sanctioned for this purpose. It is emphasised that, in documentary credit operations, banks deal exclusively with documents and not with the underlying goods or services (UCP Article 4). The bank is not directly concerned with the proper fulfilment of the contract between buyer and seller.

Advising Bank	Wherever possible, offices of the HSBC Group will be utilised unless otherwise stipulated in 'additional conditions'.
Documents	All D/C terms and conditions should be covered by the documents called for in the credit; otherwise they will be disregarded. Documents which appear on their face to comply with the D/C terms and conditions will be accepted as due presentation under the credit.
UCP	As an applicant of a Documentary Credit you should be familiar with the requirements of UCP. Copies of the current publication may be obtained directly from the ICC upon payment of a fee.

Expiry

Date of Expiry	The latest date that documents may be presented by the beneficiary at the place of expiry. This should be *less than or equal to* the latest shipment date plus the period for presentation
Period for Presentation	The number of days between the shipment and expiry dates. Usually 21 days, but may depend upon how quickly the documents need to be available to you.
Place of Expiry	D/Cs will usually expire at the counters of the advising bank in the country of the beneficiary.

Availability

Negotiation	Used primarily for D/Cs in currencies different from that of the beneficiary's country. If you select this option, the D/C will be available for negotiation at the counters of the advising bank in the country of the beneficiary until the D/C expiry date. Your account will be debited upon presentation to us of conforming documents (D/C payable at sight) or on the maturity date (D/C payable at usance). You should allow up to 21 days after expiry for the transmission of documents to the UK.
Acceptance / Deferred Payment	Select this option where you have agreed with your supplier extended terms of payment (usance period). In the case of acceptances, drafts will be drawn on the advising bank and settled by them at maturity. Deferred Payment credits have the same effect but drafts are not drawn. This can help to reduce the beneficiary's liability to stamp duty in countries where this is still levied on this type of transaction. In both cases your account is debited on the maturity date. (See also "Settlement in Foreign Currency")
Payment	The D/C will be available at the counters of the advising bank for payment of sight drafts drawn on them until the expiry date. Your account will be debited upon presentation to us of conforming documents. Allow up to 21 days after expiry for the transmission of documents to the UK. Please note that you are responsible for any interest costs between the date payment is effected in the foreign centre to the value date of our remittance in settlement of the presentation. Any such interest will be charged at the bank's current overdraft rate for the currency concerned.
	Alternatively, you may permit the advising bank to claim from us telegraphically with value date three working days after presentation of documents to them. In this case your account will be debited on the value date and you will not pay any interest costs. However, it is most unlikely that the documents will have arrived at the time your account is debited.
Other D/C Types	Appropriate advice will be provided upon request.
Transferability	Any further instructions and/or restrictions on transfer should be incorporated in "Additional Conditions".
Settlement in Foreign Currency	In order to effect timely settlement of drawings, your settlement instructions should appear on the application form. In any event, for maturing payments, we require your settlement instructions at least two working days prior to the due date. If you require advice on currency hedging products please contact your local International Banking Centre.
Beneficiaries in the UK	All such credits will be advised directly to the beneficiary. We believe this to be in the best interests of all parties.
Charges	Unless otherwise stipulated, *all* bank charges will be for account of the applicant. The most common commercial practice is for issuing bank charges to be borne by the applicant with foreign bank charges being for account of the beneficiary. Please ensure that your application form is correctly marked. Please note that Midland Bank charges will be calculated in Sterling.

Amendments to the D/C Terms and Conditions

Forms are available upon request for the provision of your amendment instructions to the bank.

Any amendment must be agreed by all parties to the credit. It should be noted that an amendment may be rejected by the beneficiary at any time prior to presentation of documents.

Any increase or reduction in the value of the credit should be fully explained. For example, an increase may reflect an increase in the quantity of goods or in the unit price.

Please ensure that any alterations made to the terms and conditions of the credit are fully reflected in amendments to the documents called for by the credit.

member HSBC **X** *group*

Form 2: Request to open, using Form 1, completed to request a negotiable credit to be advised through a foreign bank

REQUEST TO OPEN AN IRREVOCABLE DOCUMENTARY CREDIT

TO : Midland Bank plc Documentary Credits Department. Branch / IBC

Date : 13 January 1994

MIDLAND
TRADE & INTERNATIONAL
BANKING SERVICES

For Bank Use :			
L/C No.	D/T No.	CID No.	

INDICATE CHOICE WITH [X] REMAINDER TO BE TYPED OR COMPLETED IN BLACK INK IN BLOCK CAPITALS

APPLICANT'S NAME & ADDRESS
Buyers (UK) Ltd
Lower Street, London SE1

Applicant's reference (Not transmitted) PO/HK/9400123/1244

BENEFICIARY'S NAME & ADDRESS
International Sellers Limited
35th Floor, Two Exchange Square,
Connaught Place, Hong Kong

METHOD OF ADVICE [x] TELETRANSMISSION (SWIFT OR TELEX)   [ ] MAIL   [ ] COURIER

TRANSFERABILITY THIS CREDIT IS TRANSFERABLE [ ] TO .... ONLY

EXPIRY DATE 20 May 1994   **PLACE** Hong Kong

LATEST DATE FOR SHIPMENT 10 May 1994

PERIOD FOR PRESENTATION Documents to be presented within 10 days of the date of the transport document but in any event within the credit validity.

AMOUNT   CURRENCY GBP   **FIGURES** £150,000.00
WORDS One hundred and fifty thousand Pounds Sterling

AMOUNT VARIATION   + / - .... %

AVAILABLE BY [ ] PAYMENT   [ ] ACCEPTANCE   [X] NEGOTIATION   [ ] DEFERRED PAYMENT
WITH DRAFTS (if applicable) DRAWN AT Sight

PARTSHIPMENTS [ ] ALLOWED   [X] PROHIBITED
TRANSHIPMENTS [X] ALLOWED   [ ] PROHIBITED

SHIPMENT / DESPATCH / TAKING IN CHARGE
FROM Hong Kong Port   **TO** Any UK Port

INCOTERMS FOB   (ie EXW / FCA / FAS / FOB / CFR / CIF / CPT / CIP / DAF / DES / DEQ / DDU / DDP)
PLACE Hong Kong

QUANTITY & DESCRIPTION OF GOODS (avoiding excessive detail)
15000 Pieces Ladies Viscose Blouses as per Order No. 1244

member HSBC **⟨X⟩** *group*

DOCUMENTS REQUIRED	☒	Signed Commercial Invoice in .... copies

TRANSPORT DOCUMENT
EITHER : ☒ **Full set "on board" Marine Bills of Lading**
       ☒ to order & blank endorsed   ☐ to order of Applicant

OR : ☐ **Non- Negotiable Sea Waybill** evidencing goods consigned to Applicant

OR : ☐ **Full set Multimodal Transport Document**
       ☐ to order & blank endorsed   ☐ to order of Applicant

OR : ☐ **Air Waybill** evidencing goods consigned to Applicant
       ☐ Air Waybill to show actual flight number & date

OR : ☐ **CMR (Road Transport)**   }
                       } evidencing goods consigned to Applicant
OR: ☐ **Rail Consignment Note**   }

OTHER: (specify) ☐ ....

TRANSPORT DOCUMENT TO BE MARKED   ☐ Freight paid   ☒ **Freight payable at destination**

NOTIFY PARTY (if any)

INSURANCE DOCUMENT
EITHER : ☐ **Insurance Certificate**   ☐ **Insurance Policy**   ☒ **Insurance document not required**

RISKS TO BE COVERED
☐ Institute Marine Cargo Clauses (A)   ☐ Institute Air Cargo Clauses (A)   ☒ War Risks
☐ Other Risks (specify) ....

INSURED AMOUNT
☐ Gross Invoice Amount Plus 10 %   ☐ Other Amount (specify) ....

☒ Packing List in 3 copies	☐ Certificate of .... Origin in .... copies
☐ Weight List in .... copies	☒ GSP Certificate of Origin Form 'A' in .... copies

OTHER DOCUMENTS (if any)

ADDITIONAL CONDITIONS (if any)

CHARGES
Unless otherwise stipulated all charges will be for the account of the applicant and will be taken in Sterling

Midland charges payable by : ☒ Applicant   ☐ Beneficiary
Other charges payable by : ☐ Applicant   ☒ Beneficiary

DRAWINGS under this credit are to be debited to our ☒ Sterling ☐ .... Currency Account No. 12345678

Please convert currency drawings utilising ☐ Spot rate   ☐ Forward Contract   ☐ Currency Option No. ....

Please open for our account a documentary credit in accordance with the abovementioned particulars and, except so far as otherwise expressly stated, subject to the Uniform Customs & Practice for Documentary Credits in operation at the time of issuance.

SIGNED For and on behalf of the Company .... Buyers (UK) Ltd .... as Applicant

Form 3: **Advice of credit requested at 2 to advising bank, by mail, computer generated**
(Note Form 2 asks for teletransmission which is met by Form 4)

OUR REFERENCE: 09L/103733   PAGE: 1

DOCUMENTARY CREDITS DEPARTMENT   JANUARY 14, 1994
P O BOX 181
27-32 POULTRY
LONDON EC2P 2BX

IRREVOCABLE DOCUMENTARY CREDIT

TO:
HONGKONG AND SHANGHAI BKG CORP LTD
GPO BOX 64
1 QUEENS ROAD CENTRAL
HONG KONG

WE ARE PLEASED HEREBY TO ISSUE OUR IRREVOCABLE DOCUMENTARY CREDIT
09L/103733 AS DETAILED BELOW:

BENEFICIARY: APPLICANT:

INTEPNATIONAL SELLERS LIMITED   BUYERS (UK) LTD
35TH FLOOR, TWO EXCHANGE SQUARE   LOWER STREET
CONNAUGHT PLACE   LONDON SE1
HONG KONG

DATE OF EXPIRY: MAY 20, 1994   PLACE OF EXPIRY: HONG KONG

AMOUNT:GBP 150,000.00
(ONE HUNDRED AND FIFTY THOUSAND AND 00/100'S POUNDS STERLING)

PARTIAL SHIPMENTS: NOT ALLOWED   TRANSHIPMENTS: ALLOWED

SHIPMENT FROM: HONG KONG PORT
FOR TRANSHIPMENT TO: ANY UK PORT
NO LATER THAN: MAY 10, 1994

THIS CREDIT IS AVAILABLE WITH ANY BANK BY NEGOTIATION OF DRAFTS DRAWN BY
THE BENEFICIARY AT SIGHT ON MIDLAND BANK PLC P O BOX 181, 27-32 POULTRY
LONDON EC2 2BX (AND NO OTHER ADDRESS) FOR 100% OF INVOICE VALUE MARKED
"DRAWN UNDER DOCUMENTARY CREDIT NUMBER 09L/103733 OF MIDLAND BANK PLC"
ACCOMPANIED BY THE FOLLOWING DOCUMENTS:

FULL SET OF ORIGINAL CLEAN ON BOARD OCEAN BILLS OF LADING ISSUED TO ORDER
AND BLANK ENDORSED MARKED FREIGHT PAYABLE AT DESTINATION.

SIGNED COMMERCIAL INVOICE

GSP CERTIFICATE OF ORIGIN FORM A

PACKING LIST AND 2 COPIES

GOODS DESCRIPTION:

15000 PIECES LADIES VISCOSE BLOUSES AS PER ORDER NO. 1244

TERMS OF DELIVERY: FOB HONG KONG

DOCUMENTS TO BE PRESENTED WITHIN 10 DAYS AFTER THE ISSUANCE OF THE
TRANSPORT DOCUMENT(S) BUT WITHIN THE VALIDITY OF THE CREDIT.

WE ARE INFORMED THAT INSURANCE WILL BE ARRANGED OUTSIDE OF THE CREDIT
TERMS.

ALL CHARGES OTHER THAN OUR OWN ARE FOR THE ACCOUNT OF THE BENEFICIARY.

WE HEREBY ENGAGE WITH DRAWERS AND/OR BONA FIDE HOLDERS THAT DRAFTS DRAWN
AND NEGOTIATED IN CONFORMITY WITH THE TERMS OF THIS CREDIT WILL BE
HONOURED ON PRESENTATION, AND THAT DRAFTS ACCEPTED WITHIN THE TERMS OF
THIS CREDIT WILL BE HONOURED AT MATURITY.

EXCEPT SO FAR AS OTHERWISE EXPRESSLY STATED THIS CREDIT IS SUBJECT TO THE
UNIFORM CUSTOMS AND PRACTICE FOR DOCUMENTARY CREDITS 1993 REVISION,
I.C.C. PUBLICATION NO. 500

BANK TO BANK INSTRUCTIONS:

PLEASE ADVISE THIS CREDIT TO THE BENEFICIARY WITHOUT ADDING YOUR
CONFIRMATION.

REMIT ALL DOCUMENTS TO US BY REGISTERED AIRMAIL.

COMMUNICATIONS REGARDING THIS CREDIT SHOULD BE SENT TO OUR ABOVE ADDRESS.
TELEPHONE: 071 260 5978 TELEX: 8814463 MIDOCR G FAX 071 260 4640.
KINDLY ENSURE THAT YOU ALWAYS QUOTE OUR REFERENCE NUMBER FOR THIS CREDIT.

　　　　　　　　　　　AUTHORISED SIGNATURE(S)

THIS DOCUMENT CONSISTS OF 2 PAGE(S)

Registered in England (No. 14259)
Registered Office Poultry London EC2P 2BX
4183-8L (09/92) IS

member HSBC **group**

Form 4:   Advice as in Form 3, but by SWIFT, computer generated

```
SWIFT700 - ISSUE OF A DOCUMENTARY CREDIT

REF: 09L/103733                                              PAGE 1

:TO : RECEIVER`S SWIFT ADDRESS
:    : HSBCHKHHHKH
:    :
:    : RECEIVERS CID:
:    : HK1
:    :
:    : RECEIVER`S NAME AND ADDRESS:
:    : HONGKONG AND SHANGHAI BKG CORP LTD
:    : GPO BOX 64
:    : 1 QUEENS ROAD CENTRAL
:    : HONG KONG
:    :
:27 : SEQUENCE OF TOTAL
:    : 1/1
:    :
:40A: FORM OF DOCUMENTARY CREDIT
:    : IRREVOCABLE
:    :
:20 : DOCUMENTARY CREDIT NUMBER
:    : 09L/103733
:    :
:31C: DATE OF ISSUE
:    : 940114
:    :
:31D: DATE AND PLACE OF EXPIRY
:    : HONG KONG
:    : 940520
:51D: APPLICANT BANK
:    :
:    :
:    :
:    :
:50 : APPLICANT
:    : BUYERS (UK) LTD
:    : LOWER STREET
:    : LONDON SE1
:    :
:59 : BENEFICIARY
:    : INTERNATIONAL SELLERS LIMITED
:    : 35TH FLOOR, TWO EXCHANGE SQUARE
:    : CONNAUGHT PLACE
:    : HONG KONG
:    :
:32B: CURRENCY CODE, AMOUNT
:    : GBP 150,000.00
:    :
:39B: MAXIMUM CREDIT AMOUNT
:    : MAXIMUM
:    :
:41D: AVAILABLE WITH...BY...
:    : FREELY NEGOTIABLE AT ANY BANK
:    : BY NEGOTIATION
:    :
```

```
:42C: DRAFTS AT...
:   : SIGHT
:   :
:42A: DRAWEE AT ...
:   : MIDLAND BANK PLC, P O BOX 181, POULTRY, LONDON EC2P 2BX
:   :
:43P: PARTIAL SHIPMENTS
:   : NOT ALLOWED
:   :
:43T: TRANSHIPMENT
:   : ALLOWED
:   :
:44A: LOADING ON BOARD/DISPATCH/TAKING CHARGE AT/FROM ...
:   : HONG KONG PORT
:   :
:44B: FOR TRANSPORTATION TO ...
:   : AN UK PORT
:   :
:44C: LATEST DATE OF SHIPMENT
:   : 940510
:   :
:45A: SHIPMENT OF (GOODS)
:   :
:   : 15000 PIECES LADIES VISCOSE BLOUSES AS PER ORDER NO. 1244
:   : TERMS OF DELIVERY: FOB HONG KONG
:   :
:46A: DOCUMENTS REQUIRED
:   :
:   : +FULL SET OF ORIGINAL CLEAN ON BOARD OCEAN BILLS OF LADING ISSUED
:   : TO ORDER AND BLANK ENDORSED MARKED FREIGHT PAYABLE AT DESTINATION
:   :
:   : +SIGNED COMMERCIAL INVOICE
:   :
:   : +GSP CERTIFICATE OF ORIGIN FORM A
:   :
:   : +PACKING LIST AND 2 COPIES
:   :
:   :
:47A: ADDITIONAL CONDITIONS
:   :
:   : WE ARE INFORMED THAT INSURANCE WILL BE ARRANGED OUTSIDE OF THE
:   : CREDIT TERMS.
:   :
:71B: CHARGES
:   :
:   :
:   : ALL CHARGES OTHER THAN OUR OWN ARE
:   : FOR THE ACCOUNT OF THE BENEFICIARY.
:   :
:48 : PERIOD FOR PRESENTATION
:   :
:   : DOCUMENTS TO BE PRESENTED WITHIN 10
:   : DAYS AFTER THE ISSUANCE OF THE
:   : TRANSPORT DOCUMENT(S) BUT WITHIN
:   : THE VALIDITY OF THE CREDIT.
```

Registered in England (No. 14259)
Registered Office Poultry London EC2P 2BX
4183-8L (09/92) IS

member HSBC **⊕** *group*

```
:49 : CONFIRMATION INSTRUCTIONS
:   : WITHOUT
:   :
:53D: REIMBURSEMENT BANK
:   :
:   :
:   :
:   :
:   :
:78 : INSTRUCTIONS TO THE PAYING/ACCEPTING/NEGOTIATING BANK
:   : PLEASE REMIT ALL DOCUMENTS BY REGISTERED AIRMAIL
:   :
:   :
:   :
:57D: ADVISE THROUGH BANK
:   :
:   :
:   :
:   :
:   :
:72 : BANK TO BANK INFORMATION
:   : PLEASE REMIT ALL DOCUMENTS TO
:   : MIDLAND BANK PLC
:   : DOCUMENTARY CREDITS DEPARTMENT
:   : P O BOX 181
:   : 27-32 POULTRY
:   : LONDON EC2P 2BX
:   :
```

Registered in England (No. 14259)
Registered Office Poultry London EC2P 2BX
4183-8L (09/92) IS

member HSBC **⟨X⟩** *group*

Form 5:   Advice to beneficiary of in-coming confirmed credit, computer generated. Details of the credit itself are provided by means of a photocopy of the credit as issued to the bank

OUR REFERENCE: 09L/103734   PAGE: 1

DOCUMENTARY CREDITS DEPARTMENT   MARCH 14, 1994
P O BOX 181
27-32 POULTRY
LONDON EC2P 2BX

ADVICE OF CONFIRMED IRREVOCABLE DOCUMENTARY CREDIT

BENEFICIARY: ISSUING BANK:

INTERNATIONAL SELLERS LTD   ANY BANK
LOWER STREET   ANY TOWN
LONDON   ANYWHERE
SE1

                                  THEIR REFERENCE: EXP/LC/1
                                  ISSUE DATE: MARCH 10, 1994

APPLICANT:
INTERNATIONAL BUYERS LTD
35TH FLOOR, TWO EXCHANGE SQUARE
CONNAUGHT PLACE
HONG KONG

                                  AMOUNT: GBP 50,000.00
                                  (FIFTY THOUSAND AND 00/100'S POUNDS
                                  STERLING)

                                  DATE OF EXPIRY: APRIL 20, 1994
                                  PLACE OF EXPIRY: UK

WE ARE PLEASED TO ADVISE YOU OF AN IRREVOCABLE CREDIT OPENED IN YOUR
FAVOUR, DETAILS OF WHICH ARE ATTACHED.

THIS ADVICE, TOGETHER WITH ITS ATTACHMENTS, (AND ANY SUBSEQUENT
AMENDMENTS) WILL MAKE UP THE IRREVOCABLE CREDIT IN YOUR FAVOUR AND MUST
ACCOMPANY ALL PRESENTATIONS. PLEASE READ CAREFULLY ALL THE TERMS AND
CONDITIONS OF THE CREDIT AND, IF YOU DO NOT FULLY AGREE WITH ANY OF THEM,
CONTACT INTERNATIONAL BUYERS LTD 35TH FLOOR, TWO EXCHANGE SQUARE CONNAUGHT
PLACE HONG KONG IMMEDIATELY.

THIS CREDIT BEARS THE CONFIRMATION OF MIDLAND BANK PLC AND WE UNDERTAKE
THAT PRESENTATIONS TO US IN COMPLIANCE WITH THE CREDIT TERMS AND
CONDITIONS WILL BE HONOURED.

THE CREDIT IS AVAILABLE WITH MIDLAND BANK PLC BY PAYMENT OF YOUR DRAFTS AT
SIGHT ON MIDLAND BANK PLC ACCOMPANIED BY DOCUMENTS AS STIPULATED BY THE
CREDIT.

DOCUMENTS FOR THIS CREDIT MAY BE PRESENTED AT THIS OFFICE OR AT ANY OF OUR
AUTHORISED BRANCHES. WHEN PRESENTING DOCUMENTS KINDLY QUOTE OUR REFERENCE
NUMBER AND INCLUDE ONE ADDITIONAL COPY OF YOUR INVOICE FOR OUR RECORDS.

Registered in England (No. 14259)
Registered Office Poultry London EC2P 2BX
4183-8L (09/92) IS

member HSBC **(X)** *group*

MIDLAND

OUR REFERENCE 09L/103734   PAGE: 2

THE DESCRIPTION OF THE MERCHANDISE ON THE INVOICE(S) MUST APPEAR EXACTLY
AS SHOWN IN THE DOCUMENTARY CREDIT.

IF, DUE TO DISCREPANCIES, WE ARE UNABLE TO HONOUR DOCUMENTS WHEN
PRESENTED, WE RESERVE THE RIGHT TO MAKE A HANDLING CHARGE FOR THE
ADDITIONAL COSTS INVOLVED IN DEALING WITH SUCH PRESENTATIONS.

CHARGES ARE FOR YOUR ACCOUNT INCLUDING:-

ADVISING COMMISSION   GBP   40.00
CONFIRMATION COMMISION   GBP   62.50

PAYMENT COMMISSION OF 0.1% MINIMUM GBP 50.00 PER PAYMENT.

WE SHALL BE PLEASED TO RECEIVE YOUR REMITTANCE IN SETTLEMENT OF THE ABOVE
CHARGES, ALTERNATIVELY THEY WILL BE DEDUCTED FROM THE PROCEEDS FOLLOWING
PRESENTATION OF DOCUMENTS.

EXCEPT SO FAR AS OTHERWISE EXPRESSLY STATED THIS CREDIT IS SUBJECT TO THE
UNIFORM CUSTOMS AND PRACTICE FOR DOCUMENTARY CREDITS, 1993 REVISION,
I.C.C. PUBLICATION NO. 500.

COMMUNICATIONS REGARDING THIS CREDIT SHOULD BE SENT TO OUR ABOVE ADDRESS.
TELEPHONE: 071 260 5978 TELEX: 8814463 MIDOCR G FAX 071 260 4640.
KINDLY ENSURE THAT YOU ALWAYS QUOTE OUR REFERENCE NUMBER FOR THIS CREDIT.

--------------------------   ----------------------------------
                          AUTHORISED SIGNATURE(S)

                   THIS DOCUMENT CONSISTS OF 2 PAGE(S)

Registered in England (No. 14259)
Registered Office Poultry London EC2P 2BX
4183-8L (09/92) IS

                                                    member HSBC ⟨X⟩ *group*

Form 6:   Advice of amendment to advising bank, computer generated

```
OUR REFERENCE 09L/103733                                    PAGE: 1
------------------------

DOCUMENTARY CREDITS DEPARTMENT              JANUARY 28, 1994
P O BOX 181
27-32 POULTRY
LONDON EC2P 2BX

AMENDMENT TO IRREVOCABLE DOCUMENTARY CREDIT
-------------------------------------------

TO:

HONGKONG AND SHANGHAI BKG CORP LTD
GPO BOX 64
1 QUEENS ROAD CENTRAL
HONG KONG


BENEFICIARY:                        APPLICANT:

INTERNATIONAL SELLERS LIMITED       BUYERS (UK) LIMITED
35TH FLOOR, TWO EXCHANGE SQUARE     LOWER STREET
CONNAUGHT PLACE                     LONDON SE1
HONG KONG

THIS AMENDMENT IS TO BE CONSIDERED AS PART OF THE ABOVE CREDIT AND MUST BE
ATTACHED THERETO.

WE ARE PLEASED TO AMEND OUR DOCUMENTARY CREDIT NUMBER 09L/103733 DATED
JANUARY 14, 1994 AS FOLLOWS:

THE AMOUNT OF THIS CREDIT IS DECREASED BY GBP 25,000.00 TO A TOTAL OF GBP
125,000.00.

THE GOODS DESCRIPTION IS AMENDED TO READ:
12500 PIECES LADIES POLYESTER BLOUSES AS PER ORDER NO.1244


THIS AMENDMENT IS SUBJECT TO THE BENEFICIARIES CONSENT OF WHICH KINDLY
ADVISE US BY SWIFT.

ALL OTHER TERMS AND CONDITIONS REMAIN UNCHANGED.

PLEASE ADVISE THE BENEFICIARY ACCORDINGLY.

COMMUNICATIONS REGARDING THIS CREDIT SHOULD BE SENT TO OUR ABOVE ADDRESS.
TELEPHONE: 071 260 5978   TELEX 8814463   MIDOCR G   FAX: 071 260 4640.
KINDLY ENSURE THAT YOU ALWAYS QUOTE OUR REFERENCE NUMBER FOR THIS CREDIT.


-----------------------------------------------------------------------
                      AUTHORISED SIGNATURE(S)
```

Registered in England (No. 14259)
Registered Office Poultry London EC2P 2BX
4183-8L (09/92) iS

member HSBC ⟨X⟩ *group*

Form 7:   Advice of amendment as advising bank, computer generated

 **MIDLAND**

```
OUR REFERENCE 09L/103734                                    PAGE: 1
------------------------

DOCUMENTARY CREDITS DEPARTMENT                 APRIL 10, 1994
P O BOX 181
27-32 POULTRY
LONDON EC2P 2BX

ADVICE OF AMENDMENT TO CONFIRMED IRREVOCABLE DOCUMENTARY CREDIT
----------------------------------------------------------------


BENEFICIARY:                       ISSUING BANK:

INTERNATIONAL SELLERS LTD          ANY BANK
LOWER STREET                       ANY TOWN
LONDON                             ANYWHERE
SE1

                                   THEIR REFERENCE: EXP/LC/1
                                   AMENDMENT DATE: APRIL 10, 1994

APPLICANT:
INTERNATIONAL BUYERS LTD
35TH FLOOR, TWO EXCHANGE SQUARE
CONNAUGHT PLACE
HONG KONG

AT THE REQUEST OF ANY BANK, ANY TOWN, ANYWHERE WE ARE PLEASED TO
ADVISE YOU OF THE FOLLOWING AMENDMENT(S) TO THE ABOVE DOCUMENTARY CREDIT.

THE EXPIRY DATE OF THIS CREDIT IS NOW MAY 22, 1994.

THE LATEST SHIPMENT DATE IS NOW MAY 1, 1994.


THIS AMENDMENT IS CONSIDERED AN INTEGRAL PART OF THE ABOVE CREDIT AND
SHOULD BE ATTACHED TO THE ORIGINAL CREDIT.

ALL OTHER TERMS AND CONDITIONS REMAIN UNCHANGED.

CHARGES ARE FOR YOUR ACCOUNT AND ARE AS FOLLOWS:

AMENDMENT COMMISSION              GBP      40.00


COMMUNICATIONS REGARDING THIS CREDIT SHOULD BE SENT TO OUR ABOVE ADDRESS.
TELEPHONE: 071 260 5978  TELEX 8814463  MIDOCR G  FAX: 071 260 4640.
KINDLY ENSURE THAT YOU ALWAYS QUOTE OUR REFERENCE NUMBER FOR THIS CREDIT.


-----------------------------------------------------------------------
                        AUTHORISED SIGNATURE(S)
```

Registered in England (No. 14259)
Registered Office Poultry London EC2P 2BX
4183-8L (09/92) IS

member HSBC **⟨X⟩** *group*

Form 8: Advice to beneficiary of transferable credit

```
OUR REFERENCE 09L/103750                                    PAGE: 1
------------------------

DOCUMENTARY CREDITS DEPARTMENT          MARCH 14, 1994
P O BOX 181
27-32 POULTRY
LONDON EC2P 2BX

IRREVOCABLE DOCUMENTARY CREDIT
------------------------------

TO:

BUYERS (UK) LIMITED
LOWER STREET
LONDON SE1


WE ARE PLEASED HEREBY TO ISSUE OUR IRREVOCABLE TRANSFERABLE DOCUMENTARY
CREDIT 09L/103750 AS DETAILED BELOW:


APPLICANT:

ASW MUSIC SUPPLIES LIMITED
HIGH STREET
BURTON ON TRENT
STAFFS DE15 1YZ

DATE OF EXPIRY: DECEMBER 31, 1994    PLACE OF EXPIRY: UNITED KINGDOM

AMOUNT: GBP 250,000.00
(TWO HUNDRED FIFTY THOUSAND AND 00/100`S POUNDS STERLING)

PARTIAL SHIPMENTS: NOT ALLOWED     TRANSHIPMENTS: ALLOWED

SHIPMENT FROM: HONG KONG
FOR TRANSPORTATION TO: LONDON
NO LATER THAN: DECEMBER 21, 1994


THIS CREDIT IS AVAILABLE WITH ANY BANK BY NEGOTIATION OF YOUR DRAFTS DRAWN
AT SIGHT ON MIDLAND BANK PLC P O BOX 181, 27-32 POULTRY, LONDON EC2 2BX
(AND NO OTHER. ADDRESS) FOR 100% OF INVOICE VALUE MARKED "DRAWN UNDER
DOCUMENTARYCREDIT NUMBER 09L/103750 OF MIDLAND BANK PLC" ACCOMPANIED BY THE
FOLLOWING DOCUMENTS:


FULL SET OF ORIGINAL SHIPPED ON BOARD OCEAN BILLS OF LADING ISSUED TO
ORDER AND BLANK ENDORSED MARKED FREIGHT COLLECT

ORIGINAL SIGNED COMMERCIAL INVOICE AND TWO COPIES
```

Registered in England (No. 14259)
Registered Office Poultry London EC2P 2BX
4183-8L (09/92) iS

member HSBC ⊗ *group*

MIDLAND

OUR REFERENCE 09L/103750

ORIGINAL GSP CERTIFICATE OF ORIGIN FORM A

ORIGINAL AND 2 COPIES OF PACKING LIST

GOODS DESCRIPTION :

10 BABY GRAND PIANOS AS PER ORDER NO 468231 DATED 01/06/94

TERMS OF DELIVERY : FOB HONG KONG

DOCUMENTS TO BE PRESENTED WITHIN 21 DAYS AFTER THE ISSUANCE OF THE
TRANSPORT DOCUMENT(S) BUT WITHIN THE VALIDITY OF THE CREDIT.

WE ARE INFORMED THAT INSURANCE WILL BE ARRANGED OUTSIDE OF THE CREDIT
TERMS.

THIS CREDIT IS TRANSFERABLE. IN THE EVENT THAT YOU WISH US TO
TRANSFER THIS CREDIT, PLEASE COMPLETE THE ATTACHED FORM AND FORWARD IT
TOGETHER WITH YOUR REMITTANCE FOR TRANSFER COMMISSION AND THE ORIGINAL
CREDIT ADVICE FOR ENDORSEMENT, EITHER TO OURSELVES AT THE ABOVE ADDRESS
OR, IF YOU PREFER, TO ANY OF OUR AUTHORISED BRANCHES INDICATED ON THE
ATTACHED LIST.

ALL CHARGES OTHER THAN OUR OWN ARE FOR ACCOUNT OF THE BENEFICIARY.

WE HEREBY ENGAGE WITH DRAWERS AND/OR BONA FIDE HOLDERS THAT DRAFTS DRAWN
AND NEGOTIATED IN CONFORMITY WITH THE TERMS OF THIS CREDIT WILL BE
HONOURED ON PRESENTATION, AND THAT DRAFTS ACCEPTED WITHIN THE TERMS OF
THIS CREDIT WILL BE HONOURED AT MATURITY.

EXCEPT SO FAR AS OTHERWISE EXPRESSLY STATED THIS CREDIT IS SUBJECT TO THE
UNIFORM CUSTOMS AND PRACTICE FOR DOCUMENTARY CREDITS, 1993 REVISION,
I.C.C. PUBLICATION NO. 500

COMMUNICATIONS REGARDING THIS CREDIT SHOULD BE SENT TO OUR ABOVE ADDRESS.
TELEPHONE: 071 260 5978   TELEX: 8814463 MIDOCR G   FAX: 071 260 4640
KINDLY ENSURE THAT YOU ALWAYS QUOTE OUR REFERENCE NUMBER FOR THIS CREDIT.

                    AUTHORISED SIGNATURE(S)

THIS DOCUMENT CONSISTS OF 2 PAGE(S)

member HSBC **⊕** *group*

Registered in England (No. 14259)
Registered Office: Poultry London EC2P 2BX

Form 9:   Request for transfer of 8

Request for Transfer of Documentary Credit

TO: Midland Bank plc Documentary Credits Dept
London

Date   17 March 1994

MIDLAND
TRADE & INTERNATIONAL
BANKING SERVICES

Documentary Credit No. _____   **Midland Advice No. 09L/** 103750 _____

Issuing Bank   __Midland Bank plc_____

As beneficiary of the above-mentioned transferable credit, we request that you make this credit available to :

(1) International Sellers Limited, 35th Floor, Two Exchange Square
Connaught Place, Hong Kong
upon the same terms and conditions as the original credit with the exception of the following:-

(2) Amount: £200,000.00   (Words Two hundred thousand Pounds only   )

(3) Quantity (if part shipments allowed)   Unit price

(4) Valid in Hong Kong   until   20 December   1994

(5) Latest shipment date   10 December   1994

(6) Period for presentation in accordance with UCP Article 43.   10   Days.

(7) The percentage of insurance cover required under the transferred credit is increased to   %.

(8) We request you to notify the transferee by: [X] Airmail   [ ] Courier   [ ] Teletransmission

(9) We [X] intend   [ ] do not intend   to substitute our own invoices for those of the transferee
and provide our draft for the difference in value, if any.

(10) In accordance with UCP sub-article 48 (d), amendments to the original credit   [ ] require   [X] do not require
our consent before being advised to the above-mentioned second beneficiary.

(11) Any irregularities in documents presented   [X] must   [ ] need not   be referred to us before you take any action.

It is understood and agreed that these instructions are irrevocable on our part and that the transferred credit will be subject to
the Uniform Customs and Practice for Documentary Credits (1993 Revision) International Chamber of Commerce
Publication No.500, with particular reference to Article 48.

For and on behalf of   Buyers (UK) Limited

Contact Name:-   R G Preston
Telephone No:-   071-260-4017
Fax No:-   071-260-9998

Note : The following requirements must also be fulfilled before any advice of transfer is issued by Midland.

- All Requests for Transfer must be accompanied by the original L/C advice, together with any attachments and
amendments.

- Receipt by the Bank of the company's remittance (cleared funds) in respect of our charges as follows :
  - Transfer commission calculated at the rate of 0.5% of the amount transferred. Minimum £150
  - Transmission costs   -   Teletransmission £30   Courier £20
  - All other outstanding charges advised to you to date

Form 10:   Advice of credit as transferred to second beneficiary

```
OUR REFERENCE 09L/103751                                    PAGE: 1
------------------------

DOCUMENTARY CREDITS DEPARTMENT              MARCH 18, 1994
P O BOX 181
27-32 POULTRY
LONDON EC2P 2BX

IRREVOCABLE DOCUMENTARY CREDIT
------------------------------

TO:

HONGKONG AND SHANGHAI BKG CORP LTD
GPO BOX 64
1 QUEENS ROAD CENTRAL
HONG KONG

WE ARE PLEASED HEREBY TO ISSUE OUR IRREVOCABLE DOCUMENTARY CREDIT
09L/103751 AS DETAILED BELOW:


BENEFICIARY:                        APPLICANT:

INTERNATIONAL SELLERS LIMITED       BUYERS (UK ) LIMITED
35TH FLOOR, TWO EXCHANGE SQUARE     LOWER STREET
CONNAUGHT PLACE                     LONDON SE1
HONG KONG

DATE OF EXPIRY: DECEMBER 20, 1994   PLACE OF EXPIRY: HONG KONG

AMOUNT: GBP 200,000.00
(TWO HUNDRED THOUSAND AND 00/100`S POUNDS STERLING)

PARTIAL SHIPMENTS: NOT ALLOWED    TRANSHIPMENTS: ALLOWED

SHIPMENT FROM: HONG KONG
FOR TRANSPORTATION TO: LONDON
NO LATER THAN: DECEMBER 10, 1994


THIS CREDIT IS AVAILABLE WITH ANY BANK BY NEGOTIATION OF DRAFTS DRAWN BY
THE BENEFICIARY AT SIGHT ON MIDLAND BANK PLC P O BOX 181, 27-32 POULTRY,
LONDON EC2P 2BX (AND NO OTHER ADDRESS) FOR 100% OF INVOICE VALUE MARKED "DRAWN
UNDER DOCUMENTARY CREDIT NUMBER 09L/103751 OF MIDLAND BANK PLC."
ACCOMPANIED BY THE FOLLOWING DOCUMENTS:


FULL SET OF ORIGINAL SHIPPED ON BOARD OCEAN BILLS OF LADING ISSUED TO
ORDER AND BLANK ENDORSED MARKED FREIGHT COLLECT

ORIGINAL SIGNED COMMERCIAL INVOICE AND TWO COPIES
```

Registered in England (No. 14259)
Registered Office Poultry London EC2P 2BX
4183-8L (09/92) IS

member HSBC ⟨X⟩ *group*

OUR REFERENCE 09L/103751   PAGE: 2

ORIGINAL GSP CERTIFICATE OF ORIGIN FORM A

ORIGINAL AND 2 COPIES OF PACKING LIST

GOODS DESCRIPTION:

10 BABY GRAND PIANOS AS PER ORDER NO 468231 DATED 01/06/94

TERMS OF DELIVERY: FOB HONG KONG

DOCUMENTS TO BE PRESENTED WITHIN 10 DAYS AFTER THE ISSUANCE OF THE
TRANSPORT DOCUMENT(S) BUT WITHIN THE VALIDITY OF THE CREDIT.

WE ARE INFORMED THAT INSURANCE WILL BE ARRANGED OUTSIDE OF THE CREDIT
TERMS.

ALL CHARGES OTHER THAN OUR OWN ARE FOR THE ACCOUNT OF THE BENEFICIARY.

WE HEREBY ENGAGE WITH DRAWERS AND/OR BONA FIDE HOLDERS THAT DRAFTS DRAWN
AND NEGOTIATED IN CONFORMITY WITH THE TERMS OF THIS CREDIT WILL BE
HONOURED ON PRESENTATION, AND THAT DRAFTS ACCEPTED WITHIN THE TERMS OF
THIS CREDIT WILL BE HONOURED AT MATURITY.

PLEASE ADVISE THE BENEFICIARY WITHOUT ADDING YOUR CONFIRMATION.

EXCEPT SO FAR AS OTHERWISE EXPRESSLY STATED THIS CREDIT IS SUBJECT TO THE
UNIFORM CUSTOMS AND PRACTICE FOR DOCUMENTARY CREDITS, 1993 REVISION,
I.C.C. PUBLICATION NO. 500.

THE NEGOTIATING BANK MUST DESPATCH DOCUMENTS TO US BY DHL COURIER SERVICE
IN ONE LOT.

COMMUNICATIONS REGARDING THIS CREDIT SHOULD BE SENT TO OUR ABOVE ADDRESS.
TELEPHONE: 071 260 5978 TELEX: 8814463 MIDOCR G FAX: 071 260 4640
KINDLY ENSURE THAT YOU ALWAYS QUOTE OUR REFERENCE NUMBER FOR THIS CREDIT.

--   ----------------------
                               AUTHORISED SIGNATURE(S)

THIS DOCUMENT CONSISTS OF 2 PAGE(S)

Registered in England (No. 14259)
Registered Office Poultry London EC2P 2BX
4183-8L (09/92) IS

member HSBC **⟨X⟩** *group*

Index

(Notes: 1. This general index to the body of the text is by reference to paragraph numbers.
2. An index to the primary references in the text to the Articles of the Uniform
Customs appears in Appendix 2.)